Applications of Analog Integrated Circuits

PRENTICE-HALL SERIES IN SOLID STATE
PHYSICAL ELECTRONICS

Nick Holonyak, Jr., *Editor*

CHEO Fiber Optics
GREEN Solar Cells: Operating Principles, Technology, and System Applications
HAUS Waves and Fields in Optoelectronics
NUSSBAUM Contemporary Optics for Scientists and Engineers
SOCLOF Analog Integrated Circuits
SOCLOF Applications of Analog Integrated Circuits
STREETMAN Solid State Electronic Devices, 2nd ed.
UMAN Introduction to the Physics of Electronics
VAN DER ZIEL Solid State Physical Electronics, 3rd ed.
VERDEYEN Laser Electronics

Applications of Analog Integrated Circuits

SIDNEY SOCLOF

California State University
Los Angeles

PRENTICE-HALL, INC., Englewood Cliffs, NJ 07632

Library of Congress Cataloging in Publication Data

Soclof, Sidney.
Applications of analog integrated circuits.

(Prentice-Hall series in solid state physical electronics)
Includes bibliographies and index.
1. Analog electronic systems. 2. Integrated circuits. I. Title. II. Series.
TK7870.S529 1985 621.381'73 84-15026
ISBN 0-13-039173-5

Editorial/production supervision and interior design: *Ellen Denning*
Cover design: *Lundgren Graphics, Ltd.*
Manufacturing buyer: *Anthony Caruso*

Printed in the United States of America

10 9 8 7 6 5 4 3

ISBN 0-13-039173-5 01

PRENTICE-HALL INTERNATIONAL, INC., *London*
PRENTICE-HALL OF AUSTRALIA PTY. LIMITED, *Sydney*
EDITORA PRENTICE-HALL DO BRASIL, LTDA., *Rio de Janeiro*
PRENTICE-HALL CANADA INC., *Toronto*
PRENTICE-HALL OF INDIA PRIVATE LIMITED, *New Delhi*
PRENTICE-HALL OF JAPAN, INC., *Tokyo*
PRENTICE-HALL OF SOUTHEAST ASIA PTE. LTD., *Singapore*
WHITEHALL BOOKS LIMITED, *Wellington, New Zealand*

Contents

Preface

This is a book on the characteristics and applications of analog integrated circuits. The integrated circuits discussed in this book are used in a wide variety of applications in the areas of communications, control systems, signal processing, optoelectronics, digital systems interfacing, and as transducers for temperature, pressure, magnetic fields, and light sensing. There is enough material in this book for a two-semester senior or graduate-level course. By suitable selection of material, this book can also serve quite well for just a one-semester course. The background and preparation needed for this book is two semesters of basic electronics. This should preferably include some introductory material on the basic operation and characteristics of operational amplifiers.

Chapter 1 is a compendium of representative examples of the applications of operational amplifiers. Also presented in this chapter are some examples of applications of voltage comparators, which are devices that are very closely related to operational amplifiers. Only applications material is presented here since the basic characteristics of operational amplifiers are covered in many other books.

Integrated-circuit voltage regulators are discussed in Chapter 2. In addition to a presentation of the basic theory, characteristics, and the protective circuitry of voltage regulators, there are examples of various types of voltage regulators given including adjustable-positive and negative regulators, three-terminal fixed regulators, and switching-mode regulators.

In Chapter 3, integrated-circuit power amplifiers are investigated. The power conversion efficiency and distortion of power amplifiers is considered and examples are given of integrated-circuit audio power amplifiers. Examples of power-operational amplifiers are also presented.

In Chapter 4, attention is turned to the high-frequency performance of integrated circuits with a discussion of wide bandwidth or video amplifiers. First there is a discussion of the performance of common-emitter, cascode, emitter-follower, and FET circuits at high frequencies. This is followed by a presentation of examples of video-amplifier integrated circuits. Then some examples of operational amplifiers that have very wide bandwidths and high slewing rates are given. At the end of the chapter, unity gain buffers are discussed.

Modulators, demodulators, and phase-detector integrated circuits are discussed in Chapter 5. These are very closely related topics since the same basic circuit can be used for all three functions. The chapter opens with an analysis of the basic circuit configuration that is used for these three functions. Then some applications examples are given including amplitude modulation and demodulation, frequency modulation and FM detection, frequency doubling, and phase detection.

Integrated circuits that are used to generate various types of waveforms are presented in Chapter 6. Examples of voltage-controlled oscillators in which the frequency can be varied by an input voltage are considered first, followed by a discussion of waveform generators for the production of square, triangular, pulse, and sinusoidal waveforms.

The phase-locked loops of Chapter 7 are an important element of many communications and signal processing systems. The basic operation of these devices are discussed first, followed by examples of various applications such as AM and FM detection, frequency synthesis, and stereo demodulation.

The nonlinear characteristics of transistors and diodes can be used to good advatage to make circuits capable of multiplication, division, squaring, square rooting, rms-to-dc conversion, logarithmic conversion, exponential conversion, and other functions. This is the subject of Chapter 8, where the basic principles and examples of circuits to perform these various operations are presented.

Most integrated circuits have electrical inputs and outputs. In Chapter 9 integrated-circuit transducers are presented in which there is a non-electrical input such as temperature, pressure, or magnetic field. The related topic of light-sensitive devices is presented in Chapter 15.

Analog-to-digital and digital-to-analog converters are essential elements for the communication between analog and digital systems. These integrated circuits are discussed in Chapter 10 and various examples are given.

In Chapter 11, analog switches and sample-and-hold circuits are analyzed. These circuits are used in various signal processing applications such as signal multiplexing and demultiplexing and are also used in conjunction with analog-to-digital converters.

A very different type of integrated circuit considered in this book is the charge transfer device of Chapter 12. The two basic types of charge transfer devices considered are the charge-coupled device and the bucket-brigade device. After a study of the basic principles of operation of these devices, a number of applications examples are presented.

There are many monolithic and hybrid integrated circuits that are rather specialized in application and these are presented in Chapter 13. These include instrumentation amplifiers, isolation amplifiers, micropower and low-voltage integrated circuits, high-voltage integrated circuits, frequency-to-voltage converters, compandors, electronic attenuators, two-wire transmitters, tuned amplifiers, FM circuits, AM radio circuits, and integrated circuits for television.

The subject of Chapter 14 is not a specific integrated circuit, but rather the general topic of noise in integrated circuits and electronic systems. This is an important topic since electrical noise will set the lower limit on the detectibility of signals. Various noise sources in electronic devices including bipolar transistors and field-effect transistors are first considered, followed by a noise analysis of differential amplifiers. Next, operational amplifiers are considered, and at the end of the chapter some examples of low-noise operational amplifiers are discussed.

An important area of applications for integrated circuits is in optoelectronics and this is the subject of Chapter 15. Topics included in this chapter are photodiodes and phototransistors, radiation detectors and radiation damage, optically-coupled isolators, optoelectronic analog signal transmission, slotted and reflective emitter-sensor modules, and linear and area image sensors. The last topic dealing with image sensors represents an increasingly important type of integrated circuit and is discussed at length.

At the end of every chapter, (except Chapter 13), there are problems representative of the material covered in the chapter. Also at the end of every chapter is a list of general references for further reading or study.

SIDNEY SOCLOF

Applications of
Analog Integrated Circuits

Applications of Operational Amplifiers and Voltage Comparators

1

The operational amplifier (op amp) is a basic building block for many analog integrated-circuit (IC) systems and is useful in a very wide range of applications. In this chapter a number of op-amp applications are presented and briefly described. The equations presented for the op amp in this chapter are based on the assumption of an ideal op amp, with a very high open-loop gain. They do not take into account such effects as the input offset voltage, the input bias current, and the input offset current, nor is the effect of a finite open-loop gain and the frequency variation thereof considered.

A device closely related to the op amp is the voltage comparator. Some examples of circuits using voltage comparators are presented in this chapter.

A detailed description of the characteristics and internal circuitry of op amps and voltage comparators is beyond the scope of this book. Such descriptions may be found in many other books, as indicated by the references at the end of this chapter. Particular reference is made to *Analog Integrated Circuits*, by the present author, and *Analog Integrated Circuit Analysis and Design*, by Gray and Meyer.

For all the op-amp and voltage comparator circuits presented in this chapter, the usual convention with respect to inverting (−) and noninverting (+) input terminals will be used; that is, the inverting (−) input terminal is the upper input terminal and the noninverting (+) input is the lower input terminal.

1.1 OP-AMP APPLICATIONS

1. *Voltage follower* (Figure 1.1): This circuit produces a unity voltage gain with $V_O = V_S$. It is characterized by a very high input impedance Z_{IN} and a very low output impedance Z_O and is very useful as a buffer in coupling high-impedance sources to low-impedance loads.

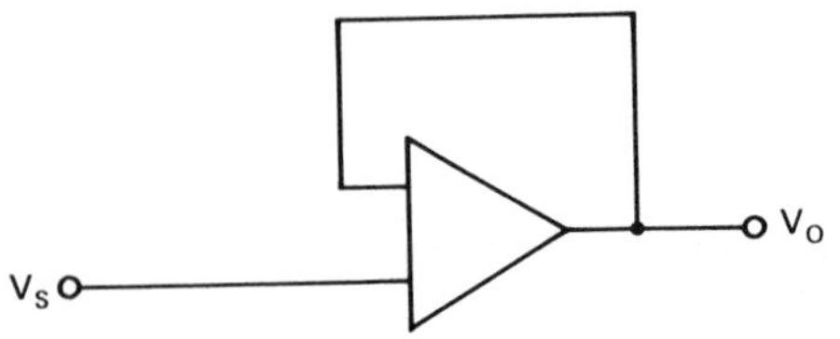

Figure 1.1 Voltage follower.

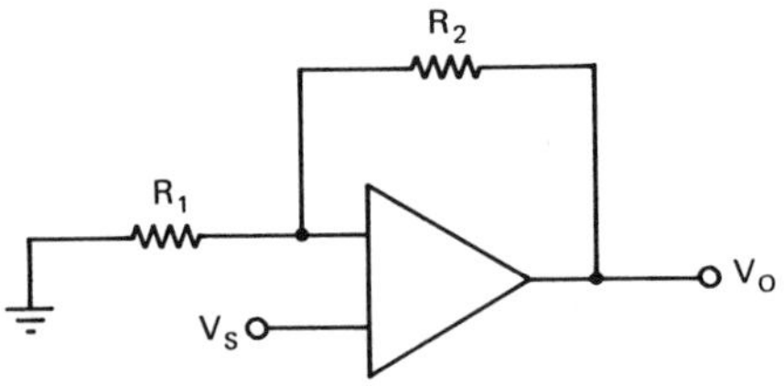

Figure 1.2 Noninverting amplifier.

2. *Noninverting amplifier* (Figure 1.2): For this circuit $V_O = (1 + R_2/R_1)V_S$. It has a very high Z_{IN} and a low Z_O.
3. *Inverting amplifier* (Figure 1.3): For this circuit $V_O = -(R_2/R_1)V_S$. It has an input impedance of $Z_{IN} = R_1$ and a very low output impedance.
4. *Summing amplifier* (Figure 1.4): For this circuit $V_O = -R_F(V_1/R_1 + V_2/R_2 + V_3/R_3 + V_4/R_4 + \cdots)$. The input impedance with respect to the various input signals V_1, V_2, V_3, . . . will be R_1, R_2, R_3, . . . , respectively.
5. *Difference amplifier* (Figure 1.5): This circuit produces an output voltage that is directly proportional to the difference of the two input signals as given by $V_O = (R_2/R_1)(V_1 - V_2)$. The input impedance with respect to the V_1 input is $R_1 + R_2$, and for the V_2 signal input it is R_1.
6. *Algebraic summation amplifier* (Figure 1.6): This circuit is an extension of the simple summing circuit, and the output voltage will represent an algebraic summation of the various input signals with coefficients determined by the resistance ratios.
7. *Current-to-voltage converter* (Figure 1.7): This circuit produces an output voltage that is directly proportional to the input current as given by $V_O = -I_S R_F$. The input impedance is equal to the feedback resistance divided by the amplifier open-loop gain A_{OL} as given by $Z_{IN} = R_F/A_{OL}$. In addition to this very low input resistance, it has a very low output impedance.
8. *Voltage-to-current converter* (Figure 1.8): The current I_L through the load resistance R_L is given by $I_L = V_S/R_1$ and is thus independent of R_L so that this circuit acts as a constant-current source. Since the current produced by

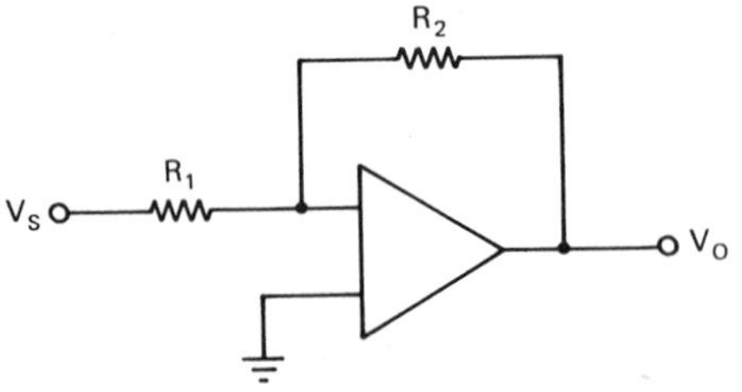

Figure 1.3 Inverting amplifier.

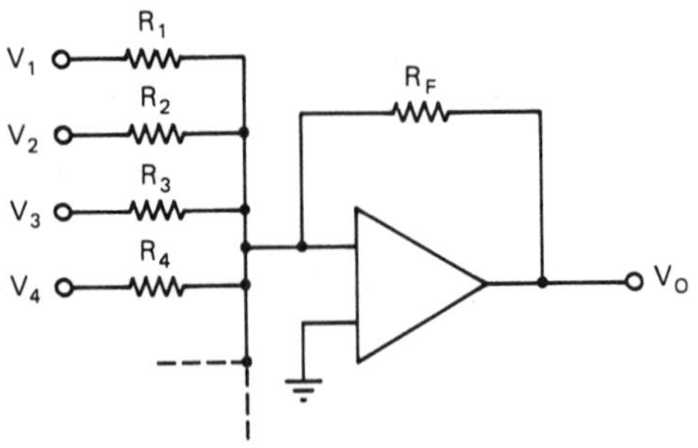

Figure 1.4 Summing amplifier.

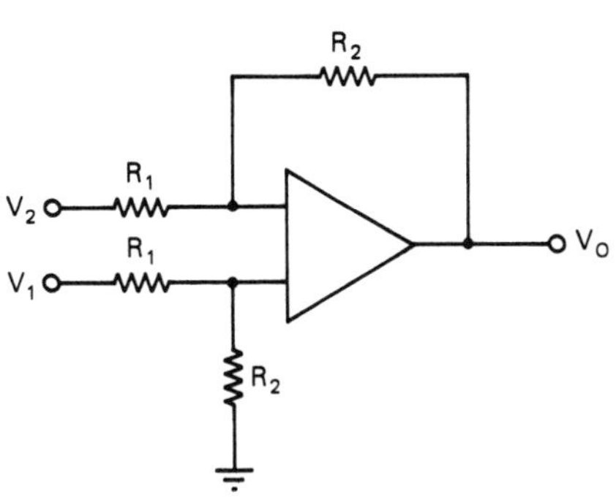

Figure 1.5 Difference amplifier.

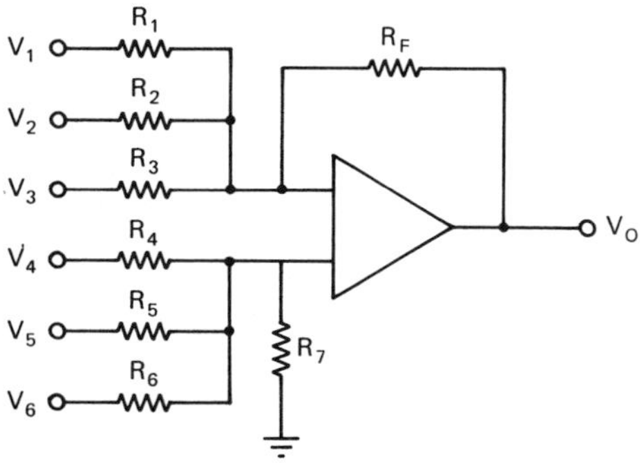

Figure 1.6 Algebraic summation amplifier.

this circuit is independent of the load resistance R_L but is directly proportional to the signal or control voltage V_S, this circuit is a voltage-controlled constant-current source. Note that neither end of the load resistance may be grounded.

9. *Constant-current source with grounded load* (*Howland current source*) (Figure 1.9): The current I_L through the load resistance R_L is given by $I_L = (V_1 - V_2)/R_1$ and is thus independent of R_L. Since the current is independent of R_L but is directly proportional to the input voltage differential, this circuit is a voltage-controlled constant-current source. Note that in this circuit a grounded load resistor may be used.

10. *Integrator* (Figure 1.10): The output voltage V_O will be proportional to the integral of the input voltage V_S over the integration period T as given by $V_O = -(1/R_1C_1)\int_0^T V_S\,dt$. The integration period is controlled by switch S_1, which opens at time $t = 0$ to start the integration process and closes at $t = T$ to terminate the integration and discharge the capacitor C_1 in preparation for the next integration cycle.

    Resistor R_1 can be omitted and this circuit can be operated as a current integrator with $V_O = (1/C_1)\int_0^T I_S\,dt = Q/C_1$, where Q is the total electrical charge delivered to the circuit over the integration period.

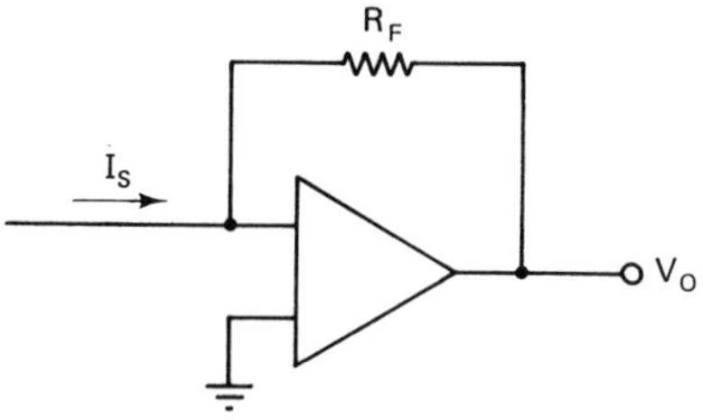

Figure 1.7 Current-to-voltage converter.

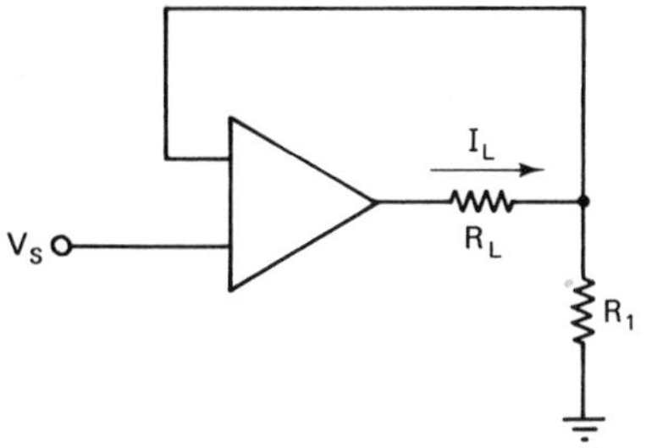

Figure 1.8 Voltage-to-current converter.

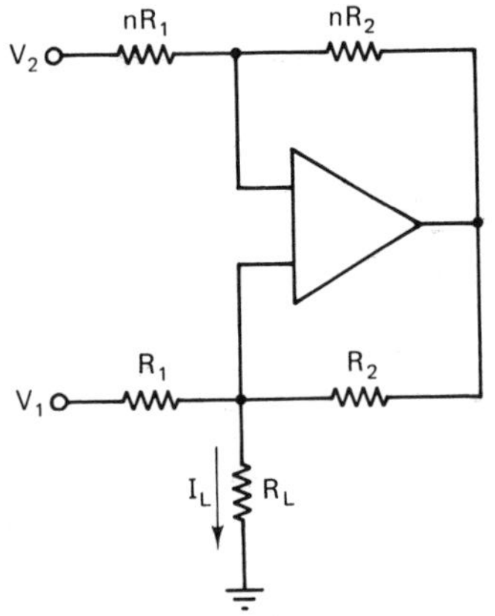

Figure 1.9 Constant-current source with grounded load (Howland current source).

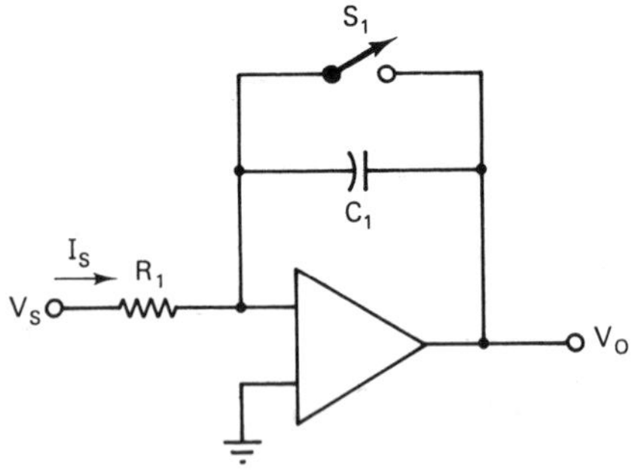

Figure 1.10 Integrator.

11. *Active low-pass filter* (Figure 1.11): In the frequency domain (sinusoidal excitation) the closed-loop gain of this circuit is given by $A_{CL} = -(R_F/R_1)/(1 + j\omega R_F C_F)$. It is a low-pass amplifier with a zero-frequency gain of $A_{CL}(0) = -R_F/R_1$ and a 3-dB bandwidth $BW = 1/(2\pi R_F C_F)$. In the time domain the response to a unit-step-function voltage input will be given by $V_O(t) = -(R_F/R_1)[1 - \exp(-t/R_F C_F)]$. For input signals whose period T is short compared to the $R_F C_F$ time constant ($T \lesssim R_F C_F/5$) the output voltage will be approximately the integral of the input voltage.
12. *Differentiator and active high-pass filter* (Figure 1.12): If $R_1 = 0$, this circuit will be an "ideal" differentiator with the output voltage being the time derivative of the input voltage as given by $V_O = -R_F C_1(dV_S/dt)$. The use of a small-value resistor for R_1 may, however, be desirable to limit the high-frequency gain. An excessively high-frequency gain can be a problem due to the amplification of the noise voltage. The value of R_1 should be chosen such that the R_1C_1 time constant will be small compared to the period of the input signal.

    In the frequency domain (sinusoidal excitation) this circuit acts as a high-pass amplifier with a gain given by $A_{CL} = V_O/V_S = j\omega R_F C_1/(1 + j\omega R_1 C_1)$.
13. *Summing integrator* (Figure 1.13): This is a simple extension of the simple

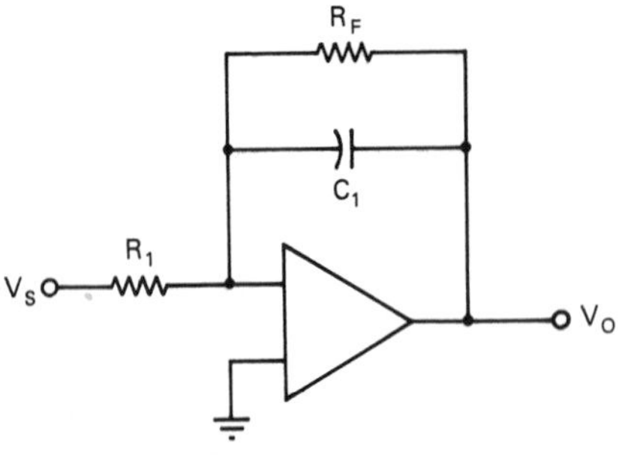

Figure 1.11 Active low-pass filter.

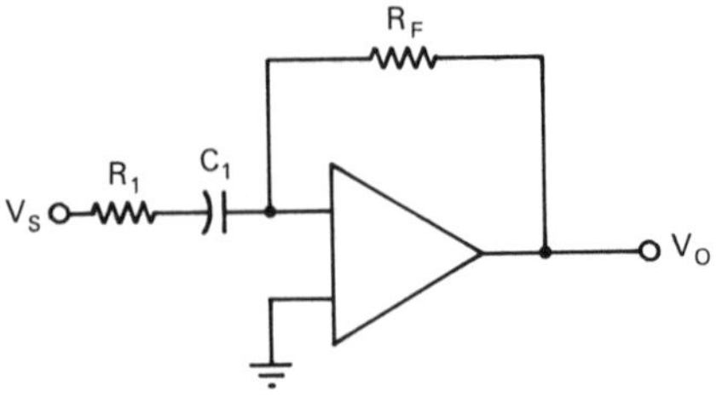

Figure 1.12 Differentiator and active high-pass filter.

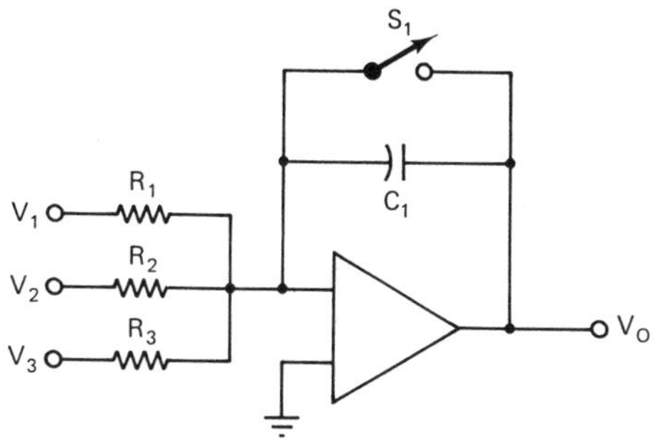

Figure 1.13 Summing integrator.

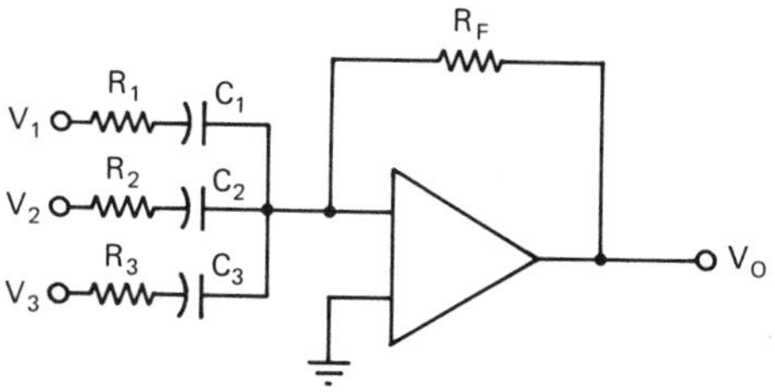

Figure 1.14 Summing differentiator.

integrator circuit. For this circuit

$$V_O = -\frac{1}{C_1}\int_0^T \left(\frac{V_1}{R_1} + \frac{V_2}{R_2} + \frac{V_3}{R_3}\right) dt$$

14. *Summing differentiator* (Figure 1.14): This is an extension of the simple differentiator circuit. For this circuit

$$V_O = -R_F\left(\frac{C_1 dV_1}{dt} + \frac{C_2 dV_2}{dt} + \frac{C_3 dV_3}{dt}\right)$$

if $R_1C_1 \ll T$, $R_2C_2 \ll T$, and $R_3C_3 \ll T$, where T is the period of the input signal.

15. *Precision half-wave rectifier* (Figure 1.15): This circuit produces $V_O = V_S$ for $V_S > 0$ and $V_O = 0$ for $V_S \leqslant 0$. It acts as a precision half-wave rectifier, or detector for communications circuits, as a result of the forward voltage drop of the diode being divided by the amplifier open-loop gain.
16. *Precision full-wave rectifier* (*absolute-value circuit*) (Figure 1.16): For this circuit $V_O = |V_S|$. Again, in this case the effect of the forward voltage drop of the diode is essentially nullified as a result of the very high open-loop gain of the amplifier.
17. *Precision peak detector* (Figure 1.17): The output voltage will be equal to the highest positive peak value of the input voltage. Amplifier A_2 is used as a unity-gain buffer for load isolation so that the current drawn by the load will not discharge C_1.
18. *Amplifier with electronic gain control* (Figure 1.18): This circuit is useful for

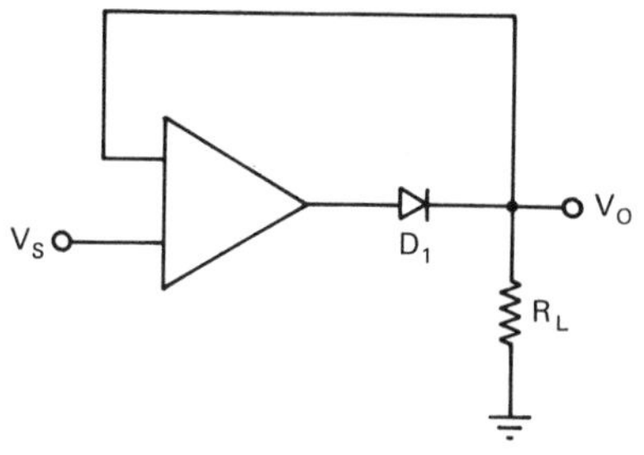

Figure 1.15 Precision half-wave rectifier.

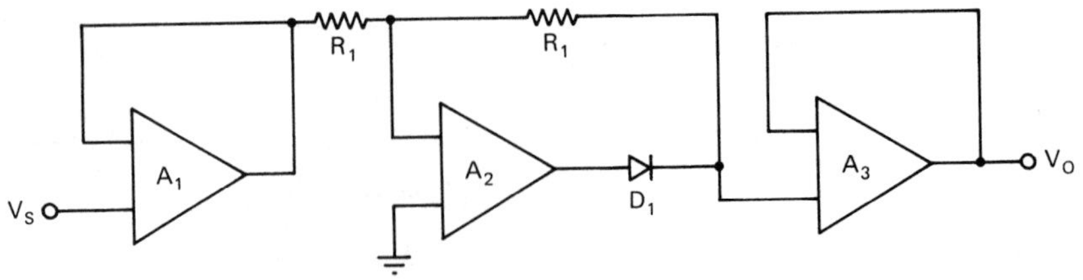

Figure 1.16 Precision full-wave rectifier (absolute-value circuit).

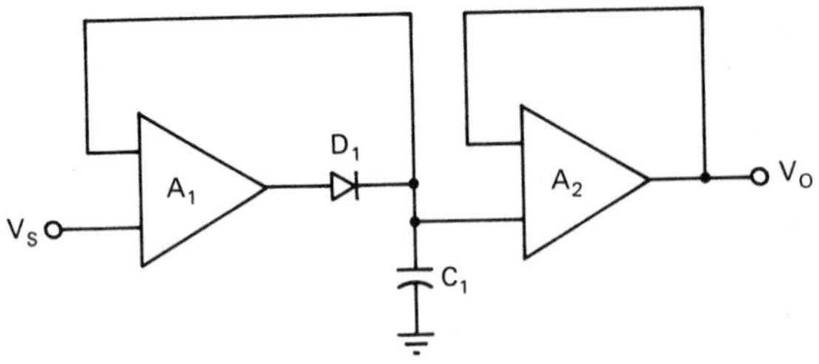

Figure 1.17 Precision peak detector.

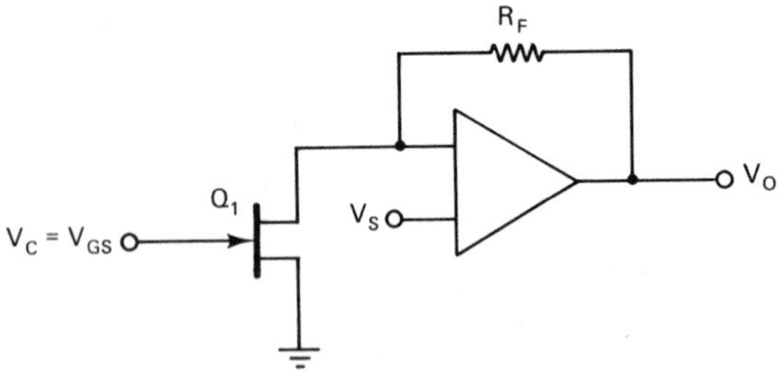

Figure 1.18 Amplifier with electronic gain control.

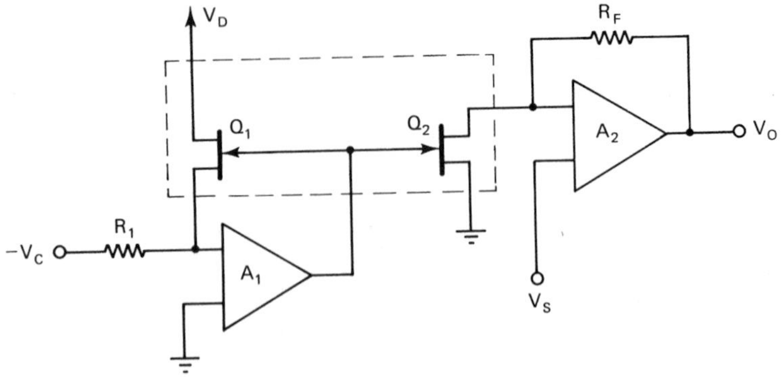

Figure 1.19 Amplifier with linear electronic gain control.

various automatic gain control (AGC) applications. The voltage gain will be given by $A_{CL} = V_O/V_S = 1 + (R_F/r_{ds})$, where r_{ds} is the drain-to-source resistance of the JFET (Q_1). Under small-signal conditions such that $V_S \simeq V_{DS} \lesssim V_p/5$, where V_p is the JFET pinch-off voltage, the drain-to-source resistance will be given approximately by $r_{ds} = r_{ds\,(\text{ON})}/(1 - \sqrt{V_{GS}/V_P})$, where $r_{ds\,(\text{ON})}$ is the "open-channel" value of r_{ds} obtained when $V_{GS} = 0$. Note that the gain will be a nonlinear function of the gain control voltage, $V_C = V_{GS}$.

19. *Amplifier with linear electronic gain control* (Figure 1.19): For this circuit transistors Q_1 and Q_2 are a pair of matched transistors. If $V_D \lesssim V_p/5$ and since $V_{GS\,1} = V_{GS\,2}$, then $r_{ds\,1} \simeq r_{ds\,2} \simeq V_D/I_{DS} = (V_D/V_C)R_1$. The closed-loop voltage gain of amplifier A_2 will be then given by $A_{CL\,2} = V_O/V_S = 1 + R_F/r_{ds\,2} = 1 + (R_F/R_1)(V_C/V_D)$. Note the linear dependence of the gain on the control voltage V_C.
20. *Amplifier with exponential gain control* (Figure 1.20): For this circuit transistors Q_1 and Q_2 should be a matched pair. The voltage gain will be an exponential function of the gain control voltage V_C as given by $A_{CL} = V_O/V_S = (R_2/R_1)\exp(V_C/V_T)$, where $V_T = kT/q \simeq 25$ mV is the thermal voltage.
21. *Logarithmic converter* (Figure 1.21): This circuit uses a matched pair of transistors (Q_1 and Q_2) in the feedback loops of A_1 and A_2 to obtain a logarithmic transfer characteristic. Amplifier A_3 is a difference amplifier with a gain of 16.7 so as to obtain the logarithmic conversion scale factor of 1.0 V/decade. The output voltage will be given by $V_O = (1.0\text{ V})\log_{10}(V_2R_1/V_1R_2)$.
22. *Exponential converter* (Figure 1.22): This is a basic circuit for an exponential converter that produces an output voltage that is an exponential function of the input voltage as given by $V_O = -I_CR_F = -I_{TO}R_F\exp(V_S/V_T)$, where I_{TO} is a parameter of the transistor.
23. *Exponential (antilogarithmic) converter* (Figure 1.23): For this circuit transistors Q_1 and Q_2 are a matched pair. The output voltage will be given by $V_O = R_3I_R\exp[-V_SR_2/V_T(R_1 + R_2)]$. The input voltage V_S can be of either po-

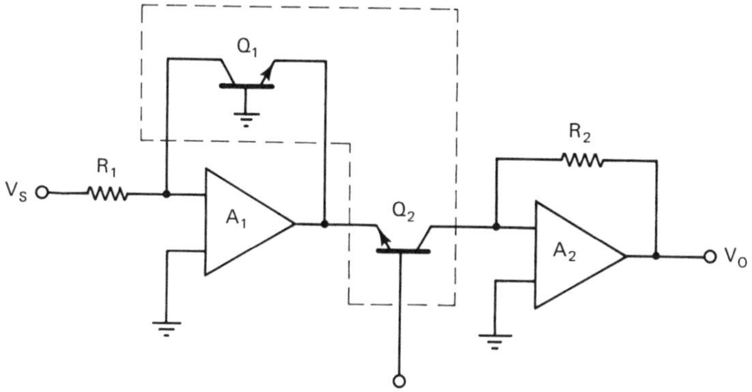

Figure 1.20 Amplifier with exponential gain control.

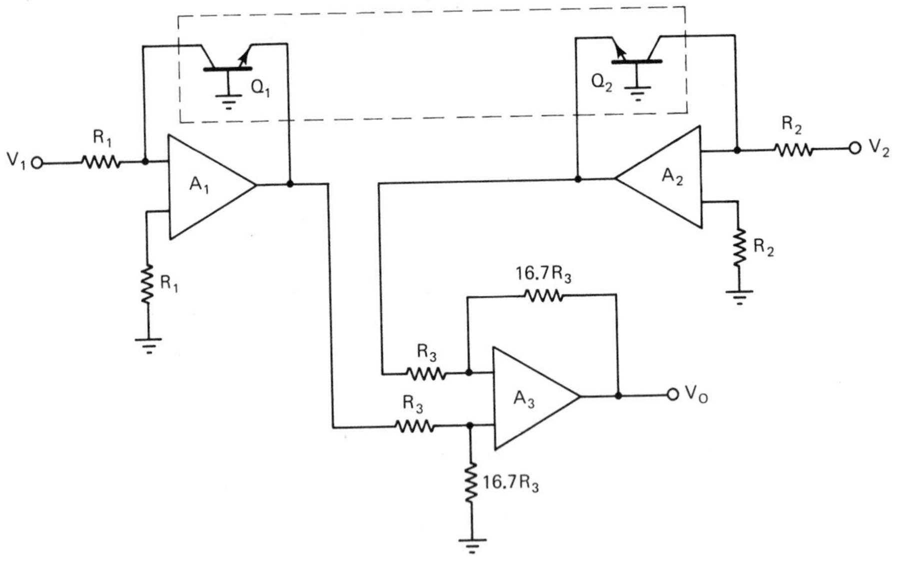

Figure 1.21 Logarithmic converter.

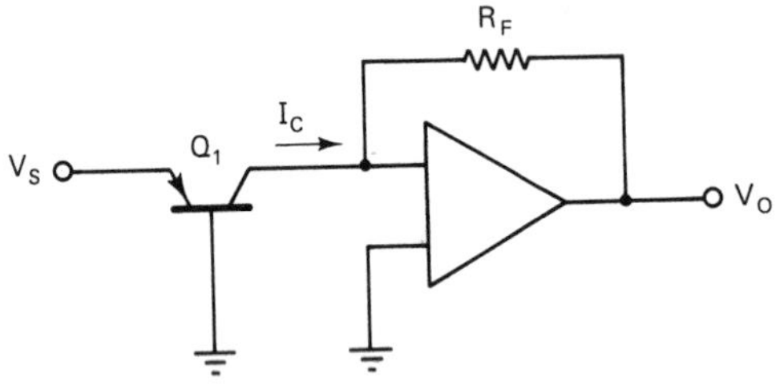

Figure 1.22 Exponential converter.

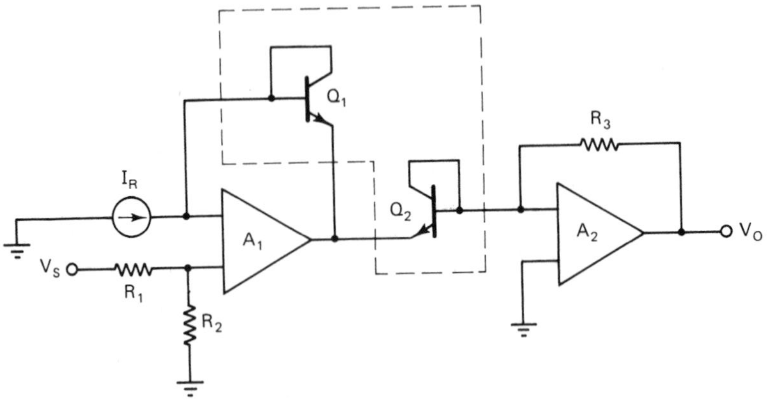

Figure 1.23 Exponential (antilogarithmic) converter.

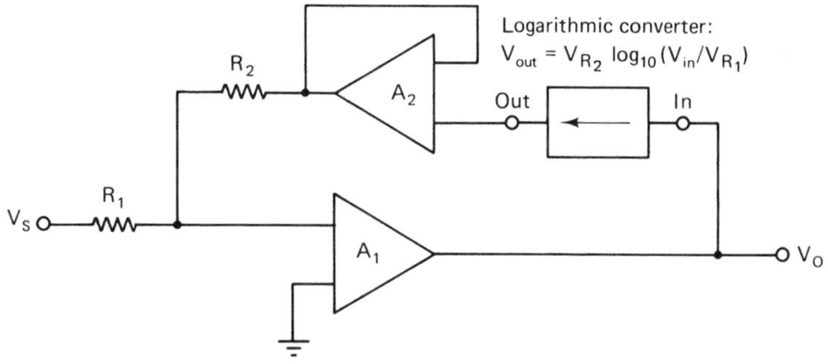

Figure 1.24 Exponential (antilogarithmic) converter.

larity, but V_O will always be of positive polarity. Note also that with a matched pair of transistors, the transistor parameter I_{TO} cancels out and does not appear in the final result for V_O.

24. *Exponential (antilogarithmic) converter* (Figure 1.24): This circuit produces an output voltage that is an exponential function of the input voltage as given by

$$V_O = V_{R1} \times 10^{-(V_S R_2 / V_{R2} R_1)}$$

where V_{R1} and V_{R2} are constants. Note that the transfer function of this circuit is the inverse function of the logarithmic converter device in the feedback loop.

25. *Exponentiating circuit* (Figure 1.25): This is a circuit for raising a variable to a fixed exponent using logarithmic techniques. The output voltage will be $V_O = (V_S)^{R_2/R_1}$. The exponent R_2/R_1 is not restricted to integer values and can be either less than unity or greater than unity.
26. *Precision phase splitter* (Figure 1.26): This circuit produces output voltages that are equal in magnitude, but of opposite algebraic sign, as given by $V_{O1} = V_S(1 + R_2/R_1)$ and $V_{O2} = -V_S(1 + R_2/R_1)$. It has a very high input impedance and a low output impedance.
27. *Instrumentation amplifier* (Figure 1.27): This is basically a difference amplifier with a high input impedance with respect to both signal inputs, and a low output impedance. The output voltage is $V_O = (V_1 - V_2)(R_2/R_1)$.
28. *Instrumentation amplifier* (Figure 1.28): This again is basically a difference

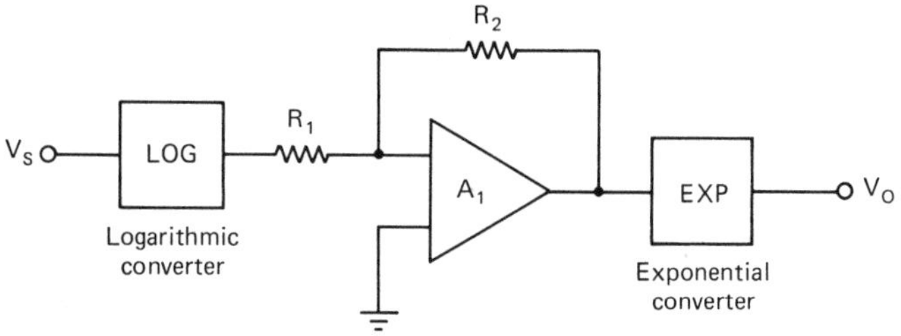

Figure 1.25 Exponentiating circuit.

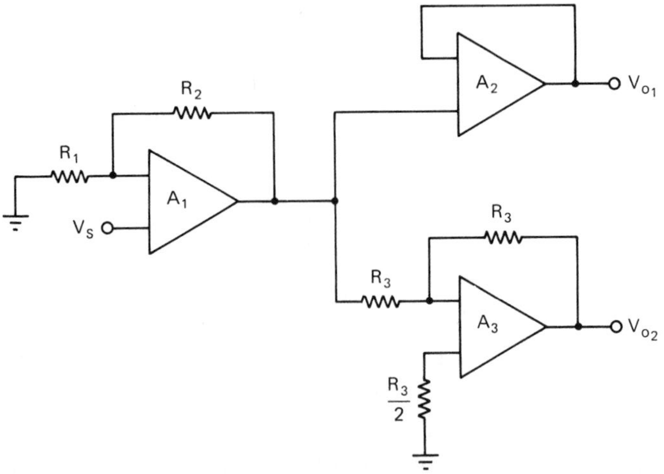

Figure 1.26 Precision phase splitter.

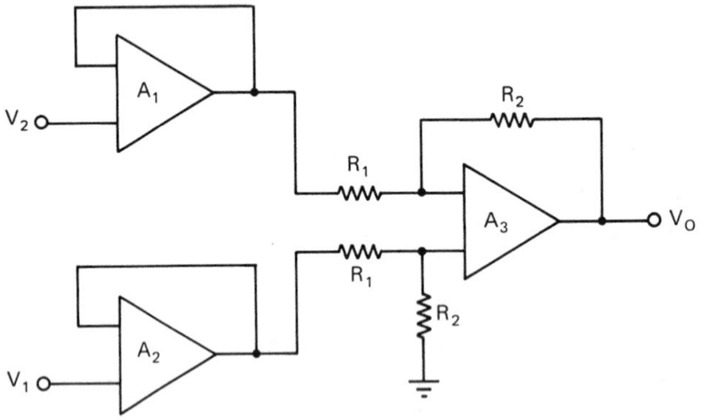

Figure 1.27 Instrumentation amplifier with high input impedance and low output impedance.

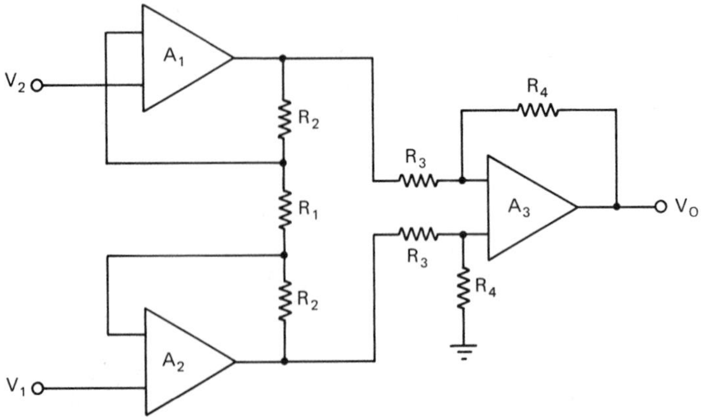

Figure 1.28 Instrumentation amplifier with high input impedance and low output impedance.

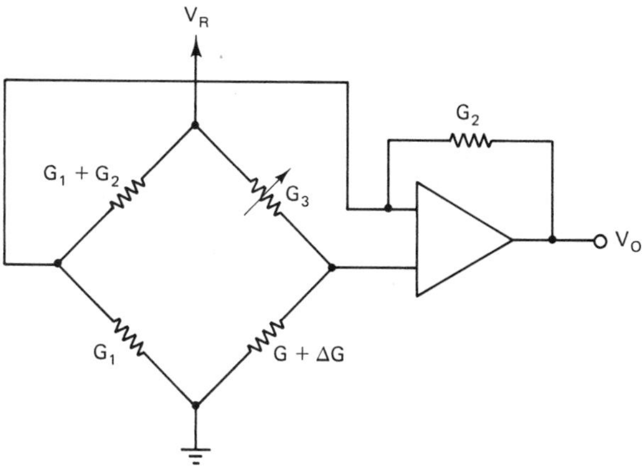

Figure 1.29 Bridge amplifier.

amplifier with a high input impedance and a low output impedance. The output voltage is given by

$$V_O = \frac{R_4}{R_3}(1 + 2R_2/R_1)(V_1 - V_2)$$

29. *Bridge amplifier* (Figure 1.29): The bridge will be balanced and the output voltage will be zero when $G_X = G_3$. If G_X then changes by an amount ΔG_X, the output voltage will be given by

$$V_O = \left(1 + \frac{G_1}{G_2}\right) \frac{-\Delta G_X}{2G_X + \Delta G_X} V_R$$

For $\Delta G_X \ll G_X$ this can be rewritten as

$$V_O \simeq -\left(1 + \frac{G_1}{G_2}\right) \frac{\Delta G_X}{2G_X} V_R \simeq -\left(1 + \frac{R_2}{R_1}\right) \frac{\Delta R_X}{R_X} \frac{V_R}{2}$$

Resistance element R_X $(= 1/G_X)$ can be a temperature-sensitive element or a piezoresistive strain transducer so that this circuit can be used in various thermometric and pressure- or strain-sensing applications.

30. *Biopolar limiting circuit* (Figure 1.30): This is a limiting or bounding circuit with the output voltage limited to a maximum of $V_{O(\text{MAX})} = V_Z + V_F = V_Z + 0.6$ V in the positive direction, and $V_{O(\text{MIN})} = -(V_Z + V_F) = -(V_Z +$

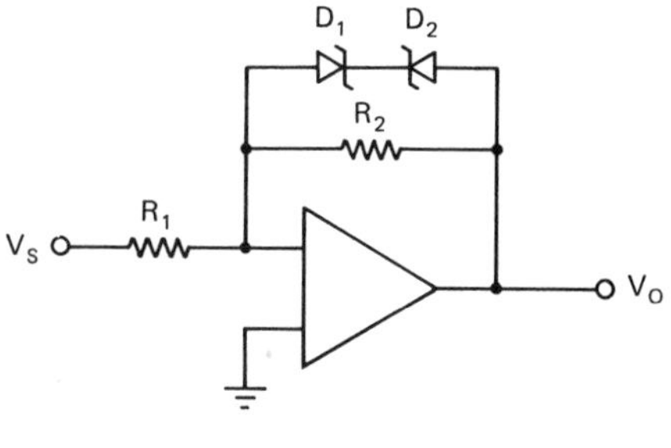

Figure 1.30 Bipolar limiting circuit.

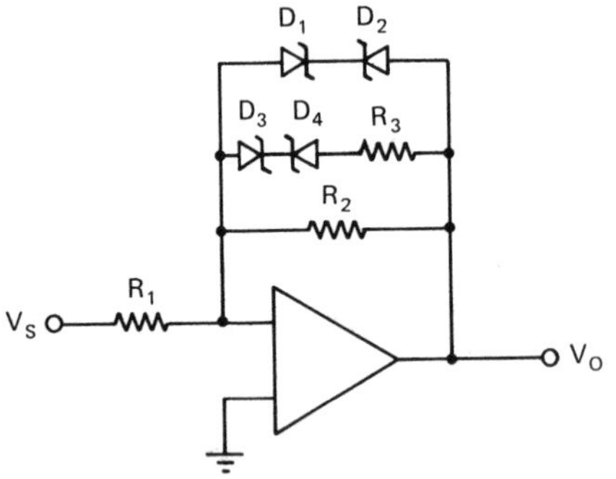

Figure 1.31 Wave-shaping circuit.

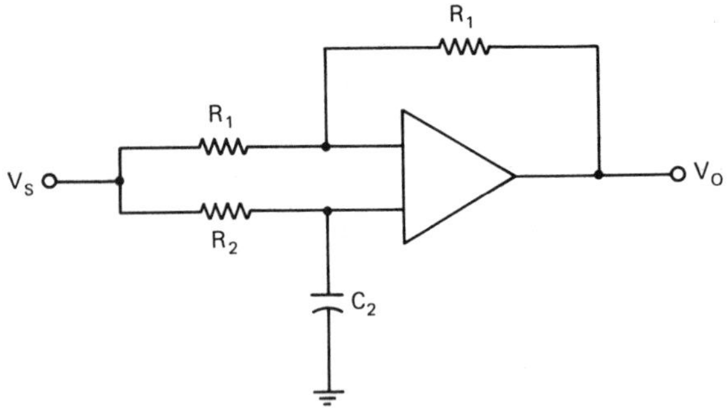

Figure 1.32 Constant-amplitude phase shifter.

0.6 V) in the negative direction, where V_Z is the zener (breakdown) voltage of diodes D_1 and D_2 and V_F is the forward voltage drop. Between these limits the output voltage will be given by $V_O = -(R_2/R_1)V_S$.

31. *Wave-shaping circuit* (Figure 1.31): This is an example of the many wave-shaping circuits that can be obtained using various combinations of resistors and diodes in the feedback loop of an op amp. The transfer function will be a piecewise linear function of the input voltage V_S.
32. *Constant-amplitude phase shifter* (Figure 1.32): This circuit produces a closed-loop gain with a magnitude of unity, independent of frequency. The phase shift, however, will change with frequency, varying from 0° at zero frequency to a value approaching −180° at high frequencies. The voltage gain will be given by

$$A_{CL} = \frac{V_O}{V_S} = 1.0 \underline{/-2 \tan^{-1}(\omega R_2 C_2)}$$

This can be used as a time-delay circuit, with the time delay T_d being given by $T_d = \phi/\omega$, where ϕ is the phase shift as given by $\phi = -2 \tan^{-1}(\omega R_2 C_2)$. For frequencies such that $(\omega R_2 C_2)^2 \ll 1$, the phase shift ϕ will be given approximately by $\phi \simeq -2\omega R_2 C_2$, so that the time delay will be $T_d \simeq -2R_2C_2$ and will thus be relatively independent of frequency.

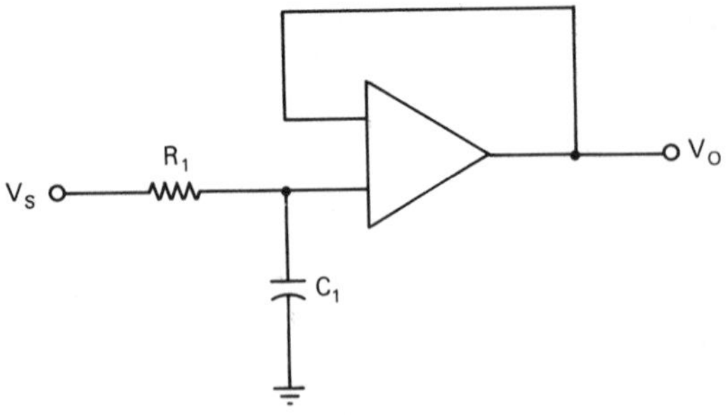

Figure 1.33 Low-pass active filter.

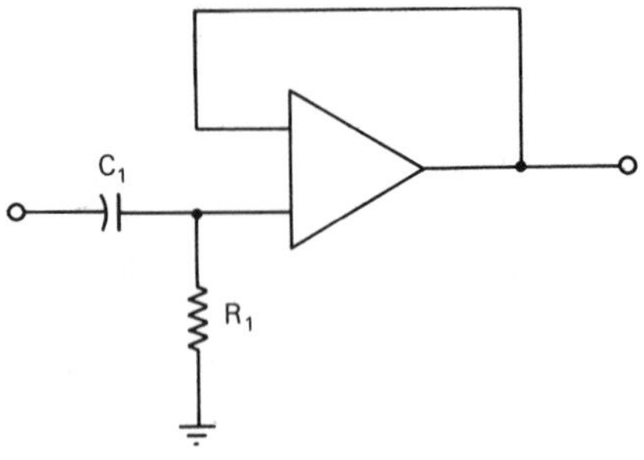

Figure 1.34 High-pass active filter.

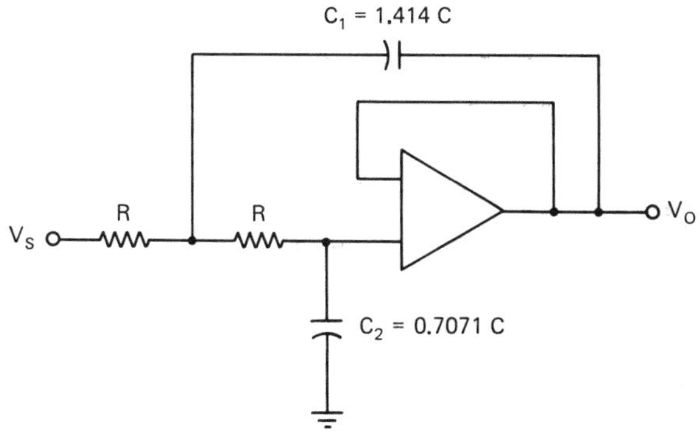

Figure 1.35 Two-pole Butterworth low-pass active filter.

33. *Low-pass active filter* (Figure 1.33): This is a simple single-pole Butterworth low-pass filter with a 3-dB bandwidth $BW = f_{3dB} = 1/(2\pi R_1 C_1)$ and a 20-dB/decade high-frequency roll-off.
34. *High-pass active filter* (Figure 1.34): This is a simple single-pole Butterworth high-pass filter with a 3-dB frequency at $f_{3dB} = 1/(2\pi R_1 C_1)$ and a 20-dB/decade low-frequency roll-off.
35. *Two-pole Butterworth low-pass active filter* (Figure 1.35): This filter has a 3-dB bandwidth $BW = f_{3dB} = 1/(2\pi RC)$. The high-frequency response has a 40-dB/decade roll-off.
36. *Two-pole Butterworth high-pass active filter* (Figure 1.36): This filter has a 3-dB frequency of $f_{3dB} = 1/(2\pi RC)$. The low-frequency response rolls off at a rate of 40 dB/decade or 12 dB/octave.
37. *Three-pole Butterworth low-pass active filter* (Figure 1.37): This three-pole active filter has a 3-dB bandwidth $BW = f_{3dB} = 1/(2\pi RC)$. The high-frequency response rolls off at a rate of 60 dB/decade or 18 dB/octave.
38. *Three-pole Butterworth high-pass active filter* (Figure 1.38): The 3-dB frequency of this high-pass filter is $f_{3dB} = 1/(2\pi RC)$. The low-frequency response rolls off at a rate of 60 dB/decade or 18 dB/octave.

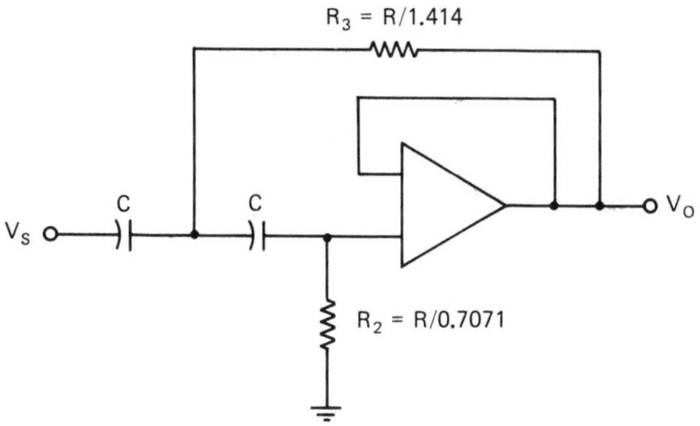

Figure 1.36 Two-pole Butterworth high-pass active filter.

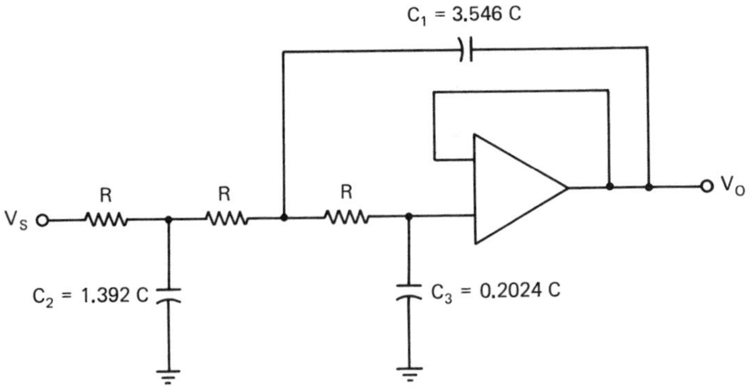

Figure 1.37 Three-pole Butterworth low-pass active filter.

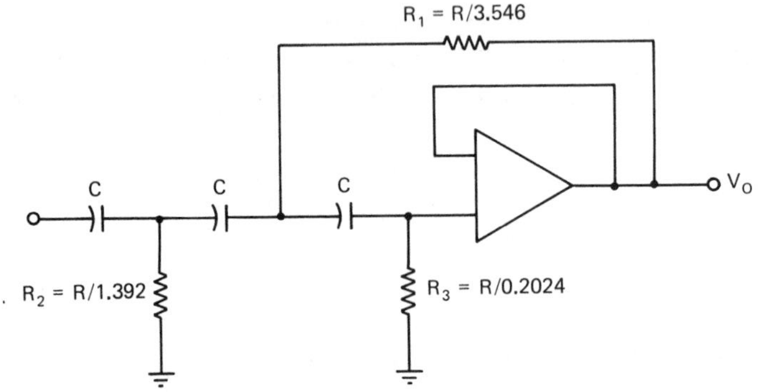

Figure 1.38 Three-pole Butterworth high-pass active filter.

Higher-order Butterworth active filters. For higher-order Butterworth active filters the two-pole and three-pole active filters can be cascaded. For an N-pole filter, where N is an even integer, $N/2$ two-pole filters can be cascaded. If N is an odd integer, one three-pole filter and $(N - 3)/2$ two-pole filters can be cascaded. The component values list in Table 1.1 should be used.

39. *Bandpass amplifier* (Figure 1.39): This is a bandpass active filter with a maximum or peak gain of $A_{V(\text{MAX})} = -R_1/R_4$ occurring at the "resonant (radian) frequency" of $\omega_o = 1/(C\sqrt{R_2R_3})$. The 3-dB bandwidth will be $BW = 1/(2\pi R_1 C)$.
40. *Bandpass amplifier* (Figure 1.40): This bandpass amplifier uses just one op amp. The maximum gain will be $A_{V(\text{MAX})} = -(R_5/R_1)C_2/(C_2 + C_3)$, occurring at the "resonant (radian) frequency" of $\omega_o^2 = (1/R_1 + 1/R_4)/(C_2C_3R_5)$. The 3-dB bandwidth is $BW = (C_2 + C_3)/2\pi R_5C_2C_3$.

TABLE 1.1 COMPONENT VALUES FOR BUTTERWORTH ACTIVE FILTERS

Number of poles	C_1/C or R/R_1	C_2/C or R/R_2	C_3/C or R/R_3
2	1.414	0.7071	
3	3.546	1.392	0.2024
4	1.082	0.9241	
	2.613	0.3825	
5	1.753	1.354	0.4214
	3.235	0.3090	
6	1.035	0.9660	
	1.414	0.7071	
	3.863	0.2588	
7	1.531	1.336	0.4885
	1.604	0.6235	
	4.493	0.2225	
8	1.020	0.9809	
	1.202	0.8313	
	1.800	0.5557	
	5.125	0.1950	
9	1.455	1.327	0.5170
	1.305	0.7661	
	2.000	0.5000	
	5.758	0.1736	
10	1.012	0.9874	
	1.122	0.8908	
	1.414	0.7071	
	2.202	0.4540	
	6.390	0.1563	

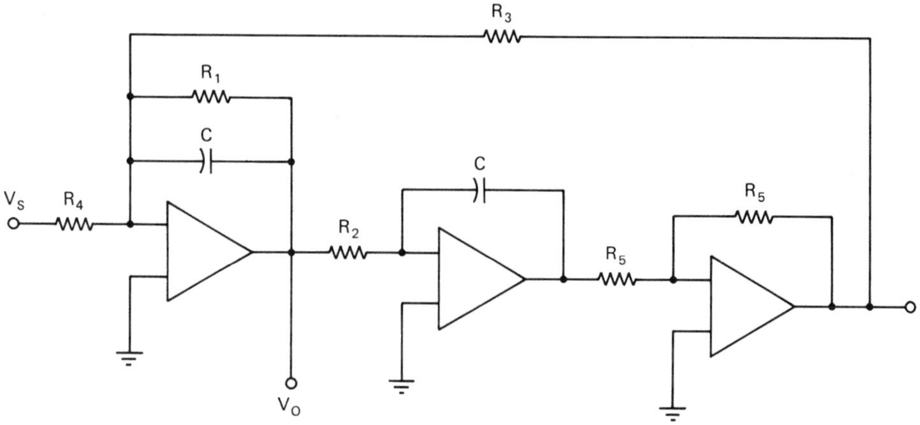

Figure 1.39 Bandpass amplifier.

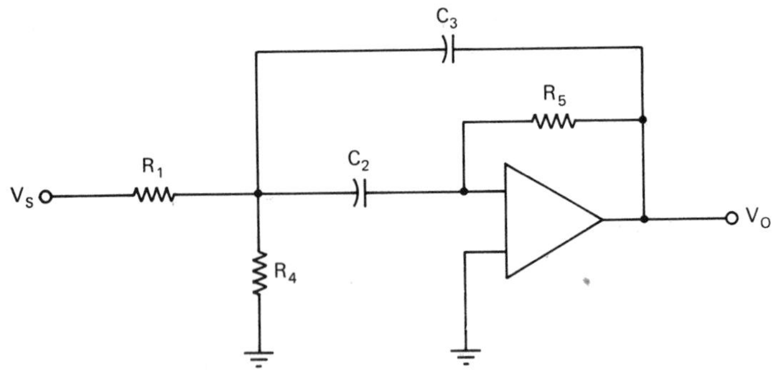

Figure 1.40 Bandpass amplifier.

41. *Band-stop active filter* (Figure 1.41): This is a band-stop or band-reject active filter that has a null or "zero signal transmission frequency" (notch frequency) at $f_o = 1/(2\pi RC)$. The 3-dB bandwidth will be $BW = 4f_o(1 - k) = 4f_oR_1/(R_1 + R_2)$.
42. *Sample-and-hold circuit* (Figure 1.42): This sample-and-hold circuit can sample an input voltage during a short time interval, and then hold this sampled value over an extended period of time. The two op amps provide source and load isolation. The input signal voltage that is sampled is V_S and the sampling control voltage is V_{sample}.
43. *Positive voltage regulator* (Figure 1.43): This is a voltage regulator or voltage source circuit with an output voltage given by $V_O = V_ZR_2/(R_1 + R_2)$ subject to the requirement that $V^+ > V_Z$, where V_Z is the zener voltage of diode D_1.

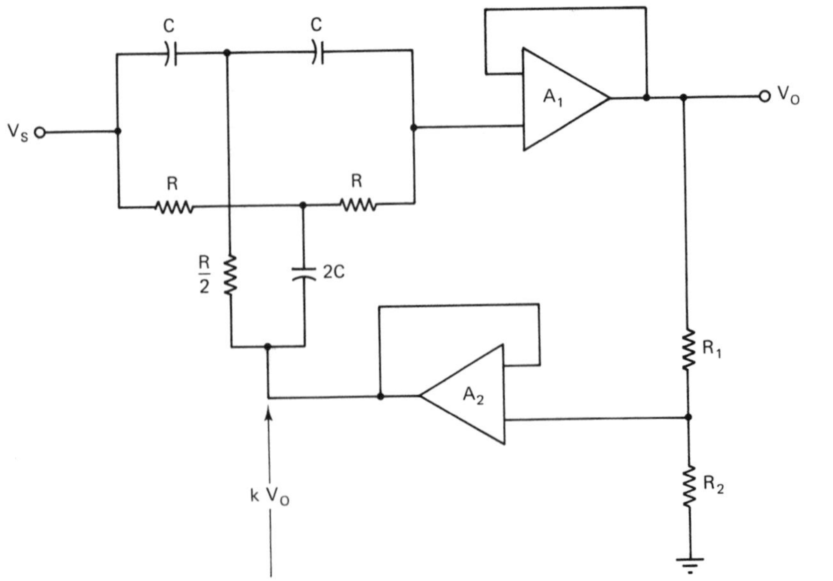

Figure 1.41 Band-stop active filter.

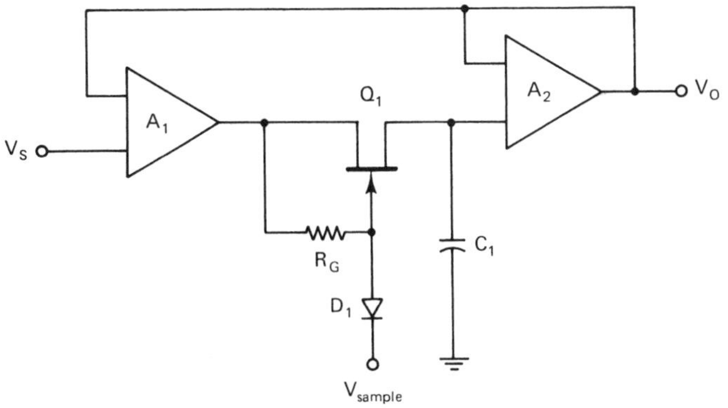

Figure 1.42 Sample-and-hold circuit.

44. *Positive voltage regulator* (Figure 1.44): In this circuit the output voltage is given by $V_O = V_Z(1 + R_2/R_1)$, so it will be greater than V_Z. Note that the current through the zener diode D_1 will be $I_Z = I_{R_3} = V_O(R_2/R_3)/(R_1 + R_2)$ and thus will be essentially independent of the supply voltage. As a result, the output voltage will be almost completely insensitive to changes in the d-c supply voltage, so that this circuit will be characterized by very good line regulation. This is, of course, subject to the requirement that the supply voltage is above the minimum value that is needed for proper operation of this circuit.
45. *High-current-voltage regulator with current limiting* (Figure 1.45): In the two preceding voltage regulator (or constant-voltage source) circuits the output current cannot exceed the maximum output current limit of the op amp. The output current of a regulator circuit can be increased considerably above this limit by using one or several transistors to boost the output current to a level considerably above that of the op amp. For the circuit of Figure 1.45 the output current of the operational amplifier is multiplied by the current gain of transistor Q_1. For even larger output currents, transistor Q_1 can be replaced by a Darlington transistor pair.

    Transistor Q_2 in conjunction with resistor R_{CL} is used for current limiting

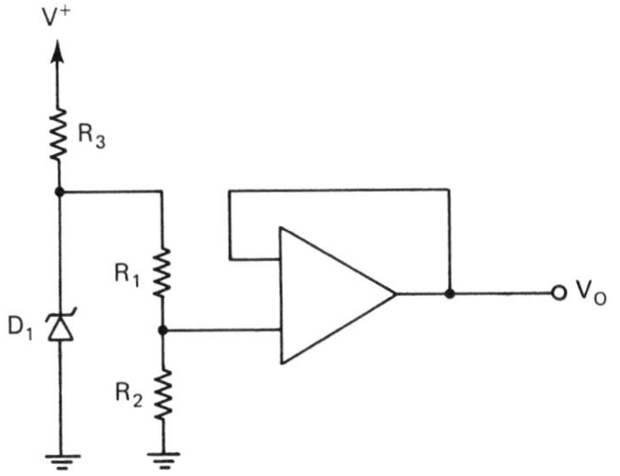

Figure 1.43 Positive voltage regulator.

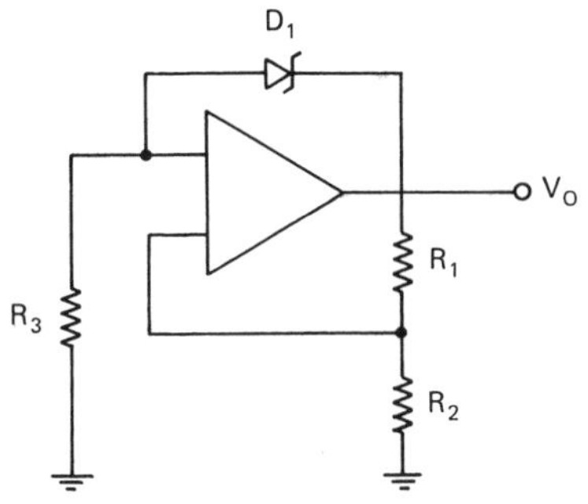

Figure 1.44 Positive voltage regulator.

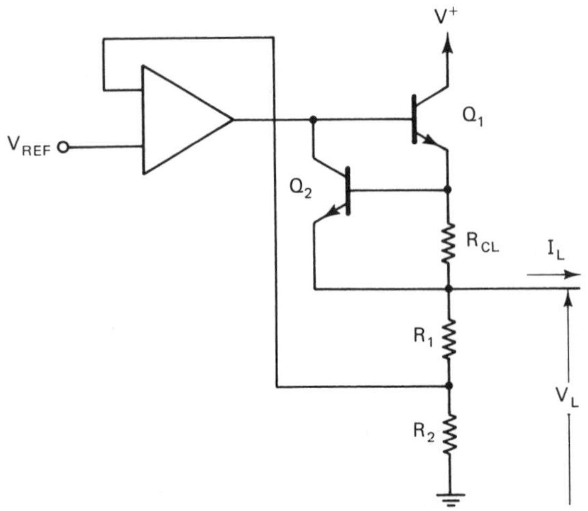

Figure 1.45 High-current-voltage regulator with current limiting.

to limit the current through the output transistor Q_1 to a safe value such that the maximum power dissipation rating of Q_1 will not be exceeded. The value of R_{CL} will be given approximately by $R_{CL} \simeq 0.65\,V/I_{L\,(\mathrm{MAX})}$.

46. *Tracking voltage regulator* (Figure 1.46): The two regulated output voltages of this circuit will be equal in magnitude but of opposite algebraic sign, as given by $V_O^+ = V_{\mathrm{REF}}(1 + R_1/R_2)$ and $V_O^- = -V_O^+$. Note that this will hold true even if the two supply voltages, V^+ and V^-, are not equal in magnitude. If the lower resistor of value R_3 is replaced by a resistor of value R_4, the equation for V_O^+ remains the same, but for V_O^- we will now have $V_O^- = -V_O^+(R_4/R_3)$.

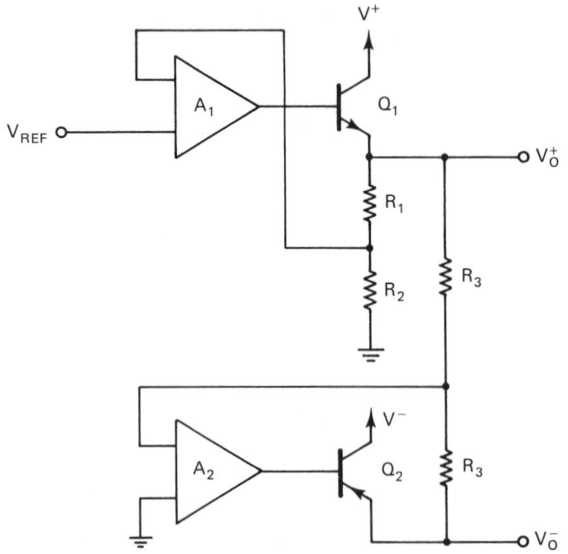

Figure 1.46 Tracking dual-voltage regulator.

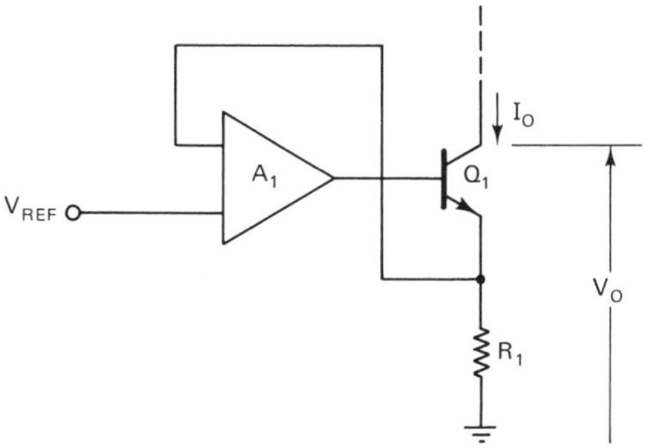

Figure 1.47 Constant-current source.

47. *Constant-current sink* (Figure 1.47): The output current of this constant-current sink will be approximately independent of the output voltage $V_O = V_{C_1}$ as long as transistor Q_1 stays in the active region. This requires that $V_{CE_1} > V_{CE(\mathrm{SAT})} = 0.2$ V, so that $V_O > V_{\mathrm{REF}} + 0.2$ V. Under these conditions, the output current I_O will be given by $I_O = V_{\mathrm{REF}}/R_1 - I_{B_1} \simeq V_{\mathrm{REF}}/R_1$, where I_{B_1} is the base current of Q_1.

The output current capability of this circuit can be greatly increased and the error due to the transistor base current can be substantially reduced by replacing transistor Q_1 by a Darlington transistor pair. As a result of the higher saturation voltage of the Darlington transistor configuration, the minimum voltage requirement now becomes $V_O > V_{\mathrm{REF}} + 0.9$ V.

An equivalent constant-current source (with I_O going out) can be obtained by simply replacing Q_1 by a PNP transistor and using an input or reference voltage V_{REF} of negative polarity.

48. *Precision constant-current source for low current levels* (Figure 1.48): For this circuit $I_O = V_{\mathrm{REF}}/R_1 - I_{GS} \simeq V_{\mathrm{REF}}/R_1$. The very small value of the JFET gate current will result in the difference or error between the output current I_O and V_{REF}/R_1 to an extremely small value, even down to very low output current levels. For the operation of this circuit as a constant-current sink the minimum output voltage V_O is given by $V_O > V_P + V_{\mathrm{REF}}$, where V_P is the pinch-off voltage of the JFET.

For an equivalent constant-current source, transistor Q_1 should be replaced

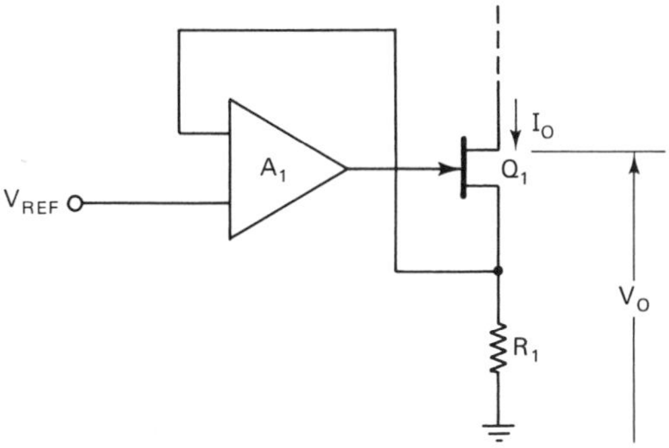

Figure 1.48 Precision constant-current source for low current levels.

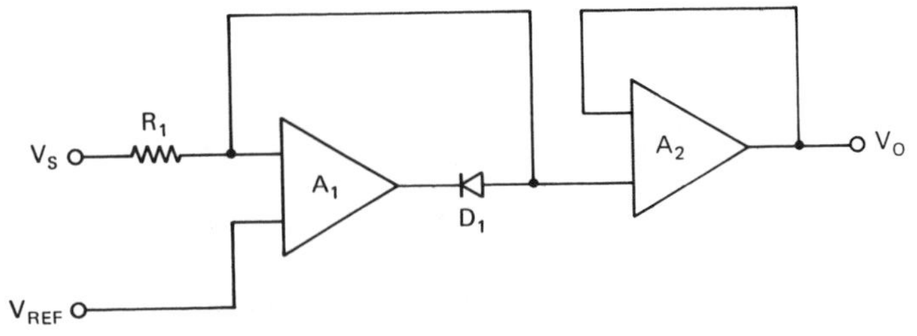

Figure 1.49 Precision voltage-controlled limiting ("clipping or "bounding") circuit.

by a P-channel JFET and the input or reference voltage $V_{\mathbf{REF}}$ should be of negative polarity. Note also that in this circuit, as well as in the preceding circuit, the input voltage $V_{\mathbf{REF}}$ can be a fixed d-c voltage or it can be some time-varying signal or control voltage, in which case this circuit will be a voltage-controlled constant-current sink (or source).

49. *Precision voltage-controlled limiting ("Clipping" or "Bounding") circuit* (Figure 1.49): This is a non-inverting unity gain amplifier circuit that clips the output voltage at $V_{\mathbf{REF}}$ such that $V_O = V_S$ for $V_S < V_{\mathbf{REF}}$ and $V_O = V_{\mathbf{REF}}$ for $V_S > V_{\mathbf{REF}}$ where $V_{\mathbf{REF}}$ can be of either polarity. The forward voltage drop of the diode is, in effect, divided by the amplifier open-loop gain such that it will have very little effect on the operation of this circuit. If diode D_1 is reversed, the transfer relationship will be $V_O = V_S$ for $V_S > V_{\mathbf{REF}}$ and $V_O = V_{\mathbf{REF}}$ for $V_S < V_{\mathbf{REF}}$.
50. *Precision voltage-controlled clamping circuit* (Figure 1.50): This circuit produces an output voltage that has the same a-c variation as the input voltage, but the d-c level is shifted such that the output voltage will not drop below $V_{\mathbf{REF}}$. The voltage $V_{\mathbf{REF}}$ can be of either polarity. If diode D_1 is reversed, the output voltage will again have the same a-c variation as the input, but the shift in the d-c level is such that the output voltage will not rise above $V_{\mathbf{REF}}$.
    The diode forward voltage drop is, in effect, divided by the open-loop gain of A_2 such that it will have a negligible effect on the performance of the circuit in most cases.
51. *Voltage-controlled gain polarity switching circuit* (Figure 1.51): This circuit is

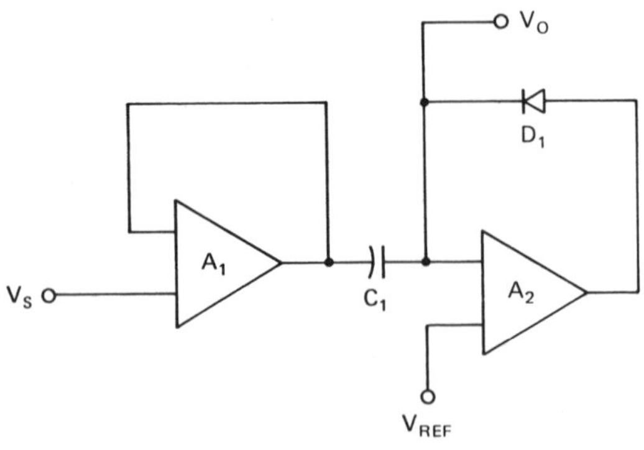

Figure 1.50 Precision voltage-controlled clamping circuit.

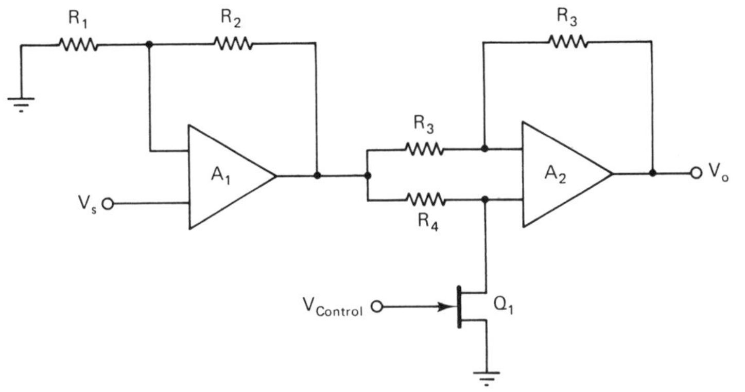

Figure 1.51 Voltage-controlled gain polarity switching circuit.

an inverting amplifier with a closed-loop gain given by $A_{CL} = -(1 + R_2/R_1)$ when transistor Q_1 is turned on ($V_{\text{control}} = 0$), and a non-inverting amplifier with $A_{CL} = 1 + R_2/R_1$ when Q_1 is turned off ($V_{\text{control}} < V_p$). The magnitudes of the two voltage gains will be approximately equal subject to the condition that $r_{ds} \ll R_4$.

52. *Voltage-controlled impedance multiplier* (Figure 1.52): The feedback impedance Z_F of this circuit is transformed to appear as an input impedance of value $Z_i = Z_F/(1 + A)$ and correspondingly, the input admittance is given by $Y_i = (1 + A)Y_F$. If the feedback impedance is a capacitor of value C_F, the input capacitance of this circuit will be $C_i = C_F\ (1 + A)$ so that this circuit can act as a capacitance multiplier. If the gain of amplifier A_2 is varied by the gain control voltage, the input capacitance will be a voltage-variable capacitance.

53. *Inductance simulator* (Figure 1.53): The input impedance of this circuit is proportional to the reciprocal of the feedback impedance Z_F, and will be given by $Z_i = R_2R_3/Z_F$. If Z_F is a capacitor of value C_F, the input impedance

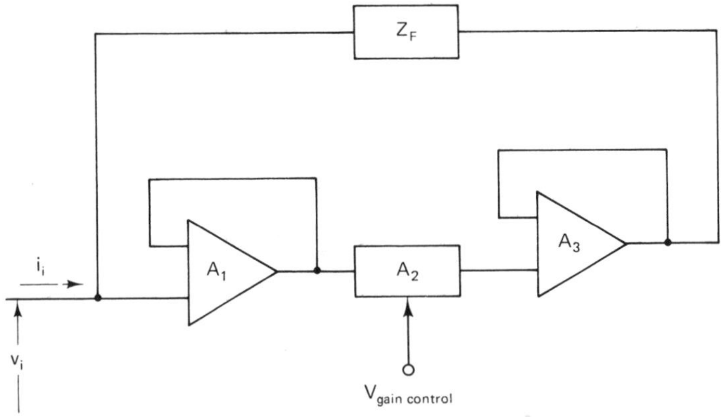

Figure 1.52 Voltage-controlled impedance multiplier.

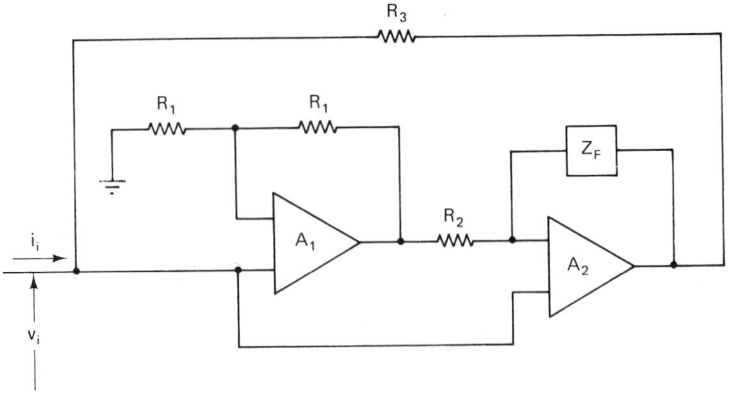

Figure 1.53 Inductance simulator.

will be given by $Z_i = j\omega R_2 R_3 C_F = j\omega L_{eq}$ so that the input impedance appears as an inductance of value $L_{eq} = R_2 R_3 C_F$.

54. *Analog signal multiplexing circuit* (Figure 1.54): For this circuit, ϕ_1 through ϕ_N are non-overlapping active low-clock pulses such that transistors Q_1 through Q_N are "on" except when the clock pulses applied to one of the transistors is

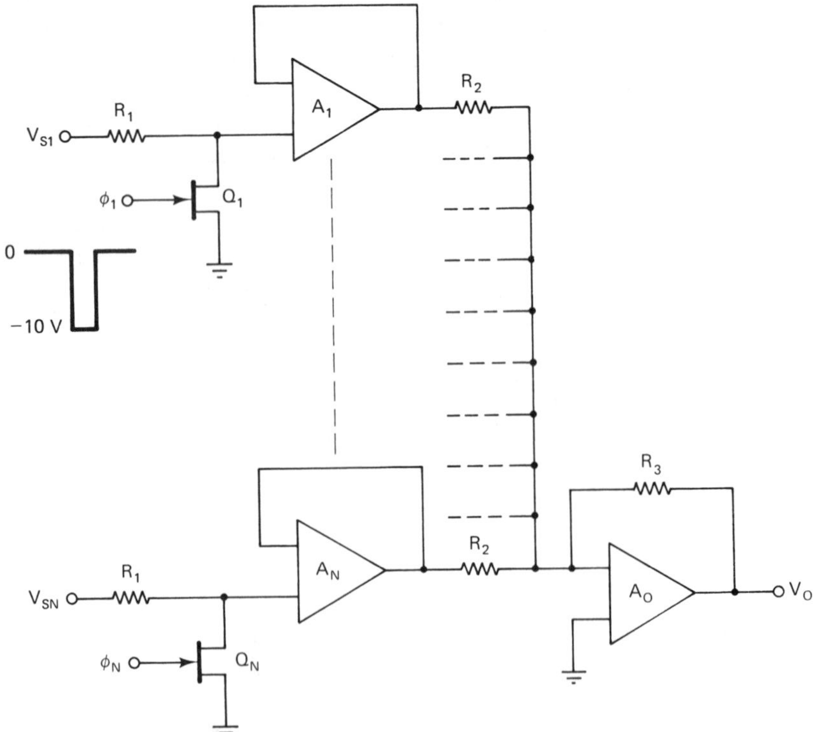

Figure 1.54 Analog signal multiplexing circuit.

active which will turn that transistor "off." This will then permit the signal transmission from the selected input to the output. The resistance R_1 should be chosen such that $R_1 \gg r_{ds(ON)}$.

One variation of this circuit is to use a series-shunt switch arrangement with additional FETs in series with R_1 and driven with active high-clock pulses such that when a shunt switch transistor is "on" the corresponding series switch transistor will be "off," and vice versa.

55. *Phase shift oscillator* (Figure 1.55): This is a feedback oscillator, and for oscillations to occur, the net gain around the feedback loop must be greater than unity at the frequency at which the net phase shift around the feedback loop is zero. The frequency of oscillation will be given by $f_{osc} = 1/(2\pi\sqrt{3}\ R_1C_1)$ and the gain condition will be satisfied if $R_3/R_2 > 8$. If the net gain around the feedback loop is adjusted to a value that is just slightly above unity, the output voltage will be a relatively undistorted sinusoidal waveform.

    This circuit will also work if voltage-followers A_2 and A_3 are omitted. The frequency of oscillation will then be given by $f_{osc} = 1/(2\pi\sqrt{6}\ R_1C_1)$ and the gain condition will require that $R_3/R_2 > 29$.

56. *Wien bridge oscillator* (Figure 1.56): This circuit has both a positive and negative feedback loop. For oscillations to occur, the net feedback must be positive with a phase angle of zero. This gives the required condition that $(R_3/R_4) > (R_1/R_2) + (C_1/C_2)$ and the corresponding frequency of oscillation will be $f_{osc} = 1/(2\pi\sqrt{R_1R_2C_1C_2})$. If the R_3/R_4 ratio is adjusted to a value that is just slightly above that required for oscillations, then a relatively undistorted sinusoidal waveform will be obtained.

57. *Optoelectronic sensor* (Figure 1.57): This simple light sensing circuit consists of a photodiode and a current-to-voltage converter op amp circuit. The photocurrent produced by the photodiode will be a linear function of the light intensity so that the resulting output voltage of this circuit will also be a linear function of the light intensity. The photodiode bias voltage could be set to zero, but a reverse bias voltage across the photodiode will have the advantage of reducing the junction capacitance and thereby decreasing the response time of this circuit.

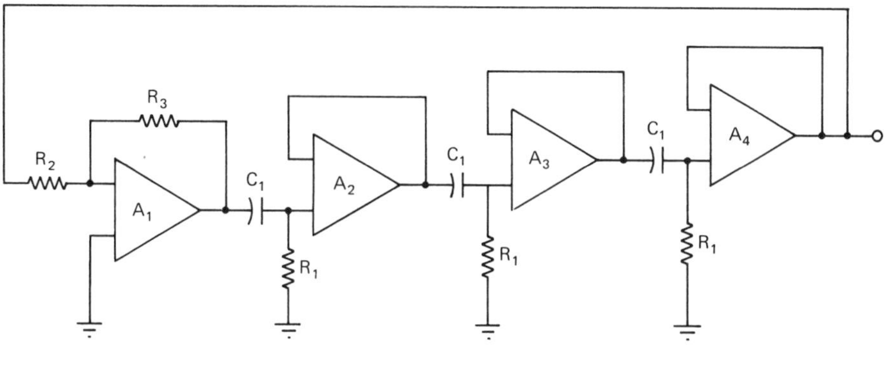

Figure 1.55 Phase-shift oscillator.

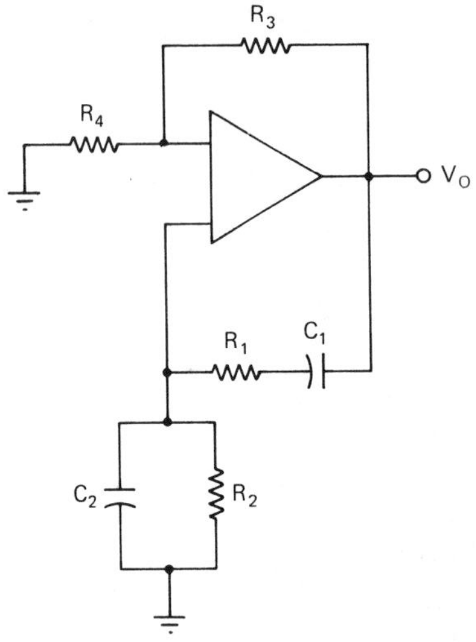

Figure 1.56 Wien bridge oscillator.

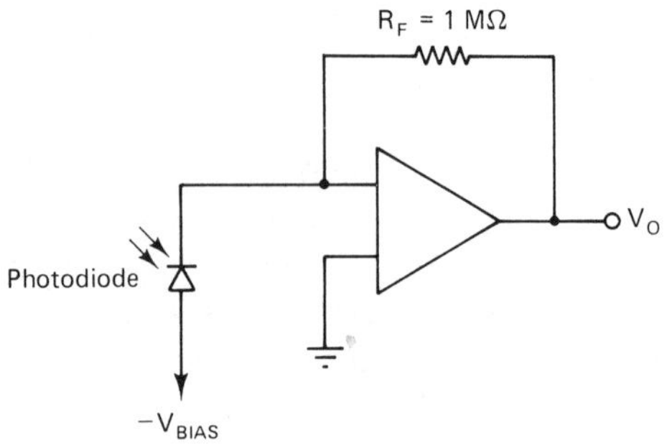

Figure 1.57 Optoelectronic sensor.

1.2 VOLTAGE COMPARATOR CIRCUIT APPLICATIONS

A number of circuits that represent applications of voltage comparators will now be presented. In these circuits an op-amp can be used in place of a voltage comparator, although better overall circuit performance will usually be obtained if a suitably chosen voltage comparator is used.

1. *Square-wave oscillator* (Figure 1.58): This simple circuit produces a square-wave output with a frequency given by $f_{osc} = 1/(2R_1C_1 \ln 3)$. The voltage across capacitor C_1 will be approximately a triangular waveform.
2. *Pulse generator* (Figure 1.59): This circuit produces an output voltage that

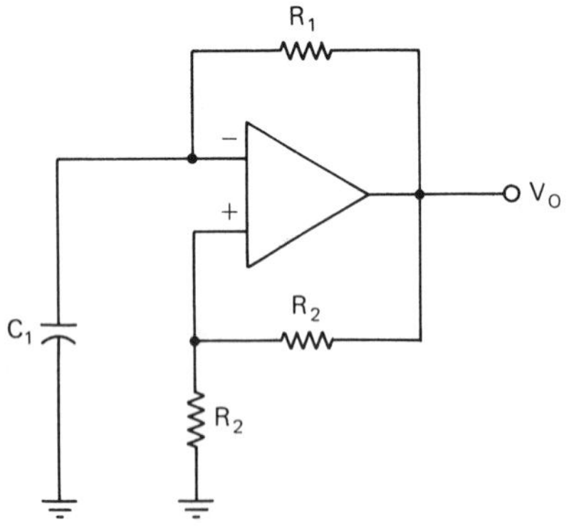

Figure 1.58 Square-wave oscillator.

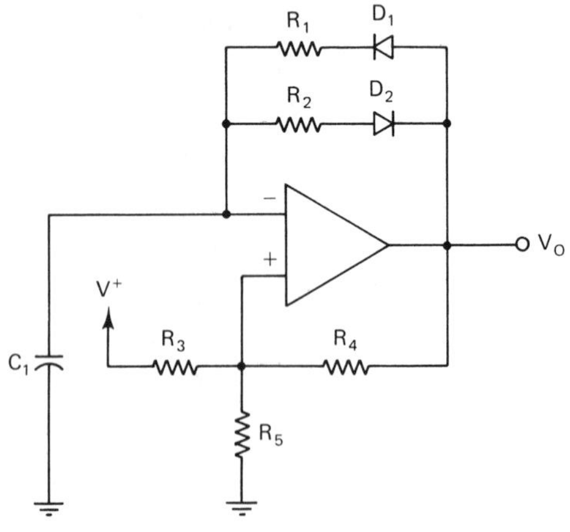

Figure 1.59 Pulse generator.

has a rectangular pulse waveform. The fraction of the period that the output voltage will be in the high state (i.e., the duty cycle) will be controlled by the ratio of R_1 to R_2 as given by duty cycle = $R_1/(R_1 + R_2)$.

3. *Time-delay generator* (Figure 1.60): The output voltage of comparator A_1 goes high when $V_S > V_{REF}$. This will cause capacitor C_1 to charge up toward the high-state output voltage of A_1 via resistor R_1. The threshold or trigger voltage levels of comparators A_2, A_3, and A_4 are set by voltage V^+ and the R_2–R_3–R_4–R_5 voltage divider. When the voltage across C_1 reaches, first, the reference voltage of A_4, the output voltage of this comparator will switch to the high state. Then, in turn, when the threshold voltage levels of A_3 and then A_2 are reached, the output voltage of these comparators will go to the high state. This therefore leads to three output pulses with leading edges that are delayed with respect to the input signal pulse V_S.
4. *Schmitt trigger* (Figure 1.61): This circuit has positive feedback from the output to the noninverting input terminal of the comparator (or operational amplifier) and will operate in the switching mode. The output voltage will have a high-to-low transition from V_{OH} to V_{OL} as the input voltage goes above the threshold level at $V_{S\,(H\text{-}L)} = V_{REF}(R_2/R_1 + R_2) + V_{OH}(R_1/R_1 + R_2)$. The low-to-high transition of the output voltage will occur as the input voltage drops below the threshold level at $V_{S\,(L\text{-}H)} = V_{REF}(R_2/R_1 + R_2) + V_{OL}(R_1/R_1 + R_2)$. The width of the resulting hysteresis loop will be $V_{S\,(H\text{-}L)} - V_{S\,(L\text{-}H)} = (V_{OH} - V_{OL})R_1/(R_1 + R_2)$.

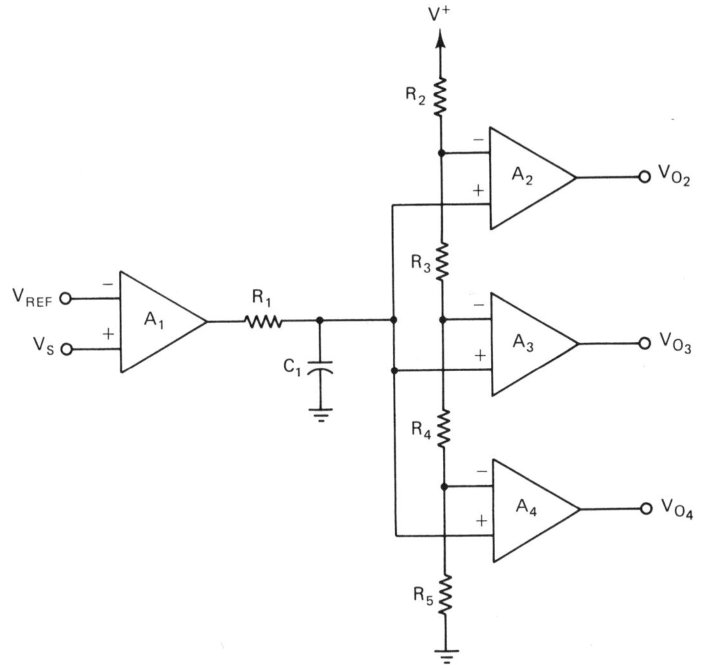

Figure 1.60 Time-delay generator.

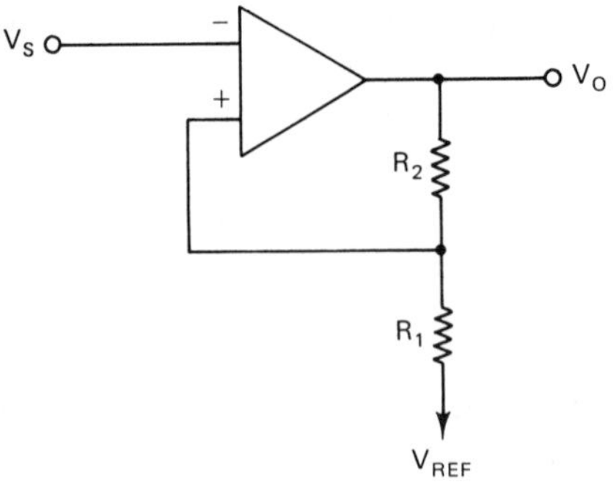

Figure 1.61 Schmitt trigger.

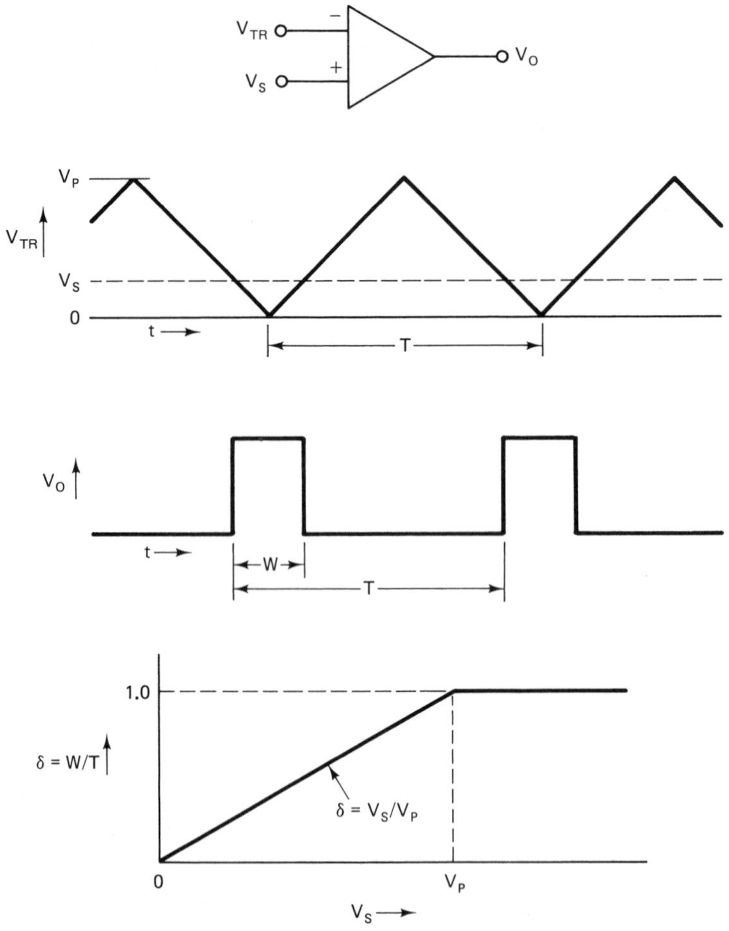

Figure 1.62 Pulse-width modulator.

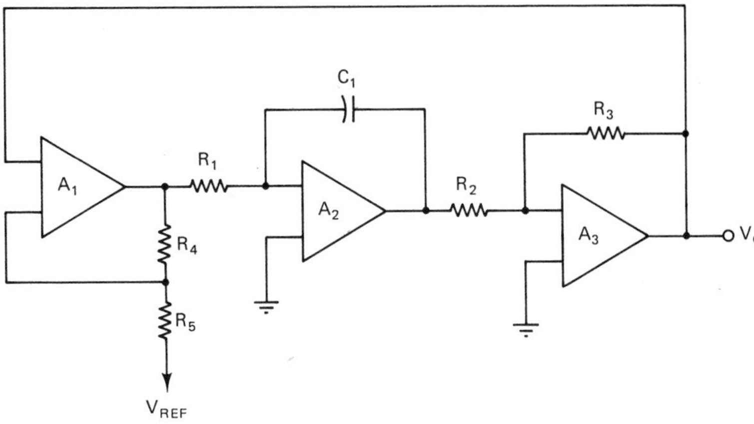

Figure 1.63 Precision linear-triangle wave generator.

5. *Pulse-width modulator* (Figure 1.62): This circuit uses a voltage comparator to compare the input or signal voltage V_S to a triangular waveform V_{TR} to produce a rectangular pulse output waveform V_O. The ratio of the pulse width W to the pulse period T (i.e., the duty cycle δ) will be directly proportional to the input signal V_S as given by duty cycle $= W/T = V_S/V_P$, where V_P is the peak value of the triangular waveform and for $0 < V_S < V_P$. For $V_S < 0$, $\delta = 0$, and for $V_S > V_P$, $\delta = 1.0$. This circuit is useful in many communications and control applications.
6. *Precision linear triangle wave generator* (Figure 1.63): This circuit produces a triangular waveform that has very straight sides. It consists of three basic elements, a Schmitt trigger using A_1 which can be either an operational amplifier or a voltage comparator, an integrator using A_2, and an inverting amplifier using A_3. It is the almost ideal integration characteristics of the integrator that is responsible for the high degree of linearity of the triangular waveform.

PROBLEMS

1.1. Verify the basic equations given in this chapter for the various op-amp circuits. Assume an ideal, infinite-gain op-amp.

1.2. Determine the effect of the following nonideal characteristics on the op-amp circuits given in this chapter.

- **(a)** Finite open-loop gain, A_{OL}
- **(b)** Input offset voltage, V_{OS}
- **(c)** Input bias current, I_B, and input offset current, I_{OS}
- **(d)** Limited frequency response, in terms of a finite unity-gain frequency, f_u, and a finite slewing rate, SR

1.3. Verify the basic equations given in this chapter for the various voltage comparator circuits. Assume an ideal, infinite-gain voltage comparator.

1.4. Evaluate the effect of the following voltage comparator characteristics on the operation of the voltage comparator circuits of this chapter.

(a) Response time (propagation delay time)

(b) Finite open-loop gain

(c) Input offset voltage

REFERENCES

BARNA, A., *Operational Amplifiers*, Wiley, 1971.

CONNELLY, J. A., *Analog Integrated Circuits*, Wiley, 1975.

FITCHEN, F., *Electronic Integrated Circuits and Systems*, Van Nostrand Reinhold, 1970.

GLASER, A. B., and G. E. SUBAK-SHARPE, *Integrated Circuit Engineering,* Addison-Wesley, 1977.

GRAEME, J. G., *Applications of Operational Amplifiers*, McGraw-Hill, 1973.

GRAY, P. R., and R. G. MEYER, *Analysis and Design of Analog Integrated Circuits*, Wiley, 1984.

GRINICH, V. H., and H. G. JACKSON, *Introduction to Integrated Circuits*, McGraw-Hill, 1975.

HAMILTON, D. J., and W. G. HOWARD, *Basic Integrated Circuit Engineering*, McGraw-Hill, 1975.

HNATEK, E. R., *Handbook of Integrated Circuits*, Wiley, 1973.

LENK, J. D., *Handbook of Integrated Circuits*, Reston, 1978.

LENK, J. D., *Manual for Integrated Circuit Users*, Reston, 1973.

MANASSE, F. K., *Semiconductor Electronics Design*, Prentice-Hall, 1977.

MILLMAN, J., *Microelectronics*, McGraw-Hill, 1979.

ROBERGE, J. K., *Operational Amplifiers*, Wiley, 1975.

SEDRA, A. S., and K. C. SMITH, *Microelectronic Circuits*, Holt, Rinehart and Winston, 1982.

SEIPPEL, R. G., *Operational Amplifiers*, Reston, 1983.

SOCLOF, S., *Analog Integrated Circuits*, Prentice-Hall, Inc., © 1985.

UNITED TECHNICAL PUBLICATIONS, *Modern Applications of Integrated Circuits*, Tab Books, 1974.

WAIT, J. V., *Introduction to Operational Amplifier Theory and Applications*, McGraw-Hill, 1975.

WONG, Y. J., and W. E. OTT, *Function Circuits*, McGraw-Hill, 1976.

Active Filters

BOWRON, P., *Active Filters for Communications and Instrumentation*, McGraw-Hill, 1979.

GARRETT, P. H., *Analog I/O Design*, Reston, 1981.

HAYKIN, S. S., *Synthesis of RC Active Filters*, McGraw-Hill, 1969.

HILBURN, J. L., and D. E. JOHNSON, *Manual of Active Filter Design*, McGraw-Hill, 1973.

Huelsman, L. P., and P. E. Allen, *Introduction to the Theory and Design of Active Filters*, McGraw-Hill, 1980.

Johnson, D. E., *Rapid, Practical Design of Active Filters*, Wiley, 1975.

Lam, H. Y.-F. *Analog and Digital Filters*, Prentice-Hall, 1979.

Tedeschi, F. P., *The Active Filter Handbook*, TAB Books, 1979.

Williams, A. B., *Active Filter Design*, Artech House, 1975.

Voltage Regulators

2

A voltage regulator is an electronic device that supplies a constant voltage to a circuit or load. The output voltage of the voltage regulator is regulated by the internal circuitry of the regulator to be relatively independent of the current drawn by the load, the supply or line voltage, and the ambient temperature. A voltage regulator may be part of some larger electronic circuit, but is often a separate unit or module, usually in the form of an integrated circuit.

A basic block diagram of a voltage regulator in its simplest form is shown in Figure 2.1. It is comprised of three basic parts:

1. A voltage reference circuit that produces a reference voltage that is independent of temperature and the supply voltage
2. An amplifier to compare the reference voltage with the fraction of the output voltage that is fed back from the voltage regulator output to the inverting input terminal of the amplifier
3. A series-pass transistor or combination of transistors to provide an adequate level of output current to the load being driven

The combination of the amplifier (often called an "error amplifier") and the series-pass transistors, together with the resistive voltage divider to tap off a portion of the output voltage, constitutes a feedback amplifier.

In the basic circuit of Figure 2.1 the closed-loop amplifier configuration acts to maintain the fraction of the output voltage fed back to the amplifier inverting input terminal equal to the reference voltage that is applied to the noninverting input terminal. As a result we have that

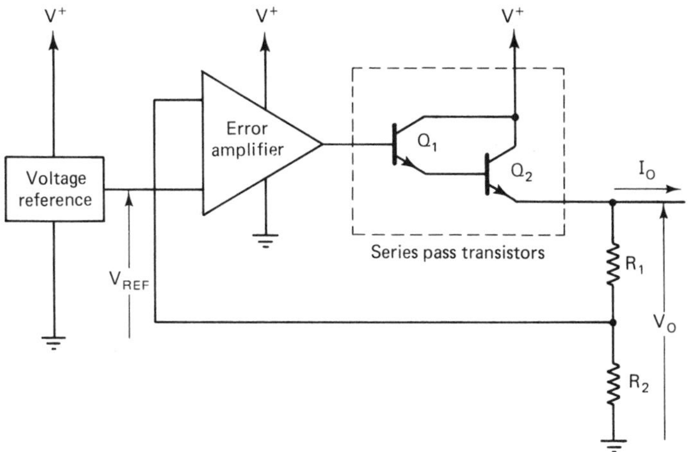

Figure 2.1 Voltage Regulator: basic block diagram.

$$V_O \frac{R_2}{R_1 + R_2} = V_{\mathbf{REF}}$$

so that

$$V_O = V_{\mathbf{REF}} \frac{R_1 + R_2}{R_2} = V_{\mathbf{REF}} \left(1 + \frac{R_1}{R_2}\right) \tag{2.1}$$

2.1 OUTPUT RESISTANCE AND LOAD REGULATION

The ideal voltage regulator would be similar to an ideal voltage source in that the output voltage would be completely independent of the output current, or equivalently of the load impedance. In an actual voltage regulator, as is the case with an actual voltage source, there will be some variation of the output voltage with load or output current. The rate of change of the output voltage with output current is defined as the output resistance as given by

$$\text{dynamic output resistance} = r_o = -\frac{\Delta V_O}{\Delta I_O} \tag{2.2}$$

The negative sign in the preceding expression is used because for the reference direction of I_O that has been chosen, an increase in I_O will lead to a decrease in V_O. Therefore, with the negative sign in front of $\Delta V_O/\Delta I_O$, the output resistance will turn out to be an algebraically positive quantity.

For a closed-loop amplifier the following relationship exists between the closed-loop output impedance and the open-loop output impedance:

$$z_{o(CL)} = z_{o(OL)} \frac{A_{CL}}{A_{OL}} \tag{2.3}$$

For the voltage regulator circuit shown in Figure 8.1, the amplifier input voltage is V_{REF} and the output voltage is V_O, so that the closed-loop voltage gain will be given by $A_{CL} = V_O/V_{REF}$. Note that the series pass transistors (the Darlington configuration) are within the feedback loop and so can be considered to be part of the amplifier. Since the voltage gain of the Darlington emitter-follower stage will be close to unity, the open-loop gain, A_{OL}, will be essentially that of the error amplifier.

The open-loop output resistance will be the dynamic resistance that is seen under open-loop conditions looking back into the voltage regulator circuit from the emitter of Q_2. This will consist of two parts. One is the dynamic resistance of the Darlington transistors, as seen looking into the emitter of Q_2 back toward the base of Q_1. This dynamic resistance will be $2V_T/I_{E_2} = 2V_T/I_O$.

Note that the dynamic resistance between the emitter and base of a single transistor, seen looking into the emitter, is V_T/I_E. Since the series pass output stage under consideration here is a Darlington compound transistor configuration in which there are two emitter–base junctions in series, V_T in the preceding expression is replaced by $2V_T$.

The second part of the open-loop output resistance will be the transformed value of the error amplifier output resistance, $r_{o\,(\text{amplifier})}$. The impedance transformation involved here is the result of the net current gain of the Darlington configuration from base to emitter, which is $(\beta_1 + 1)(\beta_2 + 1) \simeq \beta_1\beta_2$. The transformed value of the error amplifier output resistance will be $r_{o\,(\text{amplifier})}/(\beta_1\beta_2)$. Since the transistor current gains will be very large, generally of the order of 100, the product will be of the order of 10,000, so that the transformed value of the error amplifier output resistance will be very small indeed.

Combining the two resistance quantities, we now obtain for the open-loop output resistance the expression

$$r_{o\,(OL)} = \frac{2V_T}{I_O} + \frac{r_{o\,(\text{amplifier})}}{\beta_1\beta_2} \tag{2.4}$$

As a result of the large value of the beta product, the second term will generally be negligibly small so that we can write $r_{o\,(OL)} \simeq 2V_T/I_O$.

The closed-loop output resistance can now be written as

$$r_{o\,(CL)} = r_{o\,(OL)}\frac{A_{CL}}{A_{OL}} = \frac{(2V_T/I_O)(V_O/V_{REF})}{A_{OL}} \tag{2.5}$$

where A_{OL} is the gain of the error amplifier.

Since $r_{o\,(CL)} = -\Delta V_O/\Delta I_O$, we now can write

$$\frac{\Delta V_O}{\Delta I_O} = -\frac{(2V_T/I_O)(V_O/V_{REF})}{A_{OL}} \tag{2.6}$$

so that

$$\frac{\Delta V_O}{V_O} = -\frac{\Delta I_O}{I_O}\frac{2V_T}{V_{REF}}\frac{1}{A_{OL}} \tag{2.7}$$

Thus we now have a simple expression relating the fractional change in the voltage regulator output voltage to the fractional change in the output current. The *load regulation* is the change in the output voltage of a voltage regulator for a given change in the output current, generally from some no-load current condition to some specified full-load condition. Therefore, the equation above will give us some information relating to the voltage regulation, although it should be remembered that this equation will be valid only for relatively small fractional changes in the voltage and current.

If we assume a reference voltage of 1.28 V (i.e., a band-gap voltage reference), we have

$$\frac{\Delta V_O}{V_O} = \frac{-\Delta I_O}{I_O}\,\frac{50\text{ mV}}{1.28\text{ V}}\,\frac{1}{A_{OL}} = \frac{-\Delta I_O}{I_O}\,\frac{1}{26 A_{OL}} \tag{2.8}$$

Therefore, if $A_{OL} = 1000$, for example, we obtain

$$\frac{\Delta V_O}{V_O} = \frac{-\Delta I_O}{I_O} \times 3.85 \times 10^{-5} \tag{2.9}$$

Thus a 10% change in the output current of the regulator will result in only $3.85 \times 10^{-4}\%$ change in the output voltage. The load regulation for this regulator will thus be very good indeed. The corresponding value of output resistance will be given by

$$r_{O(CL)} = \frac{50\text{ mV}}{I_O}\,\frac{10/1.28}{1000} = \frac{3.9 \times 10^{-4}\text{V}}{I_O} \tag{2.10}$$

At an output current level of 100 mA, $r_{O(CL)}$ will be 3.9 mΩ, and for a current level of 1.0 A the closed-loop output resistance will be only 0.39 mΩ. These very low values of output resistance again attest to be the very good load regulation of this voltage regulator.

In looking at the expression for the regulator output resistance we see that as the output current decreases the output resistance increases, and for very small values of output current the load resistance can become unacceptably large. This can lead to a serious degradation of the load regulation characteristics of the voltage regulator. For this reason, in some voltage regulator circuits a means is provided to allow for a small output current to flow under no-load condition. To examine this in more detail we can rewrite the expression for the fractional change in the output voltage in differential form as

$$\frac{dV_O}{V_O} = -\frac{dI_O}{I_O}\,\frac{2V_T}{V_{\text{REF}}}\,\frac{1}{A_{OL}} \tag{2.11}$$

If we now integrate both sides of this expression we will obtain

$$\frac{V_{O(\text{FL})}}{V_{O(\text{NL})}} = \left(\frac{I_{O(\text{FL})}}{I_{O(\text{NL})}}\right)^{-(2V_T/A_{OL}V_{\text{REF}})} \tag{2.12}$$

Again using the values of $V_{\text{REF}} = 1.28$ V and $A_{OL} = 1000$, the exponent will be -3.9×10^{-5}. If the no-load current, $I_{O(\text{NL})}$, is chosen to be 1% of the full-load current, $I_{O(\text{FL})}$, we will have that

$$\frac{V_{O\,(FL)}}{V_{O\,(NL)}} = (100)^{-3.9\times 10^{-5}} = 0.99982 = 1 - 0.00018 \tag{2.13}$$

Thus the decrease in the output voltage in going from the no-load current of 1% of the full-load current, to the full-load current will be only 0.018%. Therefore, for many applications, a no-load current that is only 1% of the full-load value will still give acceptable load regulation results.

2.2 REGULATOR WITHIN A REGULATOR DESIGN

In the basic voltage regulator system we have seen that the output resistance is directly proportional to the closed-loop gain. If the closed-loop gain could be reduced to unity, the output resistance would be reduced to a minimum and the load regulation characteristics of the regulator can be improved.

A regulator configuration that achieves this objective is illustrated in Figure 2.2. This system is actually two regulators in one. The voltage reference, error amplifier A_1, and the R_1, R_2 resistance voltage divider constitute a voltage regulator that produces an output voltage given by $V_O = V_{REF}(1 + R_1/R_2)$. The output voltage of this regulator in turn serves as the input or reference voltage for the second regulator comprised of error amplifier A_2 and the series pass transistors. Note that this second voltage regulator has unity feedback, so that its closed-loop gain is unity.

The closed-loop output resistance of this voltage regulator will therefore be given by

$$r_{O\,(CL)} = \frac{2V_T/I_O}{A_{OL}} \tag{2.14}$$

where A_{OL} is the open-loop gain of the second error amplifier. The fractional change in the output voltage will be related to the fractional change in load current by

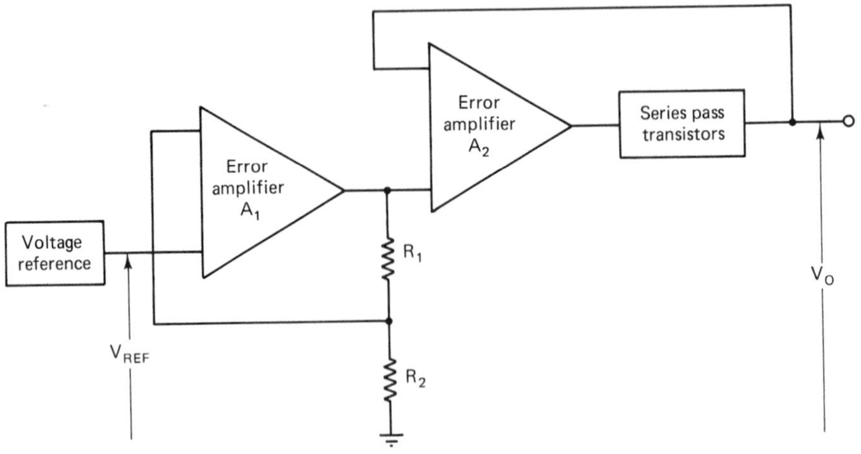

Figure 2.2 Voltage regulator using the regulator with a regulator design for improved load regulation.

$$\frac{\Delta V_O}{V_O} = -\frac{\Delta I_O}{I_o} \frac{2V_T/V_O}{A_{OL}} \tag{2.15}$$

Note that the "reference voltage" for the output regulator is V_O since it is operated in a unity-gain condition.

If we again take $A_{OL} = 1000$ for an example, and $V_O = 10$ V, we obtain

$$\frac{\Delta V_O}{V_O} = \frac{-\Delta I_O}{I_O} \frac{50 \text{ mV}/10 \text{ V}}{1000} = -\frac{\Delta I_O}{I_O} \times 5 \times 10^{-6} \tag{2.16}$$

Thus a 10% change in the load current will result in only a $5 \times 10^{-5}\%$ change in V_O, or only 5 μV, a very small change indeed.

To evaluate the change in the output voltage in going from some no-load current value to a full-load current, we have the relationship

$$\frac{V_{O(\text{FL})}}{V_{O(\text{NL})}} = \left(\frac{I_{O(\text{FL})}}{I_{O(\text{NL})}}\right)^{-(2V_T/A_{OL}V_O)} \tag{2.17}$$

For the example under consideration here, the exponent will have a value of 50 mV/(1000 $\times$ 10 V) $= 5 \times 10^{-6}$.

If we take as a no-load current a current equal to 1% of the full-load current, we obtain

$$\frac{V_{O(\text{FL})}}{V_{O(\text{NL})}} = (100)^{-5 \times 10^{-6}} = 0.99998 = 1 - (2.3 \times 10^{-5}) \tag{2.18}$$

so that the decrease in the regulator output voltage in going from the no-load condition to the full-load condition is only a very minute 0.0023%. This represents very good load regulation indeed.

2.3 VOLTAGE REGULATOR PROTECTION CIRCUITRY

In addition to the basic elements of the voltage regulator circuit that have thus far been discussed, most voltage regulators also incorporate circuitry to protect the voltage regulator from excessive power dissipation. This excessive power dissipation can lead to overheating and permanent damage. For most voltage regulators this internal protection circuit takes the form of a current-limiting circuit that senses the output current and acts to prevent the current from exceeding some preset safe limit.

2.3.1 Current Limiting

The power dissipated within the voltage regulator will be principally in the series-pass transistors, and mostly in the second transistor (Q_2) of the Darlington pair, which carries most of the current. The power dissipated in the voltage regulator will therefore be given approximately by $P_d = V_{CE_2} I_{C_2} = (V_{\text{IN}} - V_O)I_O$, wherein V_{IN} is the unregulated d-c supply voltage for the voltage regulator circuit (V^+).

The worst-case condition from the standpoint of power dissipation in the voltage regulator will occur when the output voltage is zero, for in this situation the entire d-c supply voltage will appear across Q_2 and therefore the power dissipation will be given by $P_d = V_{IN}I_O$. This worst-case situation may occur, for example, when there is an accidental short-circuit condition existing across the load.

From the standpoint of a conservative design philosophy, it would be wise to design the regulator such that it will be safe from damage even under a sustained short-circuited load condition. If the maximum allowable power dissipation of the voltage regulator is indicated as $P_{d\,(\max)}$, for short-circuit protection the protection circuitry should act to limit the current to a value given by $V_{IN}I_{CL} = P_{d\,(\max)}$, so that $I_{CL} = P_{d\,(\max)}/V_{IN}$, where I_{CL} is the value at which the output current is limited.

The circuit diagram of a simple current-limiting circuit is shown in Figure 2.3 together with the Darlington output stage of the regulator. The operation of this circuit is relatively simple. We will assume, however, that the current output of the error amplifier is limited to some maximum value by the circuit configuration of this amplifier. For a specific example let us assume that this maximum current that the amplifier can supply is 50 mA. Let us also assume that the maximum power dissipation limit of Q_2 is 50 W and that the supply voltage for the regulator will be no more than 20 V. Therefore, for short-circuit protection the value of I_{CL} should not exceed 50 W/20 V = 2.5 A. Let us assume that the two transistors that comprise the Darlington pair each have minimum current gains of 50, so that the overall current gain of the Darlington configuration will be 2500 (min).

If there were no current limiting, under short-circuit load conditions, the amplifier would be supplying its maximum available current output of 50 mA. This current, when multiplied by the overall current gain of the Darlington stage, would result in a current of at least 50 mA × 2500 = 125 A! This high current level would

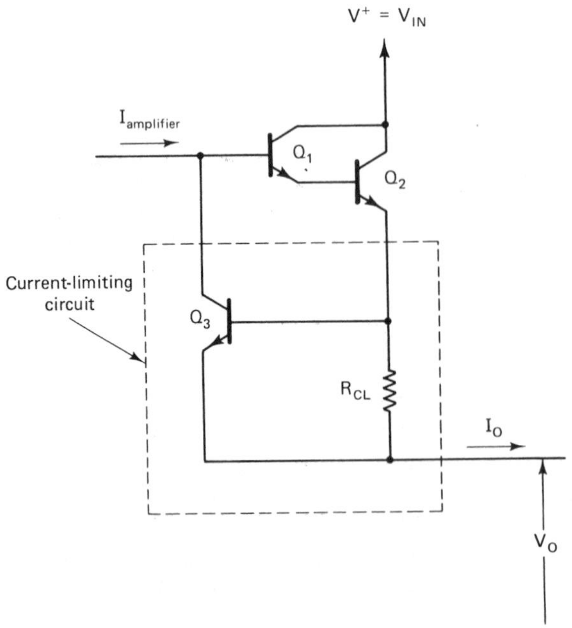

Figure 2.3 Current-limiting circuit.

most certainly irreparably damage the voltage regulator, so the use of current limiting is certainly indicated for this case.

At lower current levels such that the voltage drop across R_{CL} is less than about 500 mV, the base–emitter junction of Q_3 will be "off" and Q_3 will not shunt any base current away from Q_1. Indeed, the behavior of the circuit is essentially the same as if Q_3 were not present. At higher current levels, the voltage drop across R_{CL} is such that Q_3 starts to turn on, thereby bypassing some current from the base to Q_1 directly to the load through Q_3. Note that this bypassed current is not afforded the high current gain of the Darlington pair. Due to the action of the feedback loop, however, the output current of the amplifier will be increased to make up for the loss of the current shunted through Q_3, and thereby maintain the output voltage at its regulated value of V_O as the load current increases. Nevertheless, since the current shunted through Q_3 increases exponentially with the base-to-emitter voltage of Q_3, which is $I_O R_{CL}$, as the load current increases a point will soon be reached where the current shunted through Q_3 approaches the maximum current available from the amplifier. When this point is reached the base current of Q_1 can no longer increase, and as a result the output current reaches a limiting value known as I_{CL}.

To continue with the example, we have seen that for protection of this regulator circuit a current limit of 2.5 A is necessary. The base drive required at the base of Q_1 to supply this current is only 2.5 A/$\beta_1\beta_2$ = 2.5 A/2500 (min.) = 1.0 mA (max.). Since the amplifier is capable of supplying 50 mA, this means that in the current-limiting condition transistor Q_3 must be shunting almost 50 mA. If we assume that the base-to-emitter voltage of Q_3 is 650 mV at I_C = 1.0 mA, the V_{BE} at 50 mA will be given by V_{BE} = 650 mV + V_T ln 50 = 650 mV + 98 mV = 748 mV. Therefore, the voltage drop across R_{CL} should be 748 mV at I_O = I_{CL} = 2.5 A. The value of R_{CL} is therefore 748 mV/2.5 A = 0.30 Ω.

In Figure 2.4 the output characteristics of this voltage regulator is presented. These characteristics are for a regulated output voltage of 15 V. Load lines corresponding to several different load resistance values are shown. Note that for load resistances greater than 6.0 Ω the regulator will maintain the output voltage at 15 V. However, when the load resistance drops below 6.0 Ω, the regulator becomes current limited at I_{CL} = 2.5 A.

2.3.2 Foldback Current Limiting

In the voltage regulator circuit just considered, the current limit was set such that under the worst-case short-circuit conditions the power dissipation $V_{IN} I_{CL}$ = 20 V × 2.5 A = 50 W does not exceed the maximum power dissipation of the device. Note, however, that in the region where V_O is maintained at the regulated value of 15 V, the voltage drop across the output transistor (Q_2) will be only 5 V, so that under these conditions a maximum current of 50 W/5 V = 10 A could be allowed without exceeding the maximum power dissipation. As a result, we see that with the simple current limiting of the type considered the full potential of the voltage regulator is not utilized.

Since $P_D = (V_{IN} - V_O)I_O$, the output current limit that must be set to prevent the power dissipation from exceeding $P_{D(MAX)}$ will be given by

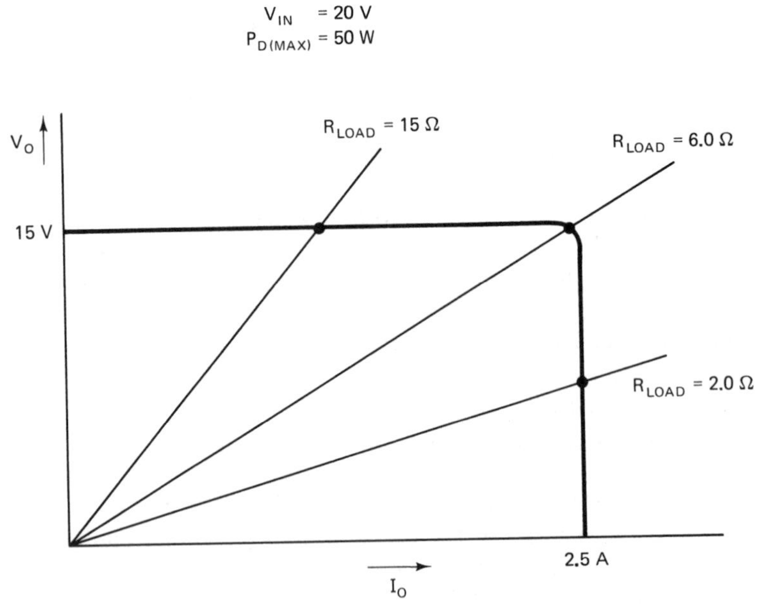

Figure 2.4 Output characteristics of a voltage regulator with simple current limiting.

$$I_{O(CL)} = \frac{P_{D(\text{MAX})}}{V_{\text{IN}} - V_O} \tag{2.19}$$

Therefore, to ensure full protection of the device, and at the same time to obtain the maximum output current possible under these conditions, a current-limiting characteristic of the type described by the equation above should be used. Note that the current limit is a function of the output voltage. As the output voltage decreases, the value of $I_{O(CL)}$ also decreases. This type of current-limiting characteristic is shown in Figure 2.5. This type of current limiting is called *foldback* current limiting, due to the shape of the regulator output characteristic curve.

For foldback current limiting the limiting circuitry must sense not only the output current but the output voltage as well. The simplest type of foldback current limiting is the linear foldback type, in which the decrease in $I_{O(CL)}$ is a linear function of V_o. This is the easiest type of foldback limiting to implement in circuit form and the characteristics of this type of current limiting are shown in Figure 2.6. The current limit when the output voltage is V_O is given by $I_{O(CL)} = P_{D(\text{MAX})}/(V_{\text{IN}} - V_O)$. For full regulator protection the regulator should not be allowed to operate in the region beyond the foldback limiting curve described by this equation. For the linear foldback case we must now determine the required short-circuit current limit.

Short-circuit current limit for linear foldback. Since $I_{O(CL)} = P_{D(\text{MAX})}/(V_{\text{IN}} - V_O)$ we have that $V_O = V_{\text{IN}} - (P_{D(\text{MAX})}/I_{O(CL)})$. The slope of the current limit curve will therefore be given by $dV_O/dI_{O(CL)} = P_{D(\text{MAX})}/(I_{O(CL)})^2$. The slope at $I_{O(CL)} = P_{D(\text{MAX})}/(V_{\text{IN}} - V_O)$ is therefore $(V_{\text{IN}} - V_O)^2/P_{D(\text{MAX})}$. The current axis intercept of the linear foldback line will therefore be at

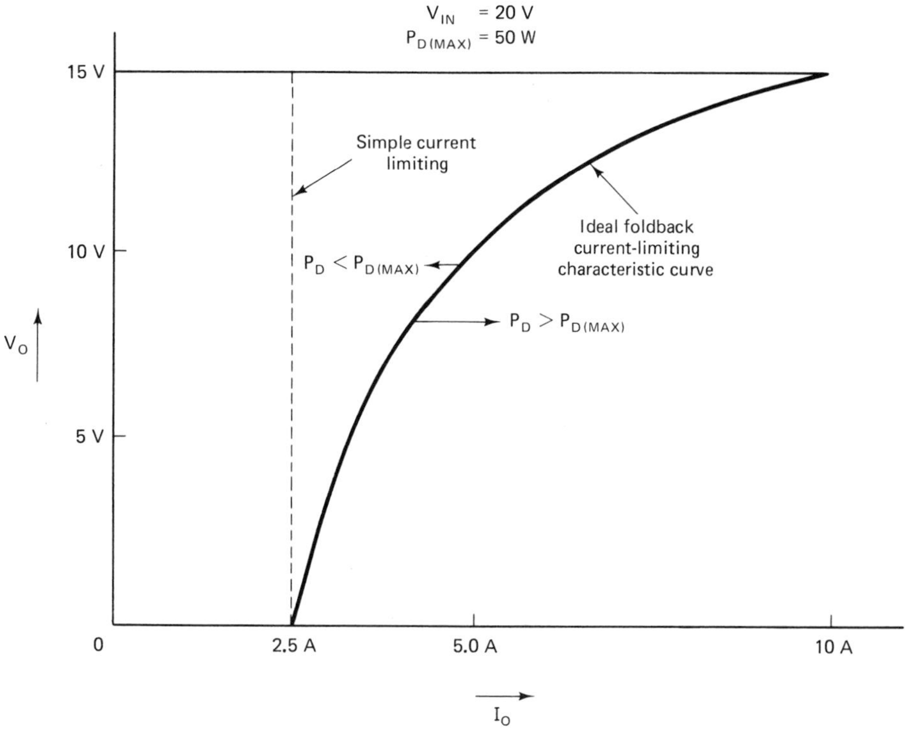

Figure 2.5 Foldback current limiting.

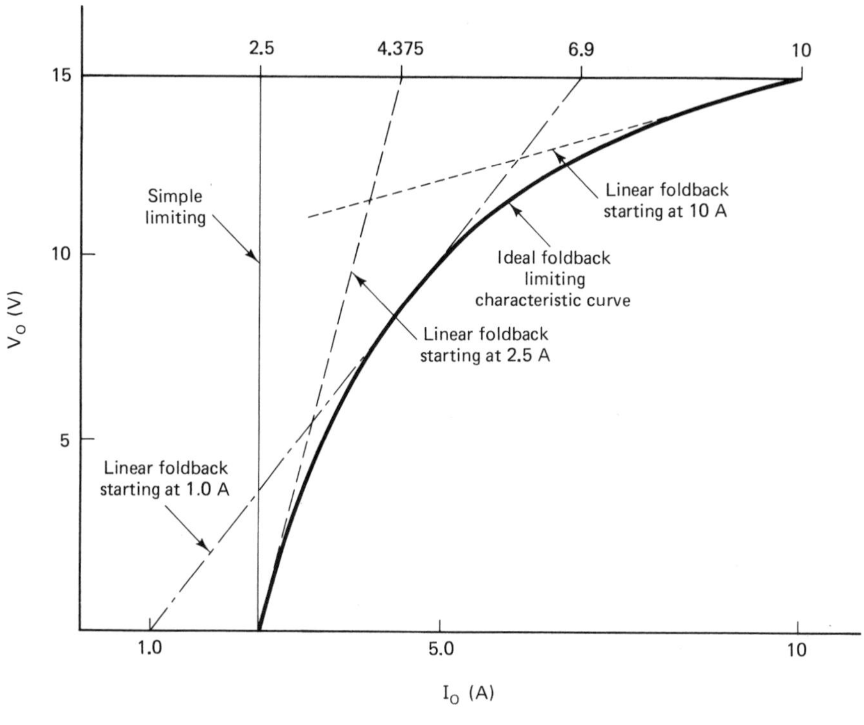

Figure 2.6 Foldback current-limiting characteristics: linear foldback.

$$I_{O(CL)}(V_O = 0) = \frac{P_{D(\text{MAX})}}{V_{\text{IN}} - V_O} - \frac{P_{D(\text{MAX})} V_O}{(V_{IN} - V_O)^2} \tag{2.20}$$

This last expression can be rewritten as

$$\begin{aligned} I_{O(CL)}(V_O = 0) &= \frac{P_{D(\text{MAX})}}{V_{\text{IN}} - V_O}\left(1 - \frac{V_O}{V_{\text{IN}} - V_O}\right) \\ &= \frac{P_{D(\text{MAX})}}{V_{\text{IN}} - V_O} \frac{V_{\text{IN}} - 2V_O}{V_{\text{IN}} - V_O} \end{aligned} \tag{2.21}$$

From this last equation we note that if the regulator supply voltage is not more than twice the output voltage, the required value for the short-circuit current limit is negative. Since this is not practical, for these cases a type of linear foldback that starts at a short-circuit current limit of $I_{O(CL)}(V_O = 0) = P_{D(\text{MAX})}/V_{\text{IN}}$ and then goes up in a straight line as shown in Figure 2.6 can be used.

Since the slope of the current-limiting characteristic curve is given by $(V_{\text{IN}} - V_O)^2/P_{D(\text{MAX})}$, the initial slope starting up from the current axis (i.e., $V_O = 0$) will be given by $V_{\text{IN}}^2/P_{D(\text{MAX})}$. Therefore, the current limit for linear foldback at V_O will be given by

$$I_{O(CL)}(V_O) = \frac{P_{D(\text{MAX})}}{V_{\text{IN}}} + V_O \frac{P_{D(\text{MAX})}}{V_{\text{IN}}^2} = \frac{P_{D(\text{MAX})}}{V_{\text{IN}}}\left(1 + \frac{V_O}{V_{\text{IN}}}\right) \tag{2.22}$$

As a result we see that for this type of current limiting the current limit when the output voltage is V_O will be $(1 + V_O/V_{\text{IN}})$ times the short-circuit value of current limit.

To return now to the values used in the preceding example, we have $V_{IN} =$ 20 V, $P_{D(\text{MAX})} = 50$ W, and a regulated output voltage of 15 V. For this case we see that we must choose the linear foldback that starts at the short-circuit current limit of 50 W/20 V = 2.5 A. The current limit will start at this value and increase linearly with voltage, and at the regulated output voltage level of 15 V, it will be 2.5 A (1 + 15/20) = 2.5 A × 1.75 = 4.375 A. Thus in this case with foldback current limiting, an output current that is almost twice the value that would be obtained with the simple current limiting can be obtained.

Looking at Figure 2.6, we note that if the linear foldback line begins at a short-circuit current that is less than $P_{D(\text{MAX}}/V_{\text{IN}} = 2.5$ A, then an even greater output current can be obtained in the voltage-regulated region where $V_O = 15$ V. For example, if the linear foldback starts at a current level of 1.0 A under short-circuit conditions, it can increase to 6.9 A at $V_O = 15$ V without exceeding the maximum power dissipation rating of the device. For this case an output current that is almost three times that which would be obtained with simple current limiting (2.5 A) can be obtained.

Linear current foldback circuit. An example of a linear curent foldback circuit is shown in Figure 2.7. The linear foldback characteristics of this circuit will be obtained by first obtaining an expression for the base-to-emitter voltage of Q_3, which will be

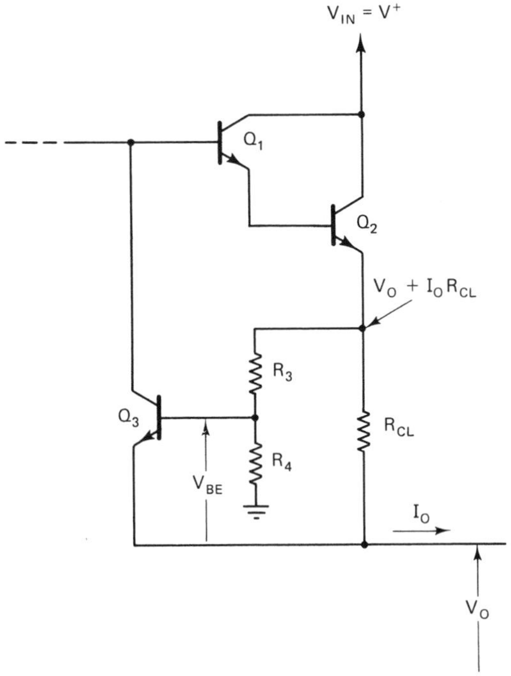

Figure 2.7 Linear foldback circuit.

$$V_{BE_3} = (V_O + I_O R_{CL})\frac{R_4}{R_4 + R_3} - V_O$$

$$= I_O \frac{R_{CL} R_4}{R_3 + R_4} - V_O\left(1 - \frac{R_4}{R_3 + R_4}\right) \tag{2.23}$$

$$= I_O \frac{R_{CL} R_4}{R_3 + R_4} - V_O \frac{R_3}{R_3 + R_4}$$

In this derivation the base current of Q_3 was assumed to be small compared to the current through R_3 and R_4. If we now solve for I_O we obtain

$$I_O = \frac{R_3 + R_4}{R_{CL} R_4}\left(V_{BE} + V_O \frac{R_3}{R_3 + R_4}\right) \tag{2.24}$$

Current limiting will occur when $V_{BE} = V_{BE(CL)}$, which is the value of the base-to-emitter voltage of Q_3 required to shunt a current approximately equal to the maximum output current of the amplifier. The value of $V_{BE(CL)}$ will generally be in the range 0.6 to 0.7 V. We will therefore have that

$$I_{O(CL)} = \frac{R_3 + R_4}{R_{CL} R_4} V_{BE(CL)} + V_O \frac{R_3}{R_{CL} R_4} \tag{2.25}$$

We see that this circuit will indeed produce linear foldback since $I_{O(CL)}$ increases linearly with V_O.

The short-circuit current limit $I_{O(CL)}$ (0), will be given by

$$I_{O(CL)}(0) = I_{O(CL)}(V_O = 0) = \frac{R_3 + R_4}{R_{CL}R_4} V_{BE(CL)} \tag{2.26}$$

The change in $I_{O(CL)}$ in going from $I_{O(CL)}$ (0) to $I_{O(CL)}$ at V_O will be given by

$$\Delta I_{O(CL)} = I_{O(CL)}(V_O) - I_{O(CL)}(0) = \frac{V_O R_3}{R_{CL}R_4} \tag{2.27}$$

Another useful design relationship is the ratio of $\Delta I_{O(CL)}$ to $I_{O(CL)}(0)$, which is

$$\frac{\Delta I_{O(CL)}}{I_{O(CL)}(0)} = \frac{V_O R_3}{(R_3 + R_4)V_{BE(CL)}} \tag{2.28}$$

Notice that R_{CL} cancels out of this relationship.

Design example. Let us consider the design of a linear foldback circuit to meet the following requirements based on the current and voltage values obtained from the previous discussion of linear foldback:

$$\begin{aligned} I_{O(CL)}(0) &= 1.0 \text{ A} \\ I_{O(CL)}(15 \text{ V}) &= 6.9 \text{ A} \end{aligned} \tag{2.29}$$

so we want to design the foldback circuit to limit the output current to a maximum of 6.9 A at the regulated output voltage of 15 V, but then as the voltage drops to zero the current limit will correspondingly drop to 1.0 A. We will assume that $V_{BE(CL)} = 0.6$ V. We will also choose a current of 50 mA through R_3 and R_4, so that the base current of Q_3 can be neglected.

For $R_3 + R_4$ we therefore will have $R_3 + R_4 \simeq 15$ V/50 mA = $\underline{300\ \Omega}$. We can now solve for R_3 using the following relationship

$$\frac{\Delta I_{O(CL)}}{I_{O(CL)}(0)} = \frac{6.9 - 1}{1} = \frac{V_O R_3}{(R_3 + R_4)V_{BE(CL)}} = \frac{15 \text{ V} \times R_3}{300\ \Omega \times 0.6 \text{ V}} \tag{2.30}$$

so that we obtain for R_3 the result

$$\begin{aligned} R_3 &= 5.9 \times 300\ \Omega \times 0.6 \text{ V}/15 \text{ V} \\ &= \underline{71\ \Omega} \end{aligned}$$

Therefore, $R_4 = 300 - 72 = \underline{229\ \Omega}$.
For R_{CL} we can now use the equation for $I_{O(CL)}(0)$ as

$$I_{O(CL)}(0) = 1.0 \text{ A} = \frac{R_3 + R_4}{R_{CL}R_4} V_{BE(CL)} = \frac{300}{R_{CL}229} \times 0.6 \text{ V} \tag{2.31}$$

so that $R_{CL} = \underline{0.79\ \Omega}$. If we now substitute these resistance values back into the equation for $I_{O(CL)}$, we obtain

$$I_{O(CL)} = 1.0 + (0.393\, V_O) \qquad \text{A} \tag{2.32}$$

Thus we can verify that with the resistance values chosen the current limit will be 1.0 A under short-circuit conditions and 6.9 A when V_O is 15 V.

We can verify that this foldback circuit will indeed protect the voltage regulator

TABLE 2.1 POWER DISSIPATION VALUES ($V_{IN} = 20$ V)

V_O (V)	$I_{O(CL)}$ (A)	P_D (W)
0	1.0	20
1.0	1.39	26.5
2.0	1.79	32.2
3.0	2.12	37.1
4.0	2.57	41.2
5.0	2.97	44.5
6.0	3.36	47.0
7.0	3.75	48.8
8.0	4.15	49.8
9.0	4.54	49.9
10.0	4.93	49.3
11.0	5.33	47.9
12.0	5.72	45.8
13.0	6.11	42.8
14.0	6.51	39.0
15.0	6.90	34.5

from excessive power dissipation by looking at the power dissipation values given in Table 2.1.

Linear foldback in which I_{CL} is a function of $V_{IN} - V_O$. The power dissipation in the voltage regulator circuit will be given by $P_D = V_{IN}I_Q + (V_{IN} - V_O)I_O$, where I_Q is the quiescent current of the regulator, generally only a few milliamperes. Since I_Q will be so very much smaller than I_O in the region where we are concerned about the power dissipation limitation, the equation for P_D can be written approximately as $P_D = (V_{IN} - V_O)I_O$. To look at it in a slightly different way, the power dissipation due to I_Q will be of the order of 5 mA $\times$ 20 V = 100 mW, so as long as the maximum power dissipation is much greater than this, we can neglect the quiescent power dissipation, $V_{IN}I_Q$, of the voltage regulator.

Since the power dissipation in the regulator will be essentially proportional to $V_{IN} - V_O$, the input–output voltage differential, the foldback current limit should be related to this voltage difference rather than on just V_O, for the greatest flexibility. For the foldback current limiting of the preceding example, the design should be based on the maximum allowable value of the input voltage, V_{IN}. If foldback current limiting based on a current limit set by $V_{IN} - V_O$, a greater maximum output current can be allowed when the input voltage is less than the maximum rated value.

An example of a linear foldback circuit in which the current limit is directly related to the input–output voltage differential is shown in Figure 2.8. Transistors Q_1 and Q_2 constitute the Darlington emitter-follower series pass output circuit, and Q_3 is the current limit transistor. The base-to-emitter voltage of Q_3, assuming the base current to be small compared to the current through R_3 and R_4, will be given by

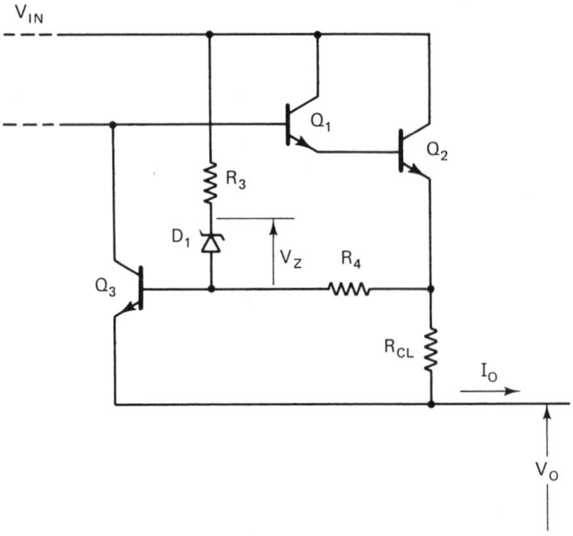

Figure 2.8 Foldback current limiting that is dependent on $V_{\text{IN}} - V_O$.

$$V_{BE_3} = I_O R_{CL} + \frac{(V_{\text{IN}} - V_Z - I_O R_{CL} - V_O) R_4}{R_3 + R_4} \tag{2.33}$$

After rearrangement we obtain

$$V_{BE_3} = \frac{I_O R_{CL} R_3}{R_3 + R_4} + \frac{[(V_{\text{IN}} - V_O) - V_Z] R_4}{R_3 + R_4} \tag{2.34}$$

Current limiting will occur when the base-to-emitter voltage of Q_3 is high enough to cause Q_3 to shunt the base drive away from the Q_1, Q_2 Darlington pair. Designating this voltage as $V_{BE(CL)}$ (generally around 0.6 to 0.7 V) and the corresponding current-limited output current as $I_{O(CL)}$, we have after rearrangement of the equation above the result that

$$I_{O(CL)} = V_{BE(CL)} \frac{R_3 + R_4}{R_3 R_{CL}} - [(V_{\text{IN}} - V_O) - V_Z] \frac{R_4}{R_3 R_{CL}} \tag{2.35}$$

From this last equation we see that $I_{O(CL)}$ will indeed be a function of the input–output voltage differential, and that as this voltage differential increases, the current limit will decrease.

To consider a design example of this type of foldback circuit, we will choose a short-circuit current limit of 1.0 A, which increases to 6.0 A at $V_{\text{IN}} - V_O = 6.0$ V. The input voltage will be 20 V and we will choose $R_3 + R_4 = 400\ \Omega$. We will assume a Vz of 6.0 volts. Upon substitution into the equation for $I_{O(CL)}$ we obtain the following resistance values:

$$\begin{aligned} R_4 &= 14.3\ \Omega \\ R_4 &= 385.7\ \Omega \\ R_{CL} &= 0.104\ \Omega \end{aligned} \tag{2.36}$$

Substitution of these resistance values back into the equation for $I_{O(CL)}$ gives

$$I_{O(CL)} = 6.0\ \text{A} - [(V_{\text{IN}} - V_O) - 6\ \text{V}]0.357 \tag{2.37}$$

At this point it should be noted that the equations above are valid only for the case in which $V_{IN} - V_O > V_Z$. If the input–output differential is less than this, the zener diode, D_1, will be off (i.e., reversed biased, but not in the breakdown region). For this case the current through R_4 will be negligible and we will have that $V_{BE_3} = I_O R_{CL}$, so that the current-limiting condition becomes simply $I_{O(CL)} = V_{BE(CL)}/R_{CL}$, current limiting. For the example above, the simple current-limiting case occurs for input–output voltage differentials of 6.0 V, or less, for which case the value of $I_{O(CL)}$ will be constant at 6.0 A.

A graph of the voltage regulator characteristics for the example under consideration is shown in Figure 2.9. At various points along the current-limit line, values of the output voltage, output current, and power dissipation are given. Note that all of the power dissipation values lie safely below the $P_{D(\text{MAX})}$ of 50 W. If just simple current limiting were to be used instead, a current limit of only 50 W/20 V = 2.5 A would have to be established.

The constant-current region that occurs for input–output differentials of less than V_Z (6 V) is useful in many cases to prevent excessive current that could damage the circuit due to such effects as electromigration of the metal-to-silicon contacts.

For a voltage regulator to operate properly a minimum value of the input–output voltage differential is required, typically around 2 V. Therefore, for this voltage regulator, operation above around 18 V is not possible, as indicated by the shaded portion of the regulator characteristics.

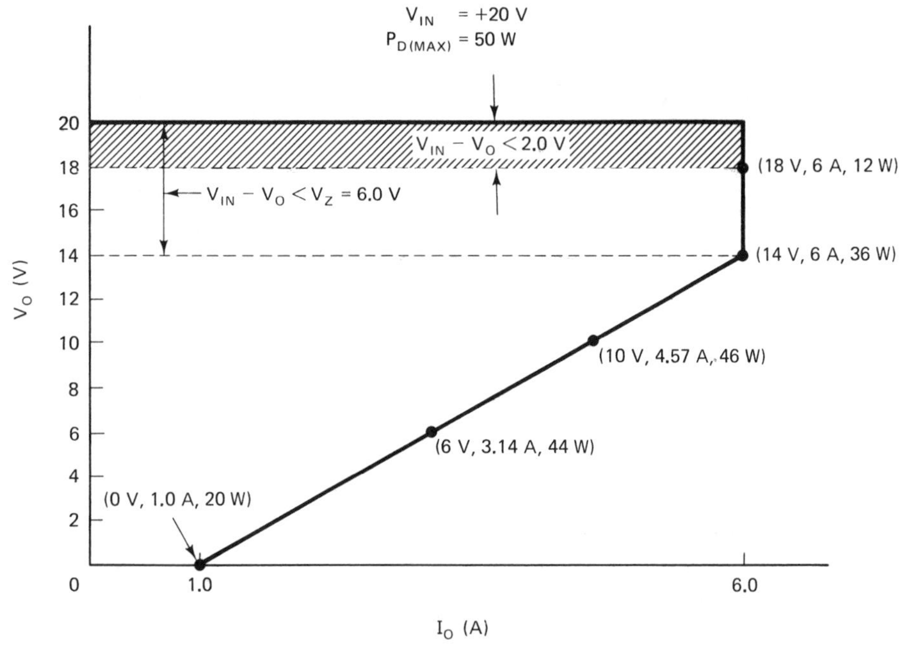

Figure 2.9 Foldback current-limiting characteristics.

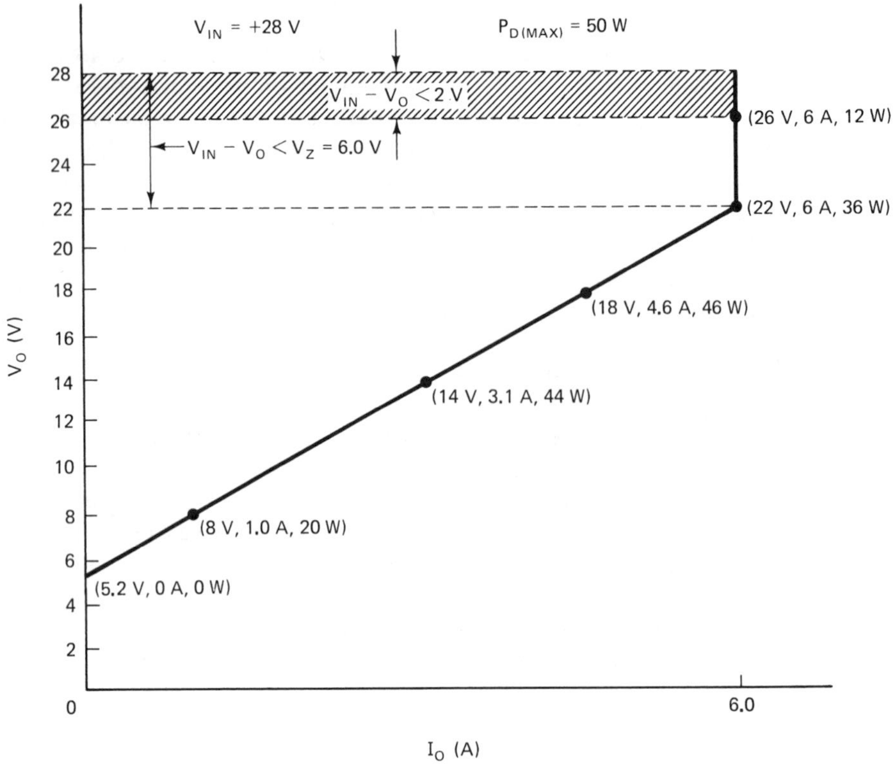

Figure 2.10 Foldback current-limiting characteristics.

In Figure 2.10 the output characteristics of the same voltage regulator circuit are shown again, except for the case in which the input voltage has been increased to 28 V. The same current-limiting circuit is that used for the preceding case with the same resistance values. Again note that at various points along the current-limit line, values of output voltage, output current, and the power dissipation are given. We see that in spite of the fact that the input voltage had been raised to 28 V, the power dissipation values are still safely below the maximum power dissipation rating of 50 W. This illustrates the versatility of this type of foldback current-limiting circuit. We may also note that if simple current limiting were to be used here, the current limit would have to be set at only 50 W/28 V = 1.8A.

2.4 THERMAL SHUTDOWN

In many IC voltage regulators and power amplifiers a *thermal shutdown circuit* is incorporated on the IC chip. The thermal shutdown circuit senses the chip temperature, and when this temperature exceeds some predetermined design limit, the circuit acts to shut down the device. Thus the thermal shutdown circuit is an additional protective circuit in addition to the current-limiting circuitry.

The basic circuitry of a thermal shutdown circuit is shown in Figure 2.11.

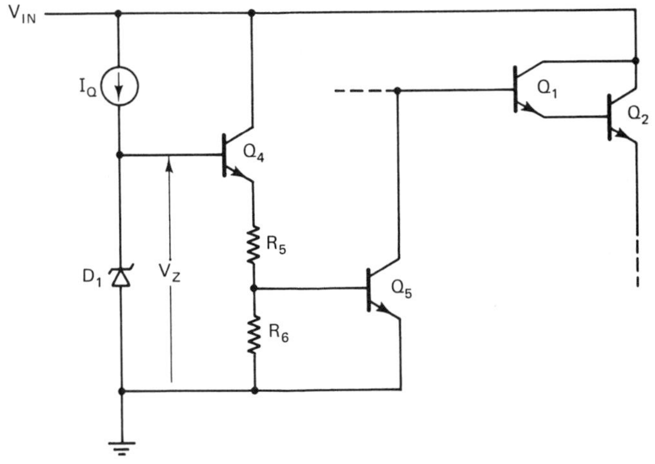

Figure 2.11 Thermal shutdown circuit.

Transistors Q_1 and Q_2 constitute the Darlington emitter-follower series pass output stage. Diode D_1 (actually a diode-connected transistor) is operated as a zener diode and biased into the reverse-bias breakdown region by current source Q_1. The voltage drop across this diode, V_Z, produce a bias voltage for transistors Q_4 and Q_5. The V_Z value for an IC zener diode is typically around 6.5 V, corresponding to the emitter–base junction breakdown voltage of the diode-connected transistor. The resistance ratio of R_6 and R_5 is such that at room temperature the base-to-emitter voltage of Q_5 is not large enough to bias Q_5 into conduction. However, as the temperature increases, the voltage across the zener diode increases due to the positive temperature coefficient of the zener voltage. At the same time, due to the negative temperature coefficient of the transistor base-to-emitter voltage, the voltage required to bias Q_5 into conduction decreases. Ultimately, a temperature will be reached at which Q_5 will be in full conduction such that it bypasses the base drive of the Darlington output stage (Q_1 and Q_2), thus preventing any further rise in temperature.

We will now obtain the basic design equations for this thermal shutdown circuit. For this analysis we will assume that the base current of Q_5 is small compared to the current through R_5 and R_6, such that R_5 and R_6 can be considered to act as a simple resistive voltage divider. As a result we will have that

$$V_{BE_5} = \frac{R_6}{R_5 + R_6}(V_Z - V_{BE_4}) \tag{2.38}$$

Rearranging this equation yields

$$V_Z = V_{BE_4} + \frac{R_5 + R_6}{R_6} V_{BE_5} = V_{BE_4} + \left(1 + \frac{R_5}{R_6}\right) V_{BE_5} \tag{2.39}$$

We must now consider the temperature dependence of V_Z and V_{BE}. Over the limited range of temperatures that we are interested in we can assume that both V_Z and V_{BE} will vary linearly with temperature as a good approximation. We can therefore write

$$V_Z(T) = V_Z + \frac{dV_Z}{dT}(T - T_R)$$
$$V_{BE}(T) = V_{BE} + \frac{dV_{BE}}{dt}(T - T_R) \tag{2.40}$$

where T_R is a reference temperature (generally 25°C) and V_Z and V_{BE} represent the values of these quantities at $T = T_R$. If we let $\Delta T = T - T_R$, we can now write

$$V_Z + \frac{dV_z}{dT}\Delta T = V_{BE_4} + \left(1 + \frac{R_5}{R_6}\right) V_{BE_5} + \left(2 + \frac{R_5}{R_6}\right)\frac{dV_{BE}}{dT}\Delta T$$
$$= V_{BE_4} + V_{BE_5} + 2\left(\frac{dV_{BE}}{dT}\right)\Delta T + \frac{R_5}{R_6}\left[\left(V_{BE_5} + \frac{dV_{BE}}{dT}\Delta T\right)\right] \tag{2.41}$$

We will now consider a design example. We will assume that $V_Z = 6.5$ V and $dV_Z/dT = +3.0$ mV/°C. For V_{BE} a temperature coefficient of -2.1 mV/°C will be used. We will assume that at $T = 25$°C, $V_{BE} = 650$ mA at $I_C = 10$ mA for Q_4 and Q_5. A quiescent current of 10 mA for Q_4 will be chosen. The maximum current available from the error amplifier will be 50 mA. The thermal shutdown circuit will be designed for complete shutdown of the regulator output when the temperature reaches 175°C, so that $\Delta T = 150$°C. At 50 mA, we will have that $V_{BE_5} = 690$ mV.

If we now substitute into the equation above we obtain

$$6.5 + (0.003 \times 150) = 0.650 + 0.690 + 2(-0.0021 \times 150) + \frac{R_5}{R_6}(0.690 - 0.0021 \times 150) \tag{2.42}$$

so that

$$6.95 = 1.34 - 0.630 + \frac{R_5}{R_6}(0.690 - 0.315)$$
$$6.95 = 0.710 + \frac{R_5}{R_6}(0.375) \tag{2.43}$$

Solving for R_5/R_6, we obtain

$$\frac{R_5}{R_6} = \frac{6.24}{0.375} = \underline{16.64} \tag{2.44}$$

The voltage across the resistive voltage divider, $R_5 + R_6$, will be $V_Z - V_{BE_4} = 6.5 - 0.65 = 5.85$ V. Since the current through R_5 and R_6 has been specified as 10 mA, we have that $R_5 + R_6 = 585\ \Omega$. Using the resistance ratio of $R_5/R_6 = 16.64$, we have that

$$1 + \frac{R_5}{R_6} = \frac{R_5 + R_6}{R_6} = \frac{585}{R_6} = 17.64 \tag{2.45}$$

so that $R_6 = 33\ \Omega$ and thus $R_5 = 585 - 33 = 552\ \Omega$.

To illustrate the sharpness of the thermal limiting characteristics we will now determine the temperature at which Q_5 shunts one-half of the base drive of Q_1 and then the temperature at which one-tenth of the base drive is shunted, the latter condition being considered as the threshold of the thermal limiting. We will first rewrite the basic equation for thermal limiting in the form

$$\Delta T = \frac{V_{BE_4} + V_{BE_5}(1 + R_5/R_6) - V_Z}{dV_Z/dt - (2 + R_5/R_6)\, dV_{BE}/dT} \tag{2.46}$$

For the condition of Q_5 shunting one-half of the base drive, the current through Q_5 will be 25 mA. The base-to-emitter voltage of Q_5 for this current at 25°C will be 690 − 17 = 673 mV. If we now substitute into the equation above, we obtain

$$\Delta T = \frac{0.650 + 0.673(17.64) - 6.5}{0.04214} = 143°\text{C} \tag{2.47}$$

so that the temperature at which "one-half shutdown" occurs will be 168°C.

For the one-tenth shutdown condition, the value of V_{BE} at which Q_5 carries 5 mA will be 632 mV at 25°C. The corresponding value of ΔT will be given by

$$\Delta T = \frac{0.650 + 0.632(17.64) - 6.5}{0.04214} = 126°\text{C} \tag{2.48}$$

so that the temperature at which one-tenth shutdown occurs will be 151°C. Thus we see that the thermal shutdown is initiated and comes to full completion over a rather narrow temperature span. This is a result of the exponential relationship between the transistor collector current and the base-to-emitter voltage.

2.5 ADJUSTABLE POSITIVE VOLTAGE REGULATOR EXAMPLE

In Figure 2.12 the circuit diagram of an adjustable positive voltage regulator is shown. This voltage regulator circuit is similar to that of the LM 376 and the LM 105/205/305/305A (National Semiconductor) series of voltage regulators. In Figure 2.12 the various functional blocks of this voltage regulator have been delineated and identified.

The current source portion of the circuit is comprised of transistors Q_6, Q_7, and Q_{13}. Transistor Q_{13} is a diode-connected field-effect transistor (JFET) and operates as a current regulator diode. For a JFET with $V_{GS} = 0$ and a drain-to-source voltage V_{DS} greater than the pinch-off voltage V_p, the drain current I_{DS} will essentially saturate at a value designated as I_{DSS}. The value of I_{DSS} is determined by the construction of the JFET, but will vary slightly with V_{DS}.

In Figure 2.13a the terminal characteristics, I_{DS} versus V_{DS}, of a JFET used as a current regulator diode are presented. Note that for values of V_{DS} above the pinch-off voltage, V_p, the drain current becomes relatively independent of V_{DS}, up to the breakdown voltage BV_{DSS}, so that the voltage compliance range can be said to extend from V_p to BV_{DSS}. The value of V_p is generally in the range 3 to 30 V,

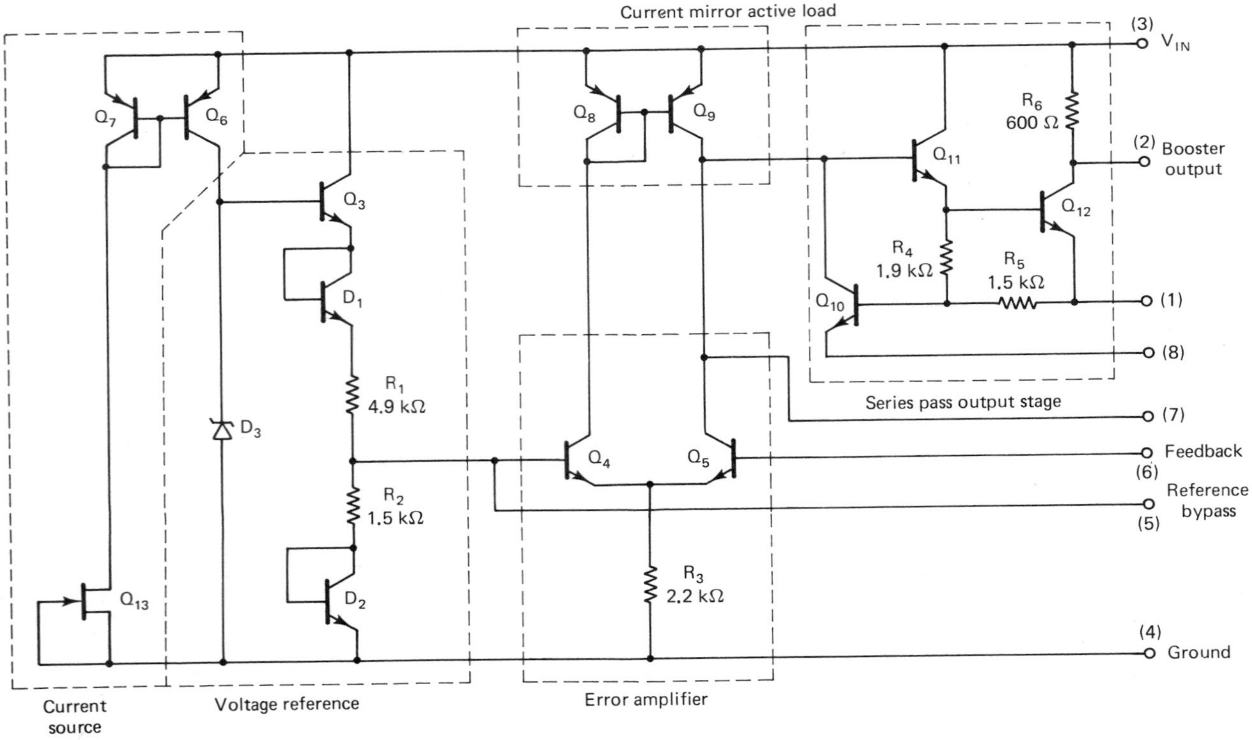

Figure 2.12 Circuit diagram of an adjustable positive voltage regulator. (LM 105 National Semiconductor).

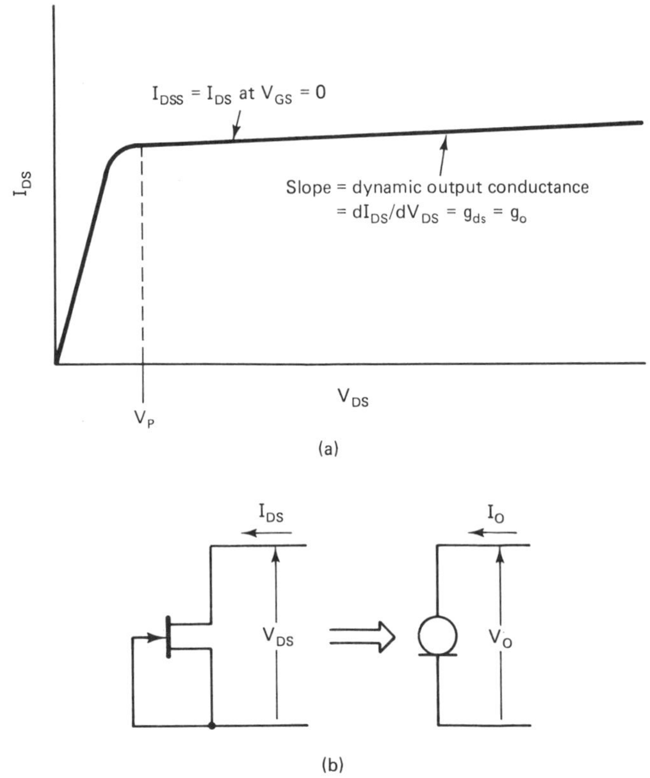

Figure 2.13 Diode-connected field-effect transistor as a current regulator diode: (a) output characteristics of diode-connected JFET; (b) diode-connected JFET and schematic symbol for current regulator diode.

with values of around 6 to 10 V being typical. The breakdown voltages will generally be in the range 30 to 300 V with most devices being in the range 50 to 100 V.

The slope of the current regulator diode characteristics within the compliance range is the dynamic output conductance as given by $g_o = g_{ds} = dI_{DS}/dV_{DS}$. The reciprocal quantity is the dynamic output resistance as given by $r_o = r_{ds} = 1/g_o = dV_{DS}/dI_{DS}$. The value of r_{ds} will generally be approximately inversely proportional to current level, and will typically be in the range 100 kΩ to 1.0 MΩ at a current of $I_{DSS} = 1.0$ mA. In Figure 2.13b a schematic representation of the current diode is shown.

The current through Q_{13} produces an approximately equal current through Q_6 by action of the Q_6–Q_7 current mirror. This in turn provides a bias current for the zener diode, D_3, which in reality is a reverse-biased diode-connected transistor with the zener voltage being the emitter–base breakdown voltage. The action of the current source circuit is to produce a current through D_3 that is relatively independent of the input voltage V_{IN}. This will, in turn, keep the voltage drop across the zener diode relatively constant and almost completely independent of the supply voltage. For example, if the zener impedance is 10 Ω and the dynamic output resistance of the current regulator diode is 100 kΩ, the rate of change of V_Z with V_{IN} will be given by

$$\frac{dV_Z}{dV_{IN}} = \frac{dV_Z}{dI_Z}\frac{dI_Z}{dI_{13}}\frac{dI_{13}}{dV_{IN}} = Z_z \times 1 \times \frac{1}{r_o} \tag{2.49}$$

$$= 10\ \Omega \times (1/100\text{k}\Omega) = 1 \times 10^{-4}$$

Therefore, a 1.0-V change in the input voltage will change the zener voltage drop by only 1×10^{-4} V = 0.1 mV. If the regulator output voltage is V_O = 12 V, the corresponding change in V_O will be approximately 0.1 mV(V_O/V_Z) = 0.2 mV. Thus the output voltage is well insulated from changes in the input or line voltage, so that this regulator should exhibit very good line-regulation characteristics.

The voltage reference circuit consists of transistors Q_1, D_1, D_2, and D_3. Thisis a temperature-compensated voltage reference in which the negative temperature coefficient of the base-to-emitter voltage drop of the diode-connected transistors, D_1, D_2, and D_3 is used to compensate for the positive temperature coefficient of the zener diode, D_3. The reference voltage that is produced at the junction of R_1 and R_2 will be approximately 1.8 V. This reference voltage is internally connected to the base of Q_4, which is part of the error amplifier. There is also an external pin tied to this point (pin 5) labeled "reference bypass." This can be used for several purposes. A capacitor can be connected between pins 5 and 4 (ground) to bypass noise that is present at the output of the voltage reference circuit. This noise is produced principally in the zener diode as a result of statistical fluctuations in the avalanche multiplication process. The bypass capacitor can also help to bypass ripple and other fluctuations that may come through the reference circuit from the input voltage. Another use of pin 5 is in switching regulators, in which case a switching waveform can be fed directly into the error amplifier.

The error amplifier is a differential amplifier consisting of transistors Q_4 and Q_5. The biasing is provided by resistor R_3. Transistors Q_8 and Q_9 serve as a current mirror active load for the differential amplifier. The quiescent current of the differential amplifier, I_Q, is determined by R_3 and the voltage drop across R_3, which is $V_{REF} - V_{BE}$. For V_{REF} = 1.8 and V_{BE} = 0.7 this becomes $I_Q = I_{R3}$ = (1.8 − 0.7)V/2.2 kΩ = 1.1 V/2.2 kΩ = 0.5 mA.

The base of Q_4 is the noninverting input of the amplifier and it is to this point that the reference voltage is applied. The base of Q_5 is the inverting input and the feedback voltage that is obtained from a resistive voltage divider across the output is fed to this point via pin 6.

The series-pass output stage consists of transistors Q_{11} and Q_{12} connected as a Darlington emitter-follower configuration. Transistor Q_{10} is used to provide current limiting in conjunction with an externally connected resistor R_{CL}, as shown in Figure 2.14.

In Figure 2.14a the basic external connections for this voltage regulator are shown. Note that output voltage of this regulator can be adjusted to the desired value by suitable choice the ratio of R_2 to R_1. The output voltage will be given by $V_{REF} = V_O R_2/(R_1 + R_2)$, so that $V_O = V_{REF}(1 + R_1/R_2)$. The minimum value of V_O will thus be V_{REF} = 1.8 V.

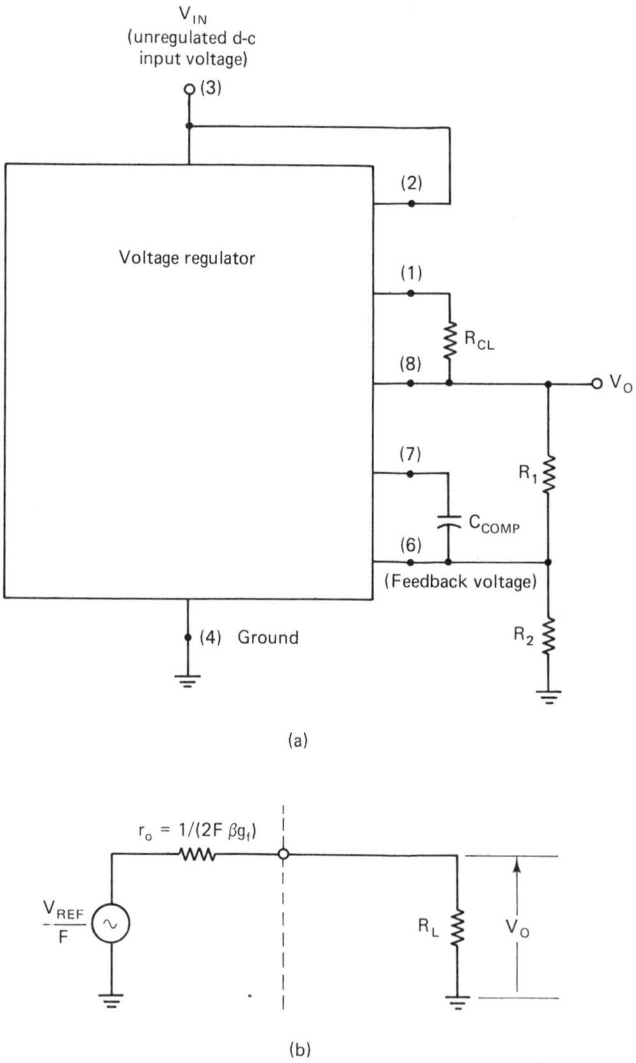

Figure 2.14 (a) Basic external connections for the adjustable positive regulator; (b) equivalent circuit for voltage regulator.

The maximum value of V_O will be determined by the minimum allowable input–output voltage differential for this regulator. Inspection of this circuit will reveal that for this regulator to operate properly such that all transistors are operating in the active mode, the minimum input–output differential will be given by

$$(V_{IN} - V_O)_{MIN} = V_{CE(SAT)}(Q_9) + V_{BE}(Q_{11}) + V_{BE}(Q_{12}) = 0.2 + 0.6 + 0.7 = 1.5 \text{ V} \tag{2.50}$$

Thus the maximum output voltage attainable will be limited to $V_{IN} - 1.5$ V.

Actually, this will be true only for low output current levels. At higher current levels the required voltage drops across the transistors will increase somewhat, and in addition there will be a voltage drop across R_{CL} of as much as 0.7 V, so that the required input–output differential may increase to about 2 to 2.5 V. Also, if no external pass transistors are to be used, resistor R_6 should be bypassed by a short-circuit between pins 2 and 3.

In the output stage resistors R_4 and R_5 constitute a voltage divider across the base–emitter junction of Q_{12}. This voltage divider will produce a small voltage to produce a prebias across the base-to-emitter junction of the current limit transistor Q_{10}, so that as a result the voltage drop that has to be produced across the current limit resistor, R_{CL}, does not have to be as large, and thus a smaller value of R_{CL} can be used.

The prebias voltage produced across R_5 will be given by

$$V_{R_5} = \frac{V_{BE\,12} R_5}{R_4 + R_5} = 0.7\ \text{V} \times \frac{1.5}{3.4} = 0.3\ \text{V} \tag{2.51}$$

Therefore, the voltage drop across R_{CL} that is required to bias Q_{10} into conduction will be only about 0.4 V. To consider an example, let us assume that $P_{D(\text{MAX})} =$ 500 mW and V_{IN} = 20 V and V_O = 10 V, so that a current limit of 50 mA is appropriate. For this current limit the value of R_{CL} that is required is 0.4 V/50 mA = 8.0 Ω. Without the prebias an R_{CL} of 0.7 V/50 mA = 14 Ω would be required. The smaller value of R_{CL} is advantageous from several standpoints, including a lower output resistance and thus better load regulation, a greater output voltage range due to a lower voltage drop across R_{CL}, and a higher overall circuit efficient due to a lower power loss in R_{CL}.

Note that the current limit chosen above of 50 mA will not provide for short-circuit protection of the regulator. For short-circuit protection a current limit of 500 mW/20 V = 25 mA would have to be chosen if simple current limiting is used. With foldback current limiting a considerably larger current limit could be obtained.

2.5.1 External Connections for Basic Positive Regulator Circuit

In Figure 2.14a a diagram of the external connections that are needed for this adjustable positive regulator are shown. Note the connection between pins 2 and 3 which places a short-circuit across the current boost resistor R_6. This resistor is needed only when external pass transistors are used, as will be seen a little later. Note also the current-limit resistor placed between pins 1 and 8. There is a resistive voltage divider placed between the output voltage pin (8) and ground to feed a fraction $R_2/(R_1 + R_2)$ of the ouput voltage back to the inverting input of the error amplifier (pin 6), where it is compared to the reference voltage.

A small compensation capacitor, C_{COMP}, is required between pins 6 and 7 to ensure stability from oscillations. The voltage regulator is basically a high-gain feedback amplifier, so it should not be surprising to find the requirement for a compensation capacitor for stability, just as in the case of an operational amplifier. C_{COMP} is a small capacitor, typically around 50 pF.

The design of the resistive voltage divider is based on two considerations. First, and foremost is that the resistance ratio be what is needed to give the required output voltage, as indicated by the relationship $V_O = V_{\text{REF}}(1 + R_1/R_2)$. The second factor is that of minimizing the effects of the differential amplifier bias (base) current. To this end the parallel combination of R_1 and R_2 should optimally be equal to the parallel combination of the R_1 and R_2 of the voltage reference circuit, which in this case is 1.15 kΩ. For example, if $V_{\text{REF}} = 1.8$ V and $V_O = 10$ V, we have that $1 + (R_1/R_2) = V_O/V_{\text{REF}} = 10/1.8 = 5.56$. Since $(R_2 + R_1)/R_1R_2 = 1/1.15$ kΩ,

$$R_1 = \frac{(1.15\ \text{k}\Omega)(R_2 + R_1)}{R_2} = 1.15\ \text{k}\Omega \times 5.56 = \underline{6.39\ \text{k}\Omega} \tag{2.52}$$

Therefore, $R_1/R_2 = 4.56$, so that

$$R_2 = \underline{1.40\ \text{k}\Omega}$$

2.5.2 Load Regulation

To evaluate the load regulation of this regulator circuit we will first obtain an expression for the dynamic output resistance. As a result of the current mirror active load, the output current of the error amplifier will be given by $2g_f(V_{\text{REF}} - V_{FB}) = 2g_f(V_{\text{REF}} - FV_O)$, in which g_f is the dynamic transfer conductance of the differential amplifier as given by $g_f = I_Q/4V_T$, and F is the feedback factor, which is the fraction of the output voltage that is fed back to the differential amplifier, $F = V_{FB}/V_O$. The factor of 2 is the result of the current-doubling action of the current mirror.

The output current of the differential amplifier supplies the base drive of the Darlington output stage, in which there is an overall current gain of $\beta = \beta_{11}\beta_{12}$. The output current will therefore be given by

$$I_O = 2\beta g_f(V_{\text{REF}} - FV_O) \tag{2.53}$$

Since $I_O = V_O/R_L$, this can be rewritten as

$$\frac{V_O}{R_L} = 2\beta g_f(V_{\text{REF}} - FV_O) \tag{2.54}$$

Collecting terms in V_O and solving for V_O gives

$$V_O = \frac{1}{F}V_{\text{REF}}\frac{R_L}{R_L + (1/2F\beta g_f)} \tag{2.55}$$

In Figure 2.14b an equivalent circuit for the voltage regulator output that is based on the equation above is presented. From this equivalent circuit and the equation that it represents, it is clear that the output resistance of the regulator will be given by $r_o = 1/2F\beta g_f$. Since $g_f = 4V_T/I_Q = 100\ \text{mV}/I_Q$ and $1/F = V_O/V_{\text{REF}}$, this equation can be restated as

$$r_o = \frac{V_O}{V_{\text{REF}}}\frac{50\ \text{mV}}{\beta I_Q}$$

Now to consider a representative example, let us use the value of $I_Q = 0.5$ mA for the differential amplifier that was determined earlier. For the Darlington output stage let us assume a typical current gain of around 70 for each transistor, so that the overall current gain will be approximately 5000. We will use a reference voltage of 1.8 V and assume an output voltage of 10 V. As a result we have that

$$r_o = \frac{10}{1.8}\left(\frac{50\text{ mV}}{5000} \times 0.5\text{ mA}\right) = \underline{0.11\ \Omega} \tag{2.56}$$

For a no-load to full-load current change of 50 mA, the corresponding decrease in the output voltage will be given by

$$\Delta V_O = \Delta I_O r_o = 50\text{ mA} \times 0.11\ \Omega = \underline{5.6\text{ mV}} \tag{2.57}$$

This is the load regulation of the voltage regulator. On a percentage basis, the load regulation will be

$$\frac{\Delta V_O}{V_O} \times 100\% = \frac{5.6\text{ mV}}{10\text{ V}} \times 100\% = \underline{0.056\%} \tag{2.58}$$

It is of interest to note that since the output resistance is directly proportional to V_O, the load regulation, on a percentage basis will not be a function of V_O.

2.5.3 Line Regulation

The line regulation is the ratio of the change in the output voltage to a given change in the regulator input voltage. We have seen from an earlier calculation that based on assuming a zener impedance of 10 Ω and a dynamic output impedance of 100 kΩ for the JFET current diode, the rate of change of the zener voltage with respect to the input voltage will be $dV_Z/dV_{IN} = 10\ \Omega/100\text{ k}\Omega = 1 \times 10^{-4}$. Since the output voltage is derived from the reference voltage, which in turn is obtained from the zener voltage, the rate of change of the output voltage with respect to input voltage, which is the line regulation, will be given by

$$\frac{dV_o}{dV_{IN}} = \frac{V_O}{V_Z}\frac{dV_Z}{dV_{IN}} = \frac{V_O}{V_Z} \times 1 \times 10^{-4} \tag{2.59}$$

For $V_O = 10$ V, this becomes

$$\frac{dV_O}{dV_{IN}} = 1.67 \times 10^{-4}\text{ V/V} = 0.167\text{ mV/V} \tag{2.60}$$

Thus the output voltage will increase by approximately 0.167 mV for every 1-V increase in the input voltage. On a percentage basis, this will be 0.00167%/V for the line regulation.

2.5.4 Ripple Rejection

The input voltage of a voltage regulator will generally be derived from a half-wave, or more commonly, full-wave rectifier circuit and associated filter. The unregulated input voltage of the regulator will accordingly not be a pure d-c waveform but will have some a-c ripple riding on it. We have just seen that the regulator will act to maintain a constant output voltage, almost completely independent of changes in the input voltage. This relative independence of the output voltage from the input voltage will hold true for the variations in the output voltage that are a manifestation of the a-c ripple voltage. As a result, the a-c ripple voltage appearing on the output of the regulator will be a very much attenuated version of the input ripple.

The *ripple rejection* of a voltage regulator is the ratio of the a-c ripple voltage on the output to the a-c input ripple voltage, and is usually expressed in decibels as

$$\text{ripple rejection} = 20 \log_{10} \frac{\text{output ripple voltage}}{\text{input ripple}} \tag{2.61}$$

Since the ratio of the output ripple to the input ripple is the same as the ratio of the change in the output voltage to the change in the input voltage, we can write the ripple rejection equation as

$$\text{ripple rejection} = 20 \log_{10} \frac{\Delta V_O}{\Delta V_{\text{IN}}} \tag{2.62}$$

so we see a very close relationship with the line regulation.

For the example under consideration above, the line regulation was 5.6×10^{-4} V/V, so that the corresponding ripple rejection should be $20 \log_{10}(5.6 \times 10^{-4}) = -65$ dB. Therefore, the output ripple will be some 65 dB below the input ripple.

For example, if the input voltage is 20 V with a 1% ripple factor corresponding to a ripple voltage of 200 mV, the output ripple voltage will be $200 \text{ mV} \times 5.6 \times 10^{-4} = 0.011 \text{ mV} = 11\ \mu\text{V}$. The output ripple factor will consequently be $11\ \mu\text{V}/10\ \text{V}) \times 100\% = 0.00011\%$, so that the output waveform will be very smooth indeed. As a result, we see that a voltage regulator with good line regulation can serve as a very useful adjunct to the filtering circuit of the rectifier in providing for a d-c output voltage with a very low ripple factor.

2.5.5 Current Boost

The maximum current output of an IC voltage regulator is limited by the maximum power dissipation rating of the device. For some IC regulators the maximum output current may be limited to as little as 50 MA.

The maximum output current can, however, be greatly increased by the use of additional series-pass transistors external to the IC. The output current will now be limited only by the maximum power dissipation rating of the external transistors, so that now output currents of several amperes, or even several tens of amperes, are possible.

An example of a "current boost" circuit is presented in Figure 2.15. The voltage regulator is the same as has been under previous analysis (Figure 2.12). The external series pass transistors are Q_A and Q_B connected in a cascade arrangement with Q_A driving Q_B.

The voltage drop across the current boost resistor R_6 of 600 Ω that is produced by the collector current of Q_{12} acts to bias Q_A on. Since the current through R_6 is limited by the V_{BE} of Q_A to about 700 mV/600 Ω ≃ 1 mA, any current through Q_{12} in excess of this will be drawn from the base of Q_A. This current therefore will become the base drive of Q_A.

The collector current of Q_A will, in turn, serve to bias Q_B on via the voltage

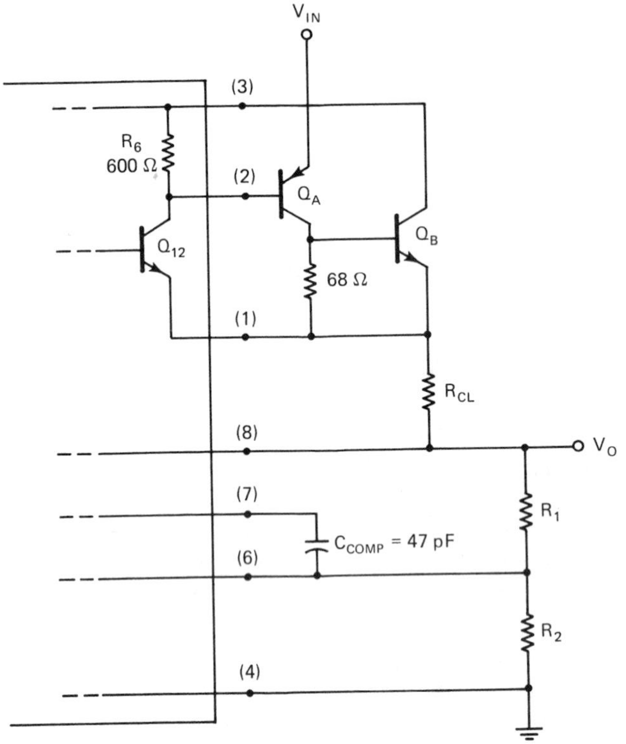

Figure 2.15 External connections for regulator with current boost.

drop across the 68-Ω resistor. Again we see that the current through this resistor will be limited by the V_{BE} of Q_B to about 700 mV/68 Ω = 10 mA. Any collector current of Q_A in excess of this will become the base drive of Q_B. This base current, when multiplied by the current gain of this transistor, will be the regulator circuit output current.

As a result of the base-to-collector current gain of Q_A, and the base-to-emitter gain of Q_B, the output current of the IC regulator can be multiplied by a very large factor. Using a representative current gain of 50 for Q_A and for Q_B, the overall current gain becomes 2500. As a result, an IC output current of 10 mA can be boosted up to 25 A by the external series-pass circuit. Nevertheless, the actual maximum output current will still be limited by considerations of maximum allowable power dissipation.

Most of the power dissipation will occur in the final transistor stage, Q_B. If, for example, Q_B has a 50-W power rating, for an input voltage of V_{IN} = 20 V, an output current of 2.5 A is possible with short-circuit protection. If foldback current limiting were to be used, for an output voltage level of 15 V, an output current of 50 W/(20 − 15) V = 10 A would be available.

The function of the 600-Ω resistor (R_6) and the 68-Ω resistor is to allow a small quiescent current to flow through Q_{12} and Q_A, respectively, under no-load conditions. This quiescent current will serve to reduce the output resistance under no-load conditions, and thus to improve the load regulation of the system, especially when the no-load current is very small.

Current boost for very large output currents. Depending on the amount of output current required, the external series-pass circuit can consist of one, two, or three transistors. In Figure 2.16 an example of a current boost circuit that is comprised of three transistors is presented. This circuit is similar to the current boost circuit just considered, except that a third transistor is added, and foldback current limiting is used. Transistors Q_A, Q_B, and Q_C are connected in cascade so that the overall current gain is now extremely large.

The 600-, 68-, and 6.8-Ω resistors are used to provide a small no-load quiescent current for transistors Q_{12}, Q_A, and Q_B, respectively. The 1.32- and 1.86-kΩ resistors across the base–emitter junction of Q_{12} is used to provide a small (~0.3 V) prebias voltage across the base–emitter junction of the current limit transistor, Q_{10}. This will allow a smaller value of R_{CL} to be used than would otherwise be the case. The foldback limiting characteristic is determined by the 47- and 160-Ω resistors in conjunction with R_{CL}.

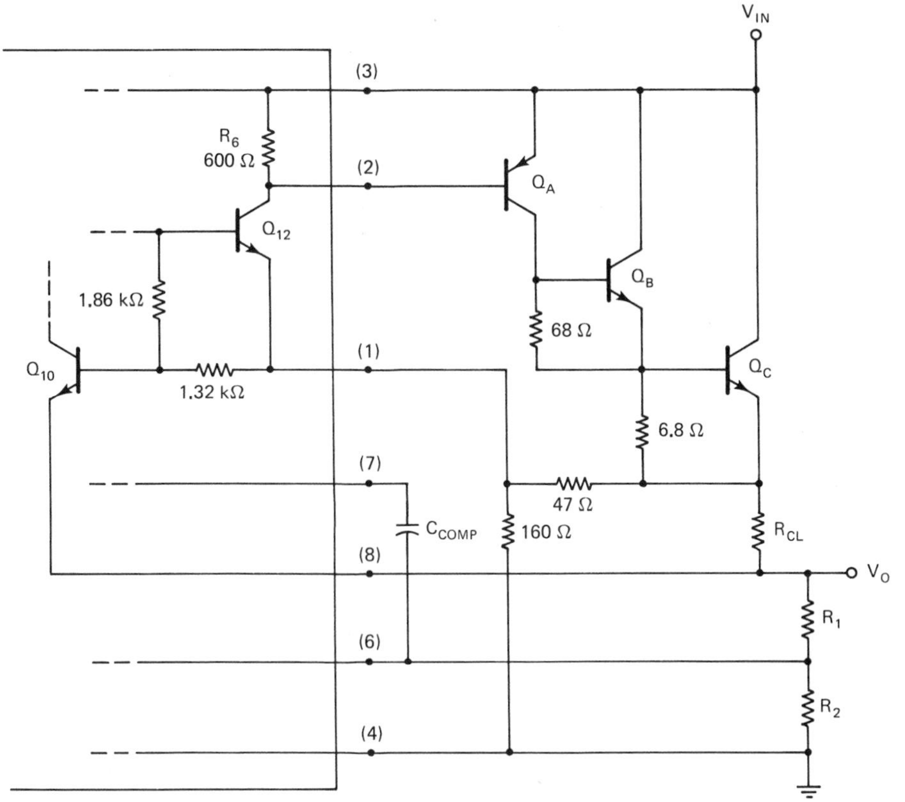

Figure 2.16 External connections for regulator with three-transistor current boost circuit with foldback current limiting.

2.6 THREE-TERMINAL REGULATORS (FIXED REGULATORS)

Three-terminal voltage regulators are voltage regulators in which the output voltage is set at some predetermined value. They therefore do not require any external feedback connections. As a result, only three terminals are required for this type of regulator: input (V_{IN}), output (V_O), and a ground terminal. Since these regulators operate at a preset output voltage, the current limit resistor R_{CL} is also internal to the regulator.

The principal advantage of three-terminal regulation is the simplicity of connection to the external circuit, with a minimum of external components required. Indeed, in many applications no external components are required. In some applications the use of filter capacitors across the input and output terminals may be desirable. In Figure 2.17 the basic circuit configuration of a three-terminal voltage regulator is shown. The simplicity and ease of application is evident. The capacitor across the input terminals is required only when the voltage regulator is located more than about 5 cm from the power supply filter capacitor such that the lead inductance between the supply and the regulator may cause stability problems and high-frequency oscillations. This capacitor should be characterized by a very low effective series resistance (ESR). Acceptable values are generally 0.2 μF ceramic disk, 2 μF or greater tantalum, or 25 μF or greater aluminum electrolytic.

A capacitor is generally not needed across the output terminals. The use of a suitable capacitor will, however, improve the regulator response to transient changes in the load conditions, and will also reduce the noise present at the regulator output.

Although, the three-terminal regulator offers only fixed output voltages, there are a wide variety of voltages available, both positive and negative. The output voltages of commercially available three-terminal voltage regulators are 5, 5.2, 6, 8, 10, 12, 15, 18, and 24 V in both positive and negative output voltage polarities. The output currents range from 100 mA to 3 A.

The three-terminal regulators generally offer a line regulation of about 0.005 to 0.02 %/V, a load regulation of 0.1 to 1.0%, and a ripple rejection of 65 to 85 dB.

2.6.1 Adjustable Voltage Output with the Three-Terminal Regulator

Although the three-terminal regulator is basically a fixed voltage regulator, with the simple addition of two resistors to the circuit an adjustable output voltage can be obtained. In Figure 2.18, a three-terminal regulator connected as an adjustable voltage regulator, is shown.

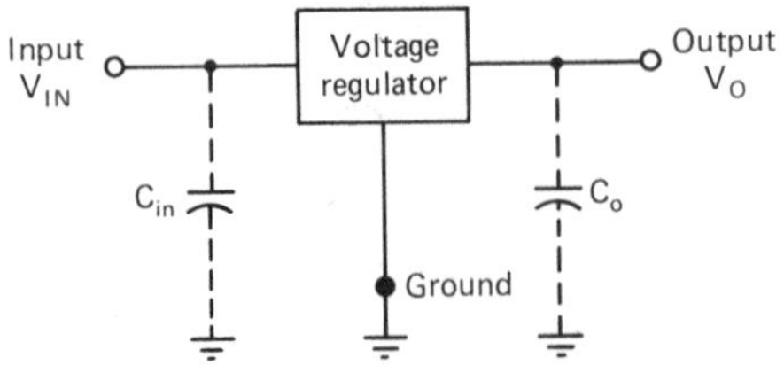

Figure 2.17 Basic three-terminal voltage regulator.

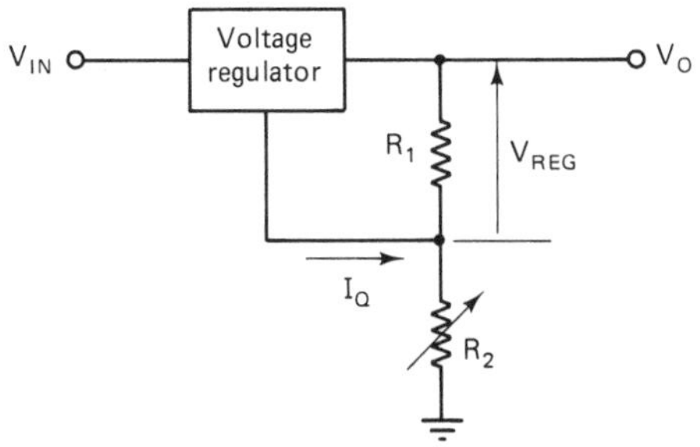

Figure 2.18 Three-terminal voltage regulator connected as adjustable regulator.

The voltage regulator will act to maintain a fixed voltage between its output and common or ground terminals. This voltage regulator output voltage is designated in Figure 2.18 as V_{REG}. The current through R_1 will therefore be V_{REG}/R_1. The current through R_2 is equal to the current through R_1 plus the voltage regulator quiescent current, I_Q. The voltage drop across R_2 will therefore be given by $V_{R_2} = (V_{\text{REG}}/R_1 + I_Q)R_2$. As a result, the output voltage of this circuit will be

$$V_O = V_{\text{REG}} + V_{R_2} = V_{\text{REG}}\,(1 + R_2/R_1) + I_Q R_2 \tag{2.63}$$

The voltage regulator quiescent current is defined as that part of the regulator input current that does not go out of the output terminal. This current will vary with changes in input voltage and in load voltage. For example, for the LM 7805 voltage regulator which has a 5.0 V output voltage, the quiescent current will be 7 mA typical, 10 mA maximum. The change in the quiescent current, ΔI_Q, for a change in the output current of from 5 mA to 1.5 A (the full load current) will be 0.5 mA maximum. The change in the quiescent current for a change in input voltage from 7 V to 25 V will be 1.3 mA maximum.

It is evident that the quiescent current, and in particular the changes in the quiescent current, will degrade the performance of the regulator, particularly with respect to the line regulation and load regulation. The line regulation of this regulator configuration will be given by

$$\Delta V_O/\Delta V_{\text{IN}} = \text{line regulation} = (1 + R_2/R_1)\Delta V_O/\Delta V_{\text{IN}} + R_2(\Delta I_Q/\Delta V_{\text{IN}}) \tag{2.64}$$

The degradation or increase in the line regulation factor due to the quiescent current will thus be equal to $R_2(\Delta I_Q/\Delta V_{\text{IN}})$. Thus we see that for good line regulation both R_2 as well as ΔI_Q should be small.

The load regulation will be given by

$$\Delta V_O/\Delta I_O = (1 + R_2/R_1)(\Delta V_O/\Delta I_O) + R_2(\Delta I_Q/\Delta I_O) \tag{2.65}$$

The degradation (increase) in the load regulation is equal to $R_2(\Delta I_Q/\Delta I_O)$, and thus again we see the importance of using a small R_2 and, if possible, choosing a voltage regulator with a quiescent current that does not change much with load current.

The quiescent current will also change with temperature so that the temperature coefficient of the adjustable three-terminal voltage regulator will be given by

$$\Delta V_O/\Delta T = (1 + R_2/R_1)\Delta V_{\text{REG}}/\Delta T + R_2 \Delta I_Q/\Delta T \tag{2.66}$$

Again we see the importance of using a small value resistor for R_2. Note, however, that as R_2 is decreased, the value of R_1 will also have to be decreased for a given output voltage. As a result of the increased current drain through R_1 and R_2, the maximum output current available from the regulator will decrease.

To consider an example of the problem arising from the quiescent current, we will use the LM 7805 three-terminal voltage regulator in an adjustable voltage regulator configuration for a range of output voltages from 5 V to 10 V. Since 5.0 V is the regulated output of the 7805, this means that resistor R_2 will have to vary from 0 to R_1.

The rated output current of the 7805 is 1.5 A so that a reasonable choice for the current through R_1 and R_2 would be around 0.2 A. Since the voltage across R_1 is 5.0 V, the value of R_1 will be 5.0 V/0.2 A = 25 Ω. As a result, we see that R_2 will range from 0 to 25 Ω. As mentioned above, the $I_Q R_2$ voltage drop will produce a degradation in the line regulation, load regulation, and temperature coefficient. For this example we will turn our attention to the temperature coefficient.

The rate of change of quiescent current with temperature for the 78XX series of regulators is approximately -7 μA/°C. Therefore, the contribution of this temperature coefficient to the temperature coefficient of the output voltage will be 7 μA/°C × 25Ω = 175 μV/°C. This is, of course, assuming that R_2 does not change appreciably with temperature. The temperature coefficient of the regulator output voltage is typically 500 μV/°C, so we see that the effect of the quiescent current can be significant.

In Figure 2.19, one very good approach to minimizing the effects of the quiescent current on the three-terminal adjustable regulator performance is shown. An operational amplifier, connected in the voltage-follower feedback configuration, is interposed between the $R_1 - R_2$ resistive voltage divider and the voltage regulator ground terminal. The voltage follower sinks the regulator quiescent current. The current flowing from the junction of R_1 and R_2 into the operational amplifier will be the bias current of the operational amplifier, I_B. By suitable choice of the operational amplifier, this bias current can be so small as to be a negligible factor in the performance of the regulator circuit. At the same time, the output impedance of the voltage follower will be so small that changes in I_Q will not affect the voltage at the ground terminal of the regulator.

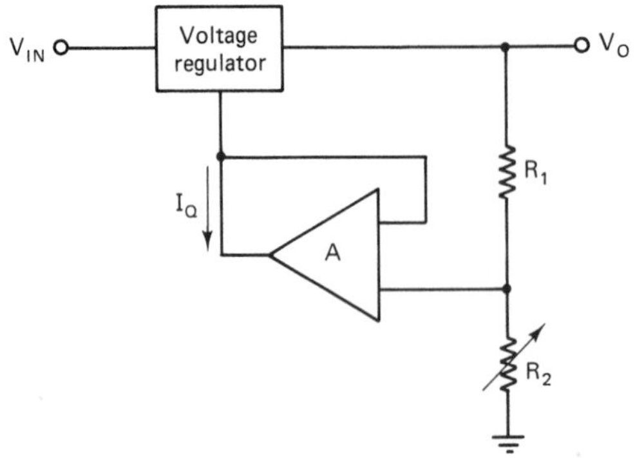

Figure 2.19 Three-terminal adjustable regulator with voltage follower to reduce effects of quiescent current.

As a result of the just-described buffering action of the voltage follower, the output voltage for this circuit can be expressed to a high degree of precision by $V_O = V_{\text{REG}}(1 + R_2/R_1)$, and there will be no degradation of the voltage regulator characteristics.

2.6.2 Three-Terminal Adjustable Regulators with Very Low Quiescent Currents

There have recently become available a series of three-terminal voltage regulators with very low quiescent currents. These voltage regulators achieve the very low quiescent currents by simply redesigning the internal circuitry of the regulator so that almost all of the biasing currents of the device go out of the output terminal rather than the ground or common terminal. As a result of almost all of the biasing currents going out the output terminal of the device, there is a minimum load current specification in order to assure proper functioning of the regulator. This minimum load current specification corresponds essentially to the total biasing currents of the device, and is typically around a few milliamperes. Since the current going out of the common, or ground terminal of the regulator is no longer the quiescent current of the device, this common terminal current is called the *adjustment pin current*, I_{ADJ}.

Examples of adjustable three-terminal voltage regulators of the type being discussed now are the following: LM 117,217, and 317; LM 117HV,217HV, and 317HV; LM 138,238, and 338; LM 150,250, and 350. The above mentioned voltage regulators all have adjustment pin current specifications of 50 μA typical, 100 μA maximum. The change in the adjustment pin current in going from a load current of 10 mA to the maximum rated current, and/or for a change in input voltage from 3 V to the maximum rated input voltage, is specified as 0.2 μA typical and 5 μA maximum for all of these voltage regulators. The minimum load current is 3.5 mA. The LM 117 and 117HV series have rated output currents of 1.5 A. For the LM 138 series there is a 5 A maximum current rating, and for the LM 150 series the current rating is 3 A. The regulated output voltage (reference voltage) of these regulators is 1.25 V.

As a result of the small values of adjustment pin current, and even more importantly, of the very small change in the adjustment pin current over the regulator operating range, precision adjustable voltage regulators can be constructed with a minimum of external components.

2.6.3 Current Regulator Based on the Three-Terminal Voltage Regulator

With the three-terminal voltage regulator, it is a relatively simple matter to construct a current regulator. A current regulator is essentially the circuit dual of a voltage regulator and is essentially a current source. With the current regulator, however, the emphasis is generally on much larger output currents than is the case with the conventional current source circuits.

In Figure 2.20 a simple current regulator is shown that is based on the use of a three-terminal voltage regulator. In this circuit, the voltage regulator acts to maintain

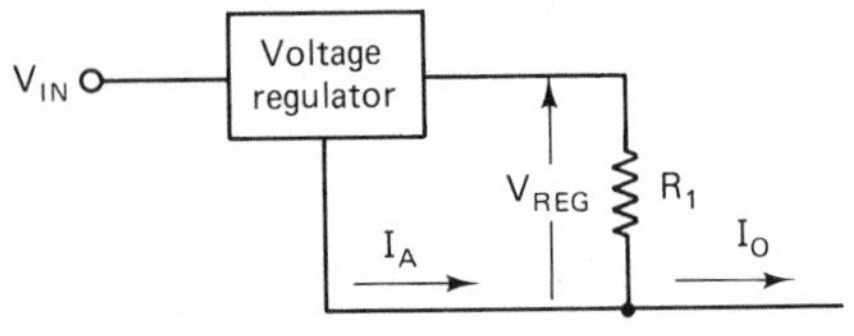

Figure 2.20 Use of a three-terminal regulator as a current regulator.

a constant voltage, V_{REG} across resistor R_1. As a result, the current through R_1 is similarly constrained to a constant value given by V_{REG}/R_1. The output current is the sum of this current and the current coming out of the common terminal of the regulator, which is the quiescent current, or the adjustment pin current, depending on the type of three terminal regulator that is used. In either case this current will be designated as I_A. Therefore, we have that

$$I_O = \frac{V_{REG}}{R_1} + I_A$$

One of the most important characteristics of a current regulator or current source is the dynamic output conductance, g_o, which in the ideal case will be zero. Since $g_o = -dI_O/dV_O$ we have

$$g_o = \frac{-dI_O}{dV_O} = -\left(\frac{1}{R_1}\frac{dV_{REG}}{dV_O} + \frac{dI_A}{dV_O}\right) \quad (2.67)$$

We must now note that the input voltage V_{IN}, as seen by the voltage regulator, is really the voltage between the input terminal and the common (ground) terminal of the regulator. For the circuit under consideration the voltage at the regulator common terminal is V_O, so that for a change in the output voltage of amount dV_O, the change in the voltage between the regulator input and common terminals will be $-dV_O$. Therefore, we can rewrite the equation for g_o as

$$g_o = \frac{1}{R_1}\frac{dV_{REG}}{dV_{IN}} + \frac{dI_A}{dV_{IN}} \quad (2.68)$$

Thus we see again that the voltage regulator common pin current, I_A, will have an influence on the overall circuit characteristics.

An appropriate example at this point is a 5-A current regulator based on the use of the LM 138 (National Semiconductor) series of three-terminal voltage regulators. For these regulators the change in the adjustment pin current is specified as 0.2 μA typical and 5 μA maximum for an input voltage range of 3 to 35 V. The rate of change of the adjustment pin current can therefore be estimated as

$$\frac{dI_A}{dV_{IN}} = \frac{200 \text{ nA}}{32 \text{ V}} = 6 \text{ nA/V (typ.)}$$
$$\frac{dI_A}{dV_{IN}} = \frac{5000 \text{ nA}}{32 \text{ V}} = 160 \text{ nA/V (max.)} \quad (2.69)$$

The line regulation is specified as 0.02 %/V (typ.). Therefore, we have that $dV_{REG}/dV_{IN} = 1.25 \text{ V} \times 0.0002/\text{V} = 250\ \mu\text{V/V}$, since the regulated output voltage is 1.25 V.

For a 5-A current regulator value of R_1 should be 1.25 V/5 A = 0.25 Ω. We consequently have for the dynamic output conductance the result

$$g_o = \frac{1}{0.25\ \Omega}(250\ \mu\text{V/V}) + \frac{dI_A}{dV_{\text{IN}}}$$
$$= 1.0\ \text{mA/V} + \frac{dI_A}{dV_{\text{IN}}} \tag{2.70}$$

Since dI_A/dV_{IN} will be no more than 160 nA/V, we see that the adjustment pin current will not be a significant factor in the output conductance. We see therefore that the dynamic output conductance of this current regulator will be 1.0 mA/V = 1.0 mS. On a percentage basis this is (1.0 mA/5 A) × 100 %/V = 0.02 %/V, so that the output current changes by only 0.02% for every 1-V change in the load voltage. This represents very good current regulation indeed.

2.6.4 Current Boost for Three-Terminal Voltage Regulators

The limited number of external pins notwithstanding, it is possible to have external transistors for the purpose of extending the output current range of the three-terminal voltage regulator. An example of a simple current boost circuit is shown in Figure 2.21.

For the circuit of Figure 2.21 we have that $I_1 R_1 + V_{EB_1} \simeq I_{\text{REG}}R_2 + V_{D_1}$, where I_{REG} is the regulator input current, and R_3 is assumed to be large enough such that it does not shunt a major amount of current from the emitter of Q_1. If diode D_1 is chosen such that its forward voltage drop is a reasonable match to the emitter–base voltage drop of Q_1, we will have that $V_{D_1} \simeq V_{EB_1}$, so that as a result $I_1R_1 \simeq I_{\text{REG}}R_2$ and thus $I_1/I_{\text{REG}} = R_2/R_1$. The output current of the circuit will therefore be given as

$$I_O \cong I_{\text{REG}} + I_1 = I_{\text{REG}}\left(1 + \frac{R_2}{R_1}\right), \text{ since } I_Q \text{ is small} \tag{2.71}$$

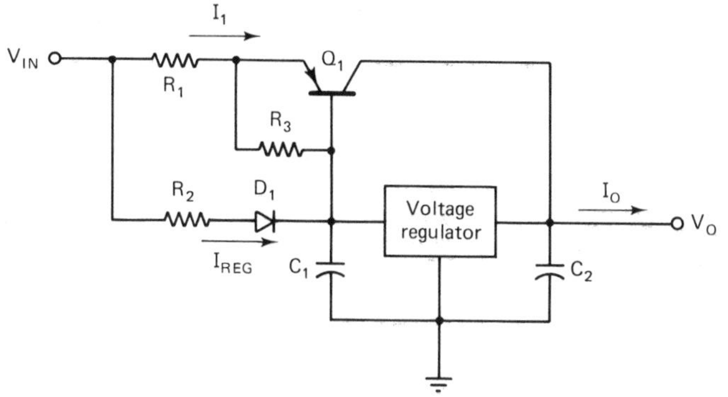

Figure 2.21 Current boost circuit for three-terminal regulator.

so that we see that by this means the output current of the circuit has been increased by a factor of $1 + R_2/R_1$.

As an example of this technique, let us consider the design of a circuit to boost the current output of a 1.5-A regulator to 6 A. The resistor ratio will therefore be $R_2/R_1 = 3$. To minimize the effects of the difference between the diode voltage drop and the emitter–base voltage drop, we want to choose resistance values large enough such that the I_1R_1 and the $I_{REG}R_2$ voltage drops are large compared to the uncertainty in the diode and transistor voltage drops. At the same time, too large a value for R_1 and R_2 should certainly be avoided because this will reduce the input voltage at the voltage regulator input pin. A reasonable choice for the $I_{REG}R_2$ and I_1R_1 voltage drops will be 0.5 V.

We will choose a target value of 1.0 A for the regulator current, to allow a reasonable safety factor. The value of R_2 is therefore $0.5\text{ V}/1.0\text{ A} = 0.5\ \Omega$. For R_1 we have that $R_1 = 0.5\text{ V}/5.0\text{ A} = 0.1\ \Omega$. Resistor R_3 should be chosen such that a low output current levels, transistor Q_3 is not turned on and the voltage regulator supplies the entire output current. A reasonable current level for this is about 50 mA, so that for R_3 we have $R_3 = 700\text{ mV}/50\text{ mA} = 14\ \Omega$.

In this circuit the current limiting of the three-terminal regulator will also act to limit the current through Q_1 and thus provide overall protection for the circuit. When the output current of the voltage regulator becomes current limited, the regulator input current will similarly be limited since the quiescent regulator current flow out the regulator common (ground) terminal is very small in comparison. Since I_{REG} thus becomes limited by the action of the voltage regulator current-limiting circuitry, the transistor current will also be limited since the ratio of these two currents is determined by the R_2/R_1 resistor ratio.

2.6.5 Three-Terminal Positive Voltage Regulator Example: LM78XX

An example of a three-terminal positive voltage regulator is shown in Figure 2.22. This is representative of the LM78XX (National Semiconductor) voltage regulator circuit and uses a band-gap type of voltage reference circuit.

The band-gap voltage reference circuit is comprised basically of transistors Q_1 through Q_8. The reference voltage generated by this circuit appears at the base of Q_6 and therefore appears across R_{18}. This reference voltage is also applied to the base of Q_1. Note, however, that the reference voltage is not available externally.

Transistor Q_{10} in the emitter-follower configuration in conjunction with resistor R_9 is used to increase the current output of the reference circuit. This current output provides the base drive for the series-pass output stage, consisting of transistors Q_{15} and Q_{16} in a Darlington emitter-follower configuration.

Transistor Q_{11} is a multiple-collector lateral PNP transistor and serves as a multiple current source. One of the collectors of Q_{11} serves as a current source active load for Q_{10}.

Foldback current limiting is provided by Q_{14} together with the current-limit resistor R_{16}. Resistors R_{13} and R_{14} and diode D_2 produce the foldback dependence on the input–output voltage differential.

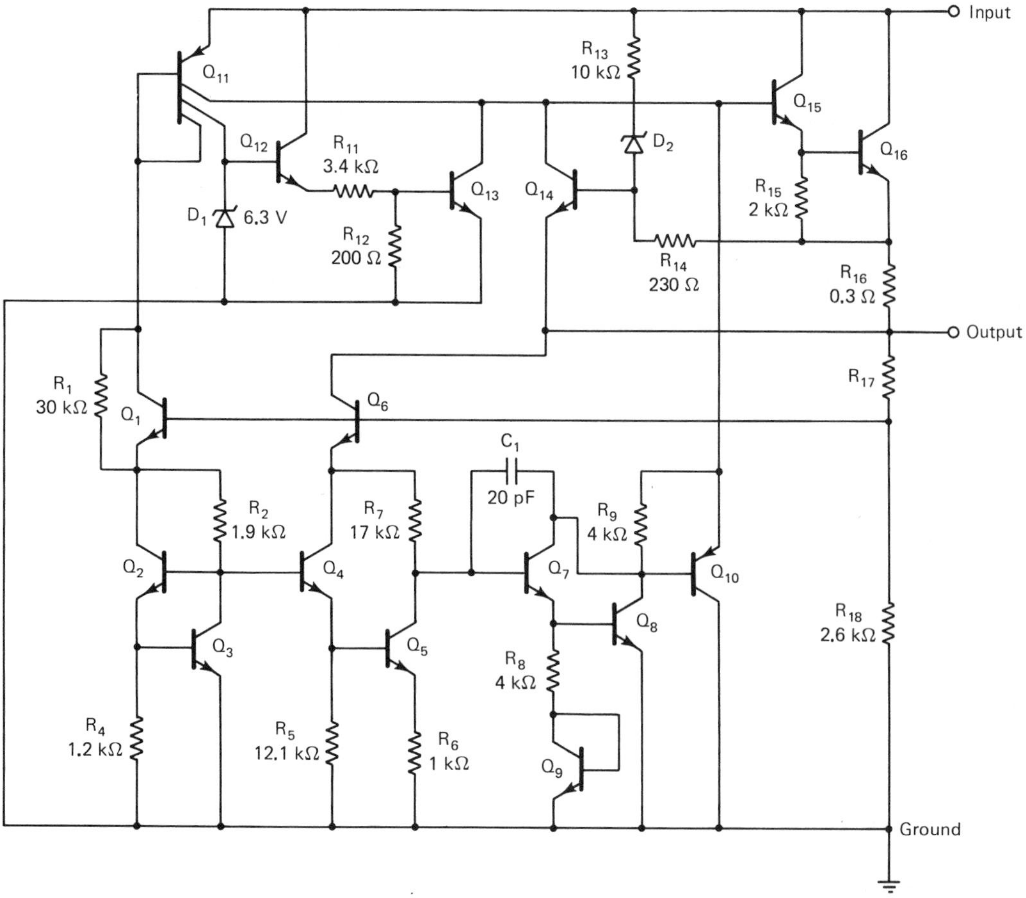

Figure 2.22 Positive voltage regulator with fixed output voltage: LM78XX (National Semiconductor).

Thermal shutdown is obtained from the circuitry of D_1, Q_{12}, Q_{13}, R_{11}, and R_{12}. One of the collectors of Q_{11} provides a current source biasing for D_1. When the thermal shutdown transistor Q_{13} is turned on, it bypasses the base drive away from the Q_{15}–Q_{16} output stage.

The output voltage is derived from the reference voltage that appears across R_{18}. Resistors R_{17} and R_{18} constitute a resistive voltage divider, and neglecting the effects of the Q_6 and Q_1 base current, the following relationship between the output and reference voltage is obtained: $V_{REF} = V_O R_{18}/R_{17} + R_{18})$. As a result we have that $V_O = V_{REF}(1 + R_{17}/R_{18})$. Note again that the reference voltage is not available externally. Since the resistive voltage divider that sets the output voltage is internal to the regulator, the regulator output voltage that appears between the output and ground terminals is not adjustable.

The biasing voltage for the reference voltage circuitry is derived from the reference voltage itself via Q_1 and Q_6. An important consequence of this is that the reference voltage will be almost completely independent of the input voltage, thus leading to very good line regulation. Since when the circuit is first turned on the reference voltage will be zero, resistor R_1 is provided to bypass Q_1 to provide a biasing current for the voltage reference circuit.

Having now described the basic operation of this voltage regulator, we will briefly return to consider the operation of the voltage reference circuit. A band-gap voltage reference circuit produces a temperature-compensated reference voltage equal to $V_{REF} = (n + 1)(E_{GO} + 3V_T) = (n + 1)1.283$ V, where $n + 1$ is the number of base-to-emitter junction drops across which V_{REF} is developed. Inspection of the LM78XX circuit reveals that V_{REF} is developed across the base–emitter junctions of Q_6, Q_7, and Q_8, so that $n + 1 = 3$, and therefore that $V_{REF} = 3.85$ V. Note that the reference voltage will be given by $V_{REF} = V_{BE_6} + I_5R_7 + V_{BE_7} + V_{BE_8}$, and it is the positive temperature coefficient of the voltage drop across R_7 that compensates for the negative temperature coefficient of the base-to-emitter voltage drops.

The voltage drop across R_2 will be $V_{REF} - V_{BE_1} - V_{BE_2} - V_{BE_3}$. Using a representative figure of 650 mV for the base-to-emitter voltage drops, the voltage drop across R_2 will be $3.85 - 3(0.65) = 1.9$ V. Therefore, the current through R_2 will be 1.0 mA. Neglecting base currents as being small, this also gives use the current through Q_3 as $I_3 = I_{R_2} = 1.0$ mA. The current through R_4 will be $I_{R_4} = 0.65$ V/1.2 kΩ = 0.5 mA.

The voltage across R_5 will be $V_{BE_2} + V_{BE_3} - V_{BE_4} = 0.65$ V, so that the current through R_5 and therefore through Q_4 will be given by $I_4 = I_{R_5} = 0.65$ V/12.1 kΩ = 0.05 mA = 50 μA.

We will now consider the current through Q_5, which is I_5, noting that it is this current that is used for the temperature compensation of the base-to-emitter negative temperature coefficients. Inspection of the circuit allows us to write that $V_{BE_2} + V_{BE_3} = V_{BE_4} + V_{BE_5} + I_5R_6$. We will assume identical transistors, all operating in the active region. We can therefore express the relationship between collector current and base-to-emitter voltage as $I_C = I_{TO} \exp(V_{BE}/V_T)$, so that $V_{BE} = V_T \ln(I_C/I_{TO})$. Solving for I_5R_6 gives

$$I_5R_6 = V_{BE_2} + V_{BE_3} - V_{BE_4} - V_{BE_5} = V_T \ln \frac{I_2 I_3}{I_4 I_5} \tag{2.72}$$

Since $I_2 = 0.5$ mA, $I_3 = 1.0$ mA, and $I_4 = 0.05$ mA, this becomes

$$I_5R_6 = V_T \ln \frac{10 \text{ mA}}{I_5} \tag{2.73}$$

This is a transcendental equation for I_5 and can be solved by an iterative technique to give a value of 0.1 mA for I_5. Corresponding to this value of I_5, the I_5R_6 voltage drop will be 25 mV ln (10 mA/0.1 mA) = 115 mV. The voltage drop across R_7 will therefore be $I_5R_7 = (R_7/R_6)(I_5R_6) = 17 \times 115$ mV = 1.96 V. Since the reference voltage is equal to the voltage drop across R_7 plus the sum of three base-to-emitter voltage drops, we obtain for the reference voltage the value $V_{REF} = 1.96 + 3(0.65) = 3.9$ V, which is close to the expected value of $3(E_{GO} + 3V_T) = 3.85$ V.

In the reference voltage circuit capacitor C_1 is used for frequency compensation to ensure stability. Resistor R_8 and diode-connected transistor Q_9 are used to prebias Q_8 to produce an acceptable quiescent current in that transistor.

The LM78XX Series of three-terminal voltage regulators are available with output voltages of 5, 6, 8, 12, 15, 18, and 24 V, with the designation of the 5-V regulator being the 7805, the 6-V being the 7806, and so on. The voltage regulators of the 78XX series all have the same internal circuitry, except for different values for R_{17}, which determines the output voltage level.

2.6.6 Three-Terminal Positive Voltage Regulator Example: LM78LXX

We will now consider another example of a three-terminal positive voltage regulator, the LM78LXX (National Semiconductor) as shown in Figure 2.23. In this circuit the voltage reference is provided by zener diode D_2 with Q_3, Q_2, and Q_1 used for temperature compensation. The temperature-compensated reference voltage appears at the junction of resistors R_1 and R_2 and is applied to the base of Q_7 which is part of the error amplifier. The zener diode D_2 is biased by Q_4 which acts as a current source.

The current source transistor Q_4 is biased by Q_5 which is a multiple emitter and multiple collector PNP transistor. Transistor Q_5 is in turn biased by the current through Q_3 which is controlled by the zener voltage drop and the base-to-emitter

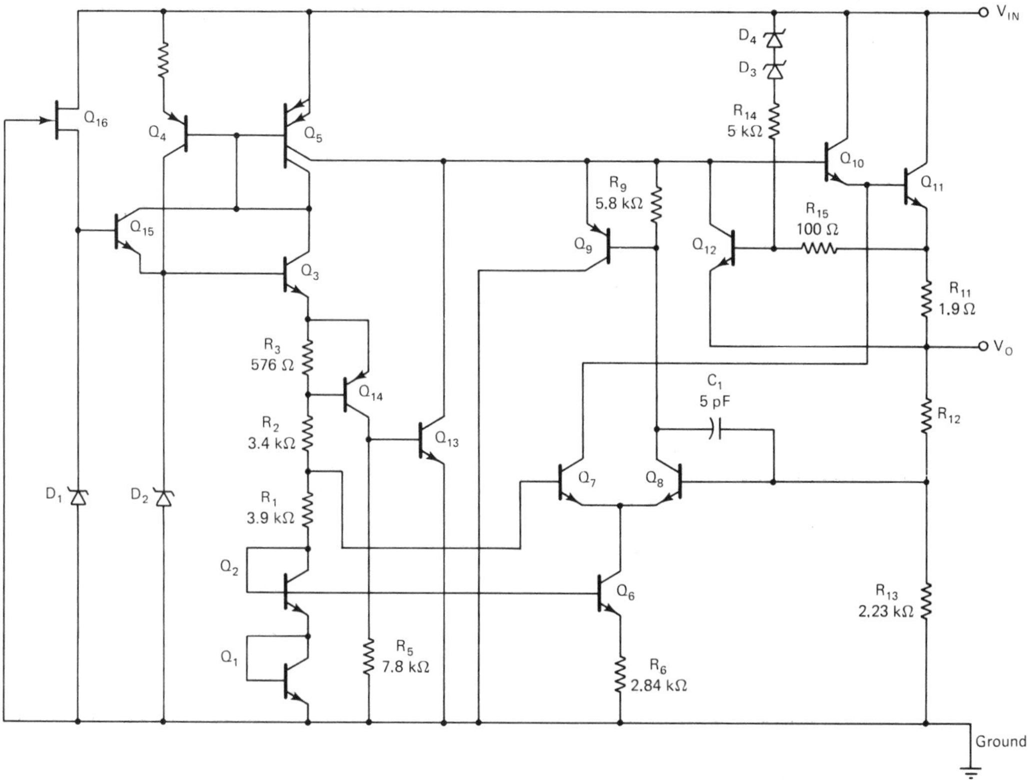

Figure 2.23 Three-terminal positive voltage regulator circuit: LM78XX (National Semiconductor).

drops of Q_3, Q_2, and Q_1. As a result, the bias current of the voltage reference circuit, and in particular of D_2, will be almost completely independent of the input voltage so that correspondingly, the reference voltage will be almost completely independent of the input voltage as well. This will result in very good line regulation for the regulator.

Transistors Q_{15} and Q_{16} and diode D_1 are used as a startup circuit to apply the initial bias to the voltage reference circuit. Once this has been achieved and the voltage across D_2 has risen to the zener voltage, transistor Q_{15} will be turned off, since its base-to-emitter voltage will now be zero, and the startup circuit will thus be disconnected from the voltage reference circuit.

The error amplifier is a differential amplifier comprised of Q_7 and Q_8 with Q_6 together with R_6 used for current sink biasing of the amplifier. The output of the differential amplifier is fed to the base of Q_9, which is in the emitter-follower configuration and drives the series-pass output stage. Capacitor C_1 connected across the collector–base junction of Q_8 is a compensation capacitor to ensure stability.

The series-pass output stage consists of Q_{10} and Q_{11} in a Darlington emitter-follower configuration. Foldback current limiting is provided by Q_{12} together with the current limit resistor R_{11}. Resistors R_{15} and R_{14}, together with diodes D_3 and D_4 will produce a foldback characteristic that is dependent on the input–output voltage differential.

A portion of the output voltage is tapped off by the resistive voltage divider, consisting of R_{12} and R_{13}, and fed back to the base of Q_8, which is the inverting input of the error amplifier. Note that this voltage divider is internal to the IC regulator, so that a fixed output voltage will result. Note also that the reference voltage is not accessible at any external terminal.

Thermal shutdown is provided by Q_{14}, Q_{13}, and R_3. The voltage across R_3 will be given by

$$V_{R_3} = \frac{(V_Z - V_{BE_3} - V_{BE_2} - V_{BE_1})R_3}{R_1 + R_2 + R_3} = (V_Z - 3V_{BE}) \times 0.073 \tag{2.74}$$

With a zener voltage of 6.5 V and a base-to-emitter drop of 0.6 V, the voltage across R_3 will be approximately 340 mV at 25°C. This is insufficient to turn Q_{14} on, and thus both Q_{14} and Q_{13} will be off. Due to the positive temperature coefficient of the zener voltage and the negative temperature coefficient of the base-to-emitter voltage drop, the voltage across R_3 will increase with temperature at a rate given by $dV_{R_3}/dT = 0.073 \times (dV_Z/dT - 3\ dV_{BE}/dT) = 0.72$ mV/°C. At the same time the voltage required to turn Q_3 on decreases at a rate of about 2.1 mV/°C. Therefore, at some elevated temperature Q_3 will indeed turn on and thereby turn Q_{13} on. This will cause the base drive of Q_{10} to be shunted through Q_{13} and thus produce the thermal shutdown.

We see that since the voltage across R_3 increases at a rate of about 0.7 mV/°C and the base-to-emitter voltage required to turn Q_{14} on decreases at a rate of 2.1 mV/°C, the temperature for thermal shutdown will be determined by the relationship $\Delta T \simeq (650 \text{ mV} - 340 \text{ mV})/2.8$ mV/°C, where ΔT is the temperature rise for thermal shutdown. Solving for ΔT gives $\Delta T \simeq 110$°C, so that thermal shutdown will occur at a chip temperature of about 135°C.

The LM78LXX series of three terminal voltage regulators is available with output voltages of 5, 8, 12, 15, 18, and 24 V, with the device designation being that the 78L05 is a 5-V regulator, and so on.

2.7 NEGATIVE VOLTAGE REGULATORS

In principle, it might be thought that negative voltage regulators could be constructed using the same circuit configuration as for positive voltage regulators, simply replacing the NPN transistors by PNP transistors, and vice versa. All of the voltages and currents would be reversed, so that the operation of the regulator would be completely equivalent to the complementary positive regulator. However, due to the fact that the performance of IC PNP transistors is in general much inferior to that of the NPN transistors, the design of the negative regulator is not the same as the positive regulator. Indeed, the design of the negative regulator is based on the preponderate use of NPN transistors, as is the case with the positive regulators. As a result of this the circuit configuration will be somewhat different, although the basic principles of operation are still the same.

An example of a three-terminal negative regulator is shown in Figure 2.24. This voltage regulator circuit is similar to that of the LM120/145/320/79XX/79LXXAC (National semiconductor) series of voltage regulators.

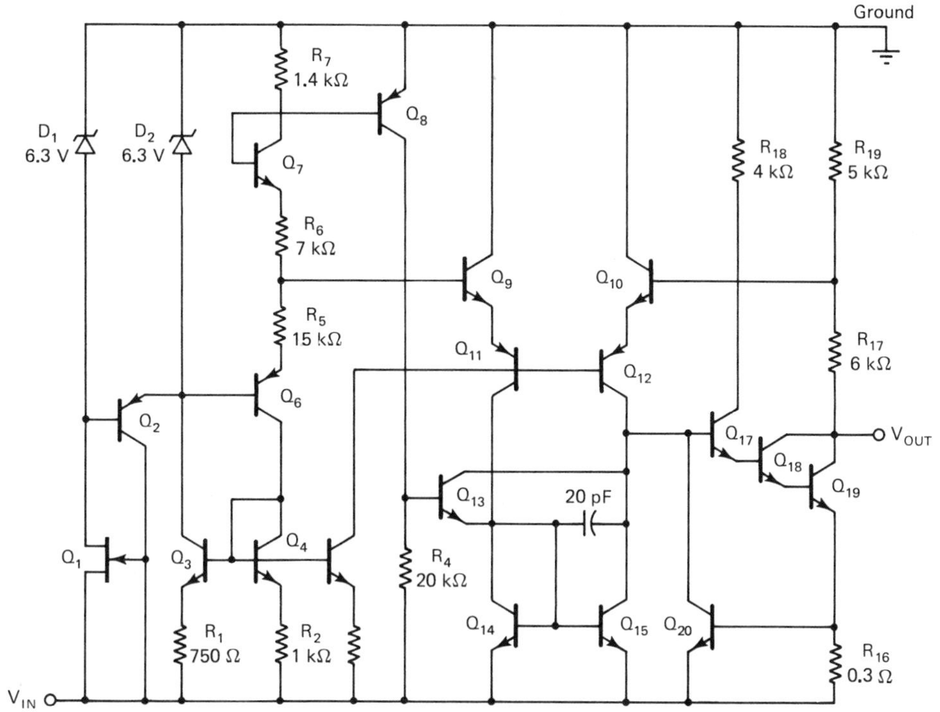

Figure 2.24 Three-terminal negative voltage regulator: LM79XX (National Semiconductor)

The voltage reference for this regulator circuit is of the temperature-compensated zener diode type. The zener diode for the voltage reference circuit is D_2 (6.3 V) and the positive temperature coefficient of this zener voltage is compensated by the negative temperature coefficients of Q_6, Q_7, and Q_8. The temperature-compensated reference voltage appears at the junction of R_5 and R_6.

The bias current for the zener diode, D_2, is supplied by Q_3, which acts as a current sink. Q_3 is in turn biased by Q_4, which is a diode-connected transistor. The current through Q_4 is supplied by the D_2, Q_6, Q_8, R_6, R_7 voltage reference circuit and is given by $I_4 = (V_Z - 3V_{BE})/R_5 + R_6$. We see, therefore, that the bias current of the zener diode is to a first approximation independent of the supply voltage, which thus leads to a very good line regulation for the voltage regulator. The startup circuit of D_1, Q_1, and Q_2 acts to supply the initial bias voltage across the voltage reference circuit. Once this has happened, the equalization of the voltage drops across D_1 and D_2 causes transistor Q_2 to turn off, thereby disconnecting the startup circuit from the voltage reference so that thereafter the voltage reference becomes self-biasing.

The reference voltage produced by the voltage reference circuit is supplied to the base of Q_9, which is the noninverting input of the error differential amplifier. This differential amplifier consists of transistors Q_9 through Q_{12}. Each half of the differential amplifier consists of a common-collector/common-base cascode direct-coupled compound transistor configuration. The bias current for this differential amplifier is the base current of Q_{11} and Q_{12} and is supplied by the current sink Q_5. Note that the current of Q_5 is determined by the current through Q_4, which is controlled by the self-biasing voltage reference. As a result the quiescent current of the differential amplifier will exhibit little dependence on the input voltage, this again leading to very good line regulation. Transistors Q_{14} and Q_{15} constitute a current mirror active load for the differential amplifier. The 20-pF capacitor from collector to base of Q_{15} is for frequency compensation.

The series-pass output stage consists of Q_{17}, Q_{18}, and Q_{19} in a Darlington emitter-follower configuration. Resistor R_{15} (2 kΩ) provides for an acceptable quiescent current for Q_{17} and Q_{18} and provides a return path for the leakage current of Q_{17} and Q_{18}.

A portion of the output voltage is tapped off by the resistive voltage divider of R_{17} and R_{19} and fed back to the base of Q_{10}, which is the inverting input of the error amplifier. Note that this is an internal feedback network, so that the output voltage is not variable.

Current limiting is accomplished by the action of Q_{20} and resistor R_{16}. When Q_{20} is turned on it diverts base drive away from the base of Q_{17} and produces current limiting.

Thermal shutdown is produced by Q_8, Q_{13}, R_7, and R_4. At 25°C the voltage drop across R_7 is given by $(V_Z - 2V_{BE})R_7/(R_5 + R_6 + R_7) = 300$ mV. This voltage is insufficient to turn Q_8 on, so that Q_{13} will also not be turned on. The voltage across R_7 will, however, increase with temperature at a rate of about 0.4 mV/°C due to the temperature coefficient of the zener diode (D_2) and the two base–emitter junctions (Q_6 and Q_7). At the same time the required base-to-emitter voltage needed to turn Q_8 on decreases at a rate of about 2.1 mV/°C. In order to turn Q_8 on, the combination of the change in the voltage across R_7 and the decrease in the required base-to-emitter voltage must add up to about 300 mV. This will require a temperature increase of 300 mV/2.5 mV/°C = 120°C. As a result, a thermal shutdown temperature of about 150°C is expected.

2.8 SWITCHING VOLTAGE REGULATORS

The voltage regulators discussed thus far have been of the "dissipative" type. In these regulators the flow of current to the load is controlled by a series-pass circuit which produces a voltage drop equal to the required input–output voltage difference, $V_{IN} - V_O$. The input voltage is the unregulated d-c voltage. In performing this function the series-pass circuit must dissipate an amount of power equal to the difference between the input power $V_{IN}I_O$ and the output power V_OI_O. As a result, the efficiency of this type of voltage regulator will be quite low, being given by

$$\text{efficiency} = \eta = \frac{P_O}{P_{IN}} = \frac{V_O I_O}{V_{IN} I_O} = \frac{V_O}{V_{IN}} \tag{2.75}$$

The fraction of the input power that is dissipated in the voltage regulator will therefore be

$$\frac{P_{IN} - P_O}{P_{IN}} = 1 - \eta = \frac{V_{IN} - V_O}{V_{IN}} \tag{2.76}$$

Since the output voltage is typically in the range $0.5\,V_{IN}$ to $0.7\,V_{IN}$, we see that the circuit efficiency will typically be in the range 50 to 70%. As a result, some 30 to 50% of the input power will have to be dissipated by the regulator.

The power dissipation in the regulator is not a serious problem for regulators supplying less than about 1 W. However, for output power levels much in excess of this, and in particular for levels above 10 W, the circuit inefficiency and in particular the power that must be dissipated by the series-pass circuit may pose serious problems. Due to the power transistor and the associated heat sinking requirements, the regulator cost, size, and weight will escalate rapidly with increasing output power requirements.

A useful alternative to the dissipative type of voltage regulator is one of the switching type. In the dissipative regulator the series-pass transistors operate continuously in the active region wherein the combination of a substantial current flow and concurrently a major voltage drop results in a large power dissipation as given by $P_d = (V_{IN} - V_O)I_O$. In contrast to this, in the switching regulator the series-pass transistors are not operated in the active mode, but rather are switched back and forth between cutoff and saturation.

In the switching regulator the power flow to the load is controlled by the duty cycle of the series-pass transistors, that is, the fraction of time that these transistors are in the "on" state. A fraction of the output voltage is supplied to the control circuitry and therein compared to the reference voltage. The difference between the feedback voltage and the reference voltage is amplified and used to control the duty cycle of the series-pass transistors. If the output voltage is too low, the control circuitry acts to lengthen the duty cycle, thus causing the output voltage to increase. If the output voltage is too high, the duty cycle is diminished and the output voltage decreases. In either case the output voltage will be stabilized at a level determined by the resistance ratio of the feedback voltage divider and the reference voltage. In Figure 2.25 a basic block diagram of a switching regulator is presented.

The power dissipation of the switching transistor will be relatively low. When the transistor is of the cutoff region of operation the current through the transistor will be negligibly small, so that the power dissipation will similarly be negligible. When the transistor is turned on, it will rapidly be driven into saturation by the control circuitry. In the saturation mode the voltage drop across the transistor will be relatively small, generally less than 1 V, and often down in the range of about 0.2 V. As a result of the small voltage drop across the transistor the instantaneous power dissipation will be correspondingly small. The only time in which there is a substantial amount of power dissipated in the transistor will be during the switching transition, when the transistor is passing through the active region in going from cutoff to saturation, or vice versa. The switching transition time will, however, represent only a very small fraction of the total time, so that the average power dissipation will be small. In Figure 2.26 the instantaneous power dissipation of the transistor as a function of time is presented.

If we now look at Figure 2.25, we see that a fraction $R_2/(R_1 + R_2)$ of the output voltage is fed back to the inverting input of the error amplifier, where it is compared to the reference voltage which is applied to the noninverting input of the error amplifier. The difference between the reference voltage and the feedback voltage is thus amplified and thence applied to the inverting input of the comparator.

The oscillator generates a triangular waveform at a fixed repetition frequency, and this voltage is applied to the noninverting input of the comparator. The output of the comparator will thus be in the high state during the time when the triangular voltage waveform is above the level of the error amplifier output, and it is during

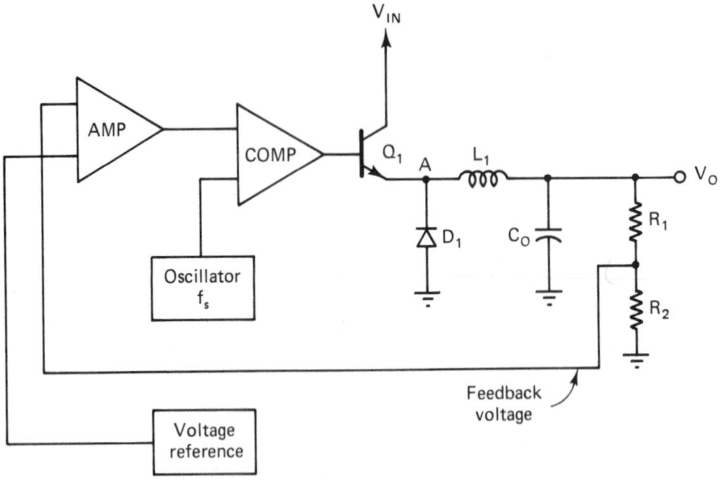

Figure 2.25 Basic diagram of a switching voltage regulator.

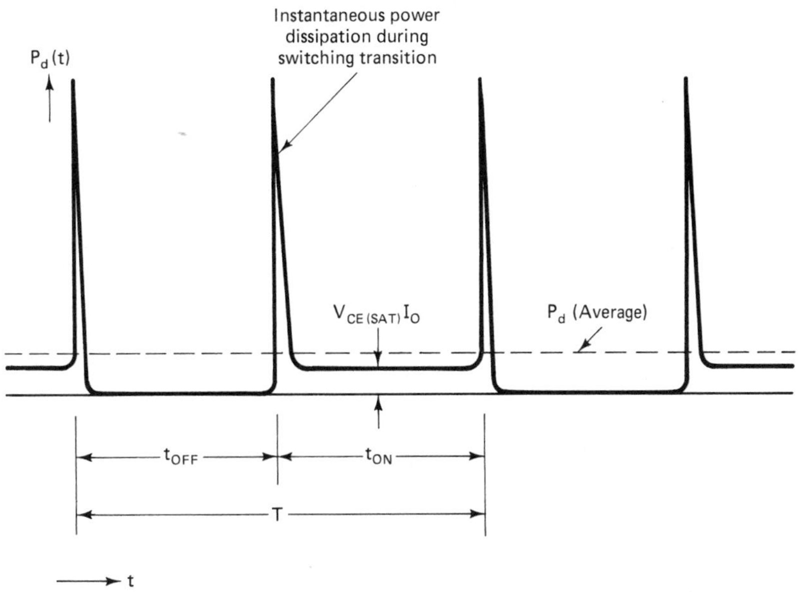

Figure 2.26 Instantaneous power dissipation of a switching transistor.

this time that the series-pass switching transistor will be turned on. During the remainder of the period the comparator output will be low and transistor Q_1 will be switched off. The output of the comparator is thus a pulse waveform, the period of which T is the same as the period of the oscillator output. The duty cycle, $\delta = t_{on}/T$, of the pulse waveform will be controlled by the difference between the feedback voltage and the reference voltage.

When Q_1 is on, the voltage applied to the inductor L_1 (at point A) will be $V_A = V_{IN} - V_{CE(SAT)} = V_{IN}$. This voltage will act to promote the flow of current through L_1. When Q_1 is turned off, the inductor L_1 will act to continue the current through itself and thus on to the load. Diode D_1 is used to provide a complete circuit during this period of time. When Q_1 is on, this diode will be biased off. Capacitor C_O acts to smooth out the voltage so that the output voltage will be a relatively smooth d-c voltage with very little a-c ripple.

During the time that Q_1 is off, the voltage at point A will be close to zero, actually one diode drop (0.7 V) below ground. The average voltage at point A will therefore be given by

$$\begin{aligned} V_A(\text{d-c}) &= (V_{IN} - V_{CE(SAT)})\frac{t_{on}}{T} + (-V_{D_1})\frac{t_{off}}{T} \\ &= V_{IN}\delta - V_{CE(SAT)}\delta - V_{D_1}(1-\delta) \qquad (2.77) \\ &\simeq V_{IN}\delta \end{aligned}$$

Since L_1 and C_O will not affect the d-c voltage, the d-c voltage at the output will be the same as at point A, namely $V_O = V_A = V_{IN}$. Thus we see that the d-c output voltage can be controlled or regulated by the control of the duty cycle by the feedback loop. The output voltage will be slightly smaller than V_{IN} due to $V_{CE(sat)}$ and the voltage drop of D_1. Both voltage drops will generally be in the neighborhood of about 0.7 V, so that we see that V_O will typically be around 0.7 V less than $V_{IN}(\delta)$. There will also be a small d-c voltage drop due to the series resistance of L_1, although this probably will not be in excess of about 0.1 V.

We have seen that the output voltage is controlled by the duty cycle $\delta = t_{on}/T$. For example, if $V_{IN} = 15$ V and V_O is to be 10 V, the duty cycle will be approximately given by $\delta = V_O/V_{IN} = 0.67$. Due to the transistor saturation voltage and the diode drop the duty cycle under steady-state conditions will actually have to be somewhat larger than this, probably around 0.70, so that Q_1 will be on for about 70% of the time (in saturation) and off (cutoff) for the remaining 30% of the time.

If the output voltage for some reason falls below 10 V, the feedback loop will act to increase the duty cycle and thereby bring the output voltage up to 10 V. Conversely, if for some reason, such as variations in load conditions or in line voltage, the output voltage goes above 10 V, the feedback loop will act to decrease the duty cycle and thereby bring the output voltage back down. The net result of the action of the feedback loop will be to regulate V_O at the design value given by $V_O = V_{REF}$ $(1 + R_1/R_2)$. The entire system acts basically as a pulse width modulator (PWM) to control the duty cycle with which the series-pass switching transistor is driven.

The optimum switching frequency f_s is generally in the range 10 to 100 kHz. A high switching frequency will allow for relatively small values of L_1 and C_O to be used, thus reducing the size, weight, and cost of the system. On the other hand, as the switching frequency goes up, the power dissipated by the switching transistor will increase as a result of the increase in the number of switching transitions per unit time. This increase in the transistor power dissipation is the result of the finite switching speed of the transistor. To maximize the circuit efficiency, therefore, a power transistor with a fast switching speed should be chosen. As a result of these considerations a switching frequency in the range 10 to 100 kHz is usually chosen, often about 20 to 50 kHz.

2.8.1 Current Waveforms

Now that we have been introduced to the basic principles of operation of the switching regulator, we will consider the current waveform through L_1 and the a-c voltage ripple across C_O, and then conclude with a design example.

The inductance value of L_1 is chosen such that there will be a continuity of current flow through the inductor throughout the entire switching cycle. Indeed, both L_1 and C_O will be large enough such that the current waveform of the inductor current I_L will have an approximately triangular waveform superimposed on a d-c current level, which is equal to the load current. This is shown in Figure 2.27.

The relationship between the voltage across L_1 and the current through L_1 is given by $V_L = L(di_L/dt)$. As a result of the approximately linear slope of the current waveform, we can express this relationship during the "on" time as

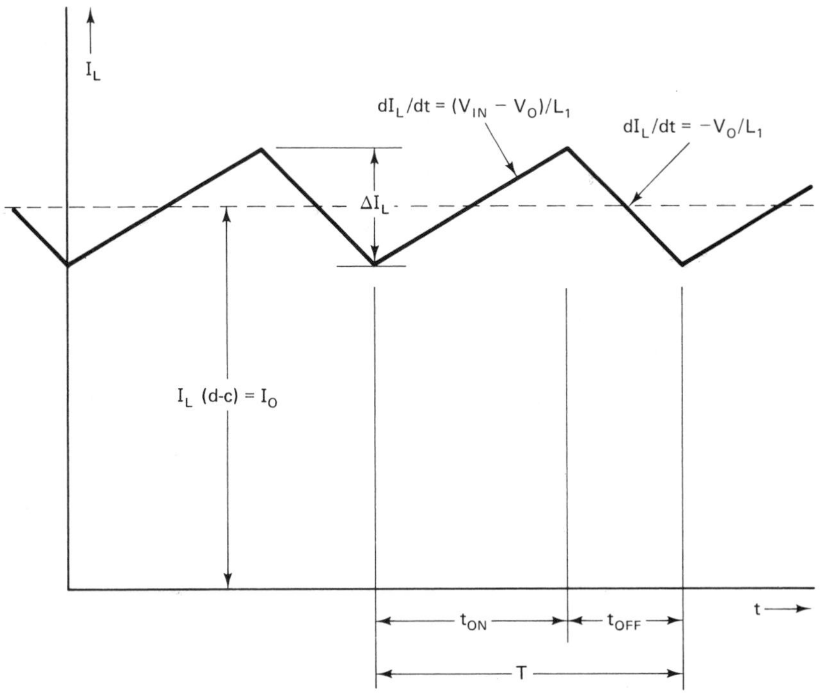

Figure 2.27 Inductor current waveform.

$$V_L = V_{IN} - V_O = L\frac{\Delta I_L}{t_{on}}$$

so that the change in the current during the "on" time will be given by

$$\Delta I_L = \frac{1}{L}(V_{IN} - V_O)t_{on} \tag{2.78}$$

During the "off" time the voltage across L_1 will be $-V_D - V_O = -V_O$, so that the change in the current through L_1 during this time period will be given by

$$\Delta I_L = \frac{1}{L}(-V_O)t_{off} \tag{2.79}$$

Since the current will be a continuous function of time, the algebraic sum of these two changes in the current must be zero, so that we have $(V_{IN} - V_O)t_{on} = V_O t_{off}$, giving $V_{IN}t_{on} = V_O(t_{on} + t_{off}) = V_O T$, and thus $V_O/V_{IN} = t_{on}/T = \delta$, which is the same as the result obtained earlier. A somewhat more rigorous analysis in which the transistor saturation voltage and the diode drop are taken into account will yield

$$V_O = V_{IN}\delta = V_{CE(SAT)}\delta - V_{D1}(1 - \delta) \tag{2.80}$$

which is again consistent with the previous results.

For the proper operation of this switching regulator, in particular for a maximally smooth output waveform, it is important that the current through the inductor never never drop to zero or even reverse direction. Therefore, we must ensure that ΔI_L never approach the d-c inductor current level, which is the same as the d-c output current I_O. To take into account variations in I_O with loading conditions, a suitable safety factor will be to have $\Delta I_L \lesssim 0.4 I_O$. Since we can express ΔI_L as $\Delta I_L = (1/L) V_{ON} t_{off}$, we can solve for L_1 as

$$L_1 = \frac{V_O t_{off}}{\Delta I_L} \gtrsim \frac{V_O t_{off}}{0.4 I_O} \tag{2.81}$$

Since $t_{off} = T(1 - \delta)$, this can be rewritten as

$$L_1 \geq \frac{(V_O/I_O)T(1-\delta)}{0.4} = R_L T(1-\delta)2.5$$

2.8.2 Output Ripple Factor

The voltage at point A will be basically a repetitive pulse waveform with a duty cycle δ and an amplitude of approximately V_{IN}. The pulse waveform is applied to L_1 and C_O, which act as a low-pass filter to smooth out this voltage waveform and produce a d-c voltage across C_O that is the average value of the input voltage, V_{IN}.

The capacitance value for C_O will be such that the reactance of C_O at the a-c frequencies of interest will be small compared to the load resistance R_L. As a result, L_1 and C_O can, to a good degree of approximation, be considered at the a-c frequencies of interest to be a simple voltage divider. The ratio of the a-c output voltage at frequency f to the a-c input voltage at the same frequency will be given by

$$\frac{v_o(f)}{v_A(f)} = \frac{1/j\omega C_O)}{j\omega L_1 + 1/j\omega C_O} \simeq -\frac{1}{\omega^2 L_1 C_O} \tag{2.82}$$

where $\omega = 2\pi f$ is the radian frequency. The negative sign for the voltage ratio is simply indicative of a 180° phase shift in the low-pass network.

To obtain an expression for the output a-c ripple voltage, we will consider the simple representative case of a 50% duty cycle for which case the d-c output voltage will be $V_O \simeq \frac{1}{2} V_{IN}$, and the voltage applied to the low-pass filter (at point A) will be a square wave of amplitude V_{IN} and period $T = 1/f_s$, where f_s is the oscillator frequency.

The Fourier series for this square wave will be given by

$$v_A(t) = V_{IN}\left(\frac{1}{2} + \frac{2}{\pi}\cos\omega t - \frac{2}{3\pi}\cos 3\omega t + \frac{2}{5\pi}\cos 5\omega t - \cdots\right) \tag{2.83}$$

where $\omega = 2\pi f_s$. We see that the input voltage to the low-pass filter will consist of a d-c component $V_{IN}/2$, a fundamental component at $f = f_s$, and various odd harmonic components at $f = nf_s$, where n is an odd integer. We further note that the amplitude of the various harmonic terms decreases as $1/n$.

The attenuation of the low-pass filter is proportional to f^2. This, together with the fact that the amplitudes of the various harmonic terms at the filter input decrease as $1/n$, will mean that the dominant component of the output a-c ripple voltage with be the fundamental term at $f = f_s$, with the other harmonics being of relatively little importance.

The a-c output ripple voltage will therefore be given approximately by

$$v_o(\text{a-c}) = v_o(f_s) = \frac{2}{\pi} V_{IN} \frac{1}{\omega_s^2 L_1 C_O} \tag{2.84}$$

Since $V_O \simeq V_{IN}/2$ and $\omega_s = 2\pi f_s$, this can be rewritten as

$$v_o(\text{a-c}) = \frac{4}{\pi} V_O \frac{1}{4\pi^2 f_s^2 L_1 C_o} \simeq \frac{1}{30 f_s^2 L_1 C_o} V_O \tag{2.85}$$

The output ripple factor is the ratio of the peak-to-peak ripple voltage to the d-c output voltage. From the preceding equation we can thus directly write the ripple factor as

$$r = \text{ripple factor} = \frac{v_o(\text{a-c})_{\text{peak-to-peak}}}{V_O} \simeq \frac{1}{15 f_s^2 L_1 C_o} \tag{2.86}$$

We thus see that the ripple factor will be inversely proportional to the square of the switching frequency and to the $L_1 C_O$ product. With a high switching frequency, therefore, a moderately small value of inductance and capacitance can be used.

2.8.3 Design Example

For a design example we will stipulate the following:

I_O = d-c output (load) current = 1.0 A
V_O = d-c output voltage = 10 V
V_{IN} = 20 V
f_s = switching frequency = 30 kHz
output ripple factor = 0.05%

For the inductor L_1 we have the following requirement:

$$L_1 = \frac{R_L T(1-\delta)}{0.4} = \frac{2.5 R_L (1-\delta)}{f_s} = \frac{2.5 \times 10\ \Omega \times 0.5}{30\ \text{kHz}} \tag{2.87}$$

so that $L_1 = 417\ \mu\text{H}$. A choice of 500 μH will therefore be adequate. From the ripple factor condition we have

$$5 \times 10^{-4} \geq \frac{1}{15 f_s^2 L_1 C_o} = \frac{1}{15(30\ \text{kHz})^2(500 \times 10^{-6}) C_O} \tag{2.88}$$

so that

$$C_O \geq 296\ \mu\text{F} \tag{2.89}$$

Therefore, a choice of 300 to 500 μF for C_O should prove satisfactory. The 0.05% ripple factor will correspond to a peak-to-peak output ripple voltage of only 5 mV, so that the d-c output waveform of this regulator circuit will be quite smooth.

2.8.4 Step-up Switching Voltage Regulator

The basic circuit of the switching regulator that has been discussed thus far is shown in Figure 2.28a. This type of switching regulator is called a step-down regulator since the output voltage is less than the input voltage (i.e., $V_O < V_{IN}$), and V_O is related to V_{IN} approximately by $V_O = \delta\ V_{IN}$, where $\delta = t_{on}/T$ is the duty cycle.

With the switching regulator it is also possible to achieve a voltage step up so that V_O will be greater than V_{IN}. The basic circuit of the step-up regulator is shown in Figure 2.28b.

It might at first be thought that it is not possible to have the output voltage greater than the input voltage. It is, however, the voltage induced in the inductor adding to the input voltage that produces an output voltage that is greater than the input voltage. During the time that Q_1 is off the reduction in the current through the inductor produces a voltage across the inductor given by $V_L = L(di_L/dt)$ that adds to V_{IN} to make V_O greater than V_{IN}. It should also be noted that even though $V_O > V_{IN}$, the output power $P_O = V_O I_O$ will not, of course, be any greater than the input power, $P_{IN} = I_{IN} V_{IN}$, since the input current will be larger than the output current.

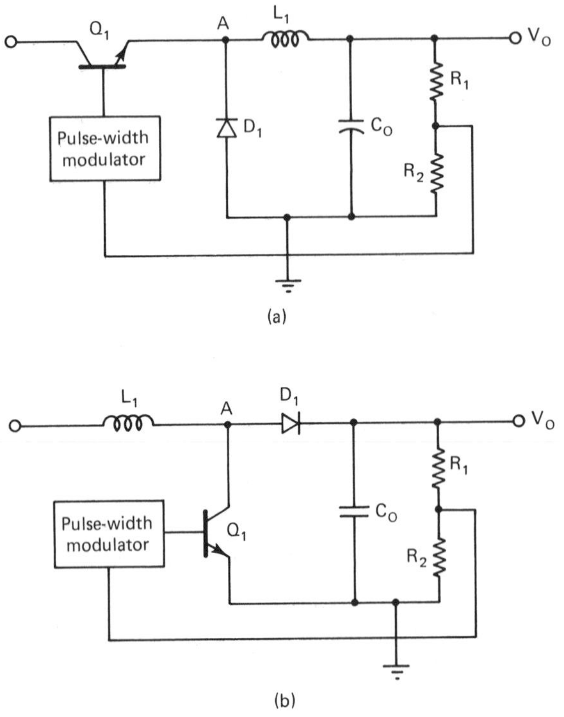

Figure 2.28 (a) Basic circuit of the step-down switching regulator; (b) basic circuit of the step-up switching regulator.

We can now easily derive the relationship between the input and output voltages of the step-up switching regulator. For this derivation we will assume that L_1 is large enough such that the current through L_1 will have a triangular waveform. During the time that Q_1 is off, the voltage across the inductor will be given by $V_{IN} - V_D - V_O = L(di_L/dt)$, where V_D is the forward-bias voltage drop of D_1 (about 0.7 V). Assuming a linear variation of current with time, we will therefore have that

$$\Delta I_L = \frac{1}{L}(V_{IN} - V_D - V_O)t_{off} \tag{2.90}$$

During the time interval that Q_1 is on (in saturation) we have that

$$V_{IN} - V_{CE(SAT)} = L\frac{di_L}{dt} \tag{2.91}$$

so that

$$\Delta I_L = \frac{1}{L}(V_{IN} - V_{CE(SAT)})t_{on}$$

Since the current flow through L_1 must be a continuous function of time, the algebraic sum of these two current changes must be zero, so that we have $\Delta I_L(t_{off}) + \Delta I_L(t_{on}) = 0$. Substituting in the equations above gives us

$$(V_{IN} - V_D - V_O)t_{off} + (V_{IN} - V_{CE(SAT)})t_{on} = 0 \tag{2.92}$$

Solving this for V_O gives

$$V_O = \frac{V_{IN}(t_{on} + t_{off}) - V_D t_{off} - V_{CE(SAT)}t_{on}}{t_{off}} \tag{2.93}$$

so that

$$V_O = V_{IN}\left(1 + \frac{t_{on}}{t_{off}}\right) - V_{CE(SAT)}(t_{on}/t_{off}) - V_D \tag{2.94}$$

Since V_D is approximately 0.7 V and $V_{CE(SAT)}$ will be less than 1 V, we see that it is quite possible to have V_O greater than V_{IN} if t_{off} is less than t_{on}. In terms of the duty cycle δ, the equation above can be rewritten as

$$V_O = \frac{V_{IN}}{1-\delta} - V_{CE(SAT)}\frac{\delta}{1-\delta} - V_D \tag{2.95}$$

For example, if we have that V_D and $V_{CE(SAT)}$ are both approximately 0.7 V, for a duty cycle of 0.7 and an input voltage of 10 V, we have

$$\begin{aligned} V_O &= \frac{10}{0.3} - 0.7\left(\frac{0.7}{0.3}\right) - 0.7 \qquad (2.96) \\ &= 31 \text{ V} \end{aligned}$$

Due to losses in L_1 and in the transistor during the switching transitions, the actual output voltage may be closer to 30 V. In any case, we see that a 3:1 voltage step-up has been achieved.

When Q_1 is on the voltage at point A will be $V_{CE(SAT)}$. When Q_1 is off, the voltage at point A will be equal to the input voltage plus the voltage induced in L_1 due to the falling current. This induced voltage will be approximately $V_{IN}(t_{on}/t_{off})$, so that the total voltage at point A during this time interval will be approximately $V_{IN}(1 + t_{on}/t_{off})$. This relationship can be readily obtained by noting that when Q_1 is on, the increase in the current through L_1 will be given by $\Delta I_L = (1/L)V_{IN}t_{on}$. When Q_1 is off, the change in the current will be $\Delta I_L + (1/L)(V_{IN} - V_A)t_{off}$. The diode drop and the transistor saturation voltage have been neglected for purposes of simplicity. Since the net change in the inductor current over the complete switching cycle must be zero, we have that $V_{IN}t_{on} + (V_{IN} - V_A)t_{off} = 0$, so that solving for V_A we have $V_A = V_{IN}(1 + t_{on}/t_{off})$.

In Figure 2.29 a diagram of the voltage waveform at point A is presented. Notice that this is a repetitive pulse waveform. The circuit to the right of point A, particularly the combination of the diode D_1 and the capacitor C_O, can be considered to be essentially a peak detector circuit giving an output waveform shown in Figure 2.29. During the pulses the capacitor will charge up via D_1 to the peak pulse amplitude $V_{IN}(1 + t_{on}/t_{off})$. Between pulses, however, the diode D_1 will be off so that the capacitor will discharge through the load. The rate of discharge of the capacitor will be $dQ_c/dt = I_O = V_O/R_L$, where R_L is the load resistance. If the circuit is designed for a low-output ripple factor V_O and therefore I_O will not change much on a percentage basis during the discharge time, the total charge lost by the capacitor during this time will be given by $\Delta Q_C = I_O t_{on} = V_O t_{on}/R_L$.

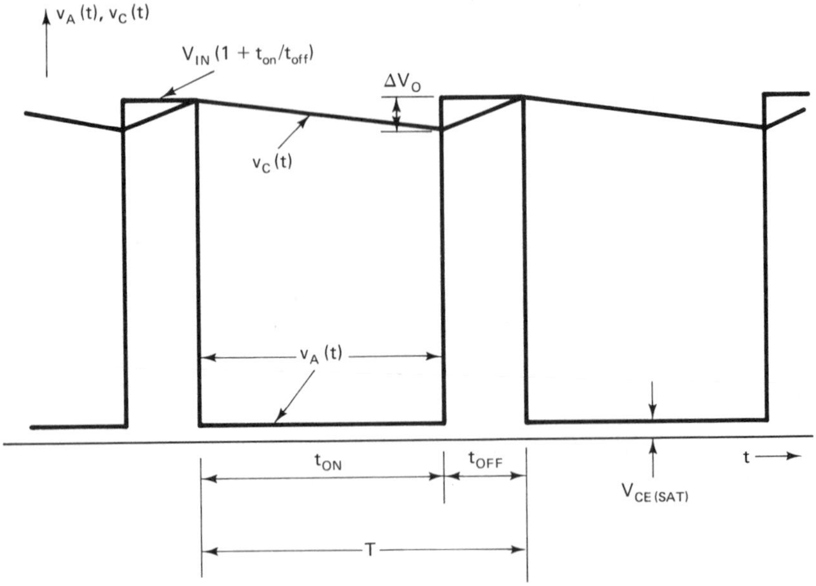

Figure 2.29 Voltage waveforms for step-up switching regulator.

The droop or sag in the output voltage at the end of the discharge time will be given by

$$\Delta V_O = \frac{\Delta Q_C}{C_O} = \frac{I_O t_{on}}{C_O} = \frac{V_O t_{on}}{R_L C_O} \tag{2.97}$$

This drop in the output voltage will be the peak-to-peak ripple voltage. The ripple factor will therefore be given by

$$\text{ripple factor} = R = \frac{\Delta V_O}{V_O} = \frac{t_{on}}{R_L C_O} = \frac{\delta T}{R_L C_O} = \frac{\delta}{f R_L C_O}$$

where f is the switching frequency.

For a representative example let us take $\delta = 0.7$, $f = 30$ kHz, $V_O = 30$ V, and $I_O = 0.5$ A. For a ripple factor at the output not to exceed 0.1%, the required value for C_O will be given by

$$C_O = \frac{\delta}{f R_L C_O} = \frac{0.7}{(30\text{ kHz} \times 60\ \Omega \times 0.001} \tag{2.98}$$
$$= \underline{389\ \mu\text{F}}$$

Thus a choice of a 500-μF, 50-V capacitor would prove to be satisfactory.

2.8.5 Effective Series Resistance

It is appropriate at this point to discuss another important factor in the capacitor selection for switching voltage regulators. This factor is the "effective series resistance" or ESR of the capacitor. Any real capacitor will exhibit together with the desired capacitance effect a parasitic series resistance, R_S, which is the effective series resistance. This series resistance will vary somewhat with frequency and with temperature.

To illustrate the importance of the ESR in the capacitor specification we will return to a consideration of the preceding example. During the discharge interval the current flowing out of the capacitor will be I_O, so that the additional drop in the capacitor voltage due to R_S will be $I_O R_S$. During the charge interval (D_1 on, Q_1 off) the charge supplied to the capacitor must make up for the charge lost during the discharge time, so that we will have

$$I_C t_{off} = I_O t_{on}$$

and thus

$$I_C = I_O \frac{t_{on}}{t_{off}} \tag{2.99}$$

where I_C is the current into the capacitor during the charging time. During this time interval there will be an additional rise in the capacitor voltage due to R_S given by $\Delta V_C = \Delta V_O = I_O R_S (t_{on}/t_{off})$. Therefore the increase in the peak-to-peak ripple voltage due to the effects of R_S will be given by

$$\Delta V_{O\,(\text{peak-to-peak})} = I_O R_S\left(1+\frac{t_{\text{on}}}{t_{\text{off}}}\right) = I_O R_S \frac{V_O}{V_{\text{IN}}} \tag{2.100}$$

For a 0.1% ripple factor and a 10-V output voltage, the corresponding peak-to-peak ripple voltage will be 10 mV. For an output current of 0.5 A and a step-up voltage ratio of 3:1, the maximum allowable value of R_S will be given by the condition that

$$10\text{ mV} = 0.5\text{ A} \times R_S \times 3 \tag{2.101}$$

so that

$$R_S = \frac{10\text{ mV}}{1.5\text{ A}} = 7\text{ m}\Omega$$

This low value of effective series resistance may be very difficult to achieve in practice so that the 0.1% ripple factor may not be readily achievable. We see therefore that the ESR may be the dominant factor in determining the ripple factor and is therefore a very important factor in the capacitor selection.

2.8.6 Self-Oscillating Switching Regulators

The switching regulators described thus far have been of the externally excited or driven type, in which an oscillator or square-wave generator external to the voltage regulator circuit is used to determine the switching frequency. The regulator circuit itself acts as a pulse-width modulator to control the duty cycle of the pulses supplied by the oscillator.

In the interest of greater overall circuit simplicity it is possible to have a self-oscillating switching regulator in which a separate oscillator circuit is not needed. The self-excited condition of the switching regulator arises by means of a positive-feedback loop, as shown in Figure 2.30.

The positive feedback is obtained via the R_3–R_4 voltage divider. A small fraction

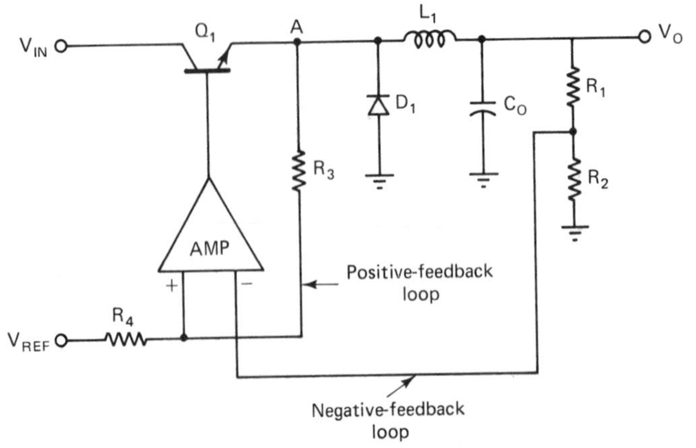

Figure 2.30 Basic diagram of the self-oscillating switching regulator.

of the voltage (typically 0.01 to 0.001) of the voltage at point A is fed back to the noninverting input of the error amplifier together with the reference voltage. There is at the same time negative feedback via the R_1–R_2 voltage divider in which a fraction of the output voltage is fed back to the inverting input of the amplifier.

To see how the self-oscillating switch regulator operates, let us start off when the input voltage is first applied, so that V_O starts off at zero. The reference voltage applied to the amplifier will cause Q_1 to turn on and go into saturation and V_O will start to increase. This will continue until the output voltage reaches a value such that the voltage fed back to the inverting input via the R_1–R_2 voltage divider equals the voltage applied to the noninverting input. These two voltages are $V_O R_2/(R_1 + R_2)$ and $V_{REF} + (V_{IN} - V_{SAT})R_4/(R_3 + R_4)$, respectively. When the voltage fed back via the negative-feedback loop approaches to voltage applied to the noninverting input of the amplifier, the output voltage of the amplifier will start to drop. This in turn will cause the voltage at point A to drop, and via the positive feedback loop, the voltage at the noninverting input terminal will also start to drop. This drop in the voltage at the noninverting input will accelerate the drop in the amplifier output voltage and thus in the drop in the voltage at point A. As a result of this positive-feedback condition Q_1 will rapidly be driven into cutoff.

With Q_1 in cutoff the output voltage will start to fall. As soon as the voltage fed back by the negative-feedback loop approaches the voltage at the noninverting input, the output of the amplifier will once again start to go up. This will cause Q_1 to turn on, raising the voltage at point A. This rise in voltage will be fed back to the amplifier via the positive feedback loop and accelerate the turn-on of Q_1, with Q_1 rapidly being driven into saturation. The output voltage will again start to go up and the cycle will then be repeated.

2.8.7 Switching Frequency

We will now derive an approximate expression for the switching frequency. We will first note that when Q_1 is on, the positive-feedback voltage will be $(V_{IN} - V_{SAT})R_4/(R_3 + R_4)$, where $V_{SAT} = V_{CE(SAT)}$ is the saturation voltage of Q_1. When Q_1 is off, the positive-feedback voltage will be $(-V_D)R_4/(R_3 + R_4)$, where V_D is the forward-bias voltage drop of D_1. The peak-to-peak swing in the positive-feedback voltage will therefore be $(V_{IN} - V_{SAT} + V_D)R_4/(R_3 + R_4) = V_{IN}R_4/(R_3 + R_4)$ since both V_{SAT} and V_D will have about the same value (0.7 V).

As a result of the switching action of Q_1, the output voltage will have some peak-to-peak ripple component. The switching of Q_1 via the amplifier occurs when the voltages at the two amplifier input terminals become equal to each other. Therefore, the peak-to-peak excursions in the positive-feedback voltage must be matched by an equal excursion in the negative-feedback voltage that is fed back to the inverting input of the amplifier via the R_1–R_2 voltage divider.

We will now turn our attention to the voltage fed back to the inverting input terminal via the negative-feedback loop. In addition to the d-c component of this feedback voltage there will be a small a-c component resulting from the a-c ripple on the output. Assuming a duty cycle of around 50% the input voltage can be considered to be a square wave with a peak amplitude of V_{IN}. The L_1–C_O network can be considered to be a simple voltage divider for the a-c frequencies of interest with a voltage division ratio of

$$\frac{v_o}{v_A} = \frac{1/j\omega C_O}{j\omega L_1 + (1/j\omega C_O)} \simeq \frac{1}{\omega^2 L_1 C_O} \tag{2.102}$$

since $\omega L_1 \gg I/\omega C_O$ for the frequencies of interest.

The voltage at point A can be analyzed using a Fourier series to give a d-c component, a fundamental term at the switching frequency and various odd harmonic terms. Due to the rapidly increasing attenuation of the L_1–C_O network with increasing frequency it will only be the fundamental term in the output that will be of any importance (except for the d-c term, of course). The fundamental term in the Fourier series has an amplitude given by $(2/\pi)V_{IN}$ at point A. At the output of the L_1–C_O low-pass filter the amplitude will be reduced by the factor $1/\omega^2 L_1 C_O$ to $v_o = (2/\pi)(1/\omega^2 L_1 C_O)V_{IN}$. The peak-to-peak voltage ripple at the output will therefore be twice this.

The peak-to-peak swing in the voltage fed back to the inverting input terminal of the amplifier will therefore be given by $(R_2/R_1 + R_2)\,(4/\pi)(1/\omega^2 L_1 C_O)V_{IN}$. If we now equate the peak-to-peak voltage excursions at the amplifier input terminals, we obtain

$$\frac{V_{IN}(4/\pi)}{\omega^2 L_1 C_O} \frac{R_2}{R_1 + R_2} = V_{IN} \frac{R_4}{R_3 + R_4} \tag{2.103}$$

so that solving for ω, we obtain

$$\omega^2 = \frac{4/\pi}{L_1 C_O} \frac{R_2}{R_1 + R_2} \frac{R_3 + R_4}{R_4} \tag{2.104}$$

The switching frequency will therefore be given by

$$(2\pi f)^2 = \frac{4/\pi}{L_1 C_O} \frac{V_{REF}}{V_O} \frac{R_3 + R_4}{R_4} \tag{2.105}$$

after noting that $V_O R_2/(R_1 + R_2) = V_{REF}$. We see that the switching frequency will be a function of the $L_1 C_O$ product as well as the feedback factors for both the positive- and negative-feedback loops.

We will now consider a representative example and we will use some of the design specifications of the switching regulator considered previously: $I_O = 1.0$ A, $V_O = 10$ V, $V_{IN} = 20$ V, $f_s = 30$ kHz, and a ripple factor of 0.05%. To meet the ripple factor specification we obtained $L_1 = 500\ \mu$H and $C_O = 300\ \mu$F. We will now use these values to determine the values of R_3 and R_4 required to make this a self-oscillating regulator. We will assume a reference voltage of 1.8 V.

If we solve the equation above for the positive-feedback factor, $R_4/(R_3 + R_4)$, we obtain

$$\frac{R_4}{R_3 + R_4} = \frac{4/\pi}{\omega^2 L_1 C_O} \frac{V_{REF}}{V_O} \tag{2.106}$$

so that

$$\frac{R_4}{R_3 + R_4} = 4.3 \times 10^{-5}$$

Thus the positive-feedback factor required is extremely small. The small value of the positive-feedback factor is due in most part to the very small ripple factor. Indeed, the positive feedback factor can be obtained more directly by expressing the peak-to-peak negative-feedback excursion directly in terms of the ripple factor as $rV_OR_2/(R_1 + R_2)$, where r is the peak-to-peak ripple factor. Since $V_OR_2/(R_1 + R_2) = V_{REF}$, this can be rewritten as rV_{REF}. Thus the peak-to-peak excursion in the negative-feedback voltage is simply equal to product of the ripple factor and the reference voltage. Since the peak-to-peak excursion in the positive-feedback voltage has previously been given as $V_{IN}R_4/(R_3 + R_4)$, we can now obtain the equation for the required positive-feedback factor by equating the two peak-to-peak excursions giving $V_{IN}R_4/(R_3 + R_4) = rV_{REF}$, so that $R_4/(R_3 + R_4) = rV_{REF}/V_{IN}$.

If we use a ripple factor of 0.05%, a reference voltage of 1.8 V, and an input voltage of 20 V, we obtain a positive-feedback factor of 4.5×10^{-5}, which is essentially the same as obtained previously. If R_4 is the source resistance of the voltage reference circuit of 1 kΩ, the value of $R_3 + R_4$ will be 22 MΩ, so that R_3 will be essentially 22 MΩ.

In practice, a ripple factor as low as 0.05% may be very difficult to achieve in a switching regulator due to the effects of the capacitor series resistance (ESR). In practice, a ripple factor in the range of 0.1 to 1% may be the best that can be achieved. For a ripple factor of 1%, the calculations above would yield a positive-feedback factor of 9×10^{-4} , so that R_3 would now be 1.1 MΩ.

One of the principal disadvantages of the switching type of voltage regulator in comparison to the linear or nonswitching type (i.e., the dissipative type) is the greater ripple factor present at the output of the switching regulator. With the linear regulator the output ripple is reduced below the input ripple level by the ripple rejection factor of the regulator. This factor is typically in the range 60 to 80 dB. For example, if the input ripple is 1% and the ripple rejection factor is 60 dB, the output ripple will be only 0.001%.

On the other hand, it must be understood that in the switching regulator the output ripple is due principally to the switching action of the regulator itself and is not due to the feedthrough of ripple from the input circuit. As a result of this a smaller filter capacitor and inductor can be used in the rectifier power supply that provides the input voltage for the switching regulator. In addition, the output ripple that does result is at a relatively high frequency, typically in the range 20 to 50 kHz as compared to the predominant output ripple component of 120 Hz for the linear type of regulator. The higher ripple frequency of the switching regulator can much more easily be filtered than that of the linear regulator by the use of low-pass filters or bandpass filters at various critical points in the circuits that are supplied by the regulator. Furthermore, with the driven switching regulator it is possible to synchronize the switching rate with some other frequency in the system supplied by the regulator such that the ripple is less of a problem.

2.8.8 Examples of Switching Regulator Circuits

We will now consider some examples of switching regulator circuits starting off with the externally driven regulators. The externally driven regulators offer the advantage of operating at a fixed switching frequency that is independent of line and load conditions. This fixed switching frequency can be chosen so as to optimize performance of the regulator. The disadvantage of the externally driven regulator is, of course, the necessity of proving for a square-wave oscillator circuit to drive the regulator.

In Figure 2.31 a circuit diagram is present of an adjustable voltage regulator that is connected as an externally driven switching regulator. The voltage regulator itself can be any of the LM105 or LM376 type, and is similar to that presented in Figure 2.12. The current boost circuitry consisting of Q_1 and Q_2 and R_5 is the same as for the linear regulator circuit. Resistor R_4 is used for current limiting, and there is a feedback of a portion of the output voltage via the R_1–R_2 voltage divider to the inverting input of the error amplifier (pin 6).

The square-wave input is integrated by the R_3–C_3 network to become a triangular waveform that is applied to the noninverting input of the error amplifier (pin 5). The internally generated reference voltage is also applied to this amplifier input so

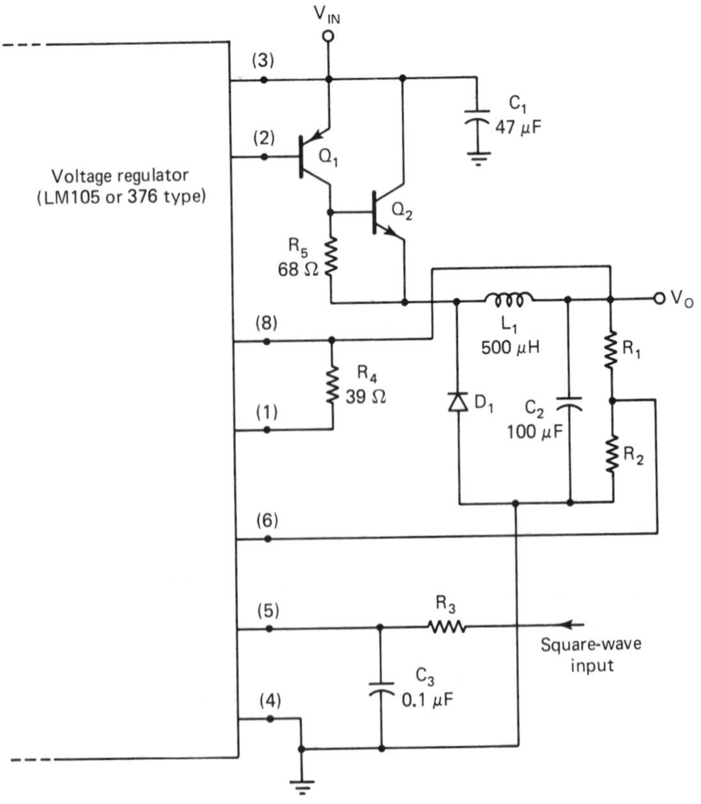

Figure 2.31 Switching regulator driven by external square-wave generator.

that the total instantaneous voltage consists of a small-amplitude triangular waveform superimposed on the reference voltage as shown in Figure 2.32. The peak-to-peak excursion of the triangular waveform is typically about 40 mV for the best performance of the circuit.

With the input voltages just described, the error amplifier operates as a pulse-width modulator. The two input voltages of the error amplifier are shown in Figure 2.32. The output of the error amplifier will be in the high state whenever $V_{\text{REF}} + v_{\text{triangular}}$ is greater than the feedback voltage, $V_{FB} = V_O R_2/(R_1 + R_2.)$ When this happens Q_1 and Q_2 will be turned on (in saturation). Conversely, when $V_{\text{REF}} + v_{\text{triangular}}$ is less than V_{FB}, the error amplifier output will be in the low state and Q_1 and Q_2 will be off. We therefore see that the series-pass transistors will be turned on and off every cycle of the input square wave. The duty cycle, $\delta = t_{\text{on}}/T$, will be a function of the value of V_{FB} relative to V_{REF}.

Under steady-state equilibrium conditions, the duty cycle will be adjusted by the feedback loop at the value necessary to maintain the desired output voltage. For example, if $V_{\text{IN}} = 20$ V and V_O is to be 5 V, a duty cycle of approximately 25% is required, essentially as is shown in Figure 2.32. Assuming a reference voltage

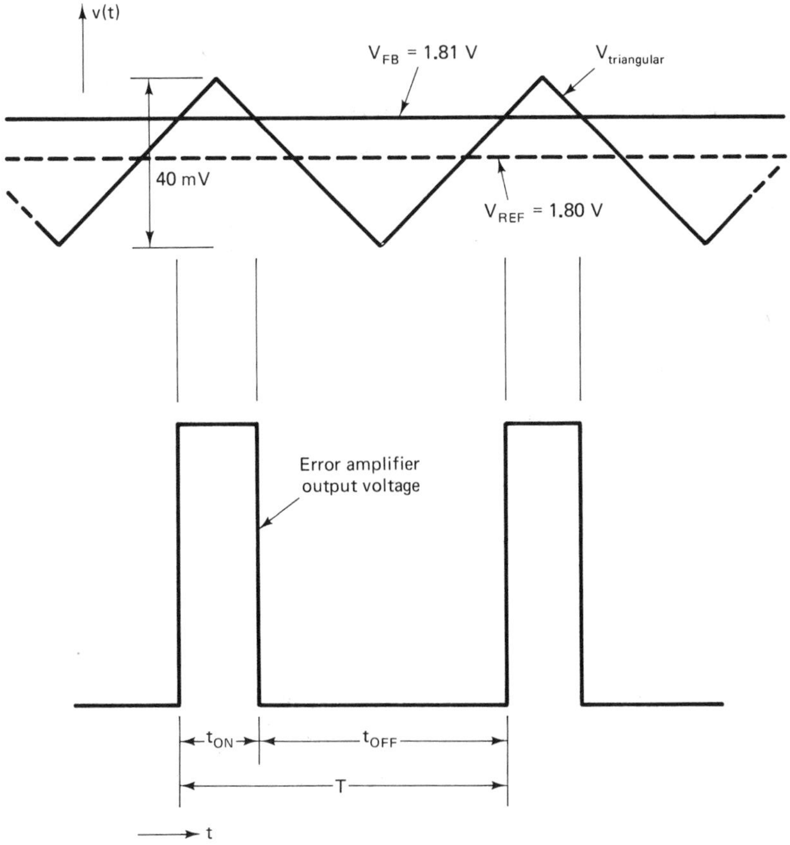

Figure 2.32 Voltage waveforms for driven switching regulator.

of $V_{REF} = 1.80$ V and a 40 mV peak-to-peak swing for the triangular waveform, the value of V_{FB} under equilibrium conditions will be $V_{FB} = V_{REF} + 10$ mV $=$ 1.81 V. For a 5.0-V output, the required resistance ratio will be given by the equation (5.0 V)$(1 + R_1/R_2) = V_{REF} + 10$ mV $= 1.81$ V.

Now if for some reason, such as an increased load current or a drop in line voltage, the output voltage drops below 5.0 V, we see that the duty cycle will lengthen and become greater than 25%. The increased duty cycle will bring V_O up back toward 5.0 V. Conversely, if for some reason, such as a sudden drop in load current V_O goes above 5.0 V, we see that the duty cycle will shorten to less than 25%. The shorter duty cycle will act to bring V_O back toward the 5.0-V equilibrium level.

We see from this example that the triangular waveform input will produce, in effect, a small shift in the reference voltage. In the example above, with a 25% duty cycle, a 10-mV shift resulted. For this reason, and the fact that the amplitude of the triangular waveform may not be temperature-compensated or well regulated, an excessively large peak-to-peak amplitude for the triangular waveform is to be avoided. On the other hand, too small an amplitude for the triangular waveform may allow the circuit to go into self-oscillation. The peak-to-peak amplitude of the triangular wave should usually be in the range 10 to 100 mV, with 40 mV generally being about the optimum value.

Self-oscillating switching regulator. A diagram of a self-oscillating switching regulator is presented in Figure 2.33. The connections shown are made to a linear voltage regulator of the LM105 or LM376 type. Most of the circuitry is the same as for the externally driven regulator that has just been discussed. The principal difference has to do with the signal fed to the noninverting input of the error amplifier (pin 5). In the externally driven regulator this was a triangular waveform obtained by the integration of a square wave input. In the self-oscillating regulator it is obtained from the emitter of Q_2 via resistor R_3. It is this connection that provides the positive feedback that is necessary to sustain oscillations.

The resistance seen looking into pin 5 is essentially the source resistance of the voltage reference of about 1 kΩ. Therefore, the positive feedback factor is approximately 1 kΩ/1 MΩ = 0.001.

From the analysis of the self-oscillating switching regulator we have obtained the simple relationship between the output ripple factor r and the positive-feedback factor as given by

$$\frac{rV_{REF}}{V_{IN}} = \frac{R_4}{R_3 + R_4} = \text{positive-feedback factor} \tag{2.107}$$

Now if for an example we let $V_{IN} = 20$ V and $V_{REF} = 1.8$ V, and for the moment neglect the effect of C_3, we have that

$$r\left(\frac{1.8}{20}\right) = \frac{1\text{k}\Omega}{1\text{M}\Omega} = 0.001 \tag{2.108}$$

so that the ripple factor will be r = 1.1%.

We will now consider the effect of C_3. Capacitor C_3 will, of course, have no influence on the d-c output voltage. If, however, the reactance of C_3 is small compared

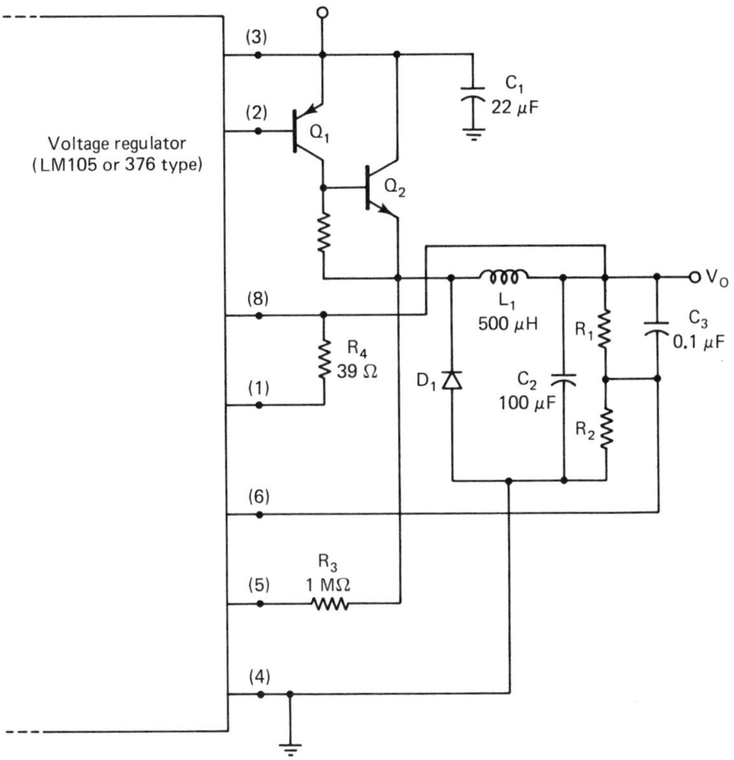

Figure 2.33 Self-oscillating switching regulator.

to the resistance of R_2, then almost the full a-c ripple voltage will appear at the noninverting amplifier input (pin 6). We must accordingly modify the relationship used above. Since the peak-to-peak excursion at pin 5 will be $V_{IN}R_4/(R_3 + R_4)$, and that at pin 6 will now be given by rV_O, we will have that

$$r\frac{V_O}{V_{IN}} = \frac{R_4}{(R_3 + R_4)} \tag{2.109}$$

Assuming an output voltage of 10 V, the ripple factor becomes

$$r = 0.001 \times \frac{20\text{ V}}{10\text{ V}} = 0.002 \quad \text{or} \quad \underline{0.2\%} \tag{2.110}$$

In practice this low a value for the ripple factor may be difficult to achieve due to the effects of the capacitor (C_2) effective series resistance.

With this type of regulator operating at an output voltage of 10 V and input voltages in the range 13 to 40 V, efficiencies in the range 85 to 90% are obtainable at an output current level of 1 A. As the output current increases, the efficiency will decrease slowly as a result of the increasing I^2R losses in the inductor and in the transistor, but even at 5-A output current the efficiency will still be up at around 72% with $V_{IN} = 28$ V.

With the component values as shown in Figure 2.32, the switching frequency will range from about 20 kHz at an output current of 0.5 A to 40 kHz at 5.0 A. The change in the switching frequency is due in large part to the decrease in the inductance of the coil with increasing current resulting from the effects of magnetic saturation of the inductor core.

2.8.9 Regulating Pulse-Width Modulator

Another switching voltage regulator that is worthy of mention is the 1524/2524/3524 (National Semiconductor, Signetics, Silicon General, etc.) type of regulating pulse-width modulator. This device is basically a switching voltage regulator with an on-chip oscillator circuit and so can be connected as a driven switching regulator without the need of any external oscillator. The frequency of oscillation is set by an external resistor and capacitor from as low as 1 kHz up to a maximum of 350 kHz.

This regulator can be connected in a variety of configurations as a step-down or as a step-up switching regulator, and with or without current boosting using external series-pass transistors.

When used as a 1-A 5-V step-down regulator with $V_{IN} = 10$ V at a 20 kHz switching frequency an efficiency of 80% is obtainable. The ripple will be 10 mV peak-to-peak, corresponding to a ripple factor of 0.2%. The load regulation for a variation in the output current of from 200 mA to 1 A will be 3 mV, corresponding to 0.06%/V. The line regulation will be 6 mV for an input voltage change of from 10 to 20 V, corresponding to a line regulation factor of 0.12%/V.

A similar type of pulse width modulator control circuit is the MC34060/35060 (Motorola). This IC contains an oscillator, 5.0 V reference, comparator, and error amplifier and can be used for step-down, step-up, and inverting voltage regulator circuits.

2.8.10 Monolithic Switching Regulator

An example of a monolithic switching regulator is the LAS6320P made by Lambda Semiconductors. This device comes in a 14-pin DIP package and contains a temperature-compensated voltage reference, sawtooth oscillator, pulse width modulator, error amplifier, and a Darlington output transistor with a 2 A rating and internal current limiting protection. The internal reference voltage is 2.25 V, the error amplifier has an open loop gain of 70 dB, and the output section current limit is set at 2.8 A. Maximum ratings include an input voltage of 35 V, and an oscillator frequency of 200 kHz. The junction-to-case and case-to-ambient (free air) thermal resistances are 13°C/W and 47°C/W, respectively, Typical performance characteristics include a line regulation of 0.015%/V and an output voltage temperature coefficient of 0.01%/°C. Both step-down and step-up modes of operation are possible. When operated as a step-down regulator with $V_{in} = 24$ V, $V_o = 5$ V, and an oscillator frequency of 50 kHz, the system conversion efficiency is 72% at an output current of 0.5 A, and is 76% for an output current of 2 A. For an output voltage of 12 V and an output current of 2 A, the efficiency will be up to 85%.

PROBLEMS

2.1. The reference voltage of a voltage regulator is $V_{REF} = 2.0$ V and has a supply voltage sensitivity of 2 mV/V. The supply voltage is +15 V with a 1% ripple factor at 120 Hz. The regulated output voltage is +10 V. Find the line regulation, the output-voltage ripple, and the output-voltage ripple factor. (*Ans.*: 10 mV/V, 1.5 mV, 0.015%)

2.2. The output voltage of a voltage regulator decreases by 10 mV as the load current increases from a no-load value of zero to a full-load value of 1.0 A. Find the average d-c output resistance. (*Ans.*: 10 mΩ)

2.3. A voltage regulator has a reference voltage of 2.0 V with a temperature coefficient of +100 ppm/°C. The regulated output voltage is +10 V. Find the temperature coefficient of the output voltage expressed in terms of ppm/°C, %/°C, and mV/°C. (*Ans.*: +100 ppm/°C, + 0.01%/°C, + 1.0 mV/°C)

2.4. A voltage regulator has a reference voltage of 2.0 V and a regulated output voltage of +10 V. The d-c output resistance of the regulator is 0.05 Ω. The error amplifier has a d-c gain of 10,000 and a unity-gain frequency of 1.0 mHz.

(a) Find the output impedance at 100 kHz.

(b) Find the value of bypass capacitor needed across the output terminals of the regulator to limit the output impedance to a maximum of 1.0 Ω over the frequency range 0 to 100 kHz. [*Ans.*: $+j50$ Ω, 1.6 μF (min.)]

2.5. A voltage regulator has a maximum supply voltage of +20 V and a maximum power dissipation rating of 10 W. The regulated output voltage is +15 V.

(a) Find the required current limit I_{CL} at $V_O = +15$ V and at $V_O = 0$ for an ideal foldback current-limiting characteristic. (*Ans.*: 2.0 A, 0.5 A)

(b) For a linear foldback current-limiting characteristic with $I_{CL} = 0.5$ A at $V_O = 0$, find I_{CL} at $V_O = +15$ V. (*Ans.*: 0.875 A)

***(c)** Use a computer to generate the ideal foldback current-limiting characteristic curve needed for this problem. Then generate linear foldback lines that are subject to the requirement that $P_d \le P_{d(MAX)}$ and that have the following current axis intercepts: 0.4 A, 0.3 A, 0.2 A, and 0.1 A. Find the corresponding values of I_{CL} at $V_O =$ +15 V.

2.6. A 5.0-V three-terminal voltage regulator is to be used as a current regulator, as shown in Figure 2.20. The voltage regulator has $V_{IN} = 20$ V and a line regulation of 10 mV/V. The regulated output current is to be 1.0 A.

(a) Find R_1. (*Ans.*: 5.0 Ω)

(b) Find the dynamic output conductance of this current source, neglecting the effect of the voltage regulator quiescent current. (*Ans.*: 2.0 mS)

(c) Find the percentage change in the output current per volt change in the output (load) voltage. (*Ans.*: 0.2%/V)

(d) The input–output voltage differential for this voltage regulator is 3.0 V (min.) and 15 V (max.). Find the voltage compliance range. (*Ans.*: from 0 to +12 V)

(e) Find the power dissipation rating needed for the voltage regulator if the output (load) voltage is to range from 0 to +5 V and the input voltage is 15 V. (*Ans.*: 10 W)

2.7. (*Switching regulator*) A switching voltage regulator operates at a switching frequency of 50 kHz and is to supply a load current I_O of 10 A at a d-c output voltage V_O of +12 V. The d-c input voltage is $V_{IN} = +18$ V and the output (peak-to-peak) ripple factor is not to exceed 0.1%.

(a) Find the value of the filter inductor L_1 such that the maximum change or ripple in the current through the inductor will not exceed 40% of the average or d-c current. [*Ans.*: 20 μH(min.)]

(b) Find the value of the output filter capacitor C_o for $L_1 = 20\ \mu$H and for $L_1 = 100\ \mu$H. (*Ans.*: 1300 μF, 267 μF)

2.8. Given: A voltage regulator circuit using an LM305 or LM376 type of voltage regulator together with the external pass transistors as shown in Figure P2.8. Assume that $V_{BE} = 0.7$ V for transistors in full conduction and $V_{BE} = 0.5$ V at threshold of conduction. Let $\beta = 100$(min.) and $V_{REF} = 1.72$ V (LM305 typ. value).

(a) Find: V_{R9}. (*Ans.*: 0.292 V)

(b) Find: I_{R9} and I_{C15}. (*Ans.*: 0.22 mA, 1.0 mA)

(c) Find: R_2 for $V_O = +15.0$ V. (*Ans.*: 719 Ω)

(d) Show that $V_1 = V_O(R_6/R_4 + R_6) + (I_O R_3)(R_6/R_4 + R_6) + (1.22 \text{ mA})(R_4 \| R_6)$.

(e) Show that current limiting will occur when

$$I_O R_3 \frac{R_6}{R_4 + R_6} - V_O \frac{R_4}{R_4 + R_6} + (1.22 \text{ mA})(R_4 \| R_6) = V_{BE_{16}} - V_{R_9} = 0.21 \text{ V}$$

(at threshold) and 0.41 V when Q_{16} is in full conduction

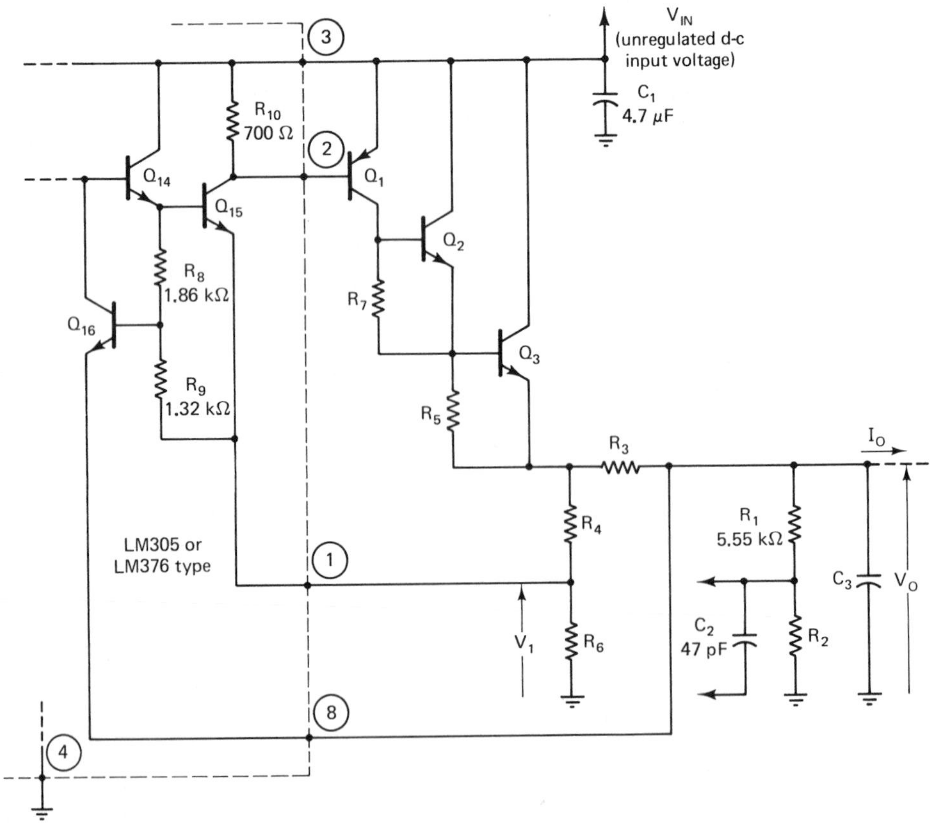

Figure P2.8

(f) If $P_{D(MAX)} = 50$ W for Q_3 and $V_{IN(MAX)} = +20$ V find $I_{O(CL)}$ for the case of $V_O = 0$, and for $V_O = +15$ V. (*Ans.*: 2.5 A, 10 A)

(g) If the parallel combination of R_4 and R_6 is set at 10 Ω and the required value of $V_{BE_{16}}$ is 0.542 V for current limiting, find the values of R_3, R_4, and R_6 for foldback current limiting to meet the conditions above for $I_{O(CL)}$. (*Ans.*: 100 mΩ, 10.5 Ω, 210 Ω)

(h) **(1)** Sketch and dimension the V_O versus I_O foldback characteristics of this circuit.

(2) What will $I_{O(CL)}$ and P_D be when $V_O = +10$ V and $V_{IN} = +20$ V? (*Ans.*: 7.5 A, 75W).

(3) Is this foldback curve suitable for the full protection of Q_3?

(i) Find R_5 for $I_2 = 100$ mA. (*Ans.*: 7.0 Ω)

(j) Find R_7 for $I_1 = 10$ mA. (*Ans.*: 70 Ω)

(k) **(1)** Find the open-loop output resistance $r_{o(OL)}$ when $I_O = 10$ A. (*Ans.*: $r_{o(OL)} = 104$ mΩ)

(2) If the voltage gain of the difference (error) amplifier is 500 (min.) including the gain of the current boost circuit, find $r_{o(CL)}$ for $V_O = +15$ V and $I_O = 10$ A. [*Ans.*: $r_{o(CL)} = 1.74$ mΩ (max.)]

(3) If the difference amplifier has a unity-gain frequency of $f_u = 1.0$ MHz, find the dynamic output impedance $z_{o(CL)}$ at $f = 20$ kHz.
(*Ans.*: $z_{o(CL)} = j17.4$ mΩ)

(l) If $TC_{V_{REF}} = +50\ \mu V/°C$, find TC_{V_O} when $V_O = +15$ V. (*Ans.*: $TC_{V_O} = 436\ \mu V/°C$ or 29 ppm/°C or 0.0029%/°C)

(m) A temperature-compensated voltage reference circuit (Figure 2.12) produces V_{REF} with $Z_z = 10$ Ω and with the dynamic output resistance of the current source I_Q being $r_o = 100$ kΩ. Find the sensitivity of the reference voltage to changes in the supply voltage, dV_{REF}/dV_{supply}. (*Ans.*: $dV_{REF}/dV_{supply} = 23\ \mu V/V = 0.00135\%/V$)

(n) Find the *line regulation* of this voltage regulator, dV_O/dV_{supply}, for an output voltage of +15 V. (*Ans.*: 202 μV/V = 0.00135%/V)

(o) Find the value of C_3 needed to keep the voltage regulator output impedance less than 50 mΩ at 200 kHz. (*Ans.*: $C_3 \geq 16\ \mu F$)

(p) Find the *load regulation* for $I_{NL} = 1.0$ A and $I_{FL} = 10$ A if $A_{OL} = 500$. The regulated output voltage is +15 V. (*Ans.*: $\Delta V_O = 2.01$ mV = 0.0134%)

(q) Find the ripple factor reduction ratio. This is the ratio of the a-c ripple voltage on the output voltage of the regulator to the a-c ripple voltage on the supply voltage. (*Ans.*: 202 μV/V)

(r) Find the value of the REF bypass capacitor required to reduce the ripple factor ratio to 20 μV/V at 120 Hz. (*Ans.*: $C_{REF\ BYPASS} \geq 17.5\ \mu F$)

(s) Find the maximum power dissipation (Q_3) that will occur for the foldback characteristics under consideration and the output voltage level at which this maximum power dissipation occurs. (*Ans.*: 78.1 W at $V_O = 7.5$ V)

(t) Choosing a power dissipation rating for Q_3 to be 80 W to provide full protection for Q_3 under all output voltage and load conditions, what thermal impedance is required for the heat sink of Q_3. The junction-to-case thermal impedance Θ_{JC} of Q_3 (2N3772) is 1.17°C/W and the maximum junction temperature $T_{J(MAX)}$ is 200°C. (*Ans.*: heat sink thermal impedance = $\Theta_{CA} \leq 1.02$°C/W)

(u) With this value of $P_{D(MAX)} = 80$ W, what would the corresponding value of $I_{O(CL)}$ be for the case of straight current limiting (i.e., no foldback)? (*Ans.*: $I_{O(CL)} = 4.0$ A as compared to 10 A available when foldback current limiting is used)

2.9. A voltage regulator circuit is designed with a linear foldback characteristic that goes to a current limit of 20 A at $V_O = +10$ V, and has a short-circuit limit of 5.0 A. The

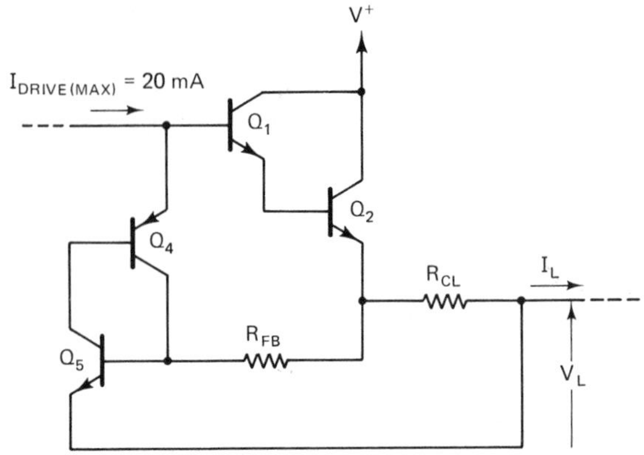

Figure P2.10

unregulated input voltage has a maximum value of +15 V. What power dissipation rating should the output transistor have for full protection and at what value of output voltage and current will the maximum power dissipation occur? (*Ans*.: 126 W, 5.83 V, 13.75 A)

2.10. (*Latching foldback circuit*)

(a) A latching foldback circuit is shown in Figure P2.10. Find R_{CL} and R_{FB} such that the current limiting circuit will be triggered at $I_{L(MAX)} = 10$ A and then will immediately reduce the load current to $I_{L(FB)} = 1.0$ A. Use $V_{BE} = 500$ mV at the threshold of conduction and $V_{BE} = 600$ mV when in full conduction. (*Ans*.: $R_{CL} = 0.050\ \Omega$, $R_{FB} = 27.5\ \Omega$)

(b) Sketch the V_L versus I_L output curve for this circuit.

2.11. (*Crowbar circuit for overvoltage protection*) In Figure P2.11 a *crowbar circuit* is shown. This circuit protects the load from excessive voltage due to various causes such as power-line voltage spikes or failure of the voltage regulator. Given: $V_z = 6.5$ V for D_1 and when $V_{REG} = 20$ V, $I_z = 1.0$ mA, and the current through resistors R_1 and R_2 will be 1.0 mA. When V_{REG} exceeds 20 V the silicon-controlled rectifier (SCR) is to turn on to protect the load from an overvoltage condition. Find:

(a) R_1 and R_2. (*Ans*.: 13.5 kΩ, 6.5 kΩ)

(b) R_3. (*Ans*.: 13.5 kΩ)

2.12. (*DC-to-DC inverter*) In Figure P2.12, a DC-to-DC inverter circuit is shown. If the

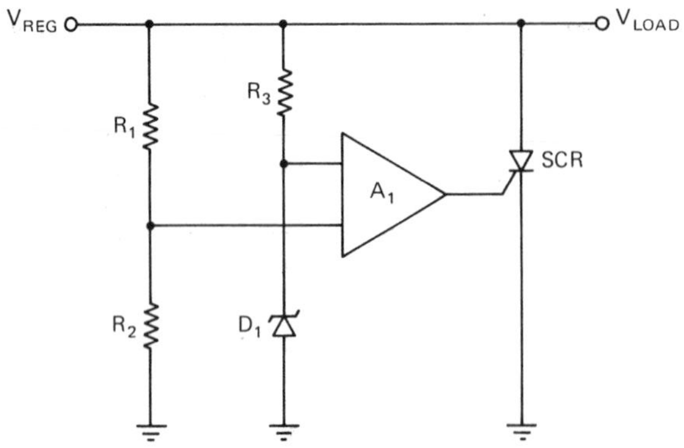

Figure P2.11

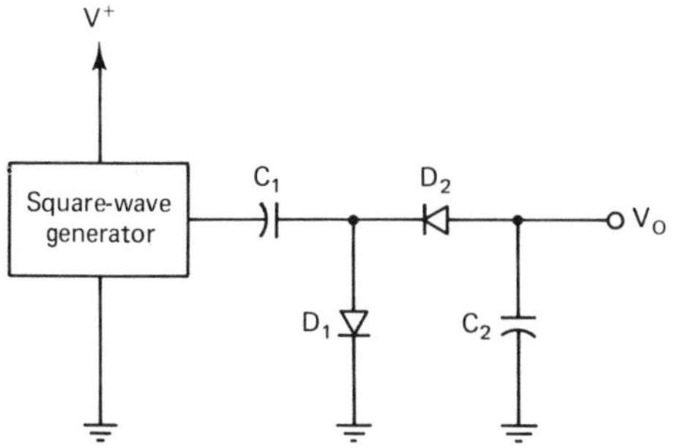

Figure P2.12

square-wave generator produces a 50 kHz square-wave voltage that goes from zero to +10 V, find the output voltage of the circuit

(a) Under no load conditions. (*Ans.*: −10 V)

(b) Under lightly loaded conditions. (*Ans.*: approx. −8.8 V).

(c) Would there be any advantage to operating this circuit at a much lower frequency, say 100 Hz? Explain. Would there be any advantage to be gained in going to a much higher frequency? Explain.

REFERENCES

COWLES, L. G., *Sourcebook of Modern Transistor Circuits*, Prentice-Hall, 1976.

GOTTLIEB, I., *Design and Operation of Regulated Power Supplies*, Howard W. Sams, 1966.

GOTTLIEB, I., *Regulated Power Supplies*, 3rd ed. Howard W. Sams, 1981.

GOTTLIEB, I., *Switching Regulators and Power Supplies*, TAB Books, 1976.

GREBENE, A. B., *Analog Integrated Circuit Design*, Van Nostrand Reinhold, 1972.

HNATEK, E. R., *Design of Solid-State Power Supplies*, Van Nostrand Reinhold, 1971.

HNATEK, E. R., *A User's Handbook of Integrated Circuits*, Wiley, 1973.

LENK, J. D., *Handbook of Integrated Circuits*, Reston, 1978.

LENK, J. D., *Manual for Integrated Circuit Users*, Reston, 1973.

OXNER, E. S., *Power FETs and Their Applications*, Prentice-Hall, 1982.

PRESSMAN, A. I., *Switching and Linear Power Supply: Power Converter Design*, Hayden, 1977.

Power Amplifiers

3

3.1 BASIC CONSIDERATIONS

For amplifiers that are designed to deliver substantial amounts of power to a load, generally greater than 1 W, the question of the amplifier power conversion efficiency becomes one of major concern. The a-c output power that the amplifier delivers to the load is derived almost entirely from the d-c power supply. The input signal acts to control the conversion of the d-c power to the a-c output power, but the signal source that drives the amplifier generally supplies a negligible amount of input power.

The amplifier power conversion efficiency, η, is defined as

$$\eta = \frac{P_O(\text{a-c})}{P_{\text{IN}}(\text{d-c})} \tag{3.1}$$

The power that must be dissipated by the power amplifier will therefore be given by $P_D = P_{\text{IN}} - P_O$, and therefore can be expressed in terms of the power conversion efficiency as

$$\begin{aligned} \text{amplifier power dissipation} = P_D &= P_{\text{IN}} - P_O \\ &= P_O\left(\frac{1}{\eta} - 1\right) \end{aligned} \tag{3.2}$$

This power dissipation will occur almost entirely in the last, or output stage of the power amplifier. From this expression we see the importance of the power conversion efficiency in determining the amount of power that must be dissipated by the power amplifier.

3.2 CLASS A POWER AMPLIFIERS

In a class A amplifier, the output stage is biased in the active region such that there is an uninterrupted flow of current during the entire cycle, and at no time does the amplifier go into the cutoff or saturation region. Thus the amplifier operates in the active region during the entire 360° cycle of the input signal.

Consider the power amplifier shown in Figure 3.1 with a supply of voltage of $+V_S$. The maximum peak-to-peak swing of the output voltage cannot exceed V_S, and in most practical cases will be limited to 1 or 2 V less than V_S, and sometimes more in part due to distortion considerations.

For a peak-to-peak output voltage swing of V_S, the peak swing will be $V_S/2$ and the rms output voltage will therefore be $V_S/2\sqrt{2}$. If the quiescent current of the output stage is I_Q, the peak output current can be no greater than I_Q, so that the rms output current will be $I_Q/\sqrt{2}$. These conditions will essentially correspond to the output transistor being biased in the middle of the active region, halfway between cutoff and saturation, the coordinates of the quiescent point being $I_C = I_{C(SAT)}/2$ and $V_C = (V_S - V_{CE(SAT)})/2 \simeq V_S/2$.

The a-c power output under conditions of maximum voltage and current swing will be given by $P_O(\text{a-c}) = v_o i_o = (V_S/2\sqrt{2})(I_Q/\sqrt{2}) = V_S I_Q/4$, where v_o and i_o are the rms output voltage and current, respectively. Since the d-c input power is $P_{IN}(\text{d-c}) = V_S I_Q$, the power conversion efficiency η will be given by

$$\eta = \frac{P_O}{P_{IN}} = \frac{1}{4} \text{ or } 25\% \qquad (3.3)$$

Thus, of the total d-c input power, a maximum of 25% can be converted to a-c power and delivered to the load, and the rest will be dissipated by the amplifier.

For example, if the a-c output power is to be 5 W, the amplifier power dissipation rating will have to be at least 15 W, and the total input power will have to be at least 20 W.

It is important to note that the 25% power conversion efficiency will be appreciated only when the amplifier is driven hard enough such that the maximum output voltage and current swings are obtained. If the input drive conditions are such that this is not the case, the efficiency will be correspondingly less. In any case it is not really possible to achieve the 25% efficiency figure in practice due in part to various other circuit losses. Most important, however, because of the nonlinearities of the amplifier output stage it is generally not desirable, based on distortion considerations, to drive the amplifier over the full span of the active region between cutoff and saturation. In order to limit distortion to an acceptable level, the output swing is

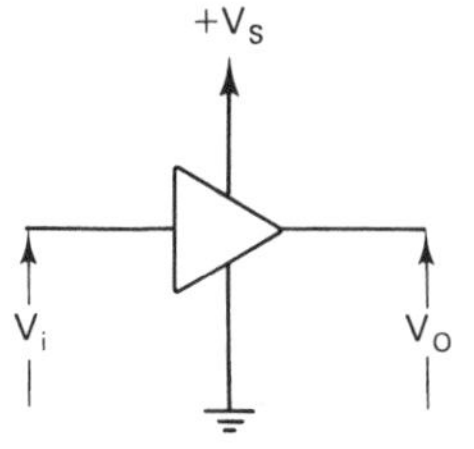

Figure 3.1 Class A power amplifier.

often limited to no more than about 50 to 80% of the total active region voltage and current spans. As a result of this the actual power conversion efficiency values of class A power amplifiers will generally fall in the range 10 to 20%, and many times even lower if a very low amount of distortion is required.

If the actual amplifier efficiency is 10%, for example, we have that $P_D = 9P_O$, so that for a 5-W power output dissipation rating of the output stage must be at least 45 W, and a total input power of at least 50 W will be required. We can thus see from these considerations the desirability of operating the power amplifier at as high a power conversion efficiency as possible, subject to the limitations imposed by distortion considerations.

3.3 CLASS B POWER AMPLIFIERS

In the class B mode of operation the output transistor is biased at, or very near cutoff, such that conduction occurs for only about one-half of the input waveform cycle, or 180° for a sinusoidal type of input signal. In this mode of operation the

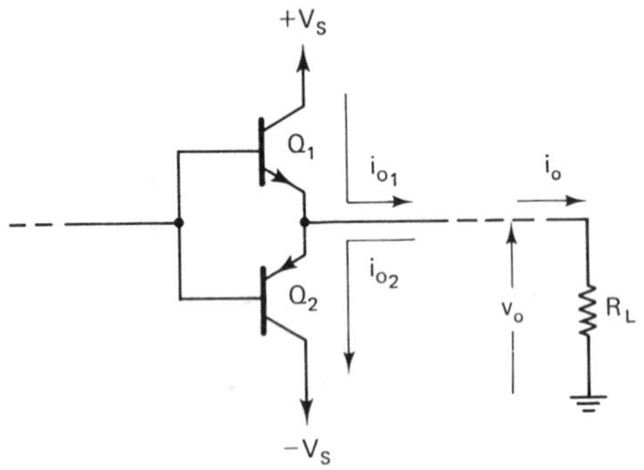

(a)

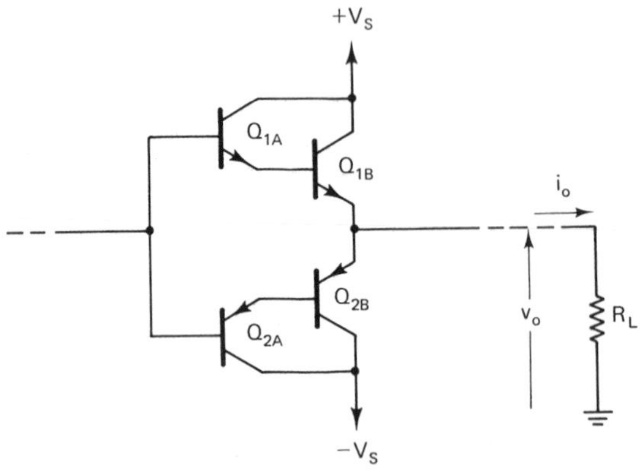

(b)

Figure 3.2 (a) Complementary emitter-follower class B push-pull output stage; (b) Darlington output stage.

quiescent current is essentially zero, and as a result of this the class B mode of operation offers the possibility of a much higher power conversion efficiency than does the class A mode.

In virtually all practical applications of a class B type of amplifier the output stage is comprised of two transistors whose outputs are combined in such a way so as to reconstruct the full 360° waveform cycle. Each transistor operates in the class B mode and conducts during alternative half-cycles of the input signal so that by combining the two outputs an amplified replica of the input signal will be obtained. The two transistors of the class B output stage are usually connected in a "push-pull" arrangement, a simple example of which is shown in Figure 3.2a.

Transistors Q_1 and Q_2 constitute a complementary push-pull emitter-follower output stage operating in the class B mode. Transistor Q_1 will conduct during the positive half-cycles of the input voltage applied to the Q_1–Q_2 output stage and will "source" or "push" current into the load. Transistor Q_2 will conduct during the negative half-cycles and will "sink" or "pull" current from the load. Each transistor thus conducts for one-half of the entire cycle and the two outputs are combined to give the full-cycle (360°) sinusoidal output current. Under quiescent condition (i.e., $v_o = 0$, $i_o = 0$) both transistors will be off and the power dissipation will be negligible.

Transistors Q_1 and Q_2 constitute a complementary pair in the sense that one is an NPN transistor and the other a PNP. Both bases are fed from the same point, so that when the base voltage goes up in the positive direction Q_1 will be turned on and conduct while Q_2 will be off. Conversely, when the base voltage goes negative Q_1 will be turned off and Q_2 will be biased into conduction. For greater current gains in the output stage Q_1 and Q_2 can be Darlington compound transistors, as shown in Figure 3.2.

3.3.1 Class B Power Output and Power Conversion Efficiency

The a-c output power of the amplifier will be P_O (a-c) $= v_o i_o = i_o^2 R_L$, where v_o and i_o are the rms output voltage and current, respectively, and R_L is the load resistance. The peak current for a sinusoidal waveform is related to the rms current by $i_{o\,(\text{peak})} = \sqrt{2}\, i_o$. During the positive half-cycles of the output current, the current is drawn from the positive supply terminal through Q_1 to the output. During the negative half-cycles of the output current, the current flow is from the load through Q_2 and then into the negative supply terminal. The average or d-c current drawn from each power supply terminal will be related to the peak and rms output current by $I_{\text{DC}} = i_{o\,(\text{peak})}/\pi = i_o\sqrt{2}/\pi$. The average of d-c power drawn from each power supply terminal will therefore be given by $V_S I_{\text{DC}} = V_S i_o \sqrt{2}/\pi$, where V_S is the d-c supply voltage, The total power that is drawn from the d-c power supply will therefore be twice this or

$$P_{\text{IN}} = 2\,V_S I_{\text{DC}} = \frac{2\,V_S i_o \sqrt{2}}{\pi} \tag{3.4}$$

The amplifier power dissipation will therefore be

$$P_D = P_{IN} - P_O = \frac{2V_S i_o \sqrt{2}}{\pi} - P_O \tag{3.5}$$

Since $i_o = \sqrt{P_O/R_L}$, this can be rewritten as

$$P_D = \frac{2V_S}{\pi}\sqrt{\frac{2P_O}{R_L}} - P_O$$

From this expression we see that the power dissipation will at first increase with P_O at a rate proportional to $\sqrt{P_O}$. It will then bend over and reach a maximum and thereafter decrease with increasing P_O.

The maximum available a-c power output is limited, however, by the peak output voltage swing, which cannot exceed the supply voltage, V_S. Since $v_{o\,(\text{peak})} = V_S$, and $P_O = v_o i_o = v_o^2/R_L = v_{o\,(\text{peak})}^2/2R_L$, we have that the a-c output power will be limited to a maximum given by

$$P_{O\,(\text{MAX})} = \frac{V_S^2}{2R_L} \tag{3.6}$$

In terms of the rms output current, this expression for the maximum output power can be expressed as

$$P_{O\,(\text{MAX})} = v_o i_o = \frac{V_S i_o}{\sqrt{2}} \tag{3.7}$$

Since $I_{DC} = i_o\sqrt{2}/\pi$, the input power will be given by

$$P_{IN} = 2V_S I_{DC} = \frac{2V_S i_o \sqrt{2}}{\pi} \tag{3.8}$$

The power conversion efficiency will therefore be given by

$$\eta = \frac{P_O}{P_{IN}} = \frac{V_S i_o/\sqrt{2}}{2V_S i_o\sqrt{2}/\pi} = \frac{\pi}{4} = \underline{0.785 \text{ or } 78.5\%} \tag{3.9}$$

Since this is the power conversion efficiency under the conditions of maximum power output, this will be the maximum possible power conversion efficiency for a class B amplifier. The value of η that is actually obtained in practice will be generally substantially less than this due to various other circuit losses, and most of all due to the fact that the peak output voltage swing will always be less than the supply voltage, typically by about several volts. Part of this is due to the saturation voltage drop of the transistor, but it also results from distortion considerations. In order to limit distortion to an acceptable value the output voltage swing is purposely limited to something considerably less than the full extent of the active region between cutoff and saturation.

The amplifier power dissipation is related to the power conversion efficiency by

$$P_D = P_{IN} - P_O = P_O\left(\frac{1}{\eta} - 1\right) \tag{3.10}$$

For a class B amplifier operating at the maximum efficiency of 78.5%, the power dissipation will be related to the a-c power output by

$$P_D = P_O\left(\frac{4}{\pi} - 1\right) = 0.273P_O \tag{3.11}$$

For example, for an a-c power output of 5 W, the input power will be $P_{IN} = P_O/\eta = 5\text{ W}/0.785 = 6.4\text{ W}$ and the power dissipation will be 1.4 W. This represents a very substantial improvement over the class A amplifier.

We will now return to the expression for power dissipation given earlier as

$$P_D = \frac{2V_S}{\pi}\sqrt{\frac{2P_O}{R_L}} - P_O \tag{3.12}$$

To determine the value of P_O at which P_D will be a maximum we will take the derivative of P_D with respect to P_O and set the result equal to zero, giving

$$\frac{dP_D}{dP_O} = \frac{V_S}{\pi}\sqrt{\frac{2}{P_O R_L}} - 1 = 0 \tag{3.13}$$

so that

$$P_O = \frac{2V_S^2}{\pi^2 R_L} \tag{3.14}$$

at the point where P_D is a maximum. To find $P_{D(MAX)}$ under these circumstances we will substitute P_O given above back into the expression for P_D and thereby obtain

$$P_{D(MAX)} = \frac{2V_S^2}{\pi^2 R_L} \tag{3.15}$$

Since P_O also has the value of $2V_S^2/\pi^2 R_L$ at this point, the power conversion efficiency will therefore be 50% at this point. In Figure 3.3 a generalized graph of P_D versus P_O is presented.

3.3.2 Crossover Distortion

The ratio of output power to power dissipation is limited to a maximum value of unity for the class A amplifier, compared to a ratio of 3.66 for the class B amplifier, so from this standpoint the class B amplifier does offer a substantial advantage over the class A circuit. The push-pull class B amplifier does, however, suffer from an important type of distortion known as *crossover distortion*. This type of distortion is due to the very low, or almost nonexistent gain of the transistors in the cutoff region.

The voltage gain of an emitter-follower stage is given as

$$A_V = \frac{g_m R_L}{1 + g_m R_L} = \frac{R_L}{R_L + 1/g_m} \tag{3.16}$$

Since $g_m = I_C/V_T = I_O/V_T$, this can be rewritten as

$$A_V = \frac{R_L}{R_L + V_T/I_O} = \frac{1}{1 + V_T/I_O R_L} = \frac{1}{1 + V_T/V_O} \tag{3.17}$$

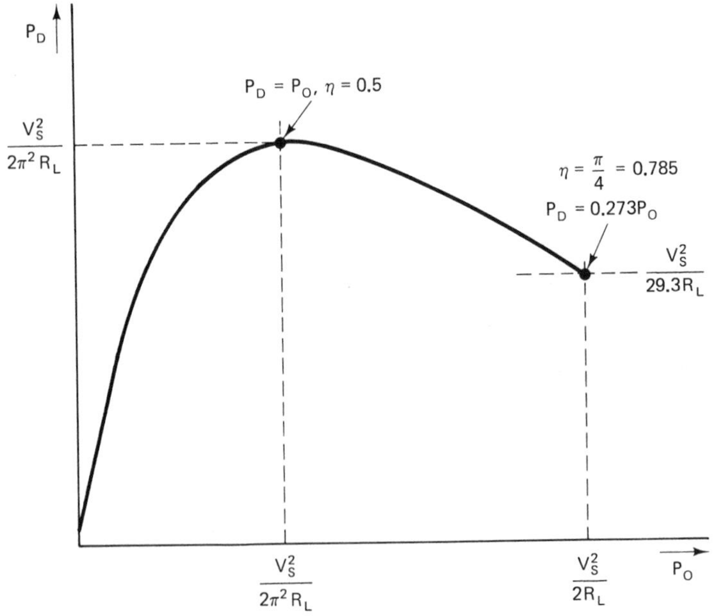

Figure 3.3 Power dissipation versus power output for a class B amplifier.

We see from this expression that in the region near cutoff, where I_O becomes very small such that $I_O R_L$ becomes comparable to, or less than V_T, the voltage gain of the emitter follower will decrease considerably below unity.

In Figure 3.4a a single complementary push-pull emitter-follower output stage is shown, and in Figure 3.4b the v_o versus v_b transfer characteristic is presented. We see that in the region where v_b is between −0.5 and +0.5 V there will be a "dead region" or "dead band" wherein both transistors will be in the cutoff region. In this region the voltage gain of both Q_1 and Q_2 is very small. In order to bring the voltage gain up toward unity for small input voltages, it is necessary to bias the transistors with a small quiescent current so as to bias the transistors at a point that is slightly into the active region.

This can be done by applying a small d-c bias voltage between the bases of the two transistors, as shown in Figure 3.5a. The resulting transfer characteristics are shown in Figure 3.5b. In order to minimize the crossover distortion, the bias voltages, V_{B1} and V_{B2}, must be sufficiently large to bias Q_1 and Q_2 enough into the active region to ensure that the emitter-follower voltage gain will be close to unity, even under quiescent condition ($v_i = 0$ and $v_o = 0$). The total bias voltage required between the two bases, $V_{B1} + V_{B2}$, will be in the range of about 1.0 V.

For the complementary push-pull emitter-follower circuit we will now derive an expression for the voltage gain under quiescent conditions. For this condition we will have that $V_O = I_O = 0$, so that the quiescent current in Q_1 and Q_2 will be equal as given by $I_1 = I_2 = I_Q$. The dynamic transfer conductances of Q_1 and Q_2 will therefore be equal, as given by $g_{m_1} = I_1/V_T = I_Q/V_T$, and $g_{m_2} = I_2/V_T =$

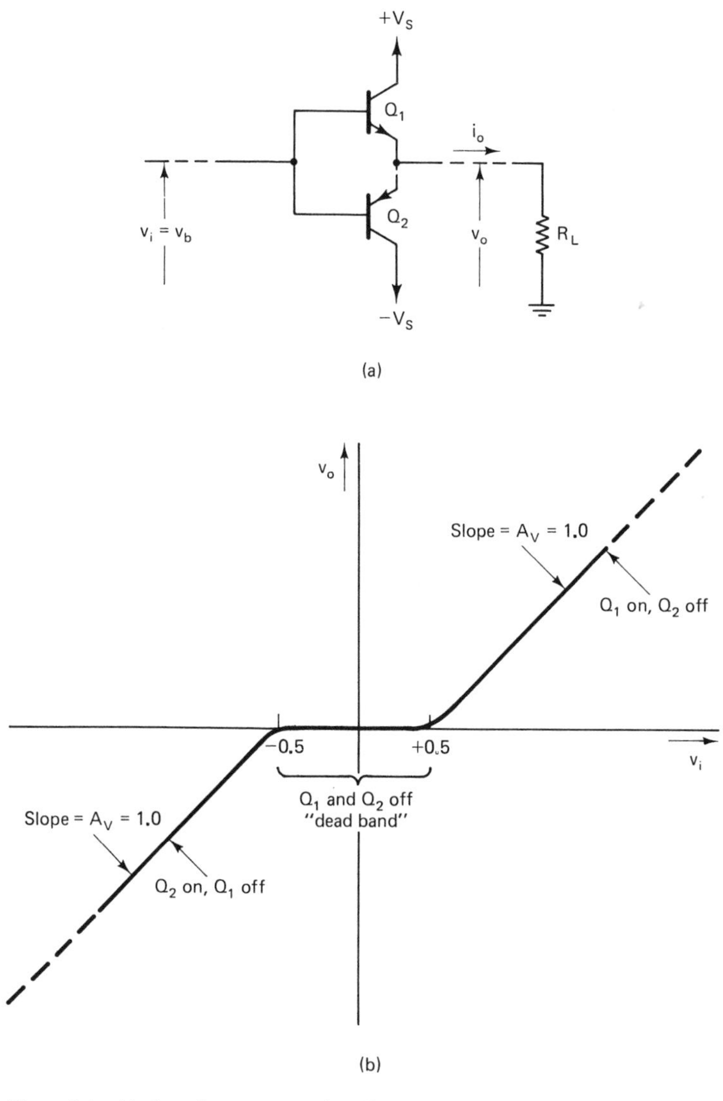

Figure 3.4 (a) Complementary push-pull emitter-follower output stage; (b) transfer characteristics.

I_Q/V_T, so that $g_{m_1} = g_{m_2} = g_m = I_Q/V_T$. The a-c small-signal output currents of the two transistors will be given by $i_{o_1} = g_m v_{be_1} = g_m(v_{b_1} - v_o)$ and $i_{o_2} = g_m v_{be_2} = g_m(v_{b_2} - v_o)$. The a-c voltage at the two bases will be the same since the two bases are separated only by a d-c voltage, V_B, so that $v_{b_1} = v_{b_2} = v_b$ and we will have $i_o = i_{o_1} + i_{o_2} = 2g_m(v_b - v_o)$. The a-c small-signal output voltage will be $v_o = i_o R_L$, so that we now have that

$$v_o = 2g_m R_L(v_b - v_o)$$

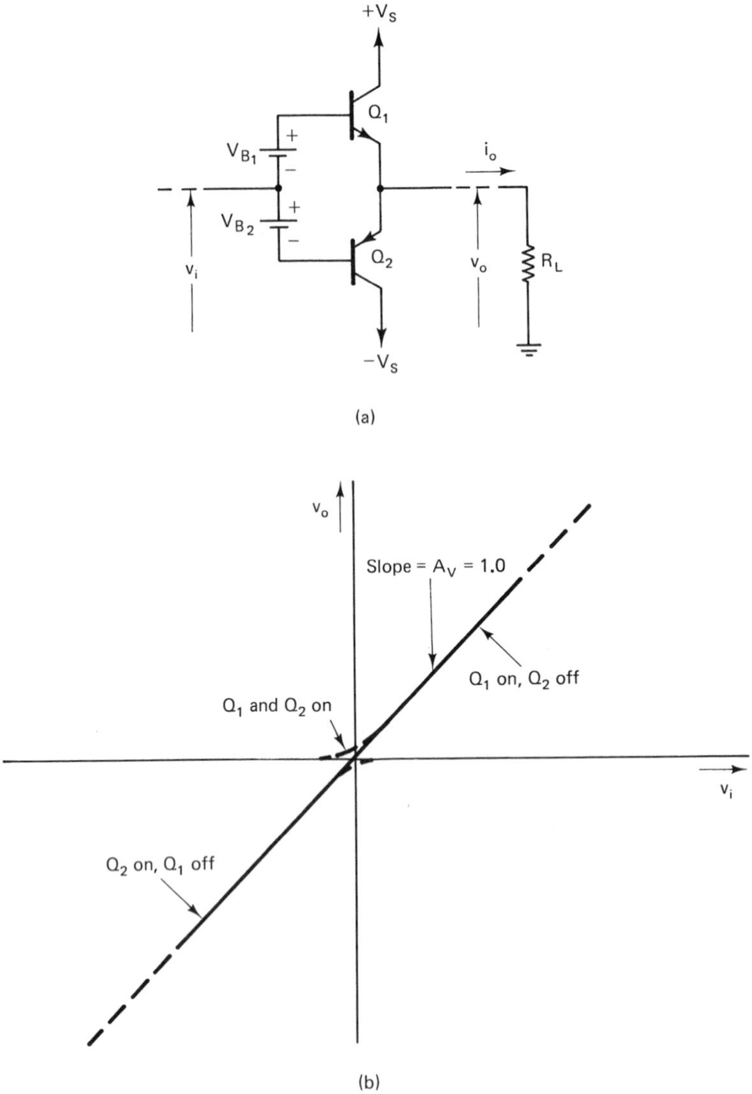

Figure 3.5 (a) Push-pull output stage biased to minimize crossover distortion; (b) transfer characteristics.

and thus

$$v_o = \frac{2g_m R_L v_b}{1 + 2g_m R_L} \tag{3.18}$$

Thus the a-c small-signal voltage gain of the output stage under quiescent conditions will be given by

$$A_V = \frac{v_o}{v_b} = \frac{2g_m R_L}{1 + 2g_m R_L} \tag{3.19}$$

This equation can be rewritten as

$$A_V = \frac{R_L}{R_L + 1/2g_m} = \frac{R_L}{R_L + V_T/2I_Q} = \frac{1}{1 + V_T/2I_QR_L} \tag{3.20}$$

Therefore, for example, for the voltage gain under quiescent conditions to be no more than 10% below the maximum gain of unity, we will have the condition that

$$V_T/2I_QR_L = (1/0.9) - 1 \leqslant 0.11$$

so that the required quiescent current flow through Q_1 and Q_2 will be given by

$$I_Q \geqslant \frac{4.5\, V_T}{R_L} \tag{3.21}$$

If the minimum expected value of load resistance, R_L, is 8 Ω, the required value of quiescent current will be $I_Q \geqslant (4.5 \times 25 \text{ mV})/8\ \Omega = 14.1$ mA. The relatively large value of required quiescent current in this case is a direct consequence of the small value of load resistance. Furthermore, to put the quiescent current into the proper perspective, let us assume a representative supply voltage of ±12 V for the amplifier so that the peak output-voltage swing will be about 10 V. The peak output current will consequently be 10 V/8 Ω = 1.25 A. Therefore, we now see that the quiescent current of 14 mA is only 1.1% of the peak output current swing, so that the resulting small loss in the overall power conversion efficiency will be a relatively small price to pay for the great reduction in crossover distortion that results from this mode of operation.

In general, we can say that in order to minimize crossover distortion we will require that the quiescent current satisfy the condition that $I_Q \geqslant 5V_T/R_L$. Since $V_{O\,(\text{peak})} = R_L I_{O\,(\text{peak})}$, this equation can be rewritten as

$$I_Q/I_{O\,(\text{peak})} = 5\,V_T/V_{O\,(\text{peak})}$$

Since $V_{O\,(\text{peak})}$ will always be somewhat less than the d-c supply voltage V_S, we can write that

$$I_Q/I_{O\,(\text{peak})} \geqslant 5\,V_T/V_S = 0.125\,V/V_S$$

Since V_S is generally in the range 10 to 30 V, we see again that the required quiescent current will be but a very small fraction of the peak output-current swing.

Since Q_1 and Q_2 are now no longer biased in the cutoff region, but slightly into the active region, the conduction angle for each transistor will be greater than 180° (i.e., one-half of a cycle), although it still will be considerably less than 360° (a full cycle). Therefore, strictly speaking, the mode of operation is no longer class B, nor is it class A. The mode of operation is called class AB, and it combines the low distortion attribute of class A operation with the high power conversion efficiency characteristics of class B operation. Since the mode of operation will generally be considerably closer to class B than to class A, the high power conversion efficiency available from class B operation can, to a large extent, still be obtained.

Along with a high power conversion efficiency a low percentage distortion figure can be obtained. Indeed, with a well-balanced push-pull amplifier the even harmonic distortion components will cancel out, leaving only the odd-numbered harmonics.

Since the amplitude of the various harmonics decrease rapidly with increasing harmonic number, the cancellation of the second harmonic term which will be the largest harmonic component, along with the other even harmonics, can lead to a very great reduction in the distortion.

Power amplifiers are usually operated under closed-loop conditions with either an internally connected or externally connected negative feedback loop. Since the closed-loop gain is related to the open-loop gain by $A_{CL} = A_{OL}/(1 + FA_{OL})$, where F is the feedback factor, it can easily be shown that the fractional or percentage variation in the closed-loop gain is related to the fractional or percentage variation in the open-loop gain by $dA_{CL}/A_{CL} = (dA_{OL}/A_{OL})(A_{CL}/A_{OL})$. Since the closed-loop gain will be less than the open-loop gain, and generally very much less, we see that any variations in the open-loop gain will result in smaller variations in the closed-loop gain.

As an example of this, let us consider a variation in the open-loop gain of 10% that is due to crossover distortion. If we take as representative values an open-loop gain of 1000 and a closed-loop gain of 50, the variation of A_{CL} due to a 10% variation of A_{OL} will be $10\% \times (50/1000) = 0.5\%$. The resulting contribution of this to the total amplifier distortion will be considerably less than 0.5% since the crossover gain variation is present only over a relatively small part of the output voltage swing.

3.4 CLASS AB PUSH-PULL OUTPUT-STAGE EXAMPLES

In Figure 3.6a an example of a simple class AB complementary push-pull emitter-follower output stage is presented. Transistor Q_3 operates as a common-emitter gain stage with a current source active load of strength I_Q. The push-pull output stage is comprised of transistors Q_1 and Q_2. The voltage drop across diodes D_1 and D_2 is the bias voltage for the class AB operation of Q_1 and Q_2. In IC applications these two diodes will actually be diode-connected transistors. The active areas of these transistors will be scaled so as to obtain the desired standby or quiescent current through Q_1 and Q_2. If, for example, D_1 and D_2 were diode-connected transistors, identical in construction to Q_1 and Q_2, respectively, but scaled in active area by a ratio of n with respect to Q_1 and Q_2, the standby current of Q_1 and Q_2 would be I_Q/n.

The voltage drop across D_1 and D_2 will of course decrease with temperature, but this temperature variation is exactly what is needed to compensate for the negative temperature coefficient of the base-to-emitter voltage of Q_1 and Q_2.

In Figure 3.6b a Darlington configuration class AB push-pull stage is shown. Transistors Q_{1A} and Q_{1B} constitute an NPN Darlington emitter follower for sourcing currents into the load. Transistors Q_{2A}, Q_{2B}, and Q_{2C} constitute a composite PNP Darlington that in effect acts like a PNP transistor with a very high current gain. The effective current gain of this compound transistor configuration will be equal to the product of the individual current gains of the three transistors involved. The PNP Darlington is made up of three transistors, as compared to the NPN Darlington,

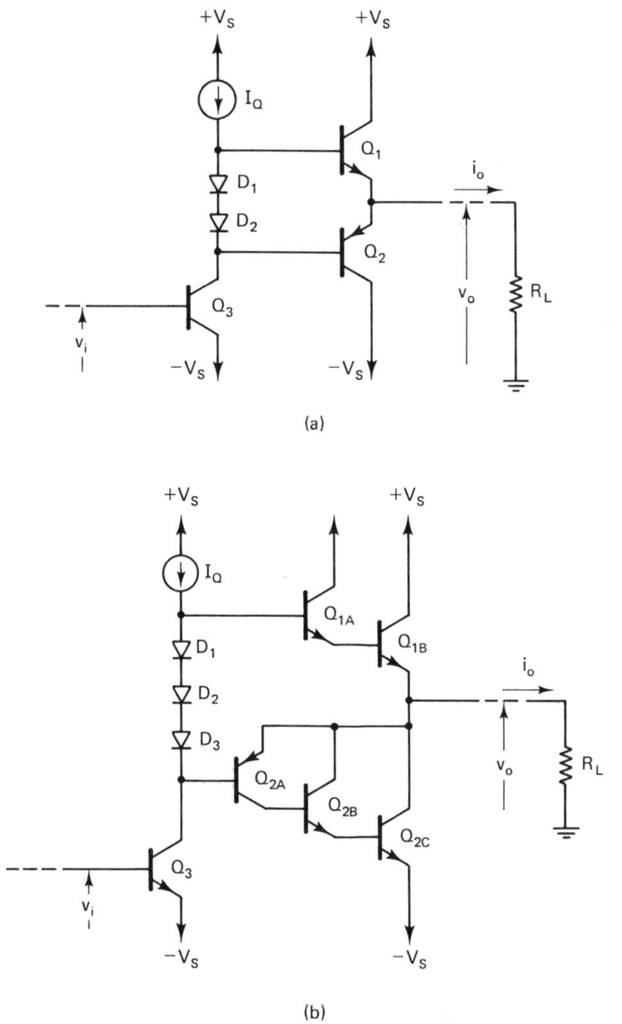

Figure 3.6 (a) Class AB push-pull output stage; (b) class AB Darlington output stage.

which is composed of two transistors. This is done to make up for the relatively low current gain of IC PNP transistors.

3.5 SINGLE-SUPPLY AUDIO POWER AMPLIFIER EXAMPLE

A simple example of a single-supply audio power amplifier is shown in Figure 3.7. This amplifier consists of a Darlington differential-amplifier input stage with a current mirror active load. The output stage is a class AB Darlington emitter-follower complementary push-pull configuration.

The input stage is a Darlington differential amplifier comprised of Q_1 through Q_4 with the current mirror active load using Q_5 and Q_6. The quiescent current of

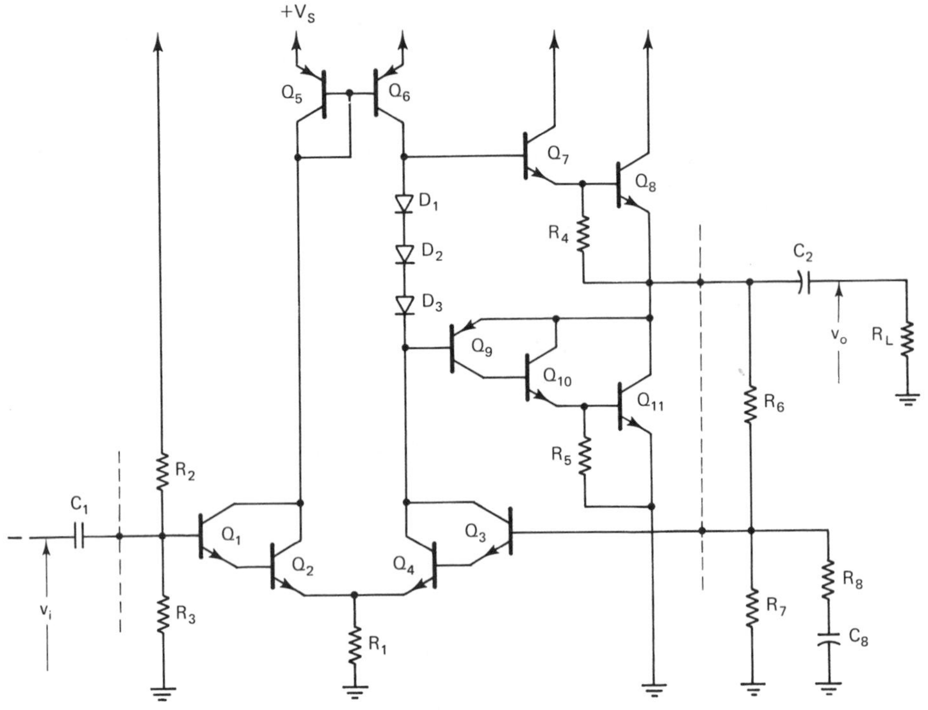

Figure 3.7 Single-supply audio power amplifier.

the differential amplifier is controlled by R_1 and the d-c voltage applied to the base of Q_1 by the R_2–R_3 voltage divider. The output of this stage is fed directly to the emitter-follower output stage, so this amplifier has only one gain stage. Nevertheless, a very high open-loop gain is possible, as will be seen.

The output stage uses Q_7 and Q_8 acting as a Darlington emitter follower to source current into the load, and Q_9, Q_{10}, and Q_{11}, which are connected as a composite PNP-Darlington emitter-follower configuration to sink current from the load. To minimize crossover distortion this output stage is operated in the class AB mode by means of the bias voltage produced across the series string of D_1, D_2, and D_3. Resistors R_4 and R_5 allow Q_7 and the Q_9–Q_{10} composite pair to operate at a higher quiescent current level than would otherwise be the case. These two resistors also provide a path for the more rapid removal of charge stored in the base region in case the above-mentioned transistors go into saturation and then have to be brought out of saturation.

The voltage divider, composed of R_6 and R_7, provides d-c feedback from the output back to the base of Q_3 so as to stabilize the quiescent output voltage level at the desired value. Under quiescent conditions the differential amplifier will be in a balanced condition with $V_{B1} = V_{B3}$. If we assume that the base currents of Q_1 and Q_3 are small compared to the currents going through the R_2–R_3 and R_6–R_7 voltage dividers, respectively, the voltage at the base of Q_1 will be given by $V_{B1} =$

$V_S R_3/(R_2 + R_3)$, and that at the base of Q_3 will be $V_{B3} = V_{O(Q)} R_7/(R_6 + R_7)$, where $V_{O(Q)}$ is the quiescent output voltage.

In order to allow this amplifier to develop the maximum possible undistorted peak-to-peak output voltage swing, the output quiescent voltage level should be midway between the positive supply voltage and ground, so that $V_{O(Q)} = V_S/2$. Since $V_{B_1} = V_{B_3}$ under quiescent conditions, we can now express the condition for the voltage-divider ratios as $(V_S/2)R_7/(R_6 + R_7) = V_S R_3/(R_3 + R_2)$ and thus $R_7/(R_6 + R_7) = 2R_3/(R_3 + R_2)$, or $2(1 + R_6/R_7) = 1 + R_2/R_3$.

A-c feedback is also established by means of feedback to the base of Q_3. Assuming that C_8 is large enough such that the capacitative reactance of C_8 is small compared to R_8 over the a-c frequency range of interest, the feedback factor will be given by $F = (R_7 \| R_8)/[(R_7 \| R_8) + R_6]$. If the loop gain, FA_{OL}, is much greater than unity the closed-loop gain will be approximately equal to $1/F$, so that we will have $A_{CL} = 1/F = 1 + R_6/(R_7 \| R_8)$.

We will now consider a simple design example for this circuit. We will use the quantities given below for this example: $V_S = +20$ V; $V_{O(Q)} = V_S/2 = +10$ V; $V_{B_1} = +5.0$ V; differential-amplifier quiescent current, $I_Q = 10$ mA; $R_L = 8\ \Omega$; $A_V = 50$; f_1 (lower 3-dB frequency) $= 20$ Hz; $\beta = 50$ (min.) for all NPN transistors; and $V_A = 200$ V (Early voltage). For R_1 we have $R_1 = (V_{B1} - 2V_{BE})/I_Q = (5 - 1.3)$ V/10 mA $-$ $\underline{370\ \Omega}$. The maximum expected base current of Q_1 and Q_3 will be given by $I_{B_1} = I_{B_3} = I_Q/2/\beta_1\beta_2 = 5.0$ mA/(50 × 50) = 2.0 μA (max.). Therefore, the current through the R_2–R_3 and the R_6–R_7 voltage dividers should be much larger than 2 μA, so as to minimize the effect of β variations on the quiescent levels. We will choose a current of 2 μA × 50 = 100 μA as satisfying this requirement, so that we will have that $R_2 + R_3 = 20$ V/0.1 mA = 200 kΩ. For $R_6 + R_7$ we will have $R_6 + R_7 = 10$ V/0.1 mA = 50 kΩ. Since $R_3/(R_2 + R_3) = 5/20$, we have that $R_3 = (1/4)(200\ \text{k}\Omega) = \underline{50\ \text{k}\Omega}$, and thus $R_2 = \underline{150\ \text{k}\Omega}$. Similarly, for the R_6–R_7 voltage divider we will have that $R_7/(R_6 + R_7) = 5/10$, so that $R_7 = R_6 = \underline{50\ \text{k}\Omega}$.

The open-loop voltage gain will be approximately just the voltage gain of the differential amplifier stage since the voltage gain of the emitter-follower output stage will be approximately unity. Accordingly, we will have $A_{OL} = A_{V_1} A_{V(EF)} = A_{V_1} = 2g_f/g_{\text{total}}$, where g_f is the dynamic transfer conductance of the differential amplifier and g_{total} is the total dynamic conductance driven by the differential amplifier at the C_3–C_4–C_6–B_7–B_9 node. For g_f we will have $g_f = I_Q/4(2V_T) = 10$ mA/0.2 V = 50 mS. During the positive half-cycles the total conductance driven by the first stage will be $g_{\text{total}} = g_{o_6} + g_{o_4} + g_{i_7}$, and during the negative half-cycles it will be $g_{\text{total}} = g_{o_6} + g_{o_4} + g_{i_9}$. Since g_{i_9} will be considerably less than g_{i_7} as a result of the greater overall current gain of the Q_9–Q_{10}–Q_{11} combination as compared to the Q_7–Q_8 combination, for a minimum-gain calculation we will use g_{i_7}. This will be given approximately by

$$g_{i_7} = \frac{1}{\beta_7 \beta_8 R_L} = \frac{1}{50 \times 50 \times 8\ \Omega} = 50\ \mu\text{S (max.)} \tag{3.22}$$

Since the transistor output conductances will be given approximately by $g_o = I_C/V_A = 5$ mA/200 V = 25 μS, the total conductance driven by the first stage will be

$g_{total} = 25\ \mu S + 25\ \mu S + 50\ \mu S$ (max.) $= 100\ \mu S$ (max.). The open-loop gain will therefore be $A_{OL} = 2g_f/g_{total} = 2 \times 50$ mS/100 μS (max.) $=$ 1000 (min.). We see therefore that a very large open-loop gain can be obtained with only one gain stage and with a load resistance of only 8 Ω.

Since the open-loop gain of 1000 (min.) is much greater than the closed-loop gain of 50, we have that $A_{OL} \gg A_{CL}$, and thus the closed-loop gain will be determined principally by the feedback factor F as given by $A_{CL} = 1/F$, so that $F = 1/A_{CL} = 1/50$. The feedback factor is given in terms of the R_6–R_7–R_8 voltage divider as $1/F = 1 + R_6/(R_7 \| R_8) = 50$, so that since $R_6 = 50$ kΩ, we have that $(R_7 \| R_8) = 50$ kΩ/49 $= 1.02$ kΩ. With $R_7 = 50$ kΩ, we obtain for R_8 a value of 1.04 kΩ.

For the required lower half-power frequency of 20 Hz, we have the condition for C_8 as $1/\omega C_8 = R_8 = 1.04$ kΩ at 20 Hz. Solving this for C_8 gives the requirement that $C_8 \geq$ 8.0 μF.

Diodes D_1 through D_3 should be designed to produce a no-load or standby current through the output transistors, Q_8 and Q_{11} that is large enough to minimize the effects of crossover distortion. This current should satisfy the condition derived earlier that $I_Q \geq 4.5 V_T/R_L$, where I_Q represents the quiescent or standby current of the output transistors. For the case under consideration here with $R_L = 8\ \Omega$, the standby current should be at least 14 mA.

3.6 IC AUDIO POWER AMPLIFIER EXAMPLES

3.6.1 The LM380

We will start off the consideration of examples of IC audio power amplifiers by looking at the LM380 (National Semiconductor). The LM380 is a fixed-gain (50) power amplifier capable of a-c power outputs of up to 5 W. In Figure 3.8a a schematic diagram of this device is presented.

The input stage is a Darlington compound differential amplifier comprised of Q_1 through Q_4 with a current mirror active load composed of Q_5 and Q_6. This differential amplifier is biased by resistors R_1 and R_2. The quiescent current through R_1 comes from the positive supply voltage, while that through R_2 is a d-c feedback current from the output terminal. Under quiescent conditions the current through each half of the differential amplifier will be approximately equal. We therefore will have that $(V^+ - 3V_{BE})R_1 = (V_O - 2V_{BE})/R_2$, where V^+ is the d-c supply voltage, V_{BE} is the base-to-emitter voltage drop of the diode connected transistor Q_{10}, and V_O represents the quiescent output voltage level. We therefore will have that

$$V_O = \frac{R_2}{R_1}(V^+ - 3V_{BE}) + 2V_{BE} = \frac{V^+}{2} - \tfrac{3}{2}V_{BE} + 2V_{BE} = \frac{V^+}{2} + \frac{V_{BE}}{2} \qquad (3.23)$$

Thus the quiescent output voltage level will be centered at approximately one-half the supply voltage. This quiescent voltage level will allow for the maximum peak-to-peak output voltage swing, and therefore the maximum a-c output voltage.

In addition to this d-c feedback loop which acts to center the output voltage at one-half the supply voltage, there will also be an a-c feedback loop via the voltage

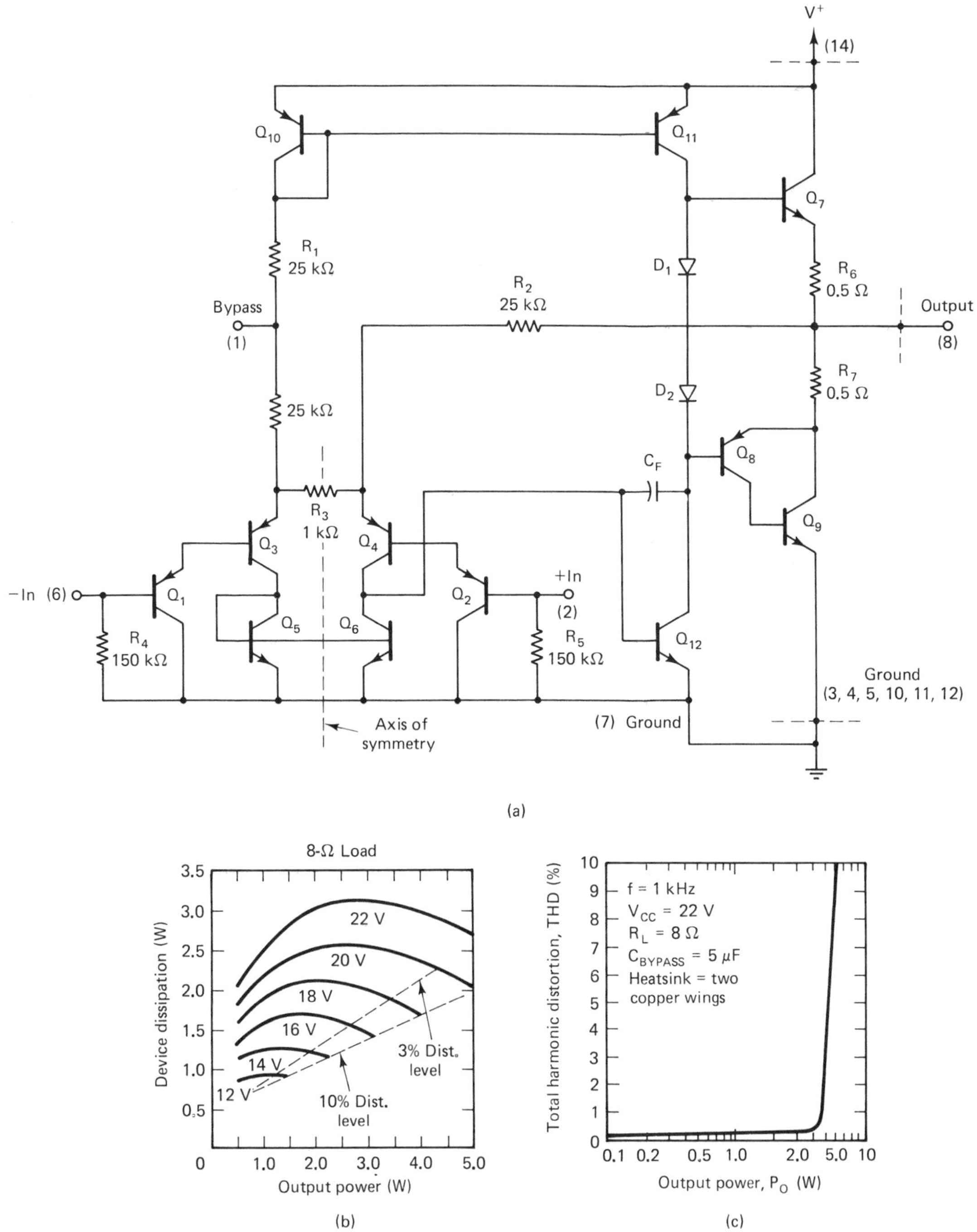

Figure 3.8 (a) LM380 IC audio power amplifier (National Semiconductor); (b) device dissipation versus output power for the LM380 (National Semiconductor); (c) total harmonic distortion versus output power for the LM380 (National Semiconductor).

divider action of R_2 and R_3. A fraction of the output voltage is fed back to the differential amplifier by this internal negative feedback loop to fix the overall voltage gain of the amplifier. If we split the differential amplifier down the axis of symmetry, we see that the feedback factor F will be given by

$$F = \frac{R_3/2}{R_2 + R_3/2} = \frac{500\ \Omega}{25\ \text{k}\Omega + 500\ \Omega} = \frac{1}{50} \tag{3.24}$$

Since the open-loop gain of the amplifier will be much greater than $1/F = 50$, the closed-loop amplifier gain will be fixed by the feedback factor to a value of $1/F = 50$, corresponding to 34 dB.

Note that the input-stage configuration of this power amplifier is similar to that of the LM124 operational amplifier, and many other operational amplifiers that can be operated with a single supply voltage. This is a direct result of the fact that the input voltage range includes ground potential, and indeed extends to about 0.5 V below ground. As a result this power amplifier can be operated with a single supply voltage, $+V_S$, and the a-c input voltage can be fed into either input terminal without the need for any d-c bias voltage superimposed on the a-c input voltage. Resistors R_4 and R_5 (150 kΩ) provides a d-c return path for the input bias (base) current so that this amplifier can be operated with either input terminal open.

The single-ended output voltage of the differential amplifier stage is fed to the second gain stage, which is comprised of Q_{12} in a common-emitter configuration with Q_{11} acting as a current source active load. Capacitor C_F, which is connected as a feedback capacitor from the output back to the input of the second stage, is used for frequency compensation to stabilize this amplifier against any type of oscillatory-response.

The single-ended output of the second gain stage drives the third, or output stage. This is a class B, complementary push-pull emitter-follower output stage, comprised of transistors Q_7, Q_8, and Q_9 and diodes D_1 and D_2. Transistor Q_7 is the NPN half of the push-pull output stage and is used to source currents into the load. Transistors Q_8 and Q_9 operate as a composite PNP-NPN transistor and are equivalent to a single PNP transistor with a current gain equal to the product of the current gains of Q_8 and Q_9. This composite configuration is used to compensate for the low current gain of the IC PNP transistors, and is used as the PNP half of the push-pull output stage to sink currents from the load. Diodes D_1 and D_2 are used to develop a small prebias voltage across the base–emitter junctions of Q_7 and Q_8 so as to minimize the crossover distortion. Resistors R_6 and R_7 are used for current limiting.

Now that we have discussed the basic circuit configuration of this power amplifier we will calculate some representative quiescent current values and voltage gains. Under quiescent conditions the current through Q_3 will be one-half of the total differential-amplifier quiescent current, I_Q, or $I_3 = I_Q/2$. This current will be given by

$$I_3 = \frac{V_S - 3V_{BE}}{R_1} = \frac{V_S - 2\ \text{V}}{50\ \text{k}\Omega} \tag{3.25}$$

For this sample calculation let us use a supply voltage of 20 V, so that

$$I_Q = \frac{2(20 - 2)\ \text{V}}{50\ \text{k}\Omega} = \underline{0.72\ \text{mA}} \tag{3.26}$$

The dynamic transfer conductance of the differential amplifier will be given by $g_f = I_Q/4(2V_T) = \underline{3.6\ \text{mS}}$.

By the symmetry of the circuit we see by inspection that the base current of Q_{12} will be equal to the sum of the base currents of Q_5 and Q_6. Therefore, on the assumption of equal current gains for all of the NPN transistors, we will have that the collector current of Q_{12} will be equal to the sum of the collector currents of Q_3 and Q_4, this sum being equal to I_Q, so that $I_{12} = I_Q = 0.72$ mA.

If we assume a representative current value of $\beta = 200$, the input conductance of Q_{12} will be given by

$$g_{i_{12}} = \frac{I_{12}}{\beta V_T} = \frac{720\ \mu\text{A}}{200 \times 25\ \text{mV}} = 144\ \mu\text{S} \tag{3.27}$$

The voltage gain of the differential amplifier stage will be given by

$$A_{V_1} = \frac{2g_f}{g_o} = \frac{2g_f}{g_{o_4} + g_{o_6} + g_{i_{12}}} \tag{3.28}$$

where the factor of 2 comes from the current doubling action of the current mirror active load. Since g_{o_4} and g_{o_6} will be given essentially by $g_o = I_C/V_A = I_Q/2V_A$, where V_A is the Early voltage, and $g_{i_{12}} = I_Q/\beta V_T$, we note that since $2V_A = 500$ V $\gg \beta V_T = 5.0$ V, we will have that $g_{i_{12}} \gg g_{o_4} + g_{o_6}$. As a result, the voltage gain of the first stage can be written approximately as

$$A_{V_1} \simeq \frac{2g_f}{g_{i_{12}}} = \frac{2I_Q/8V_T}{I_Q/\beta V_T} = \frac{\beta}{4} \tag{3.29}$$

Since $\beta = 200$, the voltage gain of the first stage will be 50. Note that this result will be essentially independent of the quiescent current level.

The voltage gain of the common-emitter second stage will be given by

$$A_{V_2} = g_{m_{12}} R'_L \tag{3.30}$$

where $g_{m_{12}}$ is the dynamic transconductance of Q_{12} as given by $g_{m_{12}} = I_{12}/V_T$ and R'_L is the transformed value of the load resistance, R_L. The impedance transformation occurs by means of the emitter-follower output stage consisting of Q_7 for the positive half-cycles and the Q_8–Q_9 composite transistor for the negative half-cycles. The transformed load resistance will be $R'_L = \beta_7 R_L$ during the positive half-cycles and $R'_L = \beta_8\beta_9 R_L$ during the negative half-cycles. For a representative load resistance value of 8 Ω (a typical loudspeaker impedance level) the transformed value of load resistance R'_L will be about 1600 Ω during the positive half-cycles, and much larger than this during the negative half-cycles. Since $g_{m_{12}} = I_{12}/V_T = 720\ \mu\text{A}/25\ \text{mV} = 29$ mS, the voltage gain of the second stage will be given by $A_{V_2} = g_{m_{12}} R'_L =$

29 mS × 1600 Ω = 46 during the positive half-cycles, and much larger during the negative half-cycles.

The voltage gain of the emitter-follower output stage will be of the order of unity so that $A_{V(EF)} = 1$, and the overall open-loop gain of the amplifier will be given by $A_{OL} = A_{V_1}A_{V_2}A_{V(EF)} = 50 \times 46 \times 1 = 2300$. The loop gain FA_{OL} will be $(1/50)(2300) = 46$. Since the loop gain is considerably greater than unity, we see that the closed-loop gain of the amplifier will be controlled principally by the feedback factor. If the open-loop gain has an actual value of 2300, as given above, the closed-loop gain will be $A_{CL} = A_{OL}/(1 + FA_{OL}) = 2300/(1 + 46) = 48.94$, compared to a closed-loop gain of 50 that would be obtained if the open-loop gain went to infinity. The gain error would thus be 2%.

Note that the gain on the negative half-cycles of the output voltage swing will be larger than during the positive half-cycles due to the greater overall current gain of the Q_8–Q_9 combination compared to that of just Q_7 alone. This imbalance in the push-pull amplifier will result in the negative half-cycles being slightly larger in amplitude than the positive half-cycles. This discrepancy in the two halves of the output voltage swing will contribute to the overall distortion of the amplifier, principally in terms of the second harmonic component. Nevertheless, in spite of this gain asymmetry, the total harmonic distortion of the output waveform can be kept to values of around 0.2% as long as the peak-to-peak output voltage swing is restricted to be at least about 8 V less than the supply voltage.

Power output characteristics. We will now look at the power output characteristics of the LM380 as shown in Figure 3.8b and c. We will consider a supply voltage of 22 V and an 8-Ω load resistance. With a 22-V supply voltage the maximum peak-to-peak output voltage swing that can possibly be obtained will be about 20 V, although there will be some degree of flattening of the output voltage peaks due to the output transistor being driven fairly close to saturation. The power output that will be achieved with this 20V peak-to-peak output voltage swing will be given by $P_{O(MAX)} = V^2_{O(P-P)}/8R_L = 6.25$ W. At this point the power conversion efficiency should be close to the theoretical value of the maximum possible power conversion efficiency of 78.5%. Since the power dissipation at this point is 2.5 W, the actual efficiency is about 71%. The price to be paid for this large peak-to-peak output voltage swing will, of course, be a considerable amount of distortion, which will be in the range 5 to 10%.

If the peak-to-peak voltage swing is now reduced to 18 V, the power output will be reduced correspondingly to about 5.1 W, and the distortion is about 4%, which is still an unacceptably high value for many applications. A further reduction in the peak-to-peak output swing to 16 V will reduce the output power to about 4.0 W, but will now reduce the total distortion way down to about 0.5%. The power dissipation under these conditions will be about 3.0 W, so that the power conversion efficiency is now about 57%.

In order to reduce the distortion to a minimum, the peak-to-peak output voltage swing has to be restricted to values less than about 14 V, for which case the distortion can be reduced to levels of about 0.2%. The very rapid increase in distortion that occurs for peak-to-peak output voltage swings in excess of about 16 V ($P_o = 4.0$

W) is due to the onset of the flattening or clipping of the voltage peaks due to the output transistors entering into the transition zone between the active and saturation regions.

The equation for the point at which the power dissipation will be a maximum has been given as $P_D = P_O = 2V_S^2/\pi^2 R_L$. For a total supply voltage of $2V_S = 22$ V, this gives a result of $P_D = P_O = 3.06$ W. The actual values of P_O and P_D obtained from the graph of the device dissipation versus output power for this device are very close to this.

3.6.2 The LM384

The LM384 (National Semiconductor) is identical to the LM380 except that it has a maximum voltage rating of 28 V, compared to 22 V for the LM380. With this higher supply voltage a larger peak-to-peak output voltage swing is possible, and hence a substantially larger output power is available. For a supply voltage of 26 V and an 8-Ω load resistance a peak-to-peak output voltage swing of 22 V will produce an output power of 7.6 W, but the total harmonic distortion will be up at about 5%. A reduction in the peak-to-peak swing to 20 V will reduce the power output to 6.25 W, but bring the distortion all the way down to about 0.5%. A further reduction in the output voltage swing to 18 V will reduce the output power to 5.1 W, but the distortion will now be only about 0.2%.

In Figure 3.9 the external circuitry for a 5-W audio amplifier using the LM384 power amplifier is shown. The 500-μF coupling capacitor serves to provide the a-c drive to the loadspeaker while at the same time maintaining the quiescent voltage at the output to one-half the supply voltage. The d-c voltage across the coupling capacitor will therefore be $V_{O(Q)} \simeq V_S/2 = 14$ V. This allows the power amplifier to operate with a single supply and still be able to both source and sink output currents.

This device comes in a 14-pin plastic dual-in-line package (DIP). The center three pins on either side (3, 4, 5, and 10, 11, 12) are ground pins. This availability of a multiplicity of ground pins is used to maximize the heat flow from the package

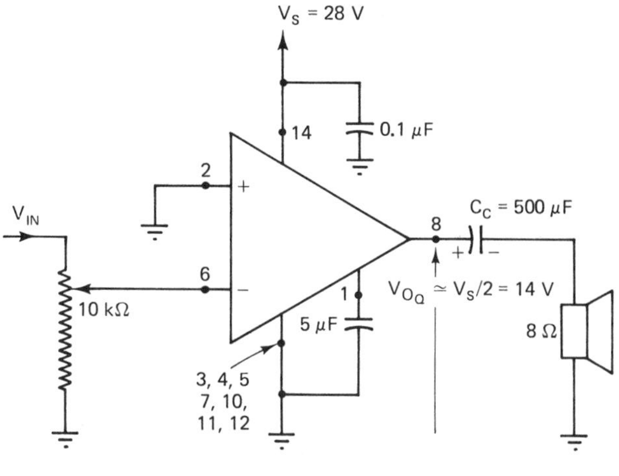

Figure 3.9 A 5-W audio amplifier.

to the heat sink, and thus to decrease the thermal impedance. The pins are of copper for good thermal conductivity and are usually soldered to a large copper foil area on a printed circuit board.

The free-air thermal impedance of this device is 82°C/W. The maximum allowable junction temperature is 150°C, so that the maximum allowable power dissipation under free-air conditions will be only 1.5 W. With the six ground pins soldered to a total copper foil area of 6 (in.)² on a printed circuit board, the thermal impedance is reduced to 35°C/W. This will increase the maximum power dissipation rating to 3.6 W. With an "infinite heat sink" the thermal impedance is reduced to 12°C/W, which corresponds to the junction-to-case thermal impedance. Under these conditions the maximum power dissipation rating will be 10.4 W.

3.6.3 Audio Power Amplifiers with External Power Transistors

The power output available from an IC power amplifier is limited by the power dissipation rating the IC itself to a maximum of generally about 10 W. Greater a-c power output levels than this can, however, be achieved by the use of external power transistors that are driven by the IC power amplifier. This is analogous to the use of current boost transistors in conjunction with IC voltage regulators for higher output currents.

An example of an IC power amplifier that is specifically designed for this type of application is the LM391 audio power driver (National Semiconductor). With this device driving suitable external power transistors, output power levels of up to 100 W are available.

In Figure 3.10 a somewhat simplified circuit diagram of this IC is presented, and in Figure 3.11 the typical external circuitry is shown. The input stage is a PNP differential amplifier (Q_1 and Q_2) with a current mirror active load (Q_3 and Q_4). The differential amplifier is biased by a current source (Q_5).

The second gain stage is transistor Q_6 in a common-emitter configuration Q_{11} acting as a current source active load. Transistor Q_6 drives the emitter-follower output transistor (Q_7), which is used for sourcing currents into the load, via externally connected transistors (Q_{20} and Q_{21}). For sinking output currents, transistor Q_6 is used directly and drives the externally connected transistors, Q_{30} and Q_{31}.

Transistor Q_{14} in conjunction with the externally connected resistors R_{31} and R_{32} produces a d-c voltage drop that biases the push-pull output stage in the class AB mode of operation. Resistors R_{31} and R_{32} act as a voltage divider, with R_{32} being across the base–emitter junction of Q_{14} (pins 6 and 5). The voltage developed across Q_{14}, from collector (pin 7) to emitter (pin 5) will be given by the relationship

$$V_{CE_{14}} \frac{R_{32}}{R_{31} + R_{32}} = V_{BE_{14}} \qquad (3.31)$$

so that

$$V_{CE_{14}} = V_{BE_{14}} \left(1 + \frac{R_{31}}{R_{32}}\right) \qquad (3.32)$$

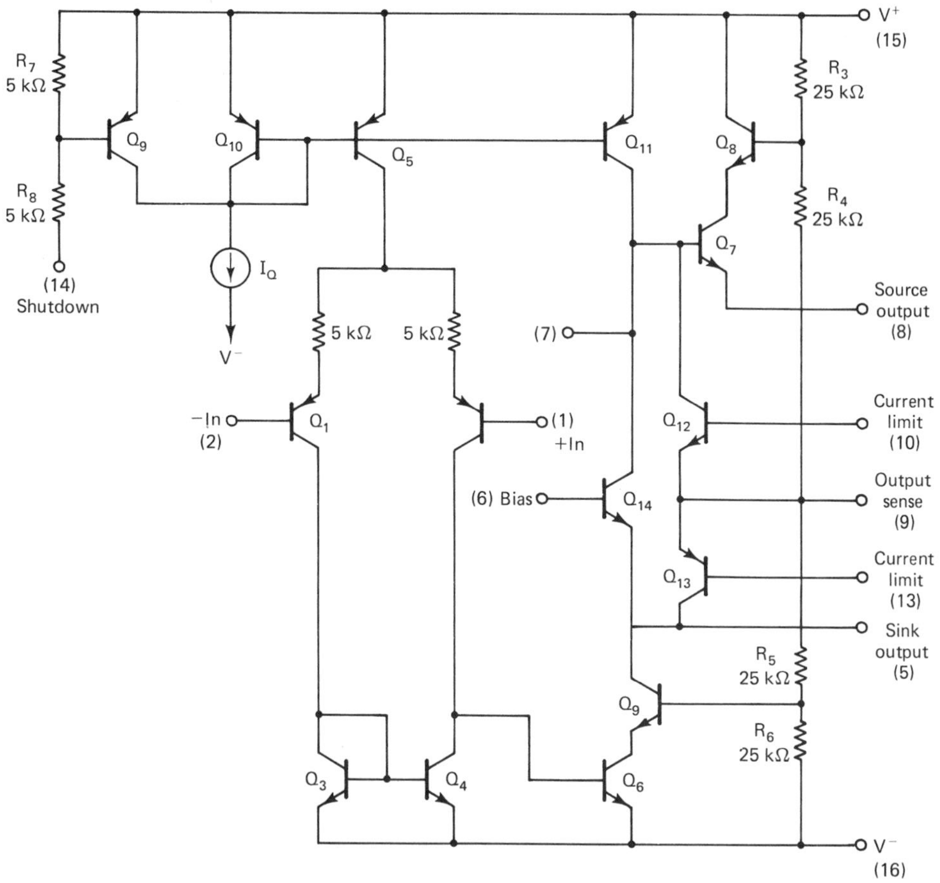

Figure 3.10 Audio power driver: LM391 (National Semiconductor).

This voltage appears in series across the base–emitter junction of Q_7, Q_{20}, and Q_{30} as

$$V_{CE_{14}} = V_{BE_7} + V_{BE_{20}} + V_{EB_{30}} \tag{3.33}$$

If V_{CE14} is designed to be of suitable magnitude (about 2.0 V), class AB operation with an acceptably low amount of crossover distortion will be achieved.

For any given quiescent or standby current for the push-pull output stage, the corresponding base-to-emitter voltages of Q_7, Q_{20}, and Q_{30} will decrease with temperature. If these three transistors share the same heat sink and are in good thermal contact, all three base-to-emitter voltages will decrease with temperature at approximately the same rate. Since the bias voltage that is developed across Q_{14} is proportional to the base-to-emitter voltage drop of Q_{14}, we see that this bias voltage will decrease at essentially the rate that is required to keep the standby current reasonably constant with increasing temperature.

This IC has a total supply voltage rating of 100 V (or ±50 V). In order to limit the collector-to-emitter voltage of Q_6 and Q_7 to voltages that are no more

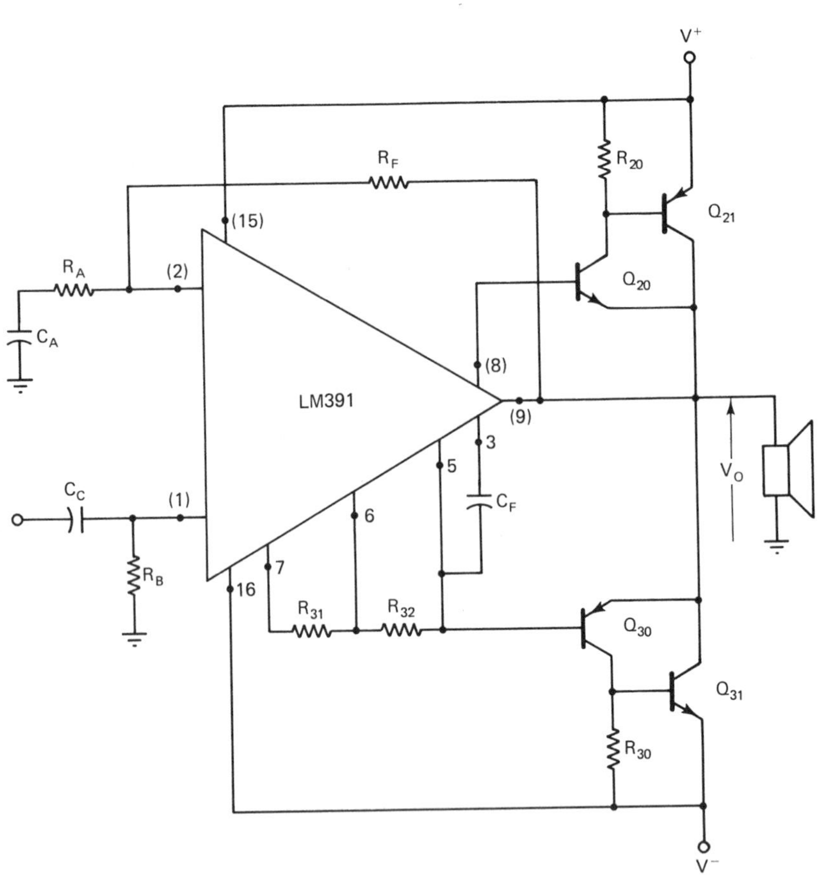

Figure 3.11 External connections for the audio power driver.

than 50 V, emitter-follower transistors Q_8 and Q_9 are used as voltage sources in conjunction with the R_3–R_4 and R_5–R_6 voltage dividers, respectively. The total voltage drop across the R_3–R_4 voltage divider is $V^+ - V_O$ so that the voltage at the base of Q_8 will be one-half of this voltage drop plus V_O or $\frac{1}{2}(V^+ - V_O) + V_O = \frac{1}{2}(V^+ + V_O)$. The voltage at the emitter of Q_8, which is the same as the collector voltage of Q_7 will be V_{BE} less than this so that we have $V_{C_7} = V_{E_8} = V_{B_8} - V_{BE} = \frac{1}{2}(V^+ + V_O) - V_{BE}$. The voltage at the emitter of Q_7 will be equal to the output voltage, V_O, plus the base-to-emitter voltage drop of Q_{20} or $V_O + V_{BE}$. Therefore, the collector-to-emitter voltage that will appear across Q_7 will be given by

$$V_{CE_7} = V_{C_7} - V_{E_7} = \tfrac{1}{2}(V^+ + V_O) - V_{BE} - V_O - V_{BE} = \tfrac{1}{2}(V^+ - V_O) - 2V_{BE} \qquad (3.34)$$

Let us now consider the operation of this circuit with the maximum rated supply voltages given by $V^+ = +50$ V and $V^- = -50$ V. Under these conditions the output voltage cannot drop below -50 V so that the maximum voltage to which Q_7 will be subject to will be $V_{CE_7(\text{MAX})} = \frac{1}{2}(50 + 50) - 2(0.7) \simeq 48$ V.

There is a similar situation for Q_6, for which $V_{CE_6} = V_{C_6} - V_{E_6} = V_{C_6} =$

$V_{B_9} - V_{BE} \simeq \frac{1}{2}(V_O - V^-)$. Since V_O cannot go above V^+, which is +50 V, the maximum voltage to which Q_6 will be subject to will be approximately 49 V.

Thus by means of the R_3–R_4 and R_5–R_6 voltage dividers in association with Q_8 and Q_9 the maximum voltage that will appear across the source and sink output transistors (Q_7 and Q_6) of the IC will be limited to no more than one-half of the total supply voltage. This makes the IC implementation of these transistors much easier, especially from the standpoint of the safe operating area (SOA) protection of these transistors based on second breakdown considerations.

3.6.4 Class B Audio Driver

Another example of an audio power driver is the MC3320P/MC3321P (Motorola) and in Figure 3.12 a circuit schematic of this IC is shown. In Figure 3.13, a typical application circuit is shown. With a 30 V d-c supply and the external power transistors, this IC is capable of delivering up to 10 W to an 8 Ω load. The feedback loop using the 100 kΩ resistor (R_4) and the 1 kΩ resistor establishes a closed-loop gain of 101 for this circuit. The quiescent output level at the emitters of the external power output transistors, Q_1 and Q_2, is set by the feedback through R_4 to pin 6 to a value closely equal to the voltage at pin 5. The d-c voltage level at pin 5 is set by the 820 kΩ and 1.0 MΩ voltage divider to a value of 0.45 V_{CC}. As a result, the quiescent output voltage level is approximately at the mid-point between the positive supply voltage and ground. This will permit the maximum symmetrical undistorted output voltage swing and therefore the maximum output power. In Figure 3.14 a graph of the total harmonic distortion versus output power for this circuit is shown. An output power of up to 8 W is available with a total harmonic distortion not exceeding 0.2%, and at a power output of 10 W the distortion level is just reaching

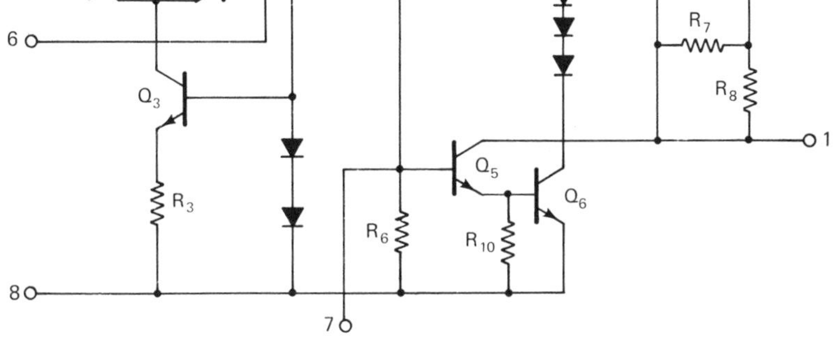

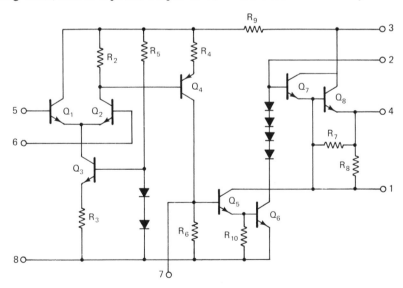

Figure 3.12 Circuit schematic of the MC3320P Audio Driver (Motorola Semiconductor Products).

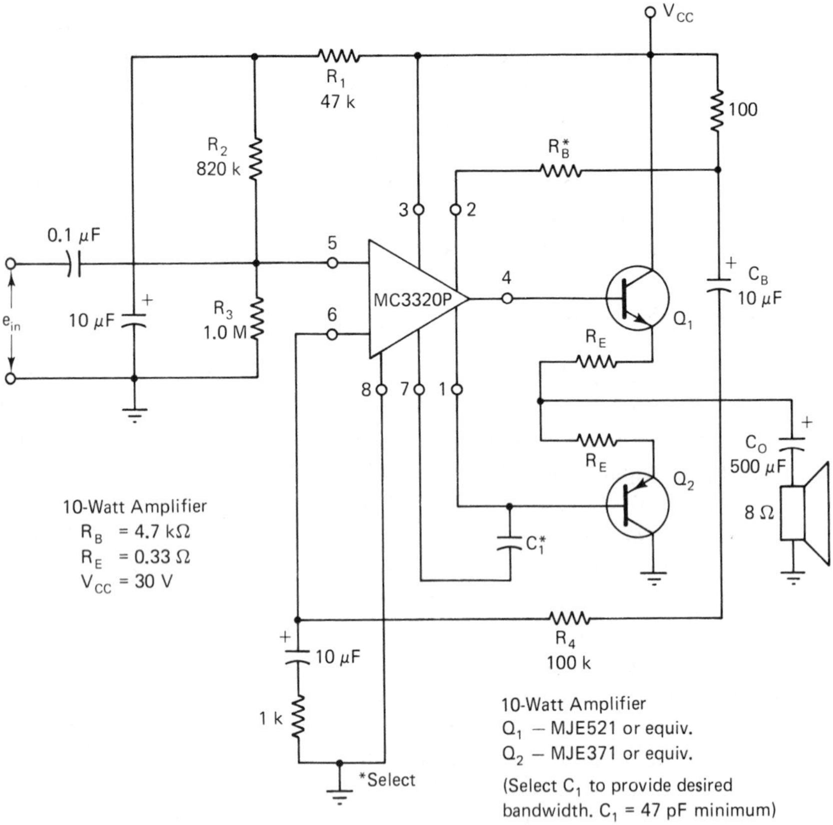

Figure 3.13 Application circuit for the MC3320P (Motorola Semiconductor Products).

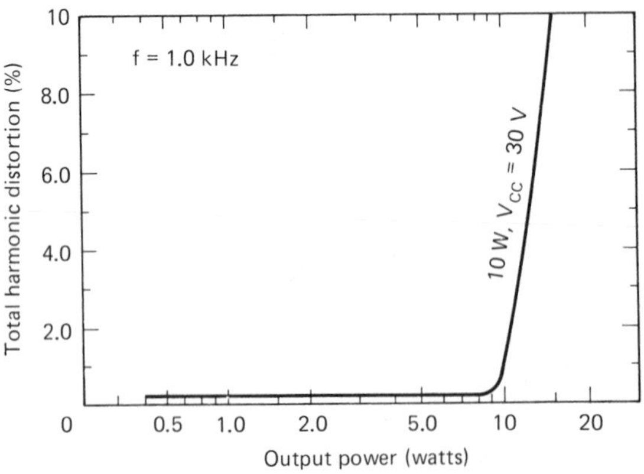

Figure 3.14 Total harmonic distortion versus output power (Motorola Semiconductor Products).

1%. Beyond this, however, the distortion increases very rapidly due to the clipping of the output voltage. At a power output of 10 W the peak-to-peak voltage swing is 25.3 V. If we add to this the base-to-emitter voltage drops of the four IC output transistors plus those of Q_1 and Q_2 which totals about 4.5 V, we obtain a total voltage very close to the 30 V d-c supply voltage so it should be expected that the distortion should increase rapidly beyond this output power level.

3.7 DISTORTION IN PUSH-PULL CLASS AB POWER AMPLIFIERS

There are two principal causes of distortion in class AB power amplifiers. One is the gain mismatch between the NPN and PNP halves of the push-pull output stage. This gain mismatch will result in an asymmetrical output waveform with the amplitude of the positive half-cycles not being the same as that of the negative half-cycles. The other possible cause of distortion is the flattening or clipping of the peaks of the output voltage waveform that will occur if the output transistors are driven from the active region into the transition zone between the active and saturation regions, or all the way into the saturation region itself.

3.7.1 Gain Mismatch

We will first look at the distortion that results from the push-pull gain asymmetry. We will use the Fourier series representation for positive half-cycles taken separately, then that for the negative half-cycles, and then we will combine the two Fourier series expressions to obtain that which will correspond to the entire output waveform. The Fourier series representation for the half-wave rectified sine wave will be used for each set of half-cycles. For a half-wave rectified sine wave of peak amplitude A the Fourier series will be given by

$$v(t) = \frac{2A}{\pi}\left(\frac{1}{2} + \frac{\pi}{4}\cos\omega t + \frac{1}{3}\cos 2\omega t - \frac{1}{15}\cos 4\omega t + \cdots\right) \qquad (3.35)$$

The peak amplitude of the positive half-cycles of the push-pull output voltage waveform will be represented by A_1, so that the positive half-cycles can be represented as

$$v_+(t) = \frac{2A_1}{\pi}\left(\frac{1}{2} + \frac{\pi}{4}\cos\omega t + \frac{1}{3}\cos 2\omega t - \frac{1}{15}\cos 4\omega t + \cdots\right) \qquad (3.36)$$

For the negative half-cycles the peak amplitude will be $-A_2$, and the negative half-cycle waveform is shifted by π radians (180°) with respect to the positive half-cycles. Since $\cos(\theta + n\pi) = \cos\theta$ for n being an even integer, and $\cos(\theta + n\pi) = -\cos\theta$ for n being an odd integer, we have for the negative half-cycles the Fourier series given by

$$v_-(t) = -\frac{2A_2}{\pi}\left(\frac{1}{2} - \frac{\pi}{4}\cos\omega t + \frac{1}{3}\cos 2\omega t - \frac{1}{15}\cos 4\omega t + \cdots\right) \qquad (3.37)$$

The total output-voltage waveform can be obtained by taking the algebraic sum of v_+ and v_-, giving

$$v_o(t) = v_+(t) + v_-(t)$$

$$= \frac{2(A_1 - A_2)}{\pi} + \frac{A_1 + A_2}{2} \cos \omega t + \frac{2(A_1 - A_2)}{3\pi} \cos 2\omega t + \frac{2(A_1 - A_2)}{15\pi} \cos 4\omega t + \cdots \tag{3.38}$$

From this expression we see that the distortion components will all be even harmonics, and the dominant distortion component will be the second harmonic term. As a result the total harmonic distortion (THD) can be expressed as

$$\%\ \text{THD} \simeq \%\ \text{2HD} = \frac{\text{amplitude of second harmonic term}}{\text{amplitude of fundamental term}} \times 100\% \tag{3.39}$$

Since the amplitude of the fundamental term is $(A_1 + A_2)/2$ and that of the second harmonic term is $2(A_1 - A_2)/3\pi$, the percentage total harmonic distortion will be given by

$$\%\ \text{THD} \simeq \%\ \text{2HD} = \frac{4}{3\pi} \frac{A_1 - A_2}{A_1 + A_2} \times 100\ \% \tag{3.40}$$

For the usual cases of interest the difference between the two amplitude values, $A_1 - A_2$, will be small compared to magnitude of either A_1 or A_2, so that if we let $A_1 = A + \Delta A$, and $A_2 = A$, for the usual case of $\Delta A \ll 1$ we will have that $A_1 + A_2 = 2A + \Delta A \simeq 2A$. Using this approximation, the expression for the percentage distortion can be written as

$$\begin{aligned} \%\ \text{THD} &\simeq \frac{4\,\Delta A}{3\pi(2A)} \times 100\% = \frac{2}{3\pi} \frac{\Delta A}{A} \times 100\% \\ &\simeq 0.2\left(\frac{\Delta A}{A}\right) \times 100\% = 20\left(\frac{\Delta A}{A}\right)\% \end{aligned} \tag{3.41}$$

To consider an example, let us take a power amplifier for which $A_{OL} = 1000$, $A_{CL} = 50$, and assume that there is a 20% open-loop gain difference between the positive and negative half-cycle output-voltage swings. The closed-loop gain difference will be given approximately by the relationship $dA_{CL}/A_{CL} = (dA_{OL}/A_{OL})(A_{CL}/A_{OL})$ so that at 20% change in the open-loop gain will result in a change in the closed-loop gain given by $dA_{CL}/A_{CL} \simeq 20\% \times (50/1000) = 1\%$. This 1% gain difference will produce a corresponding difference of 1% in the amplitudes of the positive and negative half-cycles, so that $\Delta A/A = 0.01$. As a result, the percentage distortion will be approximately 0.2%. We see in this example the beneficial action of the negative feedback in stabilizing the closed-loop gain against variations in the open-loop gain and thereby reducing the distortion produced by the open-loop gain asymmetry.

3.7.2 Distortion Due to Clipping

We now will consider the distortion that will result from a symmetrical flattening or clipping of the output waveform. If we look at Figure 3.15 we see that the waveform that results from this type of clipping can be approximated by combining a sine wave at the fundamental frequency and adding to it a sine wave at the third harmonic frequency. As we see from Figure 3.15b the third harmonic waveform will cause the net waveform to be flattened or clipped by an amount given by the amplitude of the third harmonic term, V_{O_3}. If the flattening that has been incurred by the output voltage waveform is ΔV_O, we have that $V_{O_3} = \Delta V_O$, and therefore the harmonic distortion will be given by

$$\%\ \text{THD} \simeq \%\ \text{3HD} = \frac{V_{O_3}}{V_{O_1}} \times 100\% = (\Delta V_O / V_O) \times 100\% \tag{3.42}$$

Thus, even a small amount of clipping of the output voltage can result in a very significant increase in distortion. The use of negative feedback provides only a limited amount of help in this situation since the clipping level will not be affected much by the presence of feedback. We see, therefore, that for a minimum amount of distortion

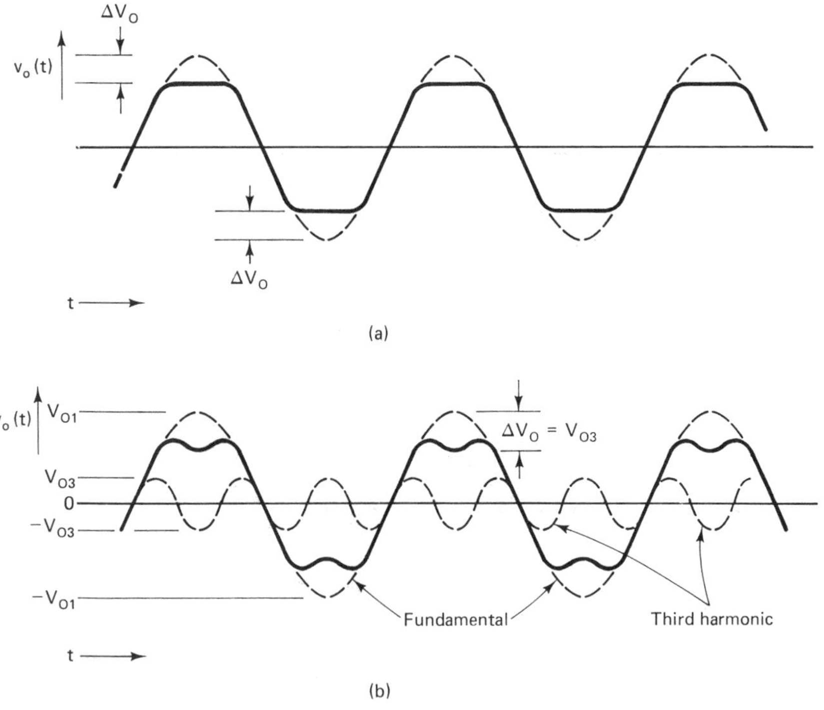

Figure 3.15 Distortion due to clipping: (a) output voltage waveform; (b) approximation of clipped output waveform using the fundamental and third harmonic sinusoidal components.

the output transistors should be kept out of the saturation region, and even well out of the transition zone between the active and saturation regions.

3.8 POWER OPERATIONAL AMPLIFIERS

Operational amplifiers can exhibit some very good performance characteristics, such as a very high open-loop gain (100,000 to several million), a very high input impedance (up into the 10^9-Ω range for some devices), and a very low input bias current. Also available are op amps with very low offset voltages (V_{OS}) and very low offset voltage temperature coefficients ($TC_{V_{OS}}$). Op amps are, however, generally limited in the amount of a-c output power available.

The current limit for most op amps is generally in the range of about 20 or 25 mA. The maximum supply voltage rating is usually around 36 V with a single supply and ± 18 V if a split supply is used. For an op amp using a ± 18-V supply, the peak output voltage swing obtainable will be about ± 15 V. For a peak output current swing of ± 20 mA and a peak output voltage swing of ± 15 V, the a-c power delivered to the load will be given by $P_O = V_{O\,(\text{peak})} I_{O\,(\text{peak})}/2 = 15 \text{ V} \times 20 \text{ mA}/2 = 150$ mW. While this power output level will be satisfactory for many applications, for some applications a considerably larger power output is required.

Larger a-c power outputs can be obtained by adding external "current boost" power transistors to the circuit in a fashion similar to that of the IC voltage regulators with external current boost transistors for greater current outputs.

In Figure 3.16a a basic circuit of an op amp with external "current boost" power transistors is shown. Transistors Q_3 and Q_5 are the current boost transistors and are driven as a complementary push-pull output stage. Transistors Q_4 and Q_6 together with the R_{CL} resistors perform the current limiting function to protect Q_3 and Q_5 against excessive current flow.

When the op amp is sourcing current to the load a voltage drop will be produced across R_1 equal to $(I_Q + I_{O_1})R_1$, where I_Q is the quiescent or biasing current of the op amp and I_{O_1} is the current sourced by the op amp. When the voltage drop across R_1 rises above 500 mV, Q_3 will start to turn on, and when the voltage drop reaches the range 600 to 700 mV, Q_3 will be in full conduction. When this happens, Q_3 will be supplying additional current to the load, I_{O_3}. A similar situation will hold true for Q_5 for sinking current from the load when the voltage drop across R_2 has risen above 500 mV. This will cause Q_5 to turn on and to sink load current.

If $I_Q = 5$ mA and the op amp output current limit is 25 mA, for example, a suitable choice for R_1 and for R_2 would be a value that will result in a voltage drop of about 600 mV when the op amp output current is 15 mA. We therefore have that $R_2 = 600 \text{ mV}/(5 + 15)\text{mA} = 150\ \Omega$, and R_1 will have the same value as R_2.

With this value for R_1 and R_2 the output stage of the op amp will supply the load current in its entirety up to a level of about 15 mA. Above that current level the external transistors, Q_3 and Q_5, will be turned on and supply any additional current required by the load. For a current gain of 50 (min.) for Q_3 and Q_5, the maximum output current available from these two transistors will be $50 \times I_{B\,(\text{MAX})}$,

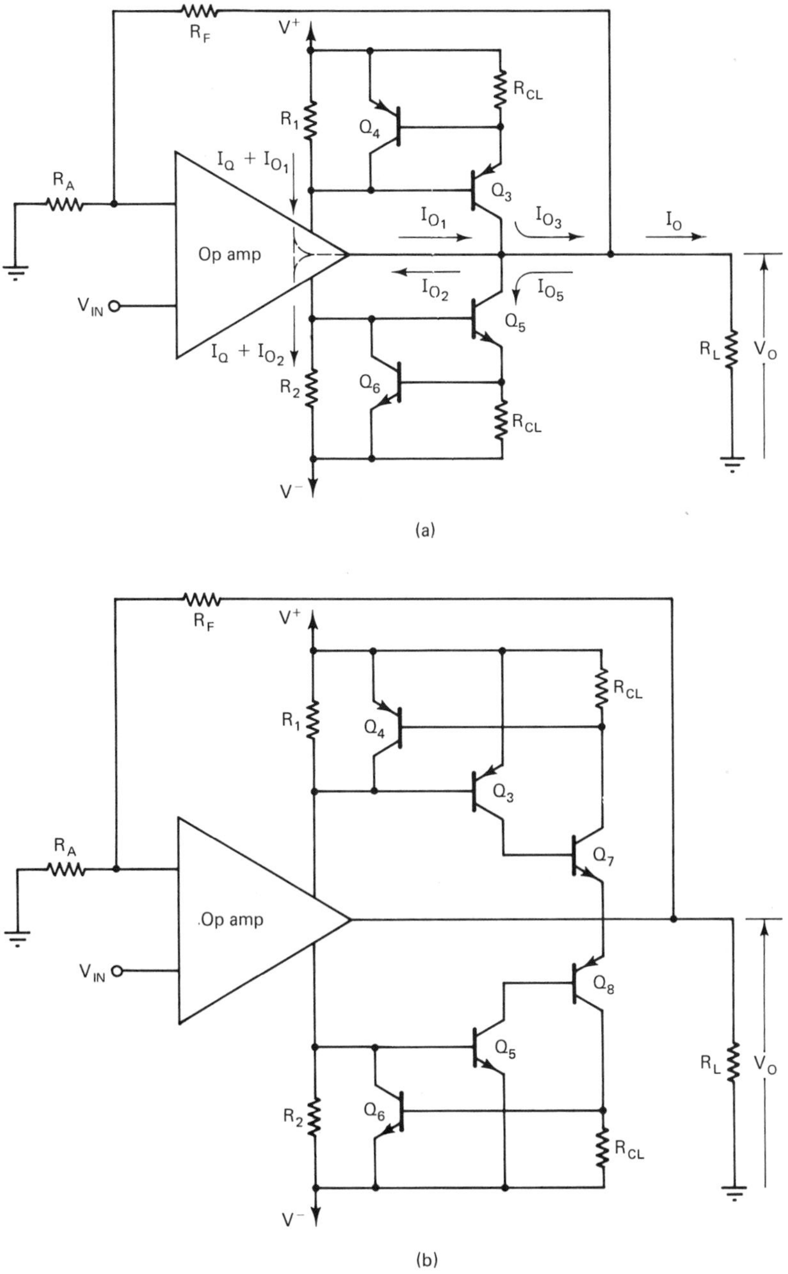

Figure 3.16 Operational amplifier with external power transistors.

where $I_{B(MAX)}$ is the maximum base drive that is available. In order to bias the transistors on, the current flow through R_1 or R_2 is 20 mA. Since the maximum output current of the op amp is limited to 25 mA, the maximum current left over to serve as the base drive for the external current boost transistors will be 10 mA, so that an output current of 525 mA (min.) will be available, with the op amp supplying 25 mA and the current boost transistor supplying 500 mA (min.). Note that Q_3 and Q_5 will operate in essentially a class B push-pull fashion, but that the operational amplifier itself will supply the output current during the transition interval between the conduction period of Q_3 and the conduction period of Q_5.

For even greater output currents than that available with the circuit just described, a Darlington configuration can be used as shown in Figure 3.16b. In this figure the Q_3–Q_7 combination is a direct-coupled PNP–NPN combination used for sourcing currents into the load. This combination will have an overall current gain equal to the product of the current gains of Q_3 and Q_7. In a similar fashion the NPN–PNP combination is used to sink load currents, and has an overall current gain equal to the product of the individual transistor current gains. With this arrangement output current levels up into the range of several amperes are now available. The maximum current that may be safely drawn from this circuit will still, of course, be limited by considerations of maximum power dissipation and of the safe operating area of Q_7 and Q_8.

3.8.1 Hybrid IC Power Operational Amplifiers

A hybrid integrated circuit that is the combination of a conventional op amp chip and current boost power transistors, all in one package, is the LH0021 and the LH0041 (National Semiconductor). A schematic diagram of this device is shown in Figure 3.17. The circuit is basically similar to that of a 741-type op amp with the addition of the current boost transistors Q_{13} and Q_{14}.

The differential amplifier input stage consists of Q_1 through Q_4 connected as a CC–CB compound differential amplifier. The differential amplifier is biased by Q_{17}, which sinks the combined base currents of Q_3 and Q_4. Transistors Q_5 and Q_6 serve as a current mirror active load for the differential amplifier. The second stage consists of Q_9 and Q_{10} connected as a Darlington common-emitter gain stage with Q_8 serving as a current source active load for this stage. Capacitor C_1 is a compensation capacitor that provides feedback around the second stage.

Transistors Q_{17} and Q_{18} serve as a complementary emitter-follower push-pull output stage, with the voltage drop provided by diodes D_3 and D_4 biasing this stage in the class AB mode in order to minimize crossover distortion.

Whenever the voltage drop across R_{10} or R_{13} exceeds approximately 500 mV, the current boost transistor, Q_{13} or Q_{14}, respectively, will be turned on. The value of R_{10} and R_{13} is 180 Ω, so that for output-current levels in excess of ± 500 mV/180 Ω $= \pm 2.8$ mA, either Q_{13} or Q_{14} will be turned on, and contribute additional current to the load. The actual turn-on threshold will be somewhat less than the value just calculated due to the standby current of Q_{17} and Q_{18} that will result from the class AB biasing condition resulting from the voltage drop across D_3 and D_4.

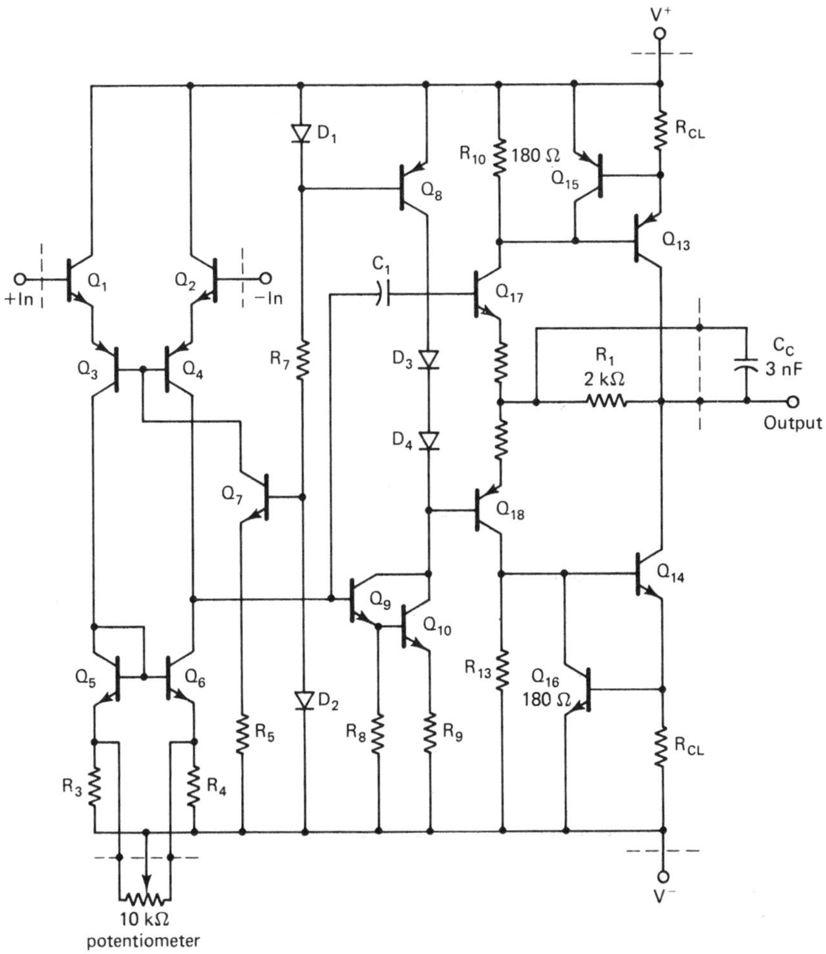

Figure 3.17 Power operational amplifier: LH0021 (National Semiconductor).

Resistor R_1 (2 kΩ) will limit the current flow through Q_{17} and Q_{18} to a maximum of about ± 18 V/2 kΩ = 6 mA, and so provides protection for these two transistors. Protection of the current boost transistors Q_{13} and Q_{14} is provided by the action of Q_{15} and Q_{16} and the voltage drop produced across the associated current-limit resistor, R_{CL}.

Capacitor C_C is an externally connected bypass capacitor (3 nF) connected across R_1. If C_C were not present, and if this device is driving a load with a substantial capacitive component, the combination of R_1 and the load capacitance would constitute an RC low-pass network. As a result of the rather large size of R_1 (2 kΩ) a large phase shift could be produced which would have a destabilizing effect on the amplifier, and could result in such effects as gain peaking or even oscillations. To eliminate this problem a capacitor of suitably large size (~3 nF) is to be connected

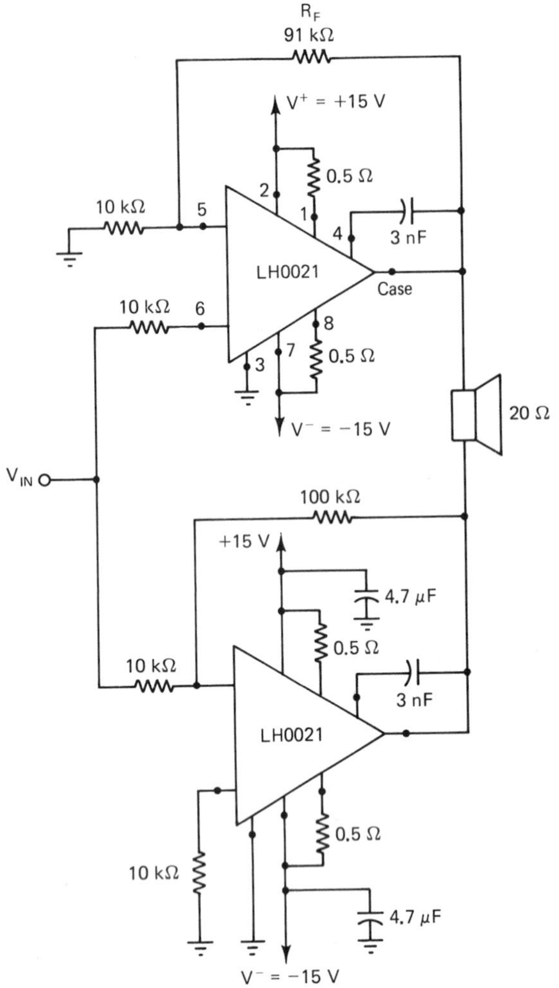

Figure 3.18 A 10-W bridge audio amplifier.

across R_1. Since it is not possible to have such a large capacitor on the chip, an externally connected capacitor is used.

The LH0021 comes in an 8-pin TO-3 type of package, and with adequate heat sinking is capable of supplying a peak current of ± 1.2 A of output current, with an output voltage swing of ± 12 V across a 10-Ω load.

In Figure 3.18 a 10-W "bridge" amplifier circuit is shown using two LH0021 power op amps. The input signal is applied to the noninverting input of one amplifier and to the inverting input of the other, so that the two output voltages will be 180° out of phase with respect to each other. For each amplifier the closed-loop gain will be $1 + (91\text{ k}\Omega/10\text{ k}\Omega) = 10$, so that the two output voltages will be $+10V_{IN}$ and $-10V_{IN}$, respectively.

With a ± 15-V split supply the LH0021 is capable of a peak output voltage swing of about 12 V into a 10-Ω load, but to limit the distortion to an acceptable value the output voltage swing should be reduced to a maximum of about 10 V.

With each amplifier supplying a peak voltage of 10 V across the load, the peak voltage across the load will be 20 V since the two amplifier output voltages are 180° out of phase with respect to each other. Note that the peak voltage that appears across the load will be *twice* the peak voltage that is supplied by each amplifier. The peak load current will therefore be 20 V/20 Ω = 1.0 A.

The average (rms) a-c power delivered to the load will be

$$P_O = \frac{V_{O\,(\text{peak})}^2}{2R_L} = \frac{I_{O\,(\text{peak})}^2 R_L}{2} = \frac{(20\ \text{V}^2)}{2 \times 20\ \Omega} = 10\ \text{W} \tag{3.43}$$

Note that if a single amplifier was used rather than the bridge arrangement shown here, the peak voltage across the load would be only 10 V, and the power delivered to the load would be limited to 2.5 W, or only one-fourth of that obtained with the bridge amplifier configuration.

The 0.5-Ω resistors are used in the current-limiting circuit (R_{CL}) and set the current limit at a value of about 600 mV/0.5 Ω = 1.2 A.

The LH0021 has a full-power bandwidth (FPBW) of 15 kHz (when driving a 10-Ω load), so this circuit will be capable of supplying the 10 W of output power over the entire audio-frequency range. The distortion will be only about 0.2% for frequencies up to 2 kHz, and then will increase to about 1.0% at 7 kHz, and 1.6% at 10 kHz. Above 10 kHz the distortion increases very rapidly as the condition of slew-rate limiting is approached at a feequency of 15 kHz. Note, however, that the distortion harmonic components produced for fundamental frequencies above 7 kHz will fall outside the audio spectrum and thus will generally not be noticeable.

3.8.2 The OPA501

An example of a power operational amplifier with a very high output power capability is the OPA501 (Burr-Brown). This hybrid op amp comes in a TO-3 package and can deliver as much as 260 W continuous (26 V at 10 A) to a load. It can operate with supply voltages as high as ±40 V and has an output current capability of ±10 A. The small-signal bandwidth of this op amp is 1.0 MHz and the full-power bandwidth is 16 kHz when delivering 40 V peak-to-peak to an 8 Ω load.

3.9 POWER MOSFETS

A device that is increasingly competing with bipolar power transistors is the MOSFET power transistor. The MOSFET power transistors are either of the vertical double-diffused type (V-DMOS) or of the V-groove double-diffused (VMOS) construction. Power MOSFETs that can handle currents as high as 25 A at voltages up to 500 V are available. Drain-to-source "on" resistances as low as 0.018 Ω have been obtained. While not strictly speaking an IC, these devices generally consist of a very large number of parallel-connected source and gate cells on a common N-type substrate which serves as the drain region. The channel length is generally of the order of 1 μm, but as a result of the thousands of parallel-connected cells the net channel width can be up in the range of 1 meter.

The power MOSFETs offer a number of substantial advantages over bipolar power transistors. First of all, the power MOSFETs have a very high input impedance so that the input current requirements are minimal, even when the output current level is up in the range of tens of amperes. The MOSFETs are a majority carrier device so that there will be no minority carrier storage time. As a result, very fast switching of large currents are possible. Also related to the fact that the MOSFET is a majority carrier device, is the negative temperature coefficient of the drain current of typically about −0.5 %/°C. This negative temperature is the result of the decrease of the electron mobility in the conducting channel with increasing temperature. The decrease of the drain current with increasing temperature will result in thermal stability for the device and there will no formation of "hot spots" and the resulting second breakdown phenomenon, as is the case for bipolar transistor. This negative temperature coefficient will also make it easy to operate MOSFET power transistors in parallel to increase the net current handling capability. Any transistor mismatch that will tend to make one transistor carry more of the current will result in an increase in the temperature of that transistor. This temperature increase will result in a decrease of the drain current of that transistor which acts to make the currents through the various transistors more equal. Finally, the power MOSFETs have an approximately linear transfer characteristic. This can be an important feature since the power MOSFETs will generally be the output stage of an amplifier and be operated under large-signal conditions. As a result, the linear transfer characteristic will result in lower distortion.

While the power MOSFET is basically a discrete device, it can be combined with bipolar transistors and with CMOS devices on a single IC substrate. Such ICs have been made with these devices on a common p-type substrate and using the conventional junction isolation process with a P+ isolation diffusion. The power MOSFETs can be of the N-channel vertical DMOS type with an N-type drain region and an N+ buried layer, together with a deep N+ drain diffusion to minimize the drain series resistance. Lateral DMOS transistors can also be used in which case the N+ buried layer is not needed. The IC power MOSFET devices offer the convenience of the high output current capability of the power MOSFET together with all the necessary driving and signal processing circuitry on one chip.

A variety of power MOSFETs are now being made by a number of manufacturers, including General Electric, International Rectifier, Motorola, RCA, Siemens, and Siliconix. As an example of power MOSFET capabilities, the Motorola MTE100N06 has a continuous current rating of 100 A and a drain-to-source "on" resistance of only 0.018 Ω at a drain current of 50 A. The drain-to-source breakdown voltage rating is 60 V minimum. Another Motorola device, the MTP1N100 has a drain-to-source breakdown voltage of 1000 V minimum, combined with a continuous current rating of 1.0 A and a drain-to-source "on" resistance of 10 Ω maximum at 0.5 A.

Power MOSFETs that combine a very high voltage rating with a very high current rating and a very low "on" resistance are available and are basically integrated combinations of an N-channel power vertical double-diffused MOSFET and a PNP transistor. The P-type body region of the MOSFET is also the collector of the PNP transistor, and the lightly doped N-type drain region is the base of the transistor.

The P+ substrate is the emitter of the PNP transistor. The PNP transistor is off when the MOSFET is off, but when the MOSFET is turned on the drain current of the MOSFET results in a base current for the PNP transistor. The PNP transistor then turns on with a heavy emission of holes from the P+ substrate region into the N-type base/drain region. The high concentration of holes injected into the N-type base/drain region results in the drawing in of an approximately equal number of electrons to maintain overall charge neutrality. The net increase in the electron and hole population in this region can result in a very substantial increase in the conductivity of this region. This effect is known as *conductivity modulation*. As a result of this conductivity modulation effect, a very lightly doped drain region can be used to obtain a very high breakdown voltage rating for the device and at the same time a very low value for the drain-to-source "on" resistance and a correspondingly high current rating can be obtained. With this type of conductivity, modulated MOSFET voltage ratings as high as 500 V together with current ratings of 25 A are available.

PROBLEMS

3.1. (*Class B audio power amplifier*) Given: A class B audio power amplifier has a positive supply voltage of $+V_S = +15$ V and a negative supply voltage of $-V_S = -15$ V. This amplifier has a closed-loop gain of 50 and is to deliver 10 W of power into an 8.0-Ω load.

(a) Find the peak output voltage swing, $V_{O(\text{peak})}$. (*Ans.*: ±12.65 V)

(b) Find the peak output current swing, $I_{O(\text{peak})}$. (*Ans.*: ±1.58 A)

(c) Find the input signal required (rms). [*Ans.*: 179 mV (rms)]

(d) Find the total power from power supply. (*Ans.*: 15.1 W)

(e) Find the power dissipated in the amplifier. (*Ans.*: 5.1 W)

(f) Find the power conversion efficiency. (*Ans.*: 66.2%)

(g) Find the power output level at which the amplifier power dissipation will be a maximum, and the maximum amplifier power dissipation. (*Ans.*: 5.70 W, 5.70 W)

(h) If the ambient temperature T_a is 25°C and the maximum allowable device temperature $T_{J(\text{MAX})}$ is 125°C, find the maximum allowable value for the case-to-ambient thermal resistance Θ_{CA} given that the junction-to-case thermal resistance Θ_{JC} is 10°C/W. (*Ans.*: 7.54°C/W)

Power Amplifiers: *Thermal Shutdown Circuits*

3.2. Refer to Figure P3.2. Given: $V_{BE} = 0.70$ V, $V_Z = 6.0$ V, $T_o = 25$ C, $TCV_{BE} = -2.1$ mV/C, $TC_{V_Z} = +3.0$ mV/°C, assume that the base-to-emitter voltage drop of all transistors at 25°C will be 700 mV when biased into full conduction, and that thermal shutdown will occur when Q_8 is biased into full conduction.

(a) Show that for thermal shutdown to occur at temperature T_{SD} the required resistance ratio will be given by $(R_6/R_5) + 2 = V_Z(T_{SD})/V_{BE}(T_{SD})$, where $V_Z(\text{T}_{SD})$ and $V_{BE}(T_{SD})$, are the values of V_Z and V_{BE} at the shutdown temperature T_{SD}, respectively.

(b) Find the resistance ratio for thermal shutdown at $T_{SD} = 175$°C. (*Ans.*: 14.75)

(c) Find R_4, R_5, and R_6 for $I_4 = I_5 = 0.5$ mA (at 25°C). (*Ans.*: 9.2 kΩ, 1.4 kΩ, 20.7 kΩ)

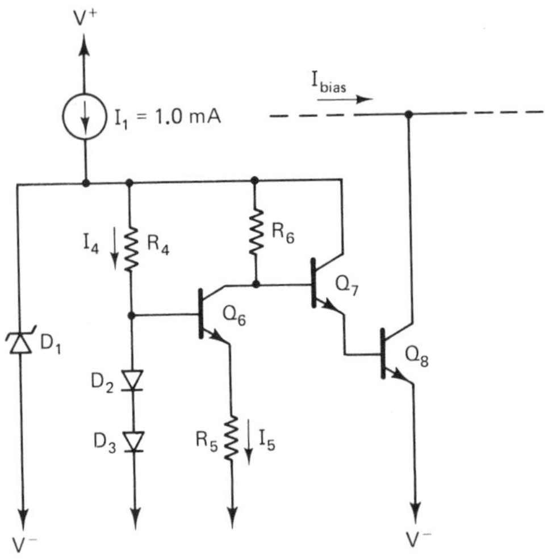

Figure P3.2

3.3. Refer to Figure P3.3. Given: $V_{\text{REF}} = 1.220$ V, $V_{BE} = 700$ mV at 1.0 mA and 25°C, $\beta = 100$ $TC_{V_{BE}} = -2.0$ mV/°C for all transistors over the range 25 to 175°C.

(a) Find the temperature at which complete shutdown (i.e., I_{bias} is reduced to zero). (*Ans.*: 123.7°C)

(b) Find the temperature at which I_{bias} has been reduced by one-half to 50 μA. (*Ans.*: 115°C)

(c) Find the temperature at the threshold of shutdown for which I_{bias} has undergone a 10% reduction to 90 μA. (*Ans.*: 95°C)

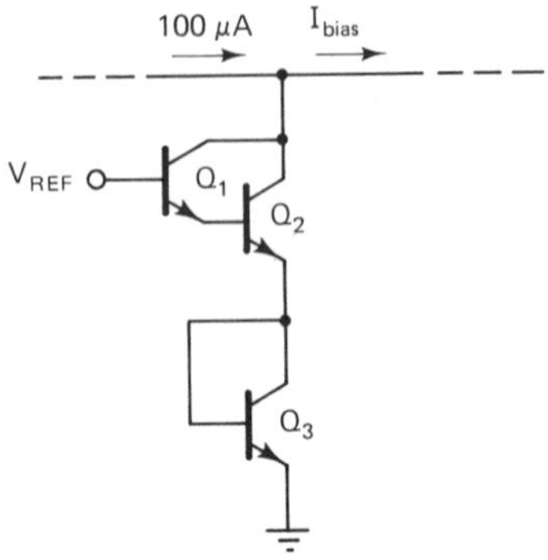

Figure P3.3

***3.4.** (*Power-amplifier distortion analysis*) Program a computer to generate the following curves: (1) $f_1(x) = \sin x$; (2) $f_2(x) = \sin x$ for $0 < x < x_1$, $f_2(x) = \sin x_1$ for $x_1 < x < \pi - x_1$, and $f_2(x) = \sin x$ for $\pi - x_1 < x < \pi$; and (3) $f_3(x) = \sin x - \alpha \sin 3x$ where $\alpha = 1 - \sin x_1$.

(a) From the computer-generated curves of $f_2(x)$ and $f_3(x)$, compare the clipped sine-wave function as given by $f_2(x)$ to the approximation given by $f_3(x)$. Have the computer plot the difference curve given by $f_2(x) - f_3(x)$. Do this for the following values of $\sin x_1$: 0.95, 0.90, 0.80, 0.70, and 0.50.

(b) Determine if other choices for the constant α will make $f_3(x)$ a better approximation to the $f_2(x)$ clipped sine-wave function. Find the value of α that will result in the smallest difference between the two functions.

(c) Have the computer plot the mean-squared difference between the $f_2(x)$ and the $f_3(x)$ functions over the range of 0 to π radians. Find the value of α that results in the smallest mean-squared difference.

(d) From the value obtained in part (c) obtain the approximate total harmonic distortion that results from the various clipping levels given in part (a).

REFERENCES

COWLES, L. G., *Sourcebook of Modern Transistor Circuits,* Chap. 8, Prentice-Hall, 1976.

EVANS, A. D., *Designing with Field-Effect Transistors,* McGraw-Hill, 1981.

GREBENE, A. B., *Analog Integrated Circuit Design,* Van Nostrand Reinhold, 1972.

KRAUSS, H. L., C. W. BOSTIAN, and F. H. RAAB, *Solid State Radio Engineering,* Wiley, 1980.

LENK, J. D., *Handbook of Integrated Circuits,* Reston, 1978.

OXNER, E. S., *Power FETs and Their Applications,* Chap. 7, Prentice-Hall, 1982.

RISTENBATT, M. P., *Semiconductor Circuits,* Chap. 7, Prentice-Hall, 1975.

Video Amplifiers

4

For operational amplifiers the emphasis is on a high open-loop voltage gain, typically of the order of 100,000 (100 dB) to 1,000,000 (120 dB) at low frequencies. Operational amplifiers are almost always operated in a closed-loop configuration and the high open-loop gain values are needed in order to obtain a high loop gain. The high loop gain is desirable in order to minimize the gain error, to produce a large input impedance, and to obtain a very small output impedance.

In order to obtain the high voltage gain, sacrifices are made in the frequency response. Indeed, in order to stabilize the amplifier against an oscillatory response, the open-loop frequency response is usually made to start rolling off at a very low frequency, often at only about 10 Hz. The resulting unity-gain frequencies are generally in the range 1 to 3 MHz, with some operational amplifiers extending up to about 10 MHz.

Video, or wideband amplifiers are designed to give a relatively flat gain versus frequency response characteristics over the frequency range that is generally required to transmit video information. This frequency range is from low frequencies, generally down in the range of about 20 Hz, up to several megahertz. For television applications bandwidths generally in the range 4 to 6 MHz are required. For some other applications bandwidths as high as 50 MHz may be needed.

In contrast with this, the bandwidths required for audio amplifiers extend only over the frequency range corresponding to that which the human ear is sensitive to, from about 50 Hz to 15 kHz. For many applications, such as telephony or AM radio, a considerably narrower bandwidth is used, typically from 100 Hz to 5 kHz. In Figure 4.1 the frequency response characteristics of video and audio amplifiers are compared.

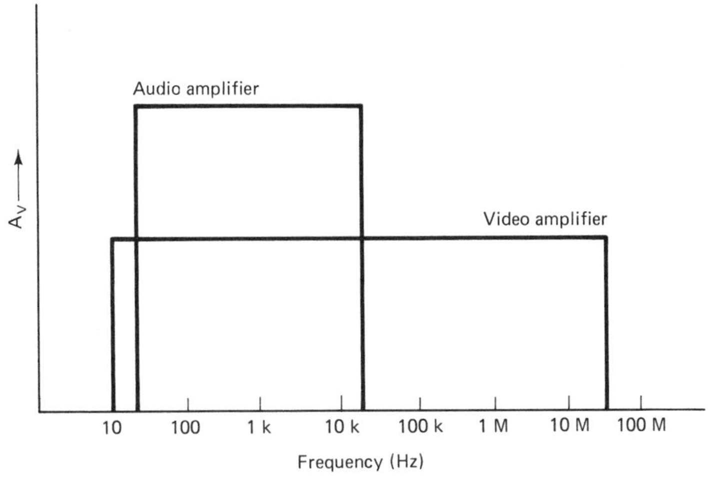

Figure 4.1 Comparison of audio and video amplifier bandwidths.

The principal technique that is used to obtain the large bandwidths that are required for video amplifiers is the trading off of gain for increased bandwidth. This trade-off is accomplished by use of reduced load resistance for the various gain stages of the amplifier and by the use of negative feedback. In many, if not most video amplifiers, the techniques of reduced load resistance and negative feedback are both employed at the same time.

4.1 TRANSISTOR FREQUENCY RESPONSE

Before we look at some representative examples of IC video amplifiers, we will first engage in a brief review of the frequency response characteristics of a single common-emitter transistor stage. The frequency response of a transistor is controlled by the interelectrode or junction capacitances, in conjunction with the various resistances in the circuit. The two transistor capacitances that are involved here are $C_{b'e}$, the emitter–base junction capacitance, and $C_{cb'}$, the collector–base capacitance. Also of interest and importance is the base spreading resistance, $r_{bb'}$, which is due to the bulk series resistance of the base region. In the discussion to follow we will analyze the frequency response of the transistor common-emitter stage to see what factors are of importance in the design of a video amplifier.

In Figure 4.2 a diagram of a basic common-emitter amplifier stage is shown, with the d-c biasing details being omitted for purposes of clarity. The transistor junction capacitances and the base spreading resistance, which are actually internal to the transistor, are shown as external elements for purposes of analysis. Also shown in this circuit are the source resistance R_S, the load resistance R_L, and the load capacitance C_L.

In Figure 4.3 a small-signal a-c equivalent circuit for the common-emitter stage of Figure 4.2 is shown. The signal source v_s and the series resistance of

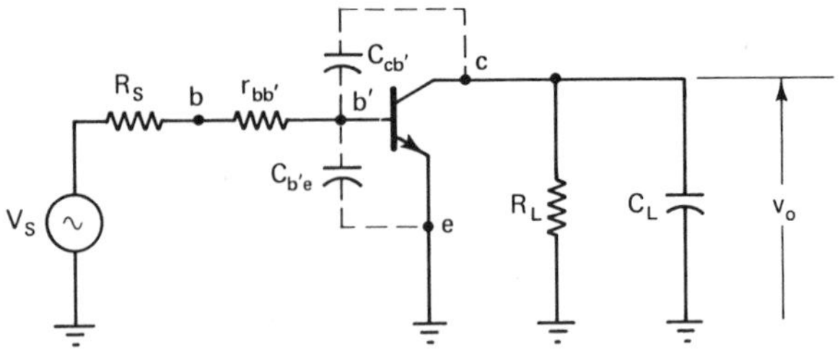

Figure 4.2 Common-emitter amplifier stage.

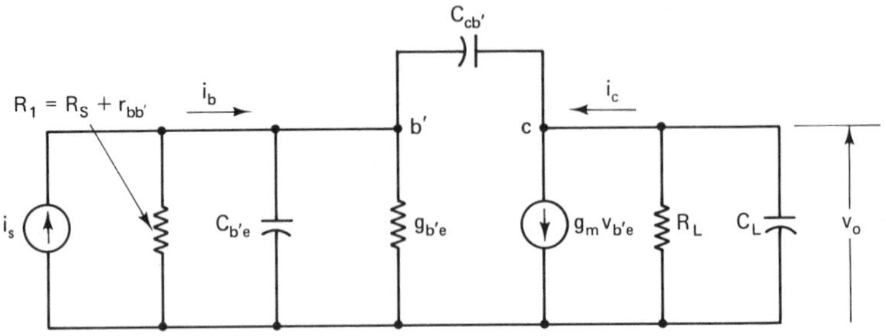

Figure 4.3 A-c small-signal equivalent circuit.

$R_S + r_{bb'}$ has been transformed into the equivalent current source/parallel resistance combination for greater ease in analysis. The parallel resistance is represented as a conductance G_1, with $G_1 = 1/(R_S + r_{bb'})$.

For the analysis to follow, the node voltage equations will be written for the two nodes of interest, b' and c, by taking the algebraic sum of the currents going into and out of these two nodes.

If we now equate the current going out of node b' to that coming into this node, we obtain

$$v_{b'}[G_1 + g_{b'e} + j\omega(C_{b'e} + C_{cb'})] = i_s + j\omega C_{cb'} v_c \tag{4.1}$$

and for node c we will similarly obtain

$$v_c[G_L + j\omega(C_{cb'} + C_L)] + g_m v_{b'} = j\omega C_{cb'} v_b \tag{4.2}$$

Solving the node c equation for v_c gives

$$v_c = \frac{-(g_m - j\omega C_{cb'})v_{b'}}{G_L + j\omega(C_{cb'} + C_L)} \tag{4.3}$$

Substitution of this expression back into the b'-node equation and rearranging yields

$$v_{b'}\left[G_1 + g_{b'e} + j\omega(C_{b'e} + C_{cb'}) + \frac{(j\omega C_{cb'})(g_m - j\omega C_{cb'})}{G_L + j\omega(C_{cb'} + C_L)}\right] = i_s \tag{4.4}$$

In these equations $g_{b'e}$ is the dynamic input conductance of the transistor looking into the base as given by

$$g_{b'e} = \frac{1}{r_{b'e}} = \frac{dI_B}{dV_{BE}} = \frac{I_B}{nV_T}$$

The constant n is a dimensionless factor between 1.0 and 2.0, typically about 1.5.

If we now solve the b'-node equation for $v_{b'}$, we obtain

$$v_{b'} = \frac{i_s}{G_1 + g_{b'e} + j\omega(C_{b'e} + C_{cb'}) + \dfrac{(j\omega C_{cb'})(g_m - j\omega C_{cb'})}{G_L + j\omega(C_{cb'} + C_L)}} \tag{4.5}$$

Going back to the c-node equation with this result allows us now to solve for v_c as

$$v_c = \frac{-(g_m - j\omega C_{cb'})}{G_L + j\omega(C_{cb'} + C_L)} \frac{i_s}{G_1 + g_{b'e} + j\omega(C_{b'e} + C_{cb'}) + \dfrac{(j\omega C_{cb'})(g_m - j\omega C_{cb'})}{G_L + j\omega(C_{cb'} + C_L)}} \tag{4.6}$$

Since $i_s = v_s/(R_s + r_{bb'}) = v_s G_1$, we can now obtain the voltage gain as

$$A_V = \frac{v_c}{v_s} = \frac{-(g_m - j\omega C_{cb'})G_1}{[G_L + j\omega(C_{cb'} + C_L)]\left[G_1 + g_{b'e} + j\omega(C_{b'e} + C_{cb'} + \dfrac{(j\omega C_{cb'})(g_m - j\omega C_{cb'})}{G_L + j\omega(C_{cb'} + C_L)}\right]} \tag{4.7}$$

This is a rather complicated expression for the frequency dependence of the voltage gain, and we will now seek to simplify it by using the following suitable approximations:

1. In the frequency range of interest it will virtually always be true that $g_m \gg \omega C_{cb'}$, so that we can replace $g_m - j\omega C_{cb'}$ by just g_m alone.
2. The input conductance $g_{b'e}$ will usually be sufficiently small compared to $G_l = 1/(R_S + r_{bb'})$ such that we can replace the sum of $G_1 + g_{b'e}$ by just G_1 alone.
3. In the frequency range of interest we will usually have that $G_L \gg \omega(C_{cb'} + C_L)$ and $g_m \gg \omega C_{cb'}$ such that the expression

$$\frac{g_m - j\omega C_{cb'}}{G_L + j\omega(C_{cb'} + C_L)} \tag{4.8}$$

can be replaced by simply $g_m/G_L = g_m R_L$.

Using these approximations, we can now write the expression for A_V as

$$A_V \simeq \frac{-g_m G_1}{[G_L + j\omega(C_{cb'} + C_L)][G_1 + j\omega(C_{b'e} + C_{cb'} + g_m R_L C_{cb'})]} \tag{4.9}$$

We will now define two breakpoint radian frequencies as

$$\omega_1 = \frac{G_1}{C_{b'e} + C_{cb'}(1 + g_m R_L)} = \frac{1}{(R_S + r_{bb'})[C_{b'e} + C_{cb'}(1 + g_m R_L)]} = \frac{1}{(R_S + r_{bb'})C_i} \quad (4.10)$$

$$\omega_2 = \frac{G_L}{C_{cb'} + C_L} = \frac{1}{R_L(C_{cb'} + C_L)}$$

Note that in the net input capacitance C_i, the collector–base capacitance C_{cb} is multiplied by $1 + g_m R_L = 1 - A_v$. This is known as the Miller effect.

The foregoing equation for the voltage gain can now be rewritten in terms of these two breakpoint frequencies as

$$A_V \simeq \frac{-g_m/G_L}{[1 + j(\omega/\omega_1)][1 + j(\omega/\omega_2)]} = \frac{-g_m R_L}{[1 + j(f/f_1)][1 + j(f/f_2)]} \quad (4.11)$$

where $f_1 = \omega_1/2\pi$ and $f_2 = \omega_2/2\pi$.

We see that the frequency response will be characterized by two breakpoint frequencies, f_1 and f_2, of which f_1 will generally be the smaller and thereby be the principal factor in determining the bandwidth of the amplifier stage. For an IC transistor there will be an additional capacitance C_{CS} between collector and substrate (a-c ground). This can be taken into account by replacing C_L by $C_L + C_{CS}$.

4.2 TRANSISTOR UNITY-GAIN FREQUENCY

The unity-gain frequency of a transistor is defined as the frequency at which the common-emitter short-circuit current gain has dropped to unity and is denoted by the symbol f_T. The current gain is defined as $A_i = i_o/i_{\text{in}} = i_c/i_b$ and the term "short-circuit" in the definition above indicates that there is an a-c short-circuit from collector to ground.

If we now consider the circuit of Figure 4.3 for the case of $R_L = 0$ we see that the a-c output or collector current will be given simply by $i_o = i_c = g_m v_{b'}$. The voltage from point b' to ground will be related to the input or base current by

$$v_{b'} = \frac{i_b}{g_{b'e} + j\omega(C_{b'e} + C_{cb'})} \quad (4.12)$$

As a result, the short-circuit current gain can be written as

$$A_{i\,(\text{s-c})} = \frac{i_o}{i_b} = \frac{g_m}{g_{b'e} + j\omega(C_{b'e} + C_{cb'})} = \frac{g_m/g_{b'e}}{1 + j\omega[(C_{b'e} + C_{cb'})/g_{b'e}]}$$

Since $g_m = dI_C/dV_{BE}$ and $g_{b'e} = dI_B/dV_{BE}$, the ratio of g_m to $g_{b'e}$ will be given by $g_m/g_{b'e} = dI_C/dI_B = \beta(\text{a-c}) = h_{fe}$ in terms of the hybrid parameters. We can therefore rewrite the current-gain expression as

$$A_{i\,(\text{s-c})} = \frac{\beta}{1 + j\omega[(C_{b'e} + C_{cb'})/(g_m/\beta)]} \tag{4.13}$$

Using the definition of the unity-gain frequency, we have that at $\omega = \omega_T$, $A_{i\,(\text{s-c})} = 1$. Since $\beta \gg 1$, for this condition we will have

$$\frac{\beta}{\dfrac{\omega_T(C_{b'e} + C_{cb'})}{g_m/\beta}} = 1$$

and thus

$$\boxed{\omega_T = \frac{g_m}{C_{b'e} + C_{cb'}} = \frac{I_C/V_T}{C_{b'e} + C_{cb'}}} \tag{4.14}$$

Note that the unity-gain frequency is independent of β and as a result of the β independence of ω_T, the unit-to-unit variation in ω_T among transistors of the same type designation will be relatively small, generally within a $\pm$ 10% range. As a result we can understand why ω_T is a very often used parameter for the characterization of transistors.

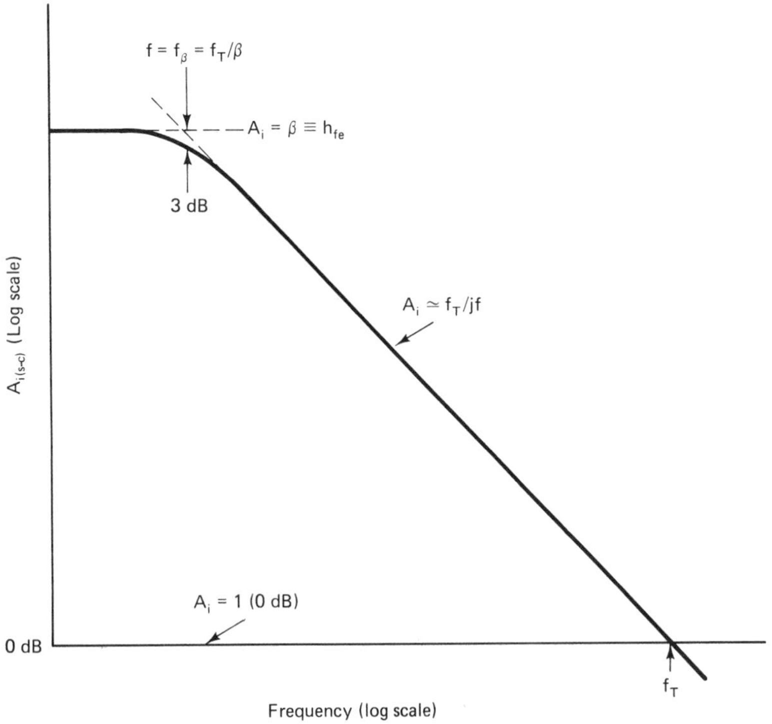

Figure 4.4 Common-emitter short-circuit current gain versus frequency.

In terms of ω_T the short-circuit current gain of the transistor can be written as

$$A_{i\,(\text{s-c})} = \frac{\beta}{1 + j(\beta\omega/\omega_T)} = \frac{\beta}{1 + j(\beta f/f_T)} = \frac{\beta}{1 + j(f/f_\beta)} \tag{4.15}$$

where $f_\beta = f_T/\beta$ is the half-power (or -3-dB) frequency of the short-circuit current gain. For frequencies that are more than one-half a decade above f_β (i.e., $f \gtrsim 3f_\beta$) we can express the current gain approximately as

$$A_{i\,(\text{s-c})} \simeq \frac{\beta}{j(f/f_\beta)} = \frac{\beta f_\beta}{jf} = \frac{f_T}{jf} \tag{4.16}$$

as in Figure 4.4. This relationship is often used for the experimental determination of f_T without the need for going all of the way up in measurement frequency to f_T. For example, if $A_{i\,(\text{s-c})} = 100$ at 10 kHz, and at 50 MHz the current gain is $A_{i\,(\text{s-dc})} = 10$, we can conclude that 50 MHz is much greater than f_β since the current gain at 50 MHz is much less than that at 10 kHz. We can therefore say that $f_T/50$ MHz $= 10$, so that $f_T = 500$ MHz. Furthermore, from the current-gain value at 10 kHz we can say that $\beta = 100$, so that f_β will be given by $f_\beta = f_T/\beta = 500$ MHz/100 $= 5$ MHz.

4.3 MULTISTAGE AMPLIFIER BANDWIDTH AND RISE TIME

A multistage amplifier can usually be modelled as a series of cascaded, but non-interacting simple R-C low-pass networks. Each low-pass network will be characterized by an R-C time constant and a breakpoint frequency (or "pole") that is related to the corresponding time constant by $f_n = 1/(2\,\pi\tau_n)$. If f_1 represents the lowest breakpoint frequency and it is at least about one decade below the next highest breakpoint frequency f_2 (i.e. $f_1 < f_2/10$), then the 3 dB bandwidth of the system will be approximately equal to (but always less than) the lowest breakpoint frequency f_1.

If the breakpoint frequencies are not well separated, then the situation is much more complicated and there is no exact simple relationship between the 3-dB bandwidth and the breakpoint frequencies. There is, however, a relatively simple approximate relationship that can be used as given by

$$\frac{1}{BW^2} \simeq \frac{1}{f_1^2} + \frac{1}{f_2^2} + \frac{1}{f_3^2} + \cdot\cdot\cdot\cdot \tag{4.17}$$

where BW is the 3-dB bandwidth of the system and f_1, etc. represent the various breakpoint frequencies in the system. Note that if the first breakpoint frequency f_1 is much smaller than the other breakpoint frequencies, the bandwidth will be approximately equal to f_1. In the special case of coincident breakpoint frequencies, there is an exact expression that can be used for the bandwidth. For a system with n coincident breakpoint frequencies there is an exact expression that can be used for the bandwidth. For a system with n coincident breakpoint frequencies the 3-dB bandwidth will be given by

$$BW = f_1\sqrt{2^{1/n} - 1} \tag{4.18}$$

For the case of two coincident breakpoint frequencies at f_1 this gives $BW = 0.6436\ f_1$, for n=3 the result is $BW = 0.5098\ f_1$, and for n=4 the bandwidth is down to $BW = 0.4350\ f_1$, so we see that there will be a considerable bandwidth shrinkage as the number of stages increases.

The 10% to 90% rise time, t_{rise}, of a system that is characterized by a single-time constant, τ, is given by $t_{\text{rise}} = 2.2\ \tau$, and in terms of the 3-dB bandwidth BW will be given by $t_{\text{rise}} = 0.35/BW$. For a system that is characterized by several time constants (i.e. a multiple pole system), the foregoing relationship between rise time and bandwidth will not be exactly true, though in almost all cases it can serve as a very good approximation. Another good approximate relationship that can be used for a multiple pole system is that the rise time will be approximately 2.2 times the largest time constant, if the largest time constant is at least twice the next largest time constant.

4.4 DESIGN CONSIDERATIONS FOR VIDEO AMPLIFIERS

For a video or wide-band amplifier it is necessary that the two characteristic or breakpoint frequencies, f_1 and f_2, be sufficiently large, since in no case can the bandwidth be any greater than either of these two frequencies. Since

$$\omega_1 = \frac{1}{(R_s + r_{bb'})(C_{b'e} + C_{cb'} + C_{cb'}g_m R_L)} \quad \text{and} \quad \omega_2 = \frac{1}{R_L(C_{cb'} + C_L)} \tag{4.19}$$

we see that in order to achieve a wide bandwidth we should do the following:

1. Trade-off gain for increased bandwidth by decreasing R_L.
2. Make the source resistance R_S as small as possible consistent with other circuit requirements. In some cases the use of an emitter-follower in the input circuit for impedance transformation may be useful.
3. Make the net load capacitance as small as possible consistent with the other circuit requirements. In this case again the use of an emitter follower on the output side of the circuit for impedance transformation may be very useful.
4. Choose a transistor with a small value of $C_{cb'}$ (i.e., a "high-frequency" transistor).
5. Choose a transistor with a small value for the base spreading resistance, $r_{bb'}$. Sometimes, transistors are characterized in terms of the $r_{bb'}C_{cb'}$ time constant, in which case a small value of this constant is the desirable feature.
6. Choose a transistor with a high unity-gain frequency f_T. Since $\omega_T = g_m/(C_{b'e} = C_{cb'})$, this will mean that $C_{b'e}$ will be small.
7. Use one or more negative feedback loops, if necessary to trade off reduced gain for increased bandwidth. The negative feedback can be done in terms of a local feedback loop around or within each gain stage, and an overall feedback loop around the entire amplifier from the output to the input.

For video amplifiers the use of local feedback is often a better choice than an overall feedback loop because of the large phase shifts that will be encountered at high frequencies with multistage amplifiers. There will consequently be stability problems with feedback loops that encompass several gain stages. In many cases both types of feedback loops are used simultaneously.

4.5 VIDEO-AMPLIFIER COMMON-EMITTER-STAGE EXAMPLE

For consideration of a simple example of a single common-emitter amplifier stage frequency response, we will use the circuit of Figure 4.2. The biasing details have been omitted for clarity. For this example we will use the following representative circuit and device parameters:

$$\begin{aligned} r_{bb'} &= 60\ \Omega & R_S &= 40\ \Omega \\ C_{cb'} &= 1.5\ \text{pF} & C_L &= 1.0\ \text{pF} \\ f_T &= 1.6\ \text{GHz at a quiescent current of 2.5 mA} \end{aligned} \tag{4.20}$$

Since $f_T = 1.6$ GHz, we will have for ω_T the value of $\omega_T = 1 \times 10^{10}\ \text{s}^{-1}$. At the quiescent current level of 2.5 mA, g_m will be given by $g_m = I_C/V_T = 2.5\ \text{mA}/25\ \text{mV} = 0.1$ S. We can now solve for $C_{b'e}$ as

$$C_{b'e} + C_{cb'} = \frac{g_m}{\omega_T} = \frac{0.1\ \text{S}}{10^{10}\ \text{s}^{-1}} = 1 \times 10^{-11}\ \text{F} = 10\ \text{pF} \tag{4.21}$$

We can now write the equations for f_1, f_2, and the midfrequency gain as

$$\begin{aligned} f_1 &= \frac{1}{(2\ \pi)(R_S + r_{bb'})(C_{b'e} + C_{cb'} + g_m R_L C_{cb'})} \\ &= \frac{1}{(2\ \pi)(100\ \Omega)(10\ \text{pF} + 0.1\ \text{S} \times R_L \times 1.5\ \text{pF})} \end{aligned} \tag{4.22}$$

$$f_2 = \frac{1}{(2\ \pi)R_L(C_{cb'} + C_L)} = \frac{1}{(2\ \pi)R_L(2.5\ \text{pF})} \tag{4.23}$$

and

$$A_{V(\text{MID})} = -g_m R_L = (0.1\ \text{S})R_L \tag{4.24}$$

For the values of load resistance, R_L, listed below we obtain the corresponding values of f_1, f_2, bandwidth, $A_{V(\text{MID})}$, and gain–bandwidth product.

R_L (Ω)	f_1 (MHz)	f_2 (MHz)	BW (MHz)	$A_{V(\text{MID})}$	$A_{V(\text{MID})} \times BW$ (MHz)
30	110	2,122	110	3	330
100	64	637	64	10	640
300	29	212	29	30	868
1,000	10	64	10	100	1,000
3,000	3.5	21	3.5	300	1,038
10,000	1.05	6.4	1.04	1,000	1,040

We see from this table that the f_1 breakpoint frequency is much lower than the f_2 breakpoint frequency for all of the load resistance values listed. Therefore, f_1 is the principal factor in determining the 3-dB bandwidth of the amplifier stage.

4.6 DIFFERENTIAL VIDEO AMPLIFIER ANALYSIS: TYPE 733

The first type of video IC that we will look at is the "733" type (μA733, LM733, etc.) of video amplifier. This video amplifier has a differential input and output, so it can accept both single-ended and balanced input signals, and either single-ended or balanced outputs can be obtained.

The circuit diagram for this device is shown in Figure 4.5. The input stage is a differential amplifier comprised of Q_1 and Q_2 with current sink biasing provided

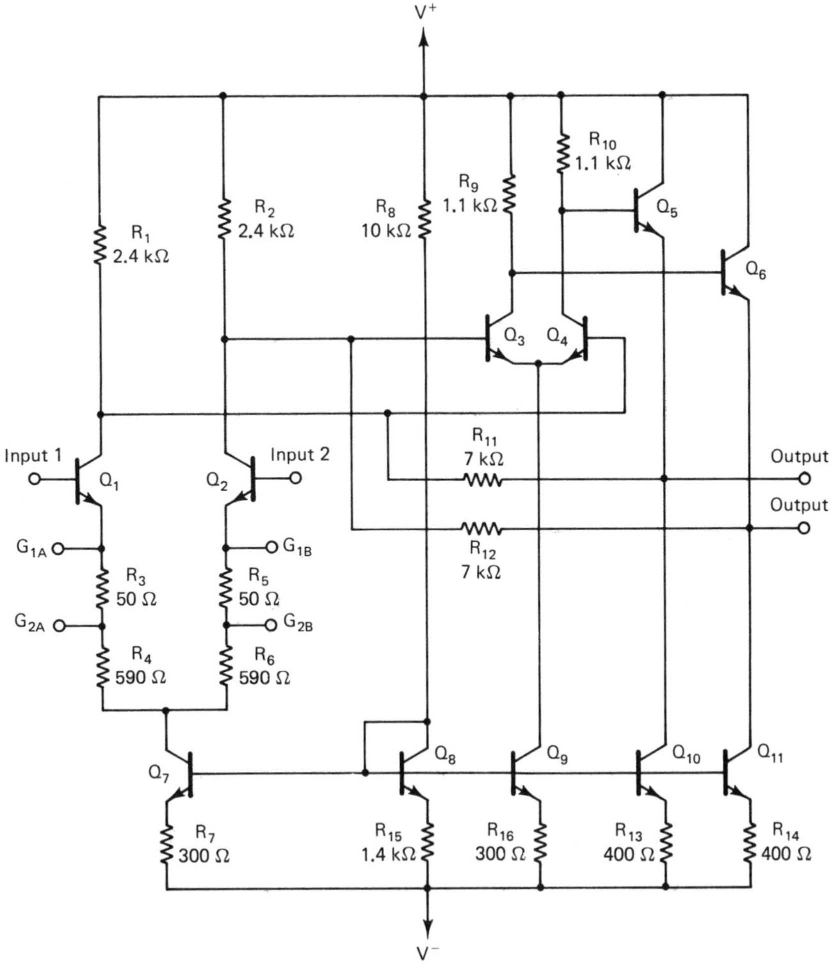

Figure 4.5 Type 733 video amplifier.

by Q_7, and with R_1 and R_2 (2.4 kΩ each) being used as the load resistors. Resistors R_3 through R_6 are used to provide local negative feedback (emitter degeneration) within the first gain stage.

A balanced output is taken from the first gain stage and drives the second gain stage, which is another differential amplifier consisting of Q_3 and Q_4 with current sink biasing provided by Q_9. Resistors R_9 and R_{10} (1.1 kΩ each) are the load resistors for the second gain stage.

The second gain stage provides a balanced output to drive a pair of NPN emitter-follower output stage transistors, Q_5 and Q_6. These emitter-follower output transistors are biased by current sink transistors Q_{10} and Q_{11}.

Resistors R_{11} and R_{12} provide negative feedback from the two output terminals back to the input terminals of the second stage. There are therefore two negative feedback loops, one within the first stage (using R_3 through R_6), and the other around the second stage using R_{11} and R_{12}.

The overall biasing for this IC is provided by the diode-connected transistor Q_8 in conjunction with resistors R_8 and R_{15}. This biasing circuit drives the current sink transistors, Q_7, Q_9, Q_{10}, and Q_{11}, and provides current sink biasing for all of the stages in the amplifier.

4.6.1 Biasing Analysis

For the biasing analysis of this device we will consider the circuit shown in Figure 4.6 showing the biasing network, and we will assume representative supply voltages of ±6.0 V. We will have for I_8 a d-c current given by $I_8 = (12 - 0.6)\text{V}/(10 + 1.4)$ kΩ = 11.4 V/11.4 kΩ = 1.0 mA. The voltage drop across R_{15} will therefore be 1.4 V. Since the base-to-emitter voltage drops of all of the transistors involved in the biasing network will be approximately equal (to within ±0.05 V), the voltage drops across all of the emitter resistors (R_{13}, R_{14}, R_{15}, R_{16}, and R_7) will be approximately

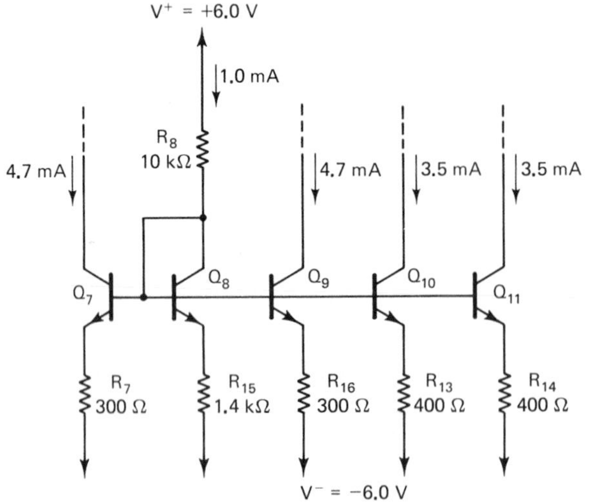

Figure 4.6 Biasing circuitry for the 733 video amplifier.

the same. Consequently, we will have that $I_7 = I_9 = 1.4\ \text{V}/300\ \Omega = 4.7$ mA, and $I_{13} = I_{14} = 1.4\ \text{V}/400\ \Omega = 3.5$ mA.

4.6.2 A-C Gain Analysis

We will perform the a-c gain analysis of this amplifier by splitting each stage down the axis of symmetry. Doing this gives the a-c circuit of Figure 4.7. The dynamic transfer conductance for each half of the first-stage differential amplifier (Q_1 and Q_2) will be given by

$$g_{f_1} = \frac{i_{c_1}}{v_{b_1}} = \frac{g_m}{1 + g_m R_E} = \frac{1}{(1/g_m) + R_E} = \frac{1}{(V_T/I_C) + R_E} \tag{4.25}$$

Note that when $R_E = 0$, this reduces to simply $g_{f_1} = g_m = I_C/V_T$. Since v_{b_1} is one-half of the total (base-to-base) input voltage V_{IN}, the a-c collector current produced by each half of the differential amplifier will be $i_{c_1} = g_{f_1} v_{b_1} = g_{f_1}(V_{IN}/2)$.

The "open-loop" voltage gain produced by each half of the second stage differential amplifier will be

$$A_{OL_2} = -g_{f_2} R_{L_2} = \frac{-I_C}{V_T}(1.1\ \text{k}\Omega) = \frac{(4.7\ \text{mA}/2)}{25\ \text{mV}} \times 1.1\ \text{k}\Omega = -103$$

The actual gain of the second stage will be slightly lower than this due to the finite input impedance presented by the emitter-follower output stage.

The voltage gain produced by each half of the emitter-follower output stage

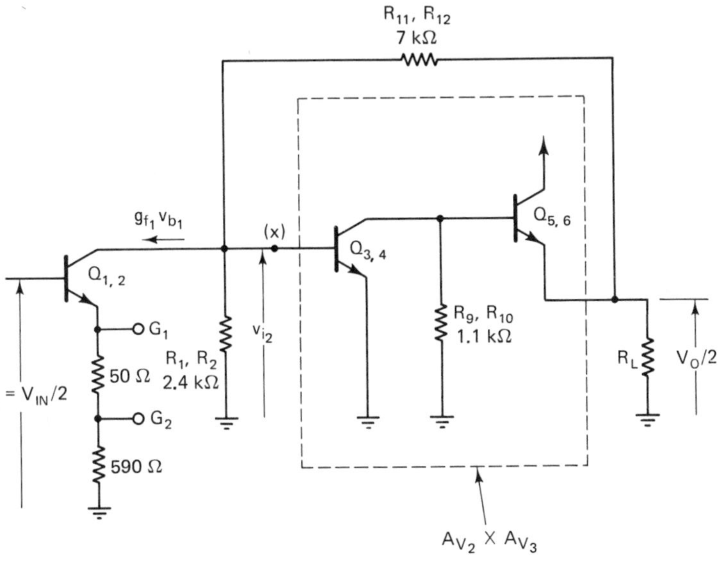

Figure 4.7 A-c circuit for the 733 video amplifier obtained by splitting amplifier down the axis of symmetry.

(Q_5 and Q_6) will be given by $A_{V_3} = R_L/[R_L + (V_T/I_C)]$, where I_C is the quiescent current of the emitter-follower transistors, 3.5 mA. We therefore will have that

$$A_{V_3} = \frac{R_L}{R_L + (25 \text{ mV}/3.5 \text{ mA})} = \frac{R_L}{R_L + 7.1\ \Omega} \tag{4.26}$$

From this we see that for any reasonable value of load resistance the voltage gain of the emitter-follower output stage will be close to unity. Therefore, the combined gain of the second and third stages, $A_{V_2} \times A_{V_3}$ will be approximately 100.

We will now write a node-voltage equation for node x in Figure 10.7 to obtain

$$-g_{f_1}\frac{V_{\text{IN}}}{2} + \frac{V_{\text{OUT}}/2}{7\text{ k}\Omega} - V_X\left(\frac{1}{7\text{ k}\Omega} + \frac{1}{2.4\text{ k}\Omega}\right) = 0 \tag{4.27}$$

Noting that $V_{\text{OUT}}/2 = A_{V_1}A_{V_2}V_X = -100V_X$, we have that $V_X = -(V_{\text{OUT}}/2)/100$, and thus the node equation can be rewritten as

$$-g_{f_1}\frac{V_{\text{IN}}}{2} + \frac{V_{\text{OUT}}/2}{7\text{ k}\Omega} + \frac{V_{\text{OUT}}/2}{100}\left(\frac{1}{7\text{ k}\Omega} + \frac{1}{2.4\text{ k}\Omega}\right) = 0 \tag{4.28}$$

Collecting terms this gives

$$V_{\text{OUT}}\left[\frac{1}{7\text{ k}\Omega} + \frac{1}{100}\left(\frac{1}{7\text{ k}\Omega} + \frac{1}{2.4\text{ k}\Omega}\right)\right] = g_{f_1}V_{\text{IN}} \tag{4.29}$$

and thus

$$A_V = \frac{V_{\text{OUT}}}{V_{\text{IN}}} = \frac{g_{f_1}}{\dfrac{1}{7\text{ k}\Omega} + \dfrac{1}{100}\left(\dfrac{1}{7\text{ k}\Omega} + \dfrac{1}{2.4\text{ k}\Omega}\right)} = \frac{g_{f_1}(7\text{ k}\Omega)}{1.04} \simeq g_{f_1}\,7\text{ k}\Omega$$

We see from this result that changes in the voltage gain of the second and third stages will have relatively little effect on the overall gain of the amplifier. Indeed, if the combined gain of the second and third stages were to go from a minimum of 100 all the way up to infinity, the net gain of the amplifier would change by only about 4%.

For g_{f_1} we have

$$g_{f_1} = \frac{1}{(V_T/I_C) + R_E} = \frac{1}{(25\text{ mV}/2.35\text{ mA}) + R_E} = \frac{1}{11\ \Omega + R_E} \tag{4.30}$$

so that the overall gain of the amplifier will be

$$A_V = g_{f_1}(7\text{ k}\Omega) = \frac{7\text{ k}\Omega}{11\ \Omega + R_E} \tag{4.31}$$

The value of R_E is determined by which, if any, of the gain pins are shorted together. If all of the gain select pins are left open, R_E will attain its maximum value of $590 + 50 = 640\ \Omega$. If G_{2A} and G_{2B} are connected together, R_E will be 50 Ω, and if pins G_{1A} and G_{1B} are shorted together, R_E will be zero. The fixed gain values corresponding to these three conditions will therefore be:

Gain 1 ($R_E = 0$): $A_V = 7\text{ k}\Omega/11\ \Omega = \underline{640}$

Gain 2 ($R_E = 50\ \Omega$): $A_V = 7\text{ k}\Omega/11 + 50\ \Omega = \underline{115}$

Gain 3 ($R_E = 640\ \Omega$): $A_V = 7\text{ k}\Omega/(11 + 640)\ \Omega = \underline{10.8}$

Values of gain that are intermediate between the maximum and minimum values given above can be obtained by connecting a fixed or variable resistor, R_{ADJ}, between the G_{1A} and G_{1B} gain select pins, for which case R_E will be given by $R_E = 640\ \Omega \parallel (R_{ADJ}/2)$. Note that $R_{ADJ}/2$ is used for R_E since when the amplifier is split down the axis of symmetry the gain adjust resustor will be cut in half.

The 3-dB bandwidth values (for a 50-Ω source resistance) that are obtained for the three gain-select options are listed below using values obtained from the specification sheet for this device.

Gain option	A_V (calc.)	A_V (spec.)	BW (MHz)	A_V BW (MHz)
Gain 1	640	400 (typ.)	40 (typ.)	16,000
Gain 2	115	100 (typ.)	90 (typ.)	9,000
Gain 3	10.8	10 (typ.)	120 (typ.)	1,200

From these values we do note that as the gain is decreased by using more feedback (i.e., increasing R_E) the bandwidth does increase. However, the increase in the bandwidth is by a far smaller factor than the decrease in the gain. This is further evidenced by the decrease in the gain–bandwidth product. Thus the decrease in the gain from a value of 400 (gain 1) to 100 (gain 2) produces an increase in the bandwidth from 40 MHz up to 90 MHz, or an increase by a factor of 2.25. The decrease in the gain from 100 (gain 2) to 10 (gain 1) results in a further increase in the bandwidth of from 90 to 120 MHz, a factor of only 1.3.

The basic reason that the decrease in the voltage gain that is produced by an increase in the negative feedback does not produce an increase in the bandwidth by the same factor that the voltage gain is decreased is the result of the multiplicity of breakpoint frequencies involved in the high-frequency region of interest (about 40 to 120 MHz). If we look at the graph of the amplifier phase shift as a function of frequency for the "733" as shown in Figure 4.8, we see that in the region 40 to 120 MHz phase shifts ranging from about 100 to 330° will be encountered. These large phase-shift values indicate that this frequency range extends from beyond the first breakpoint frequency at 40 MHz to beyond the fourth breakpoint frequency at 120 MHz. As a result, the gain versus frequency curve decreases quite rapidly in this frequency range, especially at the upper end of the range as shown in Figure 4.9. For example, if the slope is 60 dB/decade, corresponding to the effect of three breakpoint frequencies, then a sacrifice of 20 dB in gain (i.e., a 10:1 ratio) will produce an improvement in the bandwidth by only about 20 dB/(60 dB/decade) = $\frac{1}{3}$ decade, or a ratio of $(10)^{1/3} = 2.15$. We therefore see why a decrease in the gain does not lead to an increase in the bandwidth by the same factor as illustrated in Figure 4.9c.

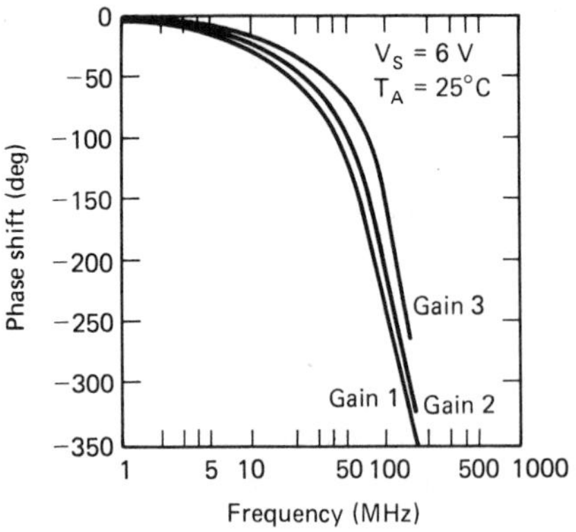

Figure 4.8 Phase shift versus frequency for the LM733 video amplifier (National Semiconductor).

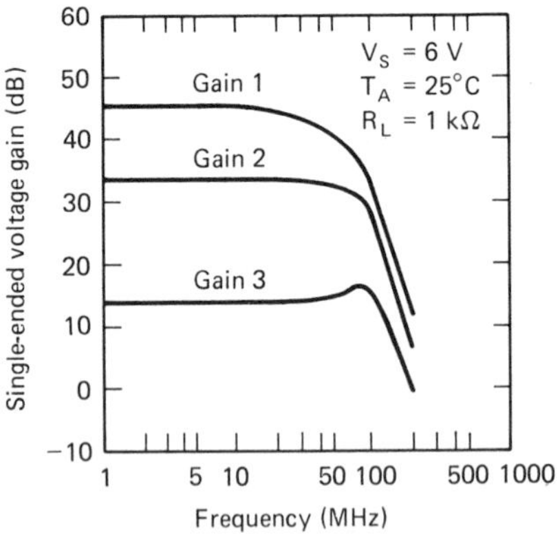

Figure 4.9 Voltage gain versus frequency for the LM733 (National Semiconductor).

The large phase shifts encountered at high frequencies will also lead to some gain peaking. This is shown by the voltage gain versus frequency curve for gain 3, where there is about 15% gain peaking at about 100 MHz. We note that at this frequency the phase shift will be approximately 180°, so this indeed corresponds to the condition in which what was negative feedback at lower frequencies has turned around to become positive feedback near 100 MHz.

If we look at the pulse response for the gain 3 condition we see that the gain peaking in the frequency domain is manifested in the time domain as overshoot in the pulse response. Indeed, not only is there about 10% overshoot, but there is also a slight amount of "ringing," or a heavily damped oscillatory response.

The voltage gain as a function of frequency characteristics of this devices are also of interest. The voltage gain for the gain 1 option ($R_E = 0$) decreases rapidly with temperature. The voltage gain for the gain 2 condition decreases at a much slower rate with increasing temperature, whereas the voltage gain for the gain 3 conditions hardly changes at all with temperature. This behavior is indeed consistent with that expected on the basis of the expression for the voltage gain as given by $A_V = g_{f_1}$ (7 kΩ) = (7 kΩ)/[$(V_T/I_C) + R_E$]. For the gain 1 condition $R_E = 0$, so that we should expect that the voltage gain will be inversely proportional to temperature since $A_V = (I_C/V_T)$(7 kΩ) for this case and $V_T = kT/q$. For the gain 3 condition, on the other hand, R_E = 640 Ω, so that A_V = (7 kΩ)/[(V_T/2.35 mA) + 640 Ω], so that the gain should indeed exhibit very little temperature dependence.

As a result of the two cascaded differential-amplifier configuration of this device and the balanced nature of the signal flow, we should expect to obtain a very good common-mode rejection ratio. This is indeed the case, and for gain 2 for which the voltage gain is 100 (typ.) or 40 dB, the common-mode rejection ratio (CMRR) will be 86 dB (typ.) for frequencies below 50 kHz. The 86-dB CMRR values correspond to a common-mode voltage gain of 40 dB − 86 dB = −46 dB, or only 0.005, compared to the difference-mode gain of +40 dB or 100. Looking at the graph of the CMRR versus frequency we see that the CMRR does decrease with frequency above about

50 kHz. Part of this decrease in the CMRR with frequency is due to the falloff of the difference-mode gain, but perhaps to a larger extent it is due to a greater capacitative feedthrough of the common-mode signal, and the decrease in the output impedance of the current sinks (Q_7 and Q_9) of the first and second differential-amplifier stages.

4.7 CASCODE–AMPLIFIER CONFIGURATION

The cascode configuration is an amplifier stage composed of a direct-coupled common-emitter/common-base combination as shown in Figure 4.10a. This configuration offers the possibility of very large bandwidths and is very often used for video and radio-frequency (RF) amplifiers.

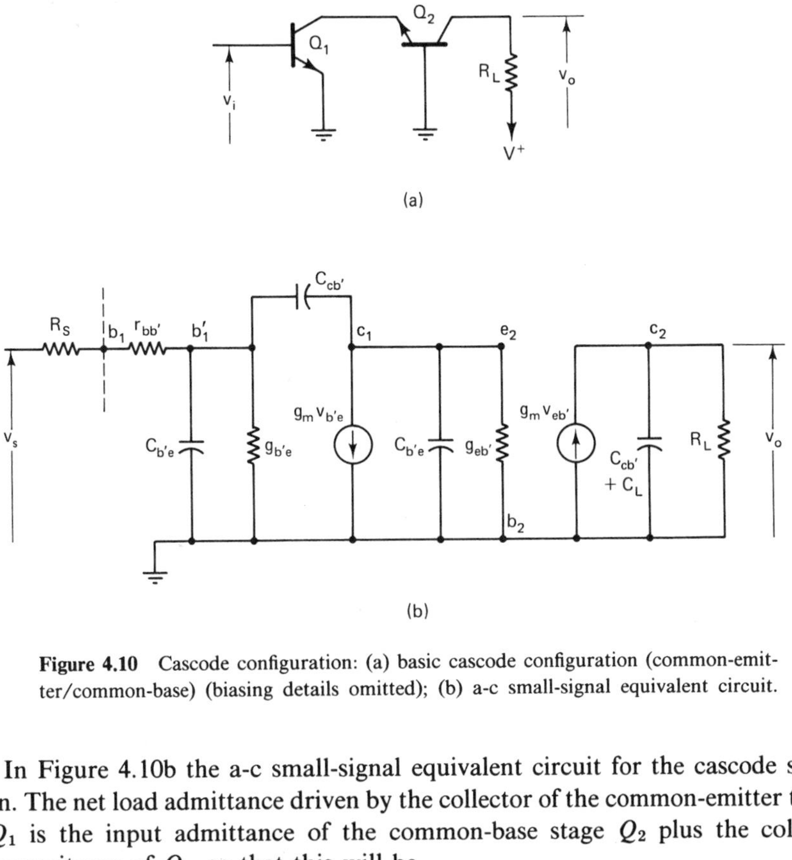

Figure 4.10 Cascode configuration: (a) basic cascode configuration (common-emitter/common-base) (biasing details omitted); (b) a-c small-signal equivalent circuit.

In Figure 4.10b the a-c small-signal equivalent circuit for the cascode stage is shown. The net load admittance driven by the collector of the common-emitter transistor Q_1 is the input admittance of the common-base stage Q_2 plus the collector–base capacitance of Q_1, so that this will be

$$Y_{L(CE)} = g_{eb'_2} + j\omega(C_{b'e} + C_{cb'}) = \frac{I_Q}{V_T} + j\omega(C_{b'e} + C_{cb'})$$

where I_Q is the quiescent current of Q_1 and Q_2. Since $I_Q/V_T = g_m$, this can be rewritten as

$$Y_{L(CE)} = g_m + j\omega(C_{b'e} + C_{cb'}) = g_m \left[1 + \frac{j\omega(C_{b'e} + C_{cb'})}{g_m}\right]$$

$$= g_m\left(1 + \frac{j\omega}{\omega_T}\right) = g_m\left(1 + \frac{jf}{f_T}\right)$$

Over the frequency range of interest we will have that $f \ll f_T$, so that $Y_{L(CE)} \simeq g_m$. The voltage gain of Q_1 will therefore be given by $A_{V1} = \dfrac{-g_m}{Y_{L(CE)}} \simeq \dfrac{-g_m}{g_m} = -1$

Since the voltage gain of Q_1 will be essentially unity, the equation for the first breakpoint (radian) frequency ω_1 will accordingly become

$$\omega_1 = \frac{G_1}{C_{b'e} + C_{cb'} + C_{cb'}g_m R_{L(CE)}} = \frac{G_1}{C_{b'e} + C_{cb'} + C_{cb'}(g_m/g_m)} \tag{4.32}$$

$$= \frac{1}{(R_S + r_{bb'})(C_{b'e} + 2C_{cb'})}$$

Since $C_{b'e}$ will usually be considerably larger than $C_{cb'}$, we can say that $C_{b'e} + 2C_{cb'} \simeq C_{b'e} + C_{cb'} = g_m/\omega_T$. This approximation will allow us the rewrite the expression for ω_1 in the form

$$\omega_1 \simeq \frac{1}{(R_S + r_{bb'})(C_{b'e} + C_{cb'})} = \frac{\omega_T}{g_m(R_S + r_{bb'})} \tag{4.33}$$

and thus

$$f_1 \simeq \frac{f_T}{g_m(R_S + r_{bb'})} \tag{4.34}$$

The second breakpoint frequency will be determined by the $g_{eb'}/(C_{b'e} + 2C_{cb'})$ time constant. Noting that $g_{eb'} = g_m$, we have for ω_2 the expression

$$\omega_2 = \frac{g_{eb'}}{C_{b'e} + 2C_{cb'}} = \frac{g_m}{C_{b'e} + 2C_{cb'}} \simeq \omega_T \tag{4.35}$$

so that

$$f_2 \simeq f_T \tag{4.36}$$

The third breakpoint frequency will be determined by the $R_L(C_{cb'} + C_L)$ time constant as

$$\omega_3 = \frac{G_L}{C_{cb'} + C_L} = \frac{1}{R_L(C_{cb'} + C_L)}$$

We should note at this point that the second breakpoint frequency f_2 is equal to the unity-gain frequency f_T, so that in virtually every case of practical interest this breakpoint frequency will be much greater than the other two breakpoint frequencies. As a result, the second breakpoint frequency will not have any significant effect in determining the overall bandwidth of the circuit.

The voltage gain of the common-base transistor Q_2 will be given by $A_{V_2} = g_m/G_L = g_m R_L$, and thus the overall voltage gain of the cascode combination will be

$$A_{V(\text{MID})} = A_{V_1} A_{V_2} = (-1)(g_m R_L) = -g_m R_L$$

Looking at the expression for the first breakpoint frequency f_1 we see that it is no longer a function of the load resistance R_L and therefore will be independent of the midfrequency voltage gain. This independence of f_1 from R_L is due to the isolation provided by the common-base transistor in that there is no longer any direct feedback from output to input via the collector–base capacitance. This isolation can be a very important consideration for RF amplifiers, for which case the stability of the amplifier from oscillations is of concern. The base of Q_2 in effect acts as an "electrostatic shield" between the input and output circuits and thus provides very good isolation from capacitative feedback effects.

We will now consider an example of the bandwidth and midfrequency gain available with the cascode configuration, and we will use the same transistor and circuit parameters as was used in the previous example of the common-emitter stage. Since $R_S + r_{bb'} = 100\ \Omega$, $f_T = 1.6$ GHz at the quiescent current of 2.5 mA, and $g_m = 0.1$ S, for f_1 we have the value

$$f_1 = \frac{f_T}{g_m(R_S + r_{bb'})} = \frac{1600\text{ MHz}}{(0.1\text{ S})(100\ \Omega)} = \underline{160\text{ MHz}} \qquad (4.37)$$

Using $C_{cb'} = 1.5$ pF and $C_L = 1.0$ pF, for f_3 we have the equation $f_3 = 1/[2\pi R_L(2.5\text{ pF})]$, and $A_{V(\text{MID})} = -g_m R_L = -(0.1\text{ S})R_L$. For the values of load resistance R_L listed below we obtain the corresponding values of f_1, f_2, f_3, 3-dB bandwidth, and midfrequency gain, $A_{V(\text{MID})}$.

R_L (Ω)	f_1 (MHz)	f_2 (MHz)	f_3 (MHz)	BW (MHz)	$A_{V(\text{MID})}$	$A_{V(\text{MID})} \times BW$ (MHz)
30	160	1,600	2,122	160	3	480
100	160	1,600	637	160	10	1,600
300	160	1,600	212	128	30	3,831
1,000	160	1,600	64	59	100	5,900
3,000	160	1,600	21	21	300	6,305
10,000	160	1,600	6.4	6.4	1,000	6,400

From these values we note the large bandwidths and gain–bandwidth products that can be obtained with the cascode circuit. Indeed, if we compare these values with those obtained for the common-emitter stage considered earlier, we see a large improvement, especially for load resistances in excess of about 300 Ω. For example, for a load resistance of 1000 Ω, for which the midfrequency gain is 100 in both cases, the bandwidth for the common-emitter amplifier stage is 10 MHz, compared to a bandwidth of 59 MHz for the cascode amplifier stage.

To be completely fair, however, we could compare the bandwidth available with the cascode stage with that obtained from two cascaded common-emitter stages with the same overall voltage gain. If we do this for the case of two cascaded common-emitter stages, each stage having a gain of 10 for an overall midfrequency voltage gain of 100 using $R_L = 100$ for each stage, the bandwidth of each stage will be 64 MHz. The net bandwidth of the cascaded combination of the two stages will be given by $BW_{\text{NET}} = BW(2^{1/2} - 1)^{1/2} = 64 \text{ MHz} \times 0.6436 = 41$ MHz. Since the bandwidth of the cascode configuration under the same voltage-gain condition of $A_{V(\text{MID})} = 100$ is 59 MHz, we see that the cascode amplifier still compares very favorably with the common-emitter amplifier.

4.8 USE OF EMITTER-FOLLOWER STAGES IN WIDE-BAND AMPLIFIERS

We have seen the important role played by the source resistance R_S and the load resistance R_L in limiting the bandwidth of video amplifiers, both for the simple common-emitter case and for the cascode configuration. In many cases the impedance transformation characteristics of an emitter-follower stage can be used to great advantage on both the source as well as the load ends of the amplifier. The emitter-follower stage interposed between the signal source and the first gain stage of the amplifier can be used to transform the source resistance R_S down to a much smaller value to be called R_S'. An emitter-follower stage interposed between the last gain stage of the amplifier and the load can be used to transform the load capacitance C_L down to a much smaller value.

In Figure 4.11 a cascode amplifier configuration is shown with the addition of emitter-follower stages for impedance transformation on both the input and output sides of the amplifier. At the source end, the transformed value of the source resistance as seen by the cascode stage (at the base of Q_1) will be $R_S' = R_S/A_{i1}$, where A_{i1} is the a-c current gain of Q_1. This will be given by the equation $A_i = \beta/(1 + jf/f_\beta)$. For frequencies more than half of a decade above f_β, this can be written approximately as $A_i \simeq \beta f_\beta/jf = f_T/jf$. Therefore, as long as the frequency range of interest is

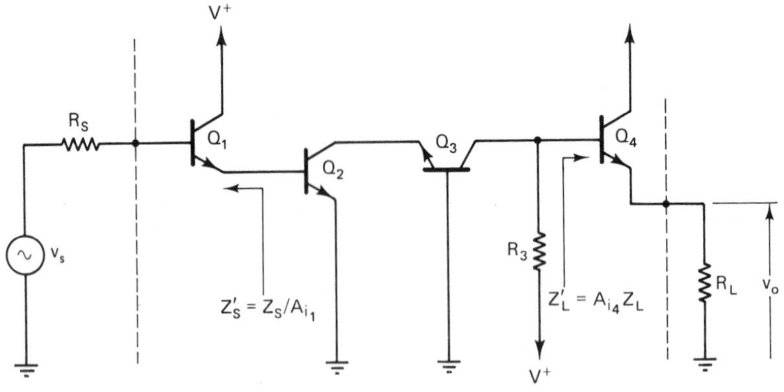

Figure 4.11 Cascode configuration with emitter-follower input and output stages (biasing details omitted).

considerably below f_T, which it will be in virtually every case, a large impedance transformation ratio can be achieved.

At the load end, the emitter follower, Q_2, will act to transform the load impedance Z_L so that the effective value of the load impedance driven by Q_3 as seen looking into the base of Q_4 will be given by $Z_L' = A_{i4}Z_L$, where A_{i4} is the a-c current gain of Q_4, and is given by the same relationships as those used above for Q_1.

The use of emitter-follower input and output stages can prove to be especially useful when large source resistances and load capacitances are present. To illustrate the efficacy of the emitter-follower stages for this purpose we will consider a cascode configuration similar to the one considered earlier, except that the source resistance will be increased by a substantial amount from 40 to 1000 Ω. The load capacitance will be changed from 1.0 pF up to 50 pF. We will consider the design of the circuit for a 50-MHz bandwidth.

Without the use of an emitter-follower stage the first breakpoint frequency f_1 would be given by $f_1 = f_T/g_m(R_S + r_{bb'}) = 1600\text{ MHz}/0.1(1060) = 15.1\text{ MHz}$. We see that we will fall far short of the bandwidth requirement with this value for f_1.

We will now interpose an emitter-follower input stage, Q_1, between the source resistance and the input base terminal (B_2) of the cascode stage, using a transistor with characteristics similar to those of the cascade configuration, so that $f_T = 1.6$ GHz at a quiescent current of 2.5 mA. At a frequency of 50 MHz, the current gain of Q_1 will be $A_{i1} = f_T/jf = 1600\text{ MHz}/j50\text{ MHz} = -j32$. The 1000-Ω source resistance will therefore be transformed to $Z_S' = Z_S/A_{i1} = 1000/-j32 = j31\ \Omega$, at 50 MHz.

With a quiescent current of 2.5 mA, the dynamic emitter-to-base resistance, $r_{eb'}$ of Q_1 will be given by $r_{eb'} = V_T/I_{CQ} = 25\text{ mV}/2.5\text{ mA} = 10\ \Omega$. The capacitative reactance present at the base of Q_2 will be given by

$$X_{C2} = \frac{1}{j\omega(C_{b'e} + 2C_{cb'})} \simeq \frac{1}{j\omega(C_{b'e} + C_{cb'})} = \frac{\omega_T}{j\omega g_m} = \frac{f_T}{jfg_m} \tag{4.38}$$

For $g_m = 0.1$ S, $f_T = 1600$ MHz, and $f = 50$ MHz, we will obtain a capacitative reactance of $X_{C2} = 1600\text{ MHz}/(j50\text{ MHz} \times 0.1\text{ S}) = -j320\ \Omega$.

We can now represent the input circuit for this cascode amplifier by the equivalent circuit shown in Figure 4.12. The voltage-gain factor $v_{b'e_2}/v_s$ can be obtained

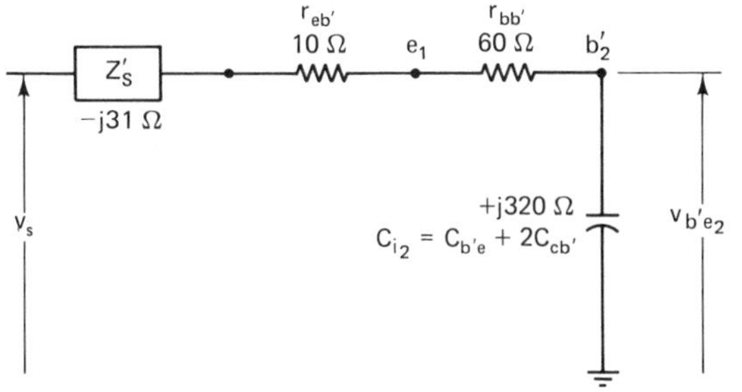

Figure 4.12 Input equivalent circuit showing transformed source resistance.

by considering this circuit to be a simple voltage divider with a voltage-division ratio given by

$$\left|\frac{v_{b'e_2}}{v_s}\right| = \left|\frac{-j320}{(+j31 + 10 + 60) - j320}\right| = \left|\frac{-j320}{70 - j289}\right| = \frac{320}{297} = 1.08 \qquad (4.39)$$

Since the $v_{b'e_2}/v_s$ factor is greater than 0.7071, we see that the bandwidth of the input circuit will be above 50 MHz. Indeed, in this case it appears that f_1 will be considerably above 50 MHz since the $v_{b'e}/v_s$ ratio is actually slightly greater than unity. This is the result of the impedance transformation of Q_1 which has resulted in the source resistance of 1000 Ω in being transformed into a reactance of $+j31$ Ω. Since the algebraic sign of this reactance is opposite to that of the capacitative reactance at the base of Q_2, the net reactance around the loop will be reduced as a result, as seen from the denominator of the $v_{b'e}/v_s$ ratio expression.

The capacitative reactance of the load capacitance of 50 pF at a frequency of 50 MHz will be given by $X_{CL} = 1/j\omega C_L = -j64$ Ω. This capacitative reactance is transformed by Q_4 to an impedance given by

$$Z_L' = Z_L A_{i4} = Z_L \frac{f_T}{jf} = (-j64\ \Omega)\frac{1600\ \text{MHz}}{j50\ \text{MHz}} = -2040\ \Omega \qquad (4.40)$$

Thus the capacitative load C_L has been transformed by Q_4 into a negative resistance of -2040 Ω.

The net capacitance driven by Q_3 will be the sum of the collector–base capacitances of Q_3 and Q_4, or $C_{cb'_3} + C_{cb'_4} = 3.0$ pF. The net conductance driven by Q_3 will be the algebraic sum of G_3 and the conductance seen looking into the base of Q_4. The breakpoint frequency f_3 obtained for this part of the circuit will be related to the net resistance R_{NET} and capacitance by $f_3 = 1/2\pi R_{\text{NET}} C_{\text{NET}}$, where $C_{\text{NET}} =$ 3.0 pF. Since f_1 will be considerably greater than the required bandwidth of 50 MHz, as will $f_2 = f_T = 1600$ MHz, we will require that $f_3 = 50$ MHz. The corresponding value of R_{NET} will be given by $R_{\text{NET}} = 1/2\pi(BW)C_{\text{NET}} = 1/2\pi(50\ \text{MHz}) \times$ 3.0 pF = 1061 Ω. Since we have that $G_{\text{NET}} = G_3 + G_{i4}$, we obtain $1/1061 = (1/R_3) + (1/-2040)$, so that $R_3 = 698$ Ω.

The midfrequency voltage gain obtained from this circuit will be given by $A_{V(\text{MID})} = -g_m R_{\text{NET}} = -0.1\ \text{S} \times 1061\ \Omega = -106$.

If there were no emitter-follower stage on the output side, the value of R_{NET} that would have to be used in order to obtain a 50-MHz bandwidth would be given by

$$R_{\text{NET}} = \frac{1}{2\pi(BW)(C_L + 2C_{cb'})} = \frac{1}{2\pi(50\ \text{MHz}) \times 51.5\ \text{pF}} = 60\ \Omega \qquad (4.41)$$

With this very small value for $R_{\text{NET}} \simeq R_3$, the midfrequency voltage gain would be given by $A_{V(\text{MID})} = -g_m R_{\text{NET}} = -(0.1\ \text{S})(60\ \Omega) = -6.0$, compared to the gain of -106 that can be obtained if an emitter-follower stage is used. Thus we see that a very substantial improvement in the gain–bandwidth product can be achieved by the use of an emitter-follower stage for the transformation of the load impedance, and we have already seen the benefits that accrue from the use of an emitter follower on the input side for source resistance transformation.

4.9 DIFFERENTIAL VIDEO AMPLIFIER EXAMPLE CA3040

We will now consider another IC video amplifier, the CA3040 (RCA) which has a differential cascode amplifier configuration. The circuit diagram for this device is shown in Figure 4.13. This is a differential video amplifier and can accept single-ended or balanced input signals, and single-ended as well as balanced output voltages can be obtained.

The input stage consists of transistors Q_1 and Q_2 in a emitter-follower configuration driving the cascode (CE–CB) differential amplifier with Q_3 and Q_4 serving as the common-emitter part of the cascode combination, and Q_5 and Q_6 serving as the common-base part. This differential amplifier has current sink biasing provided by Q_9. Resistors R_5 and R_6 (1.32 kΩ each) serve as the load resistors for this stage. Transistors Q_7 and Q_8 constitute a differential emitter-follower output stage with biasing provided by resistors R_7 and R_8.

Diodes D_1 and D_2 together with resistor R_{10} (4.5 kΩ) provide a d-c bias voltage of about 1.4 V for the proper biasing of Q_3, Q_4, Q_5, and Q_6. Since the bases of Q_1 and Q_2 will be essentially at ground potential (0 V), the bases of Q_3 and Q_4 will be at about −0.7 V and the emitters will be at about −1.4 V. Since the emitters of Q_5 and Q_6 will be at a voltage of $V_{D1} + V_{D2} - V_{BE(5,6)} = +0.7$ V, the collector-to-emitter voltage of Q_3 and of Q_4 will be approximately +2.1 V. This value of V_{CE} should prove adequate to keep Q_3 and Q_4 well out of saturation, and to ensure that these two transistors will be operating under bias conditions that will give good high-frequency performance.

The bias voltage for the current sink transistor Q_9 is supplied by the voltage divider comprised of R_{11}, and R_{12}. This bias voltage together with resistor R_9 (810 Ω) will determine the collector current of Q_9 and hence the quiescent current of the cascode differential amplifier.

4.9.1 D-C Biasing Calculations

For the d-c biasing calculations we will use a representative split supply voltage of ±6.0 V. The current through the series circuit of R_{11}, and R_{12} will be 6.0 V/2.99 kΩ ≃ 2.0 mA, so that the voltage at the base of Q_9 will be −2.0 mA × 0.82 kΩ = −1.64 V. Assuming a V_{BE} of 0.7 V, the voltage at the emitter of Q_9 will be −2.34 V, so that the voltage drop across R_9 be −2.34 − (−6.0) = 3.66 V. The current through Q_9 will therefore be I_9 = 3.66 V/0.81 kΩ = 4.5 mA, and this will be the quiescent current of the differential amplifier.

The quiescent current of Q_1 and of Q_2 will be determined by R_1 and R_2 as −0.7 − (−6.0)/4.8 kΩ = 1.1 mA. The quiescent voltage at the collectors of Q_5 and Q_6 and therefore at the bases of Q_7 and Q_8 will be given by +6.0 − (4.5 mA/2)(1.32 kΩ) = +3.0 V, so that the emitter voltage of Q_7 and Q_8 will be 2.3 V. The quiescent current of Q_7 and of Q_8 will as a result be 2.3 V/5.25 kΩ = 0.44 mA.

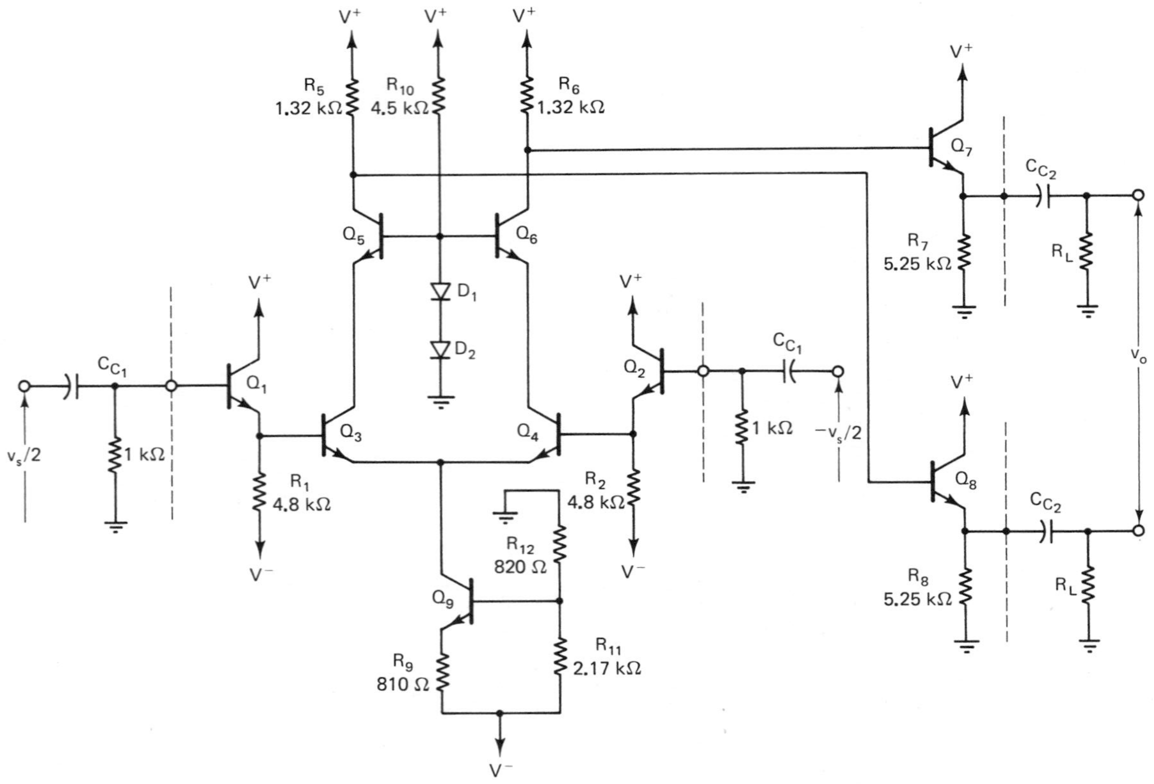

Figure 4.13 Cascode video amplifier integrated circuit: CA3040 (RCA Corporation).

4.9.2 A-C Voltage Gain Analysis

For the a-c gain analysis we will split the amplifier along the axis of symmetry producing the result shown in Figure 4.14. We see that in terms of the a-c signal flow the amplifier is basically a CC–CE–CB–CC configuration, and thus using a cascode gain stage with emitter-follower input and output stages for impedance transformation.

The midfrequency voltage gain of the cascode stage will be given by

$$A_{V(\mathrm{MID})} = -g_f R_L = -\frac{I_C R_L}{V_T} = -\frac{2.25 \text{ mA}}{25 \text{ mV}}(1.32 \text{ k}\Omega) = -\underline{119} \tag{4.42}$$

Using a representative current gain value of 100, the input resistance seen looking into the base of Q_3 and of Q_4 will be $R_{i(3,4)} = \beta V_T / I_{(3,4)} = 100 \times 25$ mV/2.25 mA $= 1.1$ kΩ. The voltage gain of the emitter-follower input stage will therefore be

$$\begin{aligned} A_{v\,1,2} &= \frac{R_{L(1,2)}}{(V_T/I_{C\,12}) + R_{L(1,2)}} = \frac{(4.8 \text{ k}\Omega \| 1.1 \text{ k}\Omega)}{(25 \text{ mV}/1.1 \text{ mA}) + (4.8 \text{ k}\Omega \| 1.1 \text{ k}\Omega)} \\ &= \frac{902\ \Omega}{(23 + 902)\ \Omega} = \underline{0.975} \end{aligned} \tag{4.43}$$

The voltage gain of the emitter-follower output stage of Q_7 and Q_8 for a load resistance of 1000 Ω will in a similar fashion be given by

$$\begin{aligned} A_{V\,7,8} &= \frac{R_{L(7,8)}}{(V_T/I_{C(7,8)}) + R_{L(7,8)}} = \frac{(1 \text{ k}\Omega \| 5.25 \text{ k}\Omega)\ \Omega}{(25 \text{ mV}/0.44 \text{ mA}) + (1.0 \text{ k}\Omega \| 5.25 \text{ k}\Omega)} \\ &= \frac{840}{57 + 840} = \underline{0.937} \end{aligned} \tag{4.44}$$

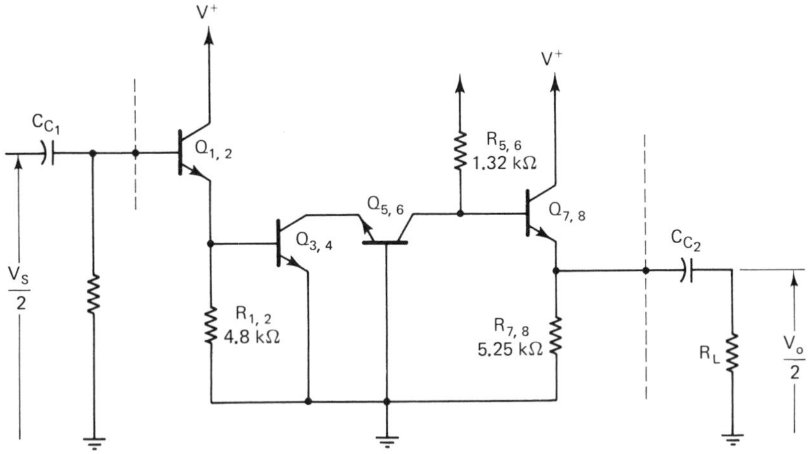

Figure 4.14 A-c circuit of 3040-type video amplifier after split along axis of symmetry.

The overall midfrequency voltage gain of this amplifier circuit will therefore be given by $A_{V(\text{MID})} = -0.975 \times 119 \times 0.937 = -109$ or 40.7 dB. This is the voltage gain that will be obtained by taking a balanced output voltage, since for a given input voltage applied as either a single-ended or balanced input, the voltage V_S will be split evenly between the two halves of the circuit. The voltage applied to each "half-circuit" will therefore be $V_S/2$ and the resultant output is $V_O/2$. By taking a balanced output, an output voltage of V_O will be obtained. If a single-ended output is taken, the output voltage will be only $V_O/2$, and the voltage gain will be only half as much as for a balanced output, or 55, corresponding to 34.7 dB.

The amplifier output impedance is the impedance seen looking into the emitter of the emitter-follower output stage (Q_7 and Q_8) and will be given by $Z_O = (V_T/I_{7,8}) + R_{1,2}/\beta = (25\text{ mV}/0.44\text{ mA}) + (1.32\text{ k}\Omega/100) = 57\ \Omega + 13\ \Omega = 70\ \Omega$. As a result, load resistances of the order of 1 kΩ or more will not have much effect on the performance of this amplifier.

4.9.3 Bandwidth Calculations

This amplifier with its cascode gain-stage configuration and its emitter-follower input and output stages should exhibit a very large gain–bandwidth product. Since the overall gain is relatively low ($A_{V(\text{MID})} = 109$) as a result of the small value of $R_{5,6}$ (1.32 kΩ), we should expect to see a relatively large bandwidth resulting.

To perform a sample calculation of the bandwidth to be expected from this circuit we will assume a representative value for the f_T of Q_3 and Q_4 of 1.0 GHz at the quiescent current level of 2.25 mA. We will also use a base spreading resistance of $r_{bb'} = 60\ \Omega$, and we will assume that the amplifier is driven from a 50-Ω source.

The effective value of the source impedance as seen looking back from the base of $Q_{3,4}$ will be

$$R'_S = R_{1,2} \| \left[\frac{V_T}{I_{1,2}} + \frac{R_S}{A_{i\,1,2}} \right]$$

$$= 4.8\text{ k}\Omega \| \left(23 + \frac{50}{A_{i\,1,2}} \right) \simeq 23\ \Omega$$

Since $A_{i\,1,2}$ will be much larger than unity in the frequency range of interest. For the first breakpoint frequency, f_1, we will have

$$f_1 = \frac{f_T}{g_m(R'_S + r_{bb'})} = \frac{1000\text{ MHz}}{(2.25\text{ mA}/25\text{ mV})(23+60)\Omega}$$
$$= \frac{1000\text{ MHz}}{(0.09)(83)} = \underline{134\text{ MHz}} \tag{4.45}$$

For the collector–base capacitance we will choose a representative value of $C_{cb'} = 1.0$ pF. Since the impedance looking into the base of $Q_{7,8}$, $R_{i\,7,8}$, will be much greater than $R_{5,6}$, the third breakpoint frequency f_3 will be

$$f_3 = \frac{1}{2\pi R_{5,6}(C_{cb\,5,6} + C_{cb\,7,8})} = \frac{1}{2\pi(1.3\text{ k}\Omega)(2.0\text{ pF})} = \underline{61\text{ MHz}}$$

Since $f_2 = f_T = 1000$ MHz and $f_1 = 134$ MHz, we see that the bandwidth will be controlled principally by f_3, and will be approximately 56 MHz. The corresponding rise time (10 to 90%) will be $t_{\text{rise}} = 0.35/BW = 6.3$ ns. The actual bandwidth (3 dB) for this video amplifier is 55 MHz (typ.) [40 MHz (min.)], so that this sample calculation has yielded a bandwidth value that agrees quite well with the actual results.

4.10 WIDE-BANDWIDTH AND FAST-SLEWING OPERATIONAL AMPLIFIERS

Most op amps have unity-gain frequencies (or gain-bandwidth products) in the range 1 to 3 MHz with slewing rates in the range 0.5 to 5 V/μs. There are many op amps that can be characterized as very wide bandwidths and fast slewing op amps. A good example is the HA2539 (Harris Semiconductor) with a gain-bandwidth product of 600 MHz and a slewing rate of 600 V/μs. This op amp will be discussed in more detail in the next section. The NE5539 (Signetics) is a very wide bandwidth monolithic bipolar operational amplifier with a gain-bandwidth product of 1200 MHz at a gain of 7 and a slewing rate of 600 V/μs. The full power bandwidth is 20 MHz with a peak-to-peak output of 3 V into a 150 Ω load. A very wide bandwidth hybrid op amp is the 3554 (Burr-Brown) with a gain-bandwidth product of 1700 MHz (at a gain of 1000) and a slewing rate of 1000 V/μs. The small-signal bandwidth is 22.5 MHz at a gain of 10, 7.25 MHz at a gain of 100, and 1.7 MHz at a gain of 1000. The full power bandwidth is 19 MHz when driving a 100 Ω load with a 20 V peak-to-peak output voltage. Another wide bandwidth hybrid op amp is the LH0032 (National Semiconductor). This JFET-input op amp has a unity-gain frequency of 70 MHZ and a slewing rate of 500 V/μs along with an input impedance of 10^{12} Ω and an input bias current of just 10 pA. A series of very wide bandwidth op amps are made by the Comlinear Corporation. The CLC200 features a 100 MHz 3-dB bandwidth for gains of from 1 to 50. The rise time is 3.6 ns and the settling time for the output voltage to settle to within 0.02% of the final value is 25 ns. The CLC210 combines a wide bandwidth with a large output voltage swing capability. It has a 50 MHz small-signal bandwidth. It can supply 50 mA to a load with a 60 V peak-to-peak output voltage swing and a full-power bandwidth of 5 MHz minimum. The CLC220 has a 200 MHz bandwidth with rise and fall times of only 1.6 ns. The slewing rate of this op amp is a very impressive 8000 V/μs. The settling time for the output voltage to settle to within 0.02% of the final value is 12 ns.

4.11 VERY WIDE-BANDWIDTH OPERATIONAL AMPLIFIER: HA-2539

An example of an operational amplifier that has a very wide bandwidth and a very high slewing rate is the HA-2539 (Harris Semiconductor). The device can be used as a video or RF amplifier in addition to the usual operational amplifier applications. This IC has a gain–bandwidth product of 600 MHz and a slewing rate of 600 V/

μs. When driving a 1000-Ω load with a ±10-V peak output voltage swing the full-power bandwidth (FPBW) is 9.5 MHz. This good high-frequency performance is, however, at the expense of the open-loop gain $A_{OL}(0)$, which is 10 V/mV.

A simplified circuit diagram of this IC is shown in Figure 4.15. The input stage consists of a complementary pair of differential amplifiers (Q_1–Q_2 and $Q_{1'}$–$Q_{2'}$). This complementary pair of differential-amplifier configuration provides for some degree of base current cancellation to produce a lower net input bias current. This allows for the biasing current I_Q of this stage to be set at a much higher value than would otherwise be the case.

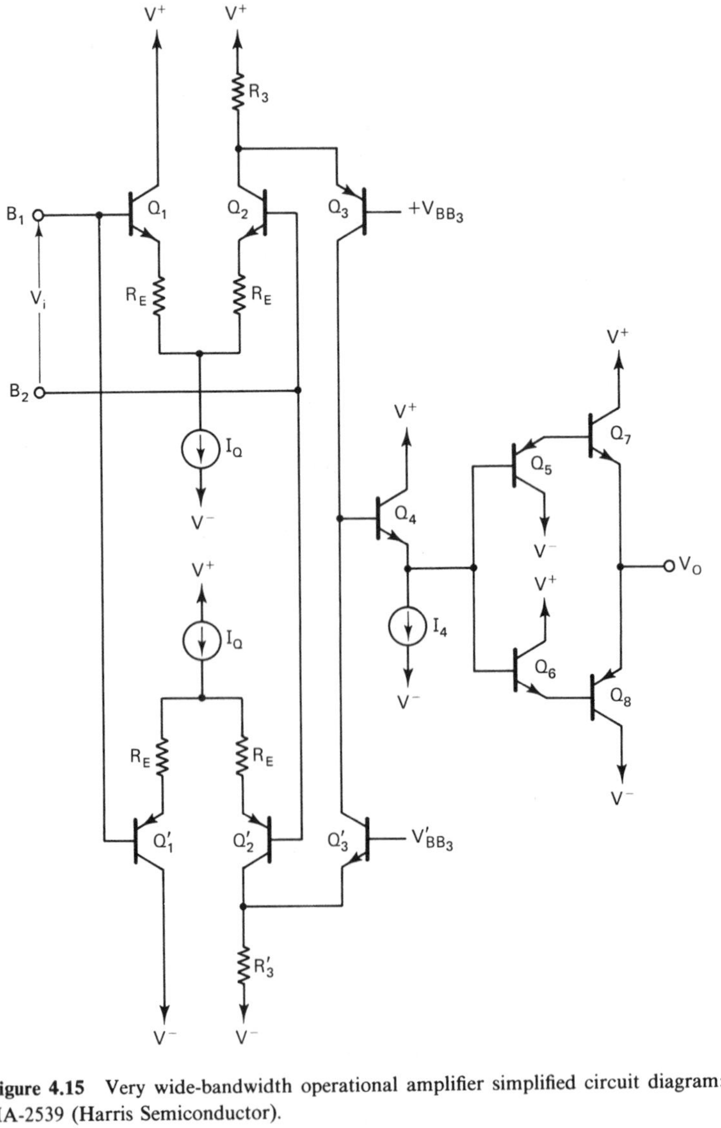

Figure 4.15 Very wide-bandwidth operational amplifier simplified circuit diagram: HA-2539 (Harris Semiconductor).

The complementary differential amplifiers drive a pair of common-base transistors (Q_3 and $Q_{3'}$). The combination of the differential amplifiers and common-base transistors essentially form a pair of CE–CB cascode stages which can be considered to constitute the single gain stage of the amplifier, and which minimizes the total amplifier phase shift.

The output stage is a complementary push-pull Darlington emitter follower using transistors Q_4 through Q_8. Transistors Q_5 and Q_6 are used as emitter followers in the output stage and also act to minimize the crossover distortion.

The very wide bandwidth and high slewing rate of this device is the result of the following design features: (1) local negative feedback (emitter degeneration) in the differential amplifiers produced by resistors R_E and $R_{E'}$; (2) a high quiescent current I_Q for the differential amplifier stage; (3) the single gain-stage configuration of the differential-amplifier/common-base cascode combination; and (4) the use of dielectric isolation to reduce the parasitic capacitances, especially the collector-to-substrate capacitance.

4.12 FET HIGH-FREQUENCY AMPLIFIERS

Most high-frequency amplifiers use bipolar transistors, but short-channel MOSFETs and GaAs MESFETs can offer very good performance for high-speed analog and digital circuits. The analysis of the frequency- and time-domain response of FET amplifier circuits follows along the same general lines as for bipolar circuits. In Figure 4.16a a common-source FET amplifier is shown and in Figure 4.16b the equivalent-circuit representation is shown. The equivalent circuit is seen to be of the form of two cascaded RC low-pass networks with time constants $\tau_i = R_S C_i$ and $\tau_o = R_L(C_o + C_L)$. Using Miller's theorem, capacitances C_i and C_o are given by

$$\begin{aligned} C_i &= C_{gs} + C_{gd}(1 - A_v) \simeq C_{gs} + (1 + g_{fs}R_L)C_{gd} \\ C_o &= C_{ds} + C_{gd}\left(1 - \frac{1}{A_v}\right) \simeq C_{ds} + C_{gd} \qquad \text{since usually } A_v \gg 1 \end{aligned} \tag{4.46}$$

The corresponding breakpoint frequencies will be given by $f_i = 1/(2\pi\tau_i)$ and $f_o = 1/(2\pi\tau_o)$.

In most wide-bandwidth amplifiers the source resistance R_S will be small such that τ_i will be substantially smaller than τ_o, so that τ_o will be the dominant time constant. For this case the 3-dB bandwidth will be given approximately by $BW \simeq f_o = 1/[2\pi R_L(C_{ds} + C_{gs} + C_L)]$ and the rise time will be $t_{\text{rise}} \simeq 2.2\ \tau_o = 2.2R_L(C_{ds} + C_{gs} + C_L)$. Since the midfrequency voltage gain will be $A_v = -g_{fs}R_L$, the gain–bandwidth product will be given approximately by $|A_v \times BW| \simeq g_{fs}/[2\pi(C_{ds} + C_{gs} + C_L)]$.

For short-channel MOSFETs a very simple relationship for the gain–bandwidth product can be obtained. The drain-to-source current can be expressed as $I_{DS} =$

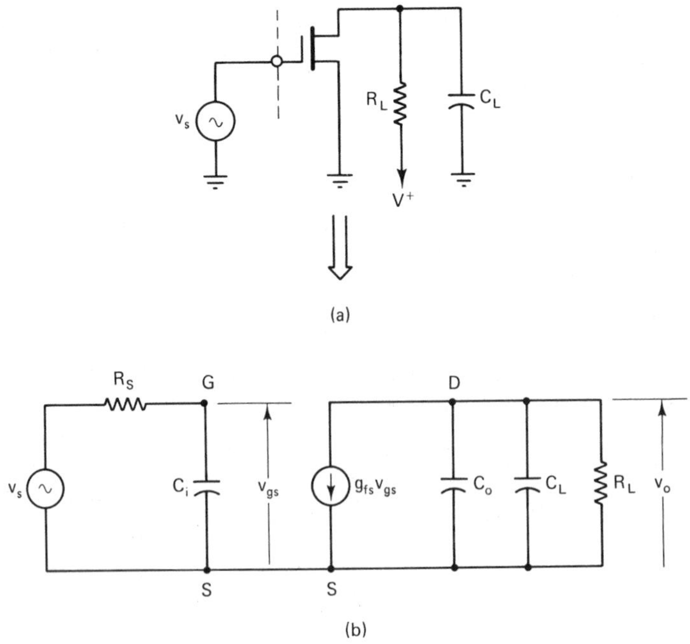

Figure 4.16 FET amplifier circuit: (a) FET common-source amplifier stage; (b) a-c small-signal equivalent circuit.

$Q_{\text{channel}}/t_{\text{transit}}$. Since $Q_{\text{channel}} = C_{gs}(V_{gs} - V_{Th})$ and $t_{\text{transit}} = L/v_{\text{sat}}$, this can be rewritten as $I_{DS} = C_{gs}(V_{gs} - V_{Th})v_{\text{sat}}/L$. The dynamic transfer conductance g_{fs} will be given by

$$g_{fs} = \frac{dI_{DS}}{dV_{gs}} = \frac{C_{gs}v_{\text{sat}}}{L} \tag{4.47}$$

Since C_{ds} is usually small compared to C_{gs}, and if we also assume C_L to be small compared to C_{gs}, the maximum gain–bandwidth product capability of the device can be expressed very simply by

$$(A_v \times BW)_{\text{MAX}} = \frac{g_{fs}}{2\pi C_{gs}} = \frac{v_{\text{sat}}}{2\pi L} \tag{4.48}$$

The saturation electron velocity v_{sat} in silicon is approximately 8×10^6 cm/s and in GaAs is approximately 2×10^7 cm/s. For a silicon MOSFET with a channel length of $L = 1.0\ \mu$m the maximum gain–bandwidth product will be about 12 GHz. For a GaAs MESFET with a 1-μm channel length the maximum gain–bandwidth product will be up to 32 GHz. Indeed, very high speed digital ICs have been developed using GaAs that offer substantial speed advantages over silicon ICs. We see therefore that short-channel field-effect transistors can indeed offer very good high-frequency performance.

4.13 UNITY-GAIN BUFFERS

A unity-gain buffer is an amplifier with an internally set gain of unity and can be considered to perform similar to a voltage-follower op amp circuit. The unity-gain buffers can, however, offer substantial performance advantages over op amp voltage-followers, especially in the areas of wide bandwidth and high slewing rate. Most unity-gain buffers consist of a JFET source-follower input stage followed by one or two emitter-follower stages. An example of a unity gain buffer circuit is shown in Figure 4.17. The input stage is a JFET source-follower with a JFET current sink active load. This drives two cascaded emitter-follower stages, both of which use JFET current sink active loads. Diode-connected transistors, Q_7 and Q_8, together with the JFET current source transistor Q_4, are used for level shifting such that $V_o = 0$ when $V_i = 0$.

An example of a high performance unity-gain buffer is the 3553 (Burr-Brown) which has a −3-dB bandwidth of 300 MHz and a slewing rate of 2000 V/μs, together with an input impedance of $10^{11}\ \Omega$, an output current capability of 200 mA, and an output resistance of only 1 Ω. The full-power bandwidth is 32 MHz for a 10 V peak output voltage swing. The voltage gain is 0.98 under no load conditions and 0.92 with a 50 Ω load. The output offset voltage is 50 mV (max) with a temperature

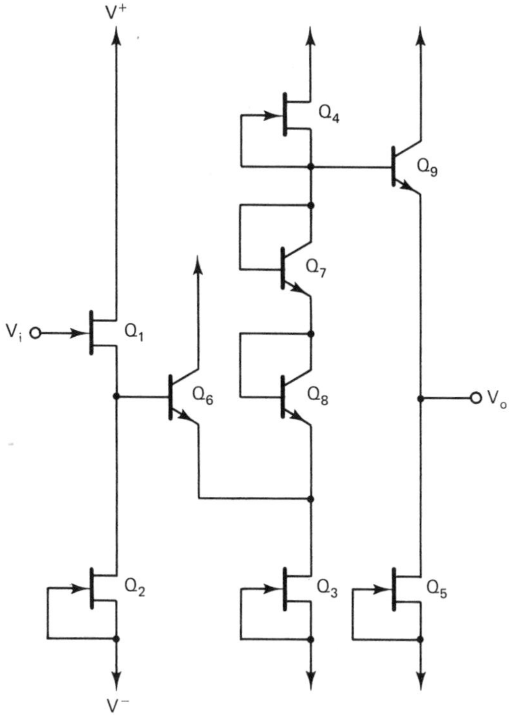

Figure 4.17 Unity-gain buffer.

coefficient of 300 $\mu V/°C$. Another fast unity gain buffer is the LH0063 (National Semiconductor) with a bandwidth of 100 MHz and a slewing rate of 6000 $V/\mu s$ with a 1000 Ω load. The input resistance is 10^{11} Ω, the output resistance is a 6 Ω, and it can supply 10 V to a 50 Ω load with a slewing rate of 2400 $V/\mu s$. The output offset voltage is 5 mV with a temperature coefficient of 50 $\mu V/°C$.

Another example of a fast unity-gain buffer is the HOS-100AH/100SH series (Analog Devices). This is a bipolar transistor buffer using a complementery set of a PNP-NPN cascaded emitter-follower pair and a cascaded NPN-PNP emitter-follower pair arranged in a push-pull configuration. The cancellation of the NPN and PNP base-to-emitter voltage drops results in an offset voltage of 5 mV with a maximum temperature coefficient of 25 $\mu V/°C$. This buffer has a bandwidth of 125 MHz and a slewing rate of 1500 $V/\mu s$. The input impedance is 200 kΩ and the output impedance is 8 Ω, and it is capable of delivering a bipolar 10 V peak output voltage into a 100 Ω load. Another bipolar video buffer of a similar configuration is the HA-5033 (Harris). This buffer has a small-signal bandwidth of 250 MHz and a rise time of 3 ns when driven from a 50 Ω source and driving a 100 Ω load. With the 100 Ω load the voltage gain is 0.93. The input resistance is 1.5 M Ω in parallel with a capacitance of 1.5 pF and the output resistance is 5 Ω.

PROBLEMS

4.1. (*Common-emitter amplifier frequency response*) Refer to Figure P4.1. Given: Common-emitter amplifier stage with $I_C = 2.5$ mA, $r_{bb'} = 100\ \Omega$ $f_T = 1.59$ GHz, and $C_{cb} = 2.0$ pF, $\beta = 100$, and $n = 1$. Find the midfrequency voltage gain, 3-dB bandwidth, and the gain–bandwidth product for the following values of load resistance:

(a) $R_L = 100\ \Omega$. (*Ans.*: 9.1, 53 MHz, 482 MHz)

(b) $R_L = 300\ \Omega$. (*Ans.*: 27, 23 MHz, 621 MHz)

(c) $R_L = 1.0$ kΩ. (*Ans.*: 91, 7.6 MHz, 691 MHz)

(d) $R_L = 5.0$ kΩ. (*Ans.*: 455, 1.6 MHz, 727 MHz)

(e) Show that the gain–bandwidth product can never be greater than $A_{V(MID)} \times BW = 1/(2\pi r_{bb'} C_{cb})$, and calculate this limiting value. (*Ans.*: 796 MHz)

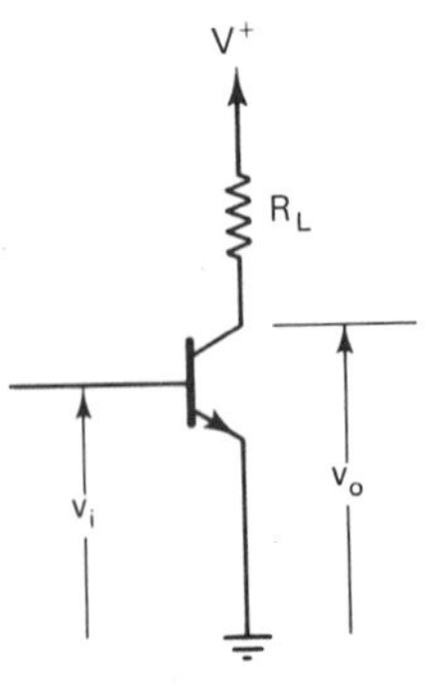

Figure P4.1

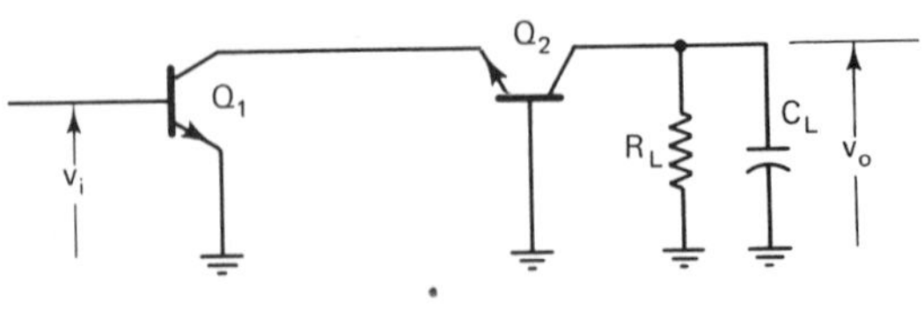

Figure P4.2

4.2. (*Cascode video amplifier*) Given: Cascode amplifier using same transistors and quiescent conditions as in Problem 4.1, and as shown in Figure P4.2.

(a) Find $A_{V(\text{MID})}$ and BW for $R_L = 100\ \Omega$ and $C_L = 5$ pF. Also calculate the gain–bandwidth product. (*Ans*.: 9.1, 130 MHz, 1183 MHz)

(b) Repeat for $R_L = 1.0$ kΩ. (*Ans*.: 91, 22 MHz, 2002 MHz)

(c) Repeat for $R_L = 100\ \Omega$ and a source resistance of 50 Ω. (*Ans*.: 8.7, 85 MHz, 740 MHz)

4.3. (*Video integrated circuit*) Given: Integrated circuit as shown in Figure P4.3 with $V^+ = +6.0$ V and $V^- = -6.0$ V. For all transistors: $f_T = 700$ MHz, $r_{bb'} = 40\ \Omega$, $C_{cb} = 1.0$ pF, $\beta = 100$ (typ.), and $V_{BE} = 0.7$ V. The circuit is driven from a 50-Ω source and drives a load resistance R_L of 1.0 kΩ. Find:

(a) $I_{C_{1,2}}$. (*Ans*.: 1.1 mA)

(b) $V_{E_{7,8}}$ and $I_{C_{7,8}}$. (*Ans*.: +2.33 V, 0.44 mA)

(c) I_{C_9}. (*Ans*.: 4.5 mA)

(d) Total quiescent supply current. (*Ans*.: 10.6 mA)

(e) Voltage gain (midfrequency) of differential amplifier stage with a balanced output. (*Ans*.: 117)

(f) Voltage gain of the emitter-follower input transistors, Q_1 and Q_2. (*Ans*.: 0.975)

(g) Voltage gain of the emitter-follower output stage, Q_7 and Q_8. (*Ans*.: 0.937)

(h) Overall voltage gain of the amplifier, v_o/v_s. (*Ans*.: 107 or 40.6 dB)

(i) Dynamic output resistance, r_o. (*Ans*.: 69 Ω)

(j) 3-dB bandwidth and rise time. (*Ans*.: 54 MHz, 6.5 ns)

(k) Coupling capacitor values C_{C_1} and C_{C_2} for a lower 3-dB frequency of 10 Hz. [*Ans*.: C_{C_1} and $C_{C_2} = 16\ \mu$F (min.) when considering the response due to C_{C_1} and C_{C_2}

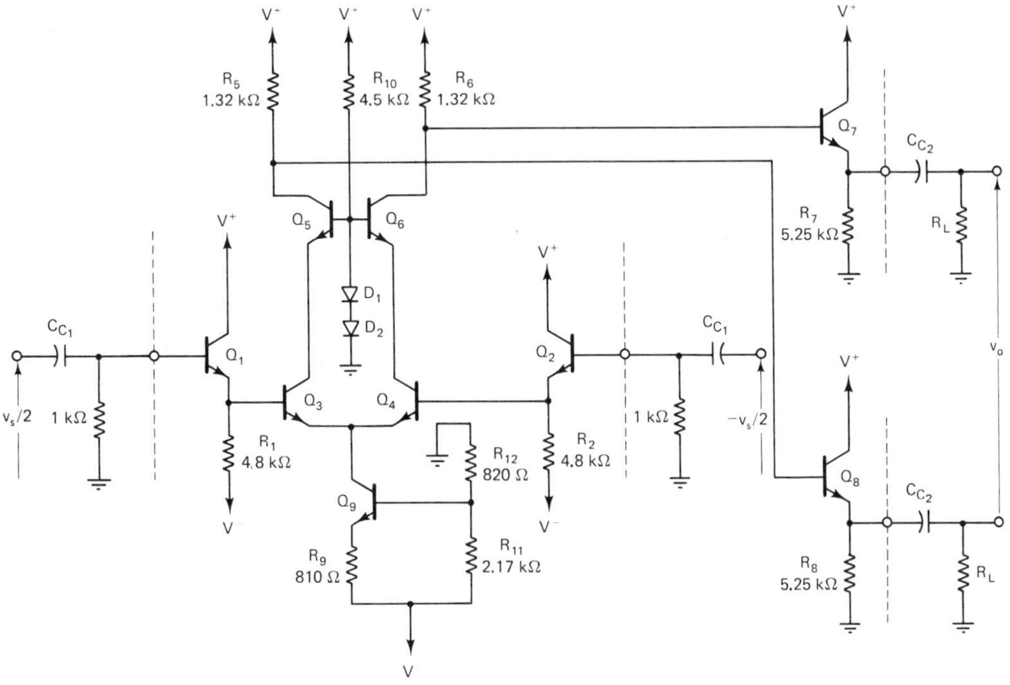

Figure P4.3

separately, and ~25 μF (min.) when considering the net effects of both coupling capacitors]

4.4. (*Wide-bandwidth operational amplifier*) Given: The very wide-bandwidth, high-slewing-rate operational-amplifier circuit (HA-2539, Harris Semiconductor) shown in Figure 4.15.

(a) Show that the open-loop gain can be expressed approximately by

$$A_{OL} \simeq \frac{g_m}{(1 + g_m R_E)(j\omega C_{\text{NET}})} \simeq \frac{1}{j\omega R_E C_{\text{NET}}} \qquad \text{if } g_m R_E \gg 1$$

where $g_m = (I_Q/2)/V_T$ and $C_{\text{NET}} = C_{CB_3} + C_{CB_{3'}} + C_{CB_4}$.

(b) Show that the gain–bandwidth product (or unity-gain frequency f_u) will be given approximately by

$$f_u \simeq \frac{g_m}{2\pi(1 + g_m R_E)C_{\text{NET}}} \simeq \frac{1}{2\pi R_E C_{\text{NET}}} \qquad \text{if } g_m R_E \gg 1$$

(c) If $I_Q = 2.0$ mA, $R_E = R_{E'} = 50\ \Omega$, and $C_{CB} = 1.2$ pF for all transistors, find the gain–bandwidth product (f_u). (*Ans*.: 590 MHz)

(d) Find the slewing rate using the parameters above. (*Ans*.: 555 V/μs)

(e) Find the full-power bandwidth for a ± 10 voltage swing. (*Ans*.: 8.83 MHz)

(f) If $\beta = 100$ and $n = 1.5$ for all transistors, find the difference-mode input resistance. (*Ans*.: 8800 Ω)

(g) Find I_{BIAS} if $\beta_{\text{NPN}} = 120$ and $\beta_{\text{PNP}} = 80$. (*Ans*.: −4.2 μA)

(h) Describe the advantage that is gained by the use of the complementary differential-amplifier configuration of this circuit.

(i) Find the values of f_u, SR, and FPBW for the preceding problems if I_Q is reduced to only 20 μA. (*Ans*.: 17 MHz, 5.6 V/μs, 88 kHz)

(j) Describe the relative advantages and disadvantages of the operation of this circuit with a large value of I_Q.

4.5. (*Multistage video amplifier*) A multistage video amplifier is to amplify an input signal of 100 μV rms up to an output voltage level of 2.0 V rms with a 30-MHz 3-dB bandwidth. This amplifier is to use wide-bandwidth operational amplifiers that have a gain–bandwidth product of 600 MHz and a slewing rate of 600 V/μs. Determine the number of cascaded op amps that are needed and the closed-loop gain needed for each op amp. (*Ans*.: five operational amplifiers, 7.25)

4.6. (*Unity gain buffer*) In Figure 4.17 a unity-gain buffer (or voltage-follower) circuit is shown. This buffer is characterized by a very high input impedance, a low output impedance, and a very wide bandwidth along with a very high slewing rate. Assume that all transistors of the same type are identical, except that transistor Q_3 has twice the channel width as the other JFETs. Also assume that the base currents of the bipolar transistors are very much smaller than the saturated drain currents of the JFETs.

(a) Show that when the input voltage V_i is zero, the output voltage will be zero.

(b) Given that the current gain of the bipolar transistors is 200 and for the JFETs, $V_P = -2$ V, $V_A = 100$ V, and $I_{DSS} = 5.0$ mA, except for Q_3 for which $I_{DSS} = 10$ mA. Find the voltage gain of this buffer under no load conditions. (*Ans*.: 0.9891)

(c) Find the output impedance. (*Ans*.: 5.08 Ω)

(d) Find the voltage gain of this buffer when driving a load resistance of 100 Ω. (*Ans.*: 0.9413)

(e) Find the quiescent supply current. (*Ans.*: 20 mA)

(f) Given that $C_{gs} = 3$ pF, $C_{gd} = 3$ pF, $C_{b'e} = 10$ pF, and $C_{cb'} = 2$ pF, find the 3-dB bandwidth. (*Ans.*: 159 MHz)

(g) Repeat parts (b) through (f) for $I_{DSS} = 1.0$ mA for all JFETs, except for Q_3 for which $I_{DSS} = 2.0$ mA. (*Ans.*: 0.9891, 25.4 Ω, 0.7888, 4.0 mA, 31.8 MHz)

4.7. (*Bipolar unity gain buffer*) In the unity-gain buffer circuit of Figure P4.7 assume all transistors of the same type to be identical and assume $\beta = 100$ for all transistors. The source resistance is 500 Ω, the load resistance is 100 Ω, and $I_Q = 2.5$ mA.

(a) Show that the quiescent current through Q_3 and Q_4 will be equal to I_Q.

(b) If the difference between the emitter-base junction voltage drops of the NPN and PNP transistors is 5 mV, show that under quiescent conditions the input-to-output offset voltage will be 5 mV.

(c) Find the dynamic output resistance, r_o. (*Ans.*: 5.1 Ω)

(d) Find the dynamic input resistance (use $n = 1.5$). (*Ans.*: 1.076 M Ω)

(e) Find the small-signal voltage gain. (*Ans.*: 0.952)

(f) If $C_{b'e} = 20$ pF and $C_{cb'} = 2$ pF for all transistors, find the input capacitance, C_i. (*Ans.*: 4 pF)

(g) Find the small-signal system 3-dB bandwidth. (*Ans.*: 80 MHz)

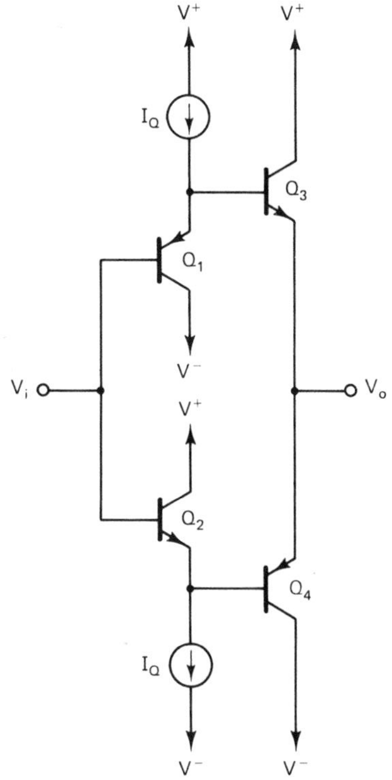

Figure P4.7

REFERENCES

Cowles, L. G., *Sourcebook of Modern Transistor Circuits*, Chap. 12, Prentice-Hall, 1976.

Fitchen, F. C., *Electronic Integrated Circuits and Systems*, Van Nostrand Reinhold, 1970.

Grebene, A. B., *Analog Integrated Circuit Design*, Van Nostrand Reinhold, 1972.

Lenk, J. D., *Handbook of Integrated Circuits*, Reston, 1978.

Manasse, F., *Semiconductor Electronics Design*, Prentice-Hall, 1977.

Millman, J., *Microelectronics*, McGraw-Hill, 1979.

Modulators, Demodulators, and Phase Detectors

5

5.1 BALANCED MODULATOR–DEMODULATOR ANALYSIS

The balanced modulator–demodulator IC can be used to perform a number of functions. These include use as a suppressed carrier double-sideband modulator, suppressed carrier single-sideband modulator, single-sideband demodulator, double-sideband demodulator, frequency modulation demodulator, frequency doubler, and phase detector.

We will first analyze the basic balanced modulator–demodulator circuit shown in Figure 5.1. For this analysis we will neglect the base currents as being very small compared to the emitter and collector currents and consider all transistors to be identical.

For the currents through Q_5 and Q_6 we have that $I_5 = I_Q + I_R$ and $I_6 = I_Q - I_R$. We also have that $I_5 = I_{TO} \exp(V_{BE_5}/V_T)$ and $I_6 = I_{TO} \exp(V_{BE_6}/V_T)$. Therefore,

$$V_{BE_5} - V_{BE_6} = (V_{B_5} - V_{E_5}) - (V_{B_6} - V_{E_6}) = V_T\left[\ln\left(1 + \frac{I_R}{I_Q}\right) - \ln\left(1 - \frac{I_R}{I_Q}\right)\right] \quad (5.1)$$

Since $V_{B_5} - V_{B_6} = v_m$ and $V_{E_5} - V_{E_6} = I_R R$, we have that

$$v_m - I_R R = V_T\left[\ln\left(1 + \frac{I_R}{I_Q}\right) - \ln\left(1 - \frac{I_R}{I_Q}\right)\right] \quad (5.2)$$

The power series expansion for $\ln(1 + x)$ is $\ln(1 + x) = x - x^2/2 + x^3/3 - \cdots$. Using this power series expansion, the equation above can be rewritten as

$$v_m - I_R R = V_T\left\{\left[\frac{I_R}{I_Q} - \frac{(I_R/I_Q)^2}{2} + \cdots\right] - \left[-\frac{I_R}{I_Q} - \frac{(I_R/I_Q)^2}{2} - \cdots\right]\right\}$$
$$\simeq 2V_T\frac{I_R}{I_Q} \qquad \text{for} \left(\frac{I_R}{I_Q}\right)^3 \ll 1 \tag{5.3}$$

Solving the I_R, we obtain $I_R\,[R + (2V_T/I_Q)] \simeq v_m$, so that $I_R \simeq v_m/[R + (2V_T/I_Q)]$.

If v_c is of large enough amplitude, the transistor pairs Q_1 and Q_2, and Q_3 and Q_4 will be switched from near cutoff to near full conduction. That is, when v_c is positive, Q_2 and Q_3 will be near cutoff, and Q_1 and Q_4 will carry almost all of the current of the differential-amplifier pair. This will be I_5 for the Q_1–Q_2 pair and I_6 for the Q_3–Q_4 pair. Therefore, $I_1 \simeq I_5$ and $I_4 \simeq I_6$ under these conditions. When v_c is negative, we will have that $I_2 \simeq I_5$ and $I_3 \simeq I_6$. The switching action of the two differential-amplifier transistor pairs will be essentially the case for signal amplitudes in excess of 200 mV, although even down to 100 mV it will be a good approximation.

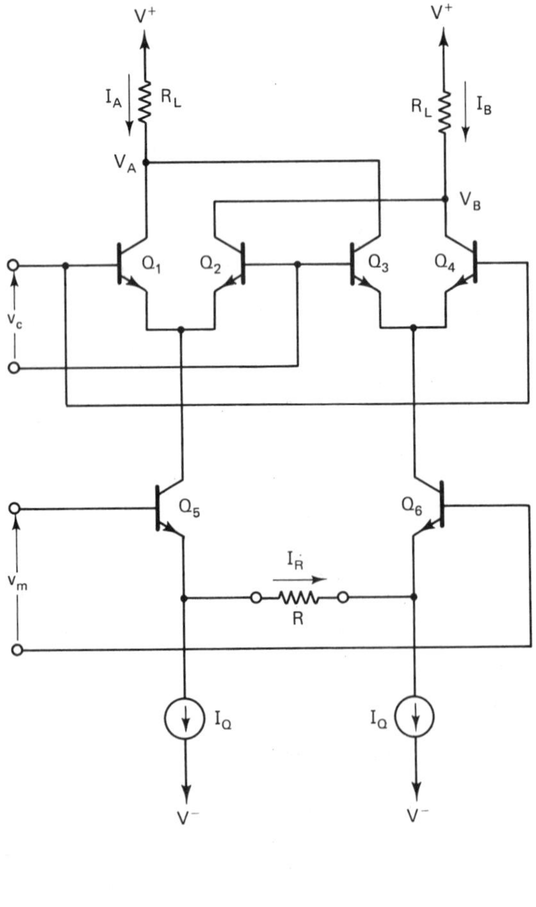

Figure 5.1 Balanced modulator–demodulator.

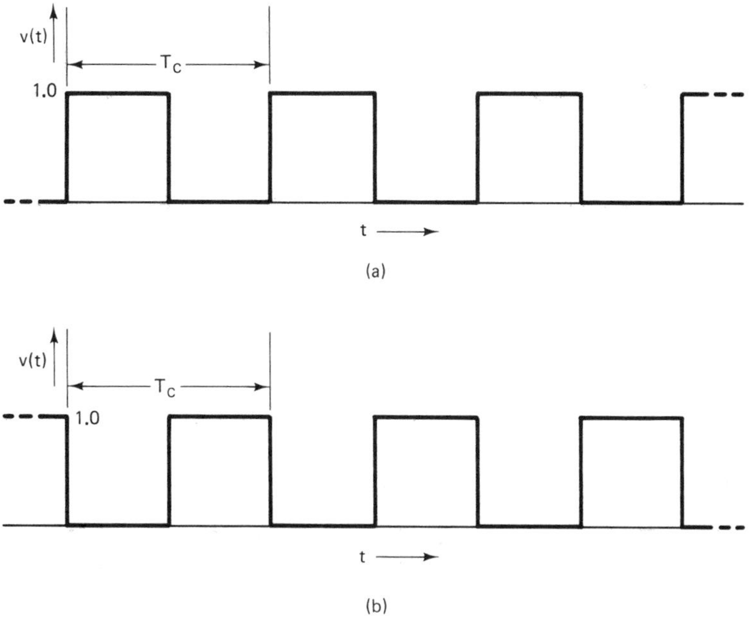

Figure 5.2 Switching functions: (a) switching function $S(t)$; (b) switching function $S(t - T_C/2)$.

5.1.1 Switching Function

The switching function $S(t)$ is shown in Figure 5.2a. It is a square wave with an amplitude of 1.0 and a period of T_C. The period of the switching function is related to the frequency of the voltage v_c applied to the "carrier" input of the modulator as $T_C = 1/f_c$. We will assume that v_c is of the form $v_c = V_C \sin \omega_c t$.

Since $S(t)$ is a square wave of unity amplitude and frequency f_c it can be represented in terms of the following Fourier series:

$$S(t) = \frac{1}{2} + \sum_{n=1}^{\infty} \frac{2}{n\pi} \sin n\omega_c t \qquad \text{where } n \text{ is an odd integer} \tag{5.4}$$

Shifting $S(t)$ by one-half of the period along the time axis will produce the function $S(t - T_C/2)$, as shown in Figure 5.2b.

If we assume a sufficiently large-signal amplitude for v_c, the collector currents of Q_1, Q_2, Q_3, and Q_4 can be expressed as

$$\begin{aligned} I_1 &= I_5 S(t) & I_3 &= I_6 S\left(t - \frac{T_C}{2}\right) \\ I_2 &= I_5 S\left(t - \frac{T_C}{2}\right) & I_4 &= I_6 S(t) \end{aligned} \tag{5.5}$$

The currents I_A and I_B will be $I_A = I_1 + I_3 = I_5S(t) + I_6S(t - T_C/2)$ and $I_B = I_2 + I_4 = I_5S(t - T_C/2) + I_6S(t)$. If we now express I_5 and I_6 as $I_5 = I_Q + I_R$ and $I_6 = I_Q - I_R$, we obtain

$$\begin{aligned} I_A &= (I_Q + I_R)S(t) + (I_Q - I_R)S\left(t - \frac{T_C}{2}\right) \\ &= I_Q\left[S(t) + S\left(t - \frac{T_C}{2}\right)\right] + I_R\left[S(t) - S\left(t - \frac{T_C}{2}\right)\right] \end{aligned} \tag{5.6}$$

and

$$\begin{aligned} I_B &= (I_Q + I_R)S\left(t - \frac{T_C}{2}\right) + (I_Q - I_R)S(t) \\ &= I_Q\left[S(t) + S\left(t - \frac{T_C}{2}\right)\right] - I_R\left[S(t) - S\left(t - \frac{T_C}{2}\right)\right] \end{aligned} \tag{5.7}$$

We now note that $S(t) + S(t - T_C/2) = 1$, and thus we have that

$$S(t) - S\left(t - \frac{T_C}{2}\right) = S(t) - [1 - S(t)] = 2S(t) - 1 = \sum_{n=1}^{\infty} \frac{4}{n\pi} \sin n\omega_c t \tag{5.8}$$

where n is an odd integer. We can now write the expressions for I_A and I_B as

$$I_A = I_Q + I_R \sum_{n=1}^{\infty} \frac{4}{n\pi} \sin n\omega_c t \tag{5.9}$$

and

$$I_B = I_Q - I_R \sum_{n=1}^{\infty} \frac{4}{n\pi} \sin n\omega_c t \tag{5.10}$$

If $v_m = V_M \sin \omega_m t$, then I_R will be

$$I_R = \frac{V_M \sin \omega_m t}{R + (2V_T/I_Q)} = \frac{V_M \sin \omega_m t}{R + 2r_{eb}}$$

where $r_{eb} = V_T/I_Q$. If we substitute this expression for I_R into the equations for I_A and I_B above, we obtain

$$I_A = I_Q + \sum_{n=1}^{\infty} \frac{4}{n\pi} \frac{V_M \sin \omega_m t \sin n\omega_c t}{R + 2r_{eb}} \tag{5.11}$$

and

$$I_B = I_Q - \sum_{n=1}^{\infty} \frac{4}{n\pi} \frac{V_M \sin \omega_m t \sin n\omega_c t}{R + 2r_{eb}} \tag{5.12}$$

If we now use the trigonometric identity that

$$\sin x \sin y = \frac{\cos (x - y) - \cos (x + y)}{2}$$

in the equation above, we obtain

$$I_A = I_Q + \sum_{n=1}^{\infty} \frac{2}{n\pi} \frac{V_M}{R + 2r_{eb}} [\cos (n\omega_c - \omega_m)t - \cos (n\omega_c + \omega_m)t] \tag{5.13}$$

and

$$I_B = I_Q - \sum_{n=1}^{\infty} \frac{2}{n\pi} \frac{V_M}{R + 2r_{eb}} [\cos (n\omega_c - \omega_m)t - \cos (n\omega_c + \omega_m)t] \tag{5.14}$$

Since $V_A = V^+ - I_A R_L$ and $V_B = V^+ - I_B R_L$, $V_O = V_B - V_A = (I_A - I_B)R_L$. Using the expressions for I_A and I_B above, we obtain for V_O the equation

$$V_O = V_B - V_A = \sum_{n=1}^{\infty} \frac{4V_M R_L}{(n\pi)(R + 2r_{eb})} [\cos (n\omega_c - \omega_m)t - \cos (n\omega_c + \omega_m)t] \tag{5.15}$$

where again we note that n is an odd integer.

5.1.2 Modulator Operation with Small Carrier Amplitudes

We will now consider the operation of this modulator–demodulator circuit for the case in which the carrier signal amplitude is small such that the Q_1–Q_2 and Q_3–Q_4 differential-amplifier transistor pairs will be operating in the approximately linear region of the transfer characteristics. For this to be the case the amplitude of the signal applied to the carrier input port v_c should not be in excess of about 25 mV.

For this case we have that the a-c collector current components of Q_1 and Q_2 will be given by $i_1 = g_f v_c$ and $i_2 = -g_f v_c = -i_1$, where g_f is the dynamic forward transfer conductance of the Q_1–Q_2 differential amplifier. Since the "quiescent" current of the Q_1–Q_2 pair is I_5, g_f will be given by $g_f = I_5/4V_T$, and $I_5 = I_Q + v_m/(R + 2r_{eb})$. We therefore have for i_1 the equation

$$\begin{aligned} i_1 = g_f v_c &= \frac{I_Q + v_m/(R + 2r_{eb})}{4V_T} v_c \\ &= \frac{I_Q v_c}{4V_T} + \frac{v_m v_c}{4V_T(R + 2r_{eb})} \end{aligned} \tag{5.16}$$

For the Q_3–Q_4 pair we will similarly have

$$i_4 = \frac{I_Q v_c}{4V_T} - \frac{v_m v_c}{4V_T(R + 2r_{eb})} \tag{5.17}$$

We again note that $i_2 = -i_1$ and also that $i_3 = -i_4$. The a-c components of $I_A = I_1 + I_3$ and $I_B = I_2 + I_4$ will therefore be

$$i_A = i_1 + i_3 = \frac{v_m v_c}{2V_T(R + 2r_{eb})} \quad \text{and} \quad i_B = i_2 + I_4 = \frac{-v_m v_c}{2V_T(R + 2r_{eb})} \tag{5.18}$$

Note here the cancellation of the $I_Q v_c/4V_T$ term in i_A and i_B.

The a-c balanced output voltage v_o of this circuit will be

$$v_o = v_b - v_a = (i_a - i_b)R_L = \frac{v_m v_c R_L}{V_T(R + 2r_{eb})} \tag{5.19}$$

If $v_c = V_C \sin \omega_c t$ and $v_m = V_M \sin \omega_m t$, we obtain

$$v_o = \frac{V_C V_M R_L}{2V_T(R + 2r_{eb})}[\cos(\omega_c - \omega_m)t - \cos(\omega_c + \omega_m)t] \tag{5.20}$$

5.2 CONVERSION TRANSFER CONDUCTANCE AND GAIN

We will define the *dynamic sideband conversion transfer conductance* y_c as the ratio of the a-c output current at the sideband frequency $nf_c \pm f_m$ to the modulation input voltage v_m at frequency f_m. We accordingly have that $y_c = i_o(nf_c \pm f_m)/v_m(f_m)$, where i_o is the a-c component of I_A or I_B. By inspection of the equations for I_A and I_B for the large carrier amplitude case ($V_C \gtrsim 50$ mV), the conversion transfer conductance will be

$$\boxed{y_c = \frac{2}{(n\pi)(R + 2r_{eb})}} \tag{5.21}$$

with respect to the sidebands at frequency $nf_c \pm f_m$. This is the conversion transfer conductance with respect to I_A. For the transfer conductance with respect to I_B the value will be the same except for a negative sign.

We note that the expressions for I_A and I_B, and therefore for V_O does not contain any term at the carrier frequency f_c. The only terms present are those of the various sidebands at $nf_c \pm f_m$.

If the output of this modulator is passed through a low-pass or bandpass filter such that only the $f_c + f_m$ and $f_c - f_m$ components of the total signal are passed through the a-c output voltage will be

$$v_o = \frac{4V_m R_L}{\pi(R + 2r_{eb})}[\cos(\omega_c - \omega_m)t - \cos(\omega_c - \omega_m)t] \tag{5.22}$$

The term at frequency $f_c - f_m$ is the lower sideband and the term at $f_c + f_m$ is the upper sideband. We again note the absence of the term at the carrier frequency. This type of signal voltage waveform is called a *double-sideband suppressed carrier* (DSB/SC) *amplitude-modulated* (AM) signal.

The dynamic sideband conversion transfer conductance for the small carrier case ($V_c \lesssim 25$ mV) can be obtained from inspection of the equations for I_A and I_B as

$$\boxed{y_c = \frac{V_C}{4V_T(R + 2r_{eb})}} \tag{5.23}$$

We note that in this case the transfer conductance will be proportional to the signal level at the carrier input port.

Inspection of the equation for v_o for the small carrier amplitude at the carrier input port situations shows that the only frequency components present will be the upper sideband frequency at $f_c + f_m$ and the lower sideband frequency at $f_c - f_m$. We therefore will have again the production of a DSB/SC AM signal.

The *sideband conversion gain* is the ratio of the output-voltage component at the sideband frequency to the modulation input voltage. In terms of the dynamic sideband conversion transfer conductance, this gain can be expressed as

$$\text{conversion gain} = \frac{v_o(nf_c \pm f_m)}{v_m(f_m)} = 2y_c R_L \tag{5.24}$$

for a balanced or double-ended output. For a single-ended (or unbalanced) output from either side of the modulator (i.e., V_A or V_B) the gain will be one-half of this or just $y_c R_L$.

5.3 AMPLITUDE MODULATION

The amplitude-modulated waveform that is produced by the modulation of the amplitude or envelope of a radio-frequency (RF) carrier can be described mathematically by $v(t) = A(t) \sin \omega_c t$, where $A(t)$ is the instantaneous amplitude of the waveform. The amplitude $A(t)$ will usually be a linear function of the modulating voltage $v_m(t)$.

If the modulating voltage is of the form $v_m(t) = V_M \sin \omega_m t$, then the amplitude function $A(t)$ can in general be written as

$$A(t) = V_C + kV_M \sin \omega_m t = V_C(1 + m \sin \omega_m t) \tag{5.25}$$

where $m = kV_M/VC$ is the *modulation index* and V_C is the amplitude of the unmodulated carrier.

As long as the modulation index m is less than unity, the envelope of the AM waveform will be a replica of the original modulating signal, and this signal can be detected or demodulated at the receiver by a simple "envelope detector." An envelope detector is a circuit that produces a voltage that is equal to or proportional to the envelope or amplitude variations of the amplitude-modulated signal. An envelope detector can be a peak detector circuit or a rectifier circuit with a suitable low-pass filter to remove the carrier frequency components of the rectified voltage.

This ease of demodulation or detection is the principal advantage of this type of amplitude-modulated waveform with $m \leqslant 1$. This type of AM waveform will be called double-sideband/large carrier (DSB/LC). The principal disadvantage of the DSB/LC signal is the inefficient use of the transmitted power.

The information in an amplitude-modulated signal is contained entirely in the sidebands. The DSB/LC voltage will be given by

$$\begin{aligned} v(t) &= A(t) \sin \omega_c t = V_C(1 + m \sin \omega_m t) \sin \omega_c t \\ &= V_C\left[\sin \omega_c t + \frac{m}{2} \cos (\omega_c - \omega_m)t - \frac{m}{2} \cos (\omega_c + \omega_m)t\right] \end{aligned} \tag{5.26}$$

The spectrum of this AM signal will consist of the carrier of amplitude V_C at f_c and the upper and lower sidebands of amplitude $mV_C/2$ at $f_c + f_m$ and $f_c - f_m$, respectively.

The amount of power contained in each spectral component of the signal is proportional to the square of the amplitude. Therefore, the ratio of the power in each sideband to the carrier power will be $m^2/4$ and the ratio of the total sideband power to the carrier power will be $m^2/2$.

Note that the carrier component is of fixed amplitude and thus carries no information. The ratio of the power in the information-carrying sidebands to the total transmitted power will thus be $(m^2/2)/[1 + (m^2/2)] = m^2/(2 + m^2)$. The maximum value that this ratio will have for the DSB/LC case will occur when $m = 1$ and will be 0.33. Thus only 33% of the total transmitted power will be in the information-carrying sidebands and the remaining 67% is in the carrier, which contains no information. In practice that maximum modulation index is often limited to a maximum value of around 0.8 to prevent any possibility of overmodulation. Overmodulation occurs whenever m exceeds unity and will lead to severe distortion of the detected signal when an envelope type of detector is used. If the maximum value of m is set at 0.8, the average value will be 0.4. For this case the sideband power will be only 7.4% of the total transmitted power. We therefore see that the system will be operated very inefficiently indeed.

In the case of the double-sideband/suppressed carrier (DSB/SC) signal, all of the power is in the sidebands, so the efficiency can approach 100% for the case of complete carrier suppression. The DSB/SC system does, however, have the disadvantage of not being able to utilize the simple envelope detection method of demodulation.

In both the DSB/SC and the DSB/LC systems the same information is contained in each of the two sidebands; that is, whatever information is contained in the lower sideband is exactly repeated in the upper sideband. As a result, the total bandwidth involved in the double-sideband systems is twice as much as is really needed for the transmission of the information. A system that uses only one sideband is called a *single-sideband suppressed carrier* (SSB/SC) system. This type of system represents the ultimate in efficiency with respect to both power and bandwidth.

5.3.1 Modulation and Demodulation Circuits for DSB/SC AM Signals

In Figure 5.3 a modulation circuit for DSB/SC AM is shown. The bandpass filter has a passband that includes the frequency range from $f_c - f_m$ to $f_c + f_m$, but does not include the sidebands of the carrier harmonic frequencies, such as $3f_c \pm f_m$, $5f_c \pm f_m$, and so on.

If the modulator is well balanced, there will be very little carrier feedthrough and there will thus be almost complete suppression of the carrier and the output will just be at the carrier sideband frequencies $f_c - f_m$ and $f_c + f_m$. The demodulator is very similar to the modulator, as shown in Figure 5.4, and indeed the same type of IC can be used.

The DSB/SC signal is applied to the modulation input port and a locally generated large amplitude ($\gtrsim$100 mV) signal at a frequency f_c' which is nominally equal

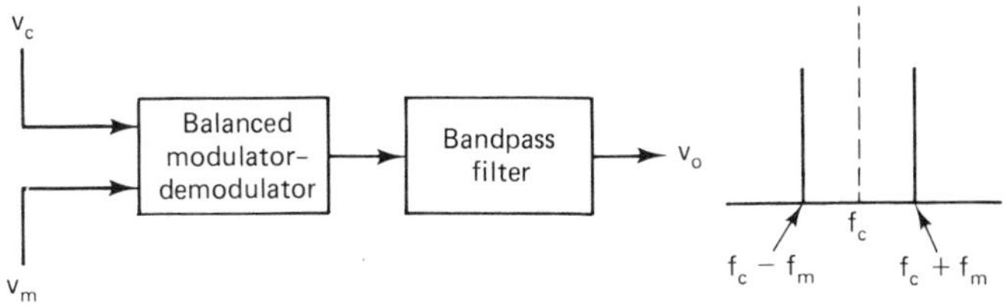

Figure 5.3 Balanced modulator circuit to produce DSB/SC AM.

to the carrier frequency is injected into the carrier input port. The nonlinear mixing action that occurs in the modulator–demodulator will result in an output voltage that includes the following frequency components: $f_c' - (f_c \pm f_m) = f_c' - f_c + f_m$ and $f_c' - f_c - f_m$, and $f_c' + (f_c \pm f_m) = f_c' + f_c + f_m$ and $f_c' + f_c - f_m$. In addition, there will also be components involving various odd multiples of f_c'.

If this output voltage now goes through a low-pass filter with a cutoff frequency f_1 such that $f_m < f_1 < 2f_c - f_m$, we obtain at the output only $f_m \pm (f_c' - f_c)$. We see that for an exact recovery of the original modulating waveform the "reinjected" carrier frequency must be exactly equal to the original suppressed carrier frequency f_c. If there is any difference between these two frequencies, the detected signal will be given by

$$v(t) = V_M \cos(\omega_m t + \Delta\omega_c t) + V_M \cos(\omega_m t - \Delta\omega_c t) = 2 V_M \cos \omega_m t \cos \Delta\omega_c t \tag{5.27}$$

where $\Delta\omega_c = \omega_c' - \omega_c$. Thus the detected signal will be amplitude modulated at the difference frequency $\Delta f_c = f_c' - f_c$. If there is exact frequency synchronism, but there is still a phase angle difference θ between the original carrier and the reinjected carrier we will have that the detected signal will be $v(t) = V_M \cos \omega_m t \cos \theta$. This will not be a serious problem as long as θ is constant and is not very large. However, if θ were to approach 90°, this would result in a severe reduction in the amplitude of the detected signal.

To facilitate the exact frequency and phase matching of the reinjected carrier at the receiver with the original carrier at the transmitter, a small-amplitude "pilot carrier" is often transmitted either at the original carrier frequency or at some integer multiple thereof. This pilot carrier serves as a reference for the locally generated carrier in order that it exactly match the original carrier in frequency and also be very close to the phase of the original carrier.

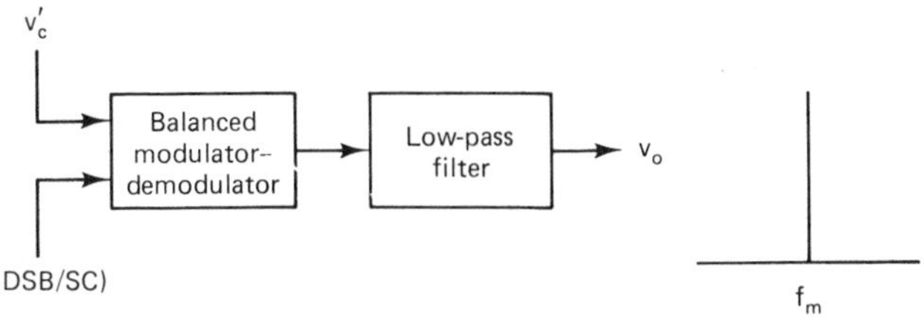

Figure 5.4 Circuit for the demodulation of a DSB/SC AM signal.

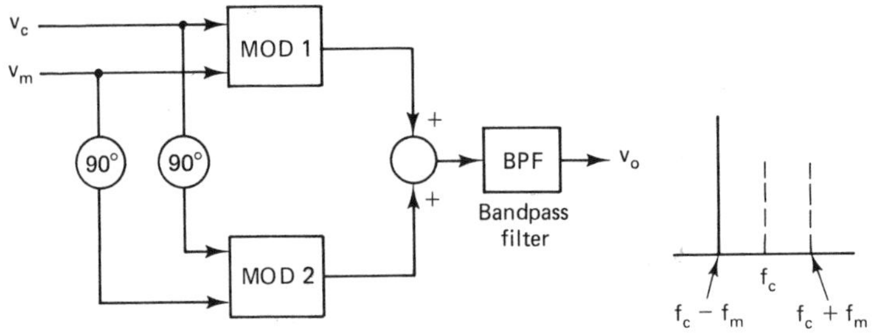

Figure 5.5 Modulator circuit for a SSB/SC signal.

5.3.2 Modulation and Demodulation Circuits for SSB/SC AM Signals

In Figure 5.5 a modulation circuit for the generation of a SSB/SC AM signal is shown. It might at first be thought that the simplest way of producing a SSB/SC signal would be to just filter out one of the sidebands using a bandpass filter. In many cases this is indeed done, especially in cases where the sidebands extend over a relatively wide frequency range.

In the case of television broadcasting this method of filtering out one of the sidebands is indeed done. Since it is not possible to have a wide bandwidth filter that will sharply cut off at the carrier frequency, part of one sideband (the lower sideband) is transmitted along with the entire upper sideband. The video bandwidth is 4.5 MHz, so that the total bandwidth that would be required if both sidebands were to be transmitted would be 9.0 MHz. The bandpass characteristic at the transmitter is such that the entire 4.5-MHz upper sideband is transmitted, but only 1.25 MHz of the lower sideband is transmitted, so that the total bandwidth required for the video portion of the transmission is now only 5.75 MHz. This technique of transmitting all of one sideband and a small part of the other sideband is called *vestigial sideband transmission*. The actual bandwidth allotted per TV channel is 6.0 MHz, to allow room for the audio portion of the signal.

In the circuit of Figure 5.5 the removal of one of the sidebands occurs not by the action of a bandpass filter, but rather by the canceling effect that results from the 90° phase shift given to both the carrier and signal input voltages supplied to one of the modulators. In many cases this method is chosen because it would be very difficult to filter out one of the sidebands without severely affecting the other sideband.

The output voltage of modulator 1 can be expressed as

$$v_{o_1} = \sum_{n=1}^{\infty} \frac{K}{n} [\cos (n\omega_c - \omega_m)t - \cos (n\omega_c + \omega_m)t] \tag{5.28}$$

where $K = 4V_M R_L/\pi(R + 2r_{eb})$ and n is an odd integer.

The output voltage of modulator 2 will be the same as that given above except for the 90° phase shift given to both the carrier and modulation input signals. Noting that $\cos (x \pm 180°) = -\cos x$ we have that

$$v_{o_2} = \sum_{n=1}^{\infty} \frac{K}{n} [\cos (n\omega_c - \omega_m)t + \cos (n\omega_c + \omega_m)t] \tag{5.29}$$

When these two voltages are added together, we obtain

$$v_o = v_{o_1} + v_{o_2} = 2 \sum_{n=1}^{\infty} \frac{K}{n} [\cos (n\omega_c - \omega_m)t] \tag{5.30}$$

We therefore see that the upper sideband has canceled out so that we obtain a SSB/SC signal with just the lower sideband.

In the single-sideband modulator circuit just discussed the 90° phase shift given to the carrier and modulating input signals of modulator 2 is of the same algebraic sign for both inputs. If the 90° phase shifts of these two signals are of opposite algebraic sign, we obtain for v_{o_2} the expression

$$\begin{aligned} v_{o_2} &= \sum_{n=1}^{\infty} \frac{K}{n} [\cos [(n\omega_c - \omega_m)t + 180°] - \cos (n\omega_c + \omega_m)t] \\ &= \sum_{n=1}^{\infty} \frac{K}{n} [-\cos (n\omega_c - \omega_m)t - \cos (n\omega_c + \omega_m)t] \end{aligned} \tag{5.31}$$

When this voltage is added to v_{o_1} we now obtain

$$v_o = v_{o_1} + v_{o_2} = -2 \sum_{n=1}^{\infty} \frac{K}{n} [\cos (n\omega_c + \omega_m)t] \tag{5.32}$$

so that now we have a SSB/SC signal with just the upper sideband present.

In Figure 5.6 a demodulator circuit for a SSB/SC signal is shown. The reinjected carrier signal is at frequency f_c', which is nominally the same as the carrier frequency f_c. The low-pass filter has a passband that cuts off somewhere beyond f_m, but well below f_c.

If the carrier and signal input voltages are $v_c'(t) = V_C' \sin \omega_c' t$ and $v_s(t) = V_S \sin (\omega_c - \omega_m)t$, respectively, at the output of the low-pass filter we will have

$$v_o(t) = \frac{4 V_S R_L}{\pi(R + 2r_{eb})} \cos (\omega_m t + \Delta\omega_c t) \tag{5.33}$$

where $\Delta\omega_c = \omega_c' - \omega_c$. Thus in order to obtain an exact replica of the original modulating signal it is necessary to have the reinjected carrier frequency exactly

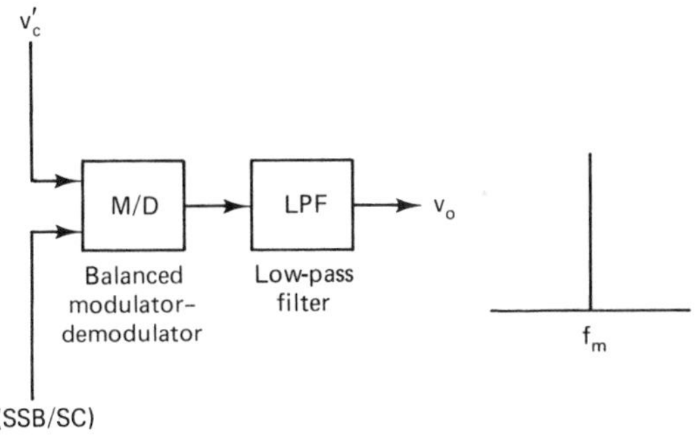

Figure 5.6 Demodulator circuit for a SSB/SC signal.

match the original carrier frequency. Any difference in the two frequencies will result in a frequency shift in the demodulated output by an amount $\Delta f = f_c' - f_c$.

5.4 FREQUENCY MODULATION

For a frequency-modulated (FM) waveform the instantaneous frequency of a carrier signal is varied or modulated by a modulating signal. The modulation is usually done in a way such that the variation or shift in the carrier frequency will be a linear function of the modulating voltage.

If the modulating signal is of the form $v_m(t) = V_M \sin \omega_m t$, the instantaneous carrier frequency will be $f(t) = f_c + k\, V_M \sin \omega_m t = f_c + \Delta f \sin \omega_m t$, where f_c is the unmodulated carrier frequency and Δf is the *peak frequency deviation*.

The radian frequency ω of a sinusoidal waveform is related to the phase angle θ by $\omega = d\theta/dt$, so that $\theta = \int_0^t \omega\, dt$. Applying this to the modulated carrier frequency, we obtain

$$\theta = \int_0^t \omega\, dt = \int_0^t (\omega_c + \Delta\omega \sin \omega_m t)\, dt = \omega_c t + \frac{\Delta\omega}{\omega_m} \cos \omega_m t \tag{5.34}$$

$$= \omega_c t + \beta \cos \omega_m t$$

where $\beta = \Delta\omega/\omega_m = \Delta f/f_m =$ *modulation index*. The frequency-modulated signal can be written as

$$v(t) = V_C \sin \theta(t) = V_C \sin (\omega_c t + \beta \cos \omega_m t) \tag{5.35}$$

If we now apply the trigonometric identity that $\sin(x + y) = \sin x \cos y + \cos x \sin y$, the equation for $v(t)$ can be written as

$$v(t) = V_C[\sin \omega_c t \cos(\beta \cos \omega_m t) + \cos \omega_c t \sin(\beta \cos \omega_m t)] \tag{5.36}$$

For small values of the modulation index such that $\beta \leqslant 0.3$, we can use the approximation that $\cos(\beta \cos \omega_m t) \simeq 1$ and $\sin(\beta \cos \omega_m t) \simeq \beta \cos \omega_m t$. We can therefore express $v(t)$ approximately as

$$v(t) \simeq V_C(\sin \omega_c t + \beta \cos \omega_m t \cos \omega_c t)$$

$$\simeq V_C\left[\sin \omega_c t + \frac{\beta}{2} \cos(\omega_c + \omega_m)t + \frac{\beta}{2} \cos(\omega_c - \omega_m)t\right] \tag{5.37}$$

This type of frequency modulation with small values of modulation index ($\beta \lesssim 0.3$) is called *narrow-bandwidth frequency modulation* (NBFM).

We will now compare the expression just obtained for the NBFM signal with that obtained earlier for the DSB/LC AM signal, which can be expressed as

$$v(t) = V_C(1 + m \cos \omega_m t) \cos \omega_c t$$

$$= V_C\left[\cos \omega_c t + \frac{m}{2} \cos(\omega_c - \omega_m)t + \frac{m}{2} \cos(\omega_c + \omega_m)t\right] \tag{5.38}$$

after noting that $\cos x \cos y = \frac{1}{2} \cos (x - y) + \frac{1}{2} \cos (x + y)$.

We see that the spectra of the two cases are the same with a carrier at f_c, an upper sideband at $f_c + f_m$, and a lower sideband at $f_c - f_m$. The principal difference in the two signals is that in the **NBFM** case the carrier is in phase quadradure with respect to the sidebands; that is, at a reference time $t = 0$ there is a 90° phase angle between the carrier and the sideband phasors.

In Figure 5.7 a number of phasor diagrams are presented showing the relation-

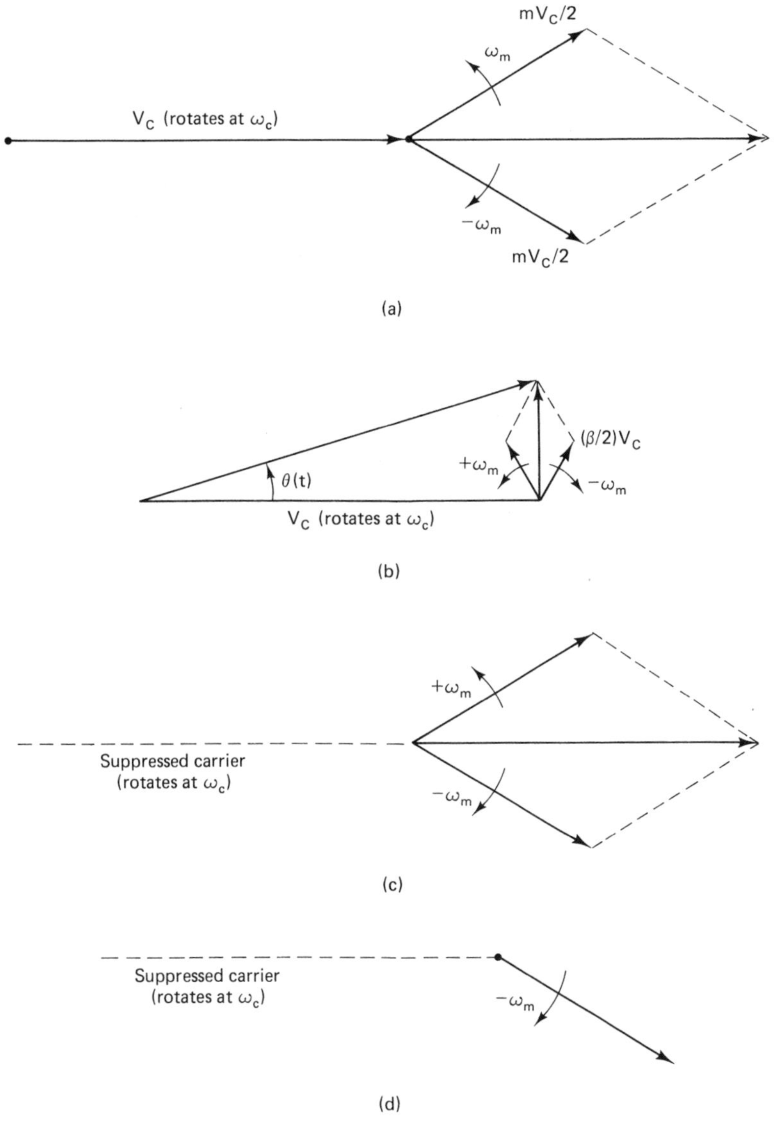

Figure 5.7 Phasor diagram for various types of modulation: (a) DSB/LC AM; (b) NBFM; (c) DSB/SC AM; (d) SSB/SC AM.

ships between DSB/LC AM, DSB/SC AM, SSB/SC AM, and NBFM. For these diagrams the phasor representing the carrier is used as the reference and the phasor rotational angular velocities are taken with respect to the carrier phasor, which itself rotates at an angular velocity of ω_c. Notice in particular the relationship between DSB/LC AM and NBFM. For the FM case note that the resultant phasor has an angular velocity that is not constant with time, but rather will fluctuate about an average value of ω_c at a rate determined by the modulating frequency ω_m.

From the phasor diagram we see that the instantaneous phase of the resultant signal with respect to the unmodulated carrier $\theta(t)$ will vary with time as $\theta(t) \simeq \beta \cos \omega_m t$. We therefore see again that there is a close interrelationship between *phase modulation* and *frequency modulation*.

5.4.1 NBFM Modulator Circuit

Narrow-bandwidth FM can be generated using a balanced modulator circuit, as shown in Figure 5.8. The modulating signal $v(t) = V_M \sin \omega_m t$ first goes through an integrator circuit to produce $\int v(t)\, dt = (V_M/\omega_m) \cos (\omega_m t)$. This modulating voltage then mixes with the carrier in the balanced modulator. The carrier signal is $v_c(t) = V_C \sin \omega_c t$, but after passing through the 90° phase shift circuit becomes $V_C \cos \omega_c t$ and is then applied to the carrier input port of the modulator.

The output voltage of the modulator then goes through a bandpass filter to remove the sidebands of the carrier harmonic frequencies, such as $3f_c \pm f_m$, $5f_c \pm f_m$, and so on. At the output of the bandpass filter we will have $v_1(t) = V_O[\cos (\omega_c - \omega_m)t + \cos (\omega_c + \omega_m)t]$. This voltage is then added to the carrier to produce the signal given by

$$\begin{aligned} v_o(t) &= V_C \sin \omega_c t + V_O[\cos (\omega_c + \omega_m)t + \cos (\omega_c - \omega_m)t] \\ &= V_C\left[\sin \omega_c t + \frac{\beta}{2} \cos (\omega_c + \omega_m)t + \frac{\beta}{2} \cos (\omega_c - \omega_m)t\right] \end{aligned} \tag{5.39}$$

where $\beta = 2V_O/V_C$ = FM modulation index. Comparison of this signal with that obtained earlier for NBFM shows that it is identical to the NBFM expression.

The circuit for NBFM can also be used as the basis for generating wide-bandwidth FM. This can be accomplished by taking the NBFM signal and feeding it into a frequency multiplier circuit. If the signal supplied to the frequency multiplier is $v_i(t) = V_C \sin (\omega_c t + \beta \cos \omega_m t)$, the output voltage will be of the form $v_o(t) =$

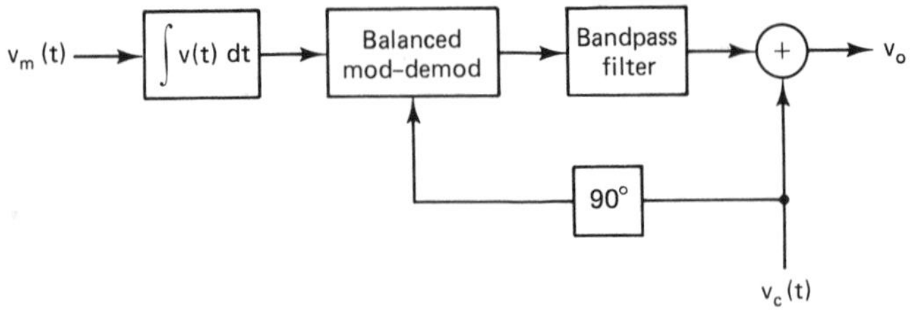

Figure 5.8 NBFM modulator circuit.

$V'_C \sin(n\omega_c t + n\beta \cos \omega_m t)$. We see that the modulation index is now $\beta' = n\,\beta$. The peak frequency deviation Δf will now be given by $\Delta f' = n\,\Delta f = n\beta f_m$.

5.4.2 FM Demodulator

The objective of an FM demodulator or detector is to produce an output voltage that is directly proportional to the instantaneous frequency deviation away from the unmodulated carrier frequency. An FM demodulator circuit is shown in Figure 5.9. The FM signal first goes through a limiter to remove any amplitude modulation that may be present. This amplitude modulation may be the result of noise, interference, variations in incoming signal strength, or variations in amplifier gain. The amplitude modulation may also be present intentionally, such as in the case of television broadcasting wherein the video signal is carried by the amplitude modulation and the sound by frequency modulation.

After the signal passes through the limiter circuit it is split, part of it going directly to the carrier input port of the balanced modulator/demodulator. The other part of the signal goes through the *quadrature circuit* and then is fed to the modulation port.

The quadrature circuit consists of a small capacitor C_2 and a parallel resonant circuit represented here by L_1, C_1, and G_1. The admittance of the resonant circuit can be written as $Y = G_1(1 + j2Q_o\delta)$, where δ is the fractional detuning as given by $\delta = (f - f_o)/f_o = \Delta f/f_o$. The voltage transfer ratio of the quadrature circuit will be

$$T = \frac{v_2}{v_1} = \frac{1/Y}{(1/Y) + (1/j\omega C_2)} = \frac{j\omega C_2}{j\omega C_2 + Y} = \frac{j\omega C_2}{G_1(1 + j2Q_o\delta) + j\omega C_2} \tag{5.40}$$

If $(\omega C_2)^2 \ll G_1^2$ the transfer ratio can be written approximately as

$$T = \frac{v_2}{v_1} \simeq \frac{j\omega C_2}{G(1 + j2Q_o\delta)} \tag{5.41}$$

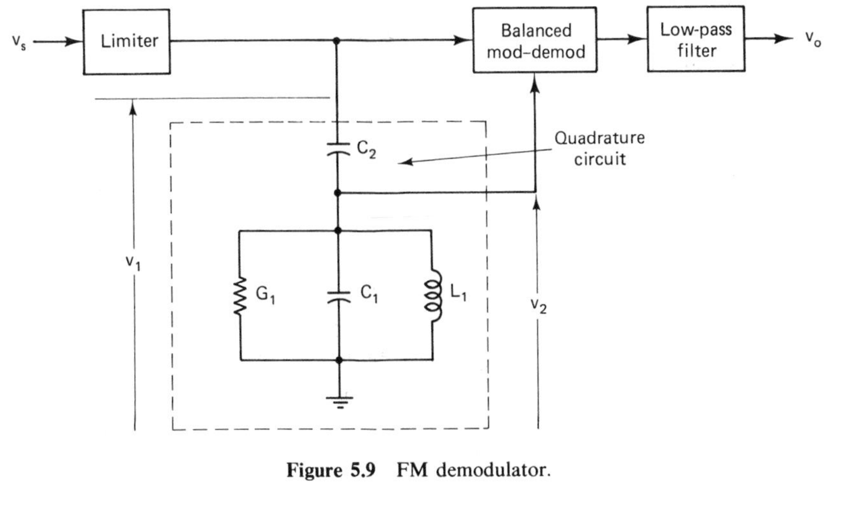

Figure 5.9 FM demodulator.

The angle of the transfer ratio $\underline{/T} = \phi$ will be $\phi = (\pi/2) - \tan^{-1}(2Q_o\delta)$. Since the 3-dB bandwidth of the tuned circuit is related to the Q-factor as $BW = f_o/Q_o$, we will have that $2Q_o\delta = 2Q_o\ \Delta f/f_o = 2\ \Delta f/BW$, where $\Delta f = f - f_o$ is the frequency deviation from the resonant frequency of the tuned circuit.

The equation for the phase shift ϕ can now be expressed as $\phi = (\pi/2) - \tan^{-1}(2\ \Delta f/BW)$. For $(\Delta f/BW)^2 \ll 1$ we can rewrite this expression as $\phi = (\pi/2) - 2\ \Delta f/BW$. We see that the phase angle ϕ will be 90° when $f = f_o$, and will vary linearly from that value as the frequency increases or decreases.

The input signals to the balanced modulator/demodulator can be expressed as $v_1 = V_1 \sin(\omega_c + \Delta\omega)t$ and $v_2 = V_2 \sin(\omega_c t + \Delta\omega t + \phi)$. We will assume that the resonant frequency of the tuned circuit f_o is equal to the unmodulated carrier frequency f_c. The output voltage of the modulator–demodulator then passes through a low-pass filter. The filter has a cutoff frequency such that the modulation frequency is passed through, but the carrier frequency and harmonics thereof are rejected.

At the output of the filter we will have only the lowest-frequency difference term as given by

$$\begin{aligned} v_o &= V_o \cos[(\omega_c + \Delta\omega)t - (\omega_c + \Delta\omega)t - \phi] \\ &= V_o \cos\phi = V_o \cos\left(\frac{\pi}{2} - \frac{2\ \Delta f}{BW}\right) \\ &= V_o \sin\frac{2\ \Delta f}{BW} \end{aligned} \tag{5.42}$$

Since $\sin x \simeq x$ for small x we will have that $v_o \simeq V_o\ (2\ \Delta f/BW)$ for $(\Delta f/BW)^2 \ll 1$. Thus we see that the objective of the FM detector has been achieved in that an output voltage is produced that is a linear function of the frequency deviation of the FM signal away from the carrier frequency.

5.5 FREQUENCY DOUBLER

The balanced modulator–demodulator can also be used as a frequency doubler. A frequency-doubler circuit is shown in Figure 5.10. The input signal represented by $v_s = V_S \sin \omega_s t$ is supplied to both the carrier and the modulation input ports. Since $f_c = f_m = f_s$ in this case, the output signal will be given by

$$v_o = \sum_{n=1}^{\infty} \frac{4V_S R_L}{(n\pi)(R + 2r_{eb})} [\cos(n\omega_s - \omega_s)t - \cos(n\omega_s + \omega_s)t] \tag{5.43}$$

where n is an odd integer. There will therefore be frequency components at d-c, $2f_s$, $4f_s$, $6f_s$, and so on.

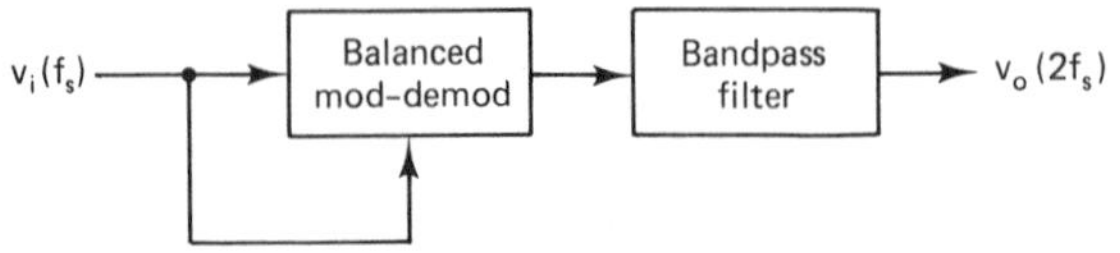

Figure 5.10 Frequency-doubler circuit.

If the output is now passed through a bandpass filter that passes the $2f_s$ component of the modulator output but rejects the higher harmonics, we obtain

$$\begin{aligned} v_o(t) &= \frac{-4V_S R_L}{\pi(R+2r_{eb})}(\cos 2\omega_s t)\left(1-\frac{1}{3}\right) \\ &= \frac{-8V_S R_L}{3\pi(R+2r_{eb})}\cos 2\omega_s t \end{aligned} \tag{5.44}$$

The voltage-doubler conversion gain will be given as

$$\text{doubler conversion gain} = \frac{v_o(2f_s)}{v_s(f_s)} = \frac{8R_L}{3\pi(R+2r_{eb})} \tag{5.45}$$

5.6 PHASE DETECTOR USING THE BALANCED MODULATOR–DEMODULATOR

The balanced modulator–demodulator circuit can be used as a phase detector. The basic phase detector circuit is shown in Figure 5.11. The two signals whose phase is to be compared are represented by $v_c = V_C \sin \omega t$ supplied to the carrier input port and $v_m = V_M \sin(\omega t + \phi)$ supplied to the modulation input port.

We will assume that the amplitude of the voltage applied to the carrier input port is large enough ($\gtrsim$100 mV) such that we have the same relationships for the currents through Q_1, Q_2, Q_3, and Q_4 as given before in terms of the switching functions $S(t)$ and $S(t - T/2)$. These relationships are $I_1 = I_5\, S(t)$, $I_2 = I_5 S(t - T/2)$, $I_3 = I_6 S(t - T/2)$, and $I_4 = I_6 S(t)$, where T is the period of the input voltage.

For this analysis we will consider the case in which there is a short-circuit connection between the emitters of Q_5 and Q_6 (i.e., $R = 0$). If the voltage applied to the modulation input port is of sufficiently large amplitude such that $V_M \gtrsim 100$ mV, the transistor pair of Q_5 and Q_6 will be operating essentially in a switching mode with I_5 and I_6 being given by $I_5 = 2I_Q S(t + \Delta t)$ and $I_6 = 2I_Q S(t + \Delta t - T/2)$, where $\Delta t = \phi/\omega$. Note that $v_m = V_M \sin(\omega t + \phi)$ can be reexpressed as $v_m = V_M \sin \omega(t + \phi/\omega) = V_M \sin \omega(t + \Delta t)$, so that a phase shift ϕ corresponds to a time delay of $\Delta t = \phi/\omega$.

If we now insert the equations for I_5 and I_6 into the equations for I_1 through I_4 given above, we obtain

$$\begin{aligned} I_1 &= 2I_Q S(t+\Delta t)S(t) & I_2 &= 2I_Q S(t+\Delta t)S\left(t-\frac{T}{2}\right) \\ I_3 &= 2I_Q S\left(t+\Delta t-\frac{T}{2}\right)S\left(t-\frac{T}{2}\right) & I_4 &= 2I_Q S\left(t+\Delta t-\frac{T}{2}\right)S(t) \end{aligned} \tag{5.46}$$

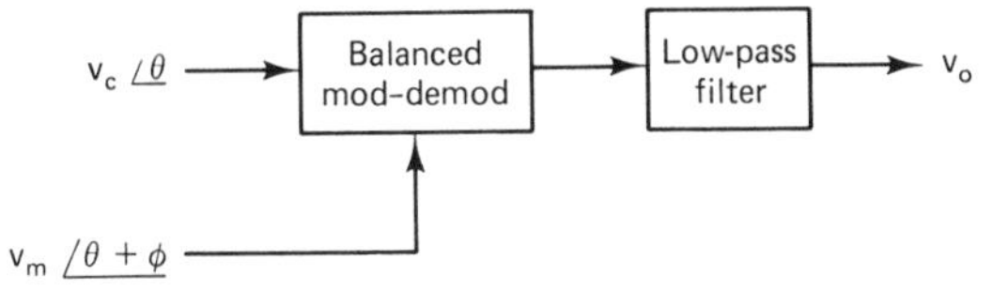

Figure 5.11 Phase detector.

Combining these four currents to obtain I_A and I_B gives

$$I_A = I_1 + I_3 = 2I_Q\left[S(t)S(t+\Delta t) + S\left(t - \frac{T}{2}\right)S\left(t + \Delta t - \frac{T}{2}\right)\right] \tag{5.47}$$

and

$$I_B = I_2 + I_4 = 2I_Q\left[S\left(t - \frac{T}{2}\right)S(t+\Delta t) + S(t)S\left(t + \Delta t - \frac{T}{2}\right)\right] \tag{5.48}$$

By inspection of the various switching functions it is easy to verify that the average value (averaged over one or an integer number of periods) of the switching functions will be given by

$$\begin{aligned} \overline{S(t)S(t+\Delta t)} &= \frac{1}{2} - \frac{|\Delta t|}{T} \\ \overline{S(t - T/2)S\left(t + \Delta t - \frac{T}{2}\right)} &= \frac{1}{2} - \frac{|\Delta t|}{T} \quad \text{for } |\Delta t| < \frac{T}{2} \\ \overline{S(t+\Delta t)S\left(t - \frac{T}{2}\right)} &= \frac{|\Delta t|}{T} \\ \overline{S\left(t + \Delta t - \frac{T}{2}\right)S(t)} &= \frac{|\Delta t|}{T} \end{aligned} \tag{5.49}$$

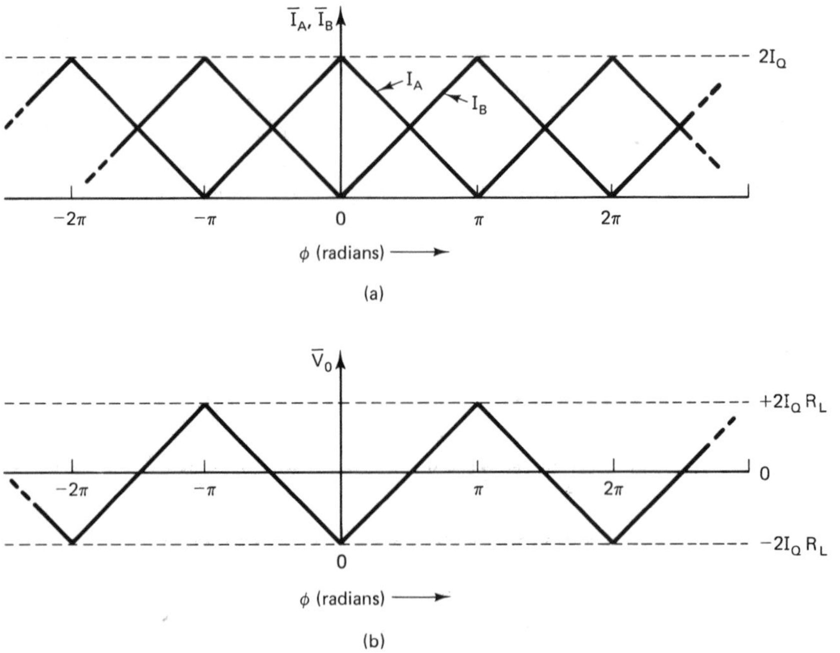

Figure 5.12 (a) $\overline{I}_A$ and $\overline{I}_B$ versus ϕ; (b) $\overline{V}_O$ versus ϕ.

As a result, we can write the average or d-c values of I_A and I_B as

$$\overline{I_A} = 2I_Q\left(1 - \frac{2|\Delta t|}{T}\right) \quad \text{and} \quad \overline{I_B} = 2I_Q\frac{2|\Delta t|}{T} \tag{5.50}$$

Since $\Delta t = \phi/\omega$ and $\omega = 2\pi f = 2\pi/T$, we have that $\Delta t/T = \phi/2\pi$. We can therefore express the average values of I_A and I_B in terms of the phase angle ϕ as

$$\overline{I_A} = 2I_Q\left(1 - \frac{|\phi|}{\pi}\right) \quad \text{and} \quad \overline{I_B} = \frac{2I_Q|\phi|}{\pi} \tag{5.51}$$

In these equations the phase angle ϕ is restricted to the range of $-\pi \leqslant \phi \leqslant +\pi$. Outside this range the correct result can be obtained by adding or subtracting $2\pi n$ to the phase angle to put the result back into the range $-\pi$ to $+\pi$, with n being an integer.

In Figure 5.12a a graph is presented showing the variation of $\overline{I_A}$ and $\overline{I_B}$ as a function of the phase angle ϕ.

If a balanced or doubled-ended output is taken such that $\overline{V_o} = \overline{V_A} - \overline{V_B} = (\overline{I_B} - \overline{I_A})R_L$, we obtain $\overline{V_O} = 2I_QR_L[(2|\phi|/\pi) - 1]$ for $-\pi < \phi < +\pi$. In Figure 5.12b the variation of $\overline{V_O}$ as a function of ϕ is shown. The *phase angle-to-voltage conversion coefficient* will be $K_\phi = |dV_O/d\phi| = (4/\pi)I_QR_L$ (V/rad).

PROBLEMS

5.1. Given a LM1496 suppressed carrier modulator circuit (Figure P5.1); $R_{\text{LOAD}} = 3.9$ kΩ.

(a) Find the quiescent currents for $V^+ = +12$ V and $V^- = -8$ V. (*Ans.*: I_5 through $I_9 = 1.0$ mA, I_1 through $I_4 = 0.5$ mA)

(b) If $R_{\text{GAIN ADJUST}} = R_{23} = 1.0$ kΩ and $V_7 - V_8 = \pm 500$ mV:

(1) Find the signal port transfer admittance at low frequencies. (*Ans.*: 0.952 mS)

(2) Find the sideband conversion transfer admittance at low frequencies and a carrier amplitude of 200 mV, or greater. (*Ans.*: 0.606 mS)

(3) Compare these values with the manufacturer's specifications.

(c) Repeat part (b) for $R_{\text{GAIN ADJUST}} = 100$ Ω. [*Ans.*: (1) 6.67 mS; (2) 4.24 mS]

(d) Find the conversion gain for a single-ended output with $R_{\text{GAIN ADJUST}} = 1.0$ kΩ and $f = 10$ kHz. (*Ans.*: $A_{V\ \text{CONVERSION}} = 2.365$ for each sideband)

(e) If $R_{\text{LOAD}} = 3.9$ kΩ and $C_{\text{TOTAL}} = 2.0$ pF, repeat part (d) for a frequency of 10 MHz. (*Ans.*: $A_{V\ \text{CONVERSION}} = 2.12$ for each sideband)

(f) If $R_{\text{GAIN ADJUST}} = 0$ and $v_c = v_s$ is a small signal (less than 30 mV), find the coefficient K in the relationship for the frequency doubler as given by $V_O(2f_i) = K[V_i(f_i)]^2$, where V_O and V_i are the peak values (amplitudes) of the output and input voltages, respectively. The load resistance R_{LOAD} is 3.9 kΩ. (*Ans.*: $K = 780\ \text{V}^{-1}$, single-ended output)

(g) For the phase detector application with $R_{\text{GAIN ADJUST}} = 0$, $v_c(t) = 100$ mV sin ωt and $v_s(t) = 100$ mV sin ωt, find R_L such that $dV_O/d\phi = 1.0$ V/rad, where $V_O = V_B - V_A = (I_A - I_B)R_L$. (*Ans.*: 785 Ω)

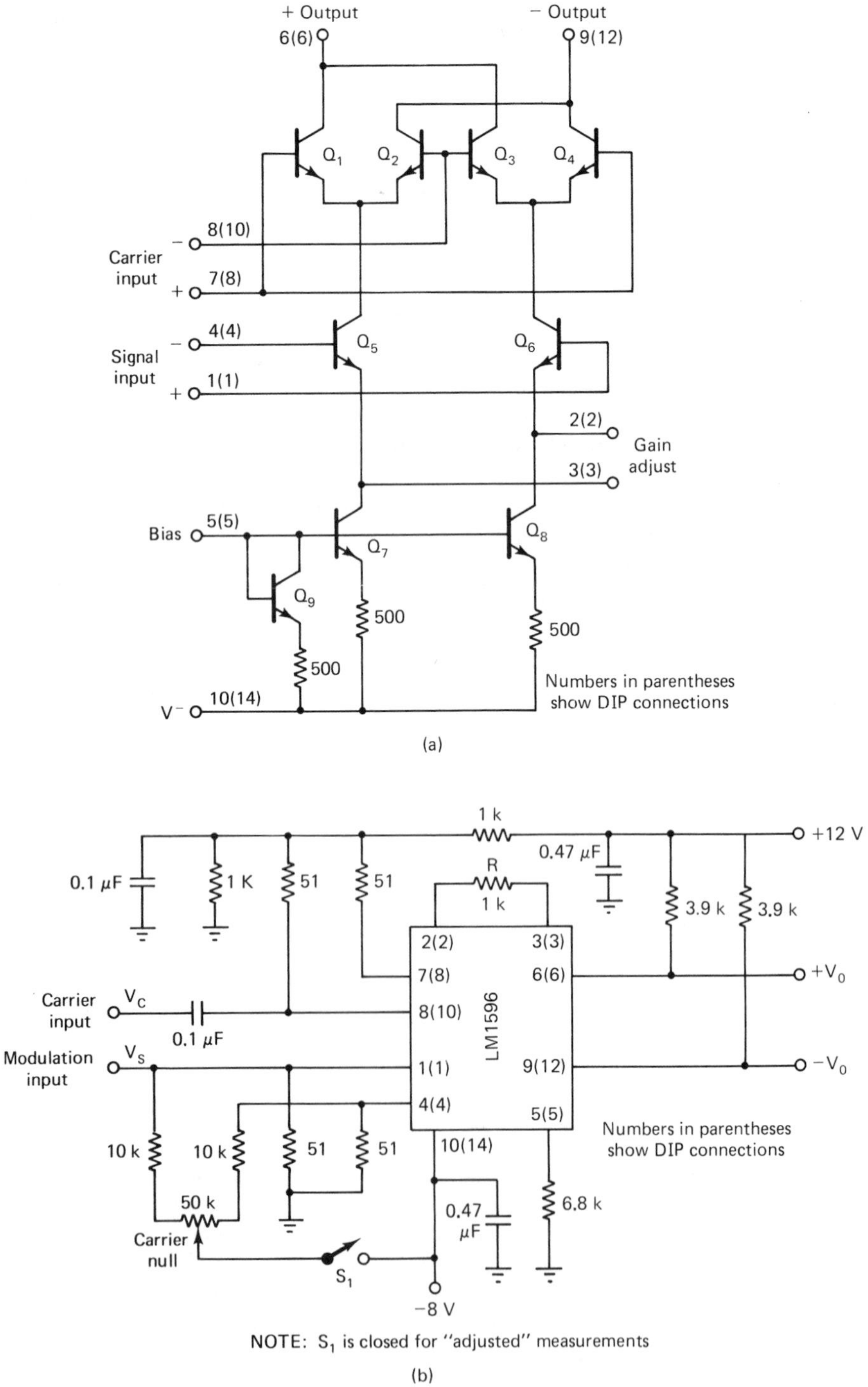

Figure P5.1 (National Semiconductor)

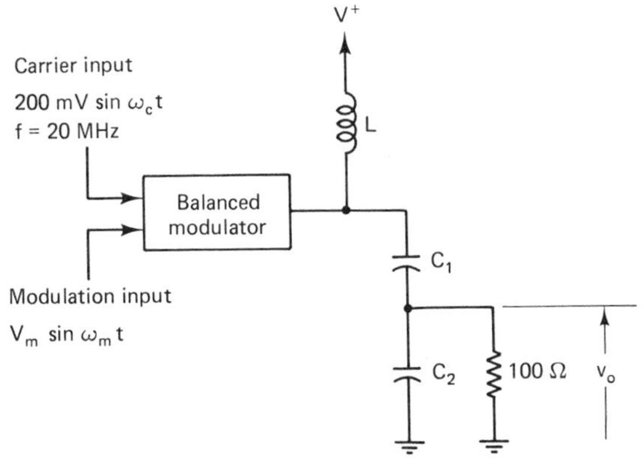

Figure P5.2

(h) Find V_O for ϕ values of 0, 45, 90, 135, and 180° for the circuit of part (g). (*Ans.*: −1.571, −0.785, 0, +0.785, +1.571 V)

(i) Repeat part (h) for a phase-to-voltage conversion coefficient of 20 mV/deg. (*Ans.*: $R_L = 900\ \Omega$)

5.2. Given at 20 MHz, the sideband conversion transfer admittance $= y_f = 2.0 + j2.0$ mS, and the output admittance $= y_o = 100 + j1000\ \mu$S (see Figure P5.2). The modulation input is a small signal with frequencies ranging up to 250 kHz.

(a) Design an output circuit for maximum sideband power to load (assuming an ideal inductor). (*Ans.*: $C_1 = 61.9$ pF, $C_2 = 557$ pF, $L = 995$ nH)

(b) Find the sideband conversion gain, $v_{o\,(\text{sideband})}/v_{\text{mod}}$. (*Ans.*: $1.414\underline{/45°}$)

5.3. (*Phase detector*) Given a phase detector circuit. Assume all transistors identical unless otherwise indicated. Use Figure 5.1 with $R = 0$ for the phase detector.

(a) If the d-c voltage drop across the load resistor R_L under quiescent conditions (i.e., no signal input) is 2.0 V, find the value of the constant in the equation $V_{O\,(\text{dc})} = -(\text{constant})\ V_M \cos \phi$, assuming that V_M is small (30 mV or less). (*Ans.*: constant = 50.9)

(b) If V_M is 10 mV rms, find the relationship between $V_{O\,(\text{dc})}$ and the phase angle ϕ. (*Ans.*: $V_{O\,(\text{dc})} = -0.720$ V $\cos \phi$)

(c) If the d-c voltage drop across the load resistance R_L under quiescent conditions is 2.0 V, and V_M is a large signal (100 mV or more), show that $V_{O\,(\text{dc})}$ will be given by $V_{O\,(\text{dc})} = 4.0\ \text{V}\ (2|\phi|\pi - 1)$.

(d) Sketch a curve of $V_{O\,(\text{dc})}$ versus ϕ for the conditions of part (c). Dimension the graph showing the positions of the maxima, minima, and so on, and the values of the peak excursions of $V_{O\,(\text{dc})}$. (*Ans.*: peak excursion = ±4.0 V)

(e) Find the value of the phase angle-to-voltage transfer coefficient, $K_{\phi-V}$ for the case of part (c). (*Ans.*: $K_{\phi-V} = 2.55$ V/rad)

REFERENCES

GRAEME, J. G., G. E. TOBEY, and L. P. HUELSMAN, *Operational Amplifiers—Design and Applications*, McGraw-Hill, 1971.

GREBENE, A. B., *Analog Integrated Circuit Design*, Van Nostrand Reinhold, 1972.

Krauss, H. L., C. W. Bostian, and F. H. Raab, *Solid State Radio Engineering*, Wiley, 1980.

Lenk, J. D., *Handbook of Integrated Circuits*, Reston, 1978.

Lenk, J. D., *Manual for Integrated Circuit Users*, Reston, 1973.

Mitra, S. K., *An Introduction to Digital and Analog Integrated Circuits and Applications*, Harper & Row, 1980.

Voltage-Controlled Oscillators and Waveform Generators

6

6.1 VOLTAGE-CONTROLLED OSCILLATORS

A *voltage-controlled oscillator* (VCO) is an oscillator circuit in which the frequency of oscillation can be controlled by an externally applied voltage. One feature that is often required for VCOs is a linear relationship between the oscillation frequency and the control voltage.

A basic block diagram of the type of VCO circuit that is used in most integrated circuit VCOs is shown in Figure 6.1. Voltage-controlled current sources are used to charge and to discharge the timing capacitor C_t. The charging and discharging time periods are controlled by the action of a Schmitt trigger circuit, the input voltage of which is the voltage across C_t. The Schmitt trigger has two threshold voltage switching levels, V_L and V_H. The width of the Schmitt trigger hysteresis curve V_W is given by $V_W = V_H - V_L$.

Since C_t is charged and discharged by current sources, the voltage across C_t will vary linearly with time. If the charging and discharging currents are of equal magnitude, the voltage waveform across C_t will be a symmetrical triangular waveform. The timing capacitor C_t will be charged from the top current source up to a voltage equal to the V_H triggering level. At this point the Schmitt trigger will be activated and cause the current sources to be switched such that the top current source is disconnected from C_t and the bottom current source is connected to C_t. The capacitor will now be discharged (or equivalently, charged in the opposite direction) by the bottom current source down to lower trigger level V_L. At this point the Schmitt trigger will be activated again to cause the current sources to be switched again, and the entire cycle will be repeated. The voltage across C_t will therefore be a symmetri-

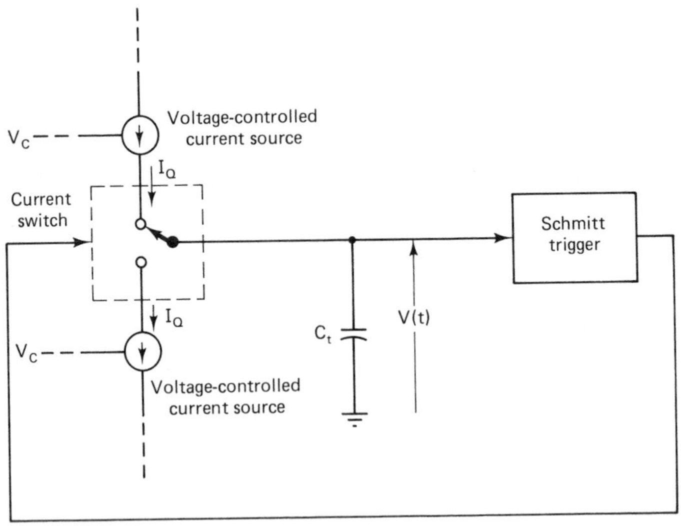

(a)

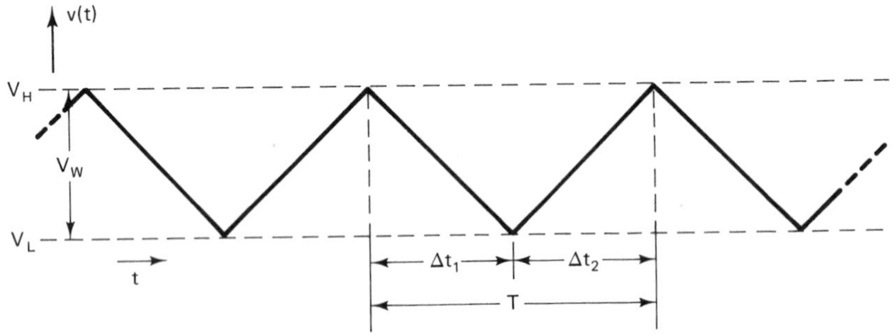

(b)

Figure 6.1 Voltage-controlled oscillator: (a) basic block diagram; (b) voltage waveform across timing capacitor.

cal triangular waveform extending between the limits of V_L to V_H for a total peak-to-peak excursion of $V_W = V_H - V_L$, as shown in Figure 6.1b.

Since the slope of the voltage across C_t is $dv(t)/dt = d(Q/C_t)/dt = (1/C_t)(dQ/dt) = \pm I_Q/C_t$, the time required to change the capacitor voltage from V_L to V_H, and vice versa, will be given by

$$\frac{V_H - V_L}{\Delta t_2} = \frac{I_Q}{C_t} \qquad \text{and} \qquad \frac{V_L - V_H}{\Delta t_1} = -\frac{I_Q}{C_t}$$

Therefore, we have that

$$\Delta t_1 = \Delta t_2 = \frac{(V_H - V_L)C_t}{I_Q} = \frac{V_W C_t}{I_Q}$$

so that the period of oscillation T will be given by $T = \Delta t_1 + \Delta t_2 = 2V_W C_t / I_Q$. The frequency of oscillation f_o will therefore be

$$\boxed{f_o = \frac{1}{T} = \frac{I_Q}{2V_W C_t}} \tag{6.1}$$

If the voltage-controlled current sources have a linear voltage-to-current transfer relationship as given by $I_Q = G_c(V_c + V_o)$, where G_c is the transfer conductance of the current source and V_c is the control voltage, we will have that

$$f_o = \frac{I_Q}{2V_W C_t} = \frac{G_C(V_c + V_o)}{2V_W C_t}$$

We therefore see that the oscillation frequency f_o will be a linear function of the control voltage V_c. The *voltage-to-frequency transfer coefficient* K_V will be given by

$$\boxed{K_V = \frac{df_o}{dV_c} = \frac{G_c}{2V_W C_t}} \tag{6.2}$$

A circuit implementation of a voltage-controlled current source is shown in Figure 6.2. Also shown in this diagram is the circuitry that produces charging and discharging currents of equal magnitude.

The voltage at the emitter of Q_2 is $V_{E_2} = V_{EB_2} + V_{EB_1} + V_C = V_C - V_{BE_1} + V_{EB_2}$. Since Q_1 is an NPN transistor and Q_2 is a PNP transistor, we will have that $V_{BE_1} \simeq V_{EB_2}$ to within something in the range 10 to 50 mV. Therefore, we have that $V_{E_2} \simeq V_C$. As a result, the current through R_1 will be $I_{R_1} = (V^+ - V_{E_1})/R_1 \simeq (V^+ - V_C)/R_1$ and the current source output current will be $I_Q = \alpha_{\text{pnp}} I_{R_1} \simeq \alpha_{\text{pnp}}(V^+ - V_C)/R_1 \simeq (V^+ - V_C)/R_1$ if $\alpha_{\text{pnp}} \simeq 1$. We thus obtain a linear relationship between the current source output current I_Q and the control voltage V_C.

Transistor Q_5 is controlled by the Schmitt trigger. When Q_5 is off, C_t will be charged with the output current of Q_2, which is I_Q via diode D_2 and D_1, Q_3, and Q_4 will be off. When Q_5 is turned on (in saturation)Q_3, Q_4, and D_1 will be on. The voltage at the anode of D_1 will be $V_{CE(\text{SAT})5} + V_{BE_3} + V_{D_1} = 0.2 + 0.65 + 0.65 = 1.5$ V. The voltage at the cathode of D_2 will be the voltage across C_t, which is $v(t)$. Since $v(t)$ will be larger than 1.0 V, we see that diode D_2 will be off.

The current through Q_4 will be equal to the current through Q_3, which will be I_Q. Since D_2 will be off, we see that C_t will be discharged through Q_4 with a current equal to I_Q. Therefore, the charging and discharging currents will be equal in magnitude and be linearly dependent on the control voltage V_C.

A diagram of a Schmitt trigger circuit is shown in Figure 6.3. To determine the high and low triggering levels, V_H and V_L, we will first examine the circuit for the case in which the Q_6–D_3–Q_7 combination is off. With Q_7 off, Q_8 will be turned on and driven into saturation. With Q_8 in saturation Q_9 will be turned off, and as a result Q_5 will also be turned off.

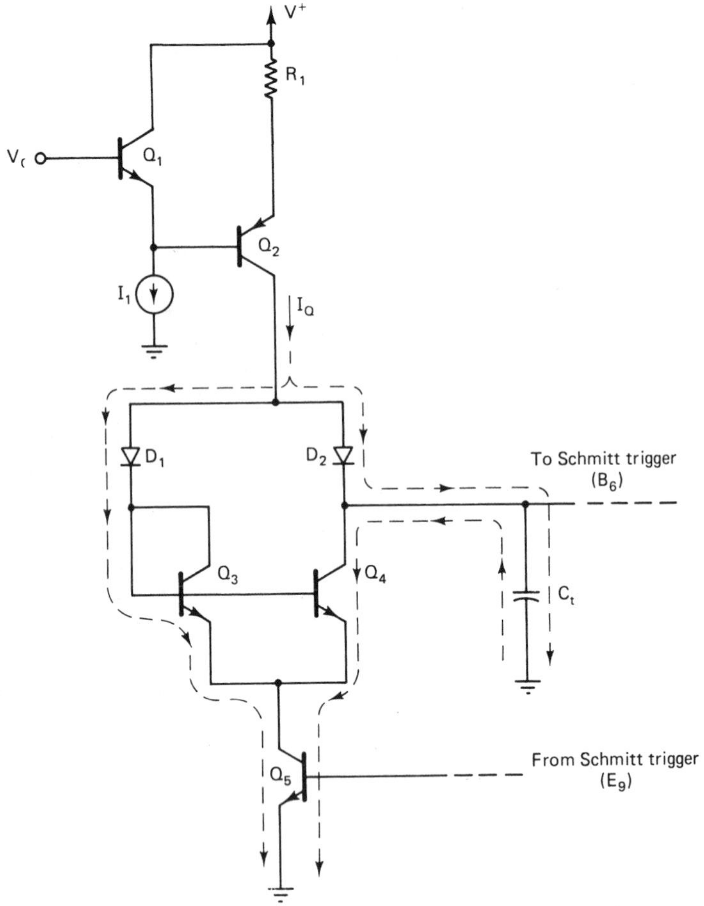

Figure 6.2 Voltage-controlled current sources for the charging and discharging of the timing capacitor.

When Q_8 is on (in saturation), the voltage across R_3 will be $V_{R_3} = V_{E_7} = V_{E_8} = (V^+ - V_{CE(\text{SAT})})R_3/(R_3 + R_4)$. The trigger or threshold voltage V_H required to switch the Schmitt trigger from this state to the other state will therefore be $V_H = V_{E_7} + V_{BE_7} + V_{D_3} + V_{BE_6} \simeq 3V_{BE} + V^+R_3/(R_3 + R_4)$.

If the voltage at the base of Q_6 goes above V_H, the Q_6–D_3–Q_7 combination will be turned on and the Schmitt trigger will rapidly go into the other state. With Q_7 on (in saturation) Q_8 will be off and as a result Q_9 will be driven into saturation. This, in turn, will drive Q_5 into saturation.

With Q_8 off, the voltage across R_3 will drop to a value given by $V_{R_3} = V_{E_7} = (V^+ - V_{CE(\text{SAT})7})R_3/(R_3 + R_2) = V^+R_3/(R_3 + R_2)$. The input voltage $v(t)$ at the base of Q_6 required to turn on Q_6, D_3, and Q_7 will be given by $V_L = V_{BE_6} + V_{D_3} + V_{BE_7} + V^+R_3/(R_3 + R_2) = 3V_{BE} + V^+R_3/(R_3 + R_2)$. The width of the Schmitt trigger hysteresis curve V_W will be given by

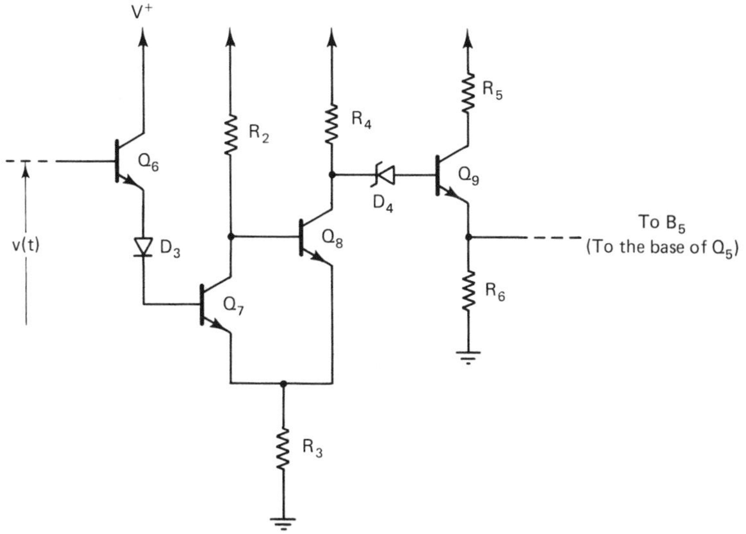

Figure 6.3 Schmitt trigger circuit.

$$V_W = V_H - V_L = \frac{V^+R_3}{R_3 + R_4} - \frac{V^+R_3}{R_3 + R_2} = V^+R_3\left(\frac{1}{R_3 + R_4} - \frac{1}{R_3 + R_2}\right) \tag{6.3}$$

To consider a representative example, let us choose the following representative values: $V^+ = +12$ V, $V_H = +8.0$ V, and $V_L = +3.0$ V for a total hysteresis span of $V_W = V_H - V_L = 5.0$ V. We will also choose $R_3 = \underline{1.0\ \text{k}\Omega}$.

We have that $V_H = 3V_{BE} + V^+R_3/(R_3 + R_4) = 1.8 + 12R_3/(R_3 + R_4) = 8.0$, so that $12R_3 = 6.2(R_3 + R_4)$ and thus $6.2R_4 = 5.8R_3 = 5.8$ kΩ, giving $R_4 = \underline{936\ \Omega}$. For R_2 we have that $V_L = 3V_{BE} + V^+R_3/(R_3 + R_2) = 1.8 + 12R_3/(R_3 + R_2) = 3.0$, so that $12R_3 = 1.2(R_3 + R_2)$, giving $1.2R_2 = 10.8R_3 = 10.8$ kΩ and thus $R_2 = \underline{10.8\ \text{k}\Omega/1.2 = 9.0\ \text{k}\Omega}$.

When Q_8 is in saturation we have that $V_{C_8} = V^+R_3/(R_3 + R_4) = 12 \times 1$ kΩ/1.935 kΩ $= 6.2$ V. Since the Zener voltage of D_4 is 6.2 V, the voltage at the base of Q_9 will be zero, and thus Q_9 and Q_5 will be off.

When Q_8 is off, Q_9 and Q_5 will be on. The base drive available to turn Q_9 on will be $I_{B_9} = (V^+ - V_Z - V_{BE_9} - V_{BE_5})/R_4 = (12 - 6.2 - 0.7 - 0.7)/935\ \Omega = 4.4\ \text{V}/935\ \Omega = 4.7$ mA. This base current will be more than sufficient to drive Q_9 and Q_5 into full saturation.

Another type of Schmitt trigger is shown in Figure 6.4. This Schmitt trigger features a differential amplifier comprised of transistors Q_{10} and Q_{11} biased by a current sink I_Q. If the voltage at the base of Q_{10} drops below the voltage at the base of Q_{11}, the action of the positive-feedback loop composed of R_7 and R_8 will be to rapidly raise the base voltage of Q_{11}. The difference in the base voltages of Q_{10} and Q_{11} that will be established will be such that almost all of current I_Q will now flow through Q_{11} and very little will go through Q_{10}.

The voltage at the base of Q_{11} will now be given by $V_{B_{11}} = (V^+ + V_R)R_8/(R_7 + R_8 + R_{10}) - V_R$. This will be the high-level trigger voltage V_H.

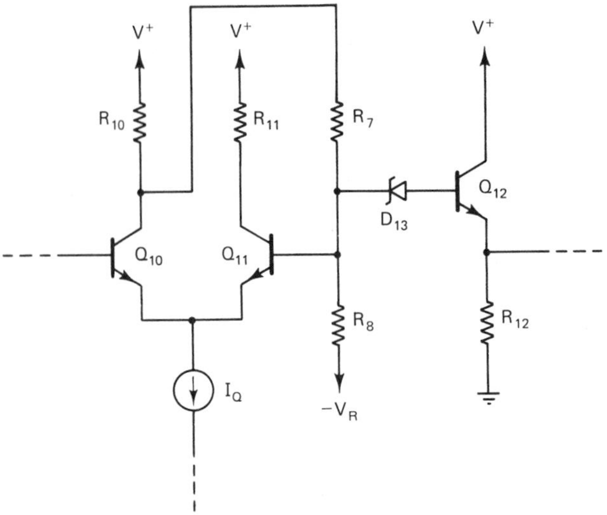

Figure 6.4 Schmitt trigger circuit using differential amplifier.

If the voltage at the base of Q_{10} now rises above $V_{B_{11}} = V_H$, the action of the feedback loop will be to very rapidly drop the voltage at the base of Q_{11} such that almost all of the current will now flow through Q_{10} and the current through Q_{11} will essentially be cut off. The voltage level at the base of Q_{11} will now be given by

$$V_L = V_{B_{11}} = \frac{(V^+ - I_Q R_{10} + V_R) R_8}{R_8 + R_7 + R_{10}} - V_R \tag{6.4}$$

and this will be the low-level trigger voltage. The difference between these two trigger voltage levels is the hysteresis width of the Schmitt trigger, as will be given by $V_W = V_H - V_L = I_Q R_{10} R_8/(R_7 + R_8 + R_{10})$.

Transistors Q_{10} and Q_{11} can be prevented from going into saturation by suitable choice of I_Q, R_{10}, and R_{11} such that the collector voltages never drop by more than 0.5 V below the base voltages. This combined with the all-NPN nature of this circuit will mean that this Schmitt trigger will have the capability of very high-frequency switching.

Another Schmitt trigger circuit closely related to the first one discussed is shown in Figure 6.5. In this circuit transistors Q_6 through Q_9 operate in the same fashion as in the circuit of Figure 3.3. When Q_6 and Q_7 are on, Q_8 will be off and the collector of Q_8 will be up near V^+, thus raising the emitter of Q_9 and the base of Q_{10} close to V^+. This will essentially turn off the Q_{10} side of the differential amplifier and Q_{11} will carry the full current. The collector current of Q_{11} will be the base drive of Q_5, turning that transistor on (to saturation). When Q_6 and Q_7 are off, Q_8 will be on. This will drop the voltage at the collector of Q_8 and therefore that at the emitter of Q_9 and the base of Q_{10} to a low value. This will cause the current in the Q_{10}–Q_{11} differential amplifier to shift to the Q_{10} side, with Q_{11} being essentially turned off. This, in turn, will turn Q_5 off.

Note that with all of these VCO circuits a square-wave output will be available

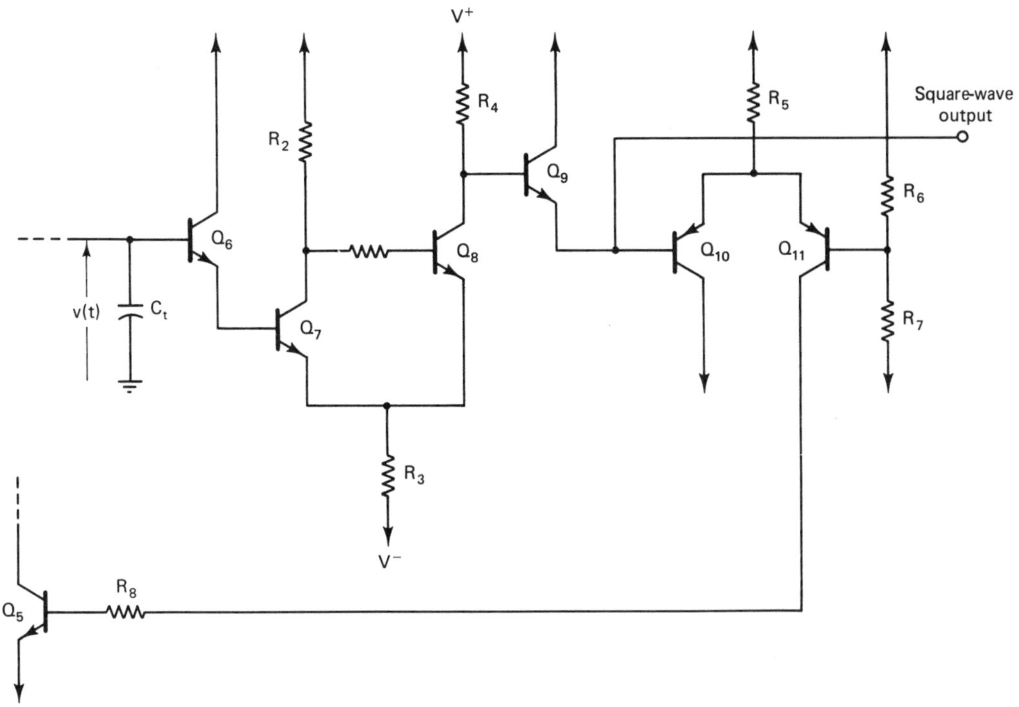

Figure 6.5 Schmitt trigger using differential-amplifier output circuit.

from the Schmitt trigger circuit. There will also be a triangular-wave output available from across the timing capacitor.

6.1.1 Emitter-Coupled Voltage-Controlled Oscillator

An emitter-coupled VCO is shown in Figure 6.6. Transistors Q_5 and Q_6 are voltage-controlled current sources, each producing a current I_Q. Transistors Q_3 and Q_4 are the switching transistors and drive loads comprised of R_1, R_2, Q_1, and Q_2. The load configuration is designed to produce a voltage drop V_D that will be relatively independent of the current level.

The voltage drop V_D can be obtained from the relationship $V_{BE} = V_D R_2/(R_1 + R_2)$. Solving for V_D, we obtain $V_D = V_{BE}(1 + R_1/R_2)$ when current is flowing through the load. Otherwise, the voltage drop will be zero.

If we now consider the condition wherein Q_3 is assumed to be on and Q_4 is off, the voltage at the base of Q_3 will be $(V^+ - V_{BE})R_6/(R_5 + R_6)$ and the voltage at the base of Q_4 will be $(V^+ - V_{BE} - V_D)R_6/(R_5 + R_6)$. The difference in the voltages between the two bases will be $V_{B_3} - V_{B_4} = V_D R_6/(R_5 + R_6) = V'_D$.

The voltage across the timing capacitor C_t will be $V_{C_t} = V_{E_3} - V_{E_4}$ and thus the difference in the base-to-emitter voltages of Q_3 and Q_4 will be $V_{BE_3} - V_{BE_4} = (V_{B_3} - V_{B_4}) - (V_{E_3} - V_{E_4}) = V_D R_6/(R_5 + R_6) - V_{C_t}$. As long as V_{C_t} is less than V_D, we will have that $V_{BE_3} > V_{BE_4}$ and Q_3 will remain on and Q_4 off.

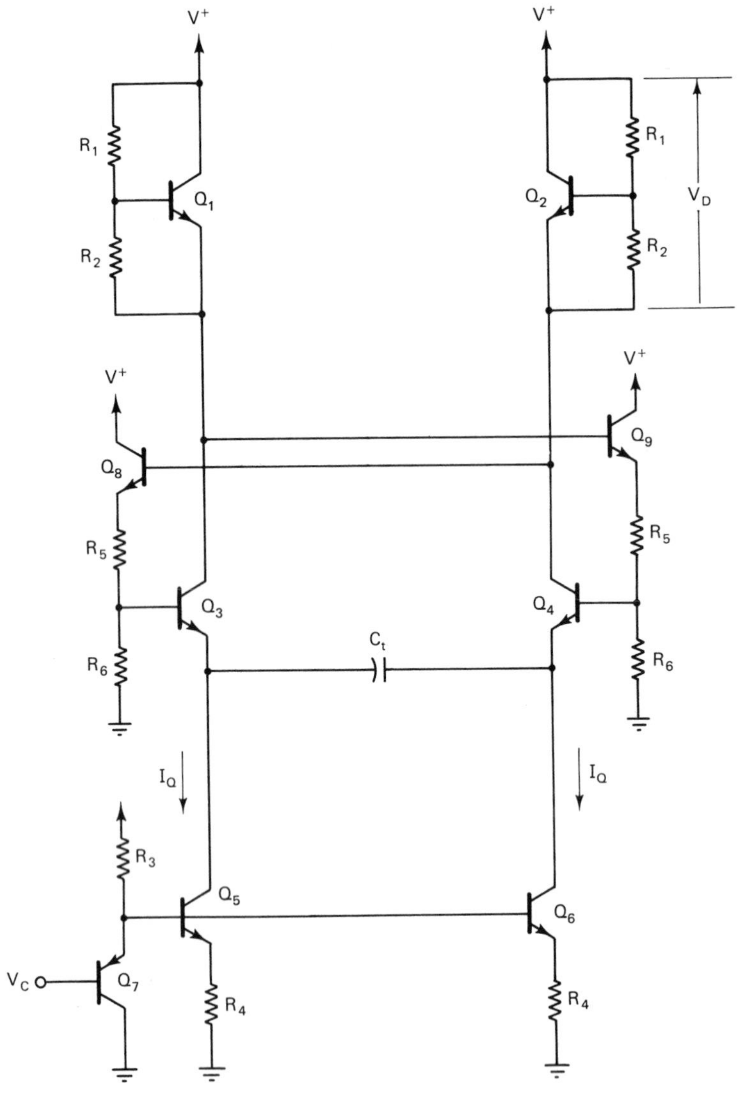

Figure 6.6 Emitter-coupled voltage-controlled oscillator.

As illustrated in Figure 6.7a, capacitor C_t is charged by current I_Q and the voltage across C_t will increase at a rate given by $dV_{C_t}/dt = I_Q/C_t$. As soon as V_{C_t} rises above V'_D, transistor Q_3 will be turned off and Q_4 will be turned on. This will result in a change in the direction of the current through C_t as shown in Figure 6.7b. This circuit will remain in this state as long as $V_{BE3} < V_{BE4}$, which requires that $V_{C_t} > -V'_D$. The voltage across C_t will now decrease at a rate given by $-dV_{C_t}/dt = -I_Q/C_t$. As soon as V_{C_t} drops below $-V'_D$, transistor Q_3 will be switched back on and Q_4 will be switched off and the cycle will be completed.

The change in the voltage across C_t that is required to cause Q_3 and Q_4 to

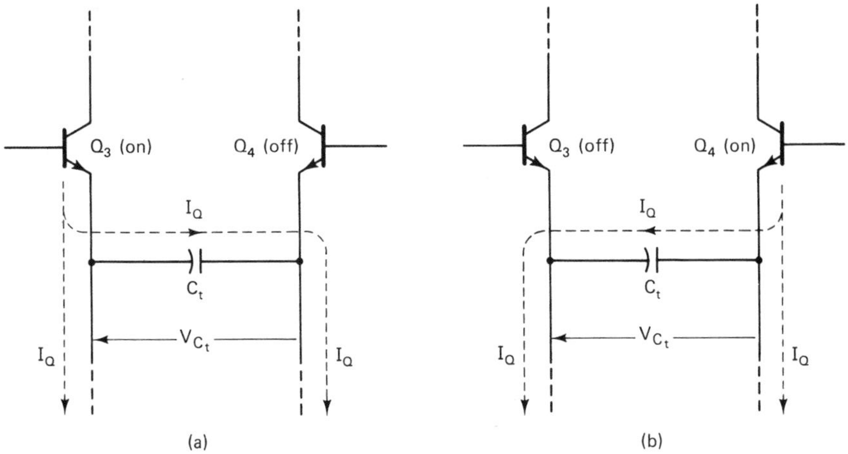

Figure 6.7 Charging and discharging cycles for C_t: (a) charging cycle with Q_3 on and Q_4 off; (b) discharge cycle with Q_3 off and Q_4 on.

switch from one state to the other is $\Delta V_{C_t} = \pm 2 V_D R_6/(R_5 + R_6) = \pm 2 V'_D$. Since $dV_{C_t}/dt = \pm I_Q/C_t$, we have that $\Delta V_{C_t} = \pm 2 V'_D = \pm I_Q \, \Delta t/C_t$, so that $\Delta t = 2 V'_D C_t / I_Q$. The oscillation period T will therefore be $T = 2\,\Delta t = 4 V'_D C_t/I_Q = 4 V_D C_t R_6 / I_Q(R_5 + R_6)$. The corresponding oscillation frequency f_o will be

$$f_o = \frac{1}{T} = \frac{I_Q}{4 V'_D C_t} = \frac{I_Q(1 + R_5/R_6)}{4 V_D C_t}$$

For the voltage-controlled current source part of the circuit we note that $V_{E_5} = V_{E_6} = V_C + V_{EB_7} - V_{BE_5} \simeq V_C$ since $V_{EB_7(\text{PNP})} \simeq V_{BE_5(\text{NPN})}$. As a result, $I_Q = V_{E_5}/R_4 \simeq V_C/_4$ and there will be a linear relationship between the current source current I_Q and the control voltage V_C. The oscillation frequency f_o can now be expressed in terms of the control voltage as

$$\boxed{f_o = \frac{V_C(1 + R_5/R_6)}{4 V_D R_4 C_t}} \tag{6.5}$$

and the voltage-to-frequency transfer coefficient will be

$$\boxed{K_V = \frac{df_o}{dV_C} = \frac{1 + R_5/R_6}{4 V_D R_4 C_t}} \tag{6.6}$$

This type of VCO has the capability of operation at relatively high frequencies ($\lesssim$50 MHz). This is the result of the fact that the switching transistors Q_3 and Q_4 can be prevented from going into saturation. The required condition for this is that the base voltage never go more than 0.5 V above the collector voltage. Thus we should require that $V^+ R_6/(R_5 + R_6) < (V^+ - V_D) + 0.5$ V.

6.2 WAVEFORM GENERATORS

A waveform generator is a device that generates the following three types of voltage waveforms: square waves, triangular waves, and sinusoidal waves. The square and triangular waves can be generated by the same types of circuits as those used for voltage-controlled oscillators. These circuits involve the charging and discharging of a timing capacitor from a current source and the use of a Schmitt trigger or comparator to switch the current source between the charging and discharging modes of operation. If the charging and discharging currents are equal in magnitude, the duty cycle will be 50%; that is, the capacitor will be charging for one-half of the total period and discharging for the other half.

A square-wave output is available from the Schmitt trigger or comparator circuit and a triangular wave is available across the timing capacitor. In the cases in which the timing capacitor has one side connected to ground, a triangular wave will appear at the high (i.e., ungrounded) side of the capacitor. In the case of the emitter-coupled VCO type of circuit, neither side of the timing capacitor is grounded. To obtain a single-ended triangular-wave output the voltage across the timing capacitor must be supplied as a balanced input to a differential amplifier. The differential amplifier will then convert this balanced or double-ended input to an unbalanced or double-ended output at the collectors of the differential amplifier.

6.2.1 Sine-Wave Generation

For the generation of a sinusoidal waveform there are two basic techniques that can be used. One approach is to use a feedback amplifier circuit using an *LC* tuned circuit or *RC* phase-shift network in the feedback loop, as shown in Figure 6.8a. The other approach is to use a nonlinear wave-shaping circuit to convert the triangular waveform into a sinusoidal waveform. The feedback oscillator circuit will be discussed first.

For a closed-loop system of the type shown in Figure 6.8a, the condition for oscillations to occur is that the magnitude of the loop gain FA_{OL} be greater than unity at the frequency $f_{180°}$ at which the angle of the loop gain is 180°. This condition can be written as $FA_{OL}| > 1$ at $f_{180°}$, where $f_{180°}$ is the frequency at which $\angle FA_{OL} = 180°$. The frequency of oscillation f_o will be determined by the phase-shift condition and will be equal to $f_{180°}$.

6.2.2 *RC* Phase-Shift Oscillator

An example of a feedback oscillator that uses an *RC* phase-shift network in the feedback loop is the *RC* phase-shift oscillator shown in Figure 3.8b.

The transfer function of the *RC* phase-shift network is given by

$$F = \frac{1}{1 - 5\alpha^2 - j(6\alpha - \alpha^3)} \qquad \text{where } \alpha = \frac{1}{\omega RC} \tag{6.7}$$

The phase shift θ of the feedback network will be given by

$$\theta = \underline{/F} = \tan^{-1}\frac{6\alpha - \alpha^3}{1 - 5\alpha^2}$$

Assuming that the amplifier phase shift is zero, we will have that $\angle FA_{OL} = \angle F = \theta$. For a 180° phase shift the argument of the inverse tangent function will be zero, so that $6\alpha - \alpha^3 = 0$. After noting that the $\alpha = 0$ case corresponds to a 0° phase shift, we see that for a 180° phase shift, $\alpha^2 = 6$. Therefore, the 180° phase-shift frequency, which will also be the frequency of oscillation f_o, will be given by the condition that $\alpha = 1/\omega_o RC = \sqrt{6}$, so that $\omega_o = 1/(\sqrt{6}\ RC)$ and $f_o = 1/(2\pi\sqrt{6}\ RC)$.

When $\alpha^2 = 6$ the value of the feedback factor F will be $F = 1/(1 - 5\alpha^2) = 1/(1 - 30) = -1/29 = (1/29)\ \angle 180°$. For oscillations to occur the magnitude of the loop gain must be greater than unity at $f = f_{180°} = f_o$. Therefore, we require that $|F(f_{180°})| \times (R_F/R) > 1$, so that $R_F/R > 29$.

If the loop gain is substantially in excess of the minimum value required for oscillations, however, the amplitude of the oscillations will be limited only by the amplifier going into saturation (or cutoff) and there will be clipping of the peaks of the output voltage. The voltage waveform produced will therefore be a clipped sine wave and there will be a large amount of distortion present. To produce a relatively undistorted sine wave, the loop gain should be adjusted or controlled to a value

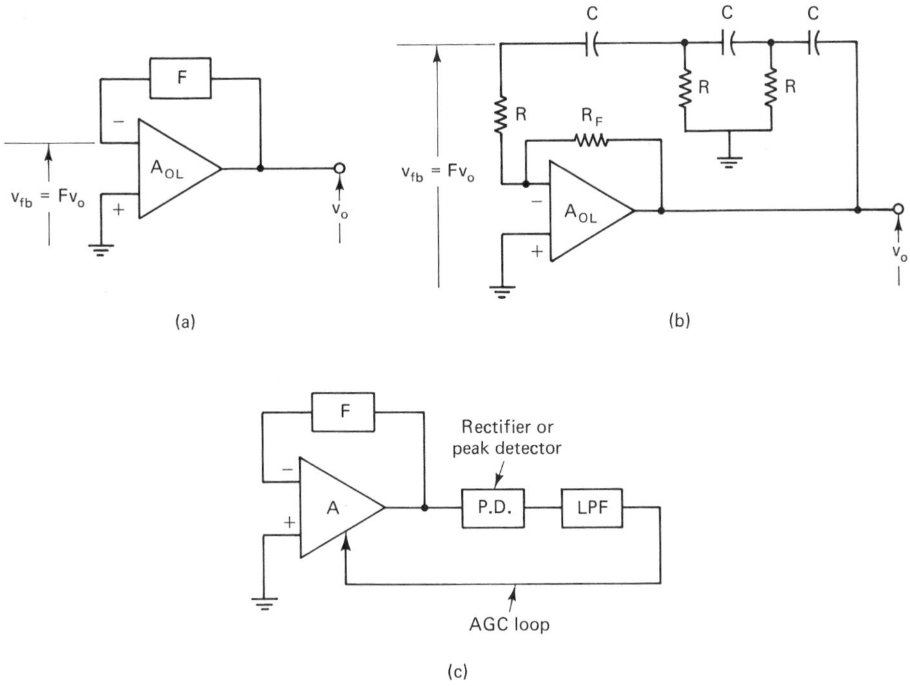

Figure 6.8 Feedback sinusoidal oscillators: (a) basic diagram of feedback oscillator; (b) *RC* phase-shift oscillator; (c) low-distortion sinusoidal oscillator using AGC.

that is just slightly greater than unity at f_o. The closer that the loop gain is to unity, the less distortion there will be.

For the phase-shift oscillator just considered a relatively undistorted sine wave can be produced by adjusting R_F to a value that is just slightly larger than that needed to initiate oscillations. This approach, however, suffers the possible drawback that changes in operating conditions such as the temperature or supply voltage may change the amplifier gain so that the optimum value of R_F may drift with time, and R_F may require periodic readjustment.

Another approach for obtaining an undistorted sine-wave output is shown in Figure 6.8c. In this case an automatic gain control (AGC) feedback loop is used to control the gain of the amplifier to the value corresponding to an output voltage that has a peak value that is substantially less than that which would produce clipping. The cutoff frequency of the low-pass filter should be much less than f_o. With this circuit a sine-wave output of very low distortion can be produced.

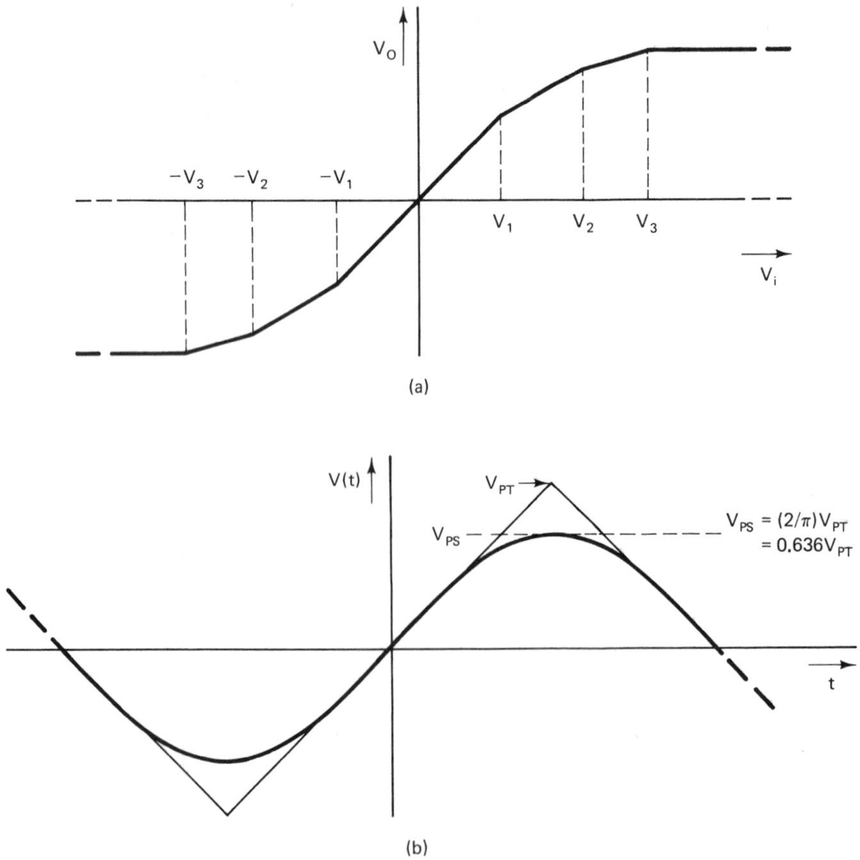

Figure 6.9 Transfer characteristics for triangular waveform-to-sine wave converter circuit: (a) seven-segment converter; (b) comparison of triangular wave and sine wave.

6.2.3 Sinusoidal VCO Output: Triangle to Sine-Wave Converter

The feedback oscillator can produce a very low-distortion sine wave, but it is difficult to modulate the oscillation frequency by means of a control voltage, especially with respect to a large-frequency sweep range. The VCO, on the other hand, is capable of a frequency sweep ratio as large as 100:1 with very good linearity between the frequency and the control voltage. A sine wave can be obtained from a VCO by using a wave-shaping network to convert the triangular-wave output to a sine wave.

A triangle wave-to-sine wave converter uses a nonlinear circuit to convert a triangular wave to a sine wave, as shown in Figure 6.9. In this figure a seven-segment piecewise linear transfer characteristic that can be used for this purpose is shown together with the corresponding sine-wave output, as shown in Figure 6.9b.

The Fourier series representation of a triangular wave is given by

$$v_T(t) = \frac{8}{\pi^2} V_{PT}\left(\sin \omega t - \frac{1}{9}\sin 3\omega t + \frac{1}{25}\sin 5\omega t - \frac{1}{49}\sin 7\omega t + \cdots\right) \tag{6.8}$$

We see that the triangular wave has a large component at the fundamental frequency, and can be considered to be a very distorted sine wave with about 12% total harmonic distortion (THD). By the use of a nonlinear wave-shaping network to modify the

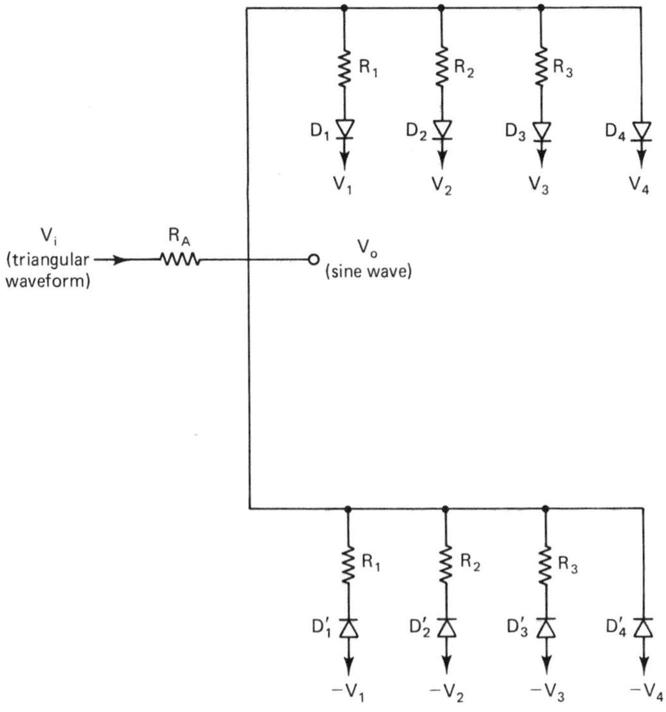

Figure 6.10 Triangular waveform-to-sine wave converter circuit.

shape of the triangular wave, particularly by rounding off of the sharp peaks of the triangular wave, a sine wave with a THD of less than 1% can easily be obtained.

In Figure 6.10 a simple example of a waveform converter circuit is shown. This circuit produces a nine-segment piecewise-linear transfer characteristic. The slope dV_o/dV_i of the transfer curve for various values of V_i will be as follows:

$$
\begin{array}{llll}
 & & & \textit{Slope} = dV_o/dV_i \\
(1) & -V_1 < V_i < +V_1 & & 1 \\
(2) & +V_1 < V_i < +V_2, & \text{or} & \dfrac{R_1}{R_1 + R_A} \\
 & -V_2 < V_i < -V_1 & & \\
(3) & +V_2 < V_i < +V_3, & \text{or} & \dfrac{R_1 \| R_2}{(R_1 \| R_2) + R_A} \\
 & -V_3 < V_i < -V_2 & & \\
(4) & +V_3 < V_i < +V_4, & \text{or} & \dfrac{R_1 \| R_2 \| R_3}{(R_1 \| R_2 \| R_3) + R_A} \\
 & -V_4 < V_i < -V_3 & & \\
(5) & +V_4 < V_i, \quad \text{or} & & \approx 0 \\
 & V_i < -V_4 & &
\end{array}
\tag{6.9}
$$

The last case should occur at a voltage level of approximately $V_4 = V_{PS} = 0.636\,V_{PT}$ to produce the final flattening of the triangular waveform to produce the rounded peak of the sine wave.

In Figure 6.11 a practical waveform converter circuit (Intersil 8038) is shown. The reference voltages V_1, V_2, V_3, and so on, are produced by a voltage divider connected between the positive and negative supply voltages as shown in Figure 6.12. The PNP–NPN transistor combinations are used to transform the impedance of the voltage divider down to a very low value that is small compared to R_1, R_2, and R_3. The voltage level that appears at the output emitters of the PNP–NPN pairs will be approximately equal to the reference voltages (V_1, V_2, etc.) since the base-to-emitter voltage drops of the PNP and NPN transistors are of opposite algebraic sign.

The effective source resistance due to the voltage divider will be reduced by a factor equal to the product of the PNP and NPN current gains and thus will be reduced to a negligibly small value ($\lesssim 1\ \Omega$). We note, however, that due to the finite voltage change needed to bias the various transistor pairs into full conduction there will not be a sharp transition between the linear segments of the transfer characteristic, but rather somewhat of a "rounded-off" transition. The rounded-off or smooth transition between the piecewise-linear segments is actually beneficial in producing a less distorted sine wave.

For the circuit of Figure 6.11, the value of R_3 (not shown) is 800 Ω and $R_4 = 0$. The complete voltage-divider circuit is shown in Figure 6.12. These reference voltage levels are suitable for the conversion of a symmetrical triangular wave with a peak-to-peak amplitude $2V_{PT}$ of $\frac{1}{3}(V^+ - V^-) = 20/3 = 6.7$ V, or $V_{PT} = 3.33$ V. A sine wave with an amplitude of $V_{PS} = V_4 = 0.247\,V^+ = 2.47$ V will be produced.

In Figure 6.13 a buffer amplifier circuit for this converter is shown. Note that in taking the algebraic summation of all of the base-to-emitter voltage drops going

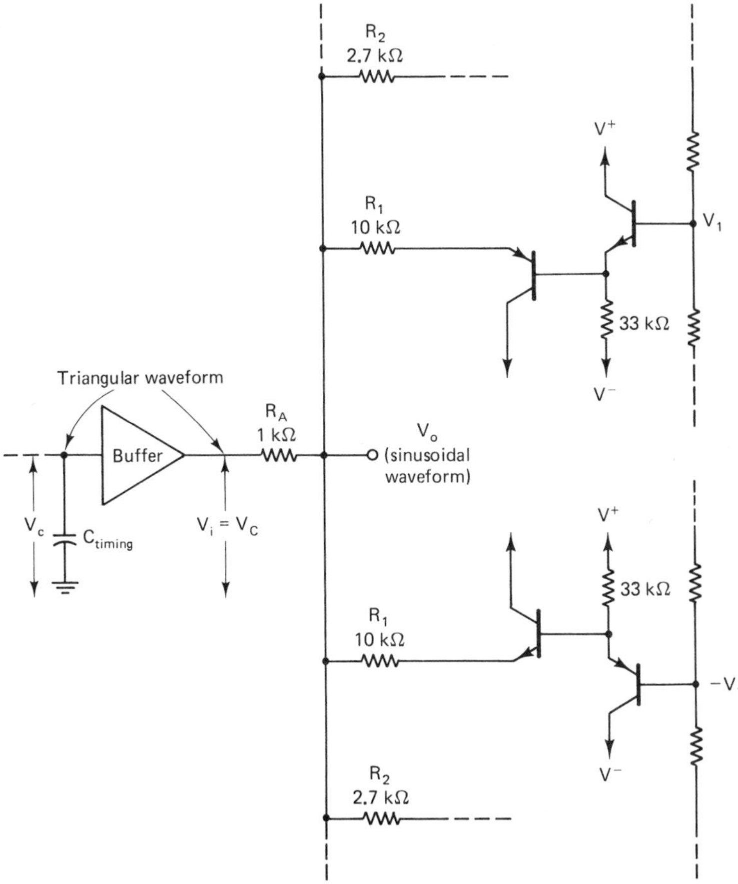

Figure 6.11 Triangular-to-sinusoidal waveform converter circuit.

from C_{timing} to the output of the buffer circuit, we will obtain the result that the output voltage of the buffer will be approximately equal to the voltage across the timing capacitor. The principal function of the buffer is to act as a unity-gain, low-output-impedance amplifier for driving the waveform converter circuit.

6.2.4 IC Timer Example: 555 Type

The 555 type of IC timer is a very versatile and popular device. This device is also available as a dual timer (556). It can be used as a monostable multivibrator (a "one-shot") for the generation of pulses ranging in duration from 1 μs to 100 s. It can also be used as an astable multivibrator with oscillation frequencies ranging from 0.01 Hz to 1 MHz.

The basic block diagram of this device is shown in Figure 6.14. It consists of two comparators that drive the set (S) and reset (R) terminals of a flip-flop, which in turn controls the on and off cycles of the discharge transistor Q_{14}. The comparator

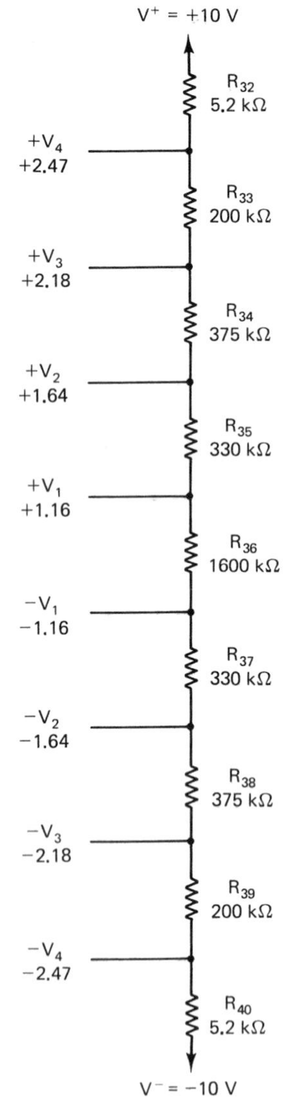

Figure 6.12 Voltage divider for breakpoint voltages.

reference voltages are fixed at $\frac{2}{3}V^+$ for comparator 1 and $\frac{1}{3}V^+$ for comparator 2 by means of the R_3, R_4, and R_5 (5 kΩ each) voltage divider.

In the operation of this circuit an external timing capacitor C is charged through an external resistor from the positive supply voltage. When the voltage across the capacitor reaches the threshold voltage level of comparator 1, which is $\frac{2}{3}V^+$, the comparator output goes *high*. This causes the flip-flop to reset so that $\overline{Q}$ is latched into the *high* state, which turns the discharge transistor Q_{14} *on*. This results in the discharge of the capacitor. In the monostable mode of operation the capacitor discharges very rapidly through Q_{14} and this terminates the action of the circuit until the next triggering pulse comes along. In the astable mode the capacitor is connected

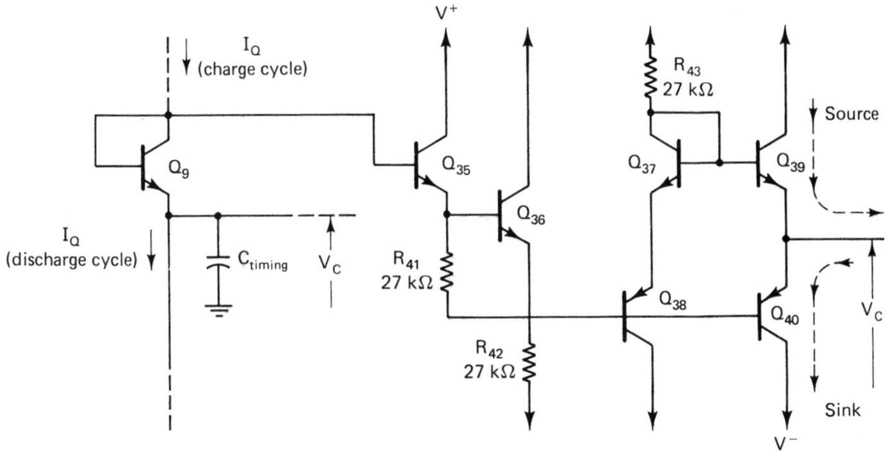

Figure 6.13 Buffer amplifier for waveform converter.

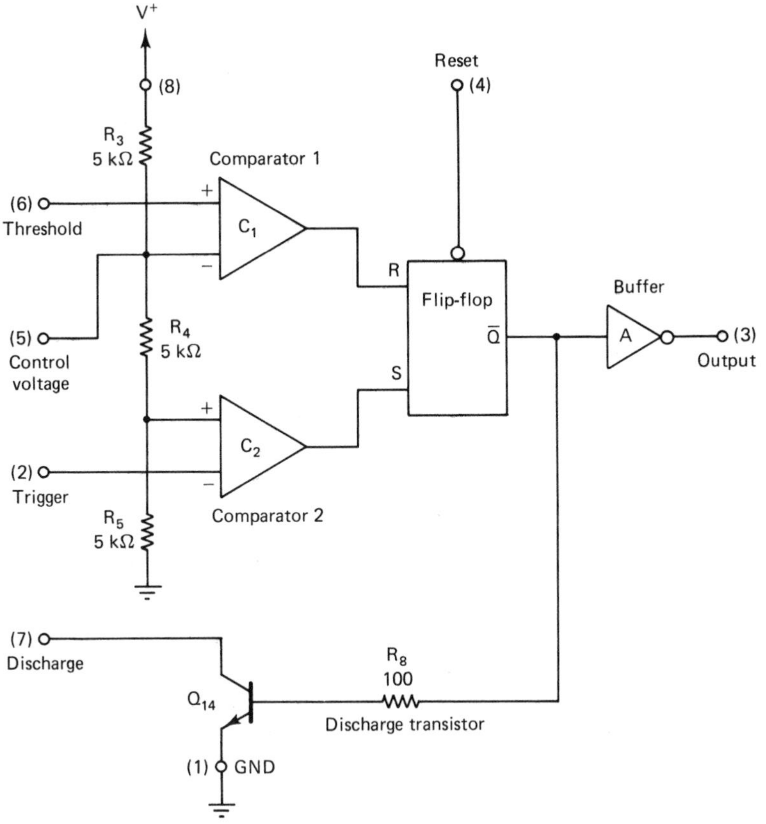

Figure 6.14 Basic block diagram of 555-type timer.

to both comparators so that when the capacitor voltage drops below the trigger level of comparator 2, which is $\frac{1}{3}V^+$ the comparator output goes *high*. This causes the flip-flop output $\overline{Q}$ to go *low*, turning off the discharge transistor thus terminating the discharge cycle. The capacitor will then once again start charging, completing the full cycle.

The capacitor charges from the trigger level of $\frac{1}{3}V^+$ up toward V^+, but the charging cycle is interrupted at the threshold voltage level of $\frac{2}{3}V^+$. At this point the capacitor starts discharging toward ground potential. When the capacitor voltage reaches $\frac{1}{3}V^+$ the discharge cycle is interrupted and the capacitor starts charging again.

In Figure 6.15 the full schematic diagram of the 555-type timer is shown. Comparator 1 is comprised of transistors Q_1 through Q_6 with Q_{15} and Q_{16} in conjunction with Q_5 and Q_6 serving as an active load. Comparator 2 is composed of transistors Q_7 through Q_{10} biased by current source transistor Q_{11}, and Q_{12} and Q_{13} serve as the active load for this comparator.

The flip-flop is comprised of Q_{19} and Q_{20}, which act as two cascaded inverters, with positive feedback from the collector of Q_{20} back to the base of Q_{19} being provided by R_7 (4.7 kΩ). The reset voltage R for the flip-flop is obtained from comparator 1 via its active load Q_{15} and Q_{16} and buffered by Q_{17}. When the voltage applied to the base of Q_{17} goes *high*, Q_{19} goes *on* and Q_{20} goes *off* and the output of the flip-flop $\overline{Q}$ goes *high*.

The set voltage S for the flip-flop is obtained from comparator 2 and is applied to the base of Q_{18}. When the voltage at the base of Q_{18} goes *high*, Q_{18} turns *on* and goes into saturation. This turns Q_{19} *off* and Q_{20} *on* (in saturation), so that the flip-flop output voltage $\overline{Q}$ is now *low*.

The flip-flop drives Q_{23}, which in conjunction with R_{11} (6.2 kΩ) and R_9 (3.3 kΩ) acts as a phase splitter which drives the "push-pull" (or "totem-pole") output stage of the Q_{27}–Q_{28} Darlington pair for sourcing currents into the load, and Q_{24} and Q_{26} for sinking load currents.

The discharge transistor Q_{14} is driven by the emitter of Q_{23} via R_8 (100 Ω). When the flip-flop output $\overline{Q}$ (at the collector of Q_{20}) is *high*, Q_{14} is turned *on* and discharges the timing capacitor. When $\overline{Q}$ is *low*, Q_{23} will be *off* and therefore Q_{14} will also be *off*. This condition allows the timing capacitor to charge up.

This circuit may be reset or cleared at any time by means of the reset transistor Q_{25}. With the base of Q_{25} (pin 4) *high* at V^+ or open, Q_{25} will be *off* and the circuit will operate in the normal fashion. When the base of Q_{25} goes *low* (<0.4 V), Q_{25} will be turned on, which will then drive Q_{14} on; this causes the discharge of the timing capacitor and also causes the output voltage of the circuit (pin 3) to go *low* (~0 V) for as long as the reset voltage is held low.

Monostable multivibrator. The external circuit connections for the 555 timer operating as a monostable or "one-shot" multivibrator are shown in Figure 6.16. With the voltage at the trigger input pin 2 *high* (at V^+), the output of comparator 2 will be *low*, causing the flip-flop output $\overline{Q}$ to be *high*. The discharge transistor Q_{14} will be *on* and the voltage across the timing capacitor will be essentially zero. The output voltage (pin 3) will be *low* (~0 V) and this will be the quiescent state of the device.

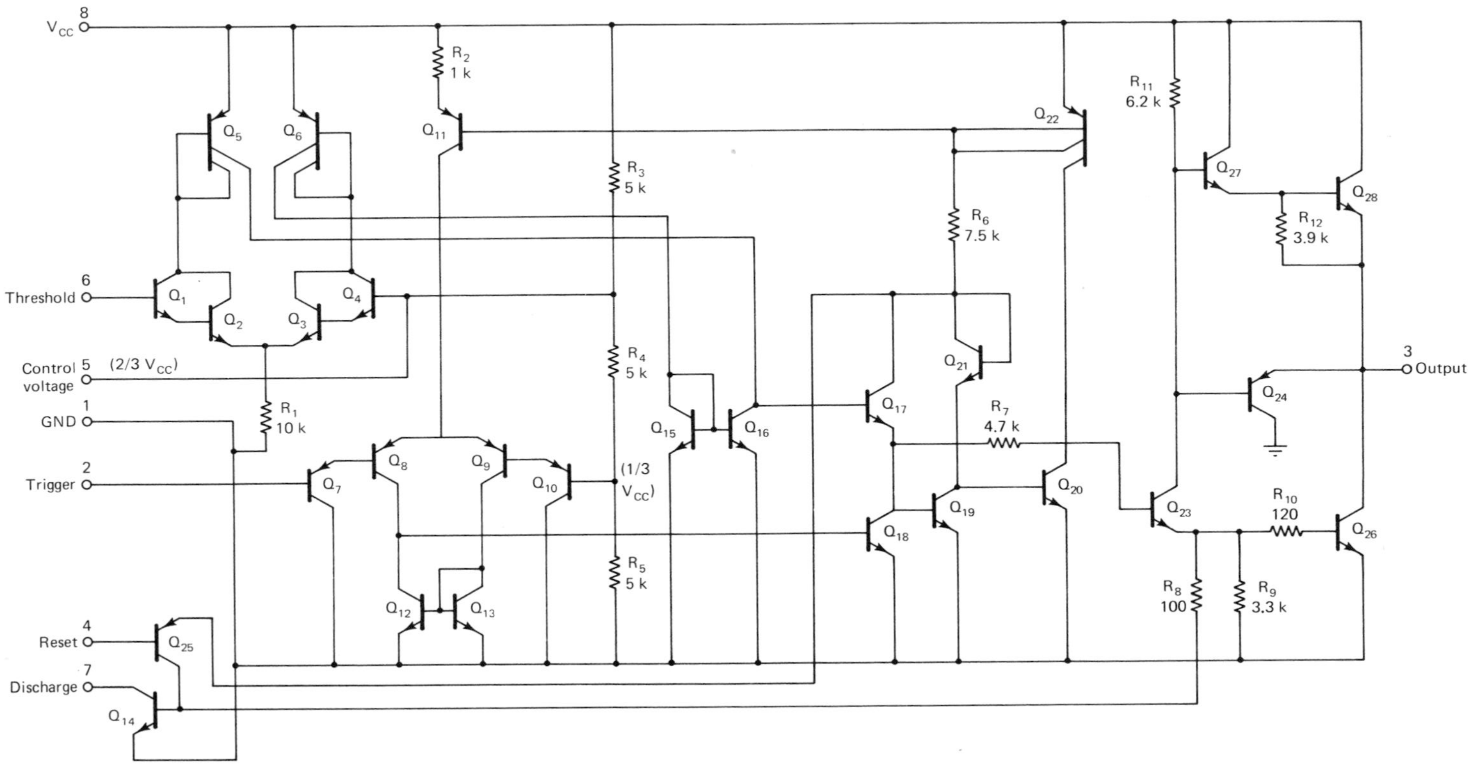

Figure 6.15 Circuit diagram of the LM555 timer (National Semiconductor).

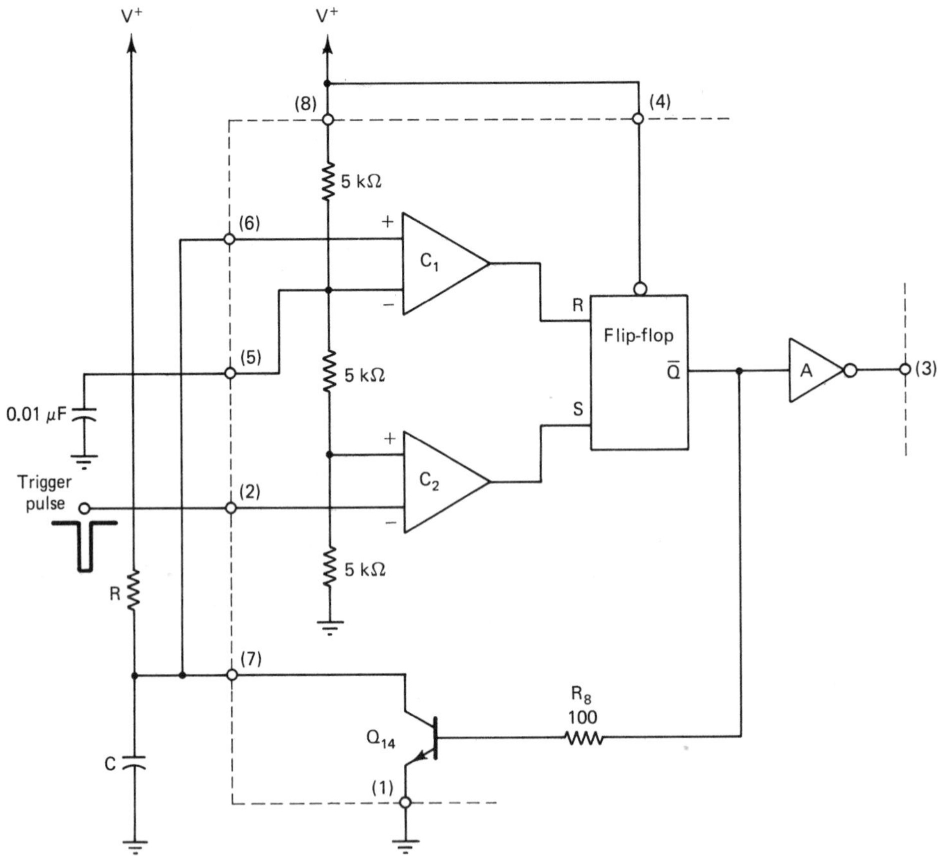

Figure 6.16 555-type monostable multivibrator.

When a negative polarity trigger pulse is applied to the trigger input pin 2 such that the voltage at this pin drops below $\frac{1}{3}V^+$, the output of comparator 2 will go *high*. This will cause the flip-flop to switch to the opposite state with $\overline{Q}$ now *low* and the discharge transistor will be turned off. Note that after the termination of the trigger pulse the flip-flop will remain in the $\overline{Q}$ low state. The timing capacitor can now charge up toward V^+ via resistor R. The voltage across the capacitor will be given by $v(t) = V^+[1 - \exp(-t/RC)]$. When $v(t)$ reaches the threshold voltage level of $\frac{2}{3}V^+$, however, comparator 1 will switch states and its output voltage will now go *high*. This causes the flip-flop to reset so that $\overline{Q}$ will go *high*. This turns on the discharge transistor Q_{14} and the voltage across the capacitor will rapidly drop to zero. The circuit will be back in its quiescent state with the output voltage *low* (~0 V).

The end of the output pulse occurs at time $t = T$, at which point $v(t) = \frac{2}{3}V^+$, so that $\frac{2}{3}V^+ = V^+[1 - \exp(-T/RC)]$, where T is the pulse duration. Solving for T gives

$$T = RC \ln 3 = 1.1RC \tag{6.10}$$

During the pulse the output voltage will be *high* at $V_{O(\text{HIGH})} = V^+ - V_{BE_{28}} - V_{BE_{27}} - I_{11}R_{11} \simeq V^+ - 1.7$ V. Note that the pulse duration T is independent of the supply voltage V^+. Note also that the trigger pulse must be shorter in duration than T.

Astable multivibrator. In Figure 6.17 the external connections are shown for the operation of the 555 timer as an astable multivibrator. In this mode of operation the timing capacitor charges up toward V^+ through $R_A + R_B$ until the voltage across the capacitor reaches the threshold level of $\frac{2}{3}V^+$. At this point comparator 1 switches states causing the flip-flop output $\overline{Q}$ to go *high*. This turns *on* the discharge transistor Q_{14} and the timing capacitor then discharges through R_B and Q_{14} (pin 7). This discharge continues until the capacitor voltage drops to $\frac{1}{3}V^+$, at which point comparator 2 switches states causing the flip-flop output $\overline{Q}$ to go *low*, turning off

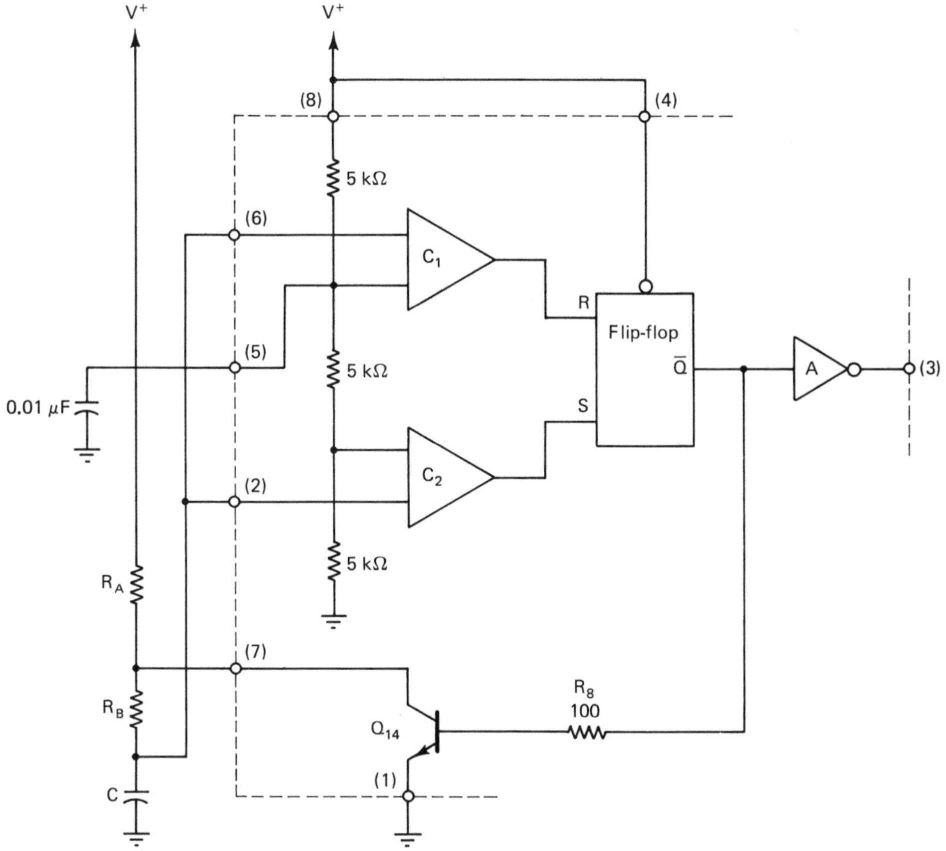

Figure 6.17 555-type astable multivibrator.

the discharge transistor Q_{14}. At this point the capacitor starts to charge again, thus completing the cycle.

During the charging period, $0 \leq t \leq T_C$, the voltage across the capacitor will be given by $v(t) = \frac{2}{3}V^+[1 - \exp(-t/R_A + R_B)C)] + \frac{1}{3}V^+$. At time $t = T_C$ the capacitor voltage reaches the threshold level of $\frac{2}{3}V^+$, so that $\frac{2}{3}V^+ = \frac{2}{3}V^+[1 - \exp(-T_C/(R_A + R_B)C)] + \frac{1}{3}V^+$. Solving for the charging time T_C gives $T_C = (R_A + R_B)C \ln 2 = 0.693(R_A + R_B)C$.

During the discharge interval $0 < t' < T_D$ we have that $v(t) = \frac{2}{3}V^+ \exp(-t'/R_BC)$. At time $t' = T_D$ the voltage across the capacitor reaches the trigger level of $\frac{1}{3}V^+$, so that we have that $v(t = T_D) = \frac{1}{3}V^+ = \frac{2}{3}V^+ \exp(-T_D/R_BC)$. Solving for T_D, we obtain $T_D = R_BC \ln 2 = 0.693R_BC$, where T_D is the discharge time.

The total period T will be $T = T_C + T_D = 0.693(R_A + 2R_B)C$ and the frequency of oscillation will be

$$\boxed{f = \frac{1}{T} = \frac{1}{0.693(R_A + 2R_B)C}} \tag{6.11}$$

The output voltage (pin 3) will be high during the charging time T_C at a value of $V_{O(\text{HIGH})} = V^+ - V_{BE_{28}} - V_{BE_{27}} - I_{11}R_{11} \simeq V^+ - 1.7$ V. During the discharge interval T_D the output voltage will be low at $V_{O(\text{LOW})} \simeq 0$. The duty cycle of the output pulse waveform will be given by

$$\text{duty cycle} = \frac{T_C}{T} = \frac{R_A + R_B}{R_A + 2R_B} \tag{6.12}$$

Note that the duty cycle will always be greater than 50% for this circuit.

For duty cycles of 50% and less, the circuit of Figure 6.18 can be used. In this circuit the capacitor C is charged only through R_A. During the charging interval the voltage across the timing capacitor will be $v(t) = \frac{2}{3}V^+[1 - \exp(-t/R_AC)] + \frac{1}{3}V^+$ for $0 < t < T_C$. At $t = T_C$ the threshold level of $\frac{2}{3}V^+$ is reached and the charging of the capacitor ceases. The charging time can therefore be obtained from the relationship that $\frac{2}{3}V^+ = \frac{2}{3}V^+[1 - \exp(-T_C/R_AC)] + \frac{1}{3}V^+$. Solving this for T_C gives $T_C = R_AC \ln 2 = 0.693R_AC$.

During the subsequent discharge period the discharge transistor Q_{14} is on (in saturation), so that the voltage at pin 7 is near ground potential. In Figure 6.19 a diagram for the discharge period is shown together with a Thévenin equivalent-circuit representation. The discharge cycle starts with $v(t') = \frac{2}{3}V^+$ at $t' = 0$ and ends at $t' = T_D$ with $v(T_D) = \frac{1}{3}V^+$. From the circuit of Figure 6.19 the voltage across the timing capacitor during the discharge interval can be written as

$$v(t') = \left(\frac{2}{3}V^+ - \frac{V^+R_B}{R_A + R_B}\right) \exp\left(\frac{-t'}{\tau_d}\right) + \frac{V^+R_B}{R_A + R_B} \tag{6.13}$$

where $\tau_d = (R_A \| R_B)C$ = discharge time constant. At $t' = T_D$, $v(T_D) = \frac{1}{3}V^+$, so that solving for T_D gives

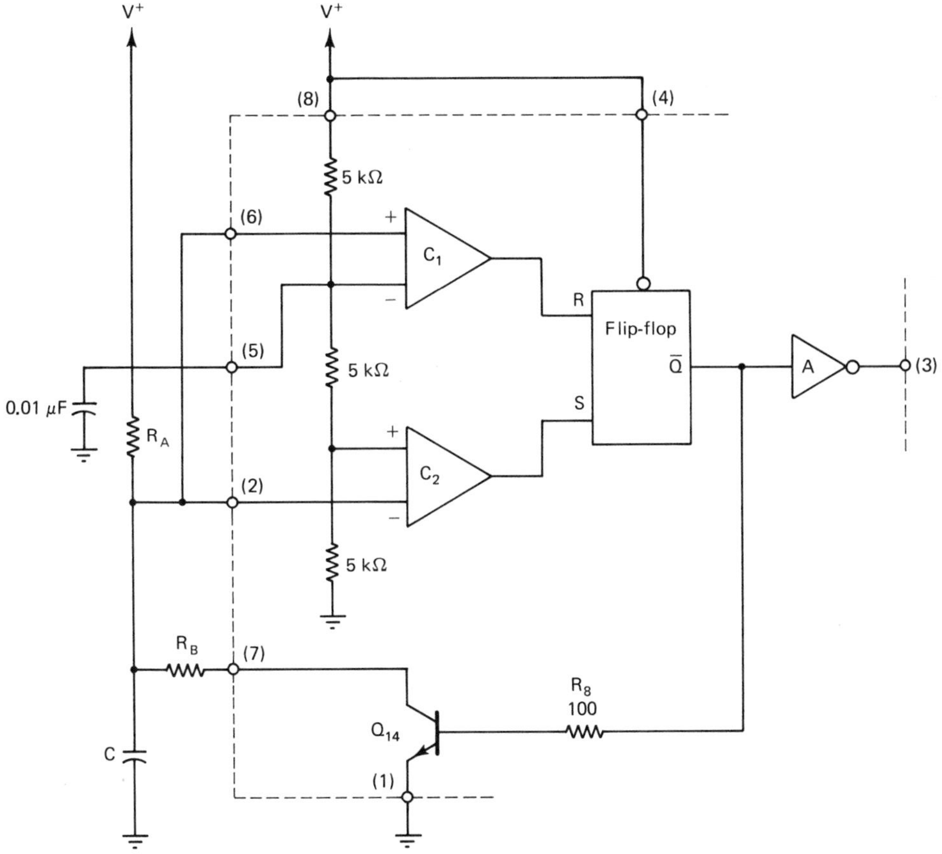

Figure 6.18 555-type monostable multivibrator for shorter duty cycles.

$$T_D = (R_A \| R_B)C \ln \frac{2R_A - R_B}{R_A - 2R_B}$$

The ratio of T_C to T_D will be

$$\frac{T_C}{T_D} = \frac{0.693(1 + R_A/R_B)}{\ln \dfrac{2(R_A/R_B) - 1}{(R_A/R_B) - 2}} \tag{6.14}$$

For a 50% duty cycle, $T_C/T_D = 1$. The corresponding resistance ratio, R_A/R_B, can be obtained by an iterative solution of the equation above to give

$$\boxed{\frac{R_A}{R_B} = 2.362} \tag{6.15}$$

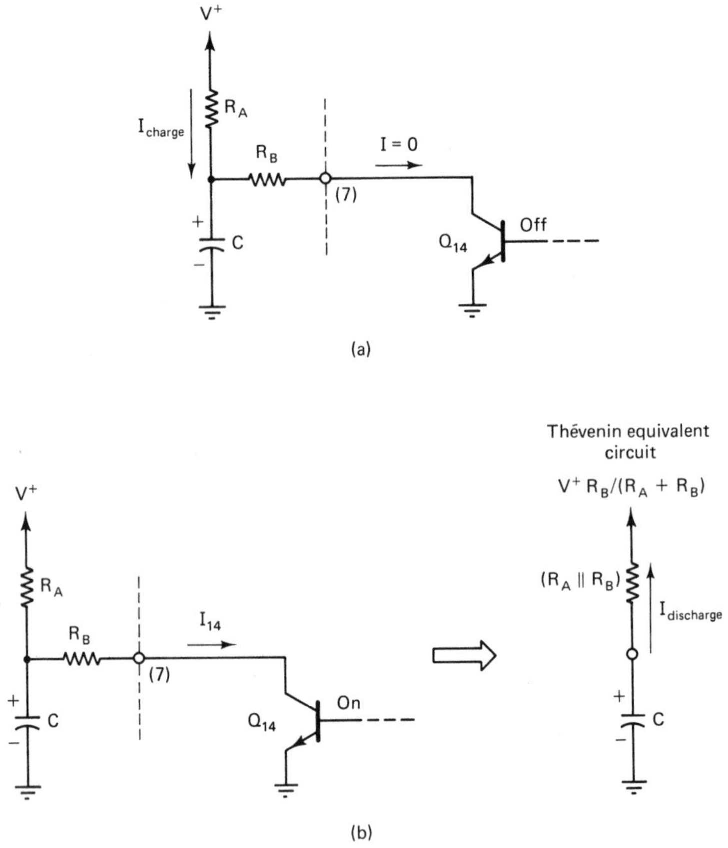

Figure 6.19 Charging and discharging cycles of astable multivibrator: (a) charging cycle; (b) discharging cycle.

For the case of a 50% duty cycle, the total period will be $T = 2T_C = 2R_AC \ln 2 = 1.386R_AC$ and the corresponding oscillation frequency will be

$$\boxed{f = \frac{1}{T} = \frac{0.721}{R_AC}} \tag{6.16}$$

The lowest value that the voltage across the timing capacitor can drop to during the discharge period will be $V^+R_B/(R_A + R_B)$, as seen from the Thévenin circuit representation. To reach the trigger level of comparator 2 and so to end the discharge cycle, the capacitor voltage must drop to $\frac{1}{3}V^+$. Therefore, we see that R_B should not be any greater than $R_A/2$ in order to satisfy this requirement, so that oscillations will occur.

Modulation capability. The voltage at pin 5 is nominally $\frac{2}{3}V^+$ and is the voltage applied to the inverting input of comparator 1. This voltage can, however, be varied by means of an externally applied voltage at this pin. Since the upper limit of the voltage across the timing capacitor (pin 6) is equal to the threshold voltage at pin 5, the charging time can be varied by means of a control or modulation voltage applied to pin 5. Thus for monostable operation if this device is triggered by a continuous pulse train, the pulse width of the output voltage can be varied or modulated to produce a *pulse-width-modulated* (PWM) signal.

The voltage across the timing capacitor will be given as before as $v(t) = V^+[1 - \exp(-t/RC)]$ during the charging time $0 < t < T_C$. The output pulse will end when the voltage across the capacitor reaches the voltage level at pin 5, which is V_M, so that at time $t = T$ we will have that $v(T) = V_M = V^+[1 - \exp(-T/RC)]$. Solving this equation for the pulse duration T gives $T = RC \ln [V^+/(V^+ - V_M)]$. Thus by varying V_M the pulse width can be modulated, although the relationship between pulse width and modulating voltage will not be linear. Note also that for triggering the voltage level at the trigger input, pin 2 must drop to less than $V_M/2$.

If this device is operated as an astable multivibrator as shown in Figure 6.17, the modulation voltage applied to pin 5 will again act to vary the upper limit of the capacitor voltage and thereby modulate the charging time. The capacitor will now charge from a lower limit of $\frac{1}{2}V_M$ up toward V^+, but will reach the upper limit of the charging cycle when $v(t) = V_M$. Note that if the voltage at pin 5 is V_M, the trigger level voltage will be $\frac{1}{2}V_M$.

The voltage across the timing capacitor during the charging cycle of $0 < t < T_C$ will be

$$v(t) = \left(V^+ - \frac{V_M}{2}\right)\left[1 - \exp\left(\frac{-t}{(R_A + R_B)C}\right)\right] + \frac{V_M}{2} \tag{6.17}$$

At $t = T_C$, $v(T_C) = V_M$, so that solving for T_C gives $T_C = (R_A + R_B)C \ln [V^+ - (V_M/2)/(V^+ - V_M)]$. Note that when $V_M = \frac{2}{3}V^+$, we obtain $T_C = (R_A + R_B)C \ln 2$, as before.

For the discharge period of $0 < t' < T_D$ we have that $v(t) = V_M \exp(-t/R_BC)$. At time $t' = T_D$ we have that $v(T_D) = \frac{1}{2}V_M$, so that solving for T_D gives $T_D = R_BC \ln 2 = 0.693R_BC$.

Note that the discharge time T_D is not a function of the modulation voltage. We see that the width of the pulse, and therefore the position of the pulse trailing edge (i.e., the negative-going transition) with respect to the leading edge can be varied. This device therefore can form the basis of a pulse-position modulator (PPM).

6.2.5 Linear Ramp Waveform Generator

In both the monostable and astable modes of operation the voltage across the timing capacitor will not be a linear function of time, but rather will be characterized by an exponential type of charging and discharging curve. For the monostable mode we have obtained that the charging time or pulse width is $T = 1.1\ RC$. Since the pulse width is equal to 1.1 RC time constants, we see that the voltage waveform across the capacitor will be quite nonlinear.

For the monostable (one-shot) multivibrator a linear ramp can be obtained by

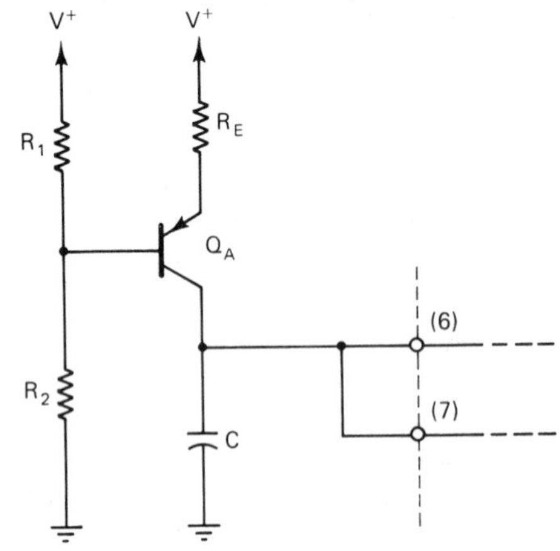

Figure 6.20 Current-source circuit for linear ramp.

charging the timing capacitor by a constant-current source rather than by a resistor. A linear ramp-generating one-shot is shown in Figure 6.20. In this circuit transistor Q_A in conjunction with resistors R_E, R_1, and R_2 acts as a constant-current source of strength $I_S = [V^+R_1/(R_1 + R_2) - V_{EB}]/R_E$.

The voltage across the timing capacitor during the charging period will be given by $v(t) = I_S t/C$, and at $t = T$ we will have the end of the charging period at which time $v(T) = \frac{2}{3}V^+$. This is the threshold voltage for comparator 1, and at this point the discharge transistor will be turned on due to the action of comparator 1 and the flip-flop. This action will rapidly discharge the capacitor and end the charging period. Setting $v(T) = \frac{2}{3}V^+$ equal to $I_S T/C$, and solving for T gives

$$T = \frac{\frac{2}{3}V^+C}{I_S} = \frac{\frac{2}{3}V^+R_EC}{[V^+R_1/(R_1 + R_2)] - V_{EB}} \tag{6.18}$$

PROBLEMS

6.1. (*Emitter-coupled voltage-controlled oscillator*) Given an emitter-coupled VCO with $R_1 = 18.6$ kΩ, $R_2 = 10.0$ kΩ, $R_3 = 50$ kΩ, and $R_5 = R_6 = 100$ kΩ. The circuit is shown in Figure 6.6 with $V^+ = 12$ V.

(a) Find V_D. (*Ans.*: $V_D = 2.0$ V)

(b) Find the control voltage range (V_C) over which the VCO will operate properly. [*Ans.*: V_C from ~ 0 V (min.) to +3.75 V (max.)]

(c) Find the VCO frequency range for $R_4 = 1.0$ kΩ and $C_t = 0.01$ μF. (*Ans.*: $f_{\text{MIN}} = 0$ and $f_{\text{MAX}} = (93.75$ kHz)

(d) If $TC_{V_{BE}} = -2.2$ mV/C and $TC_R = +2000$ ppm/C, find the temperature coefficient of the VCO frequency, TC_f. (*Ans.*: $TC_f = 1.143 \times 10^{-3}$/C = 0.1143%/C = 1143 ppm/C)

(e) If the matching tolerance of the IC resistors is ±2%, find the effect on the square-wave output symmetry. (*Ans.*: the square-wave duty cycle will be 50 ± 1%)

(f) For small values of V_C (less than about 50 mV) the square-wave symmetry will become progressively worse as V_C gets smaller due to the offset voltage between Q_5 and Q_6.

Explain. Find the resulting square-wave symmetry if $V_{OS}(Q_5, Q_6) = \pm 2.0$ mV and $V_C = 10$ mV. [*Ans.*: the square-wave symmetry (duty cycle) will be 45.5% (min.), 54.5% (max.)]

(g) Sketch and dimension the voltage versus time waveforms at the collectors of Q_3 and Q_4.

(h) Sketch and dimension the waveform across the timing capacitor C_t.

6.2. (*Voltage-controlled current source for a VCO*) Given a current source circuit for a VCO (Figure P6.2). The VCO frequency will be directly proportional to I_Q. Current source I_1 is set to give $V_{EB_1} = V_{BE_2} = V_{BE_3}$ at $I_Q = 10$ mA. The VCO frequency is $f_{MAX} =$ 1.0 MHz when $V_C = V_{C(MAX)} = 10$ V.

(a) Find the voltage-to-frequency transfer coefficient, K_V. (*Ans.*: 100 kHz/V)

(b) Find the VCO frequency f at the following V_C values and the percentage departure from linearity. (*Hint*: Use the iterative technique.)

(1) $V_C = 1.0$ V (*Ans.*: 106 kHz, 6%)

(2) $V_C = 0.50$ V (*Ans.*: 57.1 kHz, 14.2%)

(3) $V_C = 0.20$ V (*Ans.*: 28.9 kHz, 44.4%)

(c) If $V_{BE_2} = V_{BE_3} = 680$ mV and $V_{EB_1} = 700$ mV, all at a current level of 10 mA, find the required value of I_1 to satisfy the condition that $V_{EB_1} = V_{BE_2} = V_{BE_3}$ at $I_Q = 10$ mA. (*Ans.*: 4.5 mA)

(d) What is the advantage of the use of a current source I_1 over the use of a resistor in its place in this application?

(e) The voltage-controlled current source under consideration here is an open-loop system. For improved linearity a closed-loop system can be used. Show a voltage-controlled current source that will operate as a closed-loop system and exhibit very good linearity down to very low current levels.

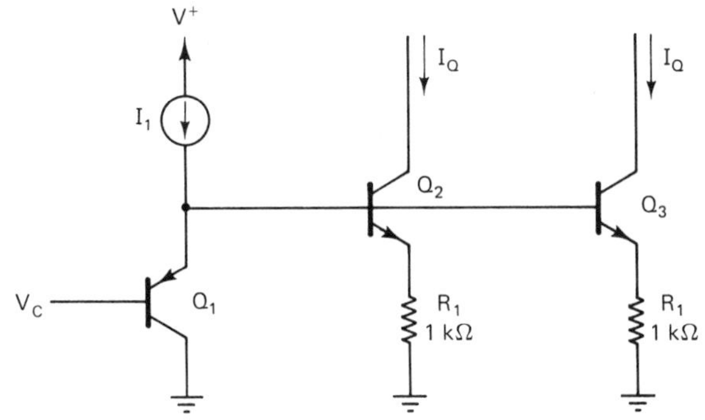

Figure P6.2

6.3. (*Low distortion Wien bridge oscillator*) In the Wien bridge oscillator circuit of Figure 1.56 a ± 15 V supply is used, $R_1 = R_2$, and $C_1 = C_2$. A small thermistor is used for R_3 to automatically adjust the negative feedback and thereby produce a low distortion sinusoidal output. The thermistor has a resistance of 4000 Ω at 25°C and a thermal resistance of 1°C/mW. The resistance of the thermistor decreases exponentially with temperature, and at 50°C has decreased by a ratio of 8 : 1. The thermistor temperature is to stabilize at 50°C due to self-heating when stable oscillations are established.

(a) Find R_4 for stable oscillations. (*Ans.*: 250 Ω)

(b) Find the rms and peak output voltage. (*Ans.*: 5.3 V rms, 7.5 V peak)

(c) Using a thermistor similar to the one described, find the thermistor resistance (at 25°C) and the value of R_4 for a 6 V peak output swing. (*Ans.*: 2560 Ω, 160 Ω)

REFERENCES

GRAEME, J. G., G. E. TOBEY, AND L. P. HUELSMAN, *Operational Amplifiers—Design and Applications*, McGraw-Hill, 1971.

MILLMAN, J., *Microelectronics*, McGraw-Hill, 1979.

STOUT, D. F., *Handbook of Microcircuit Design and Applications*, McGraw-Hill, 1980.

United Technical Publications, *Modern Applications of Integrated Circuits*, Tab Books, 1974.

Phase-Locked Loops

7

A *phase-locked loop* (PLL) is a feedback loop comprised of a phase detector, low-pass filter, amplifier, and voltage-controlled oscillator (VCO). The phase detector or phase comparator compares the phase angle of the signal to that of the VCO output voltage, as shown in Figure 7.1, and produces an output voltage that is related to this phase angle difference.

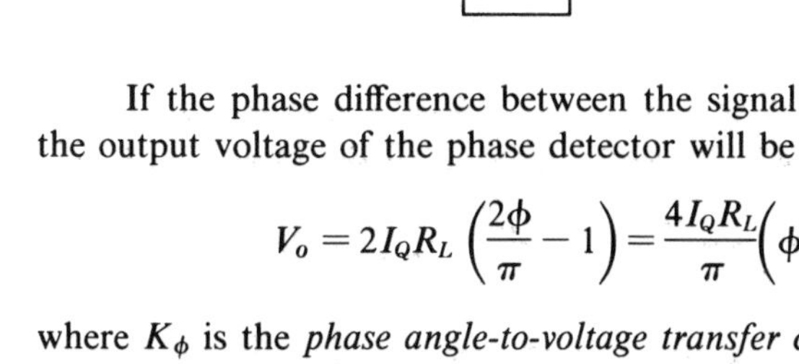

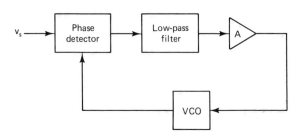

Figure 7.1 Phase-locked loop.

If the phase difference between the signal and the VCO voltage is ϕ radians, the output voltage of the phase detector will be given by

$$V_o = 2I_Q R_L \left(\frac{2\phi}{\pi} - 1\right) = \frac{4I_Q R_L}{\pi}\left(\phi - \frac{\pi}{2}\right) = K_\phi \left(\phi - \frac{\pi}{2}\right) \tag{7.1}$$

where K_ϕ is the *phase angle-to-voltage transfer coefficient* of the phase detector.

The output voltage of the phase detector is filtered by the low-pass filter (LPF) to remove the high-frequency components such as those at the signal and VCO frequencies and harmonics thereof. The output of the LPF is then amplified and applied as the input or control voltage V_C of the VCO as given by $V_C = K_\phi A(\phi - \pi/2)$, where A is the voltage gain of the amplifier.

This control voltage will result in a shift in the VCO frequency from its *free-running frequency* f_o to a frequency f given by $f = f_o + K_V V_C$, where K_V is the *voltage-to-frequency transfer coefficient* of the VCO.

7.1 LOCK-IN RANGE

When the PLL is *locked-in* to the signal frequency f_s, we have that $f = f_s = f_o + K_V V_C$. Since $V_C = (f_s - f_o)/K_V = K_\phi A\ (\phi - \pi/2)$, we will obtain that $\phi - \pi/2 = (f_s - f_o)/K_V K_\phi A$. Thus when the PLL is locked in to the signal, there will be a phase angle difference ϕ established between the signal voltage and the VCO output voltage given by

$$\phi = \frac{\pi}{2} + \frac{f_s - f_o}{K_V K_\phi A} \tag{7.2}$$

and the two frequencies will be in *exact synchronism*.

The maximum output voltage magnitude available from the phase detector occurs for $\phi = \pi$ and 0 rad and is $V_{O(\text{MAX})} = \pm 2 I_Q R_L = \pm K_\phi(\pi/2)$. The corresponding value of the maximum control voltage available to drive the VCO will be $V_{C(\text{MAX})} = \pm(\pi/2)K_\phi A$. The maximum VCO frequency swing that can be obtained will be $(f - f_o)_{\text{MAX}} = K_V V_{C(\text{MAX})} = \pm K_V K_\phi(\pi/2)A$. Therefore, the maximum range of signal frequencies over which the PLL can remained locked in on will be $f_s = f_o \pm K_V K_\phi(\pi/2)A = f_o \pm \Delta f_L$, where $2\ \Delta f_L$ will be the *lock-in frequency range*, given by

$$\boxed{\text{lock-in range} = 2\ \Delta f_L = K_V K_\phi A \pi} \tag{7.3}$$

Note that the lock-in range will be symmetrically located with respect to the VCO free-running frequency f_o.

In Figure 7.2 a graph of the VCO control voltage V_C versus the signal frequency f_s is shown. Outside the lock-in range the VCO frequency can not be brought into synchronism with the signal frequency. The resulting phase angle difference will be $\phi = (\omega_s t + \theta_s) - (\omega_o t + \theta_o) = (\omega_s - \omega_o)t + (\theta_s - \theta_o)$ and will thus change rapidly with time. The rate of change of ϕ with time will be $d\phi/dt = \omega_s - \omega_o$. The phase detector output voltage will therefore vary rapidly with time and be heavily attenuated by the low-pass filter. As a result, there will be very little voltage available to drive the VCO and the VCO frequency will revert back to essentially the free-running value of f_o. Thus we see that outside the lock-in range the VCO control voltage will essentially drop to zero.

When the VCO is locked in to the signal, we have that

$$\phi = \frac{\pi}{2} + \frac{f_s - f_o}{K_\phi K_V A} \tag{7.4}$$

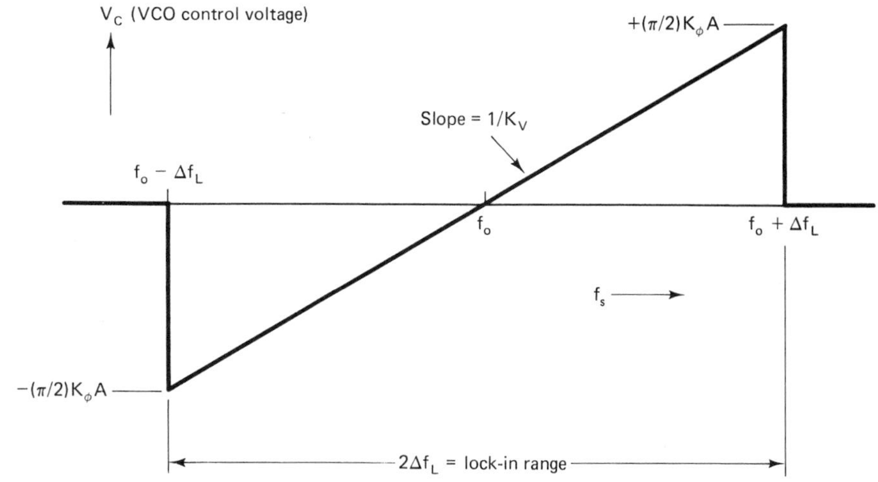

Figure 7.2 PLL lock-in range.

Note that when $f_s = f_o$ the VCO voltage will be in *phase quadrature* (i.e., 90° phase difference) with respect to the signal voltage. As f_s goes above f_o the phase angle increase from 90° toward a maximum of 180° at the upper end of the lock-in range. As f_s goes below f_o the phase angle drops from 90° toward 0° at the lower end of the lock-in range.

7.2 CAPTURE RANGE

The discussion of the lock-in range was based on the assumption that the PLL was initially locked in on the signal. We will now investigate the situation wherein this condition is not initially present to determine the span of frequencies over which the PLL can lock in on a signal. This range of frequencies over which the PLL can lock in on a signal is called the *capture range* or *acquisition range*.

When the PLL is *not* initially locked in to the signal, the frequency of the VCO will be the free-running frequency f_o. The phase angle difference between the signal and the VCO voltage will be $\phi = (\omega_s t + \theta_s) - (\omega_o t + \theta_o) = (\omega_s - \omega_o)t + \Delta\theta$ and thus not be constant, but will change with time at a rate given by $d\phi/dt = \omega_s - \omega_o$. The phase detector output voltage will therefore not have a d-c component, but rather will produce an a-c voltage with a triangular waveform of peak amplitude $K_\phi(\pi/2)$ and a fundamental frequency of $f_s - f_o$.

If the low-pass filter is a simple *RC* low-pass network it will have a transfer function given by

$$T(\omega) = \frac{1}{1 + j\omega\tau} = \frac{1}{1 + j(\omega/\omega_1)} = \frac{1}{1 + j(f/f_1)} \tag{7.5}$$

where $\tau = RC$ and $\omega_1 = 1/RC$, so that the breakpoint frequency f_1 will be $f_1 = 1/2\pi RC$. For the condition that $(f/f_1)^2 \gg 1$, the transfer function can be expressed approximately as $T(f) \simeq 1/j(f/f_1) = f_1/jf$.

The fundamental input frequency term supplied to the low-pass filter by the phase detector will be at the difference frequency $\Delta f = f_s - f_o$. If $\Delta f > 3f_1$, the LPF transfer function will be approximately given by $T(\Delta f) \simeq f_1/\Delta f = f_1/(f_s - f_o)$. The voltage available to drive the VCO will be given by $V_C = V_{o\,(\text{phase detector})} \times T(f) \times A$ and will have a maximum value of $V_{C\,(\text{MAX})} = \pm K_\phi(\pi/2)(f_1/\Delta f)A$. The corresponding value of the maximum VCO frequency shift will be given by

$$(f - f_o)_{\text{MAX}} = K_V V_{C\,(\text{MAX})} \simeq \pm K_V K_\phi \frac{\pi}{2} A \frac{f_1}{\Delta f} \tag{7.6}$$

For the acquisition of the signal frequency f_s we must have that $f = f_s$ so that the maximum signal frequency range that can be acquired by the PLL will be

$$(f_s - f_o)_{\text{MAX}} \simeq \pm K_V K_\phi \frac{\pi}{2} A \frac{f_1}{\Delta f_c} = \Delta f_c$$

where $\Delta f_c = (f_s - f_o)_{\text{MAX}}$. We therefore will have that $(\Delta f_c)^2 \simeq K_V K_\phi(\pi/2)Af_1$. Since $\Delta f_L = K_V K_\phi(\pi/2)A$, we can express Δf_c as $(\Delta f_c)^2 \simeq f_1\,\Delta f_L$ and thus $\Delta f_c \simeq \pm\sqrt{f_1\,\Delta f_L}$.

This gives the range of frequencies that can be "captured" by the PLL. The total *capture range* is given by

$$\boxed{\text{capture range} = 2\,\Delta f_c \simeq 2\sqrt{f_1\,\Delta f_L}} \tag{7.7}$$

for the usual case of $\Delta f_L \gg f_1$. Note that the capture range will be located symmetrically with respect to the VCO free-running frequency f_o.

In Figure 7.3 a graph of the VCO control voltage V_C versus the signal frequency is given again, but this time showing both the capture range and the lock-in range. the PLL cannot acquire a signal outside of the capture range, but once the PLL

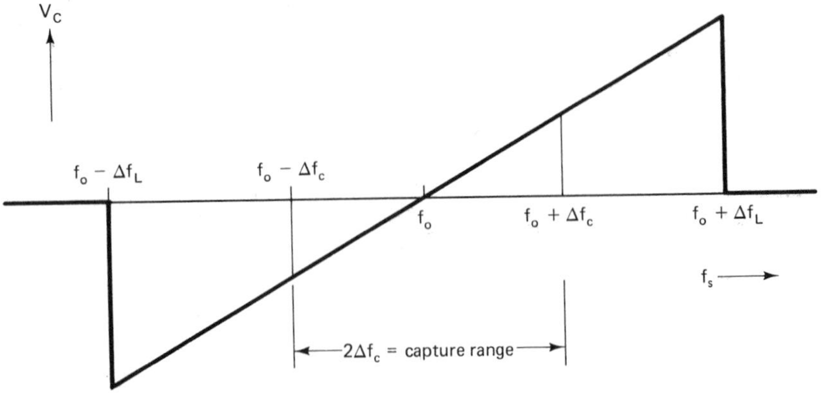

Figure 7.3 PLL capture range.

captures the signal it will hold on to it until the signal frequency goes beyond the limits of the lock-in range.

A large capture range is desirable from the standpoint of the ability of the lock-in on a signal. However, a large capture range will make the PLL more susceptible to interference by undesired signals and noise. For the maximum amount of rejection of interference and noise a small capture range is desirable. In many cases a suitable compromise is reached between these two opposing requirements for the capture range.

In some cases where a suitable compromise cannot be reached, the low-pass filter bandwidth is first set to a large value for the initial acquisition of the signal. Once the signal has been captured and the PLL is locked in on the signal the bandwidth of the low-pass filter will be reduced substantially. This will minimize the effects of interfering signals and noise. Indeed, one of the key features of a PLL is the ability to remain locked in on a signal even under very adverse noise conditions in which the signal-to-noise ratio may be less than unity. The PLL is used very often in very low-level signal applications.

7.3 THE PLL AS AN FM DETECTOR

The PLL can be very easily used as an FM detector or demodulator. A diagram of a PLL FM detector is shown in Figure 7.4.

When the PLL is locked in on the FM signal we will have that the VCO frequency $f_o + K_V V_C$ will be equal to the instantaneous frequency of the FM signal f_s so that $f_s = f_o + K_V V_C$ and thus the VCO control voltage voltage V_C will be given by $V_C = (f_s - f_o)/K_V$. If the instantaneous frequency of the FM signal is given by $f_s(t) = f_c + \Delta f \sin \omega_m t$, where f_c is the (unmodulated) carrier frequency, Δf is the peak frequency deviation, and ω_m is the radian frequency of the modulating signal, we will have that

$$V_C(t) = \frac{f_s(t) - f_o}{K_V} = \frac{f_c - f_o - \Delta f \sin \omega_m t}{K_V} \tag{7.8}$$

The a-c component of $V_C(t)$ will be $v_c(t) = \Delta f \sin \omega_m t/K_V$, so that we see that this will represent a true replica of the modulating voltage that is applied to the FM carrier at the transmitter. We see that the VCO control voltage will be a linear function of the instantaneous frequency deviation so that the FM signal will be demodulated with little or no distortion.

For a maximum symmetrical lock-in range the VCO free-running frequency f_o should be set as close as possible to the FM carrier frequency f_c.

The maximum VCO control voltage that will be available to drive the VCO will be given by $V_{C(\mathrm{MAX})} = \pm K_\phi(\pi/2)A|T(f_m)|$, where $T(f_m)$ is the low-pass filter transfer function at the modulation frequency f_m. For values of f_m such that $f_m > 3f_1$ we will have that $|T(f_m)| \simeq f_1/f_m$, where f_1 is the breakpoint frequency of the low-pass filter. Note that when the PLL is locked in on the FM signal, the VCO control voltage will vary with time as $v_C(t) = \Delta f \sin \omega_m t/K_V$. This is the voltage that is supplied to the VCO input from the low-pass filter.

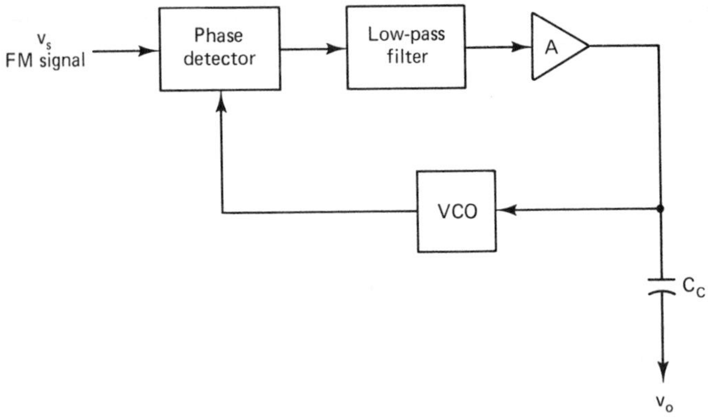

Figure 7.4 PLL FM demodulator.

For the case of $f_m > 3f_1$, we have that $V_{C(\text{MAX})} \simeq \pm K_\phi(\pi/2)A(f_1/f_m)$. If $f_o \simeq f_c$, the limiting combination of FM frequency deviation and modulation frequency that the PLL can remain locked in to will be given by $V_{C(\text{MAX})} = \Delta f/K_V \simeq K_\phi(\pi/2)A(f_1/f_m)$, so that $\Delta f \simeq K_V K_\phi(\pi/2)A(f_1/f_m)$. We therefore will have that

$$(f_m \Delta f)_{\text{MAX}} \simeq K_V K_\phi \frac{\pi}{2} A f_1 \qquad (7.9)$$

$$\simeq \Delta f_L f_1 = (\Delta f_c)^2$$

If the product of the modulation frequency f_m and the frequency deviation Δf exceeds this value, the VCO will not be able to follow the instantaneous frequency variations of the FM signal. The output voltage of this FM detector will no longer be an exact replica of the FM modulation signal and there will be distortion. The amount of distortion will be very high whenever there is a combination of a large modulation signal amplitude which produces a large Δf and a large modulating frequency f_m. Nevertheless, under conditions in which the PLL can remain locked in on the FM signal, a very linear demodulation characteristic will be obtained and there will be very little distortion of the demodulated signal.

7.3.1 Frequency-Shift Keying

Frequency-shift keying (FSK) is a type of frequency modulation in which the frequency of the FM signal is varied between two fixed levels. This can be considered to be a binary digital type of information transmission system in which one frequency f_1 represents a "0" and the other frequency level f_2 represents a "1," the "0"-to-"1" frequency deviation Δf being $\Delta f = f_2 - f_1$.

A PLL can be used as an FSK demodulator, as shown in Figure 7.5. It is similar to the PLL demodulator for analog FM signals except for the addition of a comparator to produce a reconstructed digital output signal.

If the PLL remains locked in to the FSK signal at both f_1 and f_2, the VCO control voltage which is also supplied to the comparator will be given by $V_{C_1} =$

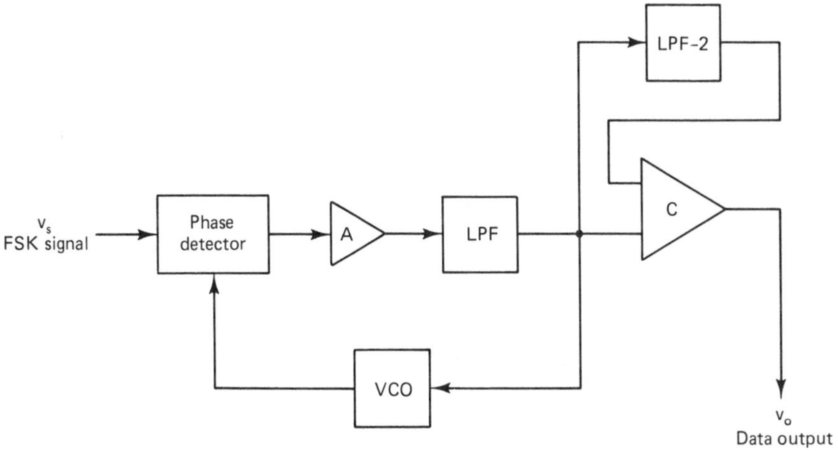

Figure 7.5 Frequency-shift keying demodulator.

$(f_1 - f_o)/K_V$ and $V_{C_2} = (f_2 - f_o)/K_V$, respectively. The difference between the two control voltage levels will be $\Delta V_C = (f_2 - f_1)/K_V$.

The reference voltage for the comparator is obtained by passing the VCO control voltage through an additional low-pass filter (LPF-2). This low-pass filter has a very long time constant compared to the FSK pulse period such that an essentially d-c voltage is obtained. This d-c voltage will have a level that is midway between V_{C_1} and V_{C_2}, and therefore is at the optimum value to produce a minimum bit error rate.

7.3.2 PLL Response Time

For an FSK demodulator the response time of the PLL to a step-function type of frequency change is of importance. For an approximate analysis of the PLL response time for a step-function frequency change from f_1 to $f_2 = f_1 + \Delta f$ we will assume that both f_1 and f_2 fall within the PLL capture range.

For the VCO frequency to change from f_1 to f_2 the required change in the VCO control voltage will be $\Delta V_C = \Delta f/K_V$. The VCO control voltage is obtained from across the capacitor of the RC low-pass filter. The time required for the voltage across this capacitor to change by an amount ΔV_C will be given approximately by $\Delta V_C = \Delta Q/C = I\,\Delta t/C \simeq (K_\phi(\pi/2)A/R)\,(\Delta t/C)$. We therefore will have that

$$\Delta t \simeq \frac{RC\,\Delta V_C}{K_\phi(\pi/2)A} \simeq \frac{RC\,\Delta f}{K_V K_\phi(\pi/2)A} \tag{7.10}$$

Since $K_V K_\phi(\pi/2)A = \Delta f_L$ and $RC = \tau$ is the RC time constant of the low-pass network, we have that $\Delta t = \tau\Delta f/\Delta f_L$. The breakpoint frequency of the low-pass network is related to the time constant τ by $f_1 = 1/(2\pi\tau)$, so that $\Delta t \simeq \tau\Delta f/\Delta f_L = \Delta f/(2\pi f_1\,\Delta f_L)$. After noting that $(\Delta f_c)^2 = f_1\,\Delta f_L$, we can also express Δt as $\Delta t \simeq \Delta f/2\pi(\Delta f_c)^2$. The ratio $\Delta f/\Delta t \simeq 2\pi(\Delta f_c)^2 = 2\pi f_1\,\Delta f_L$ can be considered to be essentially the "slewing rate" of the PLL in response to a step-function frequency change, and represents the maximum rate at which the VCO frequency can change with time. Note that the PLL slewing rate is a function of the RC time constant of the low-pass network and the loop gain $K_V K_\phi A$ around the feedback loop.

The same PLL that is used for the demodulator of the FSK signal can also be used for the production of an FSK signal. This is done by just using the VCO portion of the circuit and driving the VCO by a binary digital input voltage so that the VCO is switched between two fixed frequency levels. The PLL can thus serve very conveniently as a *modem* (or modulator–demodulator) for data communications systems using FSK, such as for the transmission of digital data over telephone lines.

7.4 PLL FREQUENCY SYNTHESIZER

The PLL can be used as the basis for frequency synthesizers that can produce a precise series of frequencies that are derived from a stable crystal-controlled oscillator. A basic diagram of a PLL frequency synthesizer is shown in Figure 7.6. The frequency of the crystal-controlled oscillator is divided by an integer factor M by a counter circuit to produce a frequency f_{osc}/M, where f_{osc} is the frequency of the crystal-controlled oscillator.

The VCO frequency f_{VCO} is similarly divided by a counter circuit by an integer factor N to become f_{VCO}/N. When the PLL is locked in on the divided-down oscillator frequency, we will have that $f_{osc}/M = f_{VCO}/N$, so that $f_{VCO} = (N/M)f_{osc}$.

The frequency counters or dividers can be programmed to produce a number of different frequency-division factors so that a large number of frequencies can be produced, all derived from the crystal-controlled oscillator.

7.5 THE PLL AS AN AM DETECTOR

The use of a PLL for AM detection is shown in Figure 7.7. When the PLL is locked in on the AM signal, the VCO frequency will be equal to the AM carrier frequency f_c. The phase angle of the VCO output voltage with respect to the AM carrier will be given by

$$\phi = -\left(\frac{\pi}{2} + \frac{f_c - f_o}{K_V K_\phi A}\right) = -\frac{\pi}{2}\left(1 + \frac{f_c - f_o}{\Delta f_L}\right) \tag{7.11}$$

where f_o is the VCO free-running frequency and Δf_L is the one-half of the lock-in range. If the PLL free-running frequency f_o is close to the AM carrier frequency such that $|f_c - f_o| \ll \Delta f_L$, the VCO output voltage will be approximately in phase quadrature (i.e., 90° out of phase) with the carrier of the AM signal.

The VCO output voltage is passed through a 90° phase-shift network to produce a large level signal that will be in frequency synchronism with the original carrier and is also approximately in phase with the carrier. It is then supplied to one input port of a product detector, such as a balanced modulator–demodulator. The other input port is supplied with the AM signal. The output of the demodulator is then filtered by a low-pass filter to remove all the higher-frequency components such as

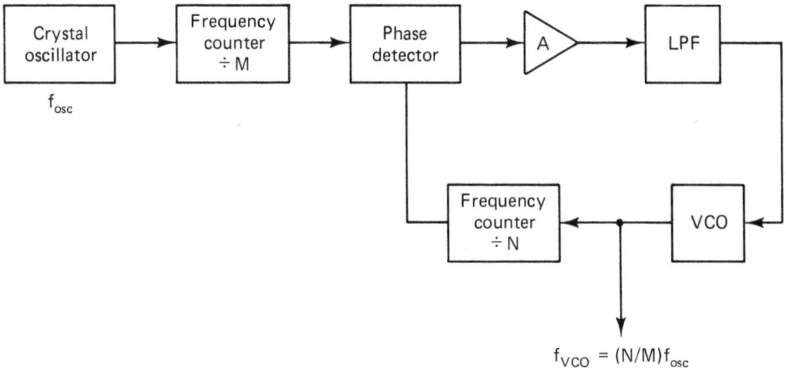

Figure 7.6 PLL frequency synthesizer.

those at $nf_c \pm f_m$, and passing through only the lowest-frequency difference terms that are obtained from the AM signal sidebands being heterodyned with the VCO frequency at f_c. For the upper sideband at $f_c + f_m$ this gives $(f_c + f_m) - f_c = f_m$, with the same result being obtained for the lower sideband.

Note that for this AM demodulation system the carrier does not have to be transmitted at the full amplitude that would be characteristic of the DSB/LC signal. For the demodulation of a DSB/LC signal with an envelope or peak detector the carrier amplitude must be such that the modulation index will never go above unity, for if it does, severe distortion will result. As a result of the large carrier amplitude a substantial fraction of the total transmitted power is used in transmitting just the carrier.

For the system under consideration the PLL can regenerate a carrier that has

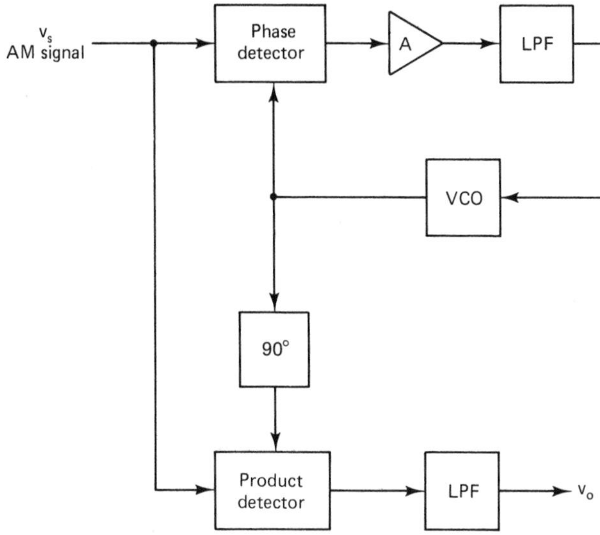

Figure 7.7 PLL amplitude-modulation detector.

been transmitted at a much reduced level and produce a large-amplitude signal in frequency synchronism with the original carrier. It will not work, however, in most cases with a DSB/SC or SSB/SC signal in which there has been complete suppression of the carrier. The required amplitude of the carrier for the PLL to lock in on will be a function of the PLL feedback loop parameters. In general, the smaller the PLL capture range and the closer the VCO free-running frequency is to the carrier frequency, the lower the minimum carrier signal amplitude can be for accurate carrier regeneration by the PLL.

7.6 STEREO DEMODULATION

An interesting application in which a PLL is used to regenerate a carrier is the PLL stereo demodulator as shown in Figure 7.8. For FM stereo broadcasting, a total modulation bandwidth of 75 kHz is available and is divided up as shown in

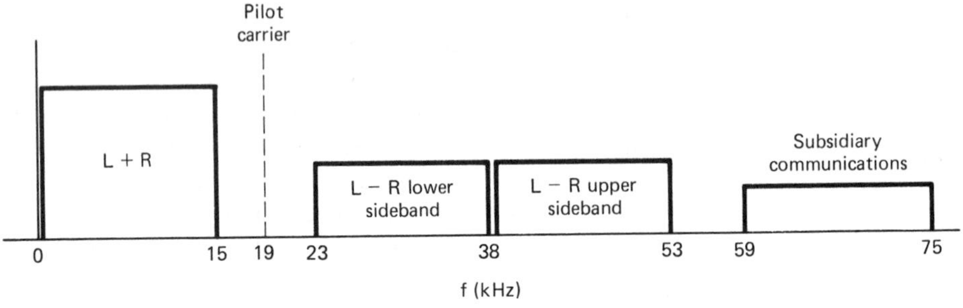

(a)

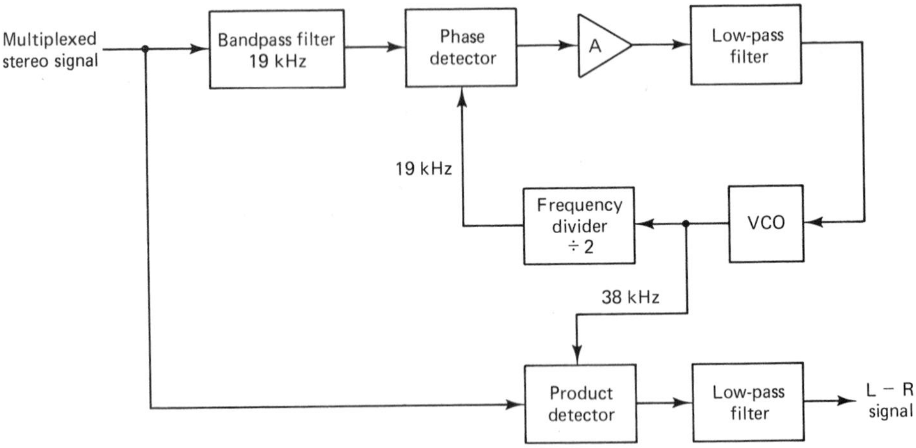

(b)

Figure 7.8 PLL stereo demodulator: (a) stereo modulation spectrum; (b) PLL demodulator for L − R signal.

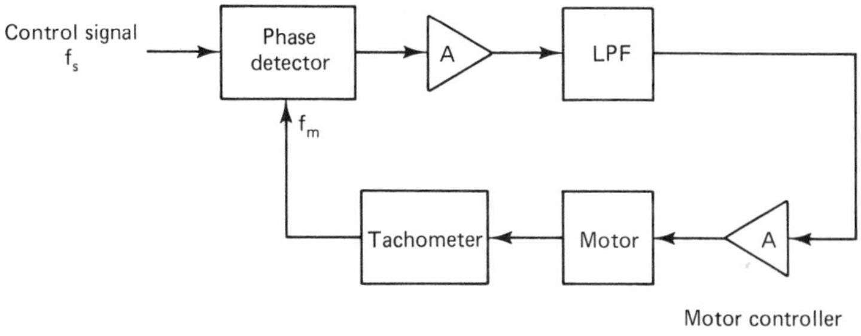

Figure 7.9 Motor speed control.

Figure 7.9. The range 0 to 15 kHz is used for the L + R (left + right) audio signal for monoaural (nonstereo) reception. The L − R difference signal is sent as a double-sideband/suppressed carrier (DSB/SC) signal using a 38-kHz suppressed carrier. A small-amplitude "pilot carrier" at exactly one-half of the carrier frequency (19 kHz) is also transmitted.

At the receiver a PLL operates on the 19-kHz pilot carrier to produce a 38-kHz signal. This 38-kHz signal will be in frequency synchronism with the original 38-kHz carrier and is combined with the multiplexed stereo signal in a product detector. The output of the product detector then passes through a low-pass filter to produce the demodulated L − R signal, the heterodyned L + R signal being rejected by the low-pass filter. the L − R signal can then be combined with the L + R signal to produce the L and R signals for stereo sound.

7.7 IC PLL EXAMPLE: LM565

An example of an IC PLL is the LM565 (National Semiconductor). In Figure 7.10 a diagram of this PLL is presented. The phase detector is comprised of the Q_1–Q_2, Q_3–Q_4, and Q_5–Q_6 differential amplifier pairs with Q_{37} together with R_3 (200 Ω) serving as a current sink bias source. Resistors R_1 and R_2 (7.2 kΩ) serve as the load for the phase detector. The output voltage of the phase detector is limited by the diode-connected transistors Q_7 and Q_8 to a maximum of ±0.7 V. This limiting action helps to minimize the effect of high-amplitude noise pulses and other transient effects on the operation of the PLL.

A balanced output is taken from the phase detector and supplied to the Q_{10}–Q_{11} differential-amplifier pair, which is biased by the Q_{39} current sink. The Q_{10}–Q_{11} differential amplifier serves as an amplifier stage in amplifying the output voltage of the phase detector. A single-ended output is taken from this stage from across the load resistor R_{12} (3.6 kΩ) and connected internally to the VCO. Resistor R_{12} serves as part of the low-pass filter. Connection of an external capacitor between pin 7 and ground will produce a simple low-pass (lag) network. A capacitor C_2 and a resistor R_2 connected in series between pin 7 and ground will result in a lag-lead network with a transfer function given by $T(s) = (1 + s\tau_2)/1 + s(\tau_1 + \tau_2)$, where $\tau_1 = R_{12}C_2$ and $\tau_2 = R_2C_2$.

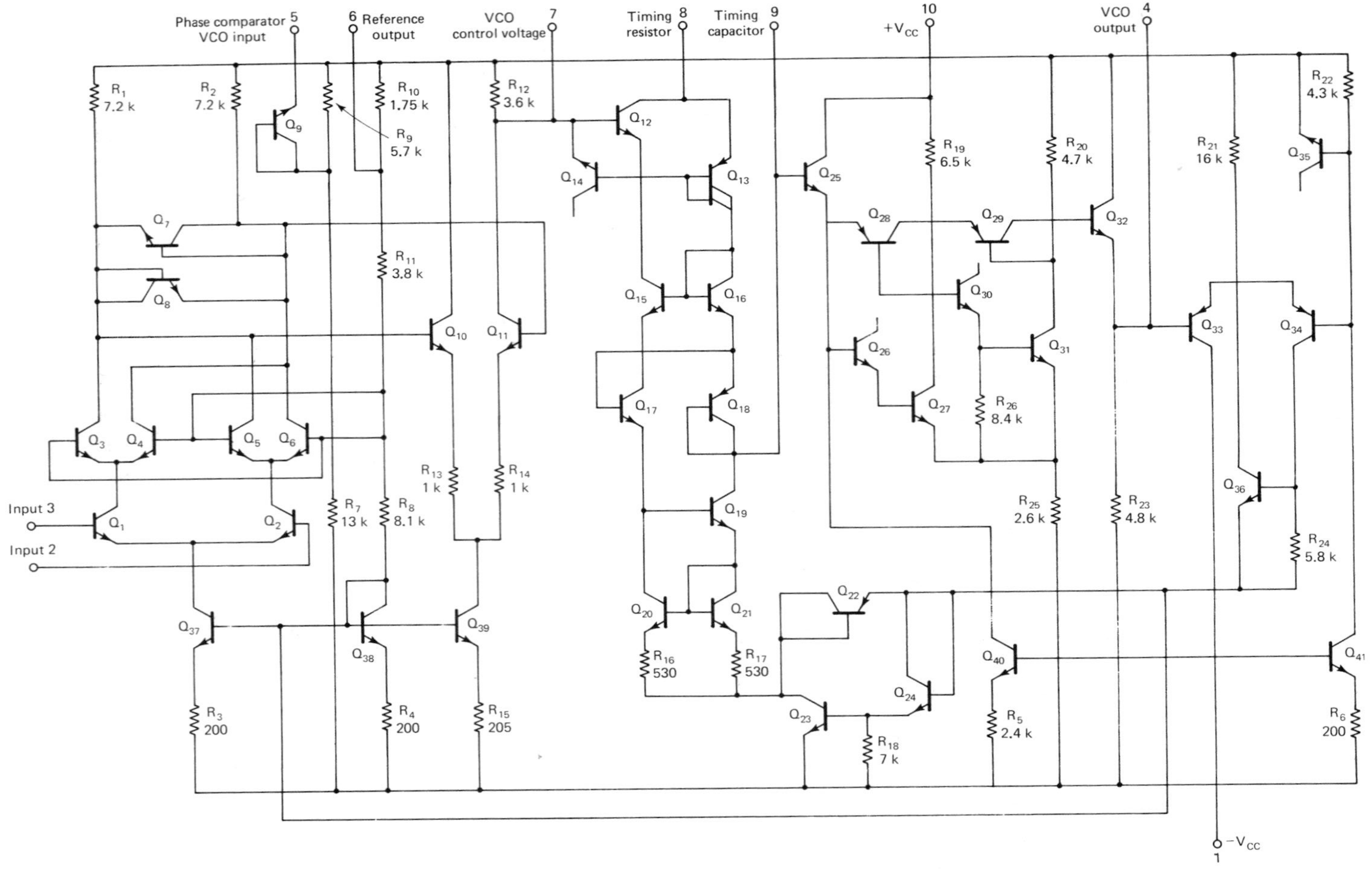

7.10 Circuit diagram of the LM565 phase-locked loop (National Semiconductor).

The VCO consists of a voltage-controlled current source (Q_{12} through Q_{23}) which supplies equal magnitude charging and discharging currents to an externally connected (pin 9) timing capacitor C_t. A timing resistor R_t is connected between pin 8 and the positive supply V^+.

The rest of the VCO circuit is a Schmitt trigger (Q_{25} through Q_{36}) with a differential-amplifier output circuit (Q_{33} and Q_{34}). This controls the turn-on and turn-off of Q_{23} and Q_{24} for the switching action of the current source for the charging and discharging cycles.

At a supply voltage level of $\pm$ 6 V the phase detector has a phase angle-to-voltage transfer coefficient (including the gain of the Q_{10}–Q_{11} differential amplifier) of $K_\phi = 0.68$ V/rad. The VCO has a voltage-to-frequency transfer coefficient or sensitivity of $K_V = 0.65 f_o$ Hz/V or $4.1 f_o$ rad/s-V, where f_o is the VCO free-running frequency.

The lock-in range will be given by $\Delta f_L = K_V K_\phi A(\pi/2) = 0.694 f_o$, so that the lock-in range will extend from $0.31 f_o$ to $1.69 f_o$, for a total extent of $2\ \Delta f_L = 1.39 f_o$.

The loop gain $\omega_L = 2\pi K_\phi A K_V$ will be $\omega_L = 2.8 f_o$ (s^{-1}). The VCO in this PLL has a maximum free-running frequency of 500 kHz. If $f_o = 100$ kHz, for example, the loop gain will be $\omega_L = 2.8 \times 10^5\ s^{-1}$ and the lock-in range will extend from 31 to 169 kHz.

7.8 PLL DESIGN EXAMPLE

We will now consider an example of a 565 type of PLL used as an FSK demodulator for telephone line data transmission. We will consider a data channel for which $f_L = 1070$ Hz represents a "0" and $f_H = 1270$ Hz represents a "1," for a total frequency deviation of 200 Hz between the low and high states and a center frequency of 1170 Hz. We will assume a keying rate (i.e., bit rate) of 150 Hz.

The "slewing rate" of a PLL in response to a step-function frequency change of amount Δf has been given as approximately $\Delta f_{VCO}/\Delta t = 2\pi f_1\ \Delta f_L$, where f_1 is the breakpoint frequency of the low-pass filter and Δf_L is the lock-in range. For the 565 PLL we have that $\Delta f_L = 0.694 f_o$, where f_o is the free-running frequency of the VCO. If f_o is set to the FSK center frequency of 1170 Hz, we obtain $\Delta f_L =$ 812 Hz.

For a keying rate of 150 Hz (i.e., 150 bits/s), let us set the maximum value of the frequency transition time Δt at $\frac{1}{4} f_{\text{keying}} = 1/(4 \times 150/\text{s}) = 1.7 \times 10^{-3}$ s. We therefore will have that $\Delta f_{VCO}/\Delta t = 2\pi f_1 \times 812\ \text{Hz} = 200\ \text{Hz}/1.7 \times 10^{-3}\ \text{s} =$ $1.2 \times 10^5\ \text{Hz}^2$. Solving for f_1 gives $f_1 = 24$ Hz. Since $f_1 = 1/2\pi\tau_1 = 1/2\pi R_{12} C_2$ where $R_{12} = 3.6\ \text{k}\Omega$, we obtain that for $f_1 = 24$ Hz, the corresponding requirement that $C_2 \leqq 1.9\ \mu F$.

7.8.1 Capture Range

The capture range is given approximately by $\Delta f_c = \sqrt{f_1\ \Delta f_L} = \sqrt{\Delta f_L / 2\pi\tau_1}$. For the case at hand we have that $\Delta f_L = 812$ Hz and $\tau_1 = 3 \times 10^{-3}$ s, so that $\Delta f_c =$ $\sqrt{812\ \text{Hz}/2\pi \times 3 \times 10^{-3}\ \text{s}} = 208$ Hz. The total capture range will thus extend from

$1170 - 208 = 962$ Hz to $1170 + 208 = 1378$ Hz. Since this total capture range encompasses both the low- and high-state frequencies of the FSK signal, we see that the FSK signal can indeed be acquired, and if subsequently lost, can be reacquired.

PROBLEMS

7.1. If the frequency of a VCO varies with the VCO input voltage, V_i, as $f = (\text{constant})(V_i + V_o)$, show that the normalized voltage-to-frequency conversion factor is given by $(1/f_o)(df/dV_i) = 1/(V_o + V_i)$, where V_o is a constant voltage.

7.2. If a VCO has a free-running frequency f_o of 50 kHz, and $V_o = 2.0$ V in the equation in Problem 7.1, find the VCO voltage-to-frequency conversion coefficient for the relationship $\Delta f = K_V \, \Delta V_i$. (*Ans.*: $K_V = 25$ kHz/V)

7.3. Given that a phase-locked loop has a VCO (Figure P7.3) with $K_V = 25$ kHz/V and $f_o = 50$ kHz. The amplifier gain is $A = 2.0$, and the phase detector has a maximum output voltage swing of ± 0.70 V. Find the *hold-in range* of the PLL. (*Ans.*: $\Delta f_{MAX} = \pm 35$ kHz, so that the hold-in range is from 15 to 85 kHz)

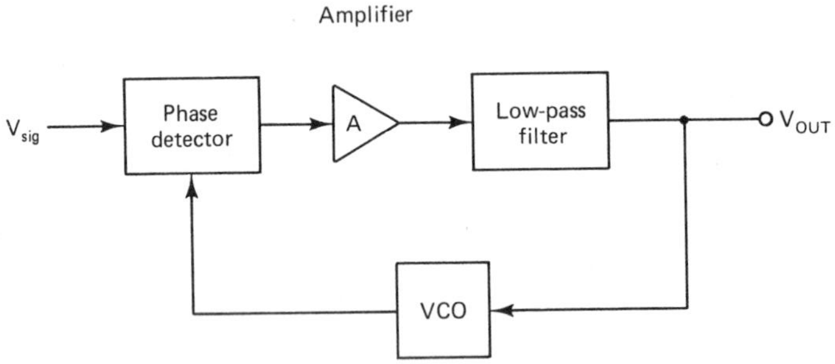

Figure P7.3

7.4. Find the approximate *capture* range of the PLL if the loop low-pass filter time constant is $\tau = RC$, where R is 3.6 kΩ for the following values of filter capacitors. (Note that C will be an external element.)
(a) 0.01 μF (*Ans.*: ±12.4 kHz)
(b) 0.03μF (*Ans.*: ±7.2 kHz)
(c) 0.10 μF (*Ans.*: ±3.9 kHz)
(d) 0.30 μF (*Ans.*: ±2.3 kHz)
(e) 1.0 μF (*Ans.*: ±1.24 kHz)

7.5. Under small-signal input conditions ($V_{\text{signal}} = 25$ mV, or less) the phase detector output voltage will become proportional to the signal voltage amplitude, so that we will have $V_{O(\text{DC})\text{phase detector}} = -(\text{constant})\, V_{\text{signal}} \cos \phi$. If for a signal voltage of 1.0 mV rms the phase detector output voltage is given by $V_{O(\text{DC})} = -50 \text{ mV} \cos \phi$, find the hold-in range using the same PLL as for Problem 7.3. (*Ans.*: $\Delta f_{\max} = \pm 2.5$ kHz, so that the hold-in range runs from 47.5 to 52.5 kHz)

7.6. If the input signal to the PLL is a frequency-modulated (FM) signal, and the PLL is in "lock," find the frequency modulation to output-voltage conversion coefficient ($\Delta V_O/$

Δf_{signal}) if the VCO characteristics are given by f = (constant)($V_i + V_o$) where V_o = 2.0 V and the free-running frequency of the VCO is 400 kHz. (*Ans.*: FM conversion coefficient = 5 mV/kHz)

7.7. Given that the input signal to the PLL is an FM signal of frequency $f_s = f_o(1 + m \sin \omega_m t)$, show that the maximum modulation frequency for which the PLL will remain in lock will be given approximately by $f_{m\,(MAX)} = (\Delta f_L/mf_o)(1/2\pi\tau)$, where $\pm\Delta f_L$ is the lock-in range, f_o is the VCO free-running frequency, and τ is the low-pass filter RC time constant.

7.8. A PLL has a VCO free-running frequency of f_o = 100 kHz and a hold-in range of Δf_H = ±50 kHz. A frequency-modulated (FM) signal has a center frequency of f_c = 100 kHz (carrier frequency) and a frequency deviation of ±10 kHz. Find the maximum modulating frequency for which the PLL will stay in "lock" for the following values of low-pass filter capacitance (R_L = 3.6 kΩ).

(a) C = 0.01 μF (*Ans.*: 22.1 kHz)
(b) C = 0.03 μF (*Ans.*: 7.4 kHz)
(c) C = 0.10 μF (*Ans.*: 2.2 kHz)
(d) C = 0.3 μF (*Ans.*: 737 Hz)
(e) C = 1.0 μF (*Ans.*: 221 Hz)

7.9. A signal that is applied to a PLL occurs in short bursts, between which the signal is absent. The signal frequency is f_s = 1.0 MHz and the signal bursts occur at intervals of 1.0 ms and have a duration of 10 μs. The PLL has a crystal controlled VCO with a free-running frequency f_o that is within 0.1% of the signal frequency. It is required that the PLL remain continuously locked in on the signal and that the phase angle of the VCO output voltage not drift by more than 0.1 rad in the interval between the signal bursts.

(a) Find the maximum allowable drift in the VCO frequency between the signal bursts. (*Ans.*: 15.9 Hz)

(b) A simple lag low-pass filter is used in this PLL. Find the maximum value of the filter time constant. (*Ans.*: 62.3 ms)

(c) If the net resistance of the filter is 4.0 kΩ, find the maximum value that the filter capacitor can have. (*Ans.*: 15.6 μF)

REFERENCES

BERLIN, H. M., *Design of Phase-Locked Loop Circuits with Experiments*, Howard M. Sams, 1978.

BLANCHARD, A., *Phase-Locked Loops*, Wiley, 1976.

CONNELLY, J. A., *Analog Integrated Circuits*, Wiley, 1975.

EGAN, W. F., *Frequency Synthesis by Phase Lock*, Wiley, 1981.

GARDNER, F. M., *Phaselock Techniques*, Wiley, 1979.

GLASER, A. B., and G. E. SUBAK-SHARPE, *Integrated Circuit Engineering*, Addison-Wesley, 1977.

GREBENE, A. B., *Analog Integrated Circuit Design*, Van Nostrand Reinhold, 1972.

KLAPPER, J., and J. T. FRANKLE, *Phase-Locked and Frequency Feedback Systems*, Academic Press, 1972.

KRAUSS, H. L., C. W. BOSTIAN, and F. H. RAAB, *Solid State Radio Engineering*, Wiley, 1980.

LENK, J. D., *Handbook of Integrated Circuits*, Reston, 1978.

STOUT, D. F., *Handbook of Microcircuit Design and Applications*, McGraw-Hill, 1980.

United Technical Publications, *Modern Applications of Integrated Circuits*, TAB Books, 1974.

Multipliers, Dividers, and Function Converters

8

8.1 CHARACTERISTICS OF MULTIPLIERS

A *multiplier* is a device that produces an output voltage that is proportional to the product of two input quantities. A general representation of a multiplier is shown in Figure 8.1, where x and y are the two input quantities and $z = Kxy$ is the output, with K being the multiplier scale factor. For electronic multipliers the input and output quantities are either voltages or currents. For example, for a voltage multiplier we can have $V_Z = KV_XV_Y$, where V_X and V_Y are the two input voltages, V_Z is the output voltage, and the scale factor K will have units of V^{-1}.

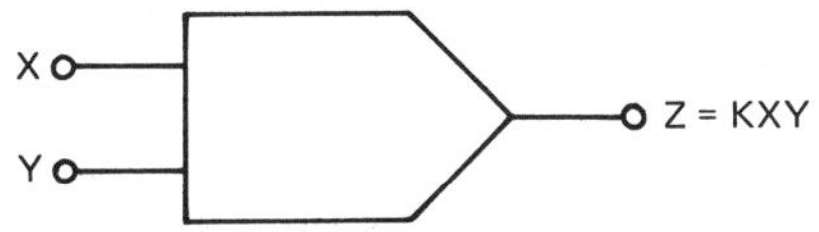

Figure 8.1 Analog multiplier.

A *four-quadrant multiplier* can accept input voltages of either polarity and can produce output voltages of both positive and negative polarity. In Figure 8.2 an example of the transfer characteristics of a four-quadrant multiplier is shown. In this figure graphs of V_Z as a function of V_X is shown for various constant values of V_Y. Note that similar results would be obtained for V_Z versus V_Y for various constant values of V_X.

In contrast to this, a *one-quadrant multiplier* can operate with only one polarity of the input voltages, and consequently the output voltage will have only one possible polarity.

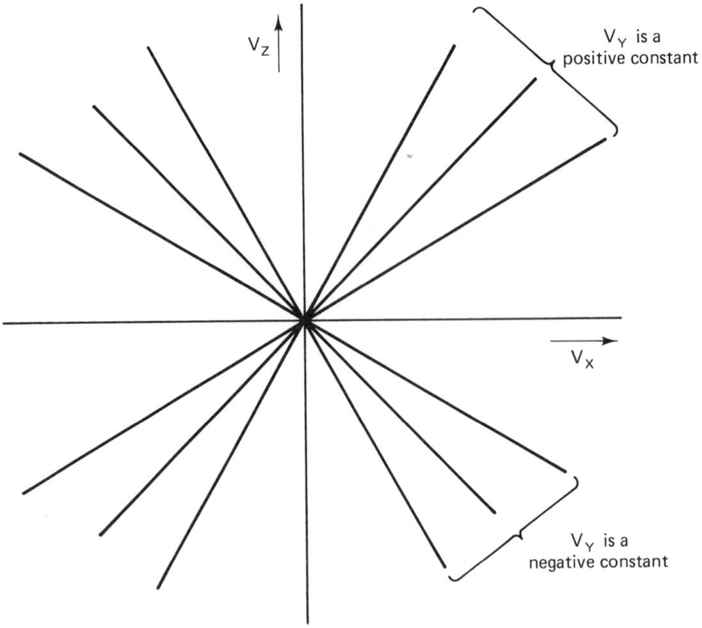

Figure 8.2 Four-quadrant multiplier transfer characteristics.

A typical range of the x and y input voltages of an analog multiplier is ± 10 V, and the output voltage range corresponding to this is generally ± 10 V. For this case the scale factor K will be $K = 1/(10\text{ V})$ and the resulting transfer relationship will be given by $V_Z = KV_XV_Y = V_XV_Y/(10\text{ V})$.

An ideal analog multiplier with a scale factor of $K = 1/(10\text{ V})$ will have a transfer relationship given by $V_Z = KV_XV_Y = V_XV_Y/(10\text{ V})$. An actual multiplier will have an output voltage given by

$$V_Z = \frac{(V_X + V_{OSX})(V_Y + V_{OSY})}{(10\text{ V})(1 + \epsilon)} + V_{OS} + (\text{nonlinear terms in } V_X^n V_Y^m) \tag{8.1}$$

Most multipliers have provision for trimming or nulling out the offset voltages (V_{OSX}, V_{OSY}, V_{OS}) and the scale factor so that the various error terms can be reduced down to the range of 0.1%. The offset voltages can be nulled out at a given operating temperature so that only the subsequent drift in the temperature and the long-term offset voltage drift will contribute to the offset error. The nonlinear terms, however, are much more difficult to compensate for, and will represent the ultimate limitation on the accuracy of the multiplier.

The accuracy of a multiplier is usually expressed in terms of its *linearity*. A graph of the output voltage V_Z as a function of one of the input voltages such as V_X is obtained, with the other input voltage kept at some constant value as shown in Figure 8.3. The input voltage that is kept constant is usually set to its maximum or full-range value. The linearity is expressed in terms of the maximum deviation of the output voltage from a "best-fit" straight line or linear transfer characteristic,

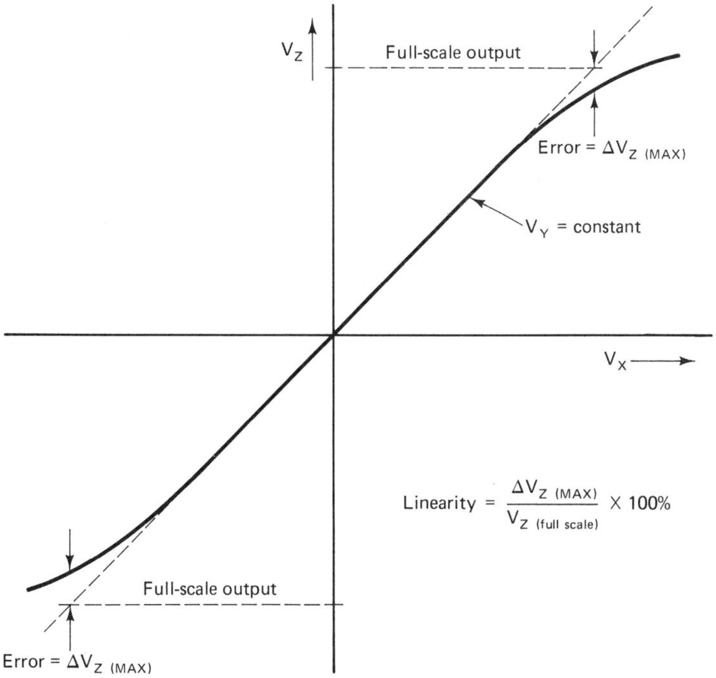

Figure 8.3 Multiplier linearity.

and is usually given as a percent of the full-scale output voltage. The maximum deviation of the output voltage from a linear characteristic usually occurs at the full-scale output voltage as shown in Figure 8.3.

Typical linearity error values for IC analog multipliers with a full-scale output voltage of 10 V are generally in the range 0.1 to 1.0%, with the lower figure being representative of multipliers in which the offset voltages have been trimmed.

Another index of multiplier accuracy is the *squaring-mode accuracy*. In this case both inputs are tied together (i.e., $V_X = V_Y$) and a graph of V_Z versus $V_i = V_X = V_Y$ is obtained as shown in Figure 8.4. The squaring-mode accuracy is the maximum deviation of the output voltage from an ideal "best-fit" square-law curve, usually expressed as a percentage of the full-scale output voltage.

The response time and frequency response characteristics are another important characteristic of a multiplier. For analog multipliers 3-dB multiplication bandwidths of up to 4 MHz are available.

8.2 MULTIPLICATION TECHNIQUES

There are a number of ways of performing the multiplication of two electrical input quantities. They can be divided first of all into analog and digital techniques. If the quantities to be multiplied are already in digital form, digital multiplication can offer

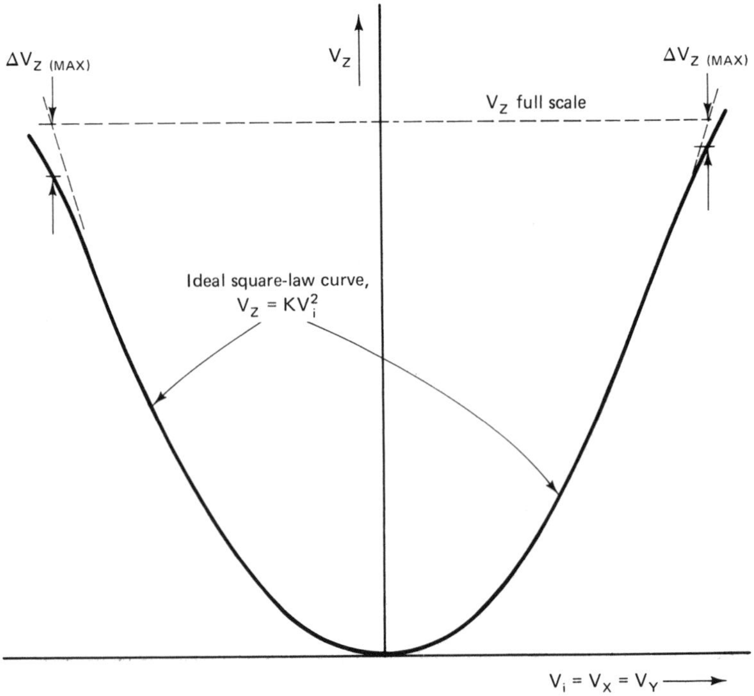

Figure 8.4 Squaring-mode accuracy.

an accuracy that is far beyond that available from any analog technique, although the speed may be considerably less.

If the quantities to be multiplied are in analog form and the output is also to be supplied in analog form the most convenient way to perform the multiplication would be by means of an analog multiplier. To do the multiplication by digital means would require an analog-to-digital converter (A/D converter), a digital multiplier, and a digital-to-analog (D/A) converter. The accuracy of the system will now be limited by the A/D and D/A converters, and would probably not be any better than that available from an analog multiplier. In addition, the speed will be considerably less. Thus for an analog input–analog output system an analog multiplier will be the best choice in most cases based on considerations of accuracy, speed, and cost.

For analog multiplication there are several basic techniques that can be used. Most high-speed analog multipliers use some form of nonlinear signal processing usually involving the exponential current–voltage relationship of transistors. Another type of analog multiplier to be discussed later is the *pulse-width modulation/pulse-amplitude modulation* (PWM/PAM) multiplier, in which the pulse width of a repetitive train of pulse is made to be proportional to one input voltage, and the pulse amplitude is made to be proportional to the other input voltage. By then passing the pulses through an integrating circuit or low-pass filter, an output voltage that is proportional to the pulse area and thus to the product of the two input voltages is obtained.

An example of a multiplier that uses nonlinear signal processing is the *quarter-square* multiplier. This multiplier uses two square-law devices to produce an output voltage given by

$$V_O = \tfrac{1}{4}[K(V_X + V_Y)^2 - K(V_X - V_Y)^2] = KV_XV_Y \tag{8.2}$$

where V_X and V_Y are the two input voltages as shown in Figure 8.5. Although this is basically a very simple technique and capable of very high-speed operation, it is difficult to obtain devices that have transfer characteristics that are close enough to an exact square-law characteristic to produce an accuracy that is comparable to that obtainable using other techniques.

The *variable transconductance* type of multiplier makes use of the transfer relation of a differential amplifier as given by

$$I_1 = \frac{I_Q}{1 + \exp(-V_i/V_T)} \quad \text{and} \quad I_2 = \frac{I_Q}{1 + \exp(V_i/V_T)} \tag{8.3}$$

where V_i is the difference-mode input voltage, and $I_Q = I_1 + I_2$ is the total current of the differential-amplifier pair. Note that the currents I_1 and I_2 are functions of both V_i and I_Q.

For small values of input voltage V_i such that $V_i < \pm V_T$, the collector currents of the differential-amplifier pair can be expressed as $I_1 = I_Q/2 + g_fV_i$ and $I_2 = I_Q/2 - g_fV_i$, so that $I_1 - I_2 \simeq 2g_fV_i$, where g_f is the dynamic forward transfer conductance of the differential amplifier as given by $g_f = I_Q/4V_T$. We therefore will have that $I_1 - I_2 \simeq I_QV_i/2V_T$. If the current I_Q is made to be proportional to one input voltage V_X such that $I_Q = k_XV_X$, and the voltage V_i is made to be equal to, or proportional to, the other input voltage V_Y such that $V_i = k_YV_Y$ we will have that $I_1 - I_2 = \Delta I \simeq k_XV_Xk_YV_Y/2V_T = KV_XV_Y$. Thus the output quantity ΔI will be proportional to the product of the two input voltages. To improve the accuracy of this type of multiplier and to increase the dynamic range of the V_Y input voltage, the V_Y input voltage often goes through a logarithmic type of processing circuit before being applied to the input terminals of the differential amplifier as V_i. A circuit showing this type of multiplier circuit will be presented and discussed later.

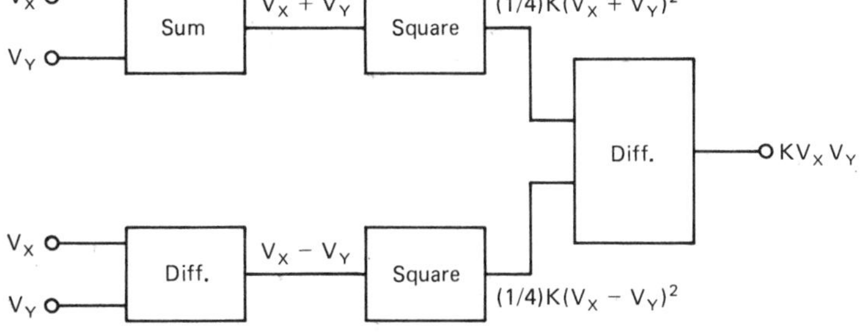

Figure 8.5 Quarter-square multiplier.

The *logarithmic-exponential* type of multiplier makes use of the relationship than $\ln V_X + \ln V_Y = \ln V_X V_Y$. The input voltages are first acted on by a logarithmic converter to produce $\ln V_X$ and $\ln V_Y$. These logarithmic voltages are then added together and then go through an exponential (or antilogarithmic) converter to produce an output voltage given by $V_Z = \ln^{-1} \ln V_X V_Y = V_X V_Y$ together with the appropriate scale factor.

For the logarithmic and exponential conversions the simple exponential relationship between the collector current and the base-to-emitter voltage of a bipolar transistor in the active mode of operation can be very conveniently used. This relationship is given by $I_C = I_{TO} \exp(V_{BE}/V_T)$ and is followed very precisely by the transistor over many decades of collector current, from down in the low-nanoampere range (10^{-9} A) up to about 10 mA (10^{-2} A) for a dynamic range of seven decades of current. Significant deviations start to occur at current levels in excess of about 10 mA. The derivation that occurs from the simple exponential relationship at the larger current levels is due mainly to the effect of the bulk series resistances in the transistor, principally that of the base spreading resistance r'_{bb}. This resistance is generally in the range 30 to 300 Ω for most small-signal transistors. It is possible to provide some degree of compensation or cancellation for the effects of the base spreading resistance, as will be seen later, and the effective current range can be extended up to about 100 mA, and in some cases even as high as 1.0 A for a total dynamic range of 9 decades of current for the logarithmic and exponential conversion processes.

8.3 LOGARITHMIC-EXPONENTIAL MULTIPLIER

We will now consider a logarithmic-exponential type of analog multiplier as shown in Figure 8.6. This circuit is available in monolithic IC form as the RC4200 (Raytheon).

To analyze the operation of this circuit we will assume that transistors Q_1

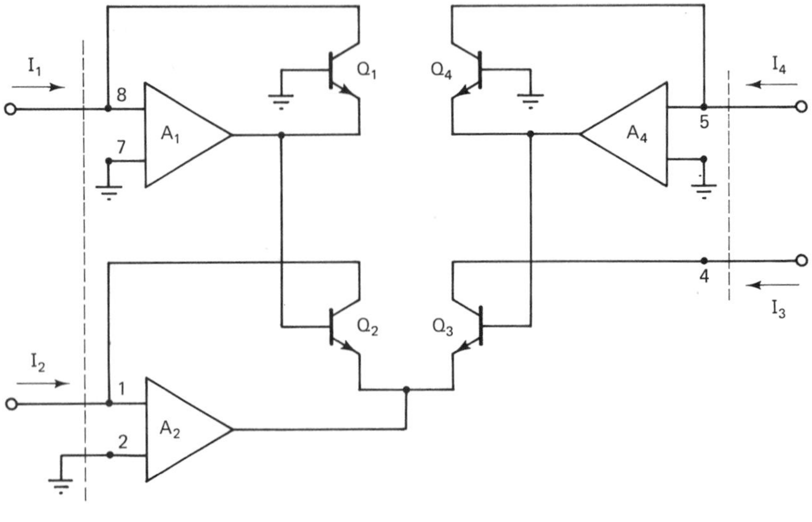

Figure 8.6 Logarithmic-exponential multiplier-divider circuit.

through Q_4 are identical, and we will consider the operational amplifiers to be ideal (i.e., $V_{OS} = 0$, $V_{\text{BIAS}} = 0$) infinite-gain devices.

Taking the algebraic summation of the base-to-emitter voltage drops around the loop (from B_1 to B_4), we obtain $V_{BE_1} + V_{BE_2} - V_{BE_3} - V_{BE_4} = 0$. Since $V_{BE_1} = V_T \ln (I_1/I_{TO})$, $V_{BE_2} = V_T \ln (I_2/I_{TO})$, and so on, we obtain

$$V_T \ln \frac{I_1}{I_{TO}} + V_T \ln \frac{I_2}{I_{TO}} - V_T \ln \frac{I_3}{I_{TO}} - V_T \ln \frac{I_4}{I_{TO}} = 0 \tag{8.4a}$$

Combining all of the logarithmic terms, we obtain $\ln (I_1 I_2/I_3 I_4) = 0$, and thus

$$\boxed{I_1 I_2 = I_3 I_4} \tag{8.4b}$$

We thus obtain a very simple relationship for the four currents. These four currents, however, are restricted to being algebraically positive values.

This circuit can, nevertheless, be the basis of a four-quadrant multiplier as shown in Figure 8.7. For this circuit we have that $I_1 = (V_X/R_1) + (V_R/R_2)$, $I_2 = (V_Y/R_1) + (V_R/R_2)$, $I_3 = (V_X/R_1) + (V_Y/R_1) + (V_R/R_2) + (V_O/R_O)$, and $I_4 = V_R/R_2$. Using the relationship given above as $I_1 I_2 = I_3 I_4$, and after rearrangement and cancellation of terms, we obtain

$$\boxed{V_O = \frac{R_O R_2}{R_1^2} \frac{V_X V_Y}{V_R}} \tag{8.5}$$

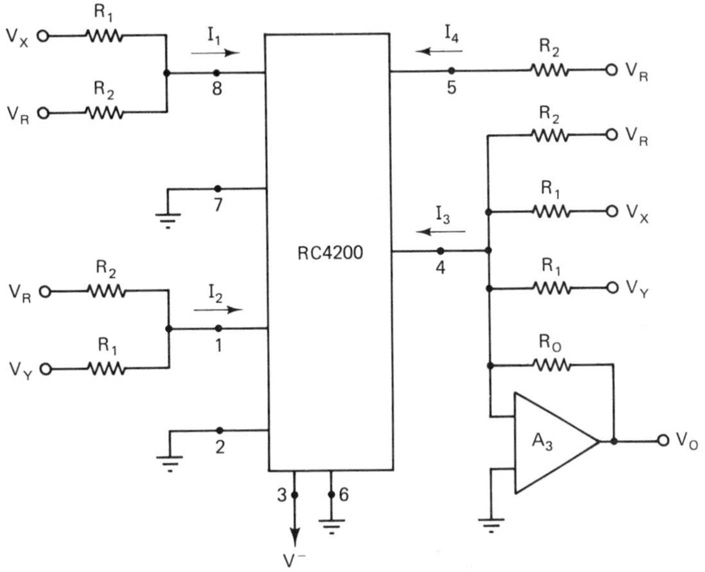

Figure 8.7 Four-quadrant multiplier circuit.

The restriction that all four currents be algebraically positive is still in effect. Thus for I_1 we have that $I_1 = (V_X/R_1) + (V_R/R_2) > 0$, and similarly for the other currents. We see that by virtue of the presence of the V_R/R_2 terms which will provide a positive component of current, voltages V_X, V_Y, and V_Z can be allowed to go negative.

Together with the restriction with respect to the algebraic sign of the four currents, for the greatest accuracy the currents should not be allowed to be excessively large, or to drop to too small a value. At large values of current the base spreading resistance of the transistors will result in a loss of accuracy, and at very small values of current the input bias current of the operational amplifier will become a significant source of error. For the RC4200 the range of currents for the specified accuracy is from +1.0 μA to +1.0 mA.

For an input voltage range of ±10 V for both V_X and V_Y, and for a full-scale output voltage of ±10 V, the scale factor $K = R_O R_2/R_1^2 V_R$ will be 1/(10 V). If $V_R = +10.0$ V, then $R_O R_2 = R_1^2$. If we set $I_{MAX} = 0.4$ mA and $I_{MIN} = 0.1$ mA for the greatest overall linearity, we will have that $(10/R_1) + (10/R_2) = 0.4$ mA, and $(-10/R_1) + (10/R_2) = 0.1$ mA. Therefore, $20/R_2 = 0.5$ mA, so that $R_2 = 20$ V/ 0.5 mA = 40 kΩ. For R_1 we have that $20/R_1 = 0.3$ mA, so that $R_1 = 20$ V/0.3 mA = 66.67 kΩ. For the scale factor we have that $R_O R_2 = R_1^2$, which gives for R_O the value of R_O = 88.89 kΩ.

To check I_3 we have that $I_{3(MAX)} = 10\ \text{V}(1/R_1 + 1/R_1 + 1/R_2 + 1/R_O) = +0.663$ mA, and $I_{3(MIN)} = 10\ \text{V}(1/R_1 - 1/R_1 + 1/R_2 - 1/R_O) = 0.1375$ mA. These maximum and minimum limits for I_3 are well within the current range for the accuracy specifications of this device.

The logarithmic-exponential multiplier circuit can also be used as a *divider*, as shown in Figure 8.8. For this circuit we have that $I_1 = V_X/R_1$, $I_2 = V_R/R_2$,

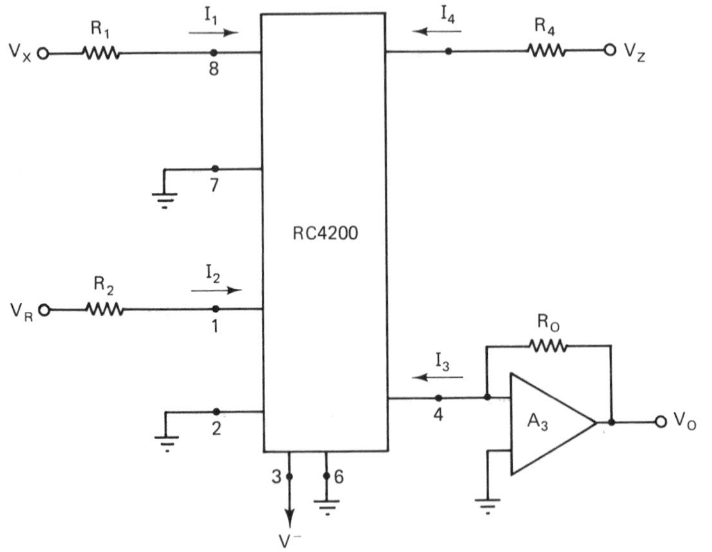

Figure 8.8 One-quadrant divider.

$I_3 = V_O/R_O$, and $I_4 = V_Z/R_4$, so that since $I_1I_2 = I_3I_4$ we obtain that $V_XV_R/R_1R_2 = V_OV_Z/R_OR_4$. Solving for V_O gives

$$V_O = \frac{V_X}{V_Z} V_R \frac{R_OR_4}{R_1R_2} \tag{8.6}$$

Thus we can obtain the quotient or ratio of two voltages, V_X and V_Z. By making V_R a third variable or applied voltage we can obtain the product of two voltages, V_X and V_R, divided by a third voltage V_Z.

Note that this will be a *one-quadrant divider* since V_X, V_Z, and V_R must be restricted to positive values. Note also that since the input currents (I_1, I_2, and I_4) should not become too small (such as the 1.0 μA limitation for the RC4200) for accurate operation of this circuit, the V_X, V_Z, and V_R input voltages will be similarly restricted with respect to their minimum allowable values.

In Figure 8.9 a *square-rooting circuit* is shown. For this circuit we again have that $I_1I_2 = I_3I_4$, so that $(V_X/R_1)(V_R/R_2) = (V_O/R_O)(V_O/R_4) = V_O^2/R_OR_4$. Solving for V_O gives

$$V_O = \sqrt{V_XV_R \frac{R_OR_4}{R_1R_2}} \tag{8.7}$$

We again note the restriction of the voltages to positive values only as well as the limitation on the minimum values of voltage for accurate operation of the circuit.

The logarithmic-exponential multiplier circuit can also be used as the basis

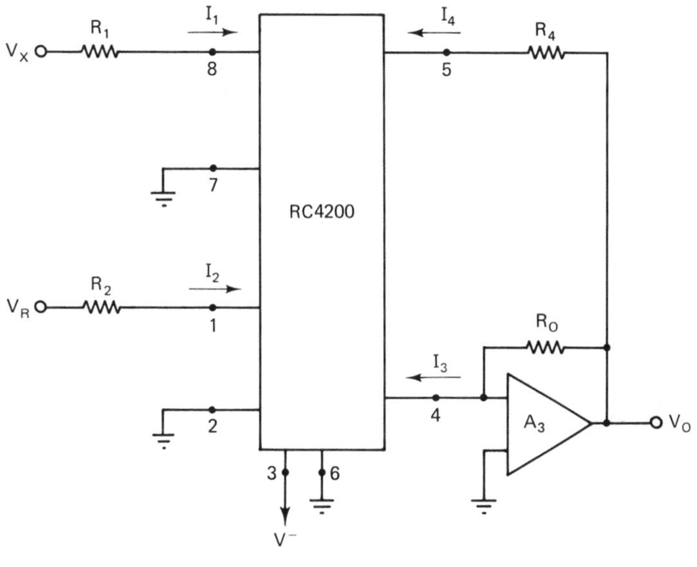

Figure 8.9 Square-rooting circuit.

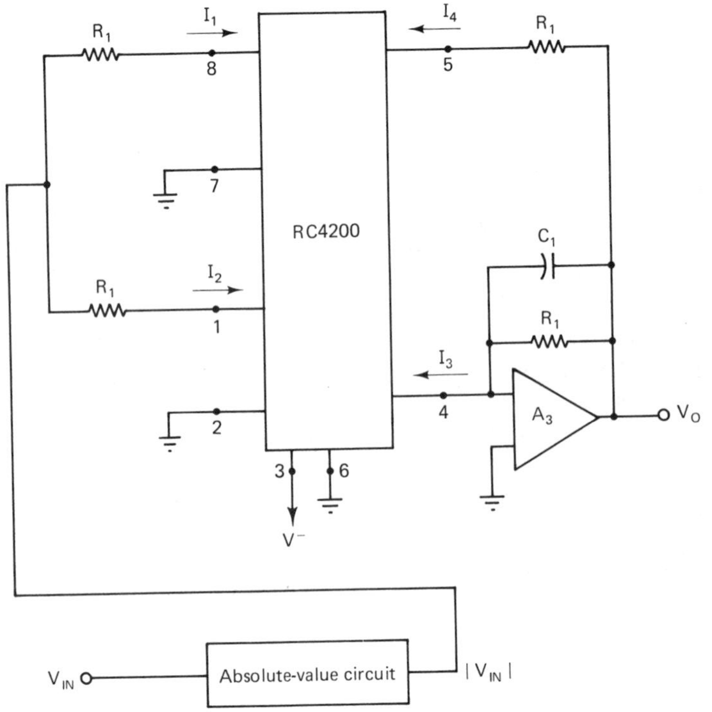

Figure 8.10 Rms-to-dc converter.

for an *rms-to-dc converter* as shown in Figure 8.10. The absolute-value circuit is essentially a precision full-wave rectifier that produces an output voltage that is equal to $|v_{IN}|$ and is thus always of positive polarity.

Starting again with the basic relationship that $I_1 I_2 = I_3 I_4$, we have that $[|V_{IN}|/R_1][|V_{IN}|/R_1] = (V_O/R_1)[V_O/R_1 + C_1(dV_O/dt)]$ and thus $|V_{IN}|^2/R_1^2 = V_O^2/R_1^2 + (R_1C_1)/R_1^2 V_O(dV_O/dt)$. Since $V_O(dV_O/dt) = (1/2)(dV_O^2/dt)$, the expression for V_O can be written as $|V_{IN}|^2 = V_O^2 + (R_1C_1/2)(dV_O^2/dt)$. Expressing $|V_{IN}|^2$ and V_O^2 in terms of the Laplace transformation variable s, we now have that $|V_{IN}|^2 = V_O^2\,(1 + sR_1C_1/2)$ and thus $V_O^2 = |V_{IN}|^2/[1 + s(R_1C_1/2)]$. As a test signal we will consider a sinusoidal voltage given by $V_{IN}(t) = A \cos \omega t$, so that $|V_{IN}|^2 = |(A^2/2)(1 + \cos 2\omega t)|$ and thus

$$V_O^2 = \frac{(A^2/2)|(1 + \cos 2\omega t)|}{1 + j\omega R_1 C_1/2} \tag{8.8}$$

If the $R_1C_1/2$ time constant is large enough such that $(\omega R_1 C_1/2)^2 \gg 1$, the 2ω term will be heavily attenuated and we will have that $V_O^2 = A^2/2$, so that $V_O = A/\sqrt{2} = V_{IN(RMS)}$. It can be shown that similar results will be obtained for nonsinusoidal waveforms, subject to the condition that the $R_1C_1/2$ time constant be at least about four times the period of the waveform.

In Figure 8.11 a diagram is presented showing the offset voltage nulling circuitry for the logarithmic-exponential (RC4200) multiplier circuit. Also shown is the scale

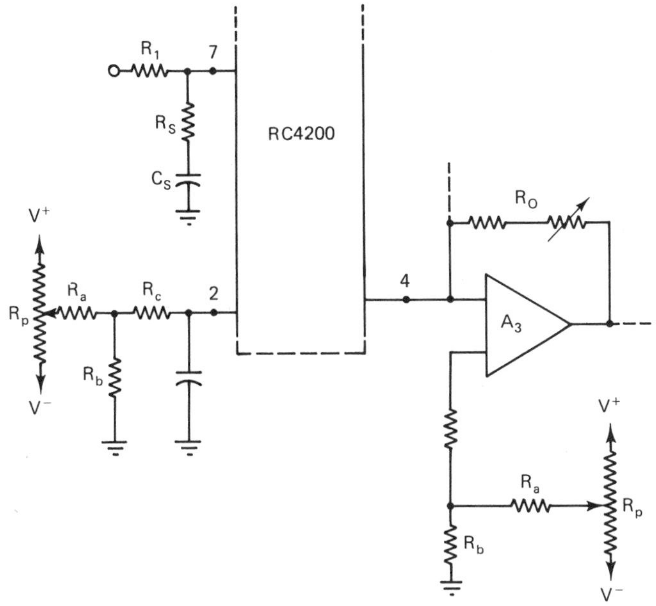

Figure 8.11 Offset and gain adjustments.

factor adjustment by means of a trimming potentiometer part of the feedback resistor R_O. When untrimmed the error of the RC4200 multiplier is rated as ±3.0% (max.), but when properly trimmed the error can be reduced to only ±0.5% (max.).

In this type if circuit there are active devices (transistors Q_1, Q_2, and Q_4) in the feedback loop of operational amplifiers A_1, A_2, and A_4. From the standpoint of the signal feedback from the operation amplifier output back to the input these transistors are in the form of common-base amplifiers so that small-signal a-c feedback factors of considerably greater than unity are possible. As a result of the large feedback factor special thought and care must be given to the question of feedback stability. In Figure 8.11 resistors R_S and capacitor C_S are used to provide an adequate measure of stability for the op-amp circuit.

8.3.1 True rms-to-dc Converter ICs

In the discussion of the logarithmic-exponential circuit, it was shown that it could perform the function of producing a d-c output voltage proportional to the rms value of an input voltage. Monolithic ICs are available that are complete rms- to d-c converters with only a few external resistors and capacitors required. An example of a monolithic IC rms-to-dc converter is the AD637 (Analog Devices). This device contains an absolute value voltage-to-current converter circuit, a logarithmic-exponential multiplier, and a low-pass active filter all on one chip, except for the feedback capacitor of the low-pass filter. There is also available from this device an output voltage that is proportional to the logarithm of the rms voltage which is convenient for decibel measurements. This IC has an 8 MHz bandwidth for input signal levels above 2 V rms and the bandwidth is 600 kHz with a 100 mV rms input. Other examples of monolithic true rms-to-dc converters are the AD536A and AD636 (Analog Devices). The AD536 has laser trimmed resistors for improved accuracy, with a maximum conversion error of just 0.5% for the AD536AK and 0.2% for the AD536AK. The AD536A like the AD637 has a decibel output with 60 dB dynamic range.

8.4 MULTIFUNCTION CONVERTER

The basic circuit of a logarithmic-exponential multifunction converter is shown in Figure 8.12. It is seen to be closely related to the logarithmic-exponential multiplier-divider circuit just considered.

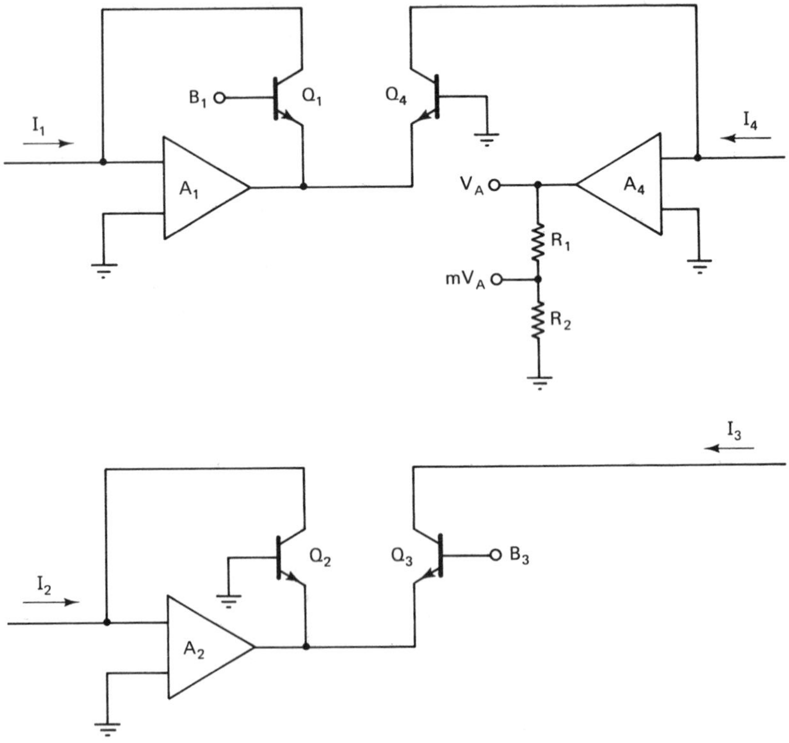

Figure 8.12 Multifunction converter.

If we again assume ideal operational amplifiers and matched transistors we have that $V_{B_1} = V_{BE_1} - V_{BE_4} = V_T \ln (I_1/I_{TO}) - V_T \ln (I_4/I_{TO}) = V_T \ln (I_1/I_4)$, and $V_{B_3} = V_{BE_3} - V_{BE_2} = V_T \ln (I_3/I_{TO}) - V_T \ln (I_2/I_{TO}) = V_T \ln (I_3/I_2)$. If $V_{B_1} = V_A$ and $V_{B_3} = mV_A$ where $m = R_2/(R_1 + R_2)$, we have that $V_{B_3} = mV_{B_1}$

and thus $V_{B_3} = V_T \ln (I_3/I_2) = mV_{B_1} = mV_T \ln (I_1/I_4) = V_T \ln (I_1/I_4)^m$. We will therefore have that $I_3/I_2 = (I_1/I_4)^m$, so that

$$\boxed{I_3 = I_2 \left(\frac{I_1}{I_4}\right)^m} \tag{8.9}$$

If we now let $V_{B_3} = V_A$ and $V_{B_1} = mV_A = mV_{B_3}$, we will have that $V_{B_1} = V_T \ln (I_1/I_4) = mV_{B_3} = mV_T \ln (I_3/I_2) = V_T \ln (I_3/I_2)^m$, so that $I_1/I_4 = (I_3/I_2)^m$. Solving for I_3, we now obtain

$$\boxed{I_3 = I_2 \left(\frac{I_1}{I_4}\right)^{1/m}} \tag{8.10}$$

Note that by suitable choice of m, I_3 can be made to be a linear ($m = 1$), sublinear, or superlinear function of the I_1/I_4 quotient.

By use of the voltage-divider circuit of Figure 8.13, the value of the exponent m in the equation $I_3 = I_2(I_1/I_4)^m$ can be varied in a continuous fashion from a minimum value of $m = R_B/(R_A + R_B)$ to a maximum value of $m = (R_A + R_B)/R_B$. The value of m will be a linear function of the position of the potentiometer wiper arm as given by

$$m = \frac{V_{B_3}}{V_{B_1}} = \frac{R_B + aR_A}{R_B + (1-a)R_A} \tag{8.11}$$

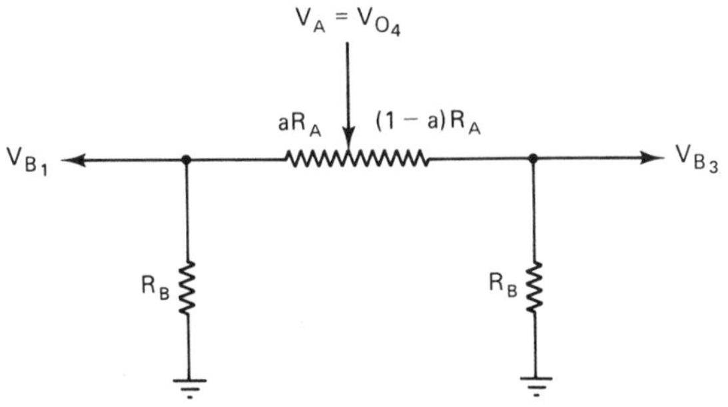

Figure 8.13 Circuit for variation of exponent in multifunction converter.

8.4.1 Monolithic Multifunction Converter Example

An example of a commercially available monolithic multifunction converter is the 4301 and 4302 (Burr-Brown). These devices are identical except that the 4301 is in a metal DIP package and the 4302 comes in a 14-pin plastic DIP package. This multifunction converter can be used for the following functions:

Function	Accuracy
Multiplication	±0.25%
Division	±0.25%
Squaring	±0.03%
Square root	±0.07%
Exponentiate	±0.15% (for $m = 5$)
Roots	±0.2% (for $m = 0.2$)
Sine θ	±0.5%
Cosine θ	±0.8%
Arctangent (V_Y/V_X)	±0.6%
Vector sum, $(V_X^2 + V_Y^2)^{1/2}$	±0.07%

The basic transfer function of this device is $V_O = V_Y(V_Z/V_X)^m$. The input voltage range (V_X, V_Y, V_Z) is 0 to +10 V (typ.), +18 V (max.) and the rated output is +10 V and 5.0 mA. In Figure 8.14 the basic block diagram of this device is shown.

8.4.2 Sine-Function Generator

The multifunction converter can be very conveniently used for the generation of the sine function. The Taylor series expansion of the sine function is given by $\sin x = x - x^3/3! + x^5/5! - x^7/7! + \cdots$. Using the first three terms in this series, an approximation to the sine function can be obtained that is accurate to within ±0.5 % in the range $-\pi/2 \leq x \leq +\pi/2$.

With the use of the multifunction converter with its noninteger exponent capability, the following two-term approximation to the sine function can be used: $\sin x \simeq x - x^{2.827}/6.28$. This approximation is accurate to within ±0.25% in the first quadrant ($0 \leq x \leq +\pi/2$).

For a sine-function generator that produces a peak output voltage of $V_{O(\text{peak})} = +10$ V at an input voltage level of $V_i = +10$ V the transfer function is $V_O = 10$ V $\sin 9V_i$ and the corresponding two-term approximation will be $V_O = 1.57V_i - 1.592(V_i/6.366)^{2.827}$. In Figure 8.15 a circuit is shown using the 4301/4302 multifunction converter for the generation of this transfer function. This circuit will operate with a *total conversion error* of ±50 mV (0.5%) for a full-scale output voltage of 10 V.

8.4.3 Cosine Function Generator

The Taylor series expansion of the cosine function is given by $\cos x = 1 - x^2/2! + x^4/4! - x^6/6! + \cdots$. A three-term expression using a noninteger exponent that is accurate to within ±0.8% in the first quadrant ($0 < x < \pi/2$) is given by $\cos x \simeq 1 + 0.235x - x^{1.504}/1.445$. Note that as was the case with the sine function, this function can be implemented using only one multifunction converter and one operational amplifier.

If it is desired that a full-scale output voltage of $V_O = +10$ V be obtained, and that an angle of 90° correspond to an input voltage of 10 V, the corresponding

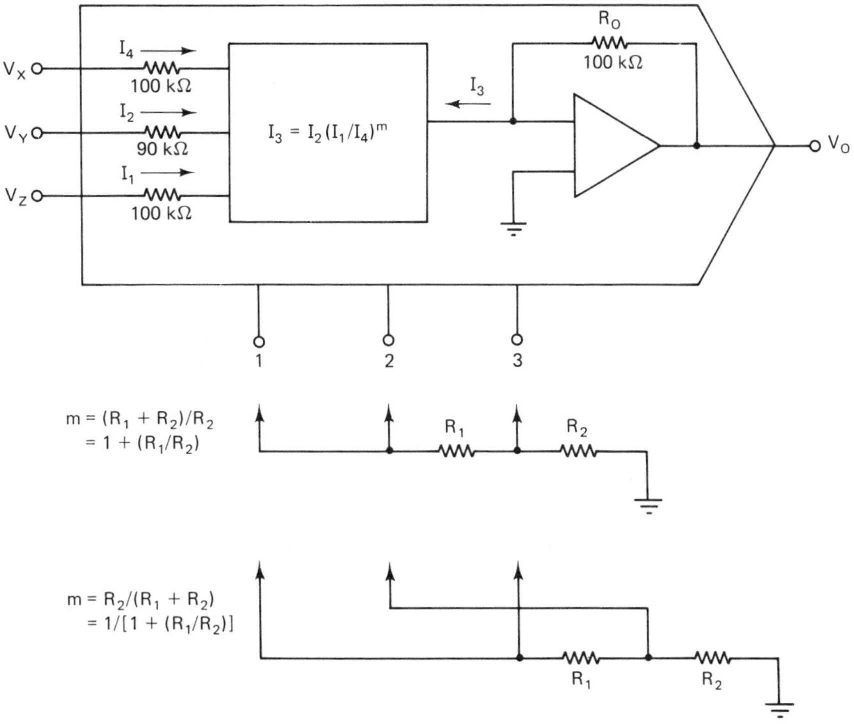

Figure 8.14 Multifunction converter integrated circuit.

cosine function will be $V_O = 10$ V cos $9\,V_i$ and the corresponding three-term approximation will be $V_O = 10 + 0.3652\,V_i - 0.4276\,V_i^{1.504}$. In Figure 8.16 a circuit implementation of this function using the 4301/4302 multifunction converter is shown. For a full-scale output voltage of 10 V this circuit provides a total conversion error of ±80 mV (typ.) or ±0.8%.

8.4.4 Arctangent Function Generator

An approximation to the arctangent function that results in an error of less than 0.75% over the total range of the variable x is given by

$$\tan^{-1}x \simeq \frac{\pi}{2}\frac{x^{1.2125}}{1 + x^{1.2125}} \quad \text{rad}$$

$$\simeq 90\frac{x^{1.2125}}{1 + x^{1.2125}} \quad \text{deg} \tag{8.12}$$

Note that in the limiting case as x goes to zero, we obtain $\tan^{-1}x = 0$, and as x goes to infinity, we have that $\tan^{-1}x = \pi/2$ or 90°, so that in these limiting cases we see that the error in the approximation expression goes to zero.

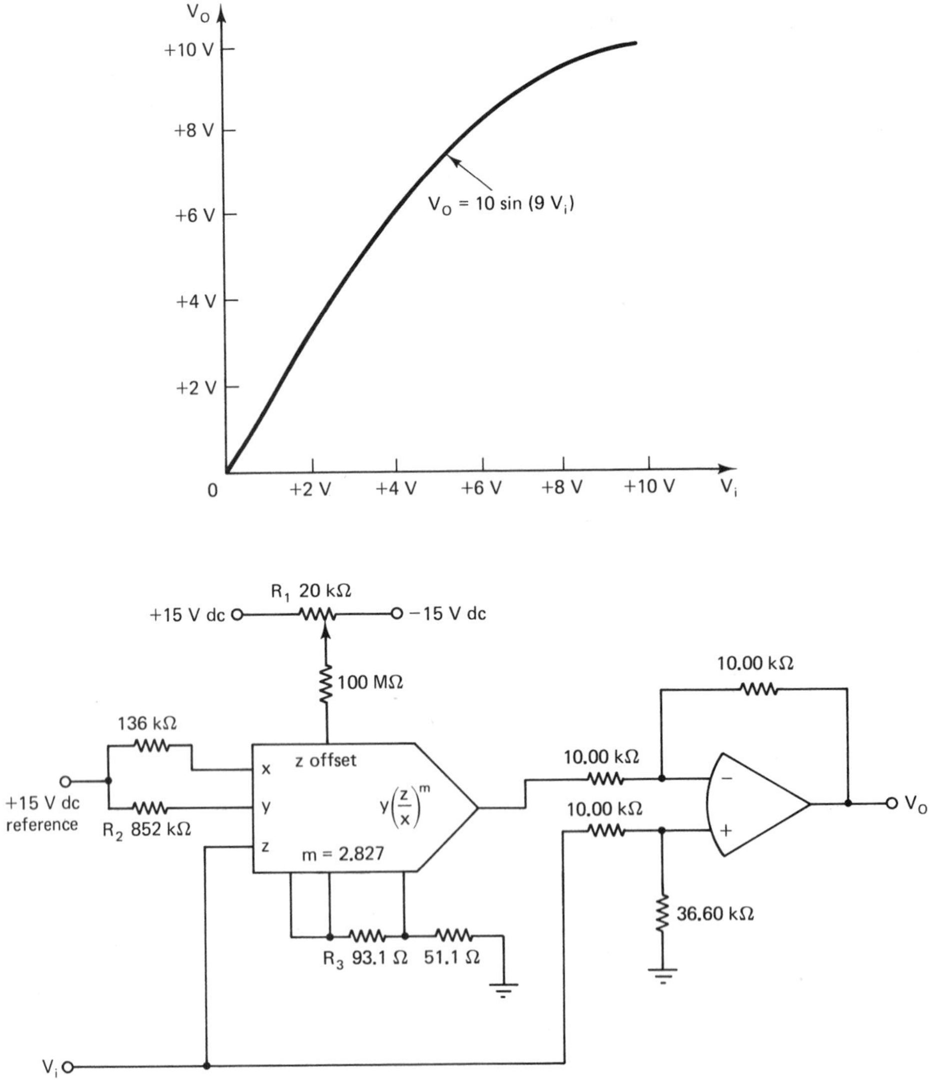

(a)

Figure 8.15 Sine-function generator: (a) sine-function circuit and transfer characteristic curve; (b) error curve for sine-function generator using two-term approximation. (From Y. J. Wong and W. E. Ott, *Function Circuits;* copyright 1976, Burr-Brown Corporation.)

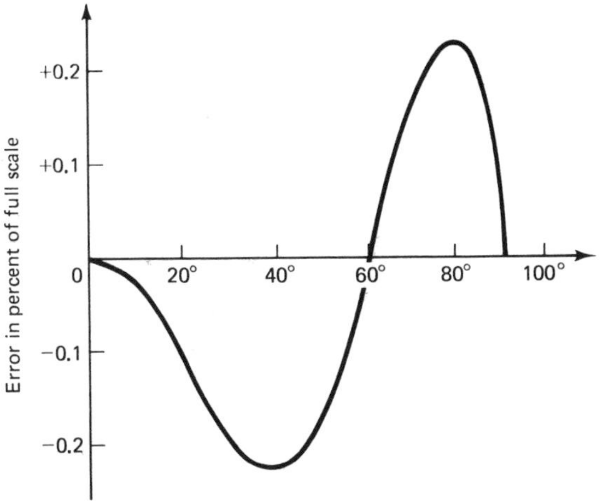

(b)

Figure 8.15 ***(cont)***

In Figure 8.17 a circuit that produces the arctangent of a voltage ratio is shown. The transfer function for this circuit is given by

$$V_o = (9.0\text{ V})\frac{|V_1/V_2|^{1.2125}}{1+|V_1/V_2|^{1.2125}} \tag{8.13}$$

as an approximation to the desired conversion function of $V_O = 9.0\text{ V}\tan^{-1}(V_1/V_2)$. When $V_1 = V_2$ the output voltage will be 4.5 V, corresponding to an angle of 45°. As the V_1/V_2 ratio becomes very large, the output voltage V_O will approach the full-scale value of 9.0 V, which will correspond to an angle of 90°.

One major application of this kind of a circuit is in the conversion of a quantity from rectangular coordinates to polar coordinates. In this regard this circuit would be used in conjunction with a vector magnitude conversion circuit, which will be considered next.

8.4.5 Vector Magnitude Conversion

The vector magnitude circuit produces the function $V_O = \sqrt{V_1^2 + V_2^2}$. An implementation of this function using a log-exponential multiplier (or a multifunction converter) and two operational amplifiers is shown in Figure 8.18. The multiplier produces the transfer relationship of $V_{O_1} = V_Y V_Z/V_X$. Since $V_Y = V_Z = V_1$, $V_X = V_O - V_2$, and $V_O = V_{O_1} - V_2$, we have that $V_O + V_2 = V_{O_1} = V_1^2/(V_O - V_2)$. From this we obtain that $V_O^2 - V_2^2 = V_1^2$, and therefore we end up with the desired result that $V_o = \sqrt{V_1^2 + V_2^2}$.

The vector magnitude circuit can be implemented with the 4301/4301 multifunction converter (Burr-Brown). For a circuit that has a full-scale input voltage range of 0 to +10 V for V_1, −10 to +10 for V_2, and produces a full-scale output voltage of +10 V, the total conversion error will not exceed 7 mV or 0.07%.

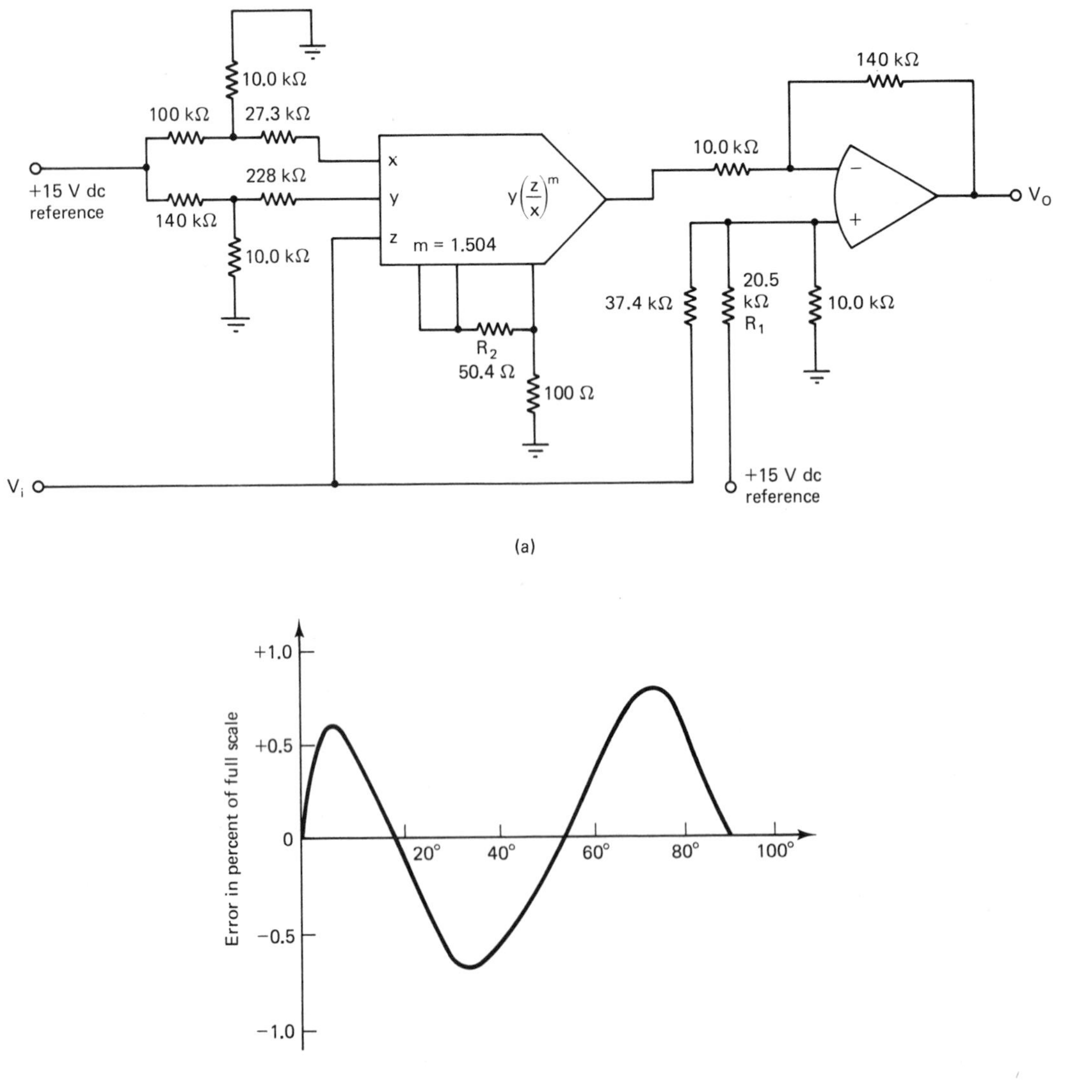

Figure 8.16 Cosine function generator: (a) cosine function circuit; (b) error curve for three-term cosine function approximation. (From Y. J. Wong and W. E. Ott, *Function Circuits;* copyright 1976, Burr-Brown Corporation.)

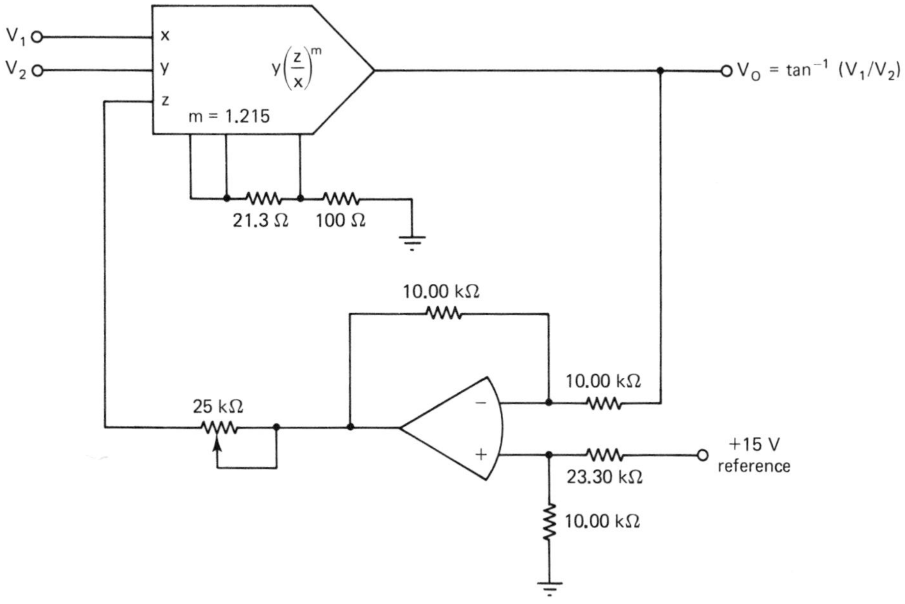

(a)

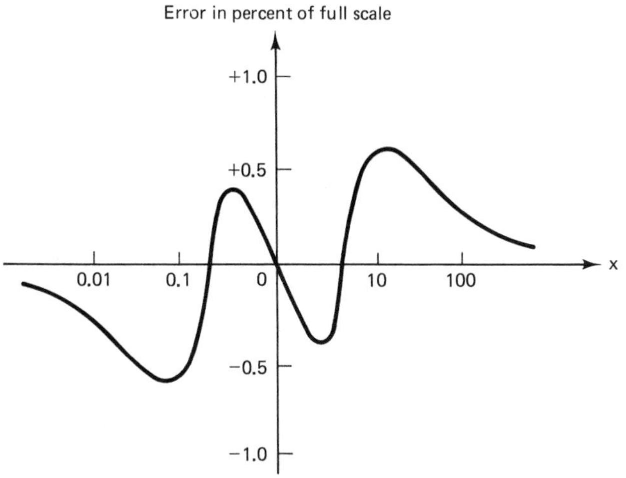

(b)

Figure 8.17 Arctangent function generator: (a) arctangent function circuit; (b) error curve for arctangent function approximation. (From Y. J. Wong and W. E. Ott, *Function Circuits;* copyright 1976, Burr-Brown Corporation.)

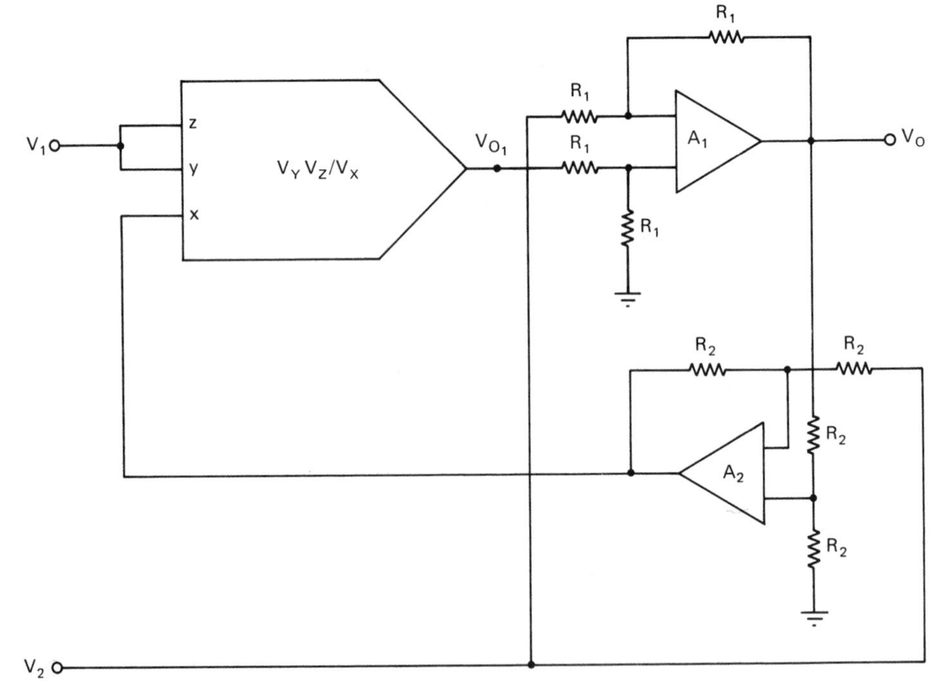

Figure 8.18 Vector magnitude circuit. (Adapted from Y. J. Wong and W. E. Ott, *Function Circuits;* copyright 1976, Burr-Brown Corporation.)

8.5 ANALYSIS OF THE FOUR-QUADRANT VARIABLE TRANSCONDUCTANCE MULTIPLIER

We will now analyze the four-quadrant variable transconductance multiplier circuit shown in Figure 8.19. For this analysis we will assume all transistors to be identical. The difference-mode input voltage of Q_6–Q_8 and Q_5–Q_7 differential-amplifier pairs will be

$$V_{BE_6} - V_{BE_8} = V_{BE_5} - V_{BE_7} = (V_1^+ - V_{D_1}) - (V_1^+ - V_{D_2}) = V_{D_2} - V_{D_1} \qquad (8.14)$$

where V_{D_1} and V_{D_2} are the base-to-emitter voltage drops of the diode-connected transistors D_1 and D_2, respectively. Letting $m = (V_{D_2} - V_{D_1})/V_T$ in the transfer relationships for a differential amplifier, we have that

$$I_6 = \frac{I_3 + I_Y}{1 + \exp(-m)}, \qquad I_8 = \frac{I_3 + I_Y}{1 + \exp(m)}, \qquad I_5 = \frac{I_4 - I_7}{1 + \exp(-m)}, \qquad I_7 = \frac{I_4 - I_7}{1 + \exp(m)}$$

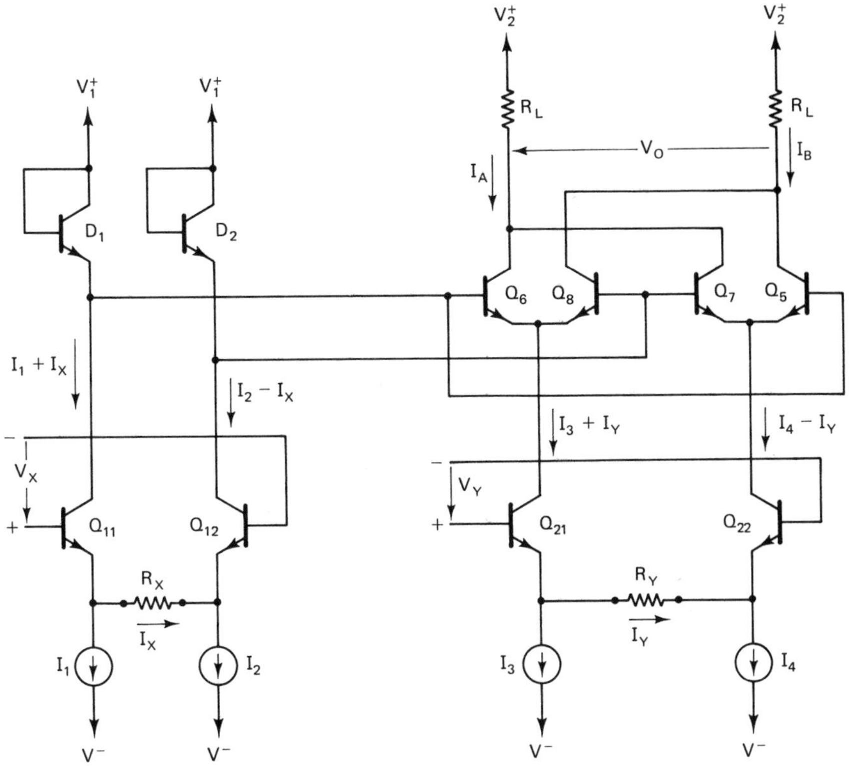

Figure 8.19 Four-quadrant variable transconductance multiplier circuit.

For $I_A = I_6 + I_7$ and $I_B = I_5 + I_8$, we will therefore have

$$I_A = I_6 + I_7 = \frac{I_3 + I_Y}{1 + \exp(-m)} + \frac{I_4 - I_Y}{1 + \exp(m)} \quad \text{and}$$

$$I_B = I_5 + I_8 = \frac{I_4 - I_Y}{1 + \exp(-m)} + \frac{I_3 + I_Y}{1 + \exp(m)} \tag{8.15}$$

For the output voltage V_O we have that $V_O = (V_2^+ - I_A R_L) - (V_2^+ - I_B R_L) = -(I_A - I_B)R_L = -\Delta I \, R_L$, where

$$\Delta I = I_A - I_B = \frac{I_3}{1 + \exp(-m)} - \frac{I_3}{1 + \exp(m)} + \frac{I_4}{1 + \exp(m)}$$

$$- \frac{I_4}{1 + \exp(-m)} + \frac{2I_Y}{1 + \exp(m)} - \frac{2I_Y}{1 + \exp(-m)} \tag{8.16}$$

Putting this equation under a common denominator gives

$$\Delta I = \frac{I_3\,[\exp(m) - \exp(-m)] + I_4\,[\exp(-m) - \exp(m)] + 2I_Y\,[\exp(m) - \exp(-m)]}{[1 + \exp(m)][1 + \exp(-m)]} \tag{8.17}$$

Factoring out the $\exp(m) - \exp(-m)$ term in the numerator gives

$$\Delta I = \frac{[\exp(m) - \exp(-m)](I_3 - I_4 + 2I_Y)}{[1 + \exp(m)][1 + \exp(-m)]} \tag{8.18}$$

Since $V_{D_1} = V_T \ln[(I_1 + I_X)/I_O]$ and $V_{D_2} = V_T \ln[(I_2 - I_X)/I_O]$, we obtain for m the expression

$$m = \frac{V_{D_2} - V_{D_1}}{V_T} = \frac{V_T[\ln[(I_2 - I_X)/I_O)] - \ln[(I_1 + I_X)/I_O)]}{V_T} = \ln\frac{I_2 - I_X}{I_1 + I_X} \tag{8.19}$$

so that

$$\exp(m) = \frac{I_2 - I_X}{I_1 + I_X} \qquad \text{and} \qquad \exp(-m) = \frac{1}{\exp(m)} = \frac{I_1 + I_X}{I_2 - I_X}$$

Upon substitution of these expressions for $\exp(m)$ and $\exp(-m)$ into the equation for ΔI, we obtain first that

$$\begin{aligned}
&\frac{\exp(m) - \exp(-m)}{[1 + \exp(m)][1 + \exp(-m)]} \\
&= \frac{\dfrac{I_2 - I_X}{I_1 + I_X} - \dfrac{I_1 + I_X}{I_2 - I_X}}{\left(1 + \dfrac{I_2 - I_X}{I_1 + I_X}\right)\left(1 + \dfrac{I_1 + I_X}{I_2 - I_X}\right)} = \frac{(I_2 - I_X)^2 - (I_1 + I_X)^2}{(I_1 + I_2)^2} \\
&= \frac{(I_2 - I_X)^2 - (I_1 + I_X)^2}{[(I_1 + I_X) + (I_2 - I_X)]^2} = \frac{[(I_2 - I_X) - (I_1 + I_X)][(I_2 - I_X) + (I_1 + I_X)]}{[(I_2 - I_X) + (I_1 + I_X)]^2} \\
&= \frac{(I_2 - I_X) - (I_1 + I_X)}{(I_2 - I_X) + (I_1 + I_X)} = \frac{I_2 - I_1 - 2I_X}{I_1 + I_2}
\end{aligned} \tag{8.20}$$

For ΔI we now obtain

$$\Delta I = \frac{I_2 - I_1 - 2I_X}{I_1 + I_2}(I_3 - I_4 + 2I_Y) \tag{8.21}$$

If we now set $I_1 = I_2$ and $I_3 = I_4$, the expression for ΔI reduces to

$$\Delta I = \frac{(-2I_X)(2I_Y)}{2I_1} = \frac{-2I_X I_Y}{I_1} \tag{8.22}$$

and thus

$$V_O = -\Delta I\, R_L = \frac{2 I_X I_Y\, R_L}{I_1} \tag{8.23}$$

We see that the output voltage V_O will be proportional to the product of two currents, I_X and I_Y. We will now investigate the relationships between I_X and I_Y and the two input voltages, V_X and V_Y. We will determine the conditions under which an approximately linear relationship will be present.

For I_X we have that

$$I_X = \frac{V_{E\,11} - V_{E\,12}}{R_X} = \frac{(V_{B\,11} - V_{BE\,11}) - (V_{B\,12} - V_{BE\,12})}{R_X} = \frac{V_X - (V_{BE\,11} - V_{BE\,12})}{R_X}$$

The difference in the base-to-emitter voltages of Q_{11} and Q_{12} (with $I_1 = I_2$) will be given by

$$\Delta V_{BE} = V_{BE\,11} - V_{BE\,12} = V_T \ln \frac{I_{11}}{I_{12}} = V_T \ln \frac{I_1 + I_X}{I_1 - I_X} = V_T \ln \frac{1 + (I_X/I_1)}{1 - (I_X/I_1)} \tag{8.24}$$

Since $\ln(1 + x) = x - x^2/2 + x^3/3 - x^4/4 + \cdots$, we will have that $\ln(1 + x)/(1 - x) = 2x + \frac{2}{3}x^3 + \cdots$. Using this in the expression for ΔV_{BE} gives $\Delta V_{BE} = 2V_T(I_X/I_1) + \frac{2}{3}V_T(I_X/I_1)^3 + \cdots$. The expression for I_X can now be written as

$$I_X = \frac{V_X - 2V_T(I_X/I_1) - \frac{2}{3}V_T(I_X/I_1)^3 + \cdots}{R_X} \tag{8.25}$$

Solving this for I_X gives

$$I_X = \frac{V_X}{R_X + (2V_T/I_1) + (2V_T/3I_1)(I_X/I_1)^2 + \cdots} \tag{8.26}$$

For good linearity between V_X and I_X we see that the $(I_X/I_1)^2$ term in the denominator of this expression should be small compared to the $R_X + (2V_T/I_1) \simeq R_X$ term. Generally, this condition will be very well satisfied for I_X values restricted to being no more than $\frac{2}{3}$ of I_1.

To consider an example, let us choose for I_1 (and I_2) a value of 1.0 mA and for I_X a maximum value of $\frac{2}{3}I_1 = 0.67$ mA. We will have that $2V_T/I_1 = 50\ \Omega$. For a maximum input signal swing of ± 10 V, the corresponding value of R_X will be given by $R_X + 50\ \Omega = 10\ \text{V}/I_{X\,(\text{MAX})} = 10\ \text{V}/0.67\ \text{mA} = 15\ \text{k}\Omega$, so that $R_X \simeq 15\ \text{k}\Omega$.

The value of the term containing $(I_X/I_1)^2$ will be $(2V_T/3I_1)(I_x/I_1)^2 = (50\ \text{mV}/3.0\ \text{mA})(2/3)^2 = 7.4\ \Omega$. This is only 0.05% of the value of R_X so that good linearity (i.e., within 0.05%) will be assured. The same result will also hold true with respect to I_Y and R_Y.

Since $I_X = V_X/(R_X + 2V_T/I_1) \simeq V_X/R_X$ and $I_Y = V_Y/(R_Y + 2V_T/I_3) \simeq V_Y/R_Y$, the expression for V_O can now be written in terms of V_X and V_Y as

$$\boxed{V_O = \frac{2V_X V_Y R_L}{I_1 R_X R_Y} = K V_X V_Y} \tag{8.27}$$

where the multiplier scale factor K is given by $K = 2R_L/(I_1 R_X R_Y)$. Note that K will have units of V^{-1}.

8.5.1 Transconductance Multiplier Example

An example of a transconductance multiplier IC, is the MPY100 (Burr-Brown). This IC has a complete transconductance multiplier circuit and an output amplifier that produces a single-ended output voltage given by $V_O = V_X V_Y/10$ V. This device can be used for many applications including multiplication, division, square rooting, and true rms-to-dc conversion. This IC has laser trimmed thin film resistors on the chip and the multiplier nonlinearity is specified as 0.08% of the full scale range (±10 V) for frequencies up to 1000 Hz.

8.6 LOGARITHMIC CONVERSION

The basic circuit of a logarithmic converter is shown in Figure 8.20. Transistor Q_1 will have its base–emitter junction forward biased by the action of the operational amplifier, and since the collector-to-base voltage will be essentially zero, this transistor will be operating in the active mode. As a result there will be a simple exponential relationship between the collector current I_C and the base-to-emitter voltage V_{BE} as given by $I_C = I_{TO} \exp(V_{BE}/V_T)$, where the preexponential constant I_{TO} is a constant of proportionality.

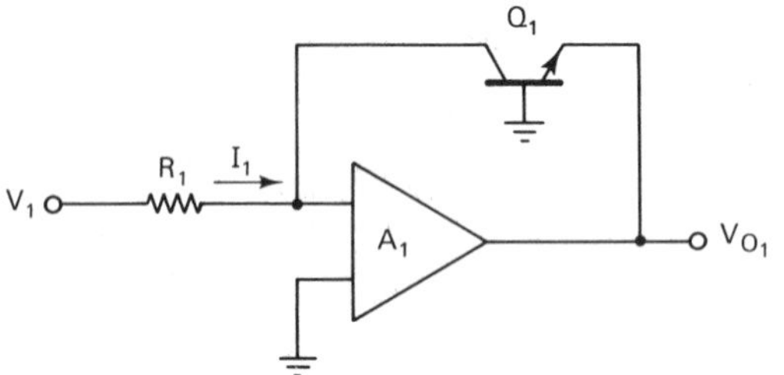

Figure 8.20 Basic logarithmic converter circuit.

Assuming that A_1 is an ideal infinite-gain operational amplifier we will have that $V_{O_1} = V_{EB} = -V_{BE} = -V_T \ln(I_C/I_{TO}) = -V_T \ln(I_1/I_{TO})$. In terms of V_1 this will be $V_{O_1} = -V_T \ln(V_1/R_1 I_{TO})$. Thus we will have a logarithmic relationship between the input quantity (I_1 or V_1) and the output voltage V_{O_1}.

The dependency of the logarithmic converter transfer characteristics on I_{TO} can be removed by using the circuit of Figure 8.21, in which transistors Q_1 and Q_2 are matched (identical) transistors. For this circuit we have that $V_{O_1} = -V_T \ln(V_1/R_1 I_{TO})$ and similarly $V_{O_2} = -V_T \ln(V_2/R_2 I_{TO})$, and thus

$$V_O = \frac{R_4}{R_3}(V_{O_1} - V_{O_2}) = -\frac{R_4}{R_3} V_T \ln \frac{V_1}{V_2}\frac{R_2}{R_1} \tag{8.28}$$

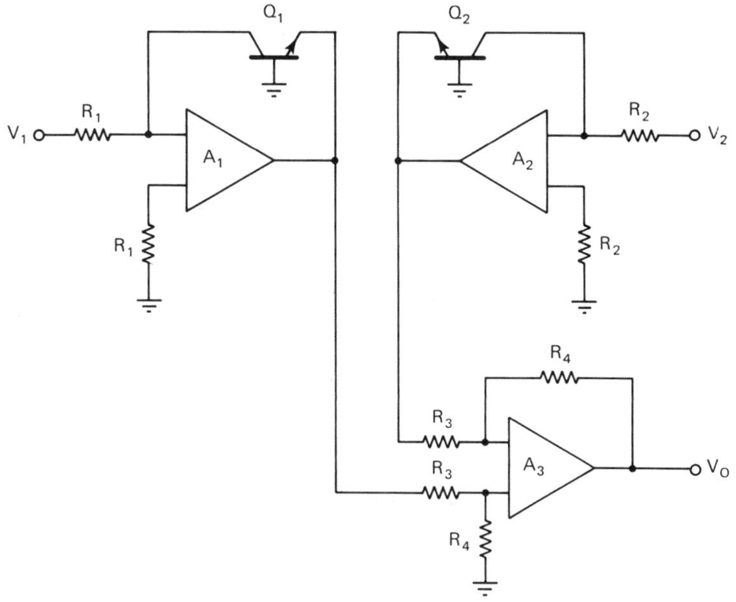

Figure 8.21 Logarithmic converter.

To express this result with respect to the base 10 logarithmic function we note that $\ln x = 2.303 \log_{10} x$, so that

$$V_O = 2.303 \times 25 \text{ mV} \times \frac{R_4}{R_3} \log_{10} \frac{V_1}{V_2} \frac{R_2}{R_1} \tag{8.29}$$

If we set $R_4/R_3 = 17.37$, the logarithmic conversion scale factor becomes 1.0 V/decade and we will have that

$$\boxed{V_O = -1.0 \text{ V} \log_{10} \frac{V_1}{V_2} \frac{R_2}{R_1}} \tag{8.30}$$

A suitable choice for R_3 and R_4 will be $R_3 = 1.0$ kΩ and $R_4 = 17.4$ kΩ. The V_O versus V_1/V_2 transfer characteristics (with $R_1 = R_2$) of this logarithmic converter is shown in Figure 8.22. Note that V_1 and V_2 will be restricted to positive values, although V_O can take on values of both positive and negative polarity.

8.6.1 Logarithmic Converter Errors and Error Correction

Principal error sources for the logarithmic converter are:

1. The operational amplifier input offset voltage, V_{OS}
2. The operational amplifier input bias current, I_{BIAS}

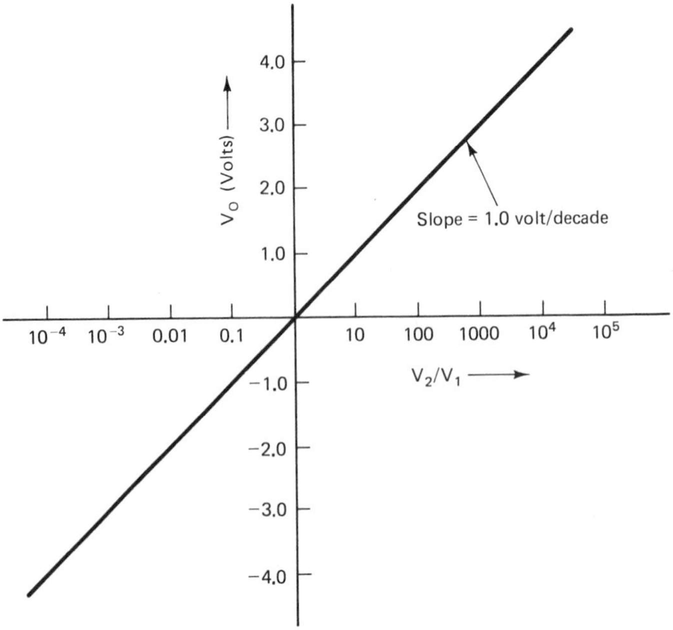

Figure 8.22 Logarithmic converter transfer characteristics.

3. The transistor pair (Q_1 and Q_2) offset voltage
4. The transistor base spreading resistance, $r_{bb'}$

The operational-amplifier offset voltage error can be minimized by suitable choice of operational amplifier (i.e., one with a very low value of V_{OS}) and by the use of a nulling circuit for V_{OS} cancellation. The bias current error can also be minimized by suitable choice of operational amplifier, such as a FET-input operational amplifier, for which case input bias currents of less than 10 pA can be obtained. In addition, the insertion of a resistor in series with the noninverting input terminal of the operational amplifier of a value equal to the resistance connected to the inverting input terminal (i.e., R_1 for A_1 and R_2 for A_2) will help to cancel out the bias currents so that only the offset current (I_{OS}) will be of concern.

The offset voltage of the Q_1–Q_2 transistor pair will produce an error voltage on the output given by $\Delta V_O = (R_4/R_3)V_T \ln(I_{TO_2}/I_{TO_1}) = (R_4/R_3)V_{OS}$. This error can be minimized by suitable choice of the Q_1–Q_2 pair, and by the introduction of a small (a few millivolts or less) offset correction voltage in series with resistor R_4 to the noninverting input terminal of operational amplifier A_3. This offset correction voltage can at the same time be used for the cancellation of the offset voltage of A_3 as well.

The base spreading resistance $r_{bb'}$ of the transistors will introduce an error term resulting from the $I_B r_{bb'}$ voltage drop as shown in Figure 8.23. For V_{O_1} we now have $V_{O_1} = V_T \ln(V_1/R_1 I_{TO}) - I_B r_{bb'}$. This error term will become of importance at the higher current levels ($I_1 = I_C \gtrsim 3$ mA). A first-order correction for this

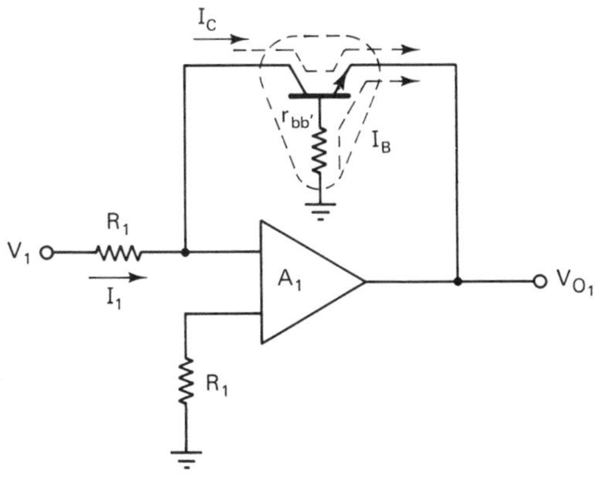

Figure 8.23 Effect of base spreading resistance on logarithmic conformity.

voltage drop can be obtained by using the circuit of Figure 8.24, where an error compensation voltage is supplied to the base of Q_1 by the R_5–R_6 voltage divider. Resistor R_6 will be very small (~3 to 20 Ω) and resistor R_5 will be very much larger than R_6. For this circuit we will now have that

$$V_{O_1} = V_T \ln \frac{V_1}{R_1 I_{TO}} - I_B(r_{bb'} + R_6) + V_1 \frac{R_6}{R_5} \tag{8.31}$$

Since $I_B = I_C/\beta = V_1/R_1\beta$, this can be rewritten as

$$V_{O_1} = V_T \ln \frac{V_1}{R_1 I_{TO}} - \frac{V_1}{R_1\beta}(r_{bb'} + R_6) + V_1 \frac{R_6}{R_5} \tag{8.32}$$

Thus if $R_6/R_5 = (r_{bb'} + R_6)/\beta R_1$, there will be cancellation of the base spreading resistance error term. For example, if $r_{bb'} = 50\ \Omega$, $R_6 = 10\ \Omega$, $\beta = 160$, and $R_1 = 1.0\ \text{k}\Omega$ we will obtain for R_5 the value given by $R_5 = \beta R_1 R_6/(r_{bb'} + R_6) = 160 \times 10 \times 1.0\ \text{k}\Omega/(60\ \Omega) = 26.7\ \text{k}\Omega$.

Note that this will produce only a "first-order" correction since the transistor current gain is not a constant, but will vary with current level.

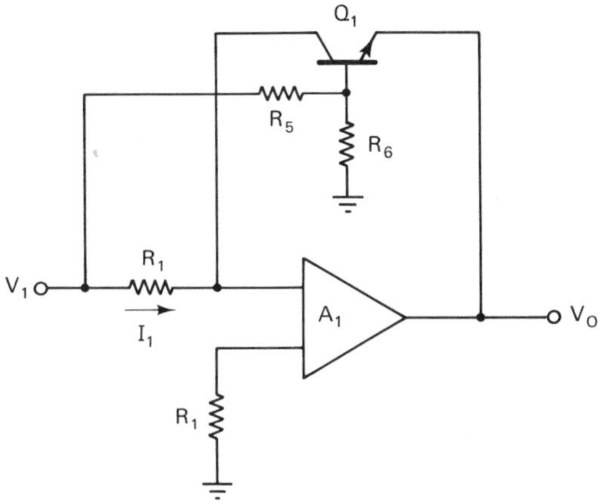

Figure 8.24 Compensation circuit for cancellation of base-spreading-resistance voltage drop.

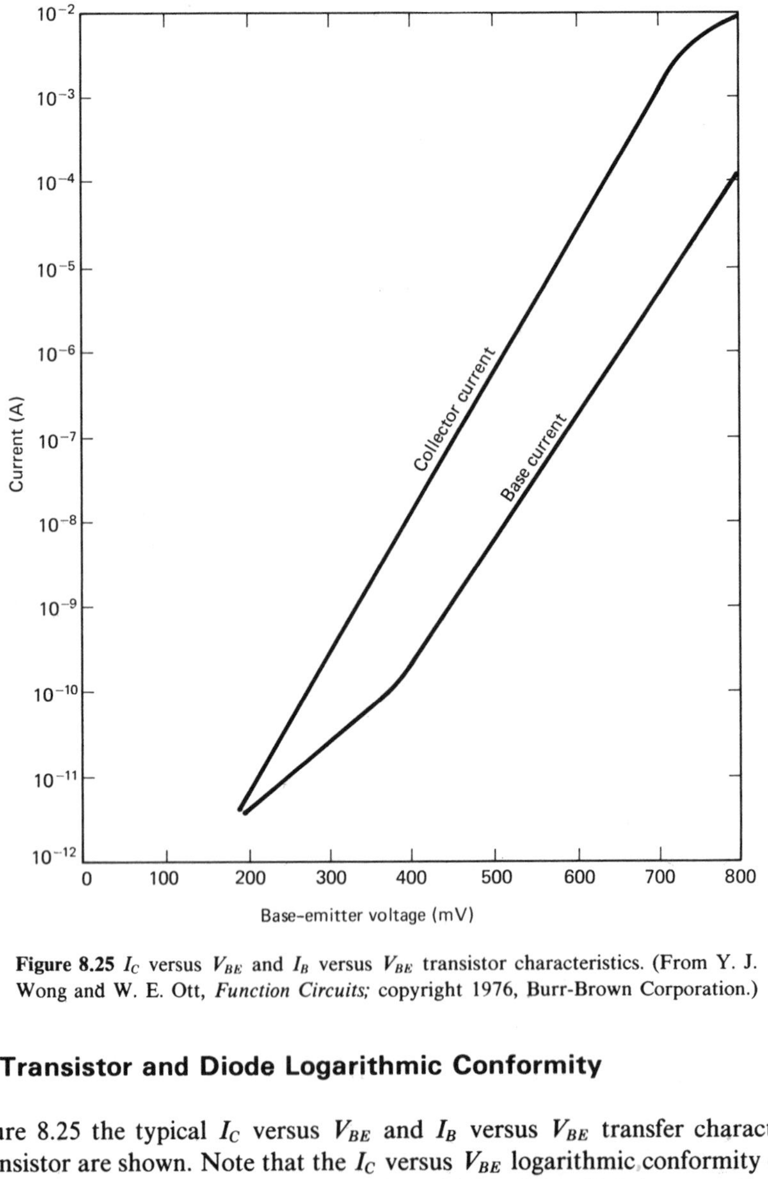

Figure 8.25 I_C versus V_{BE} and I_B versus V_{BE} transistor characteristics. (From Y. J. Wong and W. E. Ott, *Function Circuits;* copyright 1976, Burr-Brown Corporation.)

8.6.2 Transistor and Diode Logarithmic Conformity

In Figure 8.25 the typical I_C versus V_{BE} and I_B versus V_{BE} transfer characteristics of a transistor are shown. Note that the I_C versus V_{BE} logarithmic conformity extends from current levels below 10^{-11} A up to the middle of the 10^{-3} A range, for a total span of more than eight decades of current. The effect of the base spreading resistance on the logarithmic conformity, especially at current levels above 3 mA, is also apparent.

In Figure 8.26 typical results obtained from the use of the simple correction circuit of Figure 8.24 are shown. Note that the error can be reduced very substantially at the higher current levels by this circuit and the logarithmic conversion range can as a result be extended by about one decade.

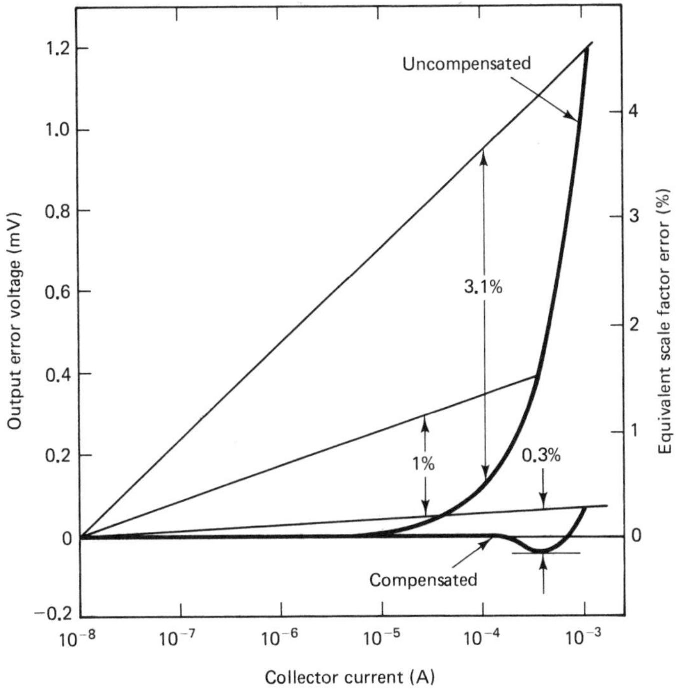

Figure 8.26 Error voltage versus collector current with correction circuit. (From Y. J. Wong and W. E. Ott, *Function Circuits*; copyright 1976, Burr-Brown Corporation.)

The advantage gained by using a transistor in the common-base (CB) configuration over the use of a diode-connected ($V_{CB} = 0$) transistor in the feedback loop can also be seen from inspection of Figure 8.25. Note that the logarithmic dependency of I_B with respect to V_{BE} is not the same as that of I_C, and can be expressed as $I_B \propto \exp(V_{BE}/nV_T)$ where n is a dimensionless constant. This quantity will have values between 1 and 2 and generally is around 1.5, but does change with current level, approaching a limiting value of 2 at very low ($\lesssim 1$ nA) current levels. Furthermore, we see that at lower currents the current gain, $\beta = I_C/I_B$ will decrease substantially, so that the base current will start to constitute a significant fraction of the total current in the diode-connected configuration for which $I_1 = I_C + I_B$. For this reason the CB configuration in which the base current is simply shunted to ground and $I_1 = I_C$ gives much greater accuracy for logarithmic conversion.

An ordinary diode can, of course, be used in place of a transistor in the feedback loop, but it will suffer exactly the same drawbacks as the use of a diode-connected transistor. The forward current versus forward voltage I_F versus V_F characteristics of diodes are very similar to the I_B versus V_{BE} characteristics of transistors, so that the resulting logarithmic conformity would not be nearly as good as that of the I_C versus V_{BE} characteristic curve.

8.6.3 Stability and Compensation

The use of a transistor (CB configuration) in the feedback loop can in some cases suffer the disadvantage of resulting in a slower response characteristics than that obtainable by the use of a diode or diode-connected transistor in the feedback loop. With a CB transistor in the feedback loop the small-signal feedback factor F will be given by $F = v_{fb}/v_{o_1} = v_c/v_{eb} = g_m R_1$ = small-signal voltage gain of transistor in CB configuration, where $g_m = I_C/V_T = I_1/V_T = (V_1/R_1)/V_T$. This can be rewritten as $F = g_m R_1 = (V_1/R_1 V_T)R_1 = V_1/V_T = V_1/25$ mV. Thus we see that as a result of having an active device in the feedback loop the feedback factor can be larger than unity, and in many cases much larger than unity.

The small-signal closed-loop gain $A_{CL}(0)$ will be given by $A_{CL}(0) = 1/F = V_T/V_1 = 25\text{ mV}/V_1$, so that correspondingly we see that the small-signal closed-loop gain can be considerably less than unity.

For stability with a 45° phase margin the condition with respect to closed-loop gain and unity-gain frequency is given by $A_{CL}(0) \geq \frac{f_u}{\sqrt{2}\,f_2}$, where f_u is the open-loop unity gain frequency and f_2 is the second breakpoint frequency of the operational amplifier. We therefore must require that $A_{CL}(0) = V_T/V_1 \geq \frac{f_u}{\sqrt{2}\,f_2}$, so that $f_u \leq \sqrt{2}\,f_2(V_T/V_1)$. If, for example, $V_1 = 10$ V (max.) and $f_2 = 1$ MHz, the requirement on f_u is $f_u \leq \sqrt{2} \times 1\text{ MHz} \times (25\text{ mV}/10\text{ V}) = \underline{3.536\text{ kHz}}$. At $V_1 = 10$ mV the closed-loop gain will be $A_{CL}(0) = 25\text{ mV}/10\text{ mV} = 2.5$ and the closed-loop small-signal bandwidth will be given by $BW_{CL} = f_u/A_{CL}(0) = 3.536\text{ kHz}/2.5 = \underline{1.41\text{ kHz}}$ and the corresponding rise time will be $\underline{248\ \mu\text{s}}$. Thus the logarithmic converter will exhibit a very slow response indeed.

The small value of f_u will require the use of a large compensation capacitor C_{COMP} so that if a C_{COMP} of 50 pF yields a unity-gain frequency of 1 MHz, for a $f_u = 3.5$ kHz, the compensation capacitor will have to be increased to 14 nF.

An alternative, and in most cases the preferable means of ensuring adequate stability is to use a resistor in series with the output terminal of the operational amplifier as shown in Figure 8.27. With this resistor (R_7) in place the small-signal feedback factor (v_{fb}/v'_{o_1}) can be written as

$$F = g_m R_1 \times \frac{r_{eb}}{r_{eb} + R_7} = \frac{I_1}{V_T} R_1 \times \frac{V_T/I_1}{(V_T/I_1) + R_7} = \frac{R_1}{(V_T/I_1) + R_7} \tag{8.33}$$

If we set $R_7 = R_1$, we see that the feedback factor F will always be less than unity, so that an internally compensated operational amplifier can be used without the need for any extra compensation.

The small-signal closed-loop voltage gain will be given by

$$A_{CL}(0) = \frac{1}{F} = \frac{R_7 + (V_T/V_1)R_1}{R_1} = \frac{R_7}{R_1} + \frac{V_T}{V_1} \tag{8.34}$$

and the small-signal closed-loop bandwidth will be

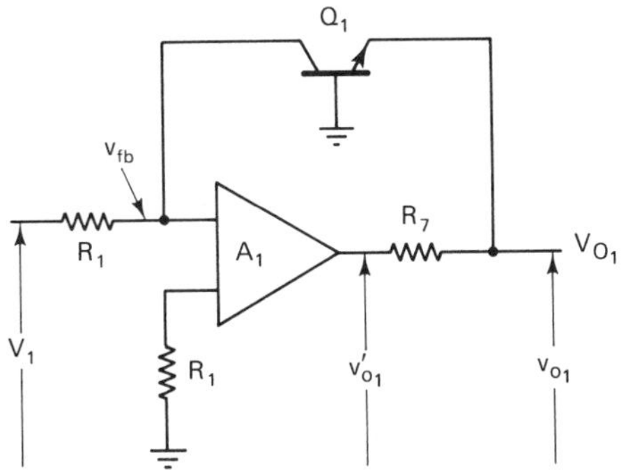

Figure 8.27 Logarithmic converter stabilization using an output series resistance.

$$BW_{CL} = \frac{f_u}{A_{CL}(0)} = \frac{f_u}{(R_7/R_1) + (V_T/V_1)} \tag{8.35}$$

We see that small values of input voltage V_1 (especially below 25 mV) will produce major reductions in the bandwidth.

If we take f_u = 1 MHz and let $R_7 = R_1$, the equation for BW_{CL} becomes BW_{CL} = (1 MHz)/[1 + (25 mV/V_1)]. If V_1 = 10 mV, we obtain BW_{CL} = 1 MHz/(1 + 25 mV/10 mV) = 286 kHz, and the corresponding small-signal rise time will be $t_{rise} = 0.35/BW_{CL} = 1.225\ \mu s$. If V_1 is down to 10 μV, the closed-loop bandwidth becomes BW_{CL} = (1 MHz)/[1 + (25 mV/10 μV)] = 1000 kHz/2.5 × 10^3 = 400 Hz and the corresponding rise time is 875 μs. We see that although there are substantial losses in bandwidth, especially at low values of V_1, the use of the series resistor R_7 does, nevertheless, allow for much higher bandwidths than in the previously considered case (i.e., $R_7 = 0$) in which a large-compensation capacitor is used for stability.

With a diode, or diode-connected transistor in the feedback loop we will have for the feedback factor the relationship

$$F = \frac{R_1}{R_1 + r_d} = \frac{R_1}{R_1 + V_T/I_1} = \frac{R_1}{R_1 + V_T R_1/V_1} = \frac{1}{1 + V_T/V_1}$$

The small-signal closed-loop gain will be given by $A_{CL}(0) = 1/F = 1 + (V_T/V_1)$, and the bandwidth will be $BW_{CL} = f_u/A_{CL}(0) = f_u/(1 + V_T/V_1)$. From this last result we see that results similar to the CB transistor case (with $R_7 = R_1$) will be obtained.

8.6.4 Exponential Converter

An exponential or antilogarithmic converter is shown in Figure 8.28. The output voltage of this circuit will be given by

$$V_O = V_R \frac{R_2}{R_1} \exp\left[\frac{V_S R_4}{V_T(R_3 + R_4)}\right] \tag{8.36}$$

so that V_O will be an exponential function of the input signal V_S. The input voltage V_S can be of either polarity, but V_R must be restricted to only a positive polarity, and consequently the output voltage V_O will always be a positive polarity voltage.

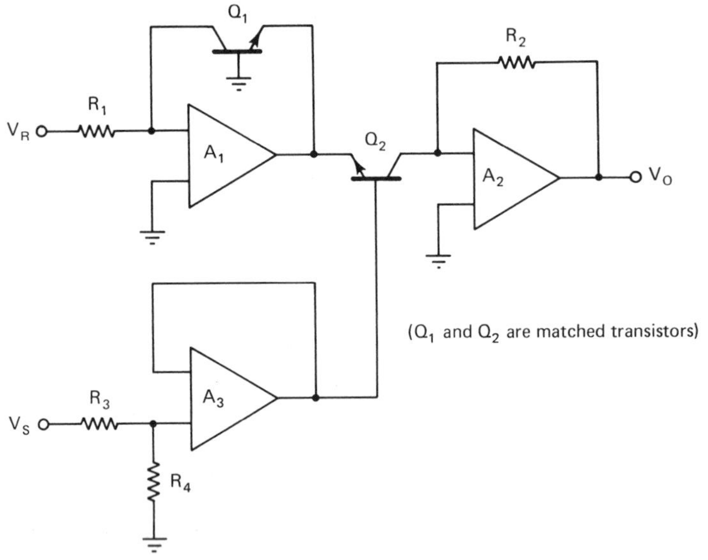

Figure 8.28 Exponential converter (antilogarithmic converter).

8.6.5 Logarithmic Converter ICs

Some examples of logarithmic amplifiers are the 4127 (Burr-Brown) and the AD755 (Analog Devices). Both devices offer a 1% maximum logarithmic conformity over an input current range of 6 decades going from 1 nA to 1 mA. Because of the effects of the input offset voltage, the logarithmic conformity range with respect to a voltage input will be less than that obtained with respect to a current input. For both devices, the 1% logarithmic conformity range for a voltage input is 4 decades, from 1 mV to 10 V. Both ICs can be operated in a log ratio mode in which the output voltage is proportional to the logarithm of the ratio of the two input currents or voltages. Another feature common to both devices is that they can easily be operated as an antilogarithmic or exponential amplifier. Because these are basically nonlinear devices, the small-signal closed-loop gain and therefore the small-signal bandwidth, will be a function of the input current level. For the AD755, for example, the small-signal bandwidth will be only 80 Hz at an input current level of 1 nA, but will increase to 10 kHz at 1 μA, 40 kHz at 10 μA, and 100 kHz at 1 mA.

PROBLEMS

8.1. Show that when the offset voltage of the four transistors, Q_1 through Q_4, of the multiplier circuit of Figure 8.6 is taken into account, the relationship obtained will be given by

$$I_1 I_2 = I_3 I_4 \exp\left[\frac{V_{OS(1,3)} + V_{OS(2,4)}}{V_T}\right]$$

where $V_{OS(1,3)}$ and $V_{OS(2,4)}$ are the offset voltages of the Q_1–Q_3 and the Q_2–Q_4 transistor pairs, respectively. What percentage error will a net offset voltage of 1.0 mV produce? (*Ans.*: 4.1%)

8.2. An analog multiplier has a 3-dB bandwidth of 5.0 MHz. Find the frequency at which this limited bandwidth will result in a multiplication error of 0.1%. (*Ans.*: 224 kHz)

8.3. (*Sine-function generator*) Verify that the sine-function generator circuit of Figure 8.15 will generate the two-term approximation to the sine function as given by $V_O = 1.57V_i - 1.59\,(V_i/6.36)^{2.82}$.

***8.4.** Write a computer program to compare the two-term sine-function approximation given in Problem 8.3 to the actual sine function given by $V_O = 10$ V sin $9V_i$. Use the computer to plot the error curve and find the maximum percentage difference between the approximate function and the actual sine function in the range of 0 to $\pi/2$ radians.

***8.5.** Write a computer program to compare the sine function with a two-term approximation obtained from the Taylor series expansion of the sine function as given by $\sin x \simeq x - x^3/3!$. Use the computer to plot the error curve and find the maximum percentage difference between the approximate function and the actual sine function in the range of 0 to $\pi/2$ radians.

8.6. (*Cosine-function generator*) Verify that the cosine-function circuit of Figure 8.16 will generate the three-term approximation to the cosine function as given by $V_O = 10 + 0.3652V_i - 0.4276V_i^{1.504}$.

***8.7.** Write a computer program to compare the three-term cosine function approximation given above to the actual cosine function given by $V_O = 10$ V cos $9V_i$. Use the computer to plot the error curve and find the maximum percentage difference between the approximate function and the actual cosine function in the range 0 to $\pi/2$ radians.

***8.8.** Write a computer program to compare the cosine function with a three-term approximation obtained from the Taylor series expansion of the cosine function as given by $\cos x \simeq 1 - x^2/2! + x^4/4!$. Use the computer to plot the error curve and find the maximum percentage difference between the approximate function and the actual cosine function in the range 0 to $\pi/2$ radian.

8.9. (*Arctangent-function generator*) Verify that the arctangent function generator of Figure 8.17 will generate the approximation to the arctangent function given by $V_O = 9.0\text{ V}\,|V_1/V_2|^{1.2125}/[1 + |V_1/V_2|^{1.2125}]$. The 25-kΩ potentiometer is set to a value of 10 kΩ.

***8.10.** Write a computer program to compare the arctangent-function approximation given above to the actual arctangent function given by $V_O = 9.0\text{ V}\tan^{-1}(V_1/V_2)$. Use the computer to plot the error curve and find the maximum percentage error between the approximate function and the actual arctangent function.

8.11. (*Vector magnitude circuit*) Verify that the vector magnitude circuit of Figure 8.18 will produce an output voltage given by $V_o = \sqrt{V_1^2 + V_2^2}$.

8.12. (*Polar-to-rectangular resolver*) Design a circuit using function generators to convert a polar function, R/θ, to a rectangular function. The two input voltages to the system are $V_R = R$ and $V_\Theta = \theta$, and the two output voltages are to be $V_x = R\cos\theta$ and $V_y = R\sin\theta$.

8.13. (*Logarithmic converter*) For the logarithmic converter circuit of Figure 8.21, show that when the input bias current and offset voltage of A_1 and A_2, and the offset voltage of the Q_1–Q_2 transistor pair are considered, the output voltage V_O of the circuit will be given by

$$V_O = -\frac{R_4}{R_3}\left[V_T \ln\left(\frac{V_1 - V_{OS_1} - I_{OS_1}R_1}{V_2 - V_{OS_2} - I_{OS_2}R_2}\frac{R_2}{R_1}\right) + V_{OS(Q_1,Q_2)}\right]$$

where V_{OS_1}, V_{OS_2}, I_{OS_1}, and I_{OS_2} are the offset voltages and currents of A_1 and A_2, and $V_{OS(Q1,Q2)}$ is the offset voltage of the Q_1–Q_2 transistor pair.

8.14. (*Logarithmic converter input voltage range*) For the logarithmic converter circuit of Figure 8.21 we have the following specifications for A_1: $I_{OS} = 100$ pA (max.), and the offset voltage of A_1 is nulled out at 25°C, but has a temperature coefficient of $TC_{V_{OS}} = 2$ μV/°C over the specified operating temperature range 0 to 50°C for this logarithmic converter. The maximum transistor current for accurate logarithmic conformity is to be limited to 1.0 mA. The maximum value of V_1 is 100 V. Find the value of R_1 and the minimum allowable value for V_1 for an error, referred to the input voltage V_1, not to exceed 1.0% over the operating temperature range. To how many decades of input voltage V_1 will this correspond? (*Ans*.: 100 kΩ, 6.0 mV, 4.22 decades)

8.15. (*Logarithmic converter error due to base resistance*) The uncompensated logarithmic converter circuit of Figure 8.23 has a transistor with $\beta = 150$ and $r_{bb'} = 75\ \Omega$. Find the error in the output voltage in absolute and percentage terms for the following values of current I_1: 1.0 mA, 3.0 mA, 10 mA, and 30 mA. The base-to-emitter voltage of the transistor is 600 mV at $I_C = 0.1$ mA. (*Ans*.: −0.076%, −0.22%, −0.70%, −2.0%)

***8.16.** (*Logarithmic converter compensation circuit*) A logarithmic converter uses the compensation circuit of Figure 8.24. The base resistance of the transistor varies with current level as $r'_{bb} \simeq 20\ \Omega + 100\ \Omega \exp(-I_C/0.5\text{ mA})$. This variation of r'_{bb} *with* I_C is due to the *current crowding* effect, which is the change in the distribution of the base current resulting from the lateral voltage drop in the base region. The transistor current gain in the higher current region of interest here is given approximately by $\beta \simeq 200 \exp(-I_C/10\text{ mA})$.

Write a computer program to obtain the output voltage error as a function of the input current I_1 and the compensation resistor R_6. Let $R_5 = R_1$. Use the computer to plot error curves for various values of R_6, and find the value of R_6 that will produce a minimum error voltage over the range of currents up to **(a)** 1.0 mA, **(b)** 3.0 mA, **(c)** 10 mA, and **(d)** 30 mA. Find the maximum value of the error voltage for each case.

8.17. (*Logarithmic converter temperature coefficient*) Given the logarithmic converter circuit of Figure 8.21

(a) Show that if all resistors have the same temperature coefficient and track each other with temperature, the output voltage V_O of this circuit will have a temperature coefficient of $TC_{V_O} = +3300$ ppm/°C $= +0.33\%$/°C.

(b) If $TC_{R_1} = TC_{R_2}$ and $TC_{R_4} = 0$, find TC_{R_3} to make $TC_{V_o} = 0$. (*Ans*.: +3300 ppm/°C)

(c) Repeat part (b) for $TC_{R_4} = +1000$ ppm/°C. (*Ans*.: +4300 ppm/°C)

(d) Repeat part (b) to obtain TC_{R_4} if $TC_{R_3} = 0$. (*Ans*.: −3300 ppm/°C)

8.18. (*Signal compression and expansion using logarithmic and antilogarithmic converters*) A transmitter has a dynamic output signal voltage range of 60 dB and the maximum output signal level is 10 V. The output signal goes through a transmission link with an attenuation of 100 dB to a receiver. The equivalent input noise voltage of the receiver is 1.0 μV.

(a) With no signal compression or expansion, find the minimum signal-to-noise ratio

(SNR) at the receiver. (*Ans.*: SNR $= 0.1$, so that the signal will be lost in the noise)

(b) A logarithmic signal compressor is to be used in the transmitter to compress the dynamic range of the signal to 10 dB with the same 10-V maximum signal output level as before. If the transfer function of the logarithmic compressor is given by $V_O = V_A \log_{10}(V_{signal}/V_B)$, where V_A and V_B are constants, find V_A and V_B. (*Ans.*: 2.278 V, 0.4083 mV)

(c) If the signal expandor at the receiver has a transfer function given by $V_O = V_C \times 10\ (V_{signal}/V_D)$, where V_C and V_D are constants, find the values of V_C and V_D necessary to restore the signal to the original 60-dB range with a maximum output level of 10 V. (*Ans.*: 0.4098 mV, 0.0228 mV)

(d) Find the signal-to-noise ratio at the receiver when the signal compression/expansion system is used, and compare the result with that obtained when there is no signal compression and expansion. [*Ans.*: SNR $= 31.6$ (min.)]

8.19. (*Signal compression and expansion*) Repeat parts (b), (c), and (d) of Problem 8.18 for the case of signal compression at the transmitter with a transfer characteristic given by $V_O = 10\sqrt{V_{signal}/V_B}$ volts and a signal expansion at the receiver with a transfer characteristic given by $V_O = 10(V_{signal}/V_D)^2$ volts, where V_B and V_D are constants. This will produce a signal compression from the original 60-dB range down to 30 dB at the transmitter, and there will be a complementary signal expansion at the receiver to restore the signal back to the full 60-dB range. Comment on the relative advantages and disadvantages of the logarithmic and square-root signal compression and complementary expansion systems in terms of the signal-to-noise ratio and the overall system linearity. (*Ans.:* $V_B = 10$ V, $V_D = 100\ \mu$V)

8.20. [*Exponential converter (antilogarithmic converter)*] Show that for the exponential converter circuit of Figure 8.28 the output voltage V_O will be given by

$$V_O = V_R \frac{R_2}{R_1} \exp\left[\frac{V_S R_4}{(R_3 + R_4)V_T}\right]$$

8.21. (*Exponential converter*) Design a circuit to produce the function $V_O = 0.1$ V exp $(V_S/1.0\ \text{V})$.

8.22. (*Hyperbolic sine-function circuit*) Design a circuit to produce the function $V_O = 0.1$ V sinh $(V_S/1.0\ \text{V})$.

8.23. (*Hyperbolic cosine-function circuit*) Design a circuit to produce the function $V_O = 0.1$ V cosh $(V_S/1.0\ \text{V})$.

8.24. (*Hyperbolic tangent circuit*) Design a circuit to produce the function $V_O = 10$ V tanh $(V_S/1.0\ \text{V})$.

REFERENCES

GLASER, A. B., AND G. E. SUBAK-SHARPE, *Integrated Circuit Engineering*, Addison-Wesley, 1977.

GREBENE, A. B., *Analog Integrated Circuit Design*, Van Nostrand Reinhold, 1972.

LENK, J. D., *Handbook of Integrated Circuits*, Reston, 1978.

Mitra, S. K., *An Introduction to Digital and Analog Integrated Circuits and Applications*, Harper & Row, 1980.

Stout, D. F., *Handbook of Microcircuit Design and Applications*, McGraw-Hill, 1980.

United Technical Publications, *Modern Applications of Integrated Circuits*, Tab Books, 1974.

Wong, Y. J., and W. E. Ott, *Function Circuits*, McGraw-Hill, 1976.

IC Transducers: Temperature, Magnetic Field, and Pressure

9

Most integrated circuits and other electronic devices and systems are used to operate on or transform an electrical input to produce an electrical output. The devices considered in this chapter and in Chapter 15 will be used to sense, measure, or detect various nonelectrical input quantities such as temperature, magnetic field, pressure, and light. These ICs and discrete devices will be *transducers* in that these various nonelectrical inputs will be converted to an electrical output.

The physical quantities mentioned above can be measured directly by the electronic transducers or can be used for a variety of other measurements, such as gas or liquid fluid flow, mechanical translational or angular position or motion, and acceleration. Other applications are in the areas of the measurement of the optical density of solids, liquids, and gases, the detection of various contaminants and impurities in gases and liquids, and for smoke and flame detection. IC transducers can also be used for measurement of relative humidity, the pH of solutions, and for the detection of various gases.

In this chapter various IC transducers are discussed, with the exception of optoelectronic devices such as photodiodes, phototransistors, and image sensors. These devices are considered in Chapter 15.

9.1 IC TEMPERATURE SENSORS

Semiconductor devices are very temperature sensitive and this temperature sensitivity can be used to make IC temperature sensors that will generate a voltage or a current that is proportional to the absolute temperature (PTAT).

There are three basic temperature-dependent effects of importance in semiconductors and semiconductor devices. The first is the thermally activated generation of free electrons and holes by the breaking loose of electrons from covalent bonds and becoming free electrons, able to freely move through the crystal structure. These electrons leave behind electron vacancies or "holes." The thermal generation rate of free electrons and holes increases exponentially with temperature. A principal device manifestation of this thermal generation phenomenon is the exponential increase of the junction reverse leakage current with temperature.

For silicon diodes and transistors the reverse current will approximately double for every 10°C increment in temperature, so that the ratio of the reverse currents at two different temperatures will be given by $I_R(T_2)/I_R(T_1) = 2^{(T_2-T_1)/10°C}$. For example, if a silicon diode or transistor has a reverse current of 1 nA at 25°C, the reverse current at 125°C will have increased to about $2^{10} \times 1$ nA = 1000 nA = μA, an increase by a factor of 1000. At 150°C the reverse current will be approximately $2^{12.5} \times 1$ nA= 6 μA, and at 175°C the reverse current will be up to around $2^{15} \times 1$ nA = 33 μA. This rapid increase in the reverse current with temperature is a principal reason for the limitation of the maximum operating temperature $T_{J(MAX)}$ for silicon devices at about 175°C.

The pronounced sensitivity of the reverse current with temperature can be used as the basis of a temperature sensor, but the value of I_R at any given temperature and its rate of change with temperature will exhibit very large variations from device to device. It generally will not be useful for temperature sensing as a result of this. In addition, the variation of the reverse current I_R with temperature will be very nonlinear, so that a simple scale factor conversion from current to temperature is not possible.

Another thermally activated process in semiconductor devices is the flow of majority carriers across the electric potential hill or barrier at a PN junction. As the temperature increases the rate of flow of electrons and holes across the potential hill will increase at an exponential rate. As a result of this, at a given forward-bias voltage level the forward current of a PN junction in a diode or transistor will increase exponentially with temperature. The forward current will increase by approximately 10% for every 1°C rise in temperature, and by a factor of approximately 2.4 for every 10°C rise in temperature.

At a given forward current level the forward voltage drop across the PN junction will correspondingly decrease at a rate of about 2.2 mV/°C. The general equation for the temperature coefficient of the forward voltage drop across a PN junction will be given by

$$TC_{V_F} = \left.\frac{dV_F}{dT}\right|_{I_F=\text{constant}} = -\left(\frac{1205\text{ mV} - V_F}{T} + 0.26\text{ mV/°C}\right) \tag{9.1}$$

This temperature coefficient can be used for temperature sensing and measurement, but there will be some unit-to-unit variations in the forward voltage drop V_F, and therefore in the temperature coefficient of V_F, TC_{V_F}. In addition, the forward voltage drop V_F (or V_{BE} in the case of a transistor) will not vary linearly with temperature.

The collector current of a transistor in the active mode of operation is related to the base-to-emitter voltage by a simple exponential relationship given by $I_C = I_{TO} \exp(V_{BE}/V_T)$. For two matched or identical transistors, Q_1 and Q_2, the ratio of the two collector currents will be given by

$$\frac{I_1}{I_2} = \frac{\exp(V_{BE_1}/V_T)}{\exp(V_{BE_2}/V_T)} = \exp\left(\frac{V_{BE_1} - V_{BE_2}}{V_T}\right) \tag{9.2}$$

$$= \exp\left(\frac{\Delta V_{BE}}{V_T}\right)$$

so that

$$\Delta V_{BE} = V_{BE1} - V_{BE2} = V_T \ln \frac{I_1}{I_2} = \frac{kT}{q} \ln \frac{I_1}{I_2} \tag{9.3}$$

If the circuit is designed such that the I_1/I_2 current ratio is constrained to be constant, we see that ΔV_{BE} will be *directly proportional to the absolute temperature (PTAT)*. This is the basis of most IC temperature sensors. Even when the two transistors are not identical, there will still be a direct proportionality between ΔV_{BE} and the absolute temperature. In the general case in which there is an offset voltage V_{OS} for the pair of transistors under consideration, the ratio of the collector currents can be written as $I_1/I_2 = \exp(\Delta V_{BE} - V_{OS})/V_T$. The offset voltage of a pair of transistors of similar construction will be due principally to the differences in the effective base widths, and can be expressed in terms of the ratio of the effective base widths as $V_{OS} = V_T \ln(W_{B_1}/W_{B_2})$, where W_{B_1} and W_{B_2} are the effective base widths of Q_1 and Q_2, respectively. For this case the base-to-emitter voltage differential of the two transistors will be given by

$$\Delta V_{BE} = V_T \ln \frac{I_1}{I_2} + V_{OS} = V_T \left(\ln \frac{I_1}{I_2} + \ln \frac{W_{B_1}}{W_{B_2}}\right) \tag{9.4}$$

We see that ΔV_{BE} will still be a precisely linear function of the absolute temperature.

The temperature dependence of the ΔV_{BE} for a pair of transistors will be the basis of most IC temperature sensors. Some examples of these IC temperature sensors will be presented in the following sections.

9.1.1 Circuit That Produces an Output Voltage Proportional to the Absolute Temperature

A simple circuit that produces an output voltage that is proportional to the absolute temperature (PTAT) is shown in Figure 9.1. Transistors Q_3, Q_4, and Q_5 are scaled such that the ratio of the active areas is $1:1:n$, respectively. Therefore, since the base-to-emitter voltages of these three transistors are equal, the collector currents will be related to each other by $I_5 = nI_4 = nI_3$. Since $I_1 = I_4$ and $I_2 = I_5$, the current ratio of I_2 to I_1 will be fixed at a value given by $I_2/I_1 = I_5/I_4 = n$.

The input voltage to the difference amplifier part of the circuit, V_i, will be given by

$$
\begin{aligned}
V_i &= V_{E_1} - V_{E_2} = (V^+ - V_{BE_1}) - (V^+ - V_{BE_2}) \\
&= V_{BE_2} - V_{BE_1} = V_T \ln \frac{I_2}{I_1} + V_{OS} \\
&= V_T \ln n + V_T \ln \frac{W_{B2}}{W_{B1}} \\
&= V_T \left(\ln n + \ln \frac{W_{B2}}{W_{B1}} \right)
\end{aligned} \tag{9.5}
$$

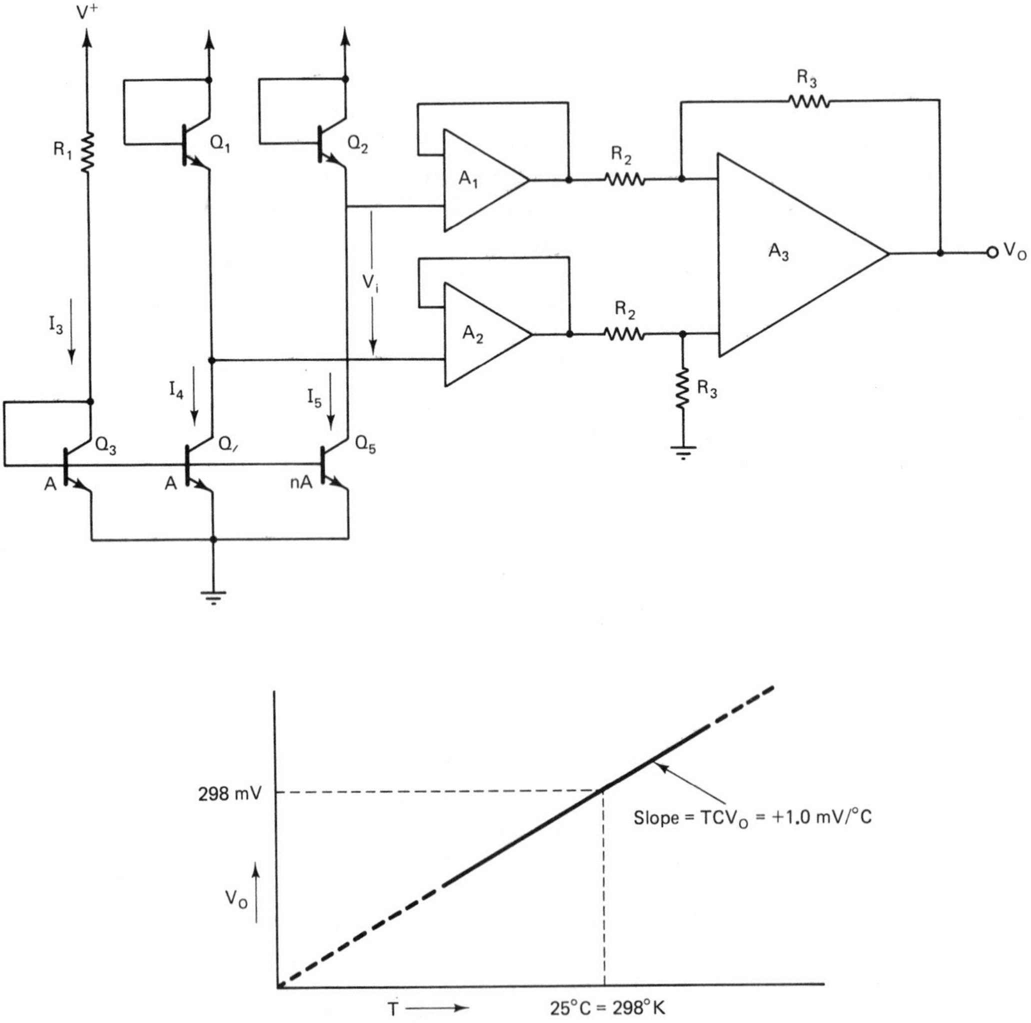

Figure 9.1 Circuit that produces an output voltage proportional to the absolute temperature.

The output voltage V_O will be related to V_i by $V_O = (R_3/R_2)V_i$, so that we now obtain

$$V_O = \frac{R_3}{R_2} V_T \left(\ln n + \ln \frac{W_{B2}}{W_{B1}}\right) \tag{9.6}$$

Noting that $V_T = kT/q$, we see that V_O will indeed be proportional to the absolute temperature. Since $d(V_T)/dT = k/q = V_T/T$, the temperature coefficient of V_O will be given by $TC_{VO} = dV_O/dT = V_O/T$.

For a temperature coefficient of $TC_{VO} = 1.0$ mV/°C at 25°C = 298°K, the required value of V_O (at 25°C) will be $V_O = 1.0$ mV/°K × 298°K = 298 mv. If we let $n = 2$ and assume that V_{OS} is small, we have that $V_O = V_T(R_3/R_2) \ln 2 =$ 25.678 mV × (R_3/R_2) × ln 2 = 298 mV. Solving for the R_3/R_2 resistance ratio, we obtain $R_3/R_2 = 16.743$.

Note that this circuit can easily be put together from standard components by using a quad op amp and IC transistor array, and five resistors. It is very important, however, that the resistors have closely matched temperature coefficients and that they track each other with temperature.

This circuit is basically a three-terminal temperature sensor, the three terminals being V^+, ground, and V_O. In the next section a two-terminal temperature sensor will be presented.

9.1.2 Two-Terminal IC Temperature Sensor with Voltage Proportional to the Absolute Temperature

In Figure 9.2 a simplified diagram of a two-terminal IC temperature sensor is shown. In this sensor the voltage drop across the device will be proportional to the absolute temperature.

This is basically a closed-loop feedback circuit involving a feedback loop consisting of amplifier A_2, the Q_3–Q_4 Darlington common-emitter stage, the R_3–R_4–R_5 voltage divider, and the Q_1–Q_2 differential amplifier. If the voltage gain around the feedback loop is very large, the input voltage of A_2, V_{i_2}, will be very small. As a result we will have that $I_1R_1 = I_2R_2$, so that the I_2/I_1 current ratio will be fixed by the action of the feedback loop at $I_2/I_1 = R_1/R_2$. Since $I_2/I_1 = \exp (\Delta V_{BE} - V_{OS})/V_T$, and $\Delta V_{BE} = V_O[R_4/(R_3 + R_4 + R_5)] = FV_O$, we have that $I_2/I_1 = R_1/R_2 = \exp [(FV_O - V_{OS})/V_T]$, where F is the feedback factor obtained from the R_3–R_4–R_5 voltage divider. Solving for V_O gives

$$V_O = \frac{V_T \ln (R_1/R_2) + V_{OS}}{F} = \frac{V_T[\ln (R_1/R_2) + \ln (W_{B_1}/W_{B_2})]}{F} \tag{9.7}$$

Since $d(V_T)/dT = k/q = V_T/T$, the temperature coefficient of V_O will be given by $TC_{V_O} = dV_O/dT = V_O/T$. Note from the preceding equations that V_O will be proportional to the absolute temperature.

For a temperature coefficient of $TC_{V_O} = 10$ mV/°C, the corresponding voltage drop V_O at 25°C = 298°K will be given by $V_O = 10$ mV/°K × 298°K = 2.98 V.

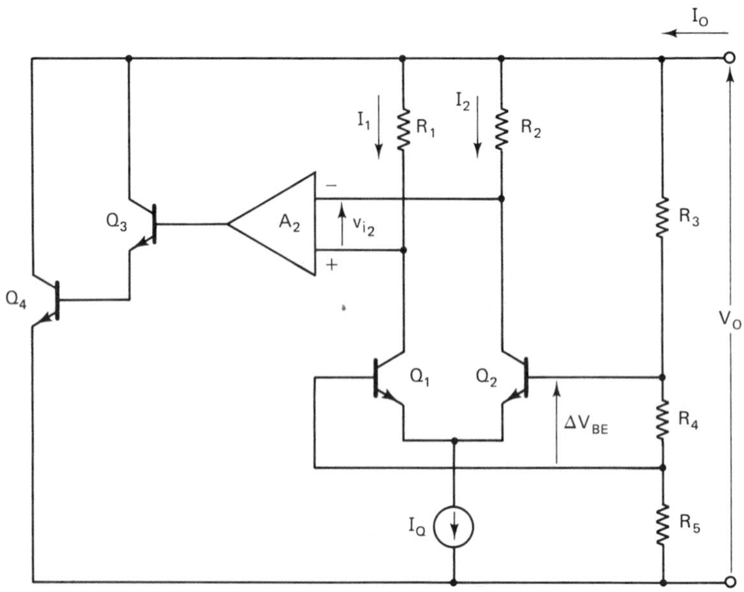

Figure 9.2 Two-terminal VPTAT temperature sensor.

If the R_1/R_2 resistance ratio is chosen such that $R_1/R_2 = 10$ and if we assume that the offset voltage is small, the required value for the feedback factor F becomes $F = V_T \ln (R_1/R_2)/V_O = 25.7 \text{ mV} \times \ln 10/2.98 \text{ V} = \underline{0.0198}$.

If $I_1 = 10\ \mu\text{A}$ and $I_2 = 100\ \mu\text{A}$, and the voltage drop across R_1 and R_2 is chosen to be 1.0 V, then $R_1 = \underline{100\ \text{k}\Omega}$ and $R_2 = \underline{10\ \text{k}\Omega}$. Since $V_O = 2.98$ V (at 25°C), and if we choose that $V_{B_2} = 1.0$ V and that the current through the R_3–R_4–R_5 series string be 1.0 mA, we have that $R_3 + R_4 + R_5 = \underline{2.98\ \text{k}\Omega}$ and $R_3 = 1.98\ \text{V}/1.0\ \text{mA} = \underline{1.98\ \text{k}\Omega}$. Since the feedback factor is $F = 0.0198$, we obtain $R_4 = F(R_3 + R_4 + R_5) = \underline{59.1\ \Omega}$, and thus $R_3 = 2.98\ \text{k}\Omega - 1.98\ \text{k}\Omega - 0.059\ \text{k}\Omega = \underline{941\ \Omega}$.

In Figure 9.3 the I_O versus V_O characteristics of this device is shown. In the region above the current level I_{MIN} the current I_O increases at an approximately exponential rate with increasing voltage V_O. At any given current level in this region the voltage drop V_O will increase linearly with increasing temperature at a rate of 10 mV/°C for this example.

Dynamic resistance. The terminal current I_O of this device will be approximately equal to the current of the Darlington output stage of Q_3 and Q_4, so that $I_O = I_3 + I_4 \simeq I_4$. The dynamic conductance of this device can be written as $g_o = dI_O/dV_O = dI_4/dV_{BE_{3,4}} \times A_1A_2F$, where A_1 is the voltage gain of the Q_1–Q_2 differential amplifier. Since the transfer conductance of the Darlington stage is $g_{f_{3,4}} = I_4/2V_T$, we obtain $g_o = (I_4/2V_T) \times A_1A_2F = (I_O/2V_T) \times A_1A_2F$ and the corresponding dynamic resistance will be $r_o = (V_T/I_O) \times (2/A_1A_2F)$.

As a representative example, let us assume that $A_1 \times A_2 = 100 \times 100 = 10{,}000$ and use the value of feedback factor obtained earlier of $F = 0.0198$. For the

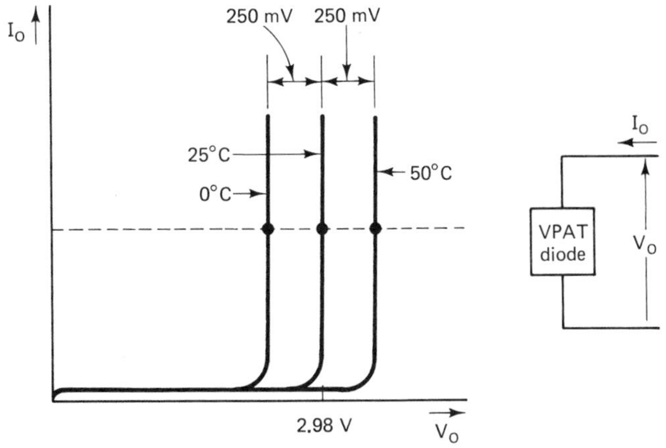

Figure 9.3 I_O versus V_O characteristics of VPAT diode.

dynamic resistance we obtain $r_o = (V_T/I_O) \times (2/(10\ \text{k}\Omega \times 0.02) = V_T/100I_O = 0.26\ \text{mV}/I_O$. Thus, at a current level of $I_O = 1.0$ mA the dynamic resistance will be only 0.26 Ω. In terms of the change in V_O resulting from a fraction change in the current, we have $r_O = dV_O/dI_O = 0.26\ \text{mV}/I_O$, so that $dV_O = 0.26\ \text{mV}(dI_O/I_O)$. Therefore, for a 10% change in I_O the resulting change in V_O will be only 0.026 mV = 26 μV. Thus if the temperature sensor is operated as shown in Figure 9.4a, a change in the V^+ supply voltage of 0.1 V will result in a change of about 1% in the device current I_O. This will produce a change in V_O of only 2.6 μV, which will correspond to only an extremely small temperature error. For even less sensitivity to supply voltage variations, the circuit of Figure 9.4b can be used in which a current source is used to bias the temperature sensor. In Figure 9.4c an equivalent circuit for the temperature sensor circuit of Figure 9.4a is shown. As long as $r_o \ll [R_1 \parallel R_L]$, the voltage across R_L will not be affected by either R_1 or R_L.

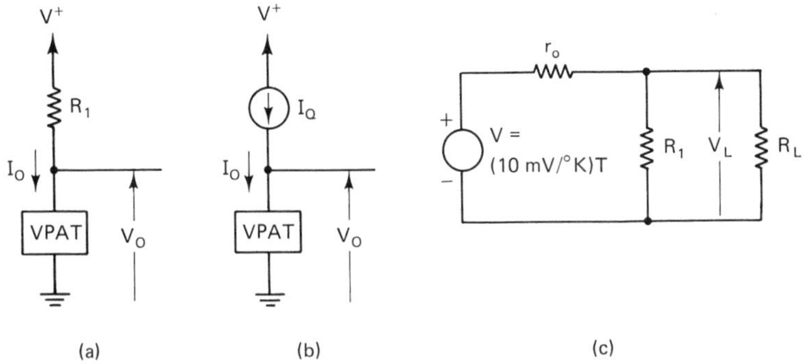

Figure 9.4 VPAT diode circuits: (a) circuit using resistor biasing; (b) circuit using current source biasing; (c) equivalent circuit.

Monolithic IC two-terminal temperature sensor with voltage proportional to absolute temperature. An example of a monolithic IC temperature sensor similar to the one just described is the LM135/235/335 series (National Semiconductor). These devices are available in a three-terminal TO-92 plastic package or a TO-46 metal can package. The voltage drop across this device will have a temperature coefficient of +10 mV/°C and will be 2.98 V at 25°C. The dynamic resistance will be less than 1.0 Ω over the operating current range 400 μA to 5 mA.

This IC has a terminal available for temperature calibration. If the device is correctly calibrated for $V_O = 2.982$ V at 25°C, the temperature coefficient will be +10 mV/°C and the maximum temperature error over the operating temperature range of the device will be 1°C for both the LM135A (−55 to +150°C) and the LM335A (−10 to + 100°).

9.1.3 Two-Terminal IC Temperature Transducer: Current Proportional to Absolute Temperature

The two-terminal temperature transducer circuits to be described produce a current flow that is directly proportional to the absolute temperature (PTAT).

The basic circuit is shown in Figure 9.5. All transistors will be assumed to be identical, except that transistor Q_3 has a larger active area (A_3) than that of Q_4 (A_4), so that the ratio of the active areas of Q_3 and Q_4 will be given by $r = A_3/A_4$.

Since Q_1 and Q_2 constitute a current mirror (i.e., equal transistors with identical base-to-emitter voltages), we have that $I_1 = I_2$ (neglecting the base currents). Since $I_3 = I_1$ and $I_4 = I_2$ (again, neglecting the base currents), we have that $I_3 = I_4$. Since Q_3 and Q_4 are of identical construction, but of different emitter areas (i.e., active areas), we have that $J_3 = J_{TO} \exp (V_{BE_3}/V_T)$ and $J_4 = J_{TO} \exp (V_{BE_4}/V_T)$, so that $J_4/J_3 = \exp (V_{BE_4} - V_{BE_3})/V_T = \exp (\Delta V_{BE}/V_T)$, where ΔV_{BE} is the voltage drop across R_1 as given by $\Delta V_{BE} = I_3 R_1$.

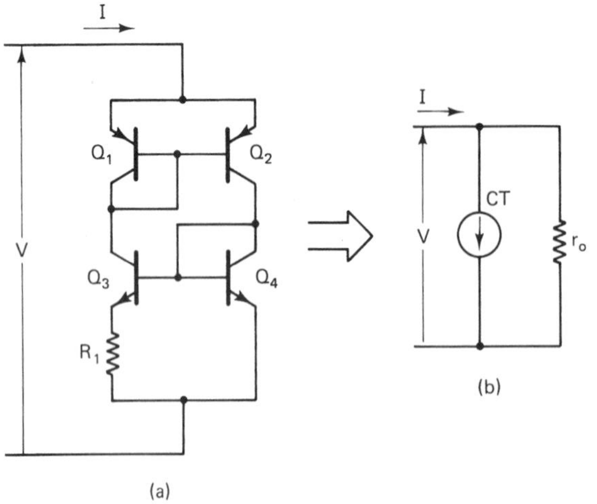

Figure 9.5 Two-terminal temperature sensor that produces a current proportional to the absolute temperature: (a) basic circuit; (b) equivalent circuit (valid for $V > 2V_{BE} \simeq 1.7$ V).

Since $I_3 = I_4$, we have that $J_4/J_3 = (I_4/A_4)/(I_3/A_3) = A_3/A_4 = r$. Thus $J_4/J_3 = r = \exp(\Delta V_{BE}/VT)$, so that $\Delta V_{BE} = V_T \ln r$. Since $\Delta V_{BE} = I_3R_1$, we obtain $I_3R_1 = \Delta V_{BE} = V_T \ln r$. Solving for I_3 gives $I_3 = (V_T/R_1) \ln r$. Since $I_4 = I_3 = I_1 = I_2$, for the total current I we have that $I = I_1 + I_2 = I_3 + I_4 = 2I_3$ so that $I = 2I_3 = (2V_T/R_1) \ln r$. Since $V_T = kT/q$ we can express I as

$$\boxed{I = \frac{2kT}{qR_1} \ln r = \left(\frac{2k}{qR_1} \ln r\right) T = CT} \tag{9.8}$$

where $C = 2k/qR_1 \ln r$ is the temperature-to-current conversion coefficient, and has units of A/°C.

We see that the terminal current, I, will be directly proportional to the absolute temperature T, as given by $I = CT$, where the constant of proportionality $C = (2k/qR_1) \ln r$.

To consider an example, since $k = 1.3804 \times 10^{-23}$ J/°K and $q = 1.602 \times 10^{-19}$ C we have that $C = (2k/qR_1) \ln r = (1.723 \times 10^{-4} \ln r)/R_1$. If the area ratio $A_3/A_4 = r = 8$, the temperature-to-current conversion coefficient becomes $C = 3.584 \times 10^{-4}/R_1$. If we want C to be some numerically convenient value such as 1.0 μA/°C, then the required value of R_1 will be $R_1 = 3.584 \times 10^{-4}/1.0 \times 10^{-6} = 358.4\ \Omega$. With this choice of resistance will will have that

$$\boxed{I = (1.0\ \mu\text{A/°K})T(\text{°K})} \tag{9.9}$$

Thus for every °C (or °K) temperature increment the current will increase by 1.0 μA. At 25°C = 298°K the current will be $I = (1.0\ \mu\text{A/°K})(298\text{°K}) = \underline{298\ \mu\text{A}}$.

The current I will be relatively independent of the terminal voltage, V, as long as V is large enough to maintain all of the transistors in the active region. For the circuit of Figure 9.5 this will correspond to $V \geqslant 2V_{BE} \simeq 1.7$ V.

The dynamic impedance of this transducer will be approximately the parallel combination of the output (or collector) impedances of Q_3 and Q_2. Since the impedance of Q_3 will be much higher than that of Q_2 due to the effect of R_1 in series with the emitter of Q_3, the net output impedance will be approximately that of Q_2. For Q_2 we will have that $g_{o_2} = g_{ce_2} = I_2/V_A = I/2V_A = g_o$, so that $r_o = 2V_A/I$. At 25°C, $I = 298\ \mu$A, so that if a typical value of about 200 V is chosen for the Early voltage, V_A, we have $r_o = 2 \times 200\ \text{V}/298\ \mu\text{A} = 1.3\ \text{m}\Omega$. As a result we can represent the two-terminal temperature transducer of this example as the parallel combination of a temperature-dependent constant-current source of strength $I = (1.0\ \mu\text{A/°K})T$, and a resistance of 1.3 MΩ (at 25°C).

A somewhat more complex temperature transducer circuit is shown in Figure 9.6. In this circuit the relative emitter areas are indicated by the numbers adjacent to the emitters.

In this circuit we note that as was the case for the circuit of Figure 9.5, $I_1 = I_2$ and $I_1 = I_3$ and $I_2 = I_4$ (again neglecting base currents) so that $I_3 = I_4$. Since $J_4/J_3 = \exp(\Delta V_{BE}/VT)$, and $J_4/J_3 = A_3/A_4$ (since $I_3 = I_4$), we have that $\Delta V_{BE} =$

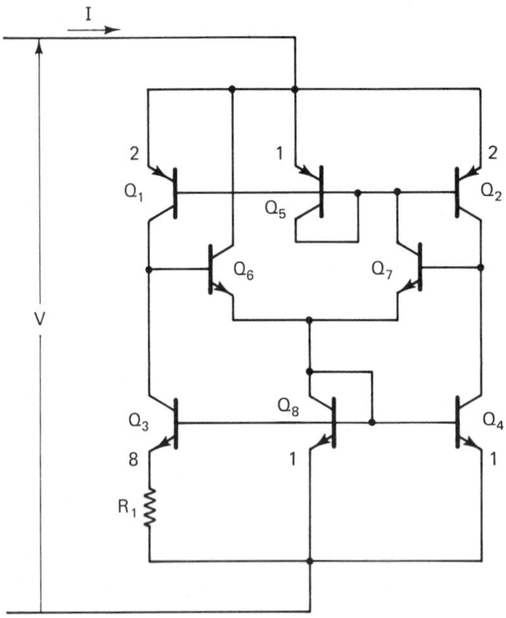

Figure 9.6 Two-terminal temperature transducer.

$V_T \ln (A_3/A_4) = V_T \ln r$. As a result, we have that $I_3 = \Delta V_{BE}/R_1 = (V_T/R_1) \ln r$.

We note that $I_3 = I_4$ and $I_8 = I_4$, so that the terminal current, I, will be given by

$$I = I_3 + I_4 + I_8 = 3I_3 = \frac{3V_T}{R_1} \ln r = \frac{3k}{qR_1} (\ln r)\, T = CT \tag{9.10}$$

Thus again we have that the total current I is proportional to the absolute temperature (PTAT).

Since $I_5 = I_7 = \frac{1}{2}I_1 = \frac{1}{2}I_2 = \frac{1}{2}I_3 = \frac{1}{6}I$. The current $I_6 + I_7 = I_8 = I_3$ so that $I_6 = I_3 - I_7 = \frac{1}{2}I_3 = I_7$. Thus Q_6 and Q_7 in effect constitute a differential amplifier in the feedback loop with $I_6 = I_7$.

In this circuit, the voltages at the collectors of Q_3 and Q_4 will be approximately equal due to the action of Q_6 and Q_7. As a result, there will be very little error due to the Early effect. In the case of the circuit of Figure 9.5, the voltages at the collectors of Q_3 and Q_4 will not be the same, with $V_{C_3} = V - V_{BE}$ and $V_{C_4} = V_{BE}$, so that $V_{C_3} - V_{C_4} = V - 2V_{BE}$. As a result of this there will a a contribution to the offset voltage of the Q_3–Q_4 transistor pair. This offset voltage contribution due to the Early effect will be approximately given by $\Delta V_{OS} = (V_T/V_A)\, \Delta V_C = (V_T/V_A)(V - 2V_{BE})$.

Monolithic IC current PTAT sensor. A two-terminal temperature sensor that produces a current proportional to the absolute temperature that is similar to the circuit just described as available as a monolithic IC (AD 590, Analog Devices). This device operates as a constant-current regulator with a current PTAT and a

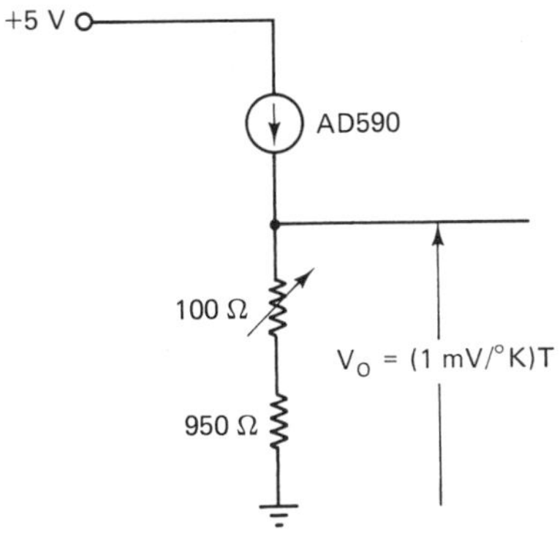

Figure 9.7 Temperature-sensing circuit using the AD590 two-terminal IC temperature sensor (Analog Devices, Inc).

temperature coefficient for the current of 1 μA/°C. This device has thin-film resistors on the chip that are laser trimmed to give the device a current of 298.2 μA at 25.0°C (298.2°K).

The voltage compliance range of this device extends from +3 V up to +30 V. The dynamic output resistance is 10 MΩ (min.) in parallel with a 100-pF capacitance. The high dynamic resistance is very advantageous in that the current of the device will be relatively independent of the voltage across the device. This will make the current relatively insensitive to supply voltage ripple or other fluctuations and the voltage drop due to line resistances in series with the device. For example, a ripple or other fluctuation in the supply voltage of as much as 1.0 V will result in a change of the device current of no more than 0.1 μA. This corresponds to a temperature measurement error of only 0.1°C.

The high dynamic resistance is a very useful feature for remote-sensing applications in which this device will be at some distance from the rest of the system. For example, a resistance of 100 Ω in the connecting wires to the device will produce an error of only 0.001% in the temperature measurement.

In Figure 9.7 a very simple temperature-sensing circuit using the IC temperature sensor is shown. If the trimming potentiometer is correctly adjusted to give $V_O =$ 298.2 mV at 25.0°C, this device will be accurate to within ±0.5°C over the temperature range −55 to +150°C (AD590K).

9.1.4 Temperature Dependence of Resistivity

A third temperature-dependent effect in semiconductors that is of interest for temperature sensing and measurement is the variation of resistivity with temperature which results from the variation of the mobility of the free electrons and holes with temperature. As the temperature increases, the amplitude of atomic vibrations in the crystal structure will increase. The increased displacement of the atoms from their equilibrium positions in the crystal structure will interfere with and impede the flow of the charge carriers. As a result, the mobility will decrease with temperature. Since the conductivity is proportional to the mobility of the free charge carriers, the conductivity will correspondingly decrease, and the resistivity will increase with temperature.

The mobility of free electrons and holes in lightly doped silicon ($\rho > 10$

Ω-cm) will vary with temperature approximately as $\mu \propto 1/T^{5/2}$. Since the conductivity σ will be directly proportional to μ and the resistivity will be inversely proportional to σ, we will have that $\rho = 1/\sigma \propto T^{5/2}$. The temperature coefficient of resistivity will therefore be given by $(1/\rho)(d\rho/dT) = \frac{5}{2}/T$, and correspondingly the temperature coefficient of resistance TC_R will be $TC_R = (1/R)(dR/dT) = \frac{5}{2}/T$, where T is the absolute temperature (°K). At temperatures near room temperature for which $T \simeq$ 300°K, we have that $TC_R = \frac{5}{2}/T = \frac{5}{2}/300°\text{K} = 8.3 \times 10^{-3}/°\text{C} = \underline{8300 \text{ ppm}/°\text{C}} = \underline{0.83\%/°\text{C}}$. Thus a small but significant temperature coefficient is obtained.

As the doping level increases above 10^{15} cm^{-3}, the temperature coefficient will decrease, and at doping levels in excess of above about 3×10^{18} cm^{-3} ($\rho \lesssim 0.01$ Ω-cm) the temperature coefficient will become negative.

A silicon resistor can be used as a temperature sensor or for temperature compensation purposes. As a temperature sensor it can be made part of a Wheatstone bridge circuit that is balanced or nulled at some reference temperature T_R. Changes in temperature from this reference temperature will unbalance the bridge and produce a small output voltage which can then be amplified by a simple op-amp circuit. For small to moderate temperature changes from the reference temperature of around 10°C or less, the output voltage will vary approximately linearly with temperature as $V_O = C(T - T_R)$, where C is a constant.

9.2 IC MAGNETIC FIELD SENSORS: THE HALL EFFECT

Most IC magnetic field sensors are based on the *Hall effect*. The Hall effect arises from the *Lorentz force* experienced by a charged particle moving in a magnetic field as shown in Figure 9.8. The Lorentz force will be given by $\overline{F}_m = q(\overline{v} \times \overline{B})$, where q is the charge, $\overline{v}$ is the velocity of the charge particle, and $\overline{B}$ is the magnetic flux density.

In Figure 9.9 a Hall plate is shown. The Lorentz force will act to produce a transverse deflection of the charge carriers. Since there can be no net current flow

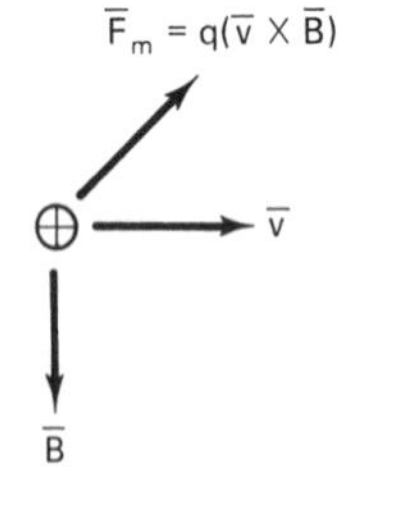

Figure 9.8 Lorentz force.

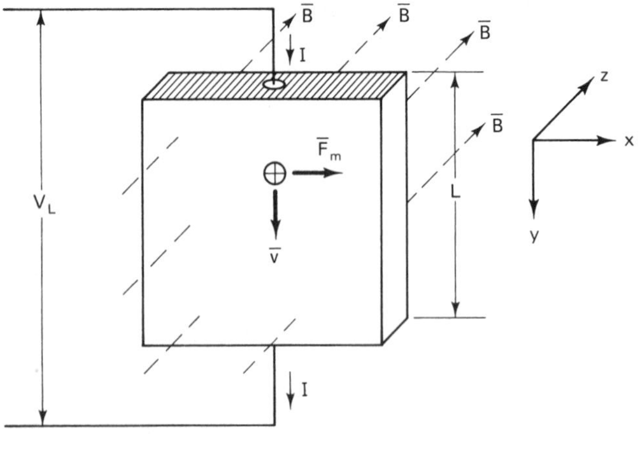

Figure 9.9 Hall effect.

in the transverse direction (x), there will be a slight shift of the charge carrier distribution with a slight accumulation of the charge carriers on one side of the plate and a depletion of charge carriers on the other side. This slight shift in the charge distribution will result in a transverse electric field E_H that will exactly balance out the Lorentz force, as shown in Figure 9.10.

With this equilibrium situations we will therefore have that the force on the charge carriers due to the electric field, $F_e = qE_H$ will be equal to the Lorentz force (but opposite in direction) so that $F_e = qE_H = F_m = q(vB)$ and thus $E_H = vB$, where E_H is the transverse or Hall electric field. The drift velocity v of the charge carriers will be given by $v = \mu E_L$, where μ is the mobility and E_L is the electric field in the longitudinal or y direction. We therefore will have that $E_H = vB = \mu E_L B$, so that the ratio of the Hall field to the longitudinal field will be given approximately by $E_H/E_L = \mu B$. The *Hall angle* θ_H as shown in Figure 9.11 is given approximately by $\tan \theta_H \simeq E_H/E_L = \mu B$. Since μB will usually be small compared to unity, we will have that $\tan \theta_H \simeq \theta_H$, so that $\theta_H \simeq E_H/E_L = \mu B$.

The voltage that is applied across the Hall plate is V_L and is related to E_L by $V_L = E_L \times L$, and the transverse or *Hall voltage* V_H is related to E_H by $V_H = E_H \times W$, where L and W are as shown in Figure 9.11. The ratio of V_H to V_L will therefore be given approximately by $V_H/V_L = E_H W/E_L L = \mu B(W/L)$. Therefore, the ratio of the transverse or Hall voltage to the applied bias voltage V_L will be directly proportional to the magnetic field strength.

In Figure 9.12 a Hall plate that is part of a monolithic IC is shown, and in Figure 9.13 a simple circuit that can be used to produce an output voltage V_O that will be proportional to the magnetic field is shown. Note that the entire circuit of Figure 9.13, including the Hall plate, can be put on a single IC chip. The output voltage V_o will be given approximately by $V_o = (R_2/R_1)V_H = (R_2/R_1)\mu B(W/L)V^+$.

We will now consider a representative example for the circuit just described, and for the Hall plate we will assume that $W = L = 200\ \mu$m. The epitaxial layer will be assumed to be 10 μm thick with a resistivity of 0.6 Ω-cm ($N_D = 1 \times 10^{16}$ cm^{-3}). The bias voltage that is applied to the Hall plate will be chosen to be +10 V. The sheet resistance of the epitaxial layer will be 0.6 Ω-cm/10 μm = 600 Ω/

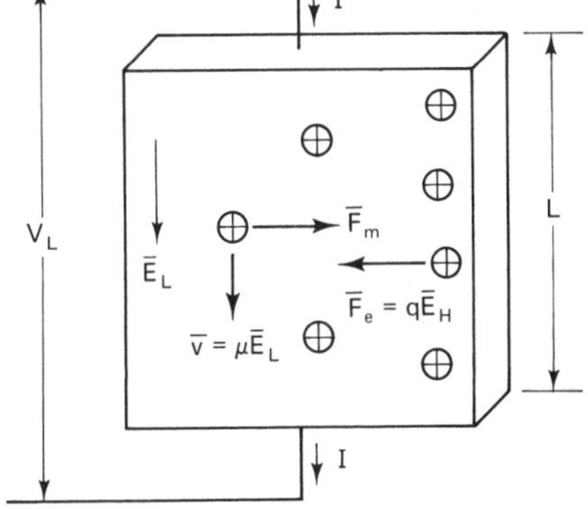

Figure 9.10 Hall effect: transverse electric field.

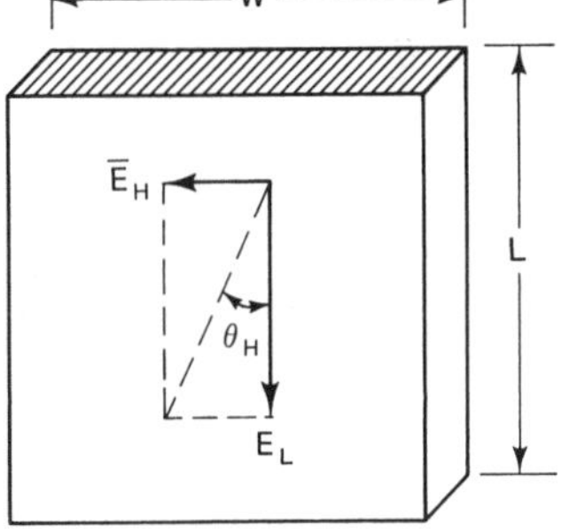

Figure 9.11 Hall angle.

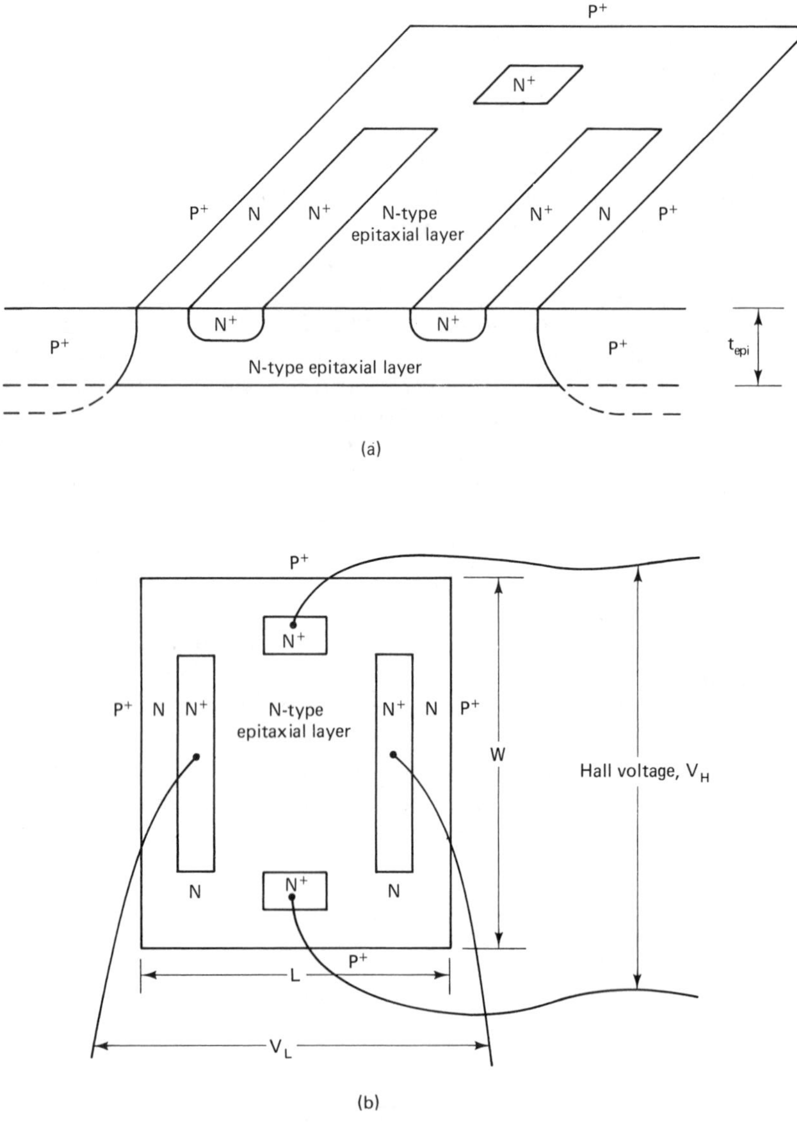

Figure 9.12 Monolithic IC Hall plate: (a) cross-sectional perspective view; (b) top view.

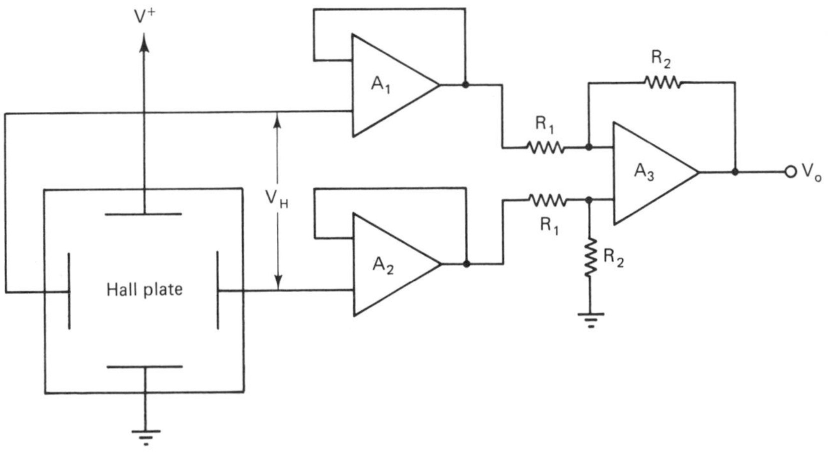

Figure 9.13 IC Hall sensor.

square, so that with a bias voltage of 10 V the current drawn by the Hall plate will be 17 mA, which is not an excessively large value.

For the moderately doped silicon of the epitaxial layer the electron mobility will be approximately 1000 cm²/V-s. The Hall voltage will be

$$V_H = \mu B(W/L)V^+ = 1000 \text{ cm}^2/\text{V-s} \times B \times 1 \times 10 \text{ V}$$

$$= 0.1 \text{ m}^2/\text{V-s} \times B \times 10 \text{ V} = 1.0(B/1 \text{ T})$$

where 1 T = 1 T = 1 Wb/m² = 1 (V-s)/m². If the magnetic flux density B is expressed in units of gauss we have that 1 T = 10,000 G = 10 kG, so that

$$V_H = 1 \times 10^{-4} \text{ V}(B/1 \text{ G})$$

$$= 100 \text{ }\mu\text{V}(B/1 \text{ G})$$

The magnetic field-to-Hall voltage transfer coefficient for this example will be 1.0 V/T = 100 μV/G.

If the net input offset voltage of the three operational-amplifiers is nulled at 25°C and the net value of $TC_{V_{OS}}$ is 4 μV/°C, the maximum change in V_{OS} over an operating temperature range of from 0 to 50°C will be ±100 μV. This will correspond to an accuracy of ±1 G for this magnetic field sensor.

The magnetic field produced by a small permanent magnet will be of the order of 1000 G or 0.1 T, and a large electromagnet will produce a magnetic field in the range of around 10,000 G (1 T). Some very large electromagnets will produce fields approaching 20,000 G (2 T). The earth's magnetic field is around 50 G, so that we see that the Hall effect sensor described above will indeed be sensitive to very small magnetic fields.

The most widely used materials for Hall effect sensors are indium arsenide (InAs) and indium antimonide (InSb), which are III–V compound semiconductors that have very large electron mobility values. The electron mobility in InSb is 80,000 cm²/V-s and in InAs is 33,000 cm²/V-s. This is to be compared to an electron mobility

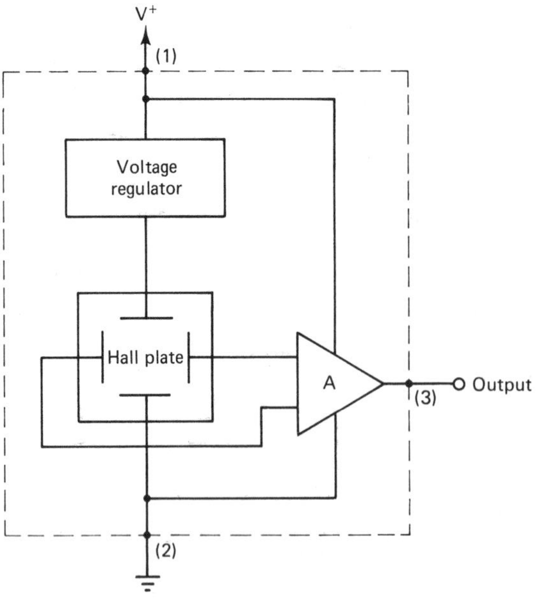

Figure 9.14 Monolithic IC magnetic field sensor (UGN-3501T). (Sprague Electric Co., I.C. Sensor Operations.)

of 1400 cm^2/V-s in lightly doped silicon. The high mobility values will produce very sensitive Hall effect sensors. Although it is not possible to make a monolithic IC Hall effect sensor with these materials, a hybrid IC is possible using an InAs or InSb Hall plate and a silicon IC chip in the same package.

9.2.1 Examples of Monolithic IC Magnetic Field Sensors

An example of a commercially available monolithic IC magnetic field sensor is the UGN-3501T (Sprague). This IC comes in a three-pin plastic package, and a block diagram is shown in Figure 9.14. This device has a magnetic field-to-output voltage transfer coefficient or sensitivity of 0.7 mV/G (7.0 V/T)(typ.) at a supply voltage of $V^+ = 12$ V and at $T = 25°C$. The magnetic field-to-voltage transfer characteristic will be reasonably linear up to magnetic fields of about 1500 G as shown in Figure 9.15.

The frequency response for this Hall effect sensor extends from 0 up to a 3-dB frequency of 25 kHz, and the output resistance is 100 Ω. The broadband output noise voltage is 100 μV (typ.) over a 10-Hz to 10-kHz 3-dB bandwidth. As a result a-c magnetic fields as small as 0.14 G in amplitude can be sensed with a unity signal-to-noise ratio.

The UGN-3501M (Sprague) is another Hall effect monolithic IC magnetic field sensor. It comes in an eight-pin "mini-DIP" package. A block diagram of this sensor is shown in Figure 9.16. This device has a differential voltage output, and also has terminals for offset voltage nulling. The magnetic field sensitivity is 1.4 mV/G (14 V/T) at a supply voltage of $V^+ = 12$ V and at $T = 25°C$.

Another monolithic IC magnetic field sensor that is of interest is the UGN-3019T (Sprague), which comes in a three-pin plastic package. A block diagram of

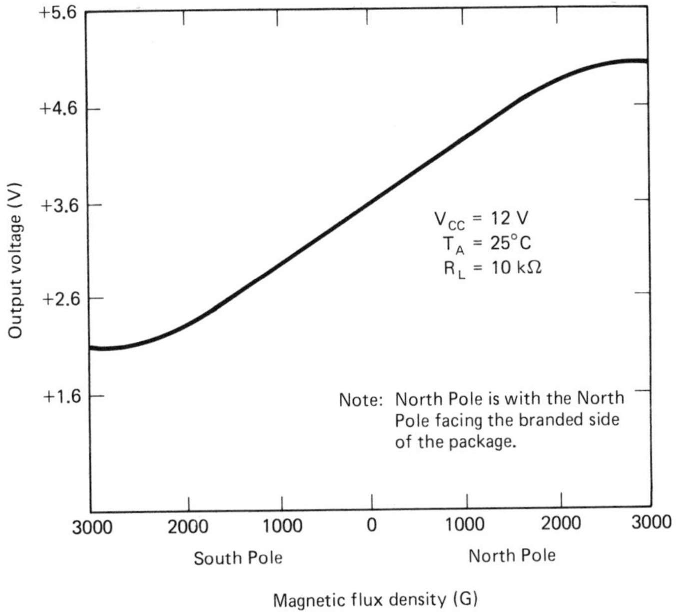

Figure 9.15 Output voltage versus magnetic flux density for the UGN-3501T (Sprague Electric Co., I. C. Sensor Operations).

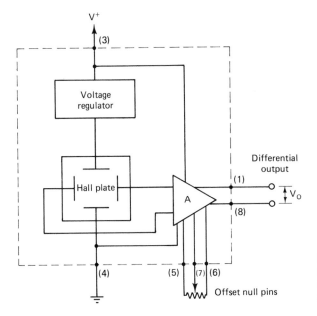

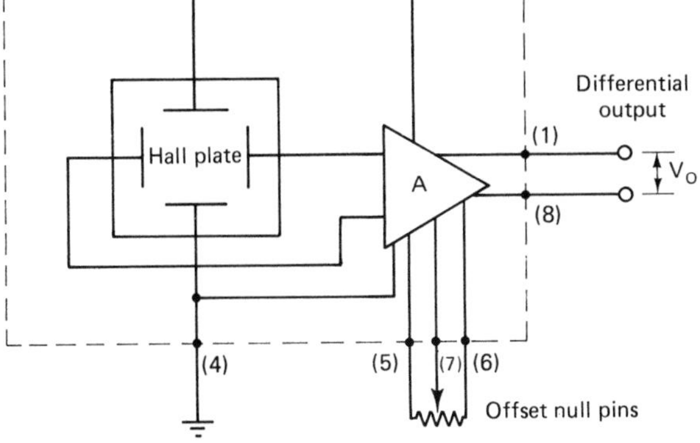

Figure 9.16 Monolithic IC magnetic field sensor with differential output (UGN-3501M) (Sprague Electric Co., I. C. Sensor Operations).

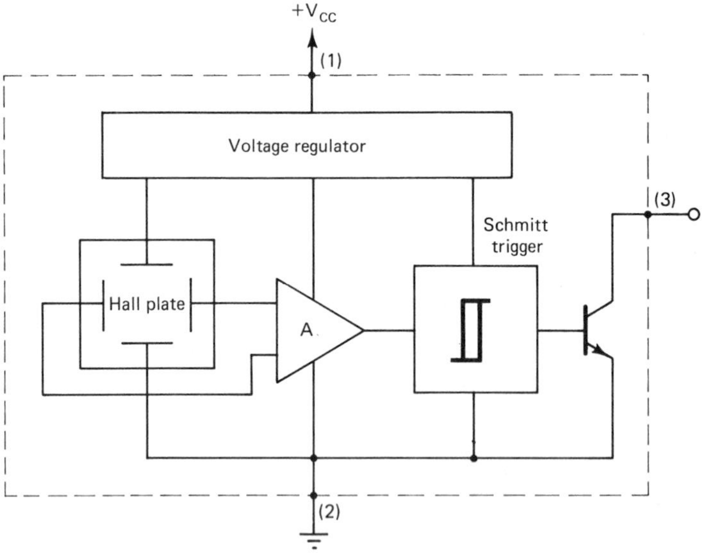

(a)

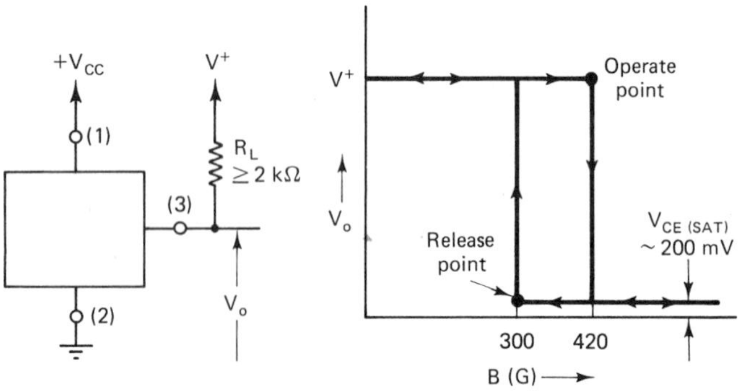

(b)

Figure 9.17 IC magnetic field sensor with digital output (UGN-3019T): (a) block diagram; (b) transfer characteristic (Sprague Electric Co., I. C. Sensor Operations).

this device is shown in Figure 9.17a and it operates as magnetic field-activated Schmitt trigger digital switch. The typical transfer characteristic of this device is presented in Figure 9.17b.

The open-collector output stage makes it easy to make the output logic levels compatible with various digital logic families by suitable choice of the power supply voltage V^+ and the pull-up resistor R_L. The supply voltage V_{CC} for the rest of the circuit can range from +4.5 to +16 V so that in most cases the same supply voltage can be used for both V_{CC} and V^+. Under the conditions of $V^+ = V_{CC} = +12$ V,

$R_L = 820\ \Omega$, and driving a load capacitance of 20 pF, the output rise time will be only 15 ns, and the fall time will be 100 ns.

9.2.2 Applications of Hall Effect Sensors

IC Hall effect magnetic field sensors can be used for the direct measurement of the magnetic field strength (as a Gauss meter), but most applications are based on using the sensor for position or motion sensing. If the position or motion of an object is to be determined or measured a small permanent magnet can be attached to, or made part of the object. The Hall effect sensor is then placed in proximity to the magnet and any change in position of the object can be sensed by a change in the strength of the magnetic field. In this way a change in position as small as 0.25 mm or 0.01 in. can be readily detected. In some cases where it is not convenient or possible to attach a small magnet to the object whose position is to be sensed, the magnet can be placed immediately behind the sensor. The position of the object can be detected by the change in the magnetic field produced as a result of the change in the reluctance in the magnetic flux path as the object moves or rotates. The change in the reluctance can be produced by a notch in the object as shown in Figure 9.18a or by a small projection as in Figure 9.18b. The notch will produce a decrease in the magnetic flux density passing through the sensor, whereas the projection will produce a small increase in the magnetic flux. This technique is useful for measuring the angular position or rotational velocity of a shaft, as, for example, in an automotive electronic ignition system.

The position or motion of small ferrous metal objects such as steel ball bearings

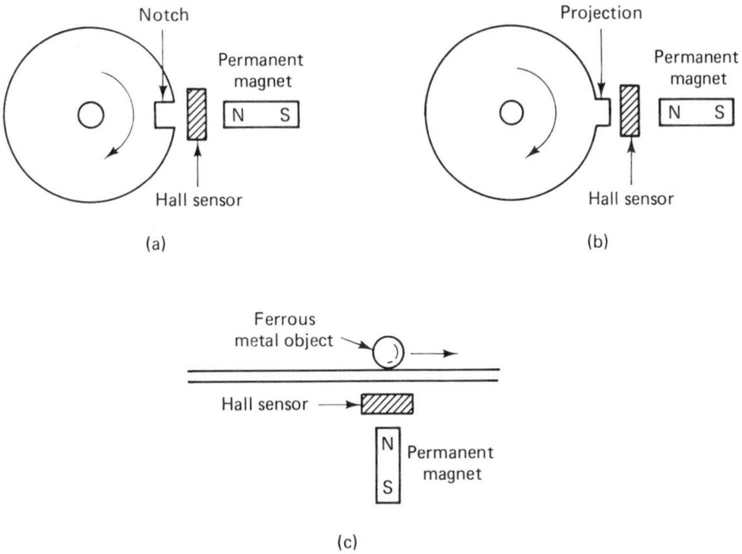

Figure 9.18 Hall effect sensing by changes in flux path reluctance: (a) notch sensing; (b) projection sensing; (c) sensor for small ferrous metal objects.

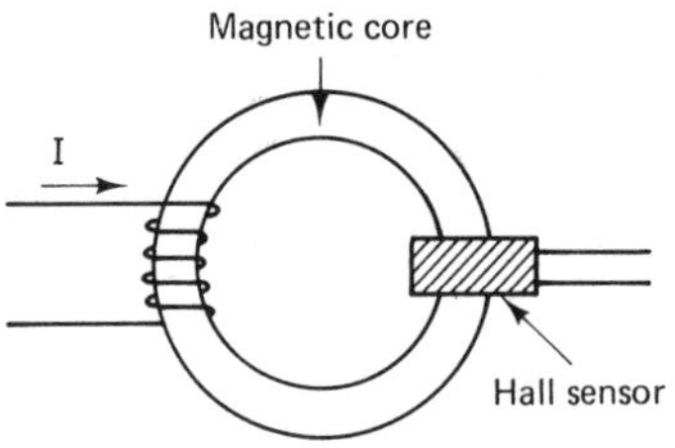

Figure 9.19 Hall sensor for current measurement.

can be measured by the change of the magnetic flux path reluctance that is produced as the object approaches the sensor as shown in Figure 9.18c. The decrease in the reluctance that occurs as the object passes by the sensor will result in a temporary increase in the magnetic flux density passing through the sensor.

The Hall effect sensors can be used to produce solid-state switches that have no moving electrical contacts that can corrode or wear out. These solid-state magnetically activated switches can be used for such applications as keyboard switches, mechanical limit switches of various types, electronic ignition systems, and applications in speed controls, speedometer pickups, and for various other applications in which the angular position and rotational velocity of shafts and other rotating parts are to be measured. The Hall sensor can be used for current sensing, especially for high current applications as illustrated in Figure 9.19.

9.3 PRESSURE TRANSDUCERS

There are two basic types of silicon pressure transducers. The first and most popular type uses the piezoresistive effect, which involves the change in the resistance produced by mechanical strain. The second basic type uses a parallel-plate capacitor in which one of the plates is a thin diaphragm. The spacing between the diaphragm and the other capacitor plate will be a function of the pressure and the resulting capacitance change can be sensed and used to determine the pressure.

Although it is possible to have a monolithic IC pressure transducer, almost all pressure transducers are either hybrid ICs with the sensor element and the amplifier in one package, or else separate sensor and amplifier modules are used.

9.3.1 Piezoresistive Pressure Sensors

The flow of free electrons and holes in a semiconductor involves a complex interaction between the free charge carriers and the atoms of the crystal lattice or structure of the solid. A very slight change in the spacing or arrangement of the atoms can produce a substantial change in the mobility of the charge carriers and therefore in the resistivity of the material. The change in the resistivity produced by a mechanical strain is called the *piezoresistive effect*.

The piezoresistive sensitivity of a material can be expressed in terms of the ratio of the fractional change in the resistivity to the mechanical strain that is the cause of the resistivity change. For lightly doped N-type silicon the fractional change in the resistivity will be related to the mechanical strain by $\Delta\rho/\rho \simeq 125\epsilon - 26{,}000\epsilon^2$, where $\epsilon = \Delta L/L$ is the strain. For lightly doped P-type silicon the corresponding equation will be $\Delta\rho/\rho \simeq 175\epsilon + 72{,}625\epsilon^2$. Usually, the strain ϵ will be very small such that the ϵ^2 term in both equations will be small compared to the first term.

The resistance of a specimen is related to the resistivity by $R = \rho L/A$ where L is the length and A is the cross-sectional area. As a result of a mechanical strain the fractional change in the resistance will be given by $\Delta R/R \simeq \Delta\rho/\rho + \Delta L/L - \Delta A/A$. The change in the cross-sectional area will be related to the change in the length by $\Delta A/A = -2\sigma\, \Delta L/L$, where σ is Poisson's ratio and has a value of approximately 0.3 for silicon. With this the equation for the resistance change can be expressed as

$$\frac{\Delta R}{R} \simeq \frac{\Delta\rho}{\rho} + \frac{\Delta L}{L} - \frac{\Delta A}{A} = \frac{\Delta\rho}{\rho} + \frac{\Delta L}{L(1+2\sigma)}$$
$$= \frac{\Delta\rho}{\rho} + \epsilon(1+2\sigma) = \frac{\Delta\rho}{\rho} + 1.6\epsilon \tag{9.11}$$

From this last result we see that the change in the resistance will be due principally to the piezoresistive effect. Thus for a strain of 10^{-6} cm/cm the change in the resistivity and therefore the change in the resistance will be approximately 125 ppm or 0.0125% for N-type silicon and 175 ppm or 0.0175% for P-type silicon.

The relatively small change in the resistance due to the mechanical strain will often be far overshadowed by the temperature coefficient of resistance (TCR), which can be as high as 2000 ppm/°C for diffused resistors. Therefore, some means of compensation or cancellation of the TCR is needed for a piezoresistive strain or pressure sensor. To do this the sensor is usually in the form of a Wheatstone bridge circuit with four diffused P-type resistors on a common silicon substrate as shown in Figure 9.20. The bridge configuration is such that resistors of diametrically opposite branches are subjected to the same mechanical stress. As a result of the monolithic construction of this sensor all four resistors will have very similar temperature coefficients and will track each other very closely with temperature.

The bridge circuit is initially nulled under unstressed conditions to give $\Delta V_o = 0$. If a mechanical stress is then applied such that the resistance of the two

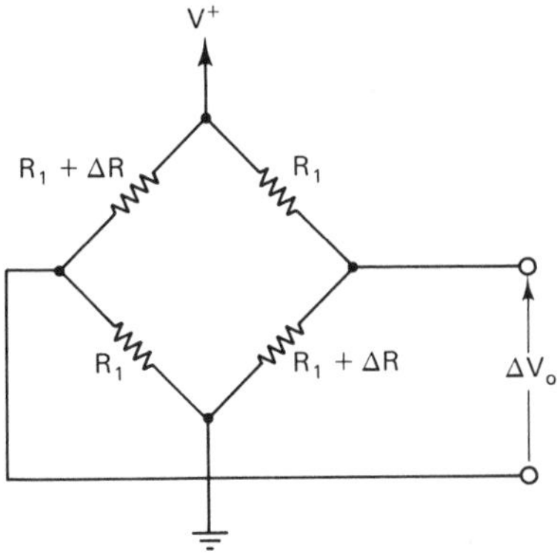

Figure 9.20 Wheatstone bridge piezoresistive pressure transducer.

diametrically opposite branches change by an amount ΔR, the resulting output voltage will be given by

$$\Delta V_o = V^+ \left(\frac{R_1 + \Delta R}{2R_1 + \Delta R} - \frac{R_1}{2R_1 + \Delta R} \right) = V^+ \frac{\Delta R}{2R_1 + \Delta R} \simeq \frac{V^+}{2} \frac{\Delta R}{R} \tag{9.12}$$

If, for example, $\Delta R/R = 175$ ppm for a strain of 10^{-6} cm/cm and $V^+ = 10$ V, the output voltage produced by the bridge will be 875 μV.

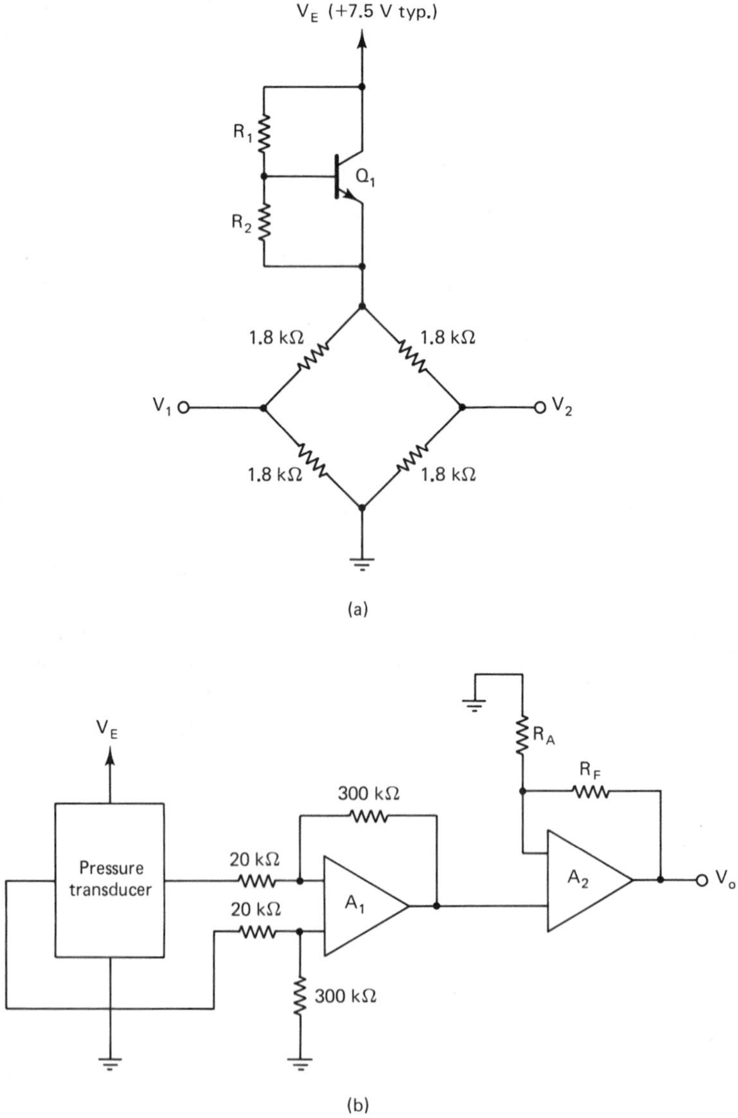

Figure 9.21 Silicon monolithic pressure transducer, LX05 and LX06 series: (a) schematic diagram; (b) pressure sensor circuit (Sensym, Inc.).

9.3.2 Examples of Silicon Pressure Transducers

Some examples of silicon piezoresistive monolithic IC pressure transducers are the LX05 and LX06 series of devices (Sensym, Inc.). A schematic diagram of these devices is shown in Figure 9.21a and in Figure 9.21b a simple pressure sensor circuit that uses the LX05 or LX06 transducer is shown. The piezoresistive elements are 1.8 kΩ diffused resistors in a Wheatstone bridge circuit. These resistors have a positive temperature coefficient in the range 1500 to 2000 ppm/°C.

Transistor Q_1 and resistors R_1 and R_2 form a temperature compensation circuit. The voltage drop across Q_1 will be given by $V_{CE} = V_{BE}(1 + R_1/R_2)$ and will be approximately 3 V. The negative temperature coefficient of the base-to-emitter voltage of Q_1 of about −2 mV/°C will result in a negative temperature coefficient of −10 mV/°C for the voltage drop across Q_1. This negative temperature coefficient will act to compensate for the positive temperature coefficient of the bridge resistors so that the bias current through the bridge circuit will be relatively constant with temperature when the excitation voltage V_E is set at 7.5 V.

The sensitivity of the LX0503 and LX0603 transducers will be in the range 0.3 to 1 mV/kPa (2 to 8 mV/psi) and the operating pressure range is 0 to 200 kPa (0 to 30 psi).

Another example of a silicon piezoresistive pressure transducer is represented by the MPX series of devices (Motorola), which uses a single P-type diffused resistor. A cross-sectional view of this devices is shown in Figure 9.22. A current flows longitudinally through the diffused resistor and a mechanical stress applied perpendicular to the current flow will produce a displacement in the current flow. This will be somewhat analogous to the shift in the current distribution produced by a magnetic field in the Hall effect. This results in the production of a transverse voltage that will be proportional to the applied stress.

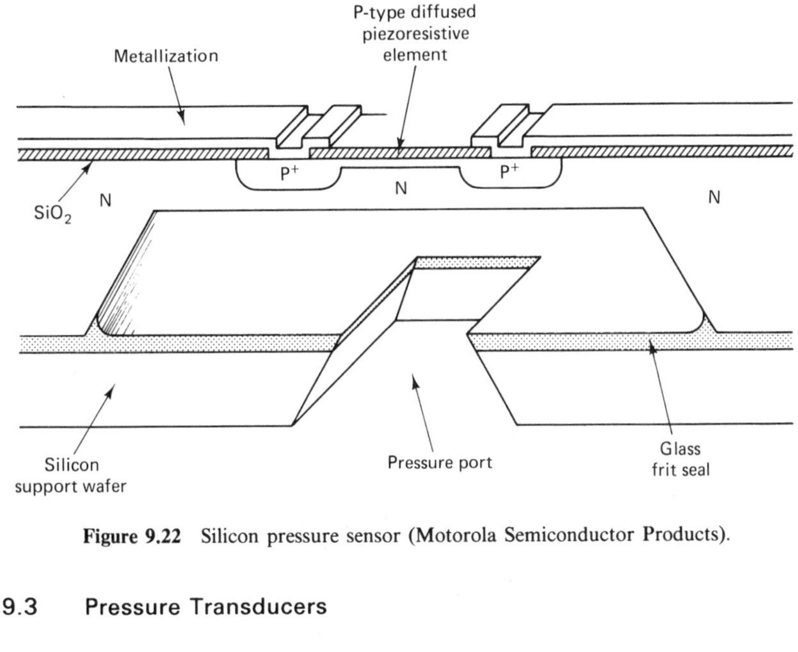

Figure 9.22 Silicon pressure sensor (Motorola Semiconductor Products).

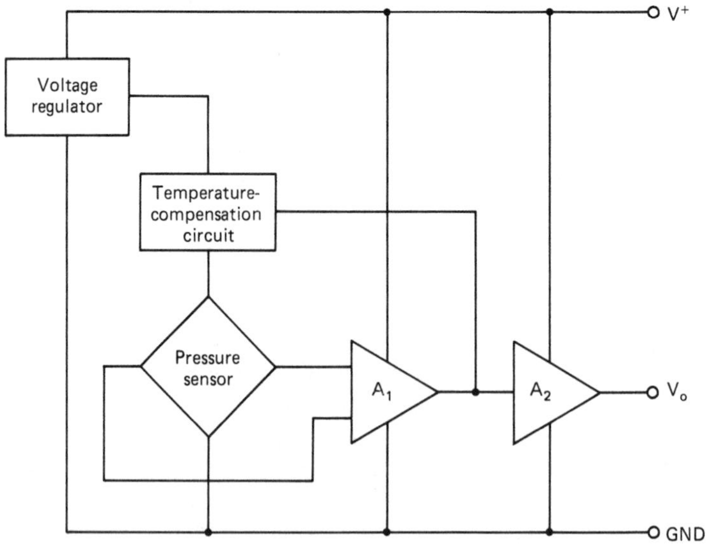

Figure 9.23 Hybrid IC pressure transducer.

The sensitivity of the MPX pressure transducers is 1.2 mV/kPa (8.3 mV/psi) for the MPX50, 0.60 mV/kPa (4.1 mV/psi) for the MPX100, and 0.30 mV/kPa (2.1 mV/psi) for the MPX200. The corresponding pressure ranges are 0 to 50 kPa (0 to 7.5 psi) for the MPX50, 0 to 100 kPa (0 to 15 psi) for the MPX100, and 0 to 200 kPa (0 to 30 psi) for the MPX200.

An example of a hybrid IC pressure transducer is the LX14 (National Semiconductor). This device contains a piezoresistive pressure sensor bridge circuit and two amplifiers in the same package as shown in Figure 9.23. Also included in the circuit are a voltage regulator and temperature-compensation circuitry.

PROBLEMS

9.1. (*True rms circuit*) The circuit of Figure P9.1 can be used to produce a d-c output voltage that is equal to the true rms value of the input voltage. The output voltages produced by the two temperature sensor ICs will be given by $V_{TS_1} = K_1T_1$ and $V_{TS_2} + K_2T_2$. The temperatures, T_1 and T_2, of the two IC chips will be given by $T_1 = \theta_1 P_{d_1} + T_A$ and $T_2 = \theta_2 P_{d_2} + T_A$, where θ_1 and θ_2 are the thermal resistances, P_{d_1} and P_{d_2} are the power dissipation values, and T_A is the ambient temperature.

(a) Show that if the two ICs are matched such that $R_1 = R_2$, $K_1 = K_2$, and $\theta_1 = \theta_2$, and using the infinite open-loop gain approximation for the operational amplifier, the d-c output voltage V_O will be equal to the *true rms value* of the input voltage V_{in}.

(b) Show that for a finite open-loop gain A_{OL} the output voltage will be given by $V_{O\,(\text{dc})} \simeq V_{i\,(\text{rms})} - R/2K\theta A_{OL}$.

(c) A mica washer is used to thermally insulate the two IC chips from the package header to increase the thermal resistance θ of IC_1 and IC_2. The IC chips are 1

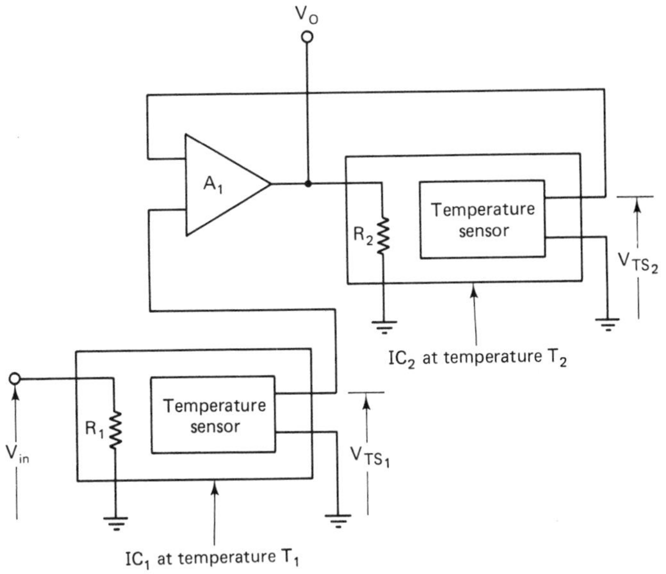

Figure P9.1

mm × 1 mm in area, and the washer is 0.25 mm thick with a specific thermal resistance of 1.7°C-m/W. The case-to-ambient thermal resistance θ_{CA} is 75°C/W. Find the junction-to-case thermal resistance θ_{JC} and the junction-to-ambient thermal resistance θ_{JA}. (*Ans.*: 425°C/W; 500°C/W)

(d) If $\theta_1 = \theta_2 = 500$°C/W, $K_1 = K_2 = 10$ mV/°C, $R_1 = R_2 = 1000\ \Omega$, and $A_{OL} =$ 10,000, find the error that results from a finite amplifier gain. What value of A_{OL} is needed for the error due to the finite grain not to exceed 1.0 mV? (*Ans.*: 10 mV; 100kΩ)

(e) What percentage output voltage errors will result from a 1% mismatch between R_1 and R_2, and θ_1 and θ_2, or K_1 and K_2, assuming that V_O is adjusted to zero when $V_{in} = 0$? (*Ans.*: 0.5% for each)

9.2. (*Hall effect*) The Hall effect can be used not only for the sensing and measurement of magnetic fields, but also as a useful analytical tool for the measurement of the mobility of charge carriers in a semiconductor. A thin N-type semiconductor sample is 10 mm long and 2 mm wide. A voltage of 1.0 V is applied across the length of the sample. A transverse voltage of 10 mV is obtained when a magnetic field of 5000 G (0.5 T) is applied perpendicular to the sample. Find the electron mobility. (*Ans.*: 1000 cm²/V-s)

REFERENCES

CHIEN, C. L., and C. R. Westgate, *The Hall Effect and Its Applications*, Plenum Press, 1980.

GARRETT, P. H., *Analog I/O Design*, Reston, 1981.

PUTLEY, E. H., *The Hall Effect and Related Phenomena*, Butterworth, 1960.

SACHSE, H., *Semiconductor Temperature Sensors and Their Applications*, Wiley, 1975.

SURINA, T., and C. HERRICK, *Semiconductor Electronics*, Holt, Rinehart and Winston, 1964.

TIMKO, M. P., "A Two-Terminal Temperature Transducer," *IEEE Journal of Solid State Circuits*, Vol. SC-11, No. 6, pp. 784–788, December 1976.

United Technical Publications, *Modern Applications of Integrated Circuits*, Tab Books, 1974. 1974.

WOLF, H. F., *Semiconductors*, Chaps. 1 and 3, Wiley, 1971.

Digital-to-Analog and Analog-to-Digital Converters

10

10.1 DIGITAL-TO-ANALOG CONVERTERS

A *digital-to-analog converter* (D/A or DAC) is a device that converts a digital input signal to an analog output voltage (or current) that is proportional to the digital signal. A simple example of an N-bit DAC for a binary digital input is shown in Figure 10.1. The output voltage will be given by

$$\begin{aligned} V_O &= -R_F\left(\frac{b_1 V_{\text{REF}}}{R} + \frac{b_2 V_{\text{REF}}}{2R} + \frac{b_3 V_{\text{REF}}}{4R} + \cdots + \frac{b_N V_{\text{REF}}}{2^{N-1}R}\right) \\ &= -2\frac{R_F}{R} V_{\text{REF}}\left(\frac{b_1}{2} + \frac{b_2}{4} + \frac{b_3}{8} + \cdots + \frac{b_N}{2^N}\right) \end{aligned} \tag{10.1}$$

where b_1 is the most significant bit (MSB), b_2 is the next significant bit, . . . , and b_N is the least significant bit (LSB).

The output voltage corresponding to the LSB input (. . . 000001) will be $V_{O\,(\text{LSB})} = 2(R_F/R)V_{\text{REF}}(1/2^N) = (R_F/R)V_{\text{REF}}(1/2^{N-1})$. The output voltage corresponding to a MSB digital input (1000 . . .) will be $V_{O\,(\text{MSB})} = V_{O\,(\text{LSB})}2^{N-1}$.

The maximum output voltage will occur when all bits are "1" (1111 . . .) and will be $V_{O\,(\text{MAX})} = 2V_{O\,(\text{MSB})} - V_{O\,(\text{LSB})} = (2^N - 1)V_{O\,(\text{LSB})} = 2V_{O\,(\text{MSB})}(1 - 1/2^N)$. The *nominal full-scale output voltage* $V_{O\,(\text{FS})}$ is defined as $V_{O\,(\text{FS})} = 2V_{O\,(\text{MSB})} = 2^N V_{O\,(\text{LSB})}$, and is thus greater than the maximum output voltage by an amount equal to $V_{O\,(\text{LSB})}$.

Many DACs are set to have a full-scale output voltage of 10.000 V. For a 4-bit ($N = 4$) DAC, $V_{O\,(\text{LSB})} = 10.00\text{ V}/2^N = 10.00/2^4 = 0.625$ V. The output voltage for a MSB input (1000) will be $V_{O(MSB)} = V_{O(FS)}/2 = 5.00$ V. The output voltage for a digital input of 1111 will be $V_{O(MAX)} = V_{O(FS)} - V_{O(LSB)} = 10.00 - 0.625 = 9.375$ V.

Similarly, for the case of an 8-bit DAC with a full-scale output voltage of 10.000 volts we will have

$$V_{O(LSB)} = \frac{10.000}{2^8} = 0.039 \text{ V}$$

$$V_{O(MSB)} = 5.000 \text{ V} \tag{10.2}$$

$$V_{O(MAX)} = 9.961 \text{ V}$$

For a 12-bit converter we have $V_{O(LSB)} = 0.00244$ V $= 2.44$ mV, $V_{O(MSB)} = 5.00$ V, and $V_{O(MAX)} = 9.9976$ V.

Another commonly used value for the full-scale output voltage for DACs is 10.24 V. With this choice of $V_{O(FS)}$ the LSB output voltage and therefore all of the voltage increments in the output voltage will be integer multiples or submultiples of 10 mV. Given below are some values for $V_{O(LSB)}$ and $V_{O(MAX)}$ for various values of N. For all cases the output voltage corresponding to a digital MSB input (1000 . . .) will be 5.12 V.

$V_{O(FS)} = 10.24$ V

N	$V_{O(LSB)}$ (mV)	$V_{O(MAX)}$ (V)
3	1280	8.96
4	640	9.60
5	320	9.92
6	160	10.08
7	80	10.16
8	40	10.20
9	20	10.22
10	10	10.23
11	5.0	10.235
12	2.5	10.2375
13	1.25	10.23875
14	0.625	10.239375
15	0.3125	10.239688
16	0.15625	10.239844

In Figure 10.2 a graph of the ideal transfer characteristic of an N-bit DAC is shown for the case of a 4-bit DAC. For the ideal DAC the envelope of the transfer characteristic will be a straight line passing through the origin (i.e., $V_O = 0$ for a digital input of 0000) and through the point $V_{O(FS)} - V_{O(LSB)}$ at a digital input of 1111.

In Figure 10.3 the envelope of the transfer characteristic of an actual, or nonideal DAC is shown and compared with that of the ideal DAC. The accuracy of a DAC is measured by the maximum error from the ideal characteristic, usually expressed as a fraction of the LSB voltage increment, $V_{O(LSB)}$. A typical accuracy specification

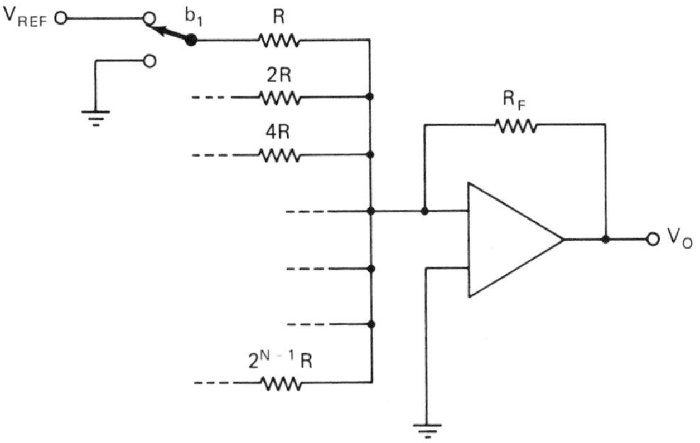

Figure 10.1 *N*-bit digital-to-analog converter.

for a DAC is $\pm\frac{1}{2}$ LSB. As long as the maximum error of the DAC is less than $\pm\frac{1}{2}$ LSB the DAC will have a monotonic transfer characteristic, that is, as the digital input increases the analog voltage output will also increase.

The ratio of the maximum resistance to the minimum resistance of the simple resistor ladder DAC of Figure 10.1 is 2^{N-1}, where N is the number of bits. For large values of $N (N \gtrsim 6)$ the resistance ratio becomes very large, and it becomes very difficult to establish accurate resistance ratios over this large a resistance ratio.

This problem can be solved by the use of cascaded resistor ladder networks

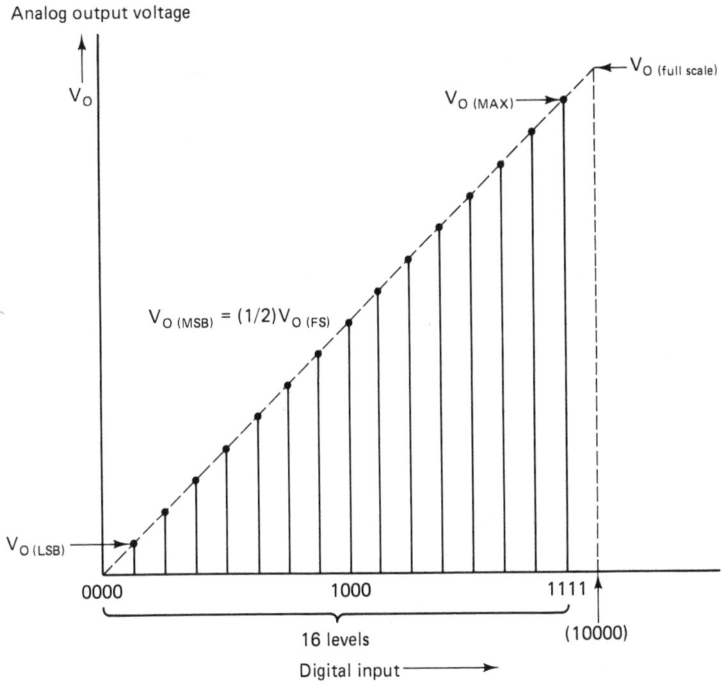

Figure 10.2 Transfer characteristic of ideal 4-bit DAC.

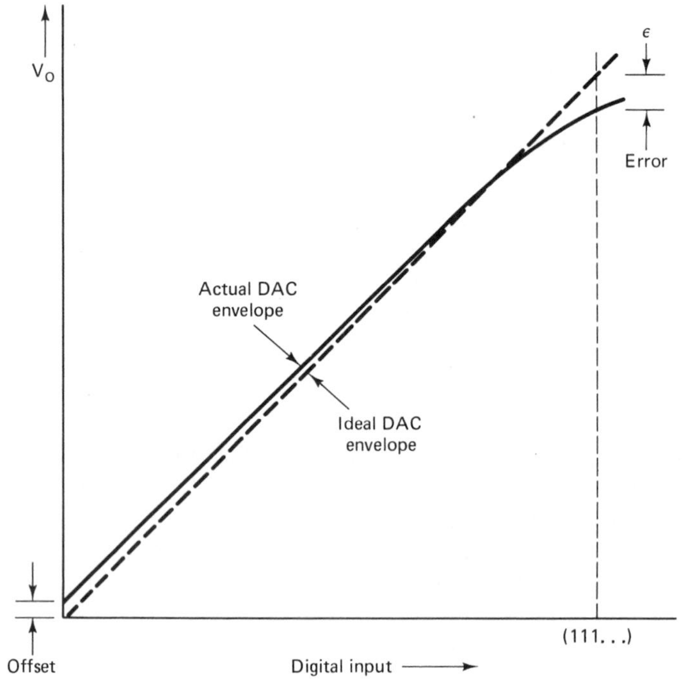

Figure 10.3 Ideal versus actual DAC transfer characteristics.

as shown in Figure 10.4. This is an 8-bit DAC using two cascaded resistor ladder quads. The resistor R_A placed between the quads for current division must produce a current division of 1:16, so that only $\frac{1}{16}$ of the current produced by the second quad will pass through R_A and appear at the operational amplifier input.

If we redraw the second quad in the form of a current source (Norton) equivalent circuit, we obtain the circuit of Figure 10.5. The resistance R_{NET} is the parallel combination of R, $2R$, $4R$, and $8R$ and will be given by $R_{\text{NET}} = 0.5333333R$. For a 16:1 current attenuation we must have that $R_A/R_{\text{NET}} = 15$, so that $R_A = 8.00R$.

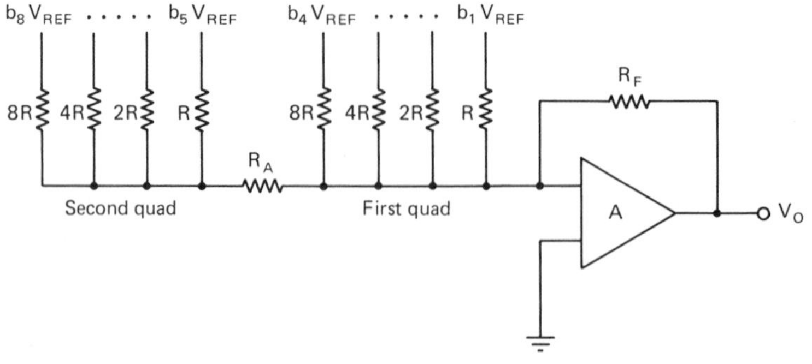

Figure 10.4 Cascaded quad DAC.

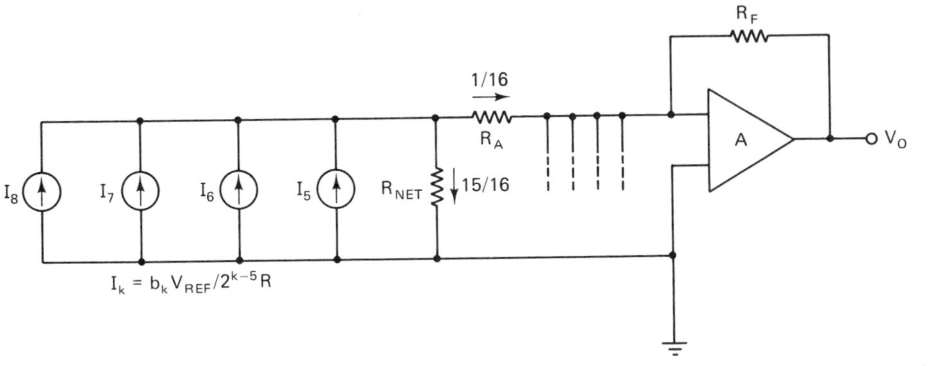

Figure 10.5 Equivalent current source-parallel resistance representation of the second quad.

If the cascaded quad DAC is driven by current sources as shown in Figure 10.6, a current divider comprised of R_B and R_C will be required. For a 15:1 current ratio between R_C and R_B we required that $R_B = 15R_C$.

To carry the cascaded quad DAC one step further, let us consider a 12-bit DAC using weighted current sources as shown in Figure 10.7. For this circuit we have two current ratio conditions to satisfy and four resistance values (R_D, R_E, R_F, and R_G). Therefore, we can arbitrarily set two conditions for the resistance values. For a representative example let us set R_D = 1.00 kΩ. For the b_5–b_8 quad we will have the requirement that $1/(R_F + R_G) + 1/R_D = 15/R_E$. Let us now set $R_F + R_G$ equal to R_E, so that we now have that $1/R_D = 15/R_E - 1/R_E = 14/R_E$, so that R_E = 14.00 kΩ.

For the b_9–b_{12} quad we have the requirement that

$$\left[\frac{R_F}{R_F + R_G + (R_E \parallel R_D)}\right]\left[\frac{R_D}{R_D + R_E}\right] = \frac{1}{16 \times 16} \tag{10.3}$$

Since $R_D/(R_D + R_E) = \frac{1}{15}$, $R_F + R_G = R_E = 14.00$ kΩ, and $R_E \parallel R_D = 1$ kΩ $\parallel$ 14 kΩ = 0.9333 kΩ, we obtain $R_F/(14\text{k}\Omega + 0.9333)$ kΩ = $15/(16)^2$, so that R_F = 0.875 kΩ and therefore R_G = 13.125 kΩ.

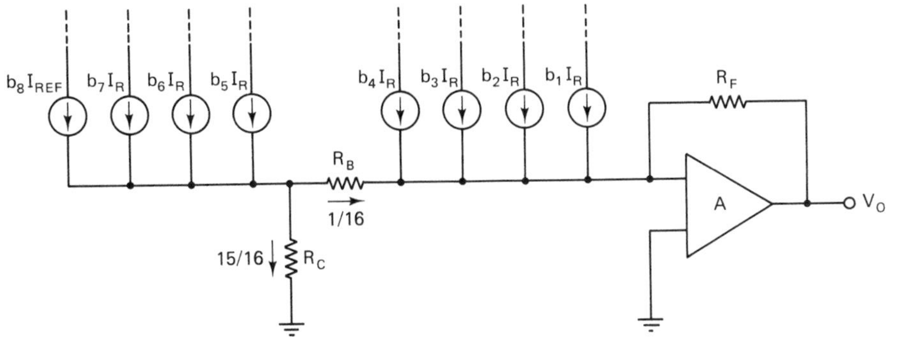

Figure 10.6 Cascaded-quad DAC using weighted current sources.

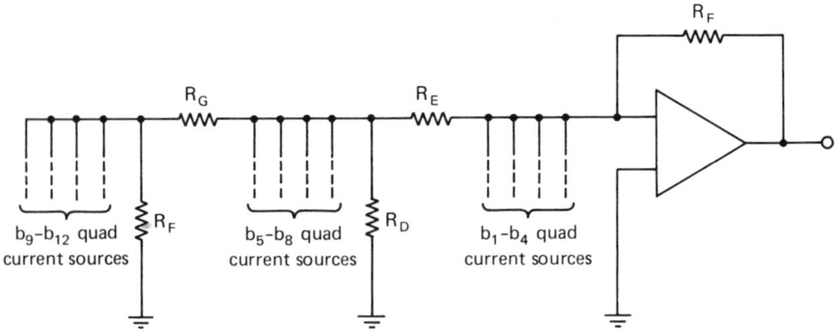

Figure 10.7 12-bit cascaded quad DAC using weighted current sources.

10.1.1 *R*-2*R* Resistor Ladder Networks

The ultimate case of a cascaded resistor ladder is the R-$2R$ ladder network shown in Figure 10.8a. This type of ladder network has the distinct feature and advantage of requiring only two resistance values, R and $2R$. For a small resistance ratio such as this, the resistance ratio tolerance of IC resistors will be much better than for the case of large resistance ratios.

At every node (1, 2, 3, . . . , N) along the R-$2R$ ladder network the resistance looking toward the left ($2R$) will be equal to the resistance seen looking toward the right ($2R$). In Figure 10.8b a view of two nodes in the R-$2R$ ladder network is shown. The current coming into node m from either the current source $b_m I_R$ or from the previous node ($m + 1$) will split into two equal parts at node m. One half of the current will go down through the $2R$ resistor and the other half will be supplied through resistor R to the $m = 1$ node. We see that the current propagating through the ladder will be split in half at every node. The output current I_O will therefore be given by $I_O = I_R\ (b_1/2 + b_2/4 + b_3/8 + \cdots + b_N/2^N)$.

In Figure 10.9 the R-$2R$ ladder network is shown connected to an operational amplifier for current-to-voltage conversion. The output voltage of this DAC will be given by

$$V_O = -R_F I_O = -R_F I_R \left(\frac{b_1}{2} + \frac{b_2}{4} + \frac{b_3}{8} + \cdots + \frac{b_N}{2^N}\right) \tag{10.4}$$

The resistor of $3R \parallel R_F$ connected between the noninverting input of the operational amplifier and ground is for the purpose of bias current cancellation.

Another R-$2R$ ladder DAC is shown in Figure 10.10. The bottom end of the $2R$ resistors will be at essentially ground potential for either position of the b_1, b_2, b_3, . . . , b_N switches since the inverting input terminal of the operational amplifier is a virtual ground. The current division at each node of the R-$2R$ ladder will be the same as that considered before and we will obtain for the output current I_O of the ladder the expression $I_O = (V_{REF}/R)\ (b_1/2 + b_2/4 + b_3/8 + \cdots + b_N/2^N)$. This "inverted ladder" DAC circuit has the advantage over the first R-$2R$ ladder circuit that the voltage level at the switching nodes remain at essentially ground potential for either position of the b_1, b_2, b_3, . . . , b_N switches. In the other

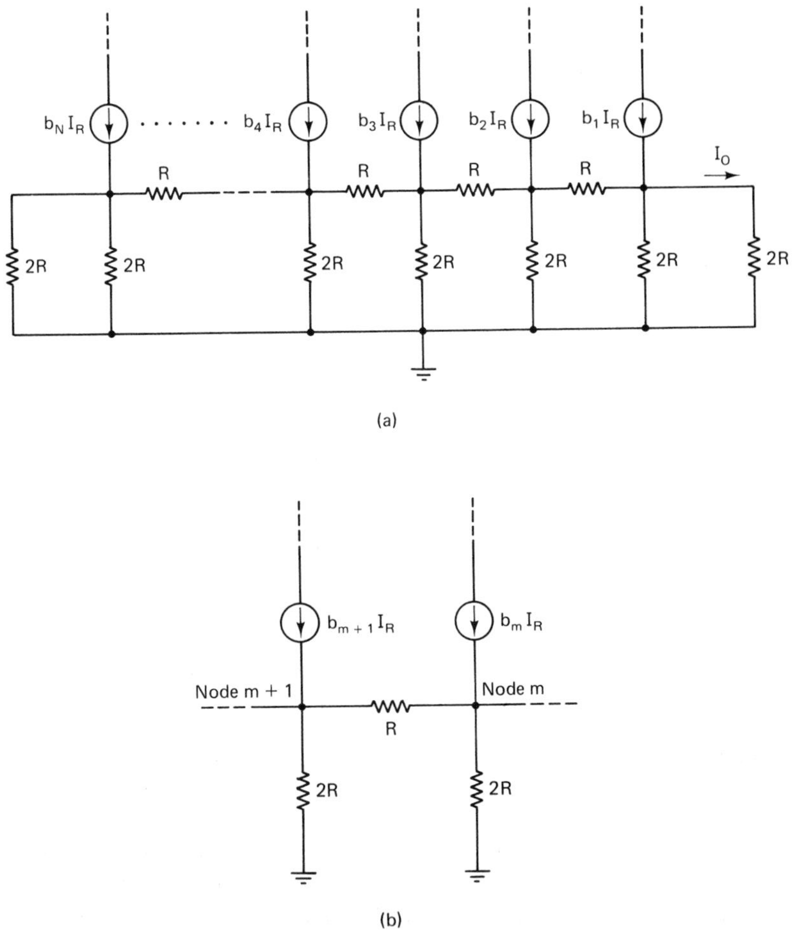

Figure 10.8 R-2R ladder with current source inputs: (a) basic circuit; (b) two nodes.

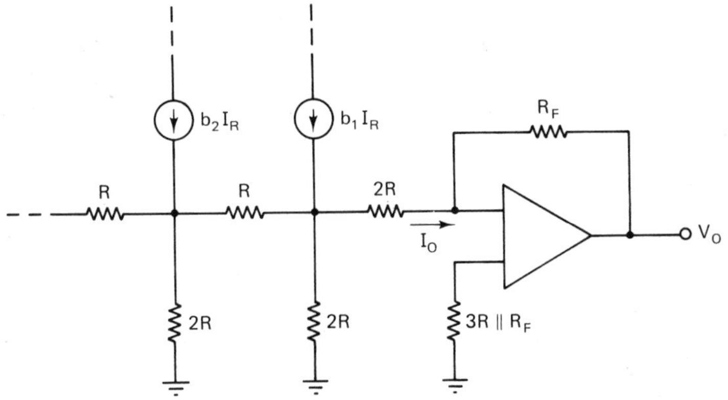

Figure 10.9 R-2R ladder DAC.

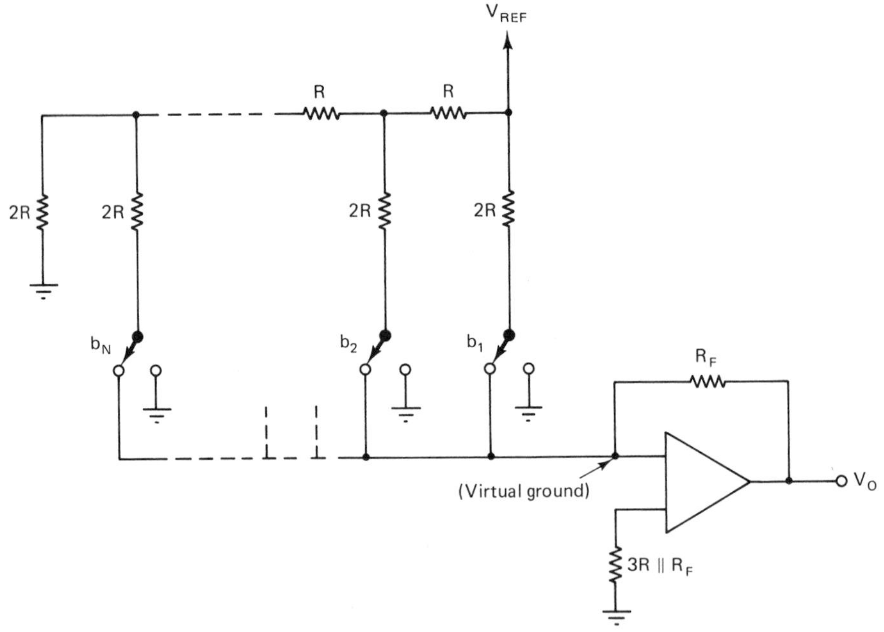

Figure 10.10 Inverted R-2R ladder DAC.

R-$2R$ ladder circuit the current switching node voltages will change depending on the values of b_1, b_2, b_3, . . . , b_N. As a result the inverted ladder DAC is capable of much faster operation since the voltage across the switching node capacitances remains at essentially ground potential.

An implementation of the inverted ladder R-$2R$ network using current source transistors is shown in Figure 10.11a. Let us first assume that all transistors are identical except that they are scaled in area such that the current densities are equal in all transistors. As a result, the base-to-emitter voltage drops will all be equal, and therefore the voltage at the top end (i.e., the emitter end) of all of the $2R$ resistors will be the same. We therefore see that the current I_1 will be equal to the current I_O through transistor Q_O (1.0 mA), current I_2 will be one-half of I_1, and so on. The last two transistors Q_N and Q_{N+1} will, however, carry equal currents. This is necessary in order to have the R-$2R$ ladder terminated at the proper resistance level.

For large numbers of bits ($N > 4$) it becomes impractical to scale the transistor areas for equal current densities since the largest transistors will become very large and take up an excessive amount of area on the IC chip. Therefore, only the four most significant bit transistors are scaled in area, and the remaining transistors are of equal active area. A method for compensating for the nonequal base-to-emitter voltage drops of the lesser significant bit transistors is shown in Figure 10.11b.

Since the current carried by every successive equal-area transistor ($Q_4 - Q_{N-1}$) decreases by a 2:1 ratio, the base-to-emitter voltage drop will correspondingly decrease by $V_T \ln 2 = 18$ mV. To compensate for this 18-mV voltage difference between transistors, the IR drop across the interbase resistors R_C is set to be 18 mV. For example, if $I_C = 200\ \mu$A, the value of R_C should be 18 mV/0.20 mA = 90 Ω.

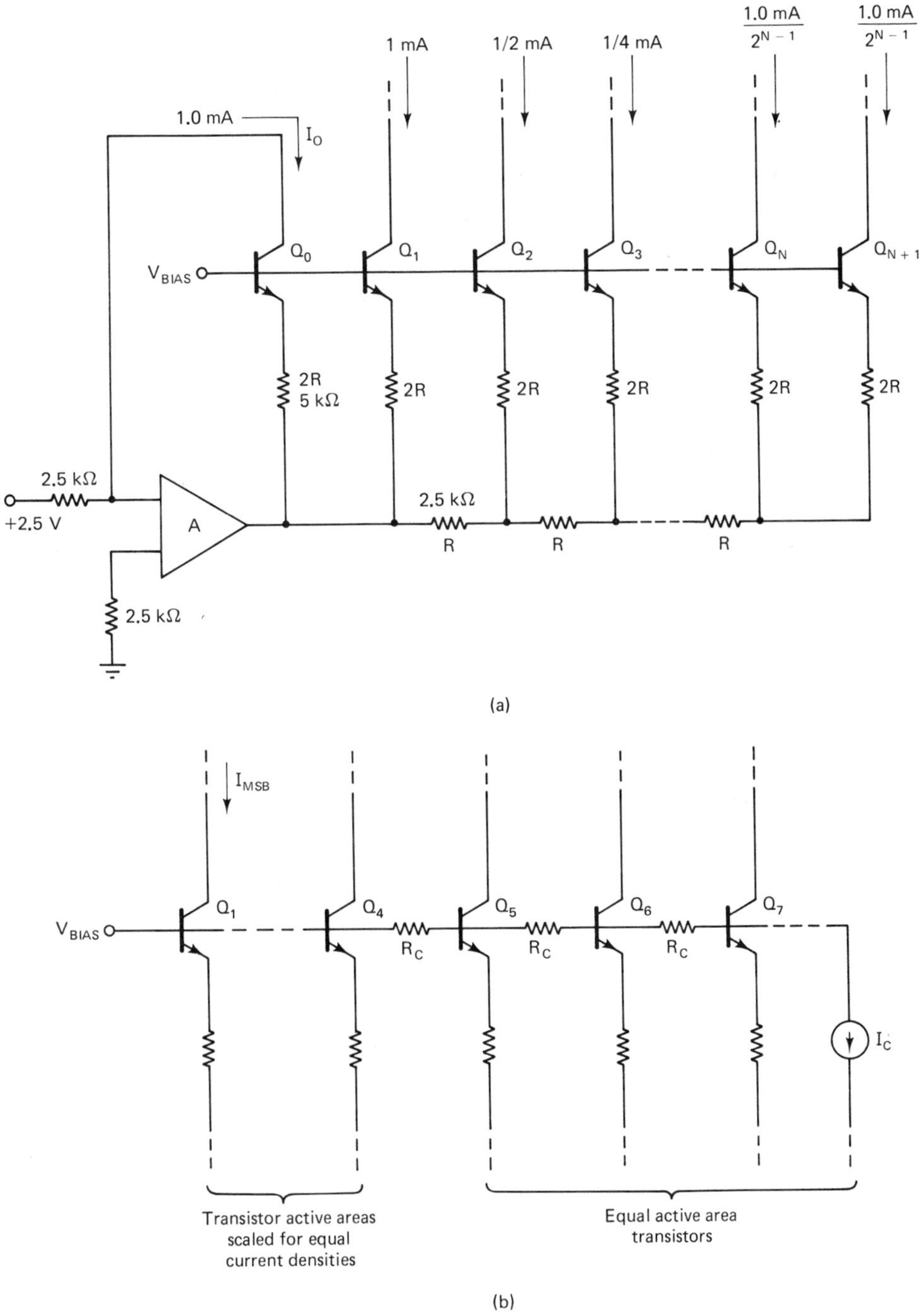

Figure 10.11 R-2R ladder with multiple current source transistors: (a) basic circuit; (b) V_{BE} compensation.

The decrease in the V_{BE} drop for transistors Q_5 through Q_N is $\Delta V_{BE} = V_T \ln 2$, and it will therefore have a temperature coefficient of $d(\Delta V_{BE})/dT = (k/q) \ln 2 = \Delta V_{BE}/T = 18{,}000\ \mu V/300°K = 60\ \mu V/°C$. This is a rather small temperature coefficient and since it affects only the lesser significant bit transistors it will generally not be a problem.

In Figure 10.12 a diagram of a current switching cell for an inverted R-$2R$ ladder is shown. This current switching cell is comprised of transistors Q_A and Q_B acting as a differential amplifier, which in turn drives the Q_C–Q_D differential amplifier. When the logic voltage level at the base of Q_B is high such that the voltage at the base of Q_B is higher than the logic reference voltage at the base of Q_A, the current in the Q_A–Q_B differential-amplifier pair will be shifted to the Q_A side. This will cause the current in the Q_C–Q_D differential-amplifier pair to shift to the Q_C side. The current from transistor Q_K is thus delivered to the DAC output current bus.

If now the input logic voltage level is low (i.e., below the logic threshold voltage level) the current in the Q_C–Q_D differential amplifier will be shifted to the Q_D side and thus will not flow into the DAC output current bus, but rather will be shunted to ground. Since the DAC output current bus is connected to the inverting input terminal of an op amp, it will remain at essentially ground potential so that the voltages at the collectors of Q_C and Q_D will be approximately the same. As a result

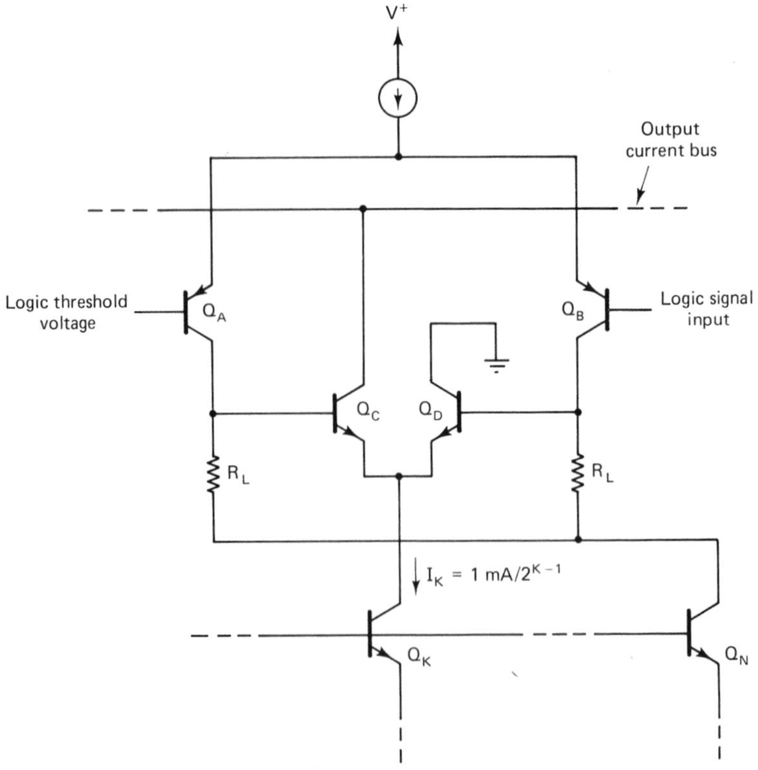

Figure 10.12 Current switching cell.

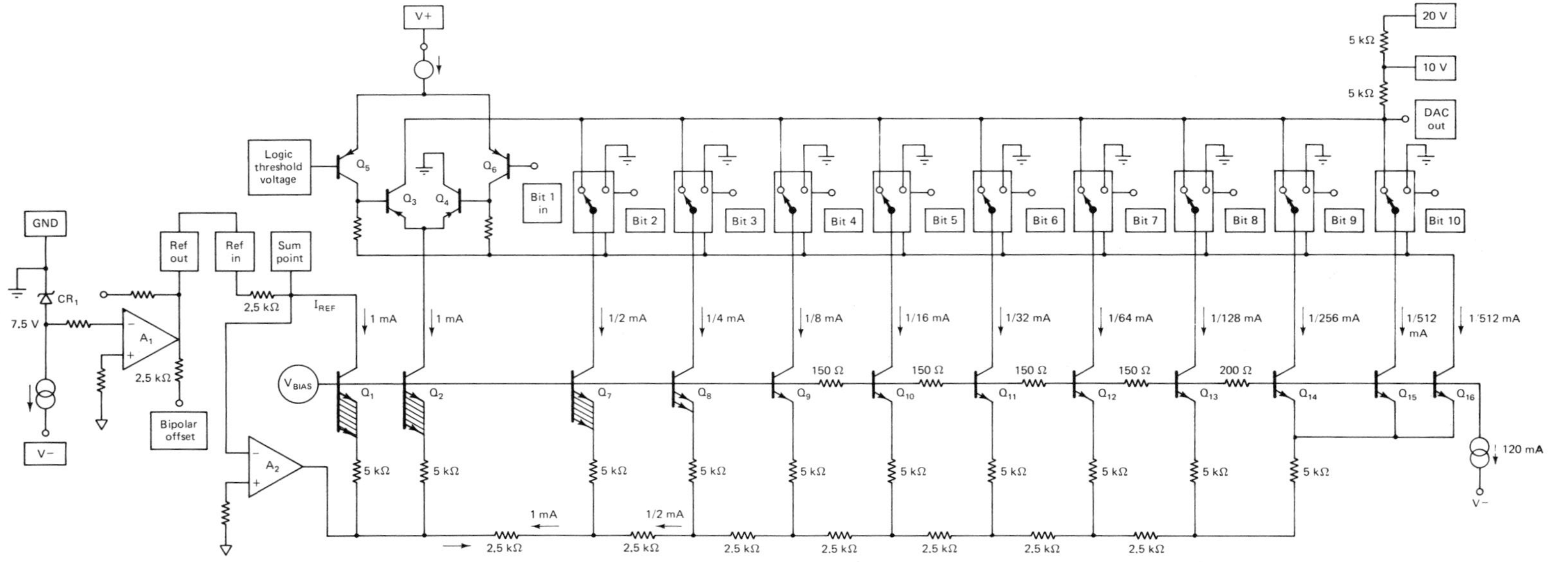

Figure 10.13 Circuit diagram of the AD561 10-bit DAC (Analog Devices Inc.).

of this and the fact that the total current through the Q_C–Q_D differential-amplifier pair remains constant at I_K and that none of the transistors involved are driven into saturation, this current switching circuit provides for a very fast (about 3 ns) switching action.

Example of 10-bit DAC: AD561. An example of a 10-bit DAC of the type just discussed is the AD561 (Analog Devices) and a circuit diagram is shown in Figure 10.13. An internally generated 7.5-V reference voltage is developed on the chip by a current-source-biased zener diode CR_1. This is a temperature-compensated diode with a net temperature coefficient in the range 0 to ±15 ppm/°C. This reference voltage is then transformed to a +2.5-V reference by amplifier A_1. This 2.5-V reference voltage is applied to the 2.5-kΩ resistor connected to the inverting input terminal of amplifier A_2 and thereby produces a current flow of 1.0 mA, which sets the MSB current level through Q_2 at 1.0 mA.

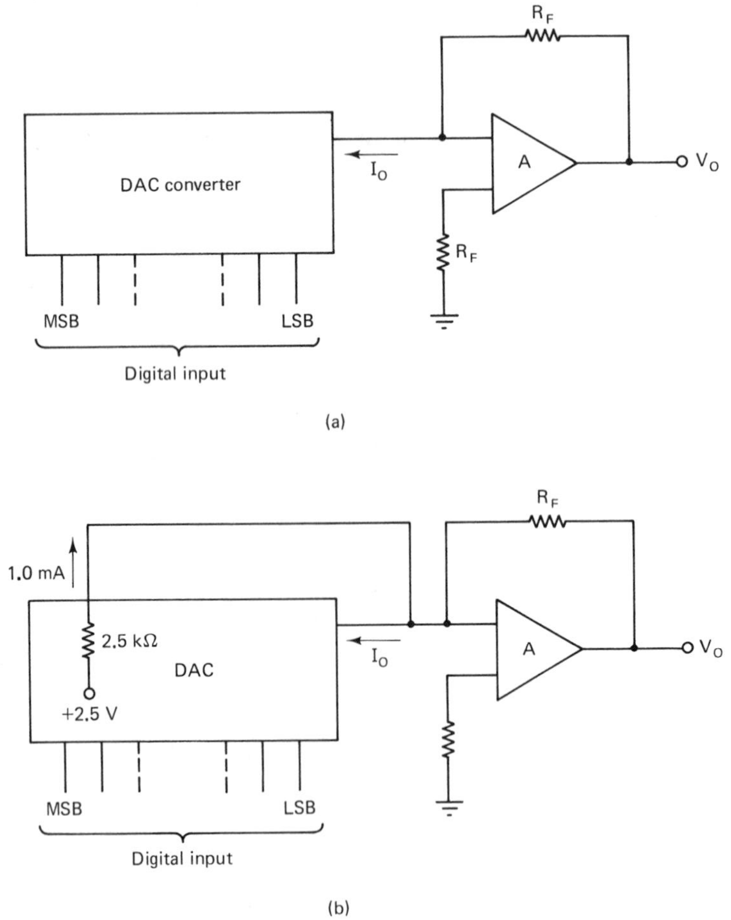

Figure 10.14 Buffered DACs: (a) with unipolar 0- to +10-V output voltage range; (b) with bipolar output voltage range.

In Figure 10.14a the basic circuit of a buffered unipolar 0- to + 10-V DAC is shown. The output current I_O is given by $I_O = 1.0\text{ mA}(b_1 + b_2/2 + b_3/4 + \cdots + b_N/2^{N-1})$, and the corresponding output voltage will be $V_O = +5.0\text{ V}(b_1 + b_2/2 + b_3/4 + \cdots + b_N/2^{N-1})$ for a nominal full-scale output voltage of +10 V. When all bits are zero (0000000000) the output voltage will be zero. For an MSB digital input (1000000000) the output voltage will be +5.0 V, and for a digital input of all "ones" (1111111111) the output voltage will be +9.990 V. The LSB voltage increment for the output voltage will be $10\text{ V}/2^{10} = 9.766\text{ mV}$.

In Figure 10.14b a buffered 10-bit DAC with a bipolar output voltage range is shown. The output voltage V_O will be given by $V_O = (I_O - 1.0\text{ mA})R_F = +1.0\text{ mA } R_F(b_1 + b_2/2 + b_3/4 + \cdots + b_N/2^{N-1} - 1)$. For a ±5.0-V output voltage range R_F should be 5.0 kΩ. The output voltage will −5.0 V for a digital of 0000000000, 0 V for a digital input of 1000000000, and $+5.0\text{ V}(1 - 1/2^{10}) = +4.995$ V for a digital input of 1111111111.

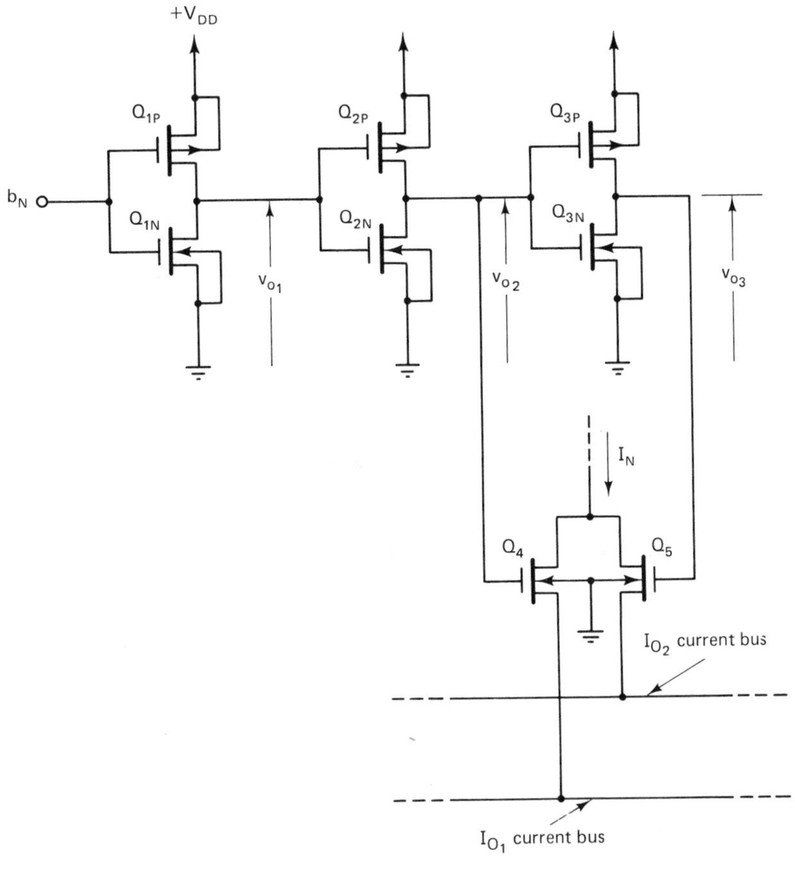

(a)

Figure 10.15 CMOS current switch: (a) basic circuit; (b) digital input low; (c) digital input high.

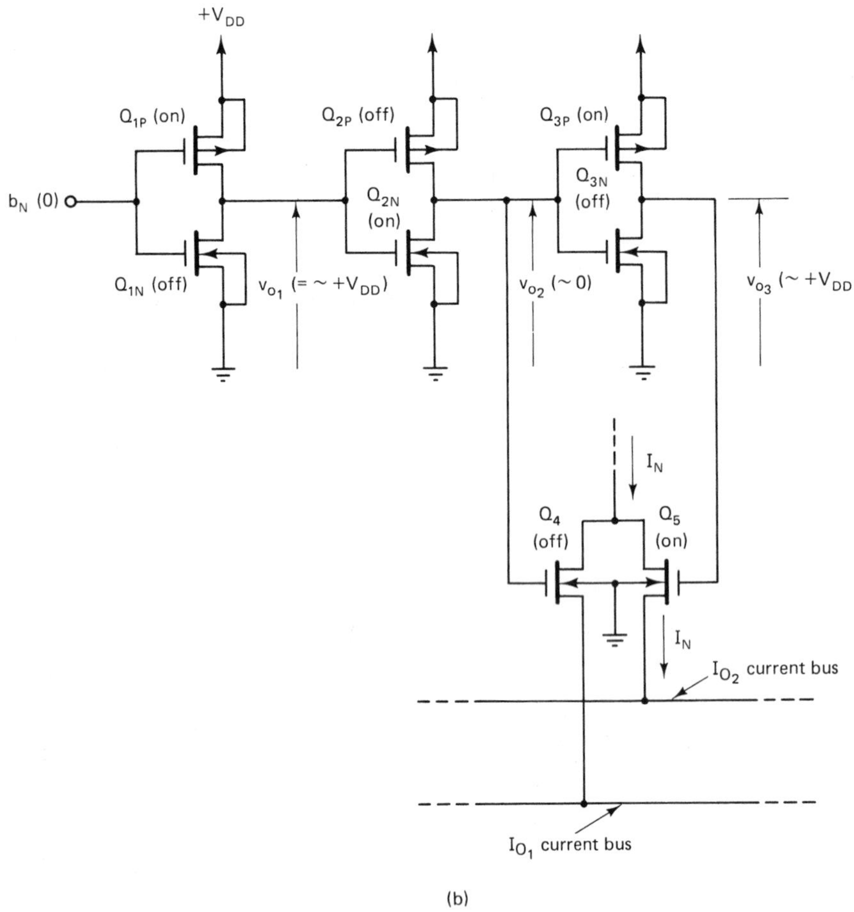

Figure 10.15 (*cont*)

10.1.2 CMOS Current Switches

In Figure 10.15a an example of a CMOS current switch for a DAC is shown. The CMOS transistor pairs will typically have a switching threshold voltage of +1.4 V, which will make this circuit compatible with any of the commonly used TTL, DTL, or CMOS logic families.

When the digital input voltage is in the low state (<1.4 V) Q_{1N} will be *off* and Q_{1P} will be *on* as shown in Figure 10.15b. The output voltage of the Q_{1N}–Q_{1P} CMOS inverter will be *high* ($= +V_{DD}$). This will cause Q_{2N} to be *on* and Q_{2P} to be *off*, so that the output voltage of the Q_{2N}–Q_{2P} inverter will be *low* (~0 V), and similarly the output voltage of the Q_{3N}–Q_{3P} inverter will be *high* ($\simeq +V_{DD}$). As a result, the current switching transistor Q_5 will be *on* and Q_4 will be *off*. This will result in the bit current I_N from the ladder network being delivered to the I_{O_2} current bus.

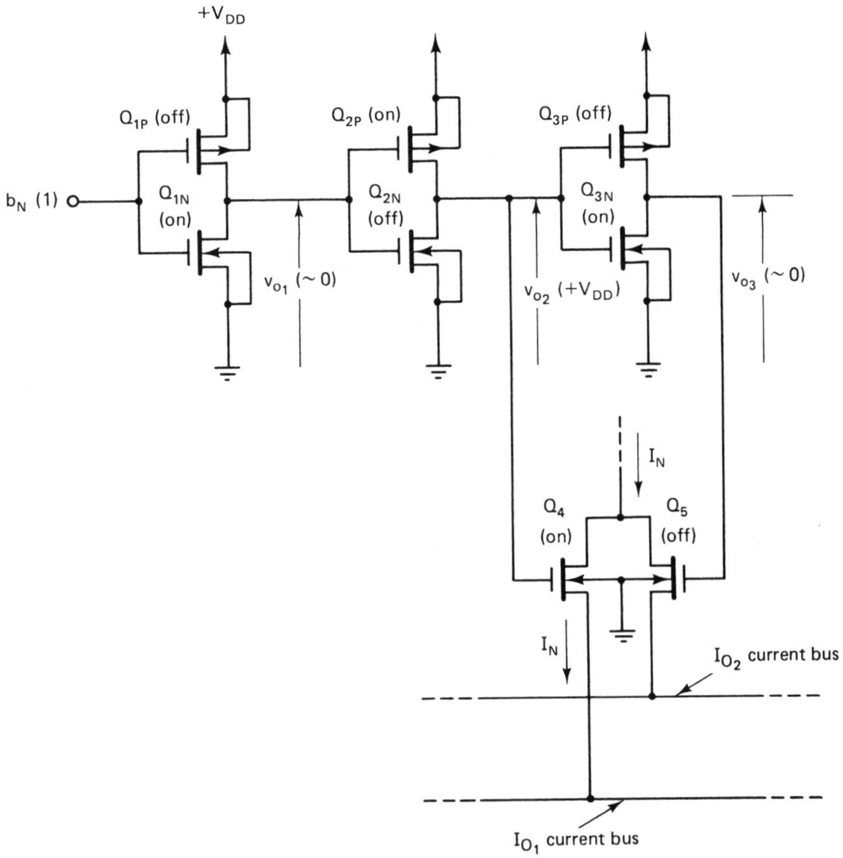

(c)

Figure 10.15 (*cont*)

In Figure 10.15c the situation for a digital bit input that is high (>1.4 V) is shown. For this case Q_4 will be *on* and Q_5 will be *off* and the current I_N will be delivered to the I_{O_1} current bus.

In Figure 10.16 a diagram of a CMOS/DAC converter is shown that uses a R-$2R$ ladder network, CMOS current switches, and a current-to-voltage converter. When the bit input (b_1, b_2, b_3, etc.) is high, the CMOS switches (S_1, S_2, S_3, etc.) will send the bit currents (I_1, I_2, I_3, etc.) into the I_{O_1} current bus. This current will be given by $I_{O_1} = (V_{REF}/10\ \text{k}\Omega)\ (b_1/2 + b_2/4 + b_3/8 + \cdots + b_N/2^N)$ and the output voltage V_O will be given by $V_O = -I_{O_1}R_F = -V_{REF}(R_F/10\ \text{k}\Omega)$ $(b_1/2 + b_2/4 + b_3/8 + \cdots + b_N/2^N)$. For a full-scale output voltage of +10 V with $V_{REF} = -10$ V, the feedback resistor R_F should be 10 kΩ.

This circuit can easily be modified for a bipolar output voltage range as shown in Figure 10.17. In this circuit both output current buses, I_{O_1} and I_{O_2}, are used. The current I_{O_2} is converted by the A_2 op-amp circuit to a voltage $-R_FI_{O_2}$, which

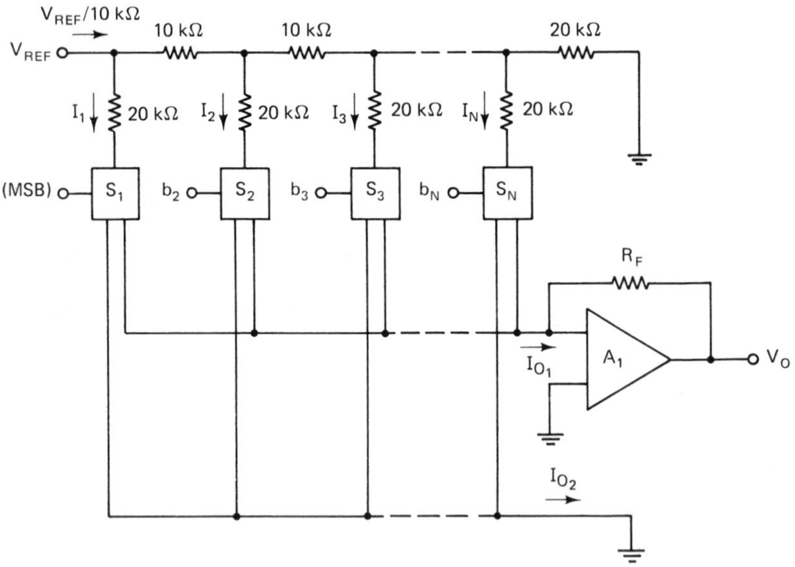

Figure 10.16 CMOS/DAC.

in turn will produce a current flow of $-R_F I_{O_2}/R_F = -I_{O_2}$ into the inverting input node of the A_1 operational amplifier circuit. The net current flowing into this circuit node will therefore be $I_{NET} = I_{O_1} - I_{O_2}$. The expression for I_{O_2} will be the same as that given earlier for I_{O_1} except for the complementation of the bits as given by $I_{O_2} = (V_{REF}/10\ k\Omega)\ (\bar{b}_1/2 + \bar{b}_2/4 + \bar{b}_3/8 + \cdots + \bar{b}_N/2^N)$, where $\bar{b}_n$ is the complement of b_N.

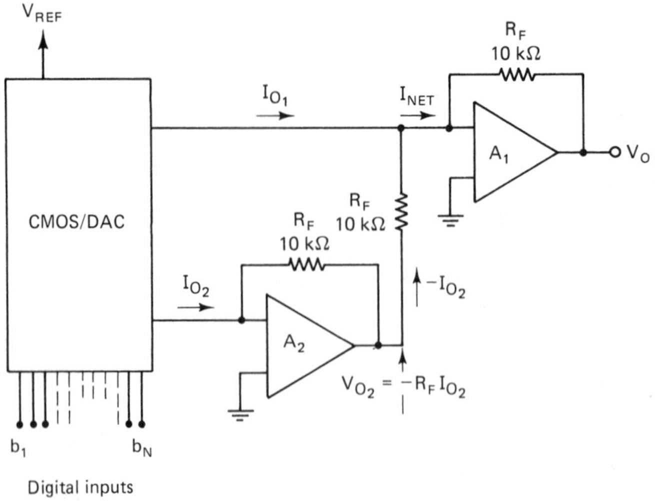

Figure 10.17 CMOS/DAC with bipolar output voltage range.

The output voltage of this circuit will therefore be given by

$$V_O = -V_{\text{REF}} \frac{R_F}{10\ \text{k}\Omega}\left(\frac{b_1 - \bar{b}_1}{2} + \frac{b_2 - \bar{b}_2}{4} + \cdots + \frac{b_N - \bar{b}_N}{2^N}\right) \tag{10.5}$$

For $V_{REF} = -10$ V and a full-scale output voltage range of ± 10 V the feedback resistor R_F should again be 10 kΩ. For a digital input of 000 . . . 000 the output voltage will be given by $V_O = -[V_{O(FS)} - V_{O(LSB)}] = -10(1 - \frac{1}{2}^N)$ V. For a digital input of 111 . . . 111 the output voltage will have its positive maximum value of $V_O = V_{O(FS)} - V_{O(LSB)} = +10\ (1 - \frac{1}{2}^N)$ V. For a digital input of 1000 . . . 000 we will have that $b_1 = 1$, $\bar{b}_1 = 0$, $b_2 = 0$, $\bar{b}_2 = 1$, $b_3 = 0$, $\bar{b}_3 = 1$, and so on. The analog output voltage V_O will therefore be given by $V_O = V_{O(MSB)} - V_{O(MAX)} - V_{O(MSB)} = 2V_{O(MSB)} - V_{O(MAX)}$. Since $V_{O(FS)} - 2V_{O(MSB)}$ and $V_{O(MAX)} = V_{O(FS)} - V_{O(LSB)}$, we will have that

$$V_O(100\ .\ .\ .\ 000) = V_{O(FS)} - [V_{O(FS)} - V_{O(LSB)}] = +V_{O(LSB)} = +10/2^N\ \text{V} \tag{10.6}$$

For a digital input of 1 LSB less than the previously considered input of 100 . . . 000, which will be 011 . . . 111, the output voltage will be

$$\begin{aligned} V_O(011\ .\ .\ .\ 111) &= -V_{O(MSB)} + V_{O(MAX)} - V_{O(MSB)} \\ &= V_{O(MAX)} - 2V_{O(MSB)} = V_{O(MAX)} - V_{O(FS)} \\ &= -V_{O(LSB)} = -10/2^N\ \text{V} \end{aligned} \tag{10.7}$$

We therefore see that there will be no digital input for which the analog output voltage will be zero. The output voltage will be $-10/2^N$ V for a digital input of 011 . . . 111, and an increase to $+10/2^N$ V for a digital input that is 1 LSB higher or 100 . . . 000. The output voltage for every 1 LSB increase in the digital input will be $2 \times 10/2^N\ \text{V} = 10/2^{N-1}$ V.

The transfer characteristic of the bipolar DAC can easily be shifted to produce an analog output voltage of zero for a "half-scale" digital input of 100 . . . 000 by supplying an offset current of magnitude $I_{OFFSET} = (V_{REF}/10\ \text{k}\Omega)\ (1/2^N) = -1.0$ mA/2^N to the inverting input node of the A_2 operational amplifier as shown in Figure 10.17. This is converted to a voltage of $(-V_{REF})\ (1/2^N)$ by this operational amplifier and produces a current flow into the inverting input node of the A_1 operational amplifier of $(-V_{REF}/10\ \text{k}\Omega)\ (1/2^N) = -I_{OFFSET}$. The net current coming into this node will now be

$$\begin{aligned} I_{NET} &= I_{O_1} - I_{O_2} - I_{OFFSET} \\ &= \frac{V_{REF}}{10\ \text{k}\Omega}\left(\frac{b_1 - \bar{b}_1}{2} + \frac{b_2 - \bar{b}_2}{4} + \cdots \frac{b_N - \bar{b}_N}{2^N} - \frac{1}{2^N}\right) \end{aligned} \tag{10.8}$$

For a "half-scale" (or 1 MSB) digital input of 100 . . . 000 this will give a current of

$$\begin{aligned} I_{NET} &= \frac{V_{REF}}{10\ \text{k}\Omega}\left[\frac{1}{2} - \left(\frac{1}{4} + \frac{1}{8} + \frac{1}{16} + \cdots + \frac{1}{2^N} + \frac{1}{2^N}\right)\right] \\ &= \frac{V_{REF}}{10\ \text{k}\Omega}\left(\frac{1}{2} - \frac{1}{2}\right) = 0 \end{aligned} \tag{10.9}$$

Examples of CMOS DACs. An example of a 10-bit DAC that uses CMOS current switches is the AD7520 (Analog Devices). Similar CMOS/DACs are the AD7523/7524 series (8-bit), the AD7530/7533/7522 series (10-bit), and the AD7521/7531/7541 series (12-bit), all made by Analog Devices, Inc.

The AD7520 and the other CMOS/DACs listed above use R-$2R$ (10 kΩ - 20 kΩ) thin-film resistor ladders deposited on the silicon CMOS chip. The resistors are silicon–chromium alloy thin-film resistors with a sheet resistance of 2 kΩ/square so that the 10-kΩ resistors will have a length-to-width ratio of 5 : 1 and the 20-kΩ resistors have a 10 : 1 ratio. As a result of the moderate values of the length-to-width ratio the resistors can be made fairly wide, which will lead to a very good absolute-value tolerance, and even more important, very close resistor ratio matching (i.e., a very small resistance ratio tolerance). These resistors have a temperature coefficient of 150 ppm/°C, and because of the very close thermal coupling between the resistors on the silicon chip, the temperature coefficient of the resistance ratio is less than 1 ppm/°C. The 10-kΩ feedback resistor R_F for the operational amplifier for the current-to-voltage conversion is also provided on the chip, so that the R-$2R$ resistors and the feedback resistor will track each other with respect to resistance changes with temperature. As a result the temperature coefficient of the DAC scale factor will be less than 10 ppm/°C.

To compensate for the "on" resistance of the CMOS switching transistors, Q_4 and Q_5, the gate geometry (channel width-to-channel length ratio) of the six most-significant-bit switches are designed so as to produce equal voltage drops of 10 mV across each switch. For a reference voltage of 10 V, the MSB current will be 0.5 mA, so this will correspond to a channel resistance of 10 mV/0.5 mA = 20 Ω for

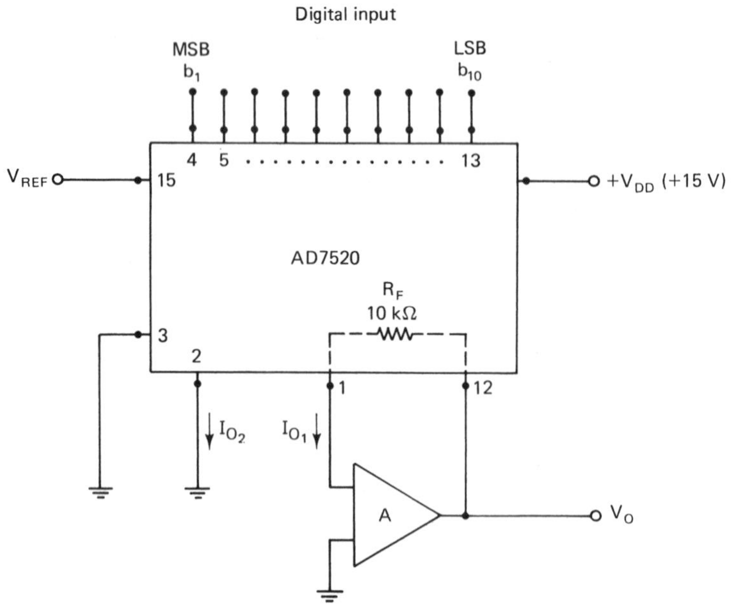

Figure 10.18 Unipolar binary 10-bit CMOS/DAC.

the MSB transistor, 40 Ω for the next significant bit (b_2) transistor, 80 Ω for the b_3 transistor, and so on. To compensate for the 10-mV drop across these switching transistors, the actual reference voltage is set at a value of 10 V + 10 mV = 10.010 V.

The four least significant bit transistors (b_7 through b_{10}) are not scaled, but this will not have a significant effect on the accuracy of the DAC due to the very small level of current through these transistors.

In Figure 10.18 the application of this 10-bit CMOS/DAC for a unipolar binary DAC with a buffered output is shown. The analog output voltages for a number of digital input codes are given below.

Digital input	Analog output
1111111111	$-V_{REF}\,(1-2^{-10})$
1000000001	$-V_{REF}\,(\frac{1}{2}+2^{-10})$
1000000000	$-V_{REF}\,(\frac{1}{2})$
0111111111	$-V_{REF}\,(\frac{1}{2}-2^{-10})$
0000000001	$-V_{REF}\,(2^{-10})$
0000000000	0

This device can be operated as a *two-quadrant multiplying DAC* since the output voltage is proportional to the product of the reference voltage V_{REF} and the analog value of the digital input code. By varying V_{REF} the gain or scale factor of the DAC can similarly be varied. Note that although V_{REF} can have both positive and negative values, the digital code is unipolar, so that as a result this multiplying DAC can operate in only two quadrants.

Another interesting DAC circuit is that of the DAC0806/7/8 series (National Semiconductor), which is an 8-bit DAC. A simplified schematic diagram of this device is shown in Figure 10.19a. It consists of two cascaded R-$2R$ ladder networks. The transistors in the first R-$2R$ section have their active areas scaled for equal current densities, and therefore the base-to-emitter voltage drops of these transistors will be equal. The second R-$2R$ ladder network is driven by a current source, which is the last transistor of the first ladder network. This transistor sinks a current equal to $\frac{1}{16}$ of the "full-scale" current.

The first transistor of the second R-$2R$ ladder network sinks a current of one-half of this, or $\frac{1}{32}$ of the full-scale current. The transistors of the second ladder network are also scaled for equal current densities.

The various currents produced by the ladder network are switched by a differential-amplifier type of current-mode switch, so that the individual currents produced by the various branches of the R-$2R$ ladder network are either delivered to the output current bus or are shunted to ground.

The reference voltage for the current-mode switches is established by the voltage drop across the two series-connected diodes and is approximately +1.4 V, which makes the bit input compatible with the TTL and CMOS logic families.

In Figure 10.19b a block diagram of this DAC is shown, and in Figure 10.19c

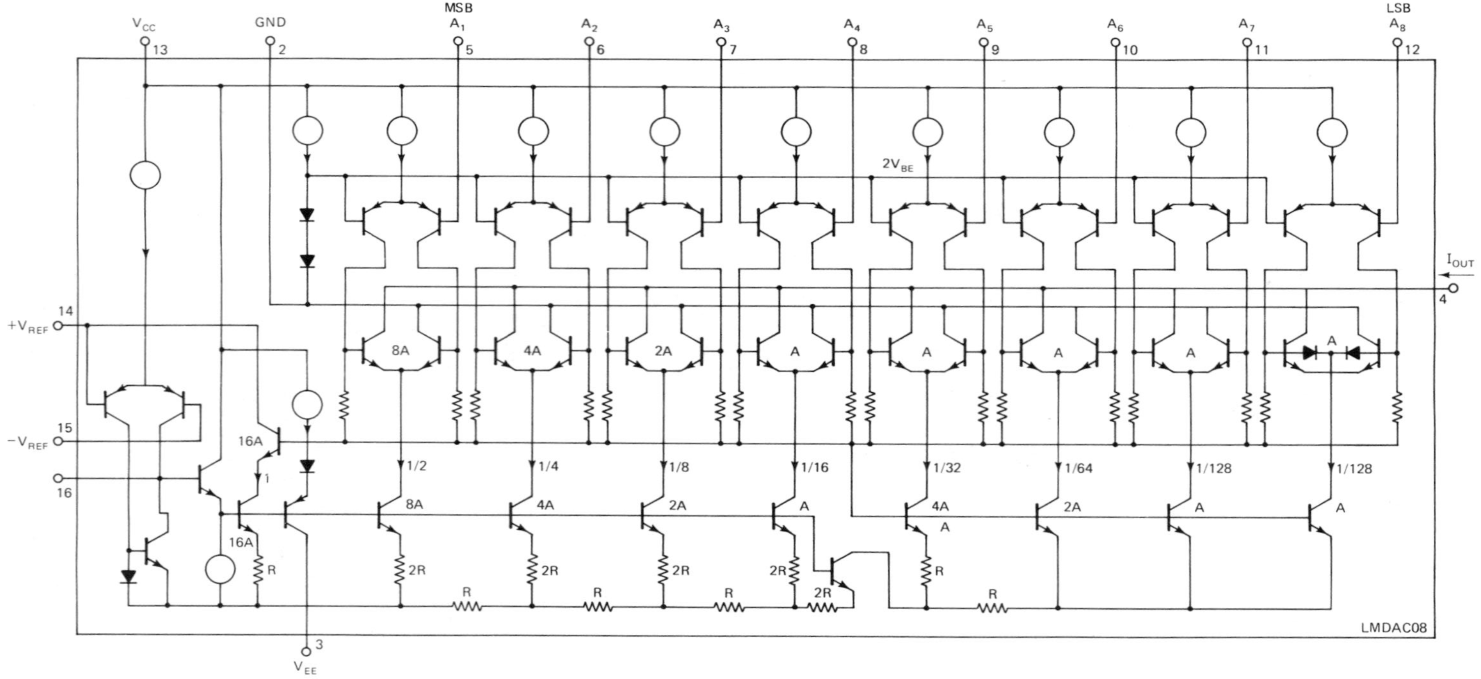

(a)

Figure 10.19 DAC0806 8-bit DAC (National Semiconductor): (a) circuit diagram; (b) block diagram; (c) unipolar DAC with +10-V full-scale output.

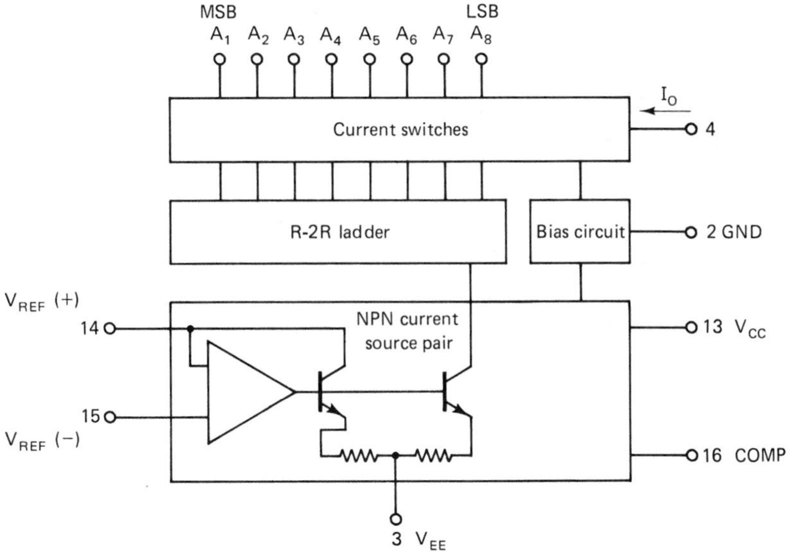

(b)

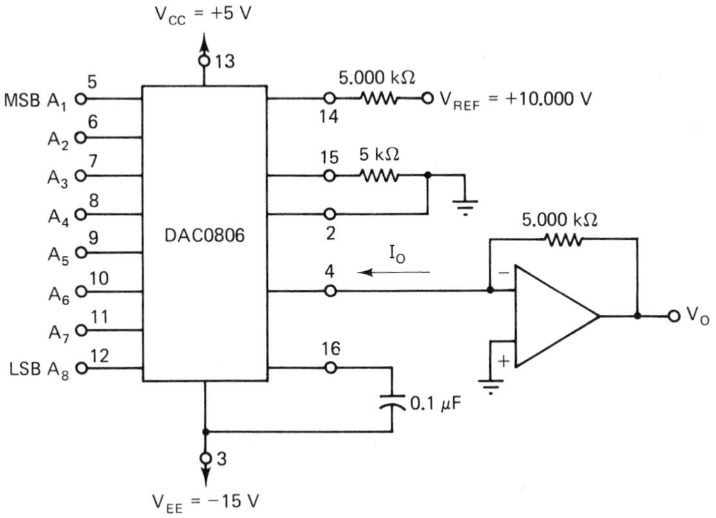

(c)

Figure 10.19 *(cont)*

a circuit for a typical application is given for a unipolar DAC with a +10-V full-scale output-voltage range.

10.1.3 16-Bit Monolithic DAC

An example of a high performance DAC is the DAC701/703 series (Burr-Brown). This is a complete monolithic 16-bit DAC that includes a low-noise buried zener voltage reference, R-$2R$ ladder resistor network, current switches, and a low-noise fast settling current-to-voltage converter op amp on a single chip. It features a linearity error of only 0.0015%. The gain error of 0.15% maximum can be adjusted to zero with an external potentiometer. The gain drift is just 10 ppm/°C and the total full scale drift is also just 10 ppm/°C. The output voltage slewing rate is 10 V/μs with a 2 kΩ load and the full scale settling time (10 V for DAC701 and 20 V for DAC703) to within 0.003% is 4μs.

10.1.4 DAC Speed and Settling Time

The speed or response time of a DAC is an important characteristic of the device. It is usually specified in terms of the *settling time*, which is the time required for the output voltage of the DAC to settle within a specified error band of the steady-state output voltage for a specified digital input change. The digital input change is usually specified as the "worst-case" condition of a change from 000 . . . 000 to 111 . . . 111, or vice versa. The corresponding output voltage change will be $\Delta V_O = V_{O(\mathrm{MAX})} = V_{O(\mathrm{FS})} - V_{O(\mathrm{LSB})}$, and the error band is usually given as $\pm \frac{1}{2} V_{O(\mathrm{LSB})}$. For a 10-bit DAC with a full-scale output voltage of $V_{O(\mathrm{FS})} = 10.24$ V we will have that $V_{O(\mathrm{LSB})} = 10.24 \text{ V}/2^{10} = 10$ mV, so that $V_{O(\mathrm{MAX})} = 10.23$ V and $\frac{1}{2} V_{O(\mathrm{LSB})} = 5$ mV or 0.05% of the full-scale output voltage.

In Figure 10.20 a graph of the output voltage versus time for a 10-bit DAC is shown in which the settling time is indicated. In Figure 10.21 an equivalent circuit of a DAC is shown in which a load resistance R_L is used for the current-to-voltage conversion. If the time-domain response of this system is controlled by the single RC time constant $\tau = R_L C_{\mathrm{NET}}$, we will have that $v_o(t) = V_{O(\mathrm{MAX})}\,[1 - \exp(-t/\tau)]$. The $\frac{1}{2}$-LSB settling time can be obtained by setting $v_o(t)$ at $t = T_{\mathrm{SETTLING}}$ equal to $V_{O(\mathrm{MAX})} - \frac{1}{2} V_{O(\mathrm{LSB})}$. Since $V_{O(\mathrm{MAX})} = V_{O(\mathrm{FS})} - V_{O(\mathrm{LSB})}$ this can be written as $v_O\,(t = T_{\mathrm{SETTLING}}) = V_{O(\mathrm{FS})} - \frac{3}{2}\, V_{O(\mathrm{LSB})}$. We therefore will have that

$$
\begin{aligned}
V_{O(\mathrm{FS})} - \frac{3}{2} V_{O(\mathrm{LSB})} &= V_{O(\mathrm{FS})}\left[1 - \left(\frac{3}{2}\right)\left(\frac{1}{2^N}\right)\right] \\
&= V_{O(\mathrm{MAX})}\left[1 - \exp\left(\frac{-t}{\tau}\right)\right] \qquad (10.10) \\
&= V_{O(\mathrm{FS})}\left(1 - \frac{1}{2^N}\right)\left[1 - \exp\left(\frac{-t}{\tau}\right)\right]
\end{aligned}
$$

Solving this for $t = T_{\mathrm{SETTLING}}$ gives

$$T_{\mathrm{SETTLING}} = \tau \ln\,[2(2^N - 1)] \simeq (N+1)\tau \ln 2 = 0.693(N+1)\tau \qquad (10.11)$$

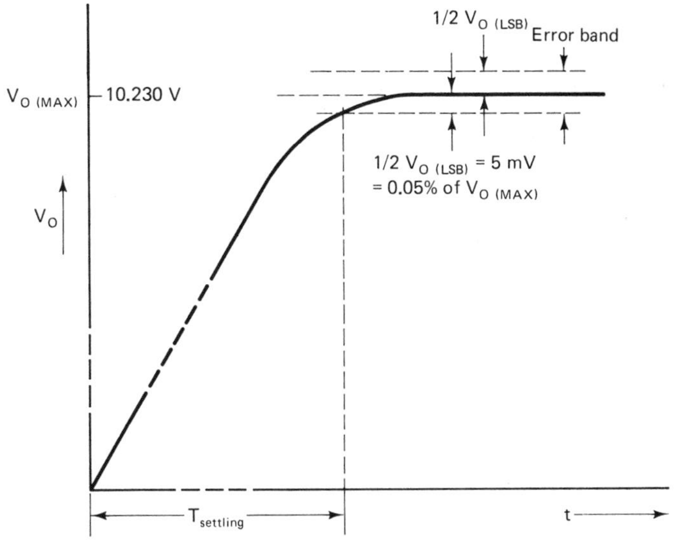

Figure 10.20 Settling time for a 10-bit DAC.

Given below are some values of $T_{SETTLING}$ for various values of N (number of bits) and the corresponding ratio of the settling time (to $\pm \frac{1}{2}$ LSB) to the 10% to 90% rise time.

N	$T_{SETTLING}$	$T_{SETTLING}/t_{rise}$
8	6.234τ	2.834
10	7.624τ	3.465
12	9.011τ	4.096
14	10.397τ	4.72

We see that the settling time will be appreciably longer than the 10% to 90% rise time.

Let us consider a 10-bit DAC that uses an inverted R-$2R$ ladder network with current switches and assume that the output capacitance (collector–base capaci-

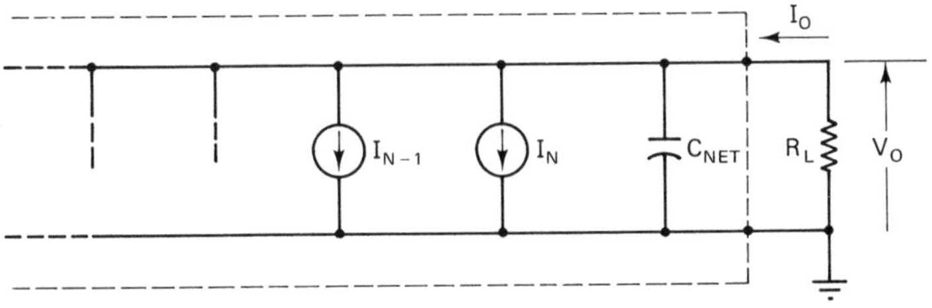

Figure 10.21 DAC using load resistance for current-to-voltage conversion.

tance, $C_{cb'}$) of each switch is 2.5 pF, so that the total output capacitance will be 25 pF. If $I_{O(MSB)} = 1.0$ mA and thus $I_{O(FS)} = 2.0$ mA and if the voltage compliance range extends down to a lower limit of -2.0 V, the maximum value of load resistance R_L that can be used will be 2 kΩ. With this value of load resistance the time constant τ will be $\tau = 2\ \text{k}\Omega \times 25\ \text{pF} = 50$ ns, and the corresponding settling time will be $T_{\text{SETTLING}} = 7.62 \times 50\ \text{ns} = 381$ ns. If the load resistance is now reduced to 1.0 kΩ, which will give a full-scale output voltage of 1.0 V, the time constant will become 25 ns and the settling time will be reduced to 191 ns.

If an operational amplifier is used for the current to voltage conversion the response-time characteristics of the system will usually be limited by the slewing rate of the operational amplifier. For example, if the full-scale output voltage is 10.24 V and the operational amplifier has a slewing rate of 1.0 V/μs, the settling time will be about 10 μs.

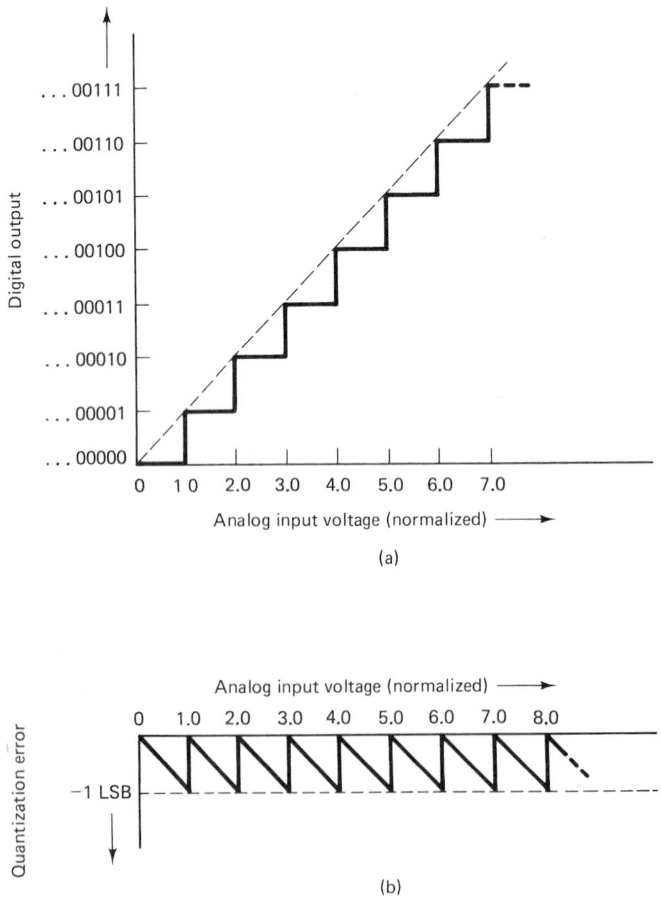

Figure 10.22 ADC transfer characteristic and quantization error: (a) transfer characteristic; (b) quantization error.

10.2 ANALOG-TO-DIGITAL CONVERTERS

ADC Transfer Characteristic and Quantization Error

In Figure 10.22a the transfer characteristic of an ADC is shown. We note that since the digital output code can take on only certain discrete values, there will be an inherent error in the system called the *quantization error*. The quantization error will be defined as the difference between the analog voltage equivalent of the digital output code and the actual analog input voltage. A graph of the quantization error corresponding to the transfer characteristic of Figure 10.22a is presented in Figure 10.22b. Note that the maximum value of the quantization error is 1 LSB.

The maximum quantization error can be reduced to $\pm \frac{1}{2}$ LSB by adding a $-\frac{1}{2}$-LSB voltage offset to the analog signal, or equivalent adding $+\frac{1}{2}$ LSB to the digital reference voltage to which the analog signal is compared. The transfer characteristic obtained with this $\frac{1}{2}$-LSB offset is shown in Figure 10.23a and the corresponding

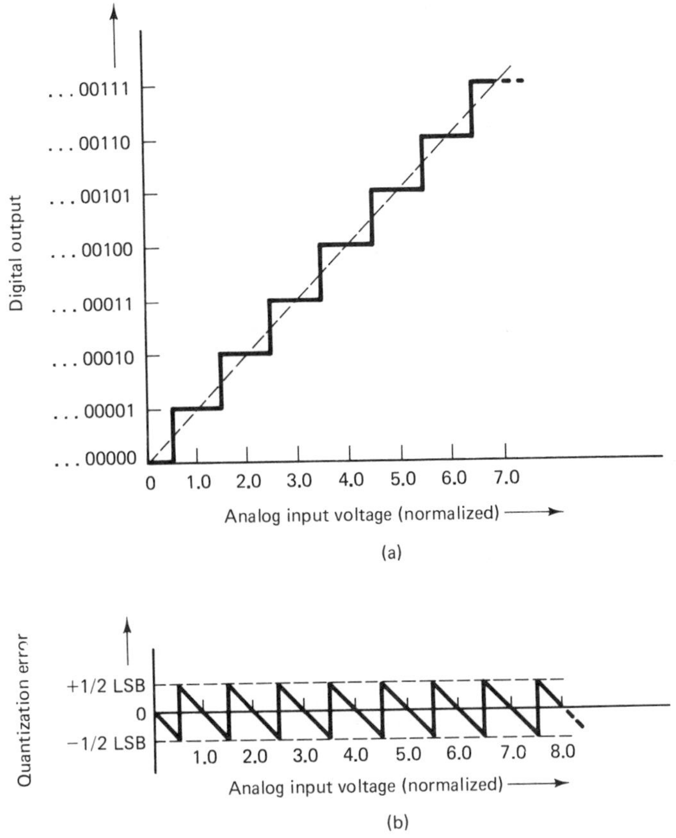

Figure 10.23 ADC transfer characteristic and quantization error with $\frac{1}{2}$-LSB offset of analog input voltage: (a) transfer characteristic; (b) quantization error.

quantization error is shown in Figure 10.23b. Note that the maximum quantization error is the same for every range of input voltage and is equal to $\pm\frac{1}{2}$ LSB.

A simple example of the effect of the $\frac{1}{2}$-LSB offset on the quantization error can be seen for the case of a 3-bit parallel comparator type of ADC. Let us assume a LSB voltage of 1.0 V and a full-scale input voltage of 8.0 V. Without the $\frac{1}{2}$-LSB offset the seven comparator reference voltages will be 1.0, 2.0, 3.0, 4.0, . . . , and 7.0 V. The digital output codes obtained will be as follows.

Analog input voltage	Digital output	Analog equivalent of output
$0 < V_A < 1.0$	000	0
$1.0 < V_A < 2.0$	001	1.0
$2.0 < V_A < 3.0$	010	2.0
$3.0 < V_A < 4.0$	011	3.0
$4.0 < V_A < 5.0$	100	4.0
$5.0 < V_A < 6.0$	101	5.0
$6.0 < V_A < 7.0$	110	6.0
$7.0 < V_A < 8.0$	111	7.0

The maximum digital output code will be 111 and the maximum quantization error will be 1 LSB in every 1.0 V (1 LSB) input voltage range. If the reference voltages are now shifted by $-\frac{1}{2}$ LSB to become 0.5, 1.5, 2.5, . . . , 6.5 V, the following transfer relationship will be obtained.

Analog input voltage	Digital output	Analog equivalent of output
$0 < V_A < 0.5$	000	0
$0.5 < V_A < 1.5$	001	1.0
$1.5 < V_A < 2.5$	010	2.0
$2.5 < V_A < 3.5$	011	3.0
$3.5 < V_A < 4.5$	100	4.0
$4.5 < V_A < 5.5$	101	5.0
$5.5 < V_A < 6.5$	110	6.0
$6.5 < V_A < 7.5$	111	7.0

The maximum quantization error is $\pm\frac{1}{2}$ LSB in every range.

10.2.1 Parallel Comparator ADC

The first type of analog-to-digital converter (ADC) that will be considered is the *parallel comparator ADC*, also known as a *simultaneous* or *flash ADC*. An example of a 3-bit ADC of this type is shown in Figure 10.24. For this ADC, seven comparators are required. In general, for an N-bit ADC of the parallel conversion type, the number of comparators required will be $2^N - 1$. Although this type of ADC has the advantage

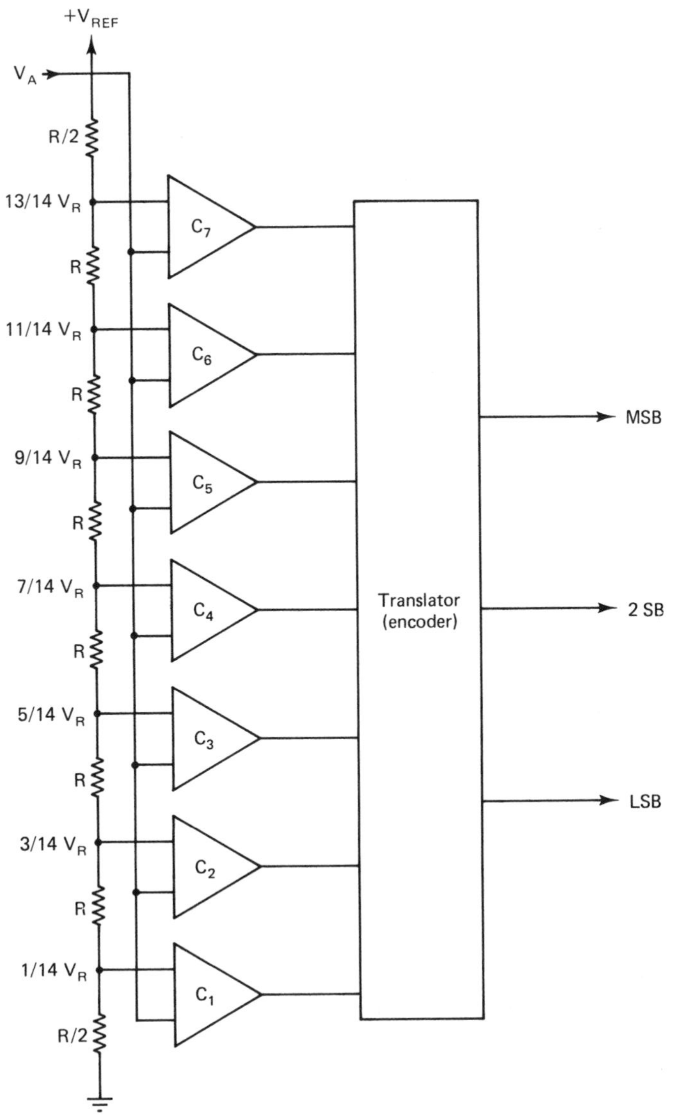

Figure 10.24 Parallel comparator analog-to-digital converter.

of being a very fast ADC, the number of comparators required increases very rapidly with the number of bits N, and usually becomes an uneconomical approach for more than 3 or 4 bits.

The reference voltage divider sets up the following reference levels for the comparators: $V_{R_1} = (R/2)/7RV_{\mathrm{REF}} = \frac{1}{14}V_{\mathrm{REF}}$, $V_{R_2} = \frac{3}{14}V_{\mathrm{REF}}$, $V_{R_3} = \frac{5}{14}V_{\mathrm{REF}}$, $V_{R_4} = \frac{7}{14}V_{\mathrm{REF}}$, $V_{R_5} = \frac{9}{14}V_{\mathrm{REF}}$, $V_{R_6} = \frac{11}{14}V_{\mathrm{REF}}$, and $V_{R_7} = \frac{13}{14}V_{\mathrm{REF}}$. The ADC transfer characteristic is as shown in Figure 10.22 with the normalized analog input voltage given by $V_A/(V_{\mathrm{REF}}/7)$.

The *quantization error* of an ADC is the range of analog input voltages that will produce a given digital output code, measured with respect to the midpoint value of the analog input. For the ADC of Figure 10.24 the choice of comparator reference voltage levels is such that the quantization error is uniformly distributed so that the quantization error is the same for every digital output level and is $\frac{1}{14}V_{REF}$. Since the total span of the analog input voltage corresponding to a 1-LSB change in the digital output is $\frac{2}{14}V_{REF}$, the quantization error of $\frac{1}{14}V_{REF}$ can be expressed in terms of the digital output as $\pm\frac{1}{2}$ LSB.

Fast CMOS ADC. For flash converters of 6-bits and up, a very large number of comparators and logic gates are required. The use of CMOS ICs can be very advantageous for these flash ADCs from the standpoint of power dissipation. An interesting example of a fast monolithic 6-bit flash CMOS ADC is the CA3300D (RCA). This device uses an array of 64 CMOS comparators and can operate at a sampling rate of 15 MHz which corresponds to a conversion time of 66 ns. In addition to 64 comparators, it contains the encoding circuits, output latches, and tri-state output gates, all on a single 2.4 mm × 3.3 mm chip. The reference voltages for the comparators are developed by a polysilicon resistor ladder with a resistance of 20 Ω between taps and a total resistance of 1250 Ω. It also produces a latched overflow bit. The overflow bit and the tri-state outputs make it possible to easily connect two of these ADCs together to produce a 7-bit ADC. In addition, the parallel connection of two of these ADCs is possible. By connecting the chip enable inputs (CE and CE) to the clock input, the two ADCs can be multiplexed such that each ADC samples the input signal on alternate half-cycles of the clock cycle. This arrangement will approximately double the sampling rate to 30 MHz. This device can operate with single supply voltages from 10 V down to as low as 3 V. When operated with a 5 V supply and at an 11 MHz clock rate, the total power dissipation is less than 50 mW.

Subranging parallel comparator ADC. The hardware needed for a parallel comparator ADC in terms of the number of comparators and logic gates for encoding the comparator outputs increases exponentially with the number of bits. For an N-bit converter $2^N - 1$ comparators are needed so that most parallel comparators or flash converters are limited to about 4 or 6 bits. There have been monolithic IC flash ADCs recently developed with 9-bit resolution and containing 511 comparators and associated circuitry on one IC chip. This flash converter has a conversion time of only 40 ns and can operate at a 25-MHz conversion rate.

For a fast high-resolution ADC a *subranging* or *cascaded* flash ADC system as shown in Figure 10.25 can be used. The first ADC produces an N_1-bit digital code that is supplied to the output as the N_1 MSBs of the digital output code. This digital signal is also supplied to a DAC which produces an analog voltage corresponding to the N_1 MSBs of the digital output code. This analog voltage is then subtracted from the analog input voltage in the difference amplifier A to produce a difference or error voltage. This difference voltage then goes to an N_2-bit ADC. The digital output of this second ADC becomes the N_2 LSBs of the digital output code, which

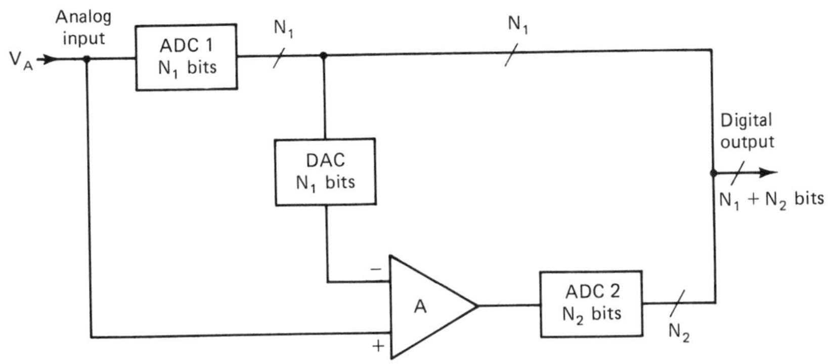

Figure 10.25 Cascaded (subranging) parallel comparator ADC.

will now have the full complement of $N_1 + N_2$ bits. Thus if two 4-bit flash ADCs are used, an 8-bit digital output can be obtained.

Although the two ADCs in the preceding example have a 4-bit output for a total of 8 bits in the digital output code, for an 8-bit accuracy the accuracy of each ADC must be such that the conversion error in each must not exceed $V_{FS}/2^8$ where V_{FS} is the full-scale analog input voltage range. This requirement will generally be no problem for the second ADC since this corresponds to a maximum error of $1/2^4$ of its full-scale voltage. It can, however, be a problem for the first comparator for which the maximum error must not exceed $1/2^8$ times its full-scale voltage. Another somewhat related problem results from the fact that the conversion process in the second ADC takes place at a slightly later time than it does in the first ADC due to the propagation delays in the first ADC, the DAC, and in the difference amplifier. This can be a significant problem for a rapidly changing analog input voltage.

Due to the effects mentioned above, the difference voltage that is supplied to the second ADC may fall outside the full-scale conversion range of the second ADC and errors will result. A means of minimizing this problem and of easing the accuracy requirements of the first ADC is shown in Figure 10.26. The range of the second

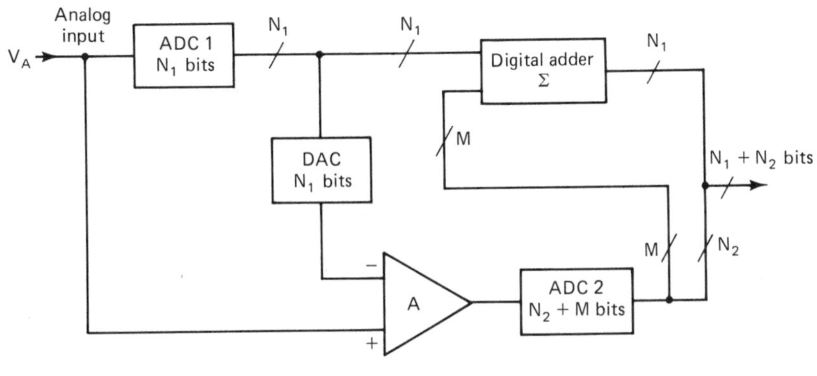

Figure 10.26 Subranging ADC with M-bit error correction.

ADC is increased from N_2 bits to $N_2 + M$ bits. The N_2 LSBs of this ADC still become the N_2 LSBs of the total digital output code. The M MSBs of this ADC are, however, combined with the N_1 bits of the first ADC in the digital adder to produce the N_1 MSBs of the digital output code, which will still have a total of $N_1 + N_2$ bits.

If there were no errors made in the first ADC or in the DAC and the analog input voltage is the same for both conversion cycles, the M MSBs of the second ADC will all be zeros and no correction will be made to the output of the first ADC in the digital adder. If this is not the case, the M bits generated by the second ADC can be used to correct the output of the first ADC.

Subranging ADC examples. An example of a fast subranging flash ADC system is the MOD-1020 (Analog Devices) which offers a 10-bit digital output at a 20 MHz conversion rate. This system consists of several ICs and other components on a single PC board. The configuration is basically similar to that shown in Figure 10.26 with the addition of a delay line placed between the analog input and the difference amplifier. This is to compensate for the conversion delay of the N_1 bits through the first ADC and the DAC. The first conversion yields 5 bits (N_1) which are then combined with the 6 bits ($N_2 + M$) of the second conversion to produce a 10-bit output, with the one extra bit being used for error correction. Another subranging flash ADC system is the MOD-1205 (Analog Devices) which offers a 12-bit output at a 5 MHz conversion rate.

10.2.2 Counting-Type

The counting type of analog-to-digital converter is one of the simplest types of ADC and a basic block diagram of this type of converter is shown in Figure 10.27a. The digital output of a modulus N binary counter goes to an N-bit digital-to-analog converter (DAC) which produces the staircase type of waveform shown in Figure 10.27b. The DAC output voltage goes up in increments of 1 V_{LSB} up to a full-scale maximum of 2^N V_{LSB}. This voltage is compared to the analog input voltage by the comparator. As long as the DAC voltage stays below the analog input voltage V_A, the comparator output voltage will stay in the *high* state. This will keep the clock gate G_1 enabled such that the clock pulses pass through to the counter so that the count will continue to increase and the DAC output voltage will continue with its incremental increases. As soon as the DAC voltage rises above the analog input voltage level, the comparator output will go *low*. This will disable the clock gate G_1, so that the count will stop at this point.

Some time after this the HOLD voltage goes *high*, which enables the N-bit digital output gate so that the binary count of the counter now becomes available as the digital output of the ADC. The HOLD pulse then terminates and the RESET pulse then resets the counter back to zero and the counter starts to count up again, thus starting another conversion cycle.

For an N-bit counting converter a total conversion time of 2^N clock cycles is required for a full-scale input voltage. As a result this type of ADC will be a relatively slow converter. For a 14-bit ADC of this type the conversion time will be

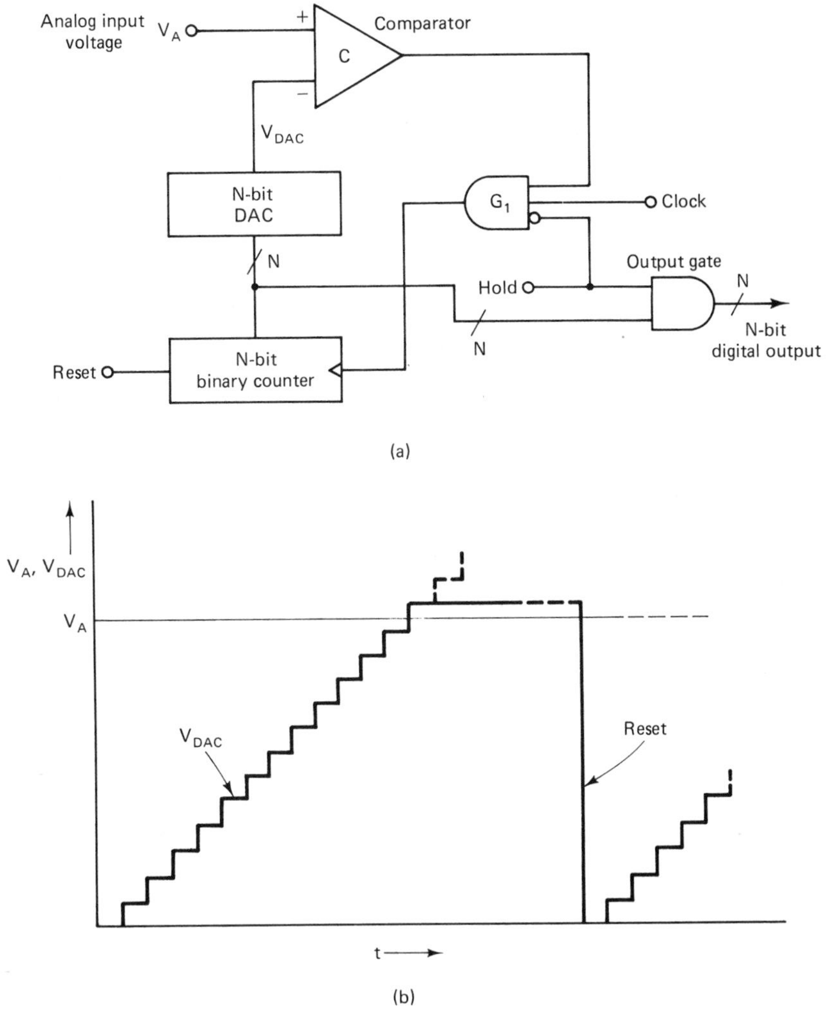

Figure 10.27 Counting analog-to-digital converter: (a) block diagram; (b) DAC output waveform.

$2^{14}T_{CLOCK} = 16{,}384T_{CLOCK}$. If $T_{CLOCK} = 100$ ns is chosen as a representative value, the resulting conversion time will be 1.64 ms and the corresponding rate will be 610 conversions per second.

The average conversion time can be reduced substantially if an up/down counter is substituted for the simple binary up counter and if the conversion cycles are terminated shortly after the counting stops. This type of counting ADC is called a *tracking* or *servo ADC*. In this type of converter the counter is not reset to zero at the beginning of every conversion cycle, but rather is given a command to either continue to count up or to count down from the previous count, this depending on whether the analog input voltage is above or below the DAC output voltage at the beginning of the conversion cycle, respectively.

For a slowly changing analog voltage the change in the count needed to match the DAC voltage with the analog input voltage will be small, so that the conversion time will be very short. For a full-scale analog voltage change occurring in a short period of time, the required conversion time will become equal to that of the simple counting ADC.

The accuracy of the counting ADC is a function of the offset voltage and voltage gain of the comparator and of the accuracy of the DAC. It will often be the DAC that will be the limiting factor in the overall accuracy of the ADC.

This type of ADC is a feedback ADC because of the presence of a feedback loop around the comparator. This feedback loop consists of the clock gate G_1, the binary counter, and the DAC. Another type of feedback ADC that has a DAC in the feedback loop is the successive approximation converter (SAR) and it will be discussed next. The SAR converter offers the same basic accuracy as the counting ADC, but it offers a much shorter conversion time and is a very widely used ADC.

10.2.3 Successive Approximation ADC

The *successive approximation register* (SAR) type of ADC is one of the most popular types of ADC because it offers the combination of high accuracy and high conversion speed. In Figure 10.28 a basic block diagram of a SAR ADC is shown. The successive approximation register for an N-bit converter contains N flip-flops (FFs) that are set to the high state ($b = 1$), one at a time to produce the bit inputs to the digital-to-analog converter (DAC). The output voltage of the DAC is compared to the analog input voltage.

The MSB FF is set to the high state ($b_1 = 1$) first so that the analog input voltage is first compared to a DAC output voltage that corresponds to the MSB voltage level of $V_{MSB} = V_{FS}/2$. If the analog voltage is greater than V_{MSB}, the MSB FF remains set ($b_1 = 1$) for the rest of the conversion period. If the analog input voltage, however, is below V_{MSB}, the MSB FF is reset to zero ($b_1 = 0$) and remains in this state for the rest of the conversion process.

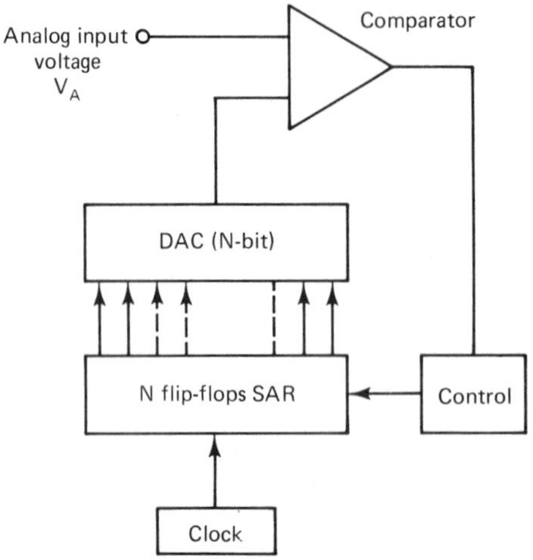

Figure 10.28 Block diagram of a successive approximation register analog-to-digital converter (SAR ADC).

The next significant bit (second bit) FF is set next ($b_2 = 1$) and the DAC output voltage now corresponds to $V_{FS}(b_1/2 + b_2/4)$ with $b_2 = 1$. If this voltage is less than the analog input voltage V_A, the second FF remains set at $b_2 = 1$. If this DAC voltage is more than the analog input voltage, the second FF is reset to give $b_2 = 0$. This process then continues for each successive FF for N clock cycles to complete the conversion process. In each case if the analog input voltage is greater than the DAC voltage, the FFs retain their present state. If the analog voltage is below the DAC voltage, the last FF to be set ($b = 1$) is reset to zero ($b = 0$).

The DAC voltage and the corresponding digital code is thus a successive approximation to the analog input voltage with each bit being tested at a time beginning with the most significant bit (b_1) and continuing one bit at a time down to the least significant bit (b_N) at the end of the conversion period.

Let us now consider the example of a 10-bit SAR ADC with a full-scale DAC output voltage of $V_{FS} = 10.24$ V, so that $V_{LSB} = 10$ mV. We will also assume that a $\frac{1}{2}$-LSB offset voltage is added to the DAC output voltage in order to minimize the conversion quantization error.

For an analog input voltage of $V_A = 7.500$ V the SAR bit outputs and the corresponding DAC output voltage values will be as given in Table 10.1.

TABLE 10.1 SAR DAC EXAMPLE

Clock cycle	Register FF states b_1(MSB)$\cdots b_N$(LSB)	DAC output voltage (+$\frac{1}{2}$-LSB offset) (V)
1	1000000000	5.125
2	1100000000	7.685 (b_2 FF now reset to $b_2 = 0$)
3	1010000000	6.405
4	1011000000	7.045
5	1011100000	7.365
6	1011110000	7.525 (b_6 FF now reset to $b_6 = 0$)
7	1011101000	7.445
8	1011101100	7.485
9	1011101110	7.525 (b_9 FF now reset to $b_9 = 0$)
10	1011101101	7.495

After 10 clock cycles the SAR conversion process is completed and the final status of the SAR FFs is 1011101101, which produces a DAC output voltage of 7.495 V. The resulting quantization error is 5 mV, which corresponds to $\frac{1}{2}$ LSB. If the $\frac{1}{2}$-LSB offset were not present, the DAC output voltage would be 7.490 V, which would result in a quantization error of 10 mV or 1 LSB.

For an analog input voltage of less than 5 mV, the digital output will be 0000000000 and the DAC output voltage (including the $\frac{1}{2}$-LSB offset voltage) will be 5 mV. For an analog input voltage between 5 and 15 mV the digital output code will be 0000000001. The maximum DAC output voltage (including the $\frac{1}{2}$-LSB offset) corresponding to a digital output code of 1111111111 will be $V_{MAX} = 10.24 - 10$ mV $+ 5$ mV $= 10.235$ V. The maximum analog voltage that can be converted with a quantization error not exceeding $\frac{1}{2}$ LSB (5 mV) is 10.240 V, which corresponds to the DAC full-scale output voltage.

The SAR ADC has the digital code output available in parallel form at the end of the conversion period. It is also possible to obtain a data output in serial form during the conversion period. As each data bit becomes valid at the end of the various clock cycle times during which the DAC output voltage is compared to the analog signal and the FFs are reset if necessary, the bits of the digital output code becomes available starting with the MSB and ending with the LSB at the end of the conversion process.

The total conversion time for an N-bit SAR ADC is approximately $(N + 2)T_{\text{CLOCK}}$, where T_{CLOCK} is the clock period, which is typically of the order of 1 μs. Therefore, for a 12-bit SAR ADC a total conversion time of around 14 μs would be required. This is to be compared to a conversion time of $2^N T_{\text{CLOCK}}$ for a digital ramp or counting type of ADC so that for a 12-bit digital ramp ADC with a 1-μs clock cycle time a total conversion time of around 4 ms will be required. Of course, a parallel comparator ADC can produce conversion times of well under 1 μs, but the hardware requirements for a 12-bit ADC (or even for an 8-bit ADC) would be quite excessive.

The two principal factors that will limit the accuracy of any of the DAC feedback type of ADCs such as the SAR ADC and the digital ramp ADCs is the precision of the DAC and the comparator offset voltage. For a 10-bit ADC with an accuracy of better than $\frac{1}{2}$ LSB and a full-scale voltage of 10 (or 10.24) V the total conversion error from all sources (but not including the inherent quantization error) must not exceed ± 5 mV. Therefore, the comparator offset voltage V_{OS} should be substantially less than 5 mV, which is not a difficult requirement to meet. However, for a 12-bit converter the total error must not exceed 1.25 mV, and for a 14-bit converter the error must not exceed 0.313 mV, which becomes a much more difficult requirement to satisfy.

The highest ADC resolution available is 16 bits. For a $\pm$1-LSB accuracy the total conversion error with a full-scale output voltage of 10 V must not exceed 10 V/2^{16} = $\underline{152\ \mu\text{V}}$ over the operating temperature range. For an operating temperature range 0 to 50°C and with the ADC calibrated at 25°C, the maximum net temperature coefficient of the reference voltage and the comparator offset voltage must not exceed 152 μV/($\pm$25°C) = $\underline{\pm 6\ \mu\text{V/°C}}$. This will indeed be a very difficult condition to satisfy.

Decision tree. Further insight into the operation of the successive approximation ADC can be obtained by looking at the "decision tree" shown in Figure 10.29 for the simple case of a 4-bit ADC with a 16-V full-scale range. In Figure 10.30 the decision tree path is shown for the case of an analog input voltage of 10.7 V as an example. The following sequence of decisions are made in the ADC:

1. MSB = 1 since $V_A > 8.0$ V.
2. 2SB = 0 since $V_A < 12.0$ V.
3. 3SB = 1 since $V_A > 10.0$ V.
4. 4SB = LSB = 0 since $V_A < 11.0$ V.

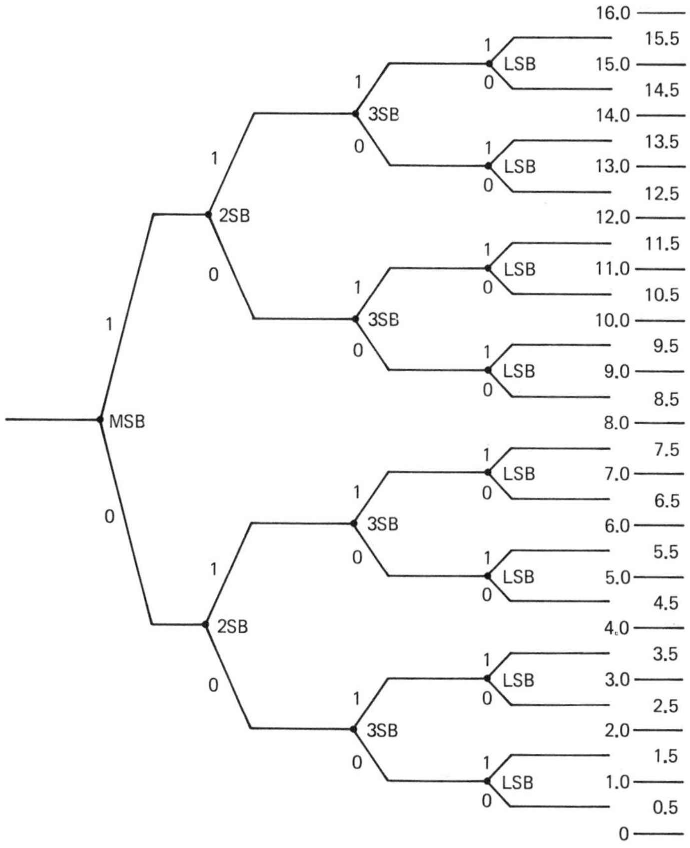

Figure 10.29 Decision tree for successive approximation ADC.

For accurate analog-to-digital conversion the analog input voltage V_A should be held constant during the conversion cycle. If the analog input voltage changes by more that $\pm\frac{1}{2}$ LSB an error in the digital output code can result. The successive approximation ADC is especially susceptible to this problem.

To illustrate the effect of a changing analog input voltage on the conversion process, let us consider a worst-case situation of a successive approximation ADC with an analog input voltage that is nominally zero, but there happens to be a large amplitude noise or interference voltage spike occurring at the time that the first (MSB) decision is being made as shown in Figure 10.31. At this decision point the MSB is set at 1 due to the presence of the voltage spike. At the remainder of the decision points the rest of the bits are set at 0 since the voltage spike is gone and the input voltage has settled back to near zero. The digital output code will be 1000 as compared to the correct value of 0000. This error in the digital output code corresponds to an input voltage error of one-half of the full-scale voltage. To minimize the occurrence of these errors *sample-and-hold* (S/H) or *tracking-and-hold* (T/H) amplifiers are often used between the analog input voltage and the ADC. These

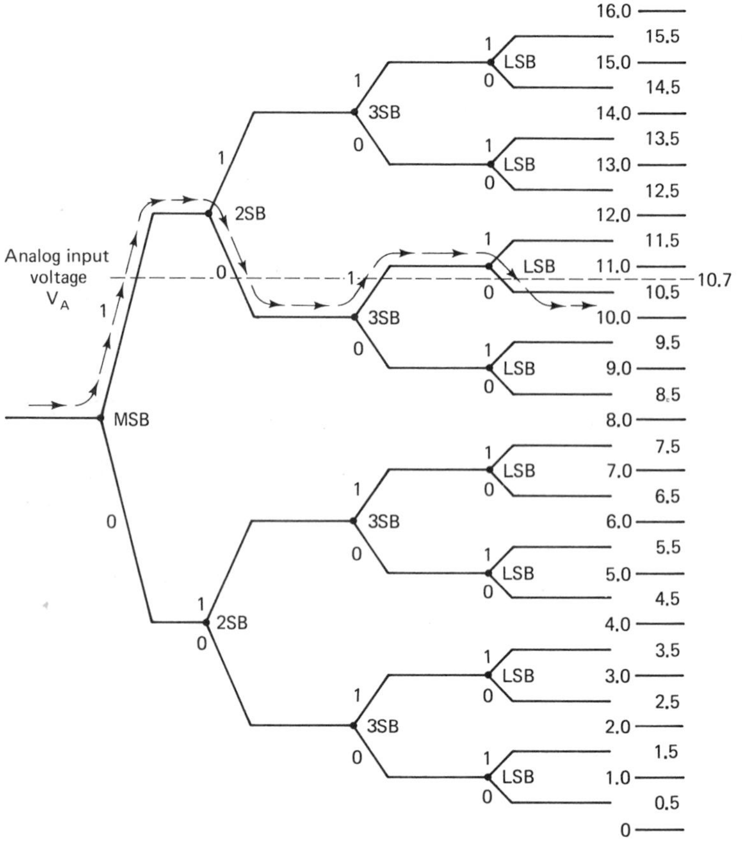

Figure 10.30 Decision tree for successive approximation ADC: example for V_A = 10.7 V.

circuits sample or track the analog input voltage before the conversion cycles begins, and then at the beginning of the conversion period will hold the value of the analog input voltage constant during the conversion process.

10.2.4 Integrating ADCs

In the integrating type of analog-to-digital converter the analog input voltage or a fixed reference voltage, or both, are integrated and the result is used to clock or gate a binary counter to obtain a digital output that represents the analog input voltage. Three basic types of integrating ADCs will be considered: the voltage-to-frequency (V/F) converter, the voltage-to-time (V/T) converter, and the dual-slope converter.

In the *voltage-to-frequency converter* the analog input voltage is integrated and the result is compared to a fixed reference voltage to produce a pulse train whose frequency is proportional to the analog input voltage. This pulse train is used to

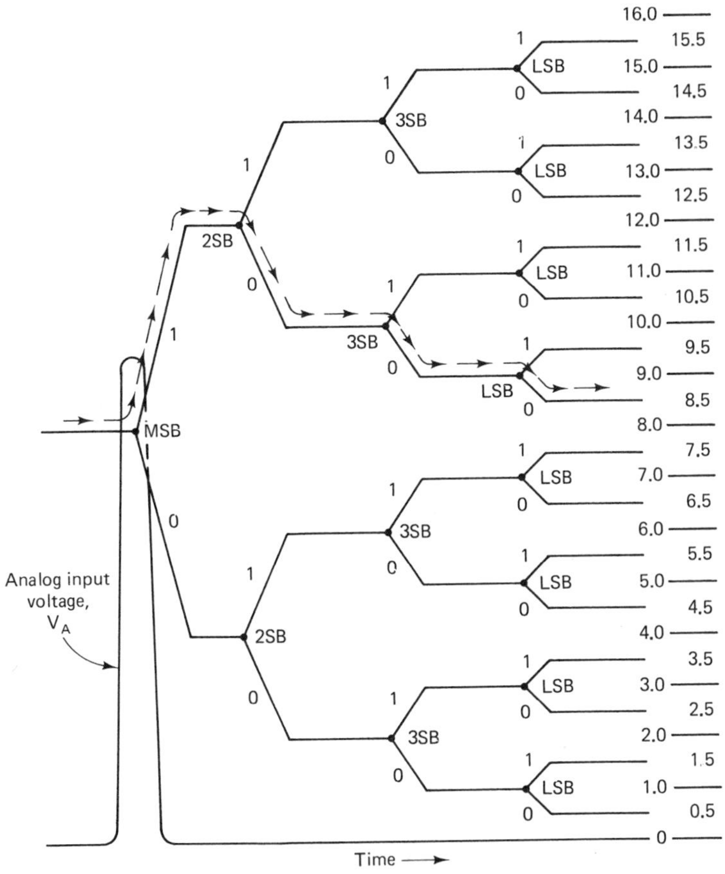

Figure 10.31 Decision tree for successive approximation ADC: effect of large voltage spike.

clock a binary counter over a fixed gate period to obtain a binary digital output that represents the analog input voltage.

In the *voltage-to-time converter* it is the reference voltage that is integrated and compared to the analog input voltage to produce a gating pulse whose length is proportional to the analog voltage. This pulse is used to gate a binary counter that is driven by a fixed-frequency clock. This produces a binary digital output that is based on the number of clock cycles in the gating period and will thus be a representation of the analog input voltage.

In the *dual-slope converter* the analog input voltage is first integrated for a fixed period of time. Then a fixed reference voltage of polarity opposite to that of the analog voltage is applied an integrated for the period of time required to bring the output voltage of the integrator circuit back down to zero. This period of time is used to gate a binary counter, and the count so produced will be a binary digital output equivalent to the analog input voltage.

The integrating converters have the advantages of offering very high resolution (up to 14 bits) and very good noise and power frequency rejection, but have the disadvantage of a very low conversion rate. We will now consider the three basic types of integrating analog-to-digital converters in somewhat more detail.

Voltage-to-frequency ADC. In the voltage-to-frequency converter the analog input voltage is used to control the frequency of a voltage-controlled oscillator (VCO) that has a very linear voltage to frequency transfer characteristic. The output pulse train of the VCO is then counted by a binary counter over a fixed sampling or gate time. The count obtained is then made available as the digital output at the end of the gate time.

A basic voltage-to-frequency ADC circuit is shown in Figure 10.32. The analog input voltage V_A produces a current $I_1 = V_A/R_1$ through the timing resistor R_1. This current is then used to charge up the timing capacitor C_1, producing an output voltage given by

$$V_{o_1} = \frac{1}{C}\int_0^t I_1\,dt = \frac{1}{R_1C_1}\int_0^t V_A\,dt = \frac{V_At}{\tau_1} \tag{10.12}$$

where $\tau_1 = R_1C_1$ and V_A is assumed to be constant during the integration period. When V_{o_1} drops below $-V_R$ the comparator output will switch to the high state, which will activate the monostable multivibrator to produce a short pulse of length T_d. This will cause switch S_1 to close, thus terminating the charging period. The charging period will terminate at time $t = T_C$ as obtained from $V_AT_C/\tau_1 = V_R$, so that $T_C = (V_R/V_A)\tau_1$. The switch will remain closed for the time period T_d to allow the capacitor to discharge completely. At the end of this short period the switch opens and the charging cycle will start again. The voltage waveforms of V_{o_1} and V_{o_2} are shown in Figure 10.32. The total period is $T = T_C + T_d$, and the corresponding frequency will be $f = 1/T = 1/(T_C + T_d)$. If $T_d \ll T_C$, then the frequency will be approximately given by $f = 1/T_C = (V_A/V_R)(1/\tau_1)$.

The pulse train produced by the monostable multivibrator becomes the clock to drive the binary counter, which will count the pulses during the fixed gate period T_G. At the end of the gate period the count stops and the output of the counter is made available as the digital output of the ADC. The total number of pulses counted at the end of the gate period will be $N = T_G \times f = T_G/T = (T_G/\tau_1)(V_A/V_R)$. The digital output will be this count in binary form.

Although this is a relatively simple ADC its accuracy and speed is limited by the requirement that $T_C = (V_R/V_A)\tau_1$ be much greater than the discharge time T_d, so that the frequency will be a linear function of the analog input voltage. The T_d pulse length is limited by the speed of the comparator or the minimum pulse available from the monostable multivibrator, as well as the capacitor discharge time constant.

The total conversion time for an M-bit ADC will be approximately $NT_{C(\text{MIN})}$, where $N = 2^M$ and $T_{C(\text{MIN})} = (V_R/V_{A(\text{MAX})})\tau_1$. Since $T_{c(\text{MIN})}$ is limited by the requirement that $T_{c(\text{MIN})} \gg T_d$, this can result in a long conversion time. For example, if $C_1 = 1$ nF and the switch "on" resistance is 25 Ω, the discharge time constant will be 25 ns. For the full discharge of C_1, a discharge time of at least 10 time constants will generally be needed so that $T_d \geq 10 \times 25$ ns $= 250$ ns. For a 6-bit ADC with

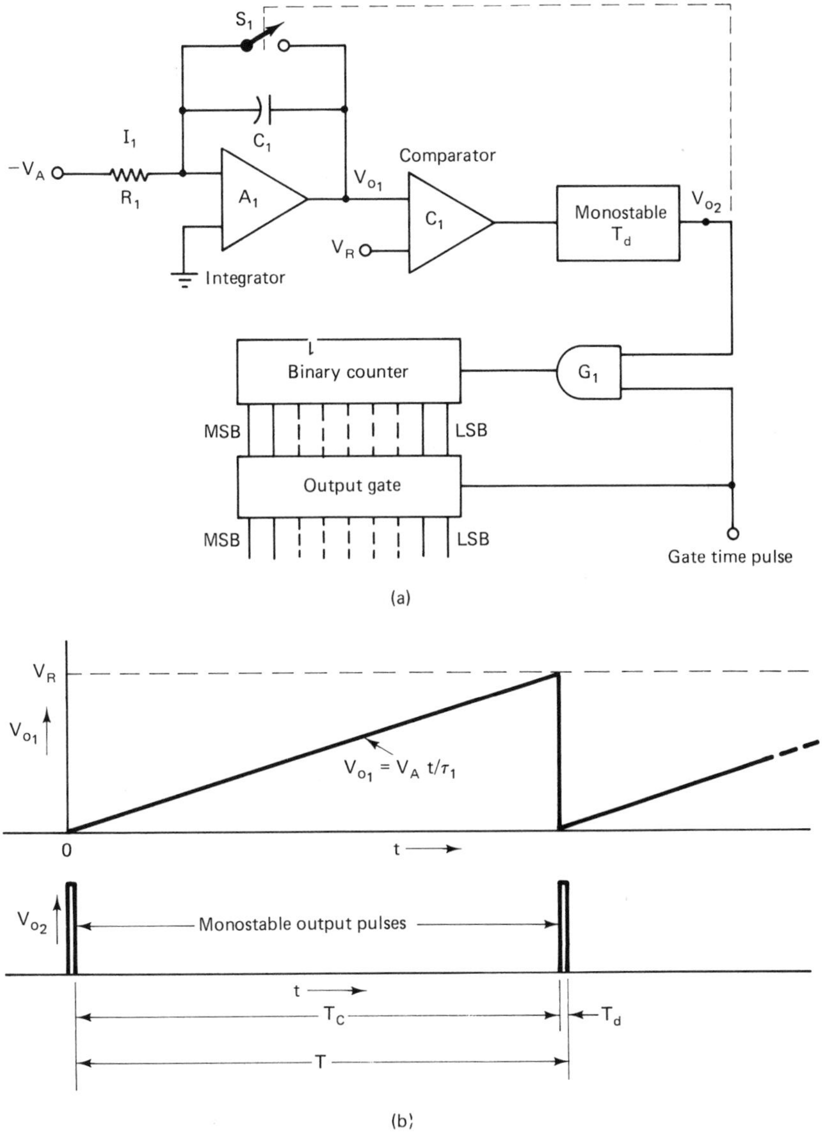

Figure 10.32 Voltage-to-frequency analog-to-digital converter: (a) basic circuit; (b) integrator and monostable output voltage.

an accuracy of $\pm\frac{1}{2}$ LSB, we should require that $T_{C(\mathrm{MIN})} = 2 \times 2^6\ T_d = 128\ T_d = 32\ \mu\mathrm{s}$. The total conversion time will therefore be approximately $NT_{C(\mathrm{MIN})} = 2^6 \times 32\ \mu\mathrm{s} = 2.05$ ms. The corresponding conversion rate will be 488 conversions per second. For an 8-bit V/F-type ADC the total conversion time will be $2 \times 2^8 \times 2^8 \times 250$ ns $= 33$ ms and the corresponding conversion rate will be only 30 conversions per second.

Voltage-to-time ADC. Another type of integrating ADC is the voltage-to-time converter. In this type of converter the reference voltage is integrated for a period of time until its integrated value reaches the analog input voltage. This time period is used to gate a binary counter that is driven by a fixed-frequency clock. The number of clock pulses counted by the counter will be proportional to the analog input voltage, and the digital output will be this number of clock pulses expressed in binary form.

In Figure 10.33 a diagram of this type of ADC is presented, together with voltage waveforms. At time $t = 0$ the switch S_1 is opened, which initiates the integration period. At the same time the AND gate G_1 is enabled so that the clock pulses can now drive the binary counter. The output voltage of the integrator circuit A_1 will be

$$V_{o_1} = -1/(R_1C_1)\int_0^t -V_R\,dt = V_R t/\tau_1,$$

where $\tau_1 = R_1C_1$. At time $t = T$ the integral of the reference voltage will be equal to the analog input voltage, so that $V_R T/\tau_1 = V_A$, and thus $T = (V_A/V_R)\tau_1$.

At time $t = T$ the comparator output voltage goes low, which disables the gate G_1, so that the counter stops counting and the binary counter outputs are gated out as the digital output of the converter. The control voltage next goes high, which resets the integrator to zero by closing switch S_1. At the same time the output gate G_2 is disabled and the clock input gate G_1 is enabled, allowing the counter to start counting again. The count will start from zero, however, since the counter will have been reset to zero shortly before switch S_1 is opened.

The digital output that is made available at the end of the integration time period T will be a binary number corresponding to N clock pulses, where $N = T/T_{\text{CLOCK}} = (V_A/V_R)(\tau_1/T_{\text{CLOCK}})$. Thus the digital output code will be proportional to the analog input voltage.

For an M-bit V/T type of ADC, the total number of clock pulses that must be available for counting in a conversion cycle must be $N_{\text{MAX}} = 2^M$, so that the conversion time will be approximately $2^M T_{\text{CLOCK}}$. Thus for a 10-bit ADC with a representative clock period of $T_{\text{CLOCK}} = 50$ ns, the conversion time will be approximately $2^{10} \times 50$ ns $= 51\ \mu$s and the corresponding conversion rate will be 20,000 conversions per second. For a 14-bit converter the conversion time will be up to 820 μs and the conversion rate will be 1220 conversions per second. Thus the V/T ADC is a relatively slow converter, although it generally will be much faster than the voltage-to-frequency (V/F) type of integrating ADC.

In both the V/T and the V/F converters the conversion accuracy will be a direct function of the accuracy and stability of the timing resistor R_1 and capacitor C_1 that establish the integrator time constant τ_1. There will usually be provision for a small trimming or adjustment resistor to be connected externally to the IC that can be used to adjust the net value of R_1 to produce the correct ADC scale factor at some reference temperature, such as 25°C. Let us consider as an example a 10-bit ADC with an accuracy of ± 1 LSB over the temperature range 0 to 50°C, and for which the net value of R_1 has been adjusted at 25°C to produce the correct ADC scale factor. Since the integrator time constant, and thus the ADC scale factor,

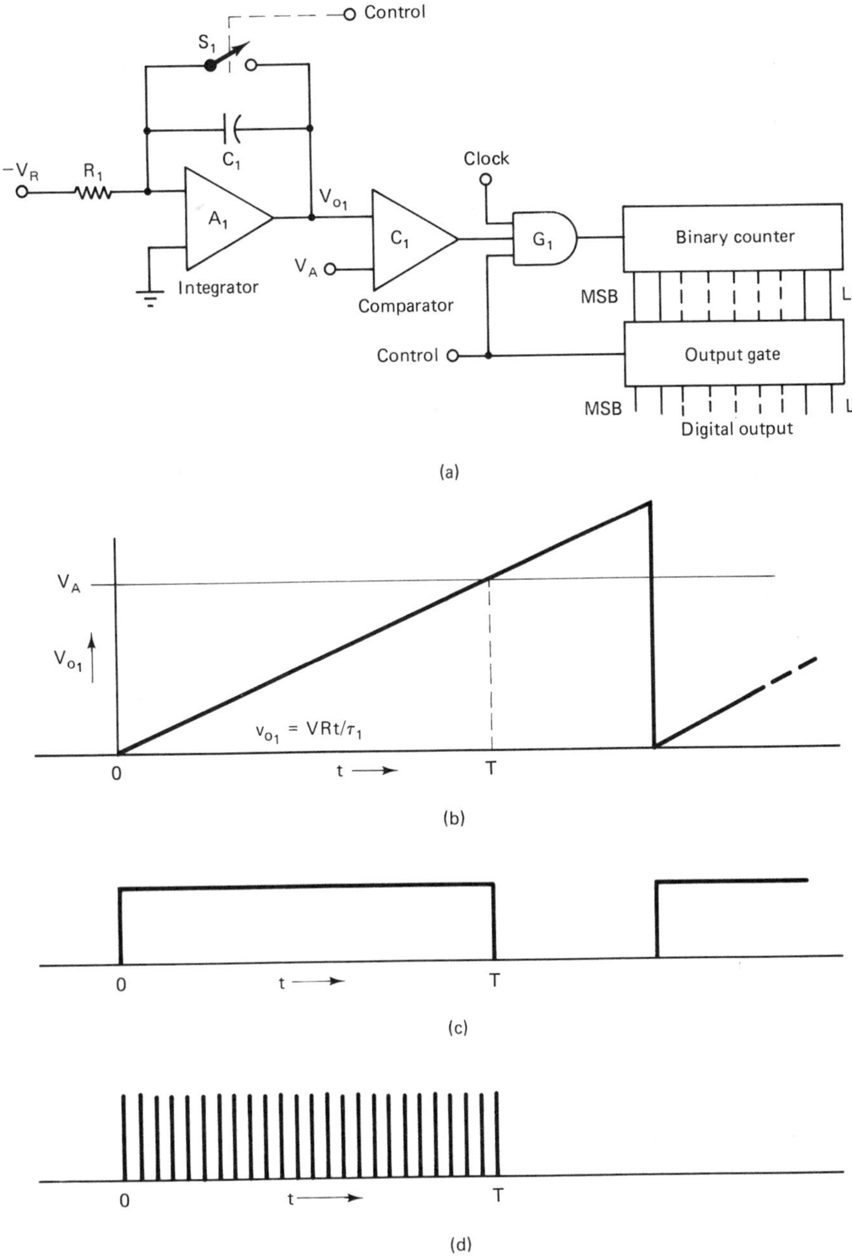

Figure 10.33 Voltage-to-time analog-to-digital converter: (a) basic circuit; (b) integrator output voltage; (c) comparator output voltage; (d) clock pulse input to counter.

will be directly proportional to R_1, the maximum fractional deviation of R_1 over the temperature range 0 to 50°C will be given by $(\Delta R_1/R_1)_{MAX} = 1/2^{10} = 1/1024 = 0.001$. The corresponding maximum allowable value for the temperature coefficient of the resistance will be given by $TC_{R\,MAX} = (1/R_1)(dR_1/dT_{MAX}) = 0.001/\pm 25°C = 4 \times 10^{-5}/°C = 40$ ppm/°C $= 0.004\%/°C$. This can be a difficult requirement to meet.

The comparator offset voltage V_{OS} can also be a factor in the accuracy of the ADC. If we assumed that the offset voltage is initially nulled or compensated for at 25°C, the maximum allowable change in V_{OS} over the operating temperature range 0 to 50°C will be given by $\Delta V_{OS}/V_A = 1/2^{10} = 0.001$. For a full-scale analog input voltage of 10 V this will give $\Delta V_{OS\,(MAX)} = 10\text{ V} \times 0.001 = 10$ mV. The corresponding maximum allowable temperature coefficient of the offset voltage $TC_{V_{OS}}$ will be $TC_{V_{OS}\,(MAX)} = dV_{OS}/dT = 10\text{ mV}/(\pm 25°C) = \pm 0.4$ mV/°C $= \pm 400$ μV/°C. This will not be a difficult requirement.

If we now consider an example of a 14-bit ADC of the V/F or V/T type with a ±1-LSB accuracy over an operating temperature range of 0 to 50°C as in the previous example, the requirement of the temperature coefficient of resistance for R_1 becomes $TC_{R\,MAX} = 2.5$ ppm/°C. This will indeed be a very difficult requirement to meet. For the offset voltage the maximum allowable temperature coefficient for this case will be given by $TC_{V_{OS}\,(MAX)} = \pm 25$ μV/°C. This will still not be a very difficult requirement, so the main problem will be with respect to the temperature coefficient of the timing resistor R_1. Other possible problem areas are the temperature coefficient of the timing capacitor C_1 and the variation with temperature of the counter gating pulse in the case of the V/F converter, and the clock frequency in the case of the V/T converter. In addition, the temperature coefficient of the reference voltage is important. For the 10-bit ADC the reference voltage V_R must have a temperature coefficient of no more than 1000 ppm/°C, and for the 14-bit converter the temperature coefficient of V_R must not exceed 61 ppm/°C.

In the next section we will investigate the dual-slope type of integrating ADC. In the dual-slope converter the only temperature coefficient that will be a factor in the accuracy of the ADC will be that of the reference voltage, so that converter resolutions are up to 14 bits become readily available.

Dual-slope ADC. The third type of integrating ADC that we will consider is the dual-slope ADC, and it will be seen that this type of converter will offer some significant advantages over the V/F and V/T converters in that the conversion scale factor will be independent of the integrator time constant and the clock frequency. A basic diagram of the dual-slope converter is shown in Figure 10.34, together with the integrator voltage versus time waveform.

At time $t = 0$ switch S_1 is connected to the analog input voltage V_A and switch S_2 is opened, so that the analog input voltage integration begins. The output voltage of the integrator will be

$$V_{o1} = \frac{-1}{R_1C_1}\int_0^t V_A\,dt = \frac{-V_At}{R_1C_1} = \frac{-V_At}{\tau_1} \tag{10.13}$$

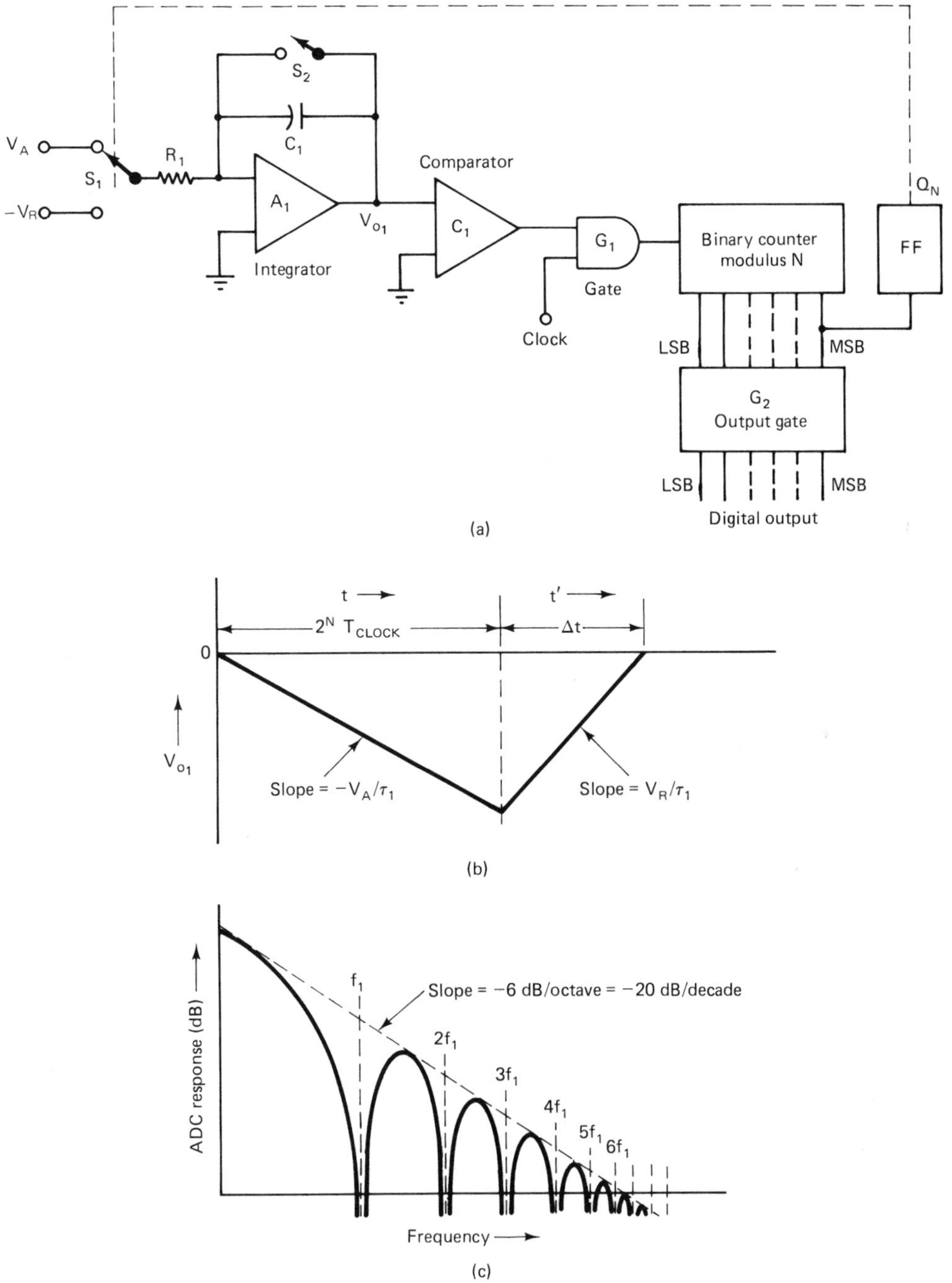

Figure 10.34 Dual-slope analog-to-digital converter: (a) basic circuit; (b) integrator output voltage; (c) frequency response characteristic.

where $\tau_1 = R_1C_1$ is the integrator time constant, and it is assumed that V_A remains constant over the integration time period. At the end of 2^N clock periods at time $t = 2^N T_{\text{CLOCK}}$ the output of the flip-flop, Q_N, goes high ($Q_N = 1$), which causes switch S_1 to be switched from V_A to $-V_R$. At this very same time the binary counter has gone through its entire count sequence and has cycled back to the 000 . . . state.

The integrator output voltage will now be given by $v_{o_1} = -V_A(2^N T_{\text{CLOCK}})/\tau_1 + V_R t'/\tau_1$, where $t' = t - 2^N T_{\text{CLOCK}}$ and is the time measured from the instant of the change of switch S_1 at the end of the binary counter cycle. This output voltage will reach zero at $t' = \Delta t$ given by $V_R \; \Delta t/\tau_1 = V_A(2^N T_{\text{CLOCK}})/\tau_1$, so that $\Delta t = (V_A/V_R)2^N T_{\text{CLOCK}}$. At this time the comparator output voltage goes low, which disables the clock AND gate G_1. This stops the clock pulse from reaching the counter, so that the counter will be stopped at a count corresponding to the number of clock pulses in time Δt as given by $n = \Delta t/T_{\text{CLOCK}} = (V_A/V_R)2^N$. Note that the clock period cancels out of this expression. The binary digital output of the counter will correspond to this count and therefore will be directly proportional to the analog input voltage.

Note that the digital conversion scale factor will be independent of the integrator time constant, which cancels out as a result of the two successive integrations of V_A and V_R. Note also that the scale factor will not be a function of the clock period, again because of the two successive integrations. Indeed, the principal factor that will control the conversion accuracy will be the temperature coefficient of the reference voltage.

To consider a representative example, let us look at a 14-bit dual-slope ADC with an accuracy of ± 1 LSB over an operating temperature range of 0 to 50°C. We will assume that the reference voltage has been adjusted to give the correct conversion scale factor at 25°C. The maximum allowable temperature coefficient for the reference voltage will be given by $(1/V_R)(dV_R/dT) = (1/2^{14})/25°\text{C} = \underline{2.44 \times 10^{-6}/°\text{C}} = \underline{2.44 \text{ ppm}/°\text{C}}$. For a 10 volt reference voltage, the maximum allowable temperature coefficient will therefore be $\pm 24\ \mu\text{V}/°\text{C}$. This is a difficult requirement and requires a well-compensated temperature reference circuit.

A very important feature of the dual-slope ADC is its rejection of frequency components that are integer multiples of $f_1 = 1/(2^N T_{\text{CLOCK}})$. Since the analog voltage integration time is fixed at $2^N T_{\text{CLOCK}}$, these frequency components will have periods that are integer submultiples of the analog signal integration time and so will execute an integer number of complete waveform cycles in this time. The contribution of these components of the analog input voltage to the integral of the analog voltage will therefore be zero.

Generally, the most troublesome interference frequency component will be the 60-Hz power-line frequency and harmonics thereof. Therefore, if the analog voltage integration period $2^N T_{\text{CLOCK}}$ is made equal to 1/60 s, there will be a very good rejection of the power-line frequency and harmonics, often with rejections of 70 dB or more for these frequencies. The total conversion time for this case will be 1/30 s for a conversion rate of 30 conversions per second. For a 14-bit converter the corresponding clock period will be $T_{\text{CLOCK}} = (1/2^{14}) \times (1/60)\ \text{s} = \underline{1.02\ \mu\text{s}}$ and the corresponding clock frequency will be $\underline{983 \text{ kHz}}$.

In Figure 10.34c a normalized frequency response graph of the dual-slope ADC is shown. Note that in addition to the strong rejection of the frequency component at integer multiples of $f_1 = 1/2^N T_{CLOCK}$ there will also be an attenuation of the higher-frequency components. This characteristic is useful for the rejection of noise and other interference.

The dual-slope ADC can also be used for voltage ratio conversions and measurements. The number of clock cycles counted to produce the digital output code is $n = (V_A/V_R)2^N$ and therefore is directly proportional to the ratio of two voltages V_A and V_R. If a second analog input voltage V_B is used in place of the fixed reference voltage V_R, the count will be proportional to the V_A/V_B ratio, so that the digital output code will correspond precisely to the voltage ratio.

The dual-slope ADC is used as the basic element of most digital voltmeters (DVMs) and digital multimeters (DMMs). For these applications a high accuracy is needed, and slow conversion rates are acceptable. A four-digit DVM or DMM

TABLE 10.2 HIGH-PERFORMANCE ANALOG-TO-DIGITAL CONVERTERS

ADC type	Resolution (bits)	Conversion rate
Parallel comparator (flash)		
CA3300D (RCA)	6	15 MHz
AD6020KD (AD)	6	50 MHz
AD9000SD (AD)	6	75 MHz
TDC1029 (TRW)	6	100 MHz
MC10315L/10317L (MOT)	7	15 MHz
TM1070 (Telmos)	7	15 MHz
TDC1025 (TRW)	8	75 MHz
TDC1019J (TRW)	9	25 MHz
Subranging Parallel Comparator Systems		
MOD-1020 (AD)	10	20 MHz
MOD-1205 (AD)	12	5 MHz
Successive Approximation		
ADC1103 (AD)	8	1 MHz
ADC60 (BB)	8	1.1 MHz
ADC1103 (AD)	10	670 kHz
ADC60 (BB)	10	530 kHz
ADC1103 (AD)	12	300 kHz
ADC60 (BB)	12	300 kHz
HS9516-6 (HS)	16	10 kHz
ADC72 (AD)	16	20 kHz
Integrating		
Dual-slope		
ADC141 (AD)	14	25 Hz
ADB1200/LF13300 (NS)	12	28 Hz
Voltage-to-frequency		
ADC100 (BB)	12	80 Hz
ADC100 (BB)	14	20 Hz
ADC100 (BB)	16	5 Hz

Manufacturer: AD, Analog Devices; BB, Burr-Brown; HS, Hybrid Systems Corp.; MOT, Motorola; NS, National Semiconductor.

with a full-scale range of 0 to 9.999 will require a resolution of 14 binary bits, so that high-resolution ADCs are indeed required for many DVM and DMM applications.

10.2.5 High-Performance Analog-to-Digital Converters

It is of interest to see what is currently available in terms of high-performance ADCs. In Table 10.2 the resolution and conversion rate of some ADCs are listed.

PROBLEMS

10.1. (*D/A converter*) Given a D/A converter using *binary-weighted quad current sources* (see Figure P10.1). Assume that the bit current transistors have their active areas scaled such that the *current density* is the same for all of the bit current transistors.

(a) Given that $R_2 + R_3 = R_1$, find R_1, R_2, and R_3 for this 12-bit D/A converter. (*Ans.*: $R_1 = 14.000$ kΩ, $R_2 = 13.13$ kΩ, $R_3 = 875$ Ω)

(b) Given that D_1 and D_2 constitute a temperature-compensated zener diode with $V_Z = 6.3$ V and $V_F = 0.7$ V, find R_8 such that $V_{REF} = 10.24$ V. (*Ans.*: $R_8 =$ 4.63 kΩ)

(c) For a minimum value of the temperature coefficient of V_{REF} it is necessary to bias the zener diode D_1 and diode D_2 at a current level of about 7.5 mA. Find the required value of R_9. (*Ans.*: $R_9 = 432$ Ω)

(d) Find the value of R_4 needed to produce a MSB current of 1.00 mA. (*Ans.*: $R_4 = 81.92$ kΩ)

(e) Find value of R_5 needed to minimize error due to I_{BIAS} (assume that $R_6 >> R_5$). (*Ans.*: $R_5 = 82$ kΩ)

(f) For the case of unipolar operation (i.e., pins 1, 2, and 3 connected together) find the value of R_F needed to give a nominal full-scale output voltage of +10.24 V. (*Ans.*: $R_F = 10.24$ kΩ)

(g) Find R_{10} for minimum error due to I_{BIAS}. (*Ans.*: $R_{10} = 3.82$ kΩ)

(h) Find V_O for the following digital inputs (positive logic, unipolar operation):
(1) 000 . . . 000; **(2)** 100 . . . 000; **(3)** 111 . . . 111 (*Ans.*: +10.2375 V; +5.1175 V; +0.0000 V)

(i) Find the change in V_O for a 1-LSB change in the digital input. (*Ans.*: $\Delta V_O =$ 2.50 mV)

(j) Find the value of R_6 required for a ±50-mV adjustment range for the full-scale voltage. (*Ans.*: $R_6 = 25$ MΩ)

(k) Find the value of R_{11} needed for a ±10-mV offset adjustment range (unipolar case). (*Ans.*: $R_{11} = 7.7$ MΩ)

(l) **(1)** Find the emitter voltage swing on the MSB transistor such that $I_{OFF} \leqslant I_{LSB}/10$. (*Ans.*: $\Delta V_E = 248$ mV)
(2) Find I' such that $\Delta V_E = 1.0$ V. (*Ans.*: $I' = 1.1$ mA)
(3) Find R_{12} for $I' = 1.1$ mA (i.e., MSB input "high"). (*Ans.*: $R_{12} = 11.8$ kΩ)

(m) For an accuracy, referred to the output voltage, of ±1 LSB over the specified temperature range, what is the maximum allowable output error voltage, and

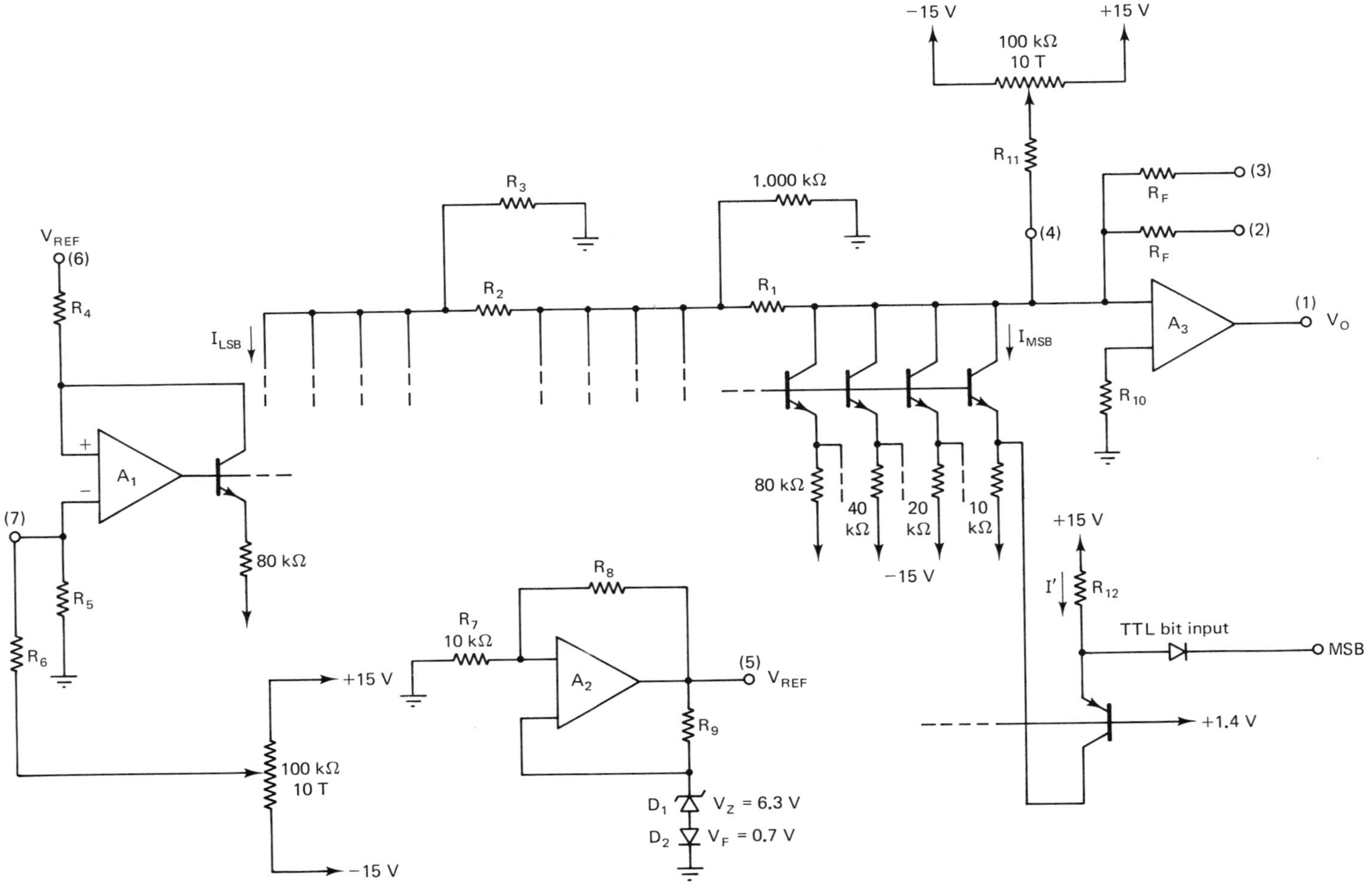

−15 V
+15 V
100 kΩ
10 T
R11
(4)
RF
(3)
RF
(2)
R3
1.000 kΩ
VREF
(6)
R4
R2
R1
ILSB
IMSB
A3
(1)
VO
R10
+
−
A1
(7)
80 kΩ
40 kΩ
20 kΩ
10 kΩ
−15 V
+15 V
R5
80 kΩ
R8
R12
I′
TTL bit input
MSB
R7
10 kΩ
R6
+15 V
A2
(5)
VREF
R9
+1.4 V
100 kΩ
10 T
D1
VZ = 6.3 V
D2
VF = 0.7 V
−15 V

Figure P10.1

the corresponding percentage error (with respect to the full-scale output voltage). (*Ans.*: ±2.50 mV, ±0.0244%)

For the following problems assume that the D/A converter is trimmed to give zero error at 25°C, and the specified operating temperature range is −25 to +75°C.

(n) **(1)** If the contribution of V_{OS} to the total maximum error is limited to $\frac{1}{5}$ of the total, what is the maximum allowable value of $TC_{V_{OS}}$? (*Ans.*: $TC_{V_{OS}}$ = 10 μV/°C)

(2) If $TC_{V_{OS}} = V_{OS}/T$, where V_{OS} is the offset voltage before trimming, what is the maximum allowable value of V_{OS}? [*Ans.*: V_{OS} = 3.0 mV (max.)]

(o) If I_{OS} is to contribute no more than $\frac{1}{5}$ of the total error, find the maximum allowable value for $TC_{I_{OS}}$. [*Ans.*: $TC_{I_{OS}}$ = 2.0 nA/°C (max.)]

(p) If the error due to the transistor leakage current is to not exceed $\frac{1}{5}$ of the total error, find the maximum allowable value for the transistor leakage current, $I_{C(\mathrm{OFF})}$. (Note that the leakage current doubles for approximately every 10°C temperature increment.) [*Ans.*: $I_{C(\mathrm{OFF})}$ = 715 pA (max.) at 25°C (corresponding to 23 nA at 75°C)]

(q) Find the maximum TCR tracking error if this tracking error is to contribute no more than one-half of the total error. Assume that the resistor network layout is such that there are no net temperature differentials between resistors. (*Ans.*: ΔTC_R = 4.88 ppm/°C)

(r) Find the resistor ratio tolerance required if this is not to contribute more than one-half of the total error. Note that the ratio tolerance of the resistors associated with the MSB and the next significant bit will be the most important, since the other bits, going down to the LSB, will contribute successively smaller amounts of current. (*Ans.*: 0.0244%)

(s) The offset voltage between the bit current transistors can produce a contribution to the total error, especially with respect to the matching between the MSB and the next significant bit (i.e., the second bit) transistor. Find the maximum allowable offset voltage is this is to contribute no more than $\frac{1}{5}$ of the total error. Note that the transistor active areas are scaled to produce equal current densities. (*Ans.*: ΔV_{BE} = 0.977 mV)

(t) If the $TC_{V_{\mathrm{REF}}}$ is to contribute no more than $\frac{1}{5}$ of the total error, find the maximum allowable value for $TC_{V_{\mathrm{REF}}}$ and for TC_{V_Z}. (*Ans.*: 1.0 ppm/°C for both $TC_{V_{\mathrm{REF}}}$ and TC_{V_Z})

(u) If pin 2 is connected to pin 1 as before, but pin 3 is now connected to V_{REF} (i.e., pins 5, 6, and 3 connected together):

(1) Show that bipolar operation is achieved with $V_O = -10.24$ for a digital input of 1111 . . . 111 and $V_O = +10.235$ for a digital input of 00000 . . . 000.

(2) Find ΔV_O for a 1-LSB change in the digital input. (*Ans.*: ΔV_O = 5.0 mV)

(v) If a $\frac{1}{2}$-LSB settling time of 1.0 μs is required for a full-scale output voltage of 10 V, what is the required slewing rate of the operational amplifier A_3? [*Ans.*: $SR \simeq$ 10 V/μs (min.)]

10.2. (*Effect of reference voltage temperature coefficient on ADC accuracy*) A 10-bit ADC has a reference voltage of 10.24 V. The maximum error of this ADC is not to exceed $\pm\frac{1}{2}$ LSB over the operating temperature range 0 to 50°C, and the error is adjusted to zero at 25°C. Find the maximum allowable value for $TC_{V_{\mathrm{REF}}}$. Express the result in terms of μV/°C and ppm/°C. (*Ans.*: ±200 μV/°C, ±19.5 ppm/°C)

***10.3.** (*ADC with reference voltage temperature compensation*) The reference voltage of an ADC has a temperature coefficient of 100 μV/°C. This reference voltage will be temperature compensated by a circuit that produces a compensation voltage given by $V_{comp} = A(\Delta T + B\Delta T^2)$ where $\Delta T = T - 25°C$ and $B = 0.05(1/°C)$. Use a computer to plot the variation of the compensated reference voltage with temperature for various values of A over the temperature range of 10 to 40°C.

(a) Find the value of A that results in the smallest change in the compensated reference voltage and find the corresponding fractional change in the reference voltage.

(b) If the compensated reference voltage is to be used for an N-bit ADC, find the maximum value for N for which the error due to the temperature variation of the reference voltage will not exceed $\pm\frac{1}{2}$ LSB.

10.4. (*Flash ADC encoder logic*)

(a) Show that a general $2^N - 1$: N encoder to go from a "thermometer code" to a binary code can be based on the following logic gate configuration:

$Q_{LSB} = (Q_1 \oplus Q_2) + (Q_3 \oplus Q_4) + (Q_5 \oplus Q_6) + (Q_7 \oplus Q_8) + \cdots$

$Q_{2SB} = (Q_2 \oplus Q_4) + (Q_6 \oplus Q_8) + (Q_{10} \oplus Q_{12}) + \cdots$

$Q_{3SB} = (Q_4 \oplus Q_8) + (Q_{12} \oplus Q_{16}) + \cdots$

$\vdots$

(b) Show that for a 4-bit flash ADC encoder this will reduce to

$Q_{LSB} = (Q_1 \oplus Q_2) + (Q_3 \oplus Q_4) + (Q_5 \oplus Q_6) + (Q_7 \oplus Q_8) + (Q_9 \oplus Q_{10}) + (Q_{11} \oplus Q_{12}) + (Q_{13} \oplus Q_{14}) + Q_{15}$

$Q_{2SB} = (Q_2 \oplus Q_4) + (Q_6 \oplus Q_8) + (Q_{10} \oplus Q_{12}) + Q_{14}$

$Q_{3SB} = (Q_4 \oplus Q_8) + Q_{12}$

$Q_{MSB} = Q_8$

10.5. (*Flash ADC encoder logic*) An N-bit parallel comparator ADC uses type D flip-flops with complementary outputs to latch the comparator output voltage levels. Show that the following logic gate configuration using AND and OR gates can be used to convert the thermometer code to a binary code.

$Q_{LSB} = (Q_1 \cdot \overline{Q}_2) + (Q_3 \cdot \overline{Q}_4) + (Q_5 \cdot \overline{Q}_6) + \cdots$

$Q_{2SB} = (Q_2 \cdot \overline{Q}_4) + (Q_6 \cdot \overline{Q}_8) + (Q_{10} \cdot \overline{Q}_{12}) + \cdots$

$Q_{3SB} = (Q_4 \cdot \overline{Q}_8) + (Q_{12} \cdot \overline{Q}_{16}) + \cdots$

$\vdots$

10.6. (*Flash ADC encoder that uses only NOR gates*) Develop a general thermometer code to binary code encoder that uses only NOR gates. This will be for an N-bit parallel comparator ADC with the comparator output levels latched by D flip-flops with complementary outputs.

10.7. (*3-Bit flash ADC encoder*) Show a logic gate diagram of a NOR gate encoder for a 3-bit parallel comparator ADC.

10.8. (*Flash ADC design*)

(a) Show that the number of comparators needed for an N-bit flash ADC is $2^N - 1$.

(b) Show that the reference voltage levels needed for the $2^N - 1$ comparators will be given by $V_{REF} = (M - \frac{1}{2})V_{FS}/(2^N - 1)$, where M takes on integer values from 1 to $2^N - 1$. This is for the condition that the quantization will not exceed $\pm\frac{1}{2}$ LSB at any point.

(c) A 4-bit flash ADC is to have a full-scale analog input voltage of +15.0 V. Find the reference voltage levels needed for the comparators such the quantization error will not exceed $\pm\frac{1}{2}$ LSB at any point.

(d) For the comparator of part (c) find the maximum allowable net error due to the comparator reference voltages and the drift in the comparator offset voltage such that the total conversion error will not exceed ±1 LSB at any point in the 0- to +15.0-V analog input voltage range. (*Ans.*: ±0.50 V)

10.9. (*Combining ADCs to increase the number of bits*) Show how two N-bit parallel comparator ADCs can be combined to produce an $N + 1$ bit ADC. Each ADC has a $-V_{REF}$ and a $+V_{REF}$ input terminal for the two ends of the reference voltage divider. Each ADC has D_O through D_{N-1} active high tri-state outputs plus an active high overange (OVR) output. There is also an active high-chip enable (CE) input that puts the D_O through D_{N-1} outputs into the high-Z state. The total conversion range is to be from −5.12 V to +5.12 V.

10.10. [*8-Bit cascaded* (*subranging*) *flash ADC*] An 8-bit subranging flash ADC uses two 4-bit ADCs. Each of the two ADCs has a full-scale input voltage range of +15.9375 V. The DAC produces a maximum output voltage of +15.0 V.

(a) Design the difference amplifier and specify its transfer function. (*Ans.*: A_v = 16)

(b) Find the number of comparators required for each of the two ADCs and the reference voltage levels needed for each comparator. The reference voltage levels should be such that the quantization error will not exceed $\pm\frac{1}{2}$ LSB at any point.

(c) Find the 8-bit digital output code and the quantization error both in absolute terms and as a fraction of an LSB voltage change for the following analog input voltages (volts):

(1) 0.000 (*Ans.*: 0000 0000, 0 V or 0 LSB)
(2) 0.1000 (*Ans.*: 0000 0010, 0.025 V or 0.4 LSB)
(3) 2.603 (*Ans.*: 0010 1010, 0.022 V or 0.352 LSB)
(4) 5.324 (*Ans.*: 0101 0101, −0.0115 V or −0.184 LSB)
(5) 7.276 (*Ans.*: 0111 0100, −0.026 V or −0.416 LSB)
(6) 12.870 (*Ans.*: 1100 1110, 0.005 V or 0.08 LSB)
(7) 14.220 (*Ans.*: 1110 0100, 0.030 V or 0.48 LSB)
(8) 15.375 (*Ans.*: 1111 0110, 0 V or 0 LSB)
(9) 15.772 (*Ans.*: 1111 1100, −0.022 V or −0.352 LSB)
(10) 15.9530 (*Ans.*: 1111 1111, −0.0155 V or −0.248 LSB)
(11) 15.9375 (*Ans.*: 1111 1111, 0 V or 0 LSB)

(d) For a $\pm\frac{1}{2}$-LSB accuracy (not including the quantization error) find the required tolerance limits for the reference voltage levels of the comparators of the LSB ADC and the MSB ADC. (*Ans.*: ±500 mV, ±31.25 mV)

***10.11.** (*Successive approximation ADC simulation*) Write a computer program to simulate the operation of an 8-bit successive approximation ADC with a full-scale analog input voltage level of 10.00 V. Using this program, obtain a plot of the ADC transfer characteristic and a plot of the quantization error versus analog input voltage.

REFERENCES

ANALOG DEVICES, INC., *Analog–Digital Conversion Notes*, Analog Devices, Inc., P.O. Box 796, Norwood, MA 02062.

CONNELLY, J. A., *Analog Integrated Circuits*, Wiley, 1975.

GARRETT, P. H., *Analog I/O Design*, Reston, 1981.

GRAEME, J. G., G. E. TOBEY, and L. P. HUELSMAN, *Operational Amplifiers—Design and Applications*, McGraw-Hill, 1971.

GREBENE, A. B., *Analog Integrated Circuit Design*, Van Nostrand Reinhold, 1972.

GRINICH, V. H., and H. G. JACKSON, *Introduction to Integrated Circuits*, McGraw-Hill, 1975.

HOESCHEL, D. F., *Analog-to-Digital/Digital-to-Analog Conversion Techniques*, Wiley, 1968.

MILLMAN, J., *Microelectronics*, McGraw-Hill, 1979.

MITRA, S. K., *An Introduction to Digital and Analog Integrated Circuits and Applications*, Harper & Row, 1980.

STOUT, D. F., *Handbook of Microcircuit Design and Applications*, McGraw-Hill, 1980.

TAUB, H., and D. SCHILLING, *Digital Integrated Electronics*, Chap. 14, McGraw-Hill, 1977.

WAIT, J. V., *Introduction to Operational Amplifier Theory and Applications*, McGraw-Hill, 1975.

Analog Switches and Sample-and-Hold Circuits

11

11.1 ANALOG SWITCHES

Analog switches use transistors to serve as fast on–off switches. The ideal analog switch will have zero resistance in the "on" state and an infinite impedance in the "off" state. Although either bipolar or field-effect transistors can be used as the active element of an analog switch most analog switches use FETs. This is because of the inherent symmetry of FETs and the offset voltage that is present in bipolar transistors as shown in Figure 11.1. While the offset voltage (V_{CE} at $I_C = 0$) of bipolar transistors will generally be only a few millivolts, it can produce significant errors in the transmission of low-level analog signals. Another advantage of FETs over bipolar transistors for analog switch applications is the very high input impedance and very small gate current of the FETs compared to those of bipolar transistors.

Bipolar transistors can offer the advantage of relatively small "on" resistance, down to as low as 3 to 30 Ω, but there are VMOS and DMOS transistors available with comparably low values of "on" resistance. Integrated-circuit analog switches generally incorporate the driving circuitry and several electrically independent JFET or MOSFET switching transistors in one package.

As mentioned above, FETs are very useful for analog switches because they are inherently symmetrical devices and they have no offset voltage (i.e., $V_{DS} = 0$ when $I_{DS} = 0$). The drain-to-source "on" resistance, $r_{ds(\mathrm{ON})}$, of a FET is, however, a function of the gate-to-source voltage, V_{GS}. If we refer to Figure 11.2, we see that if the control or gate voltage of the FET switch is kept at a constant value, the "on" resistance will vary with the analog signal level. In the extreme case, if

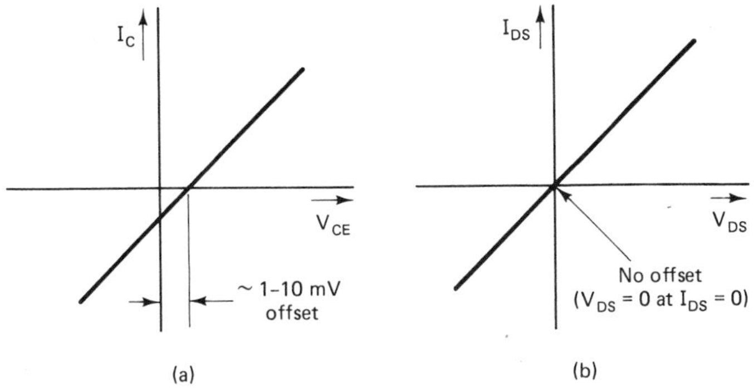

Figure 11.1 Comparison of bipolar transistor and field-effect transistor characteristics; (a) bipolar transistor; (b) field-effect transistor.

the analog input voltage swing is large enough, it can actually cause the FET to switch off during part of the analog voltage swing.

One simple solution to this problem of the variation of $r_{ds\,(\text{ON})}$ is shown by the circuit of Figure 11.3. Let us consider, for example, the case of a JFET with a pinch-off voltage of $V_P = -5.0$ V. We will assume that the control voltage is -10 V for turning the switch off and $+10$ V for the switch to be turned on. We will also assume that the analog input voltage swing does not exceed ± 5.0 V peak.

When the control voltage is -10 V diode D_1 will be turned on, and since the gate-to-source voltage of the FET is greater than the pinch-off voltage, the FET will be turned off. When the control voltage is at $+10$ V diode D_1 will be turned off. The gate-to-source voltage of the FET will be essentially zero due to the very small voltage drop across R_G that is the result of the very small gate leakage current and diode reverse leakage current. Since $V_{GS} \simeq 0$ the FET switch will be fully on, and V_{GS} will stay constant at essentially zero volts throughout the analog input voltage swing.

Although this simple circuit does offer the advantage of a fairly constant $r_{ds\,(\text{ON})}$ it does suffer the disadvantage of control signal feed-through to the output via R_G. In addition, at higher frequencies the gate voltage will no longer exactly follow the

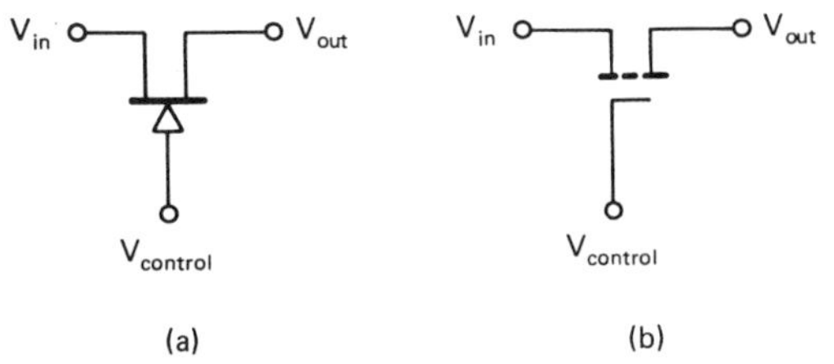

Figure 11.2 (a) JFET and (b) MOSFET analog switches.

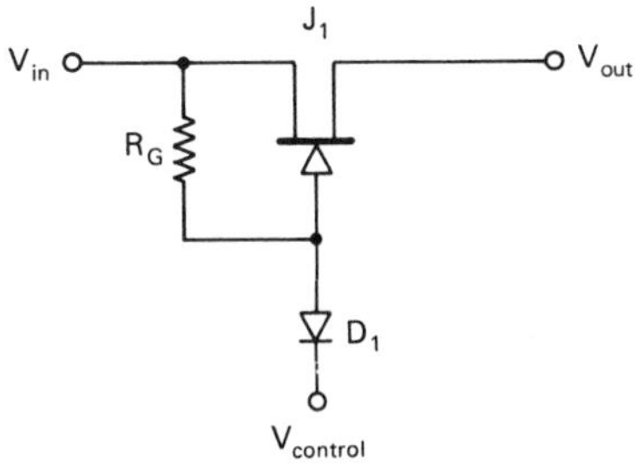

Figure 11.3 JFET analog switch with constant "on" resistance.

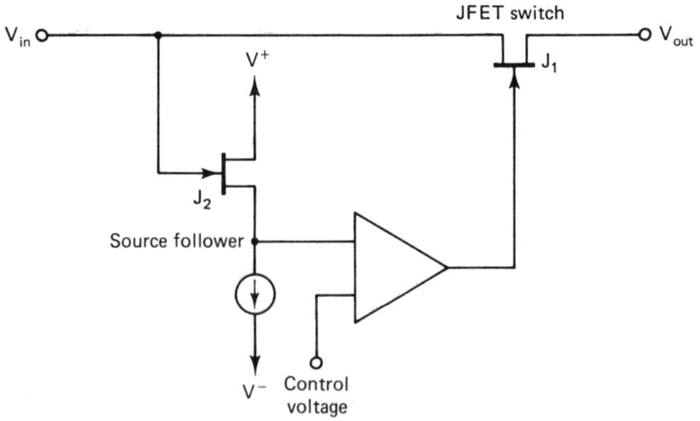

Figure 11.4 JFET analog switch with source follower to keep "on" resistance constant.

source voltage due to the effect of R_G and the combination of the diode junction capacitance and the FET gate capacitance.

Another type of FET switch circuit that acts to keep V_{GS} and therefore $r_{ds\,(ON)}$ constant is shown in Figure 11.4. A JFET source follower is used together with appropriate d-c level shifting to keep the V_{GS} of the JFET switch constant at near zero volts in the "on" state. This type of JFET analog switch configuration will be examined in more detail in the next section. A third means of minimizing the variation of the switch resistance is the CMOS analog switch to be considered later.

11.1.1 Monolithic IC Analog Switch

An example of a monolithic analog JFET switch is the LF11331/11332/11201/11202 series (National Semiconductor). This IC contains four independent SPST JFET switches and the associated control circuitry, as illustrated by the block diagram of Figure 11.5.

The control circuit of this device acts to keep the "on" resistance constant at about 150 Ω (typ.), 200 Ω (max.) over an analog signal range of from −10 to +10 V, varying by only about 10 Ω over this entire input voltage range.

In the "off" condition the switch leakage current will be less than 1 nA at 25°C and for $V_{in} - V_{out} = 20$ V. This ensures very good input-to-output isolation. The "off" state isolation will, however, decrease markedly with increasing frequency due to the parasitic drain-to-source capacitance of the FET switch. Thus at a frequency of 1.0 MHz the "off" state isolation will be −50 dB with a load resistance of 680 Ω. This corresponds to a drain-to-source resistance of about 0.7 pF.

In Figure 11.6 a simplified diagram of the control circuitry of one of the four identical analog switches of this IC is shown. When the logic input voltage at the base of Q_1 is high, Q_3 will be turned off and Q_5 will be on. Transistor J_6 has $V_{GS} = 0$ and acts as a current source of strength I_{DSS}. The current supplied by J_6 will be split between the Q_5 branch and the J_4 branch of the circuit. The current through

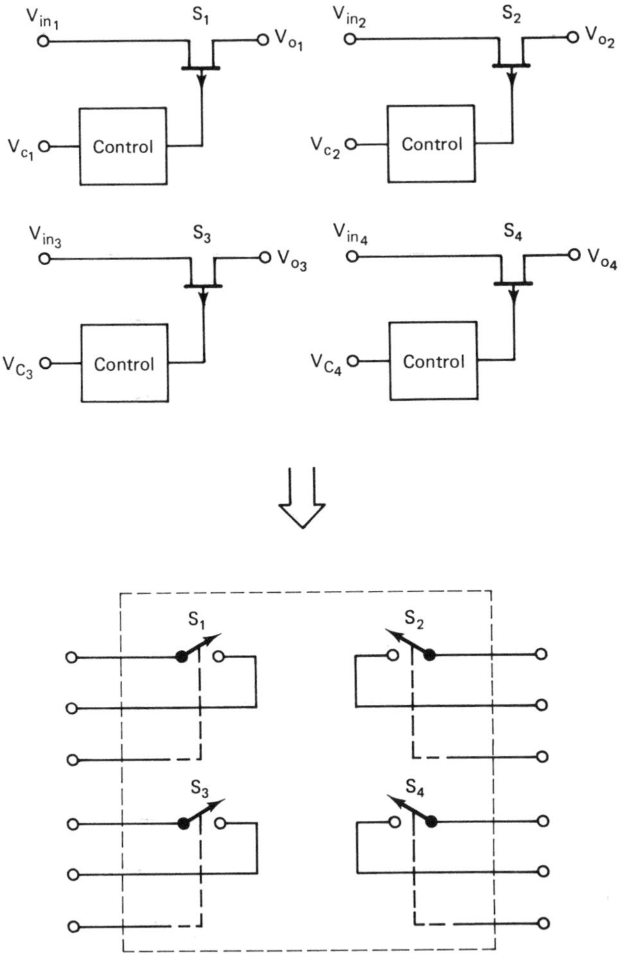

Figure 11.5 Block diagram of quad bilateral JFET analog switch: LF11331 (National Semiconductor).

J_4 will be given approximately by $I_4 = I_{DSS}(R_2/R_2 + R_3)$. If this resistance ratio is suitably chosen the gate-to-source voltage of J_4 can be made to be approximately equal to the diode drop such that $V_{GS_4} \simeq V_D \simeq +0.7$ V.

The gate-to-source voltage of the analog switch transistor J_5 will be given by $V_{GS_5} = -V_{D_4} + V_{D_5} + V_{D_6} - V_{GS_4} \simeq 0$. Thus J_4, in acting as a source follower in conjunction with the d-c level shifting resulting from diodes D_4, D_5, and D_6, will act to keep the gate-to-source voltage of the analog switch transistor J_5 approximately constant at zero volts independent of the analog signal level.

When the logic input voltage at the base of Q_1 goes low, Q_3 will be turned on. The resulting increase in the current through R_2 will raise the voltage at the emitter of Q_5 high enough to turn Q_5 off. When Q_5 is turned off, the voltage at the gate of J_5 is pulled up to near the positive supply voltage $+V_{DD}$ and J_5 is therefore turned off.

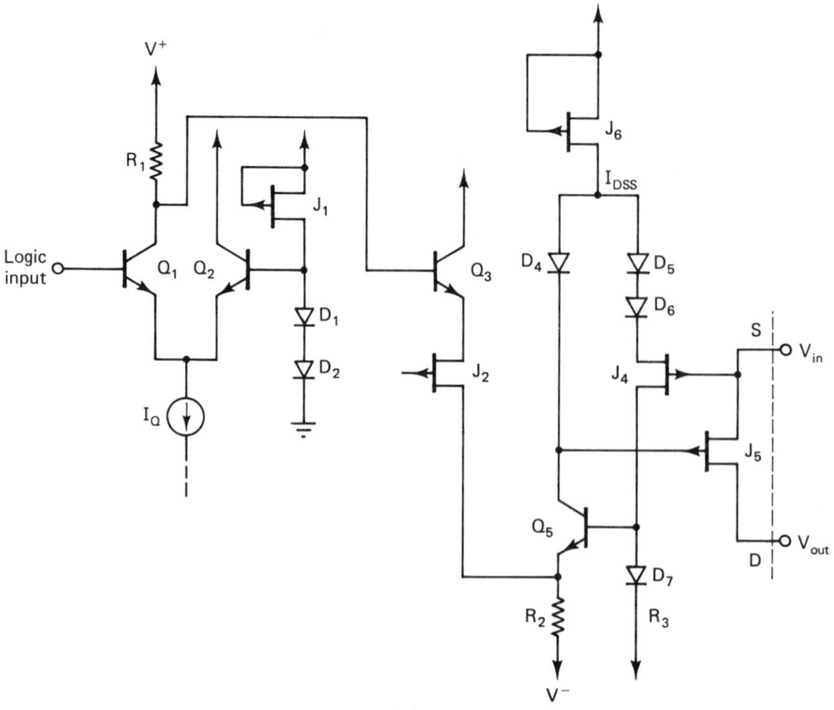

Figure 11.6 Monolithic IC analog switch: LF11331 (National Semiconductor).

11.1.2 CMOS Analog Switch

The CMOS analog switch consists of a parallel combination of an NMOS transistor and a PMOS transistor and the associated driving circuitry, which includes an inverter to provide the two opposite polarity control or gate voltages for the two MOS transistors as shown in Figure 11.7.

The drain-to-source "on" resistance, $r_{ds(\text{ON})}$, of the MOS transistors will be a function of the gate-to-source voltage $V_{GS} = V_G - V_{\text{in}}$, where V_{in} is the analog input voltage. In Figure 11.8 curves of $r_{ds(\text{ON})}$ as a function of V_{in} are given for each transistor. Also given is a curve shown the net switch "on" resistance which is the parallel combination of the $r_{ds(\text{ON})}$ values for the NMOS and PMOS transistors. Note that whereas the $r_{ds(\text{ON})}$ of each transistor will vary considerably with the input voltage level, the variations are in opposite directions such that the variation in the net switch "on" resistance r_{ON} will be much less.

As V_{in} increases in the positive direction the NMOS transistor resistance will increase substantially due to the decrease in the V_{GS} of this transistor. When V_{in} reaches a value of $V_C - V_{t(\text{NMOS})}$, where V_C is the control voltage applied to the gate of the NMOS transistor, the NMOS transistor will turn off and remain off for all higher values of V_{in}. At the same time the gate-to-source voltage of the PMOS transistor is increasing in the negative direction. This acts to increase the density of holes in the inversion-layer channel of the PMOS transistor, so that the $r_{ds(\text{ON})}$ of

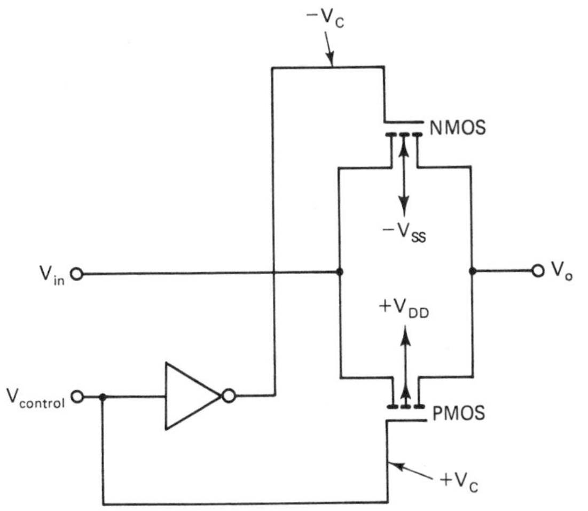

Figure 11.7 Basic CMOS analog switch.

this transistor will be decreasing. The decrease in the $r_{ds(\text{ON})}$ of the PMOS transistor will partially compensate for the increase in the resistance of the NMOS transistor. A similar process will occur for a negative-going analog input voltage, except that the roles of the two transistors will be interchanged.

Analysis of CMOS switch resistance. To gain further insight into the operation of the CMOS analog switch we will look at a simplified analysis of the switch resistance. For small values of V_{DS} ($V_{DS} \lesssim V_P/3$) the drain-to-source conductance g_{ds} will be directly proportional to the mobile charge in the inversion-layer channel that exists between the source and drain regions. The drain-to-source conductance will be given approximately by the equation $g_{ds} = Q_{\text{channel}}\mu(W/L)$, where Q_{channel} is the charge per unit area in the inversion layer, μ is the mobility of the charge carriers, L is the length of the channel, and W is the width of the channel.

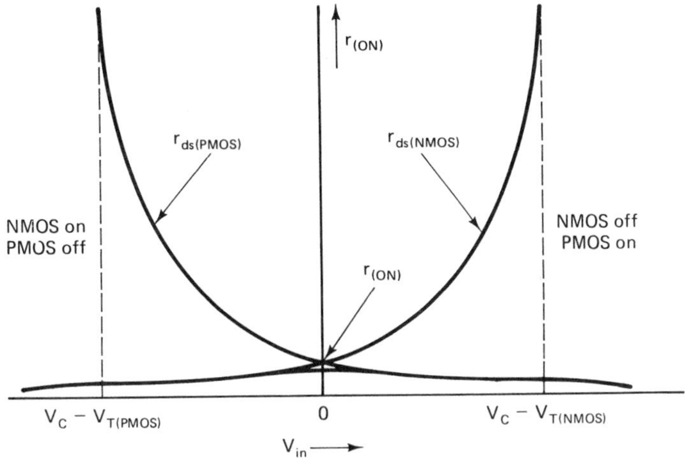

Figure 11.8 Variation of switch "on" resistance with analog input voltage.

The charge density in the inversion layer will be given by $Q_{\text{channel}} = C_{ox}(V_{GS} - V_t)$, where $C_{ox} = \epsilon_{ox}/t_{ox}$ is the capacitance per unit area between the gate and the channel, $\epsilon_{ox} = 3.8\epsilon_o$ is the dielectric permittivity of the gate oxide, and t_{ox} is the thickness of the gate oxide. Putting all of this together, we obtain

$$\begin{aligned} g_{ds} &= Q_{\text{channel}}\mu \frac{W}{L} = \mu C_{ox} \frac{W}{L}(V_{GS} - V_t) = \mu \frac{\epsilon_{ox}}{t_{ox}} \frac{W}{L}(V_{GS} - V_t) \\ &= K(V_{GS} - V_t) \end{aligned} \tag{11.1}$$

where $K = \mu(\epsilon_{ox}/t_{ox})(W/L)$ and V_t is the threshold voltage.

The net switch "on" conductance of a CMOS switch will be given by

$$g_{(ON)} = g_{ds\,(NMOS)} + g_{ds\,(PMOS)} = K_{NMOS}(V_{GS\,N} - V_{t\,N}) + K_{PMOS}(V_{GS\,P} - V_{t\,P}) \tag{11.2}$$

Since $V_{GS\,N} = V_C - V_{in}$ and $V_{GS\,P} = -V_C - V_{IN}$, the equation for $g_{(ON)}$ can be written as

$$g_{(ON)} = K_{NMOS}(V_C - V_{in} - V_{t\,N}) + K_{PMOS}(-V_C - V_{in} - V_{t\,P})$$

If we now consider the simple case of NMOS and PMOS transistors with identical characteristics such that $K_{NMOS} = -K_{PMOS} = K$ and $V_{t\,N} = -V_{t\,P} = V_t$, we obtain

$$g_{(ON)} = K(V_C - V_{in} - V_t) - K(-V_C - V_{in} + V_t) = 2K(V_C - V_t)$$

Note that the switch conductance $g_{(ON)}$ is now independent of the analog input voltage when both transistors are on, as shown in Figure 11.9. When the analog input voltage is greater than $V_C - V_t$ the NMOS transistor will be off and the switch conductance will be due only to the PMOS transistor as given by $g_{(ON)} = K(V_{in} - V_C - V_t)$. At the other extreme, when $V_{in} < -(V_C - V_t)$ the PMOS transistor will be off and the switch conductance will be due only to that of the NMOS transistor and will be given by $g_{(ON)} = K(V_C - V_{in} - V_t)$.

Let us now consider a representative sample calculation. We will choose the

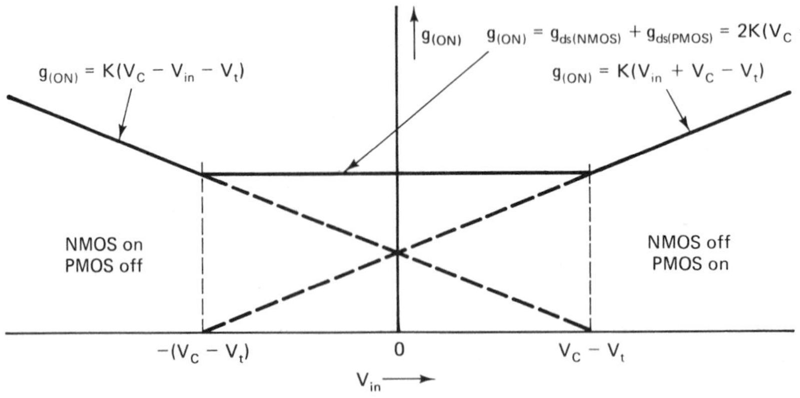

Figure 11.9 CMOS analog switch conductance versus analog input voltage: $K_{NMOS} = -K_{PMOS} = K$; $V_{t(NMOS)} = -V_{t(PMOS)} = V_t$.

following device parameters: t_{ox} = 1000 Å, = 0.1 μm, L = 3 μm, W = 300 μm, μ = 200 cm²/V-s, and V_t = 3.0 V. With these parameters the oxide capacitance becomes $C_{ox} = \epsilon_{ox}/t_{ox} = 3.363 \times 10^{-8}$ F/cm². The coefficient K becomes $K = \mu C_{ox}(W/L) = 200$ cm²/V-s $\times 3.363 \times 10^{-8}$ F/cm² $\times$ 300 μm/3 μm = $\underline{0.673 \times 10^{-3}}$ $\underline{\text{S/V}}$ = $\underline{0.673 \text{ mS/V}} \simeq \underline{1/1.5 \text{ k}\Omega\text{-V}}$.

If we again assume that the NMOS and PMOS transistor have identical parameters such that $K_N = -K_P = K$ and $V_{t_N} = -V_{t_P} = V_t$, the switch conductance will be given by

$$\begin{aligned}
&(1)\quad g_{(ON)} = 2K(V_C - V_t) &&\text{for} \quad -(V_C - V_t) < V_{in} < (V_C - V_t) \\
&(2)\quad g_{(ON)} = K(V_{in} + V_C - V_t) &&\text{for} \quad V_{in} > (V_C - V_t) \qquad (11.3)\\
&(3)\quad g_{(ON)} = K(V_C - V_{in} - V_t) &&\text{for} \quad V_{in} < -(V_C - V_t)
\end{aligned}$$

A graph of $g_{(ON)}$ versus V_{in} is presented in Figure 11.10a for the case of V_C = 5.0 V. This will require a total supply voltage of $V_{DD} - V_{SS}$ = 10 V for the CMOS switch. In Figure 11.10b a similar graph is given, but for the case of V_C = 9.0 V, which corresponds to a total supply voltage of 18 V.

Examples of CMOS analog switches. An example of a CMOS analog switch is the CD4016 (National Semiconductor), which contains four independent CMOS switches and the associated driving circuitry in one IC package. A simplified diagram of one of the four CMOS switches is shown in Figure 11.11. In Figure 11.12 the variation of the "on" resistance with the analog input voltage is shown. We note that although this switch is capable of operating with either polarity or analog input voltage, there will still be a substantial variation of the "on" resistance with input voltage. The "on" resistance will have a maximum value of 500 Ω when the total supply voltage is 15 V and will be almost 900 Ω if the supply voltage is 10 V, so that we see that the "on" resistance can be quite large.

Another example of a quad bilateral CMOS analog switch is the CD4066. Like the CD4016, this IC contains four independent switches and the associated driving circuitry. A diagram of one of the four switches is presented in Figure 11.13. Unlike the CD4016, in which the body (or "substrate") regions of the NMOS and PMOS transistors are tied to the $-V_{SS}$ and $+V_{DD}$ supplies, respectively, the body (P-type well) of the NMOS transistor in the CD4066 will not be tied to $-V_{SS}$. When the control input logic level is high, the Q_1–Q_2 and Q_3–Q_4 CMOS switches will be turned *on* and Q_5 will be turned *off*. The body (P-well) of the NMOS switch transistor Q_1 will now be connected to the analog input voltage via the Q_3–Q_4 CMOS switch. As a result, the source-to-body voltage of Q_1 will be essentially zero. This will ensure a minimum threshold voltage and a minimum "on" resistance for this transistor.

When the control input logic level is low, the Q_1–Q_2 and Q_3–Q_4 CMOS pairs will be *off* and Q_5 will be *on*. The body voltage of Q_1 will now be pulled down to near the negative supply voltage, $-V_{SS}$. This will act to minimize the capacitative input-to-output feedthrough of the Q_1–Q_2 switch in the "off" state.

We have seen that when the Q_1–Q_2 switch is on, the body (P-well) of Q_1 will be essentially equal to the source voltage. This will result in a lower threshold voltage

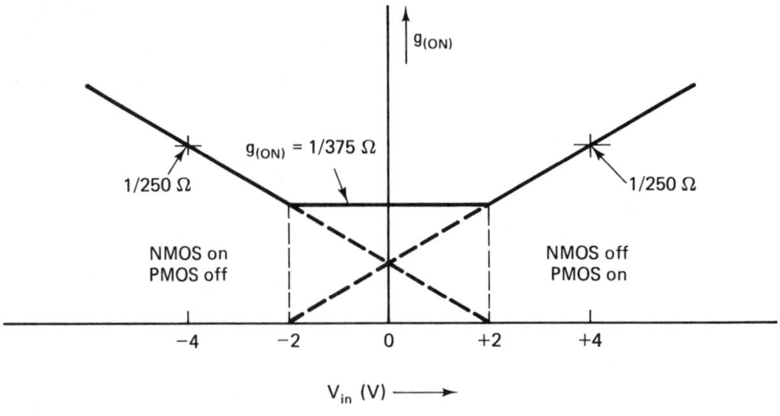

(a)

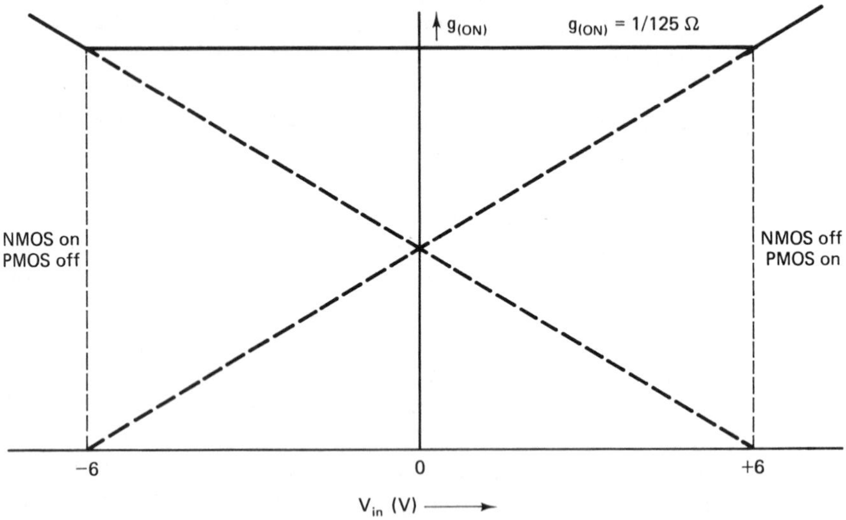

(b)

Figure 11.10 Example of CMOS switch resistance versus analog input voltage: $K_{NMOS} = -K_{PMOS} = 1/1.5\ k\Omega - V$; $V_{t(NMOS)} = -V_{t(PMOS)} = +3.0$ V: (a) $V_{DD} - V_{SS} = 10$ V; (b) $V_{DD} - V_{SS} = 18$ V.

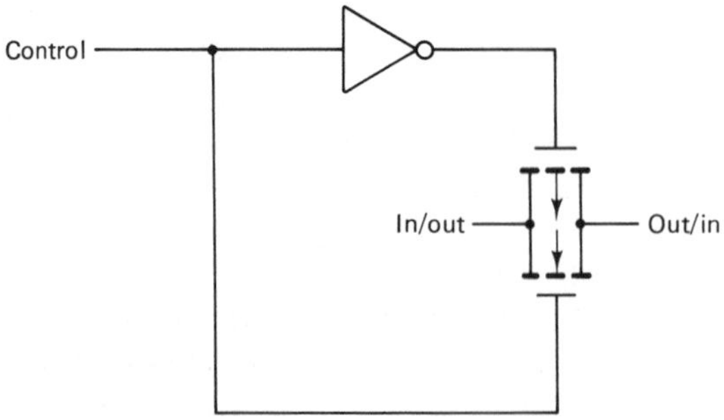

Figure 11.11 Simplified diagram of a CMOS switch (National Semiconductor).

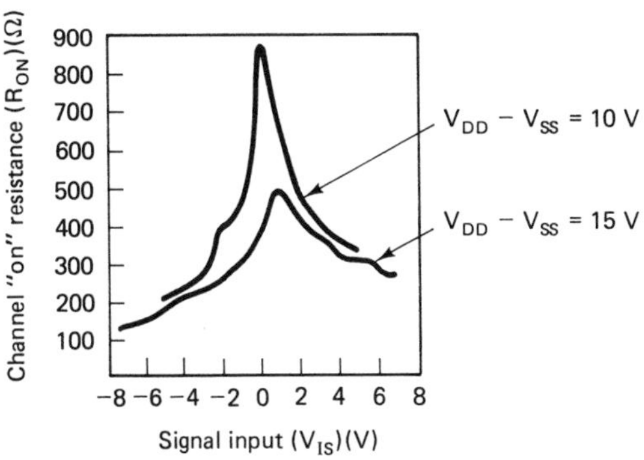

Figure 11.12 Variation of "on" resistance with analog input voltage in a CMOS switch (National Semiconductor).

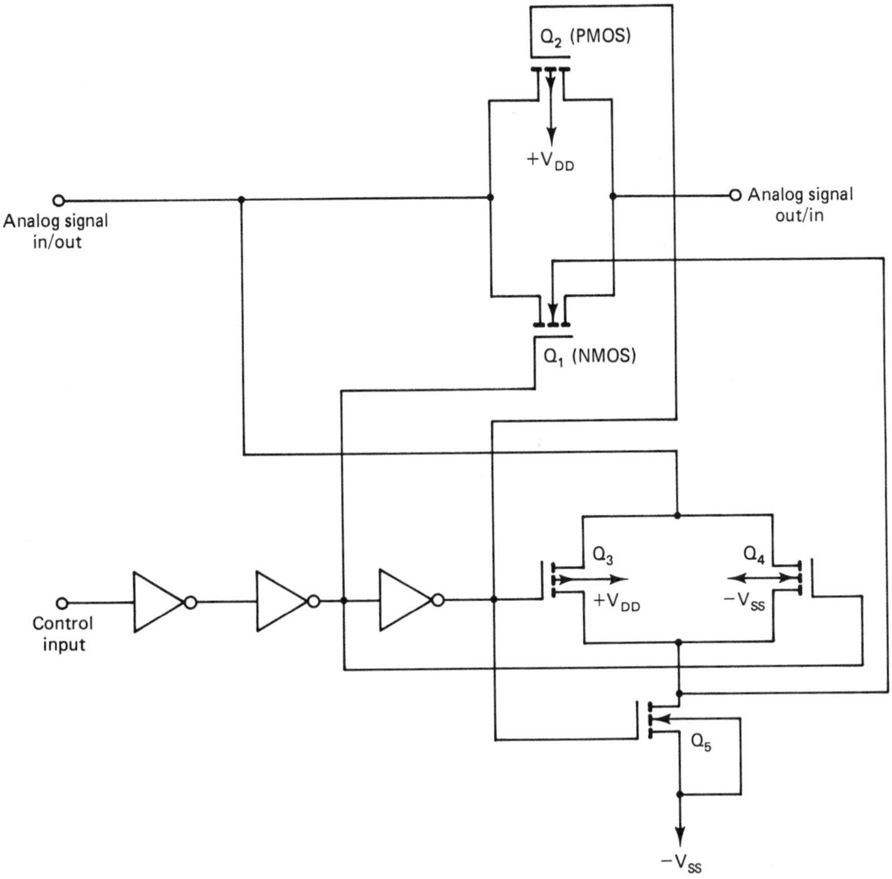

Figure 11.13 CMOS analog switch with reduced resistance variation: CD4066 (National Semiconductor).

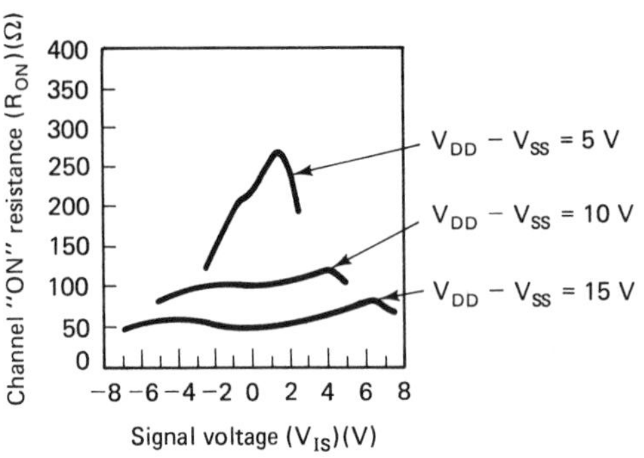

Figure 11.14 Circuit configuration for lower, more constant "on" resistance in CMOS switch.

and a smaller "on" resistance. This will be especially evident in the region when V_{in} is close to zero, for which case both transistors will be operating with a gate-to-source voltage that is just a little above the threshold voltage.

This circuit configuration produces a lower and more constant "on" resistance, as evidenced by Figure 11.14. For the case of $V_{DD}-V_{SS} = 10$ V the "on" resistance will be down in the range 80 to 110 Ω over an input voltage span of −7 to +7 V. If the net supply voltage is increased to 15 V, the "on" resistance will be down in the range of 50 to 70 Ω over the same input voltage span.

An example of a very fast, low resistance CMOS analog switch, is the HI-201HS (Harris). This monolithic IC uses dielectic isolation to achieve very low parasitic capacitances and contains four SPST analog switches in a 16-pin DIP package. The turn-on time is only 30 ns, the "on" resistance is just 30 Ω, and the leakage current in the "off" state is only 0.3 nA.

11.1.3 Applications of Analog Switches

There are many applications of analog switches, including the following:

1. Sample-and-hold (S/H) circuits
2. Analog multiplexing and demultiplexing
3. Chopper stabilization of amplifiers
4. Digital-to-analog (D/A) conversion
5. "Integrate-and-dump" circuits
6. Programmable op-amp transfer characteristics, such as digital control of gain, frequency response, and phase shift
7. Signal gating and squelch control

The subject of sample-and-hold circuits is an important one and will be treated separately in a later section of this chapter. Some of the other analog switch applications listed above will now be discussed briefly.

Programmable op-amp transfer characteristics. In Figure 11.15 an example of a programmable gain op amp is shown. The net feedback impedance can be changed by digital control of the various analog switches, which will in turn

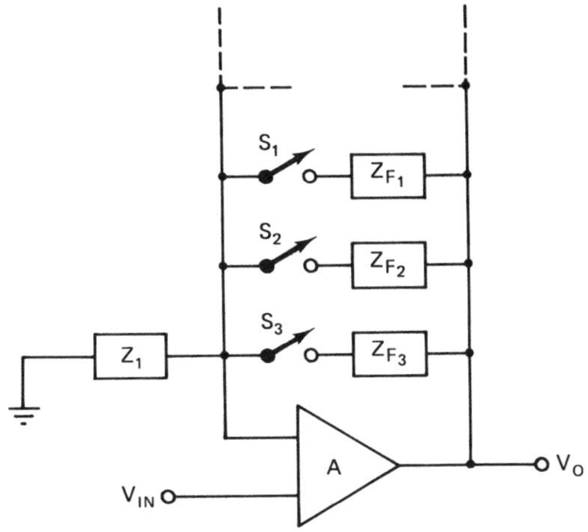

Figure 11.15 Programmable operational amplifier.

change the closed-loop gain characteristics of the operational amplifier. If the impedances are all purely resistive in nature, the principal change involved will be the magnitude of the closed-loop gain. If, however, the impedances have reactive components, the frequency response and the phase-shift characteristics can also be changed.

Integrate-and-dump circuit. In Figure 11.16 an "integrate-and-dump" circuit is shown. If the JFET switch S_1 is "off," the output voltage will be the integral of the input voltage as given by

$$V_o = \frac{1}{C}\int_0^t i_{\text{in}}\,dt = \frac{1}{RC}\int_0^t (V_{\text{in}} - V_{OS})\,dt$$
$$= \frac{1}{RC}\int_0^t V_{\text{in}}\,dt - \frac{1}{RC}\int_0^t V_{OS}\,dt \tag{11.4}$$

where $t = 0$ represents the beginning of the integration period. We see that in the absence of the JFET switch the effect of the amplifier offset voltage V_{OS} will become increasingly pronounced as time increases. To prevent this from happening it is therefore desirable to reset the circuit periodically by turning on switch S_1 to discharge the capacitor. When S_1 then turns off again, the integration process will start all

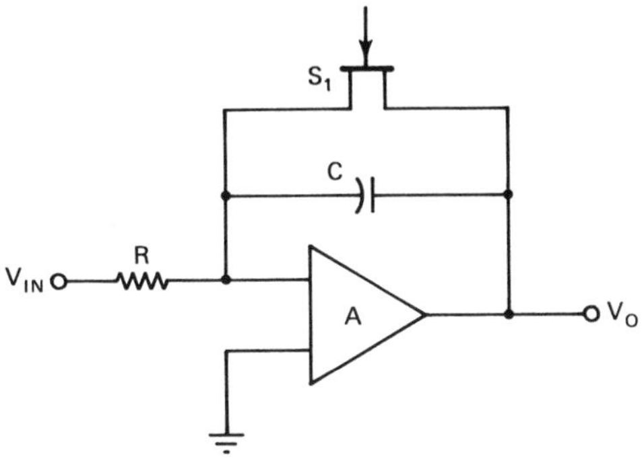

Figure 11.16 "Integrate-and-dump" circuit.

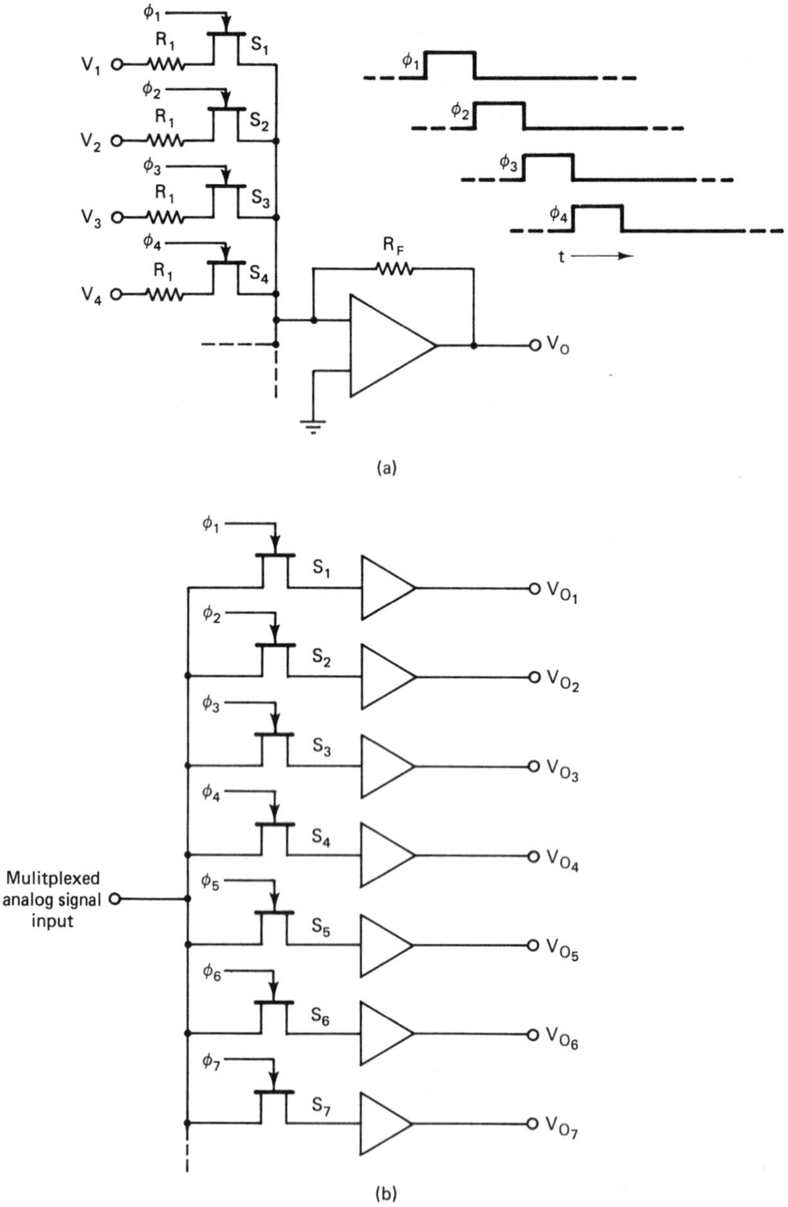

Figure 11.17 Analog (a) multiplexing and (b) demultiplexing circuits.

over again. This circuit can also be useful in applications where it is necessary to integrate an input voltage over some specified limited period of time.

Analog multiplexing and demultiplexing circuits. In Figure 11.17a an example of an analog multiplexing circuit is shown, and in Figure 11.17b a demultiplexing circuit is given. The analog switch clock waveforms are also shown and consist of repetitive pulse trains for ϕ_1, ϕ_2, ϕ_3, and so on. These pulses are nonoverlapping such that only one analog switch is on at a time. Each analog input channel is supplied to the amplifier input only during the time when the respective clock pulse is active, to produce the time-domain multiplexed output signal. Thus the analog signal from channel 1 is transmitted when ϕ_1 is active, and so on for the rest of the analog input channels.

For the demultiplexing process a similar set of nonoverlapping clock pulses are used in synchronism with the sampling pulses at the transmitting end of the system. When the signal from channel 1 is being transmitted, switch S_1 is turned on by clock pulse ϕ_1, and so on for the rest of the channels. The output from each channel can be smoothed out by a low-pass filter so that a continuous output waveform that is a good replica of the input signal will be obtained.

For the accurate reconstruction of the analog signal the sampling frequency for each channel must be at least *twice* the highest-frequency component of the analog input signal. For example, if there are 10 analog channels to be multiplexed, and the highest analog signal frequency is 5 kHz, the sampling rate for each channel must be 10 kHz and the sampling time must be limited to no more than $\frac{1}{10} \times (\frac{1}{10}\text{ kHz}) = 10\ \mu\text{s}$.

Chopper-stabilized amplifiers. Chopper-stabilized amplifiers are used for amplifying very low-level ($\lesssim$1 mV) signals that have frequency components that extend down to d-c or relatively low frequencies ($\lesssim$10 Hz). A chopper-stabilized amplifier circuit is shown in Figure 11.18. In this circuit the amplifier offset voltage will not have any effect on the output signal, due to the blocking effect of the coupling capacitors. The input voltage V_{in} is chopped by switch S_1 to produce an a-c signal with a peak-to-peak swing equal to the amplitude of the input voltage. This a-c signal is then amplified by the amplifier to produce an a-c signal of peak amplitude $AV_{in}/2$.

The second switch, S_2, is operated in synchronism with switch S_1. This second switch shorts out the negative-polarity portions of the a-c output voltage so that only the positive-going portions remain, this being an example of "synchronous detection." The output voltage then goes through a low-pass filter to produce an output voltage of amplitude $AV_{in}/4$. For the accurate reproduction of the input voltage waveform the switching frequency should be at least twice the highest-frequency component in the input voltage. Note that this circuit will work with input frequencies all the way down to d-c.

The "on" resistance of the switches should be small compared to resistances R_1 and R_2. It is also very important that the switches have no offset voltage, so that bipolar transistors cannot be used for this application, but FETs will serve quite well.

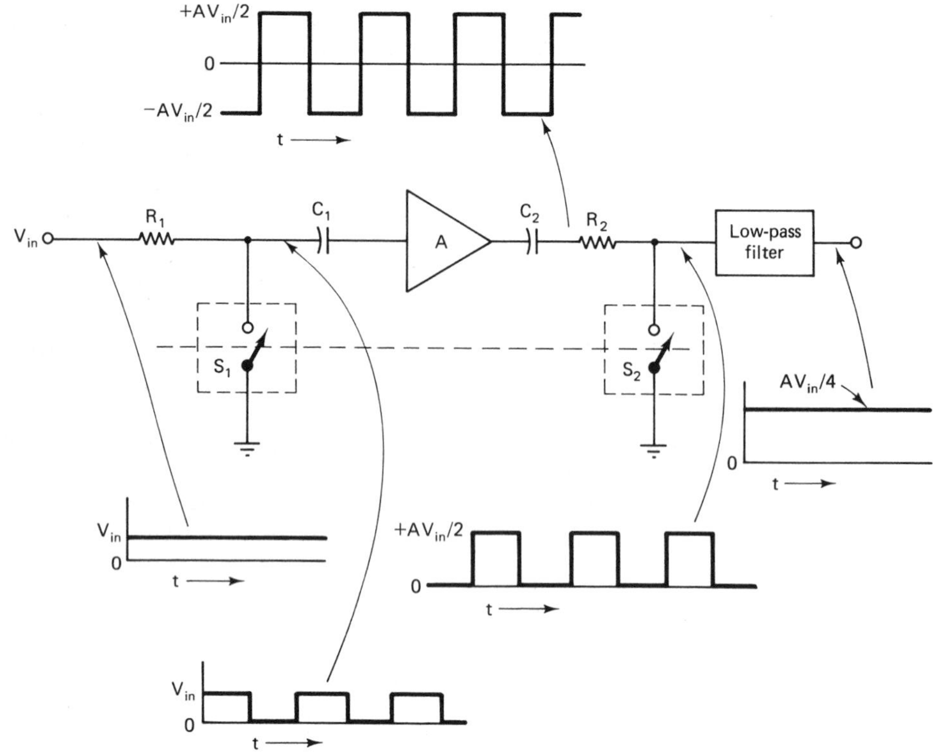

Figure 11.18 Chopper-stabilized amplifier.

11.2 SAMPLE-AND-HOLD CIRCUITS

A major applications area for analog switches is their use in sample-and-hold (S/H) circuits. Sample-and-hold circuits are used to sample an analog input voltage for a very short period, generally in the range 1 to 10 μs, and to hold the sampled voltage level for an extended period, which can range from a few millisecond to several seconds. The circuits are often used in analog-to-digital converters, especially the successive-approximation type, to hold the analog input voltage level constant during the A/D conversion period. S/H circuits are also used in analog demultiplexing circuits, reset-stabilized op-amp circuits, staircase generators, and other applications.

Three basic examples of sample-and-hold circuits are shown in Figure 11.19. In these circuits a JFET is used as an analog switch, although a MOSFET could also be used. During the sampling time the JFET switch is turned on, and in the case of Figure 11.19a and b, the holding capacitor charges up to the level of the analog input voltage. At the end of this short sampling period the JFET switch is turned off. This isolates the holding capacitor C_H from the input signal and the voltage across C_H, and therefore the output voltage V_O will remain essentially at the value of the input voltage at the end of the sampling time. There will, however, be a small drop-off or droop of the capacitor voltage during the hold period due to the various leakage currents, including the $I_{DS(OFF)}$ of the JFET, the I_{BIAS} of the operational amplifier (A_2), and the internal leakage current of the holding capacitor C_H.

The *acquisition time* of a S/H circuit is the time required for the holding capacitor C_H to charge up to a level close to the input voltage during the sampling time. In the circuit of Figure 11.19a there are three principal factors that will control the acquisition time. One is the RC time constant resulting from the "on" resistance, $r_{ds(ON)}$, of the JFET switch and the holding capacitance, C_H. A second factor is the

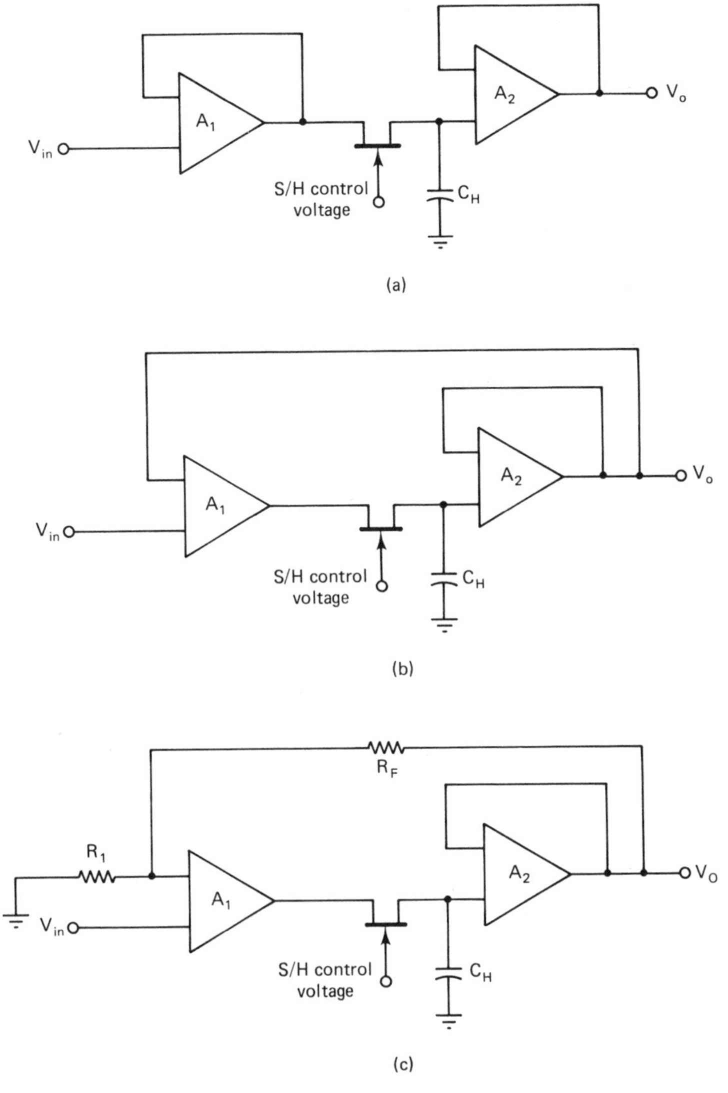

Figure 11.19 Some basic sample-and-hold circuits: (a) and (b) basic circuits; (c) circuit with voltage gain; (d) circuit using an integrating amplifier.

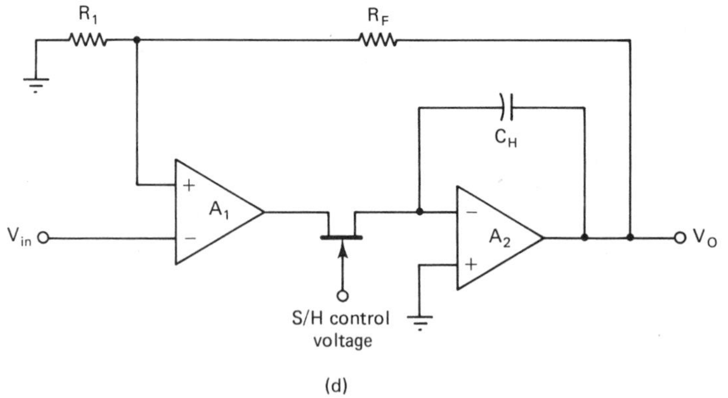

Figure 11.19 (*cont*)

maximum output current, which can be source or sunk by the operational amplifier (A_1). The third factor is the slewing rate capability of the op amp.

The circuit of Figure 11.19b can offer some advantage over that of Figure 11.19a in terms of the acquisition time since the $r_{ds(ON)}$ of the JFET switch is inside the feedback loop of A_1 and A_2. In this circuit the acquisition time will usually not be limited by the $r_{ds(ON)}$ of the JFET, but rather by the maximum output current capability of A_1 or the slewing rate of the operational amplifier. The maximum rate of change of voltage across C_H will be given by $dV_C/dt = I_{O(MAX)}/C_H$ or $dV_C/dt = (SR)_{op\ amp}$, whichever is smaller. To consider a representative example, let us assume $I_{O(MAX)} = 10$ mA, an op-amp slewing rate of 5 V/μs, and $C_H = 10$ nF. For this case we have that $I_{O(MAX)}/C_H = 10$ mA/10 nF $= 1.0$ V/μs, and since this is much smaller than the op-amp slewing rate, the "slewing rate" of the S/H circuit during the sampling time will be essentially 1.0 V/μs. For a full-scale output-voltage step of 10 V the acquisition time will be 10 μs.

If the combined leakage currents of the JFET, op amp (A_2), and the capacitor

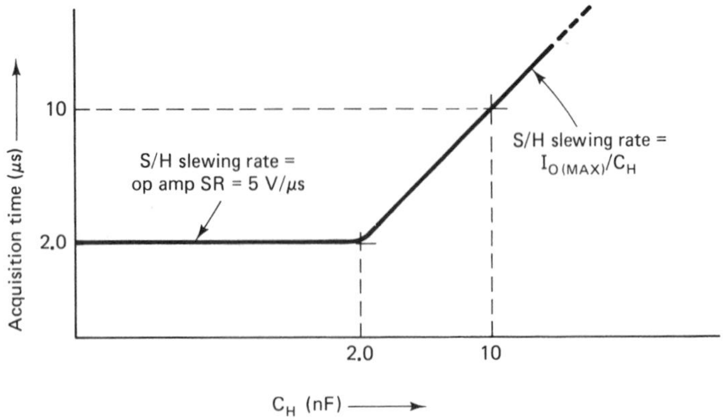

Figure 11.20 S/H acquisition time versus C_H: $I_{O(MAX)} = 10$ mA; $\Delta V_O = 10$ V.

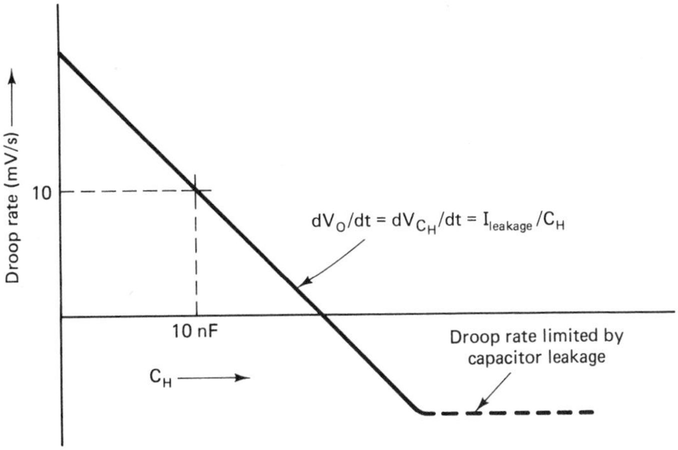

Figure 11.21 S/H droop rate versus C_H: $I_{\text{leakage}} = 1.0$ nA.

is 100 pA (max.), the voltage *droop rate* during the hold period will be $dV_C/dt = I_{\text{leakage}}/C_H = 100$ pA (max.)/10 nF = 10 mV/s.

The acquisition time can be reduced by using a smaller value of holding capacitor, but the voltage droop rate will increase. The acquisition time will ultimately be limited by the slewing rate of the op amp. If in the example above, C_H is reduced to 2.0 nF, the acquisition time will be shortened to about 2.0 μs, but the droop rate will increase to about 50 mV/s. If C_H is further reduced below this value, the acquisition time will remain at about 2.0 μs, limited now by the slewing rate of the op amp. This is illustrated in Figure 11.20, and the variation of the droop rate with C_H is shown in Figure 11.21.

The S/H circuit of Figure 11.19c performs in a fashion similar to that of Figure 11.19b but offers the additional feature of providing voltage gain. The voltage gain of this circuit will be $1 + (R_F/R_1)$, so that the output voltage during the hold period will be equal to the input voltage that is sampled during the sample period multiplied by the voltage gain factor of $1 + (R_F/R_1)$.

The integrating amplifier configuration of Figure 11.19d can offer the advantage of a faster capacitor charging rate and thus a shorter acquisition time. This is because the voltage at the inverting input terminal of A_2 is equal to the capacitor voltage divided by the open-loop gain of A_2.

In Figure 11.22 an example of the driving circuitry for the JFET switching transistor is shown. During the sampling time the control voltage will go up to near the positive supply voltage V^+. This will ensure that diode D_1 will be turned off. Under these conditions the voltage drop across R_G will be very small ($\lesssim 1$ mV) due to the very small gate leakage current of the JFET, Q_1. As a result, the gate-to-source voltage of Q_1 will be essentially zero and Q_1 will be fully on.

During the hold period the control voltage will be pulled down to near the negative supply voltage V^-. Diode D_1 will now be on and there will now be a large gate-to-source voltage drop produced across R_G. This voltage drop will be sufficient to turn Q_1 off.

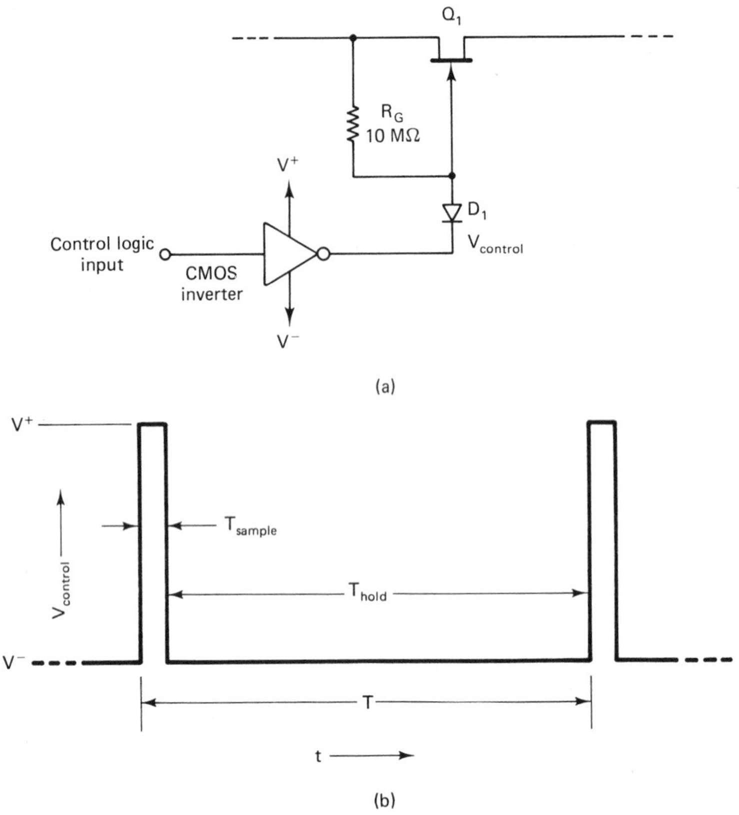

Figure 11.22 Driving circuitry for JFET S/H switching transistor: (a) basic circuit; (b) control voltage waveform.

11.2.1 Monolithic S/H Integrated Circuit

An example of a monolithic S/H integrated circuit is the LF198/298/398 (National Semiconductor). A block diagram of this IC is shown in Figure 11.23. This circuit features an acquisition time of 4 μs to bring the output voltage to within 0.1% of a 10-V output step. This is with a holding capacitance of 1 nF. If C_H is increased to 10 nF, the acquisition time will increase to 20 μs. The net leakage current flowing out of the holding capacitor is 30 pA (typ.) and 100 pA (max.) at 25°C during the hold period. With C_H = 1.0 nF the droop rate will be 30 mV/s (typ.) and 100 mV/s (max.).

The *hold step* of a S/H circuit is the voltage step produced across the hold capacitor at the beginning of the hold period due to feedthrough of the FET gate control voltage step. This feedthrough occurs via the gate-to-drain capacitance C_{gd} of the FET, as shown in Figure 11.24. This feedthrough will be manifested at the beginning of the hold period by an output voltage step of amount $\Delta V_O = \Delta V_{\text{control}} \times C_{gd}/C_H$. For the LF198 S/H IC the hold step is 10 mV for C_H = 1 nF and a

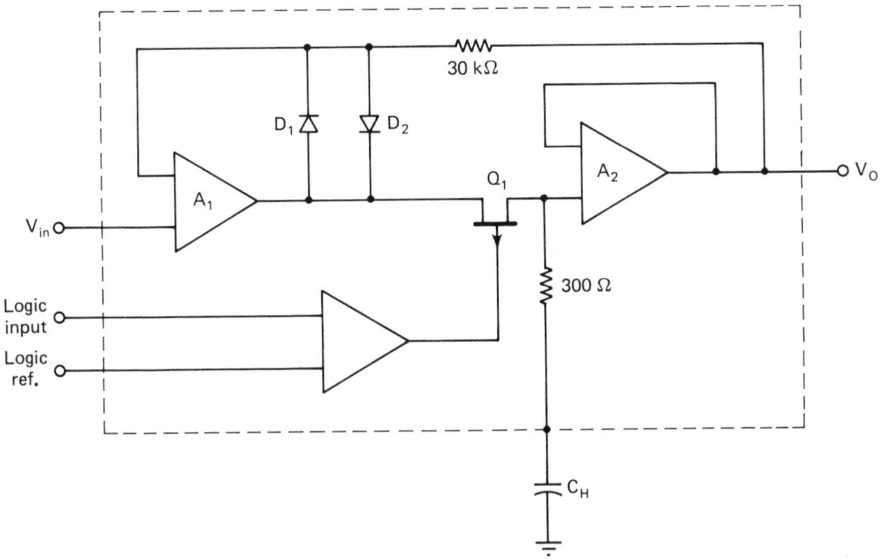

Figure 11.23 Monolithic S/H integrated circuit: LF198/298/398 (National Semiconductor).

sample-to-hold control (gate) voltage step of $\Delta V_{\text{control}} = 5$ V. This corresponds to a gate-to-drain capacitance of $C_{gd} = 1 \text{ nF} \times 10 \text{ mV}/5 \text{ V} = 2$ pF.

During the hold period (Q_1 off) there will also be some feedthrough of the analog input signal to the output through the parasitic drain-to-source capacitance (C_{ds}) of Q_1 and other small stray wiring capacitances of the circuit, as shown in Figure 11.25. The *feedthrough rejection ratio* is the fraction of the analog input signal that is fed through to the output during the hold period. With a hold capacitance of 1.0 nF the feedthrough rejection ratio for the LF198 is approximately −80 dB. This corresponds to a C_{ds} capacitance of only 0.1 pF.

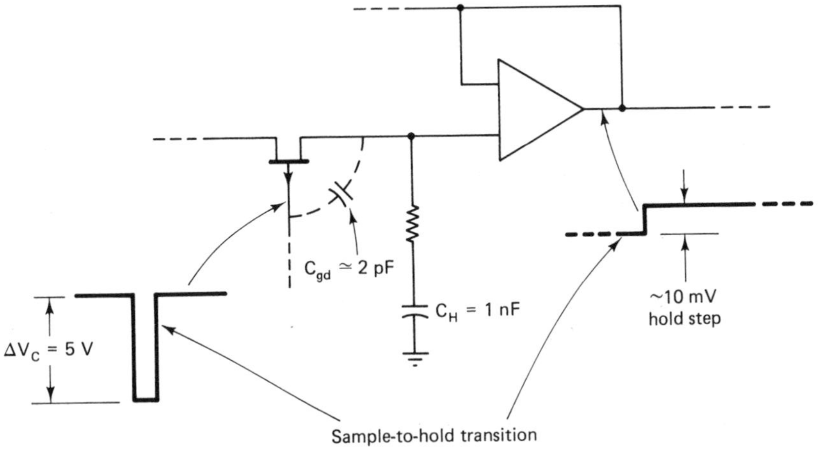

Figure 11.24 S/H hold step.

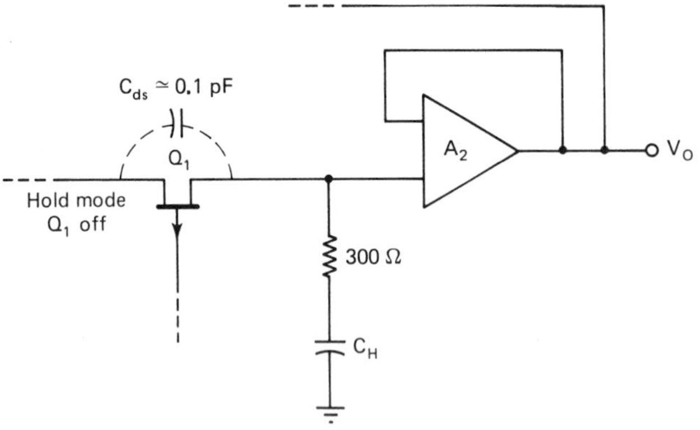

Figure 11.25 Feedthrough rejection ratio.

11.2.2 Fast Sample-and-Hold ICs

An example of a very fast sample-and-hold IC is the HA-5320 (Harris). This is a monolithic IC using dielectric isolation to minimize the parasitic capacitance and allow a very high speed operation. It uses an integrating amplifier configuration (similar to Figure 11.19d) with an internal 100 pF MOS feedback (hold) capacitor. The acquisition time for the output voltage to reach within 0.1% of a 10 V step is 0.8 μs and for 0.01% is 1 μs. The droop rate at 25°C is 0.08 μV/μs which corresponds to a net leakage current of 8 pA. An external capacitance may be added to decrease the droop rate, but this will be at the expense of an increased acquisition time.

Another very fast sample-and-hold IC is the SHC803/804 (Burr-Brown). This IC also uses an integrating amplifier configuration with an internal hold capacitor. It has an internal resistor feedback network set for unity gain. The acquisition time of this device is only 300 ns for the output voltage to respond to within 0.01% of a 10 V step.

11.2.3 Sample-and-Hold IC Using a Diode Bridge

Most sample-and-hold circuits use FET switches to control the charging of the hold capacitor. A diode bridge using four matched IC diodes can, however, offer the advantage of a faster acquisition time due to the low dynamic resistance of the forward biased diodes. An example of a sample-and-hold IC that uses a diode bridge is the SMP-10 (Precision Monolithics Inc). In addition to the diode bridge a "super charger" amplifier is used to supply currents of up to 50 mA directly to the hold capacitor during the sampling time. At the end of the sampling time, the output circuit of this amplifier is disconnected from the hold capacitor. With a hold capacitor of 5 nF the slewing rate of this IC is 10 V/μs and the acquisition time for a 10 V step to 0.1% is 3.5 μs and to 0.01% is 5 μs. The leakage current during the hold time is 250 pA and the corresponding droop rate is 50 μV/ms maximum.

11.2.4 Applications of Sample-and-Hold Circuits

As mentioned before, one of the most important applications of S/H circuits is in analog-to-digital conversion systems, in which the analog input voltage must be held constant during the conversion period. Another application of S/H circuits is for analog demultiplexing, as shown in Figure 11.26. The input signal into the demultiplexer is a time-domain multiplexed analog signal. This signal is supplied in parallel to all of the S/H circuits. The sampling times for the various S/H circuits are staggered by the nonoverlapping clock pulses ϕ_1, ϕ_2, ϕ_3, and so on. Each S/H circuit is turned on for a short period of time during which the analog signal corresponding to the particular analog signal channel is being transmitted. The sampled voltage is then held until the beginning of the next sampling time for that signal channel.

Reset-stabilized op amp using a S/H circuit. Another applications area for analog switches and S/H circuits is for reset-stabilized operational amplifiers. These circuits are useful for the amplification of very low-level signals ($\lesssim 1$ mV) that extend down to very low frequencies or have a d-c component. For these low-level signals the offset voltage and the drift of the offset voltage of the operational amplifier with temperature and time can be a serious problem. The low-frequency or d-c components of the input signal also preclude the use of coupling capacitors to block the offset voltage.

In the reset-stabilized op-amp circuit shown in Figure 11.27, the analog input voltage is periodically disconnected from the op-amp input for a very short period of time by the JFET switch S_1. At the same time the output voltage is sampled by the S/H circuit. Since the input voltage is disconnected from the operational amplifier

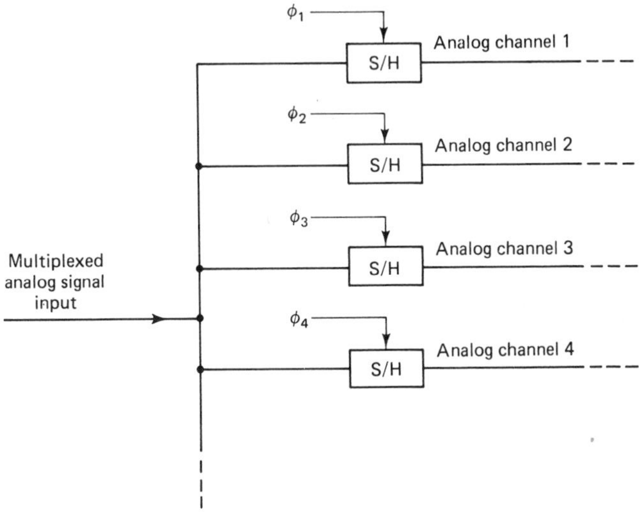

Figure 11.26 Analog signal demultiplexer using S/H circuits.

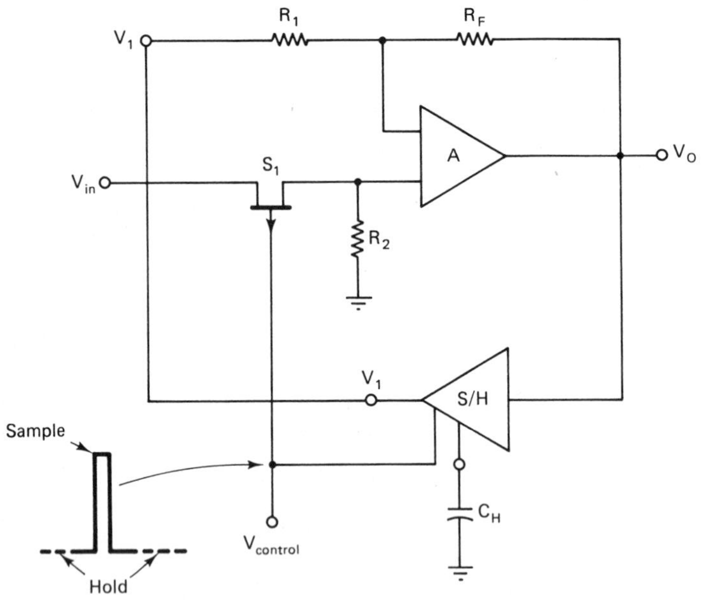

Figure 11.27 Reset-stabilized operational amplifier using a S/H circuit.

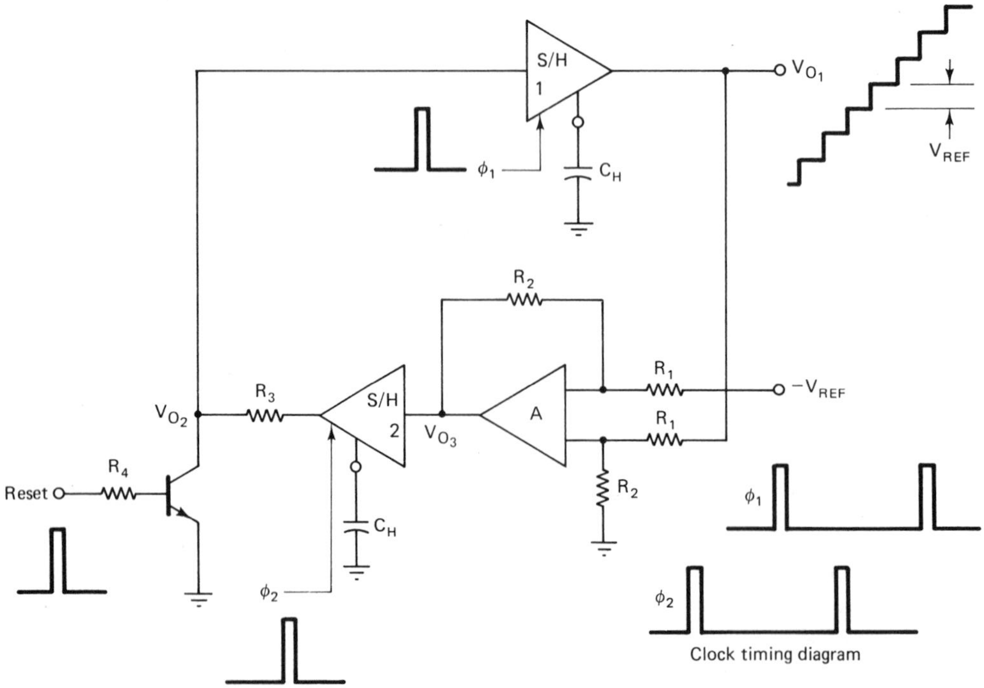

Figure 11.28 Staircase generator.

during this sampling time, the output voltage that is sampled by the S/H circuit is due only to the offset voltage of the operational amplifier. This sampled output offset voltage is then fed back to the inverting input of the operational amplifier via R_1, and this d-c feedback loop acts to dynamically null out the offset voltage. This offset nulling voltage is held by the holding capacitor C_H of the S/H circuit so that the offset voltage nulling will continue throughout the hold period.

We note that the output signal will be interrupted periodically during the offset voltage sampling time. This interruption will, however, represent a very small fraction of the total time and can be smoothed out by a low-pass filter circuit.

We will now consider a more detailed analysis of this circuit. When the control voltage, V_{control}, is *high*, S_1 will be off and the S/H will be in the sampling mode. At this time $V_1 = V_o$ and therefore we have that $V_O = -(R_F/R_1)V_1 + (1 + R_F/R_1)V_{OS} = -(R_F/R_1)V_O + (1 + R_F/R_1)V_{OS}$, so that $V_O(1 + R_F/R_1) = V_{OS}(1 + R_F/R_1)$ and thus $V_1 = V_O = V_{OS}$. Therefore, C_H will charge up to V_{OS} during the sampling period and during the subsequent hold period will remain essentially at that level.

When the control voltage then goes low, S_1 will be turned back *on* and the S/H circuit will go into the hold mode with its output voltage $V_1 = V_{OS}$. The output voltage of the circuit during this time period will be

$$\begin{aligned} V_O &= (V_{\text{in}} + V_{OS})\left(1 + \frac{R_F}{R_1}\right) - \frac{R_F}{R_1} V_1 \\ &= V_{\text{in}}\left(1 + \frac{R_F}{R_1}\right) + V_{OS}\left(1 + \frac{R_F}{R_1}\right) - \frac{R_F}{R_1} V_{OS} \qquad (11.5) \\ &= V_{\text{in}}\left(1 + \frac{R_F}{R_1}\right) + V_{OS} \end{aligned}$$

In the absence of the S/H circuit we would have that $V_1 = 0$ and therefore $V_O = V_{\text{in}}(1 + R_F/R_1) + V_{OS}(1 + R_F/R_1)$, so that we see that the action of the S/H circuit will reduce the effect of the offset voltage by a factor equal to the closed-loop gain of $1 + R_F/R_1$.

Staircase waveform generator. Two sample-and-hold circuits can be combined to produce a staircase generator, as shown in Figure 11.28. The output voltage of the first S/H circuit is combined with the reference voltage V_{REF} in the difference amplifier and then sampled and held by the second S/H circuit. This second S/H circuit, in turn, supplies a voltage that is sampled-and-held by the first S/H circuit.

If $R_1 = R_2$, then the output voltage of the difference amplifier after the nth cycle of clock pulses will be $V_{O_3}(n) = V_{O_1}(n) + V_{\text{REF}}$. This voltage will then be sampled and held by S/H-2 when the sampling clock pulse ϕ_2 is active. When the sampling clock pulse ϕ_1 then becomes active, the held output voltage of S/H-2 will be sampled and held by S/H-1. The output voltage of S/H-1 after this $(n + 1)$th cycle of clock pulses will now be $V_{O_1}(n + 1) = V_{O_2}(n) = V_{O_1}(n) + V_{\text{REF}}$.

We see that the output voltage V_{O_1} of S/H-1 will increment by an amount

$\Delta V_{O_1} = V_{O_1}(n + 1) - V_{O_1}(n) = V_{REF}$ during every sampling time for S/H-1 and then remain at that level during the hold period. The result is a staircase waveform with a uniform step size.

If R_1 is not equal to R_2, we will have that $V_{O_3} = (R_2/R_1)[V_{O_1}(n) + V_{REF}]$ and thus $V_{O_1}(n + 1) = (R_2/R_1)V_{O_1}(n) + (R_2/R_1)V_{REF}$. The step size is now $\Delta V_{O_1} = V_{O_1}(n + 1) - V_{O_1}(n) = (R_2/R_1)V_{REF} + (R_2/R_1 - 1)V_O(n)$. We see that it is now possible to generate a "nonlinear" staircase waveform with successively increasing (if $R_2/R_1 > 1$) or decreasing (if $R_2/R_1 < 1$) step sizes.

The staircase waveform will be terminated when the reset transistor Q_1 is turned on. When Q_1 then goes off, the staircase waveform will start off all over again from zero.

Fast acquisition–very low droop rate S/H circuit. For some applications it may be desirable to have a very short acquisition time for the S/H circuit, yet also have a very low droop rate during the hold period. It may turn out that there is no value of holding capacitor that can satisfy these two requirements simultaneously.

The requirements of a fast acquisition time and a very low droop rate, however, can often be met by the use of two cascaded S/H circuits, as shown, for example, in Figure 11.29. The first S/H circuit has a short acquisition time ($\lesssim$10 μs) due to the use of a small value of holding capacitor ($\sim$1 nF). The second S/H circuit then samples the output voltage of the first S/H circuit over a much longer time period ($\sim$10 ms) and has a 1-μF hold capacitor. As a result of the large value of the holding capacitor of the second S/H circuit, its droop rate will be very small. Note that the time period over which the input voltage is sampled is still limited by the first S/H circuit to only 10 μs, so that any variation in the input voltage over the 10-ms sampling time of the second S/H circuit will not affect the output voltage of the circuit.

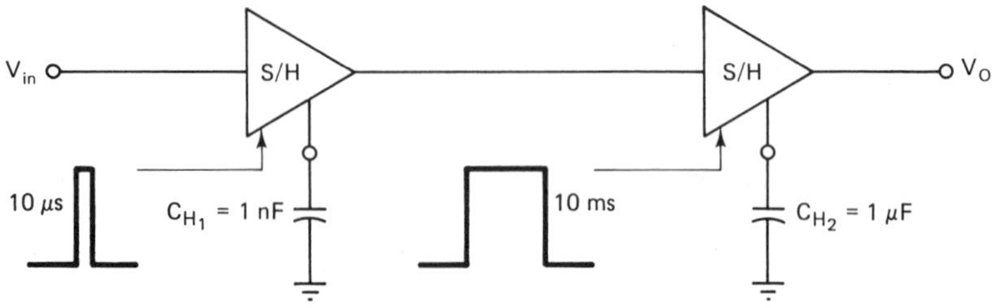

Figure 11.29 Fast acquisition—very low droop S/H circuit.

PROBLEMS

11.1. (*Analog multiplexer*) For the analog multiplexer circuit of Figure 11.17, $R_1 = 100\ \Omega$ and the switch-on resistance is 100 Ω. When the switch is off, it appears as a 10-pF capacitance. Find the crosstalk between channels at an analog signal frequency of 1.0 MHz and express the result in decibels. (*Ans.*: −38 dB)

11.2. (*Integrate-and-dump circuit*) An integrate-and-dump circuit, as shown in Figure 11.16, uses a JFET switch with an on resistance of 100 Ω. The integration period is to be 1.0 s and a full-scale output voltage of 10 V is to be obtained when a 1.0-V d-c input is integrated over this 1.0-s integration period. The integrated output is to be "dumped" down to a value of no more than 1% of the final output voltage in a time period of 1.0 ms. Find R and C. [*Ans.*: 2.172 μF (max.), R = 46.05 kΩ (min.)]

11.3. (*Chopper-stabilized amplifier*) For the chopper-stabilized amplifier circuit of Figure 11.18, the switches have an on resistance of 50 Ω.

(a) Find R_1 and R_2 such that the output voltage error due to the switch resistance will not exceed 1.0%. [*Ans.*: $R_1 = R_2 =$ 10 kΩ (min.)]

(b) If the switch capacitance (when off) is 10 pF and the amplifier input capacitance is 10 pF, find the 3-dB bandwidth of the system, assuming that it is not limited by the amplifier bandwidth. (*Ans.*: 512 kHz)

11.4. (*MOS switch resistance*) An NMOS transistor is to be used as an analog switch. The gate oxide thickness is 800 Å and the channel length is 5 μm. The threshold voltage is +2.0 V, and the gate voltage when the switch is on will be +7.5 V. Find the channel width needed to produce an "on" resistance not to exceed 250 Ω. Assume an average electron mobility of 200 cm²/V-s in the channel. (*Ans.*: $W \geqslant$ 433 μm)

11.5. (*Sample-and-hold circuits*) Given a S/H circuit, shown in Figure P11.5. The op amp A_1 has a maximum current output capability of ±10 mA. I_{BIAS} = 0.5 nA (max.) and $I_{DS(OFF)}$ = 0.5 nA for Q_1. This S/H circuit is to be used with a 12-bit ADC with a 1-μs clock period and a total conversion time of 14 μs. The acquisition (sampling) time is to be $\frac{1}{4}T_{CLOCK}$ = 250 ns and the S/H accuracy required is $\pm\frac{1}{4}$ LSB. The full-scale voltage is 10.24 V.

(a) Find maximum and minimum limits for the capacitor C_1. [*Ans.*: C_1 = 250 pF (max.), 22.4 pF (min.)]

(b) If a capacitor value of 100 pF is used for C_1, find the slew rate of the S/H circuit. (*Ans.*: SR = 100 V/μs = 100 mV/ns)

(c) With C_1 = 100 pF, find the hold decay (droop rate). (*Ans.*: 10 μV/μs)

(d) What are the slewing rate requirements for A_1 and A_2 in order to meet the requirements given above for the ADC? (*Ans.*: SR should be substantially above 40 V/μs for both A_1 and A_2)

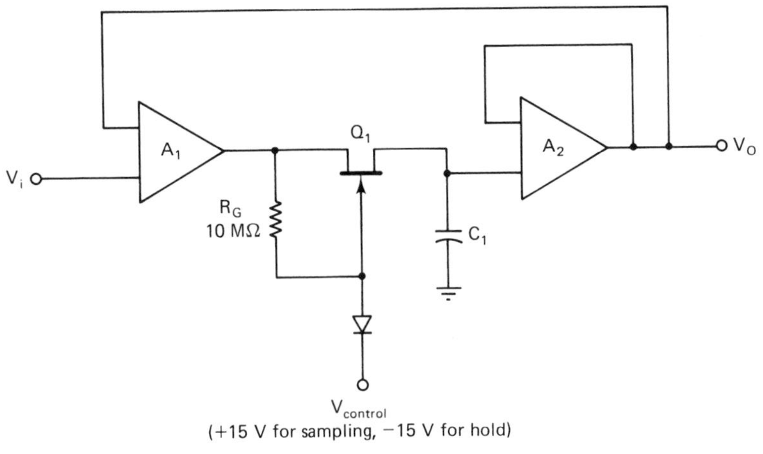

Figure P11.5

REFERENCES

CONNELLY, J. A., *Analog Integrated Circuits*, Wiley, 1975.

LENK, J. D., *Handbook of Electronic Circuit Design*, Prentice-Hall, 1976.

LENK, J. D., *Manual for MOS Users*, Reston, 1975.

MIRTES, B., *D-C Amplifiers*, Chap. 6, Butterworth, 1969.

MITRA, S. K., *An Introduction to Digital and Analog Integrated Circuits and Applications*, Harper & Row, 1980.

OXNER, E. S., *Power FETs and Their Applications*, Chap. 9, Prentice-Hall, 1982.

STOUT, D. F., *Handbook of Microcircuit Design and Applications*, McGraw-Hill, 1980.

TAUB, H., and D. SCHILLING, *Digital Integrated Circuits*, Chap. 13, McGraw-Hill, 1977.

United Technical Publications, *Modern Applications of Integrated Circuits*, Tab Books, 1974.

Charge-Transfer Devices: Analog Delay Lines

12

A very interesting and different type of integrated circuit is the charge-transfer device (CTD), of which there are two basic types: the *charge-coupled device* (CCD) and the *bucket-brigade device* (BBD). These devices are very useful for analog delay lines and can be used for a wide variety of analog signal processing applications. They can also be used for linear and area image sensor devices. The CCD can also be used as a digital shift register and a serial access memory. We will first consider the CCD.

12.1 CHARGE-COUPLED DEVICES

The basic structure of a CCD is shown in Figure 12.1. The charge storage and transfer element of a CCD is the MOS capacitor, shown in Figure 12.2. If a suitably large positive voltage of typically 10 to 15 V is applied to the gate electrode, the electric field produced will act to repel holes away from the region underneath the electrode and a depletion region will be formed. The electric field lines emanating from the gate electrode will terminate on the negatively charged acceptor ions in the depletion region, which will typically extend for several micrometers into the lightly doped ($\sim 10^{14}$ to 10^{15} cm^{-3}) P-type substrate. This depletion region will be a "potential well," as illustrated by Figure 12.3. This potential well will, however, gradually fill up due to the flow of thermally generated electrons, as shown in Figure 12.2b. The electrons will accumulate near the silicon surface and form a surface N-type inversion layer, as shown in Figure 12.2c. In Figures 12.2d and 12.3b the situation of a completely filled potential well is shown and in this case the inward

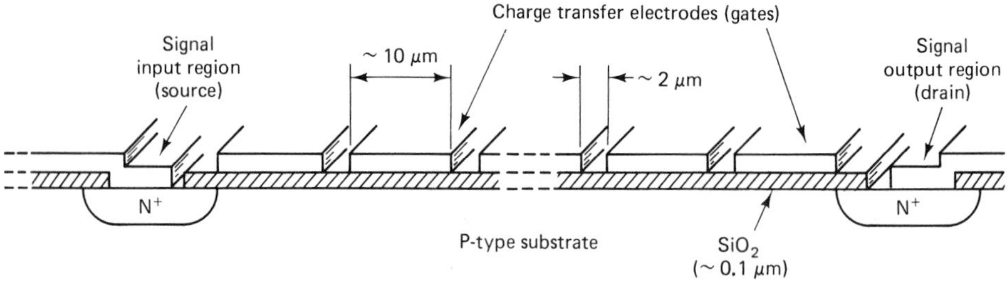

Figure 12.1 Basic structure of a charge-coupled device.

diffusion of electrons into the well will be exactly balanced by the outward flow of electrons, so that there is now no net flow of electrons into the potential well.

The filling of the potential well by the thermally generated electrons will not occur instantaneously, but will take some time, usually of the order of 0.1 s. This will set a lower limit on the speed of operation of the CCD in that the total delay time for an analog signal passing through the CCD array should be short compared to the time it takes the potential well to fill up with the thermally generated electrons.

In the CCD array a potential well is produced under the gate at the source end and a given amount of charge is injected from the source region into this potential well in the form of a given number or "packet" of electrons. These electrons can

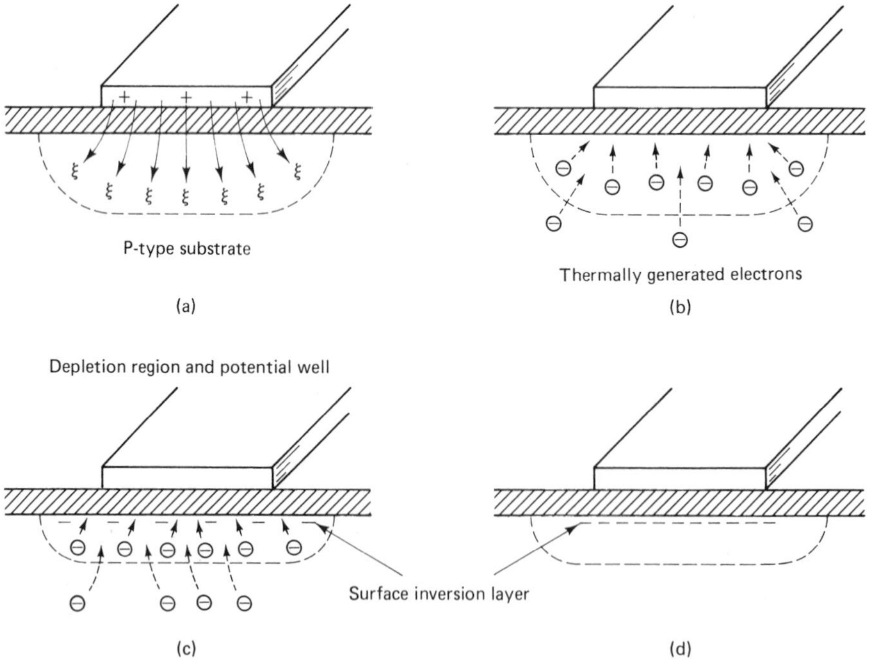

Figure 12.2 CCD potential well: (a) formation of depletion region; (b) thermally generated electrons flowing into potential well; (c) formation of inversion layer at Si/SiO_2 interface; (d) filled potential well.

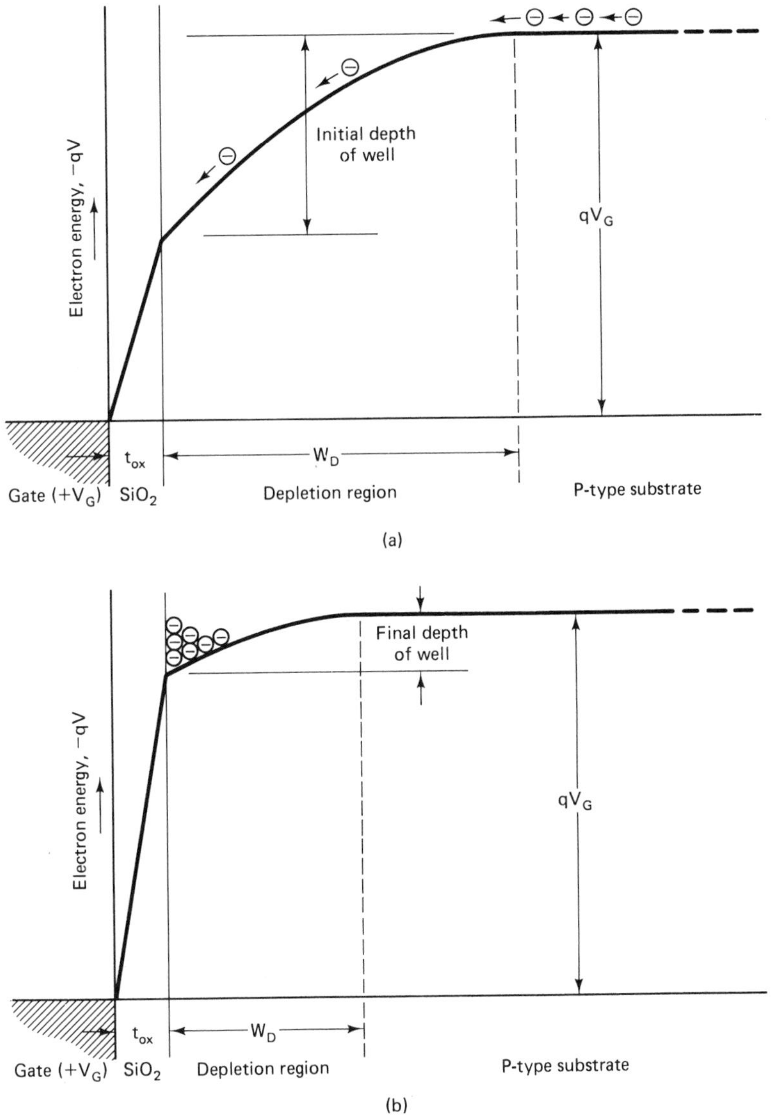

Figure 12.3 MOS capacitor potential well: (a) potential well formed immediately after application of gate voltage; (b) potential well after being filled with thermally generated electrons.

then be transferred along the array from gate to gate in successively formed potential wells from the source end of the CCD array to the drain end, where the charge is then extracted. Let us consider the situation shown in Figure 12.4. In Figure 12.4a the electron charge packet is localized in the potential well underneath the ϕ_1 electrode. As the voltage applied to the ϕ_2 electrode now goes high and at the same time the ϕ_1 decreases to zero, the electrons will move from the collapsing potential well under-

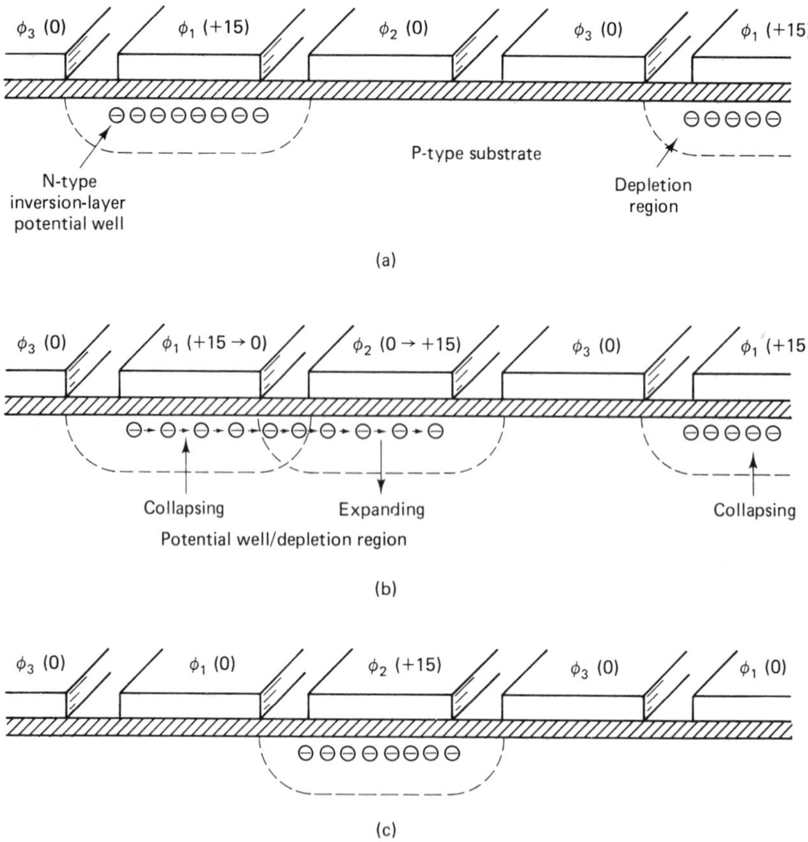

Figure 12.4 Charge transfer in a CCD: (a) electron charge packet localized in the potential well underneath the ϕ_1 electrode; (b) and (c) electrons move to the expanding well underneath the ϕ_2 electrode.

neath the ϕ_1 electrode to the now expanding well underneath the ϕ_2 electrode, as shown in Figure 12.4b and c. Note that as a result of the very close electrode spacing ($\sim$2 μm) the depletion regions and potential wells of the two electrodes will overlap during this charge-transfer process.

Next as the ϕ_2 electrode goes low and simultaneously the ϕ_3 electrode goes high, the electron packet will be transferred to the ϕ_3 electrode. Then as the next ϕ_1 goes high and ϕ_3 simultaneously goes high, the electron packet moves to the adjacent ϕ_1 electrode and the three-phase charge-transfer cycle is completed. In a similar fashion this cycle is repeated and the charge packet will be propagated along the CCD array from the source end to the drain end. This is an example of a three-phase CCD and the directionality of the charge-transfer process is established by the three-phase clocking.

The electrons are injected into the CCD array at the source or input end, and one way of doing this is shown in Figure 12.5. For the charge injection process the input gate electrode goes high, which produces an N-type surface inversion layer

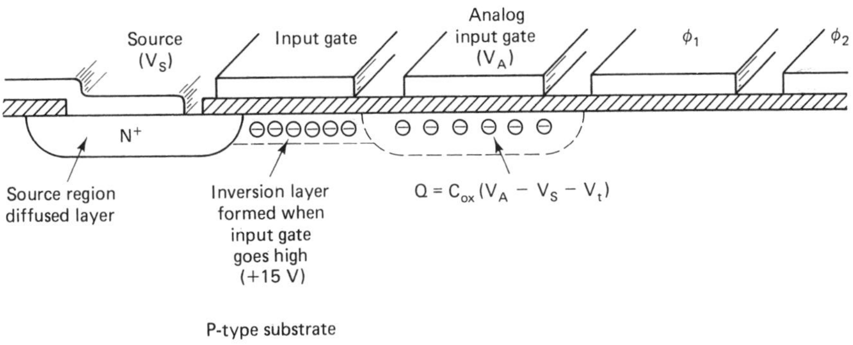

Figure 12.5 Charge injection into a CCD array.

between the N^+ source region and the potential well underneath the signal input gate electrode. This potential well will immediately be filled with electrons from the source region to a level corresponding to a net charge of $Q = C_{ox}(V_A - V_t)$, where C_{ox} is the MOS capacitance, V_A is the analog signal level, and V_t is the threshold level for surface inversion. The input gate then goes low, which now isolates the signal input potential well from the N^+ source region and the electron packet in the signal input gate potential well can then be propagated along the CCD array to the drain end.

At the output or "drain" end of the CCD array the electron packet is collected by the N^+ drain region, as shown in Figure 12.6. The collected charge is usually directly coupled to an on-the-chip MOS amplifier in order to minimize the capacitative loading effects.

A two-phase CCD is also possible, but some asymmetry in the potential wells is required to ensure the proper directionality of the charge packet transfer. Two methods of providing this asymmetry are shown in Figure 12.7. In part (a) a stepped oxide structure is shown together with the corresponding shape of the depletion region. Note that the depletion region will be wider and the corresponding potential well

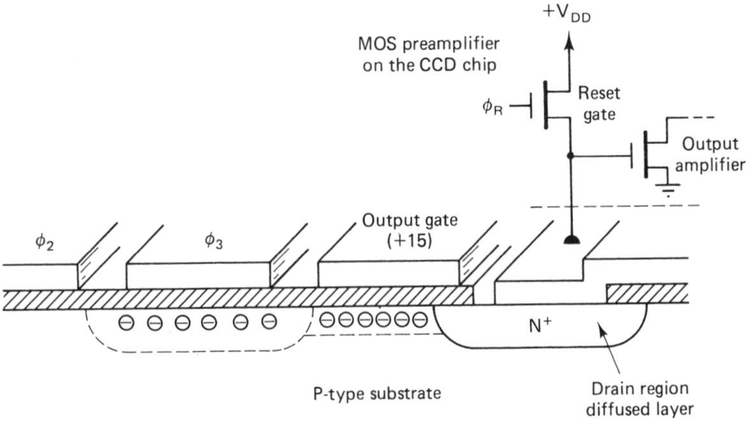

Figure 12.6 Charge extraction at the end of a CCD array.

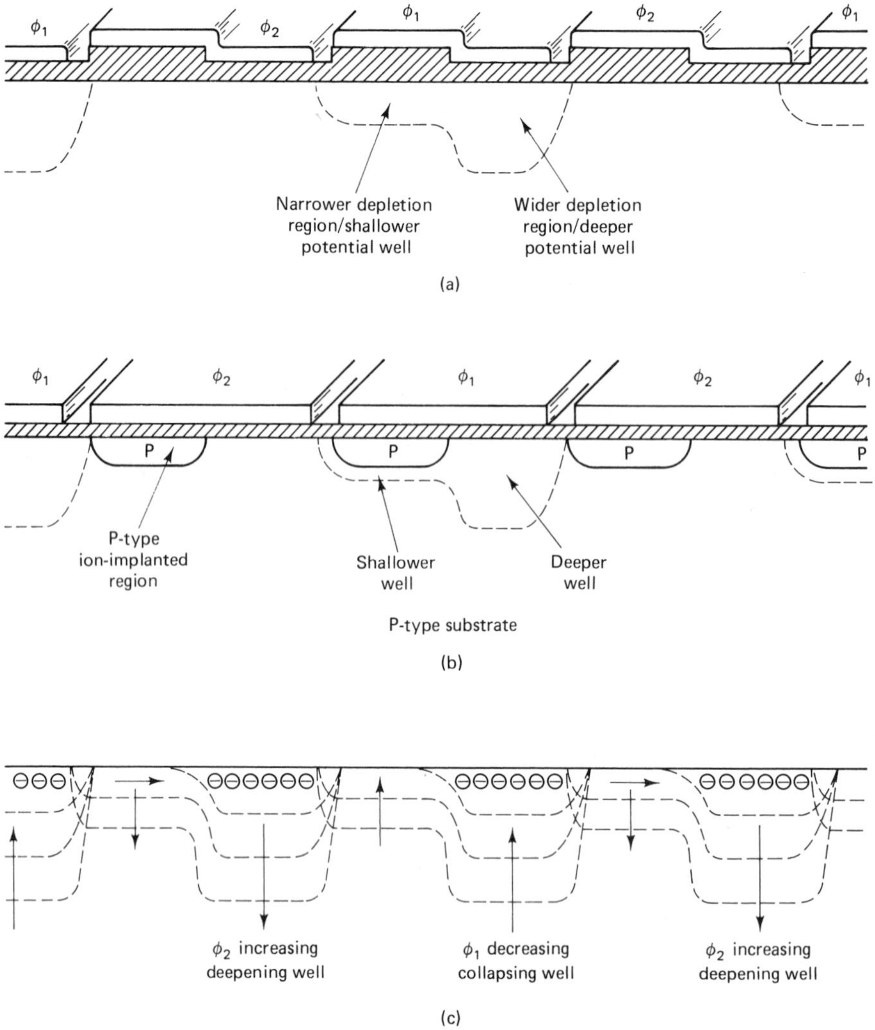

Figure 12.7 Two-phase CCDs: (a) stepped-oxide two-phase CCD; (b) P-type implantation two-phase CCD; (c) charge transfer in a two-phase CCD.

will be deeper underneath the thinner portion of the oxide as a result of the larger electric field in that region.

In Figure 12.7b the potential well asymmetry is produced by the low-dosage P-type implanted regions underneath the trailing edges of the charge-transfer electrodes. The heavier P-type doping in these regions will result in a decreased depletion layer thickness and a shallower potential well for electrons.

In Figure 12.7c the charge-transfer process in a two-phase CCD is shown. The electrons are shown to be first concentrated in the deeper part of the potential wells underneath the ϕ_1 electrodes. Now, as the ϕ_1 voltage decreases and the ϕ_2 voltage goes high, the electrons will spill over into the ϕ_2 potential well located on the right of the ϕ_1 well. Note that the channel between the ϕ_1 well and the adjacent ϕ_2 well to the left will become cut off as the ϕ_1 voltage decreases.

12.1.1 Example of a Charge-Coupled Device

A good example of a CCD is the CCD321A (Fairchild), which consists of two independent 455-bit analog shift register stages. A diagram of one of the two 455-bit CCD arrays is shown in Figure 12.8. The input charge for the CCD array is injected from the V_A source region into the potential well under the V_A electrode via the inversion-layer channel which is formed when the signal input gate electrode goes high (+13 V typ.). The amount of charge in the electron packet under the V_R electrode will be proportional to the $V_R - V_A$ potential difference. After the charge packet has been supplied to the V_R well, the input signal sampling gate goes low (+0.5 V typ.) and the V_R well is now isolated from the V_A source region. The charge packet is then propagated along the CCD array to the drain region, during which time additional charge packets are fed into the array from the source region.

This is basically a two-phase CCD, but the clock pulses are applied only to the ϕ_1 gates, the V_2 gates being held at a fixed d-c voltage. The ϕ_1 gates have a low-state voltage level of +0.5 V (typ.) and a high-state level of +13 V(typ.) and V_2 is set at a level approximately midway between the θ_1 low and high levels or about +6 V.

At the drain end of the CCD array the output charge packet is directly coupled to an on-the-chip MOS preamplifier circuit. This consists of three cascaded source-follower stages using Q_2, Q_4, and Q_6, with Q_3, Q_5, and Q_7 acting as current source active loads. The gate of the input transistor Q_2 must periodically be discharged to remove the accumulation of electrons supplied to Q_2 from the CCD array. This is done by transistor Q_1, which has its gate connected to the ϕ_1 clock line. When ϕ_1 is low and therefore V_2 is high with respect to ϕ_1, the gate of Q_2 will receive a packet of electrons from the CCD drain region. When ϕ_1 goes high, the gate of Q_2 will then be discharged through Q_1.

Transistor Q_8 can be used as a sample-and-hold switch to provide an output voltage waveform that is a smoother approximation to the analog input signal. This CCD can also be operated in the nonsampling mode by connecting the gate of Q_8 to $+V_{DD}$.

The CCD321A has a minimum clock frequency of 20 kHz, which corresponds to a maximum delay time of 455/20 kHz = 23 ms. If the two 455-bit sections are connected in series, the maximum delay time can be increased to 46 ms. The maximum clock frequency is 20 MHz, which corresponds to a minimum delay time of 23 μs. Thus by variation of the clock frequency the delay time can be varied over a 1000:1 range.

The two 455-bit analog shift register sections of the CCD321A can be connected in parallel in a multiplexed mode to produce a 910-bit shift register. In this case the analog signal sampling rate will be twice the clock rate. With a clock rate of 7.16 MHz and a sampling rate of 14.32 MHz, the 3-dB signal bandwidth will be 5 MHz (min.) for the CCD321A-1 and 4.2 MHz (min.) for the CCD321A-2 and -3 devices.

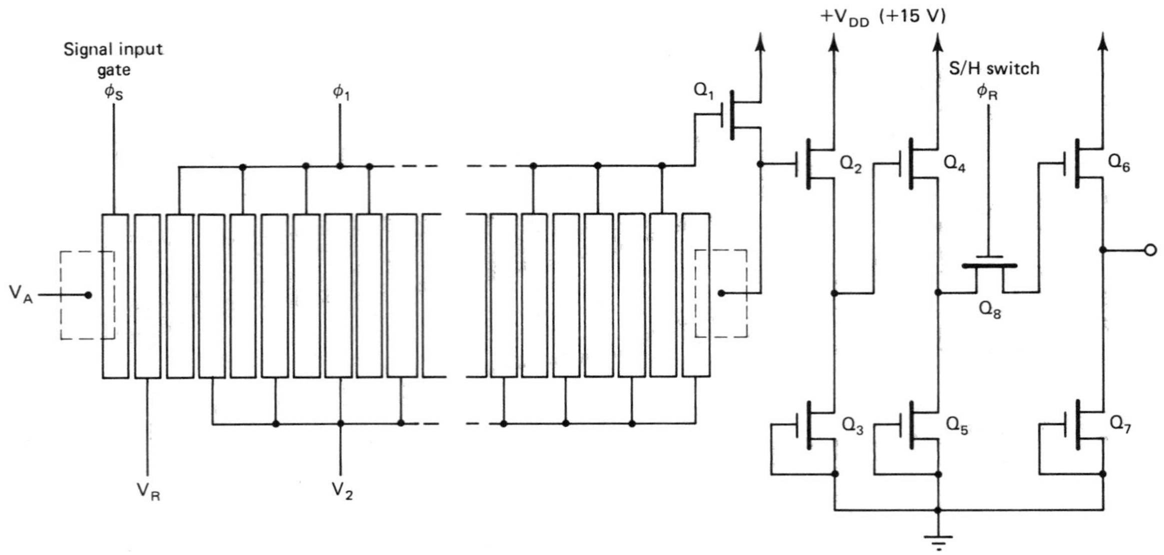

Figure 12.8 CCD circuit: CCD321A (Fairchild CCD Imaging).

The length and frequency response of this device are such that one complete horizontal TV line of 63.5 μs duration can be stored, so that this device can be used for such applications as video time-base correction and comb filtering. It can also be used for drop-out compensation for videotape systems in which if there is a momentary signal loss due to a tape defect or other causes, the preceding TV line can be substituted.

12.1.2 Buried-Channel CCDs

The high-frequency capability of the CCD321A and similar CCDs is made possible by a buried-channel structure. In the surface channel CCDs described earlier, the electron charge packets are held in surface inversion layers that are located adjacent to the Si/SiO_2 interface. As a result of the close proximity of the electrons in the potential well to the Si/SiO_2 interface, there will be a considerable amount of electron trapping at the interface. This temporary trapping of the electrons will cause some of the electrons in the potential well to trail behind the rest of the electron packet as it is being transported along the CCD array.

The fraction of charge left behind after a CCD charge transfer is called the *transfer inefficiency* ϵ. For a surface channel CCD (SCCCD) the transfer inefficiency will generally be down in the range 3×10^{-5} at low clock frequencies, becoming around 10^{-4} at 100 kHz, and will then start to increase rapidly. It will typically be on the order of 10^{-3} at 3 MHz, 10^{-2} at 10 MHz, and 10^{-1} at 30 MHz. For a 455-stage CCD the corresponding values of the overall transfer ratio will be 0.986 at low frequencies, 0.96 at 100 kHz, 0.634 at 3 MHz, and only 0.01 at 10 MHz. We see that the maximum clock frequency will be limited to around 1 or 2 MHz, and the maximum analog signal frequency will be limited to somewhat less than 1 MHz.

The charge-transfer efficiency can be improved substantially by the use of a *buried-channel CCD* (BCCCD) structure, in which the potential well is located a small distance ($\sim$1 μm) from the Si/SiO_2 interface, as shown in Figure 12.9. The BCCCD has a higher charge-transfer efficiency than the SCCCD, but because of the greater distance of the potential well from the gate electrode, the potential well will not be as deep. As a result, not as much charge can be accommodated, so that the maximum output signal and dynamic range of the device will be smaller than for the SCCCD.

The BCCCD structure is obtained by the use of a very thin ($\sim$2 μm), lightly doped ($\sim 10^{15}$ cm^{-3}) N-type epitaxial layer deposited on the P-type substrate, as shown in Figure 12.9a. Application of a reverse-bias voltage between the N-type epitaxial layer and the P-type substrate will result in the complete depletion of the N-type layer, as shown in Figure 12.9b. The free electrons have been swept out of the N-type layer, leaving behind the immobile positive charge due to the ionized donor dopant atoms. This positive charge produce an electric field distribution that points outward toward the substrate and also toward the gate electrode. This electric field and the resulting variation in the electric potential will result in a shallow potential well located a short distance from the surface ($\sim$1 μm). Application of a positive gate voltage will then make the potential well deeper and also shift the potential well minimum a little closer to the surface, as shown in Figure 12.9c.

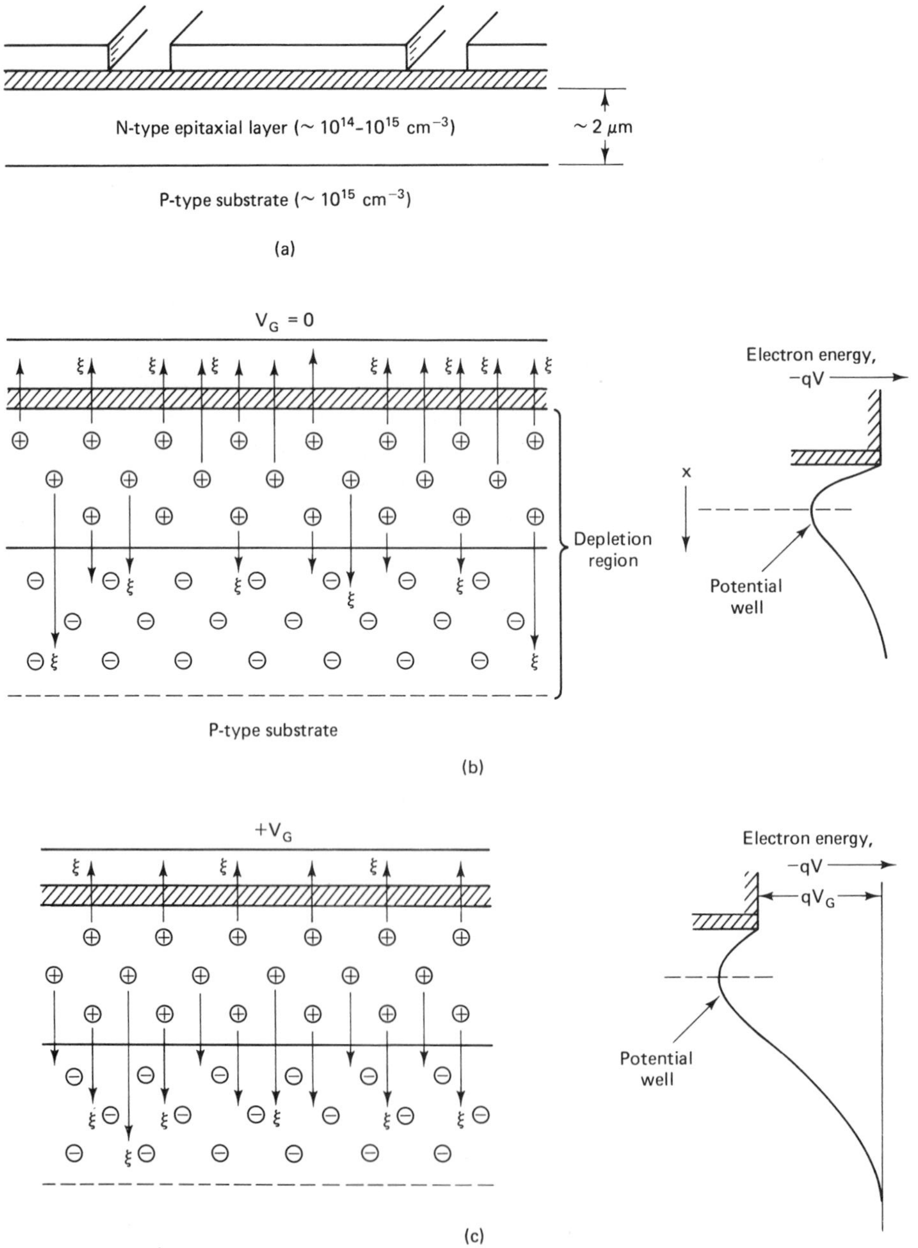

Figure 12.9 Buried-channel charge-coupled device: (a) basic structure; (b) with fully depleted epitaxial layer and $V_G = 0$; (c) with positive gate voltage.

12.2 BUCKET-BRIGADE DEVICES

An equivalent representation of a *bucket-brigade charge transfer device* (BBD) is shown in Figure 12.10. The charge that is stored on any given capacitor is transferred to the following capacitor on alternate clock pulses and thus propagates down the BBD array. The switches and other active devices in a BBD may be implemented using bipolar or MOS transistors, although MOSFETs are almost always used. Note that the number of charge packets, which represent various samples of the analog input signal that can be accommodated in the BBD array, is equal to one-half the number of charge storage capacitors because when any set of switches is closed, the same charge is on two capacitors simultaneously.

A basic diagram of a MOSFET BBD is shown in Figure 12.11 and a cross-sectional view of one BBD stage is given in the same diagram. We see that the storage capacitors are formed by the MOS gate-to-drain overlap capacitance.

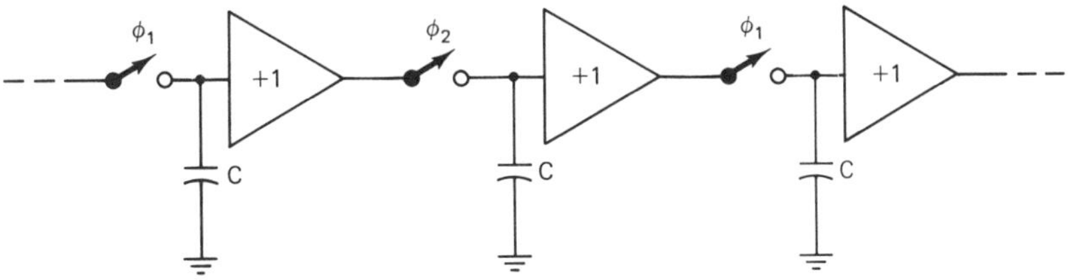

Figure 12.10 Equivalent representation of a bucket-brigade device.

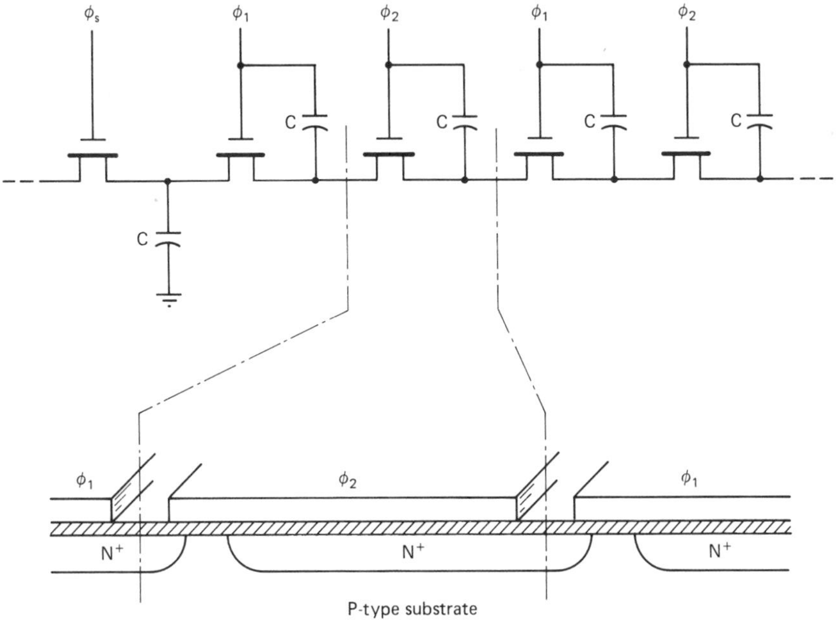

Figure 12.11 Basic diagram of a MOSFET BBD.

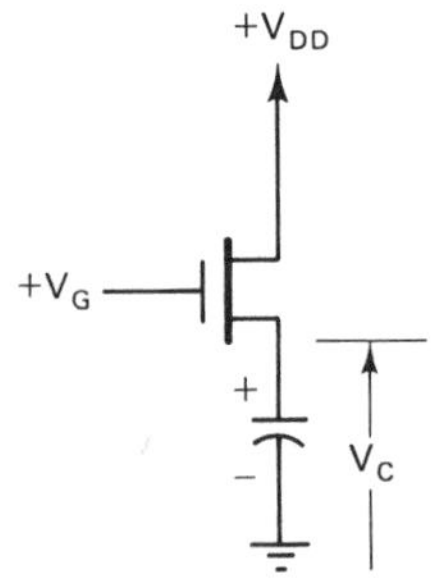

Figure 12.12 MOSFET source follower with load capacitance.

To understand the charge-transfer process in a BBD, let us first consider the circuit of Figure 12.12, showing a MOSFET source follower with a load capacitance C. If a gate voltage $+V_G$ is applied to the MOSFET, the capacitor C will charge up from the positive supply voltage via the drain-to-source channel of the MOSFET. The charging of the capacitor will continue until the gate-to-source voltage reaches the MOSFET threshold voltage level V_t, at which point the MOSFET will turn off and the charging of the capacitor will cease. The voltage level to which the capacitor charges up to will therefore be $V_G - V_t$.

Let us now look at the circuit of Figure 12.13. Since the current through both capacitors is the same, the charge transferred from one capacitor to the other will be equal. We will have that $\Delta V_{C_1} = \Delta Q_1/C_1$ and $\Delta V_{C_2} = \Delta Q_2/C_2$. Since $\Delta Q_2 = -\Delta Q_1 = \Delta Q$, we obtain $\Delta V_{C_1}/\Delta V_{C_2} = -C_1/C_2$. If $C_1 = C_2$, then $\Delta V_{C_1} = -\Delta V_{C_2}$.

With this background let us now look at the series of diagrams in Figure 12.14. The quiescent condition for the BBD will correspond to all capacitors being charged up to a voltage level of $V_G - V_t$. If this is the case, there will be no net charge transfer in the BBD array during the various clock pulses.

In Figure 12.14a we see the charging of the first capacitor from the analog signal source. The voltage of this capacitor will become equal to the analog input signal level V_A. Figure 12.14b shows the next charge-transfer process. The first capacitor will charge up to a level of $V_G - V_t$ when ϕ_2 goes high, for a voltage change of $\Delta V = V_G - V_t - V_A$. The voltage across the second capacitor will correspondingly change from the original quiescent level of $V_G - V_t$ down to $V_G - V_t - \Delta V = V_A$.

In Figure 12.14c we have the third charge-transfer process. The second capacitor will charge up from V_A to $V_G - V_t$ for a voltage change of $\Delta V = V_G - V_t - V_A$. The voltage across the third capacitor will therefore change from the quiescent level of $V_G - V_t$ to the new level of $V_G - V_t - \Delta V = V_A$. This process is repeated down the length of the bucket-brigade array. We note that the input analog voltage

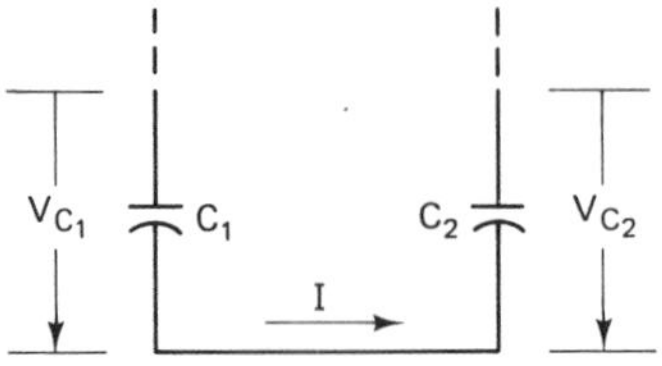

Figure 12.13 Charge transfer between capacitors.

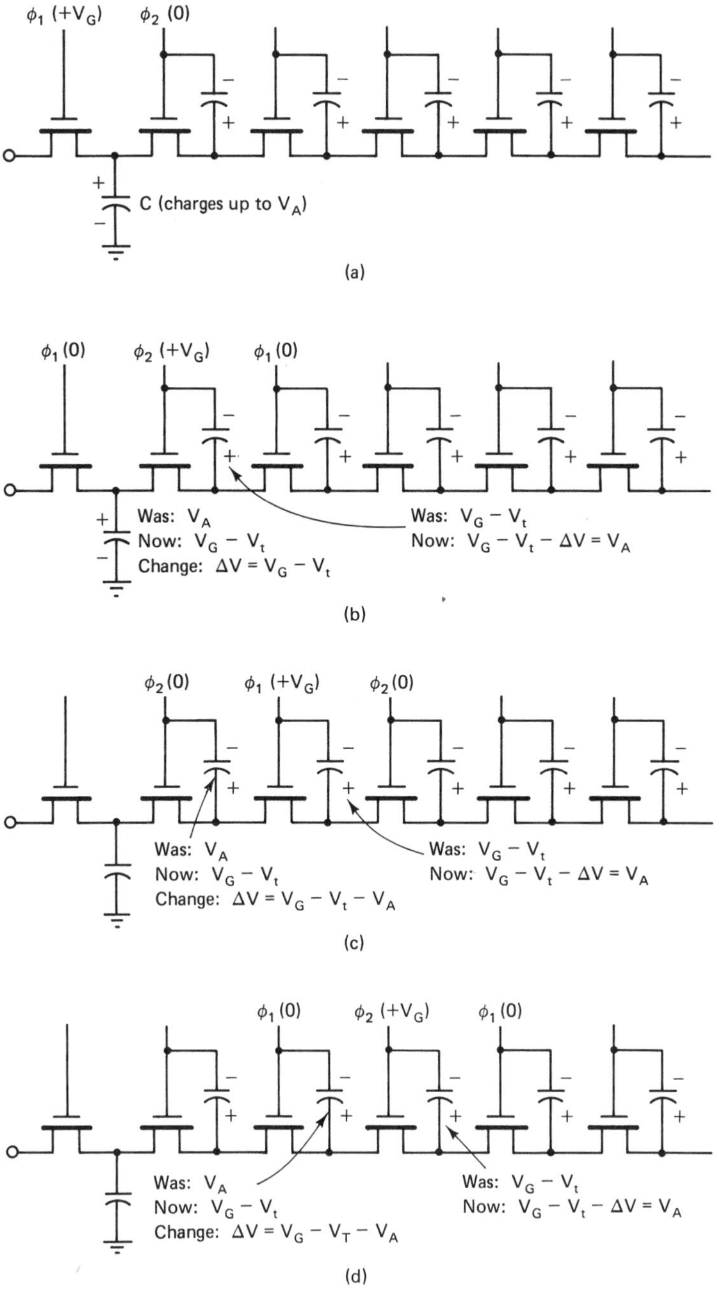

Figure 12.14 Charge-transfer process in a BBD: (a)–(d) first through fourth stages.

level V_A will propagate successively from capacitor to capacitor through the array by means of the $\phi_1 - \phi_2$ two-phase nonoverlapping clock pulses applied to the gates of the transistors.

The minimum clock rate and therefore the maximum delay time of the BBD is controlled by the capacitor leakage currents. The analog signal charge packet should be transported through the BBD in a time short compared to that in which the storage capacitors will get filled due to the leakage currents. The leakage current will be principally that across the N^+P junction and will generally be in the range 10 to 100 nA/cm² at 25°C. If the oxide thickness is 0.1 μm, the storage capacitance per unit area will be $C_{ox} = \epsilon_{ox}/t_{ox} = 3.8 \times 8.85 \times 10^{-14}$ F/cm/10^{-5} cm = 34 nF/cm². For an analog signal level of $V_A \simeq 1$ V the signal charge transferred along the BBD array will be $Q \simeq 34$ nC/cm². The capacitor filling time will be given by $t_{fill} = Q/I_{leakage}$, so that with the leakage currents given above the filling times will be in the range 0.3 to 3 s. Therefore, the maximum BBD delay time should be down in the range of about 100 ms. For a 512-stage BBD this will correspond to a minimum clock rate of 5 kHz.

The maximum clock rate and therefore minimum delay time of a BBD are limited by the rate at which charge can be transferred from one storage capacitor to the next through the finite drain-to-source resistance of the MOSFET. Bucket-brigade devices are generally slower than charge-coupled devices, so whereas CCDs can be operated in the video frequency range with clock rates as high as 20 MHz, BBDs generally are used in the audio-frequency range, but clock rates of up to 1.5 MHz are available.

12.2.1 Tetrode MOSFET Bucket-Brigade Devices

The simple BBD of Figure 12.14 suffers from the problem of the drain-to-source parasitic capacitances illustrated in Figure 12.15a. These parasitic capacitances will result in the incomplete charge transfer from one storage capacitor to the next in the BBD array and the coupling of part of the signal to storage capacitors in the adjacent stages. This will result in a reduced charge-transfer efficiency and a smearing or distortion of the output signal.

The tetrode MOSFET BBD structure of Figure 12.15b can be used to reduce the unwanted capacitative coupling very substantially. Transistors Q_{1A} and Q_{2A} throughout the array when turned off serve to isolate a bucket-brigade stage from the following stage. The gates of the isolation FETs are connected to a voltage level close to the $+V_{DD}$ supply.

When ϕ_1 goes high (+15 V) and ϕ_2 goes low (0 V), the voltage at the drain of Q_{2B} will drop to the analog signal sample level V_A. The gate-to-source voltage of Q_{1A} will be $+15 - V_A$ and Q_{1A} will therefore be on and the charge transfer from C_2 to C_1 will take place. Capacitor C_2 will charge from V_A to $V_G - V_t$ as in the preceding analysis of the BBD. The voltage at the drain of Q_{1B} will, however, increase from $V_G - V_t$ to $+15 + (V_G - V_t)$ as ϕ_1 goes high. As capacitor C_1 charges, this voltage will decrease to $+15 + (V_G - V_t) - \Delta V = +15 + V_A$. Since the voltage at the source of Q_{2A} is higher than the gate voltage, this transistor will be off during the charge-transfer process from C_2 to C_1 via Q_{1A} and Q_{1B}. This

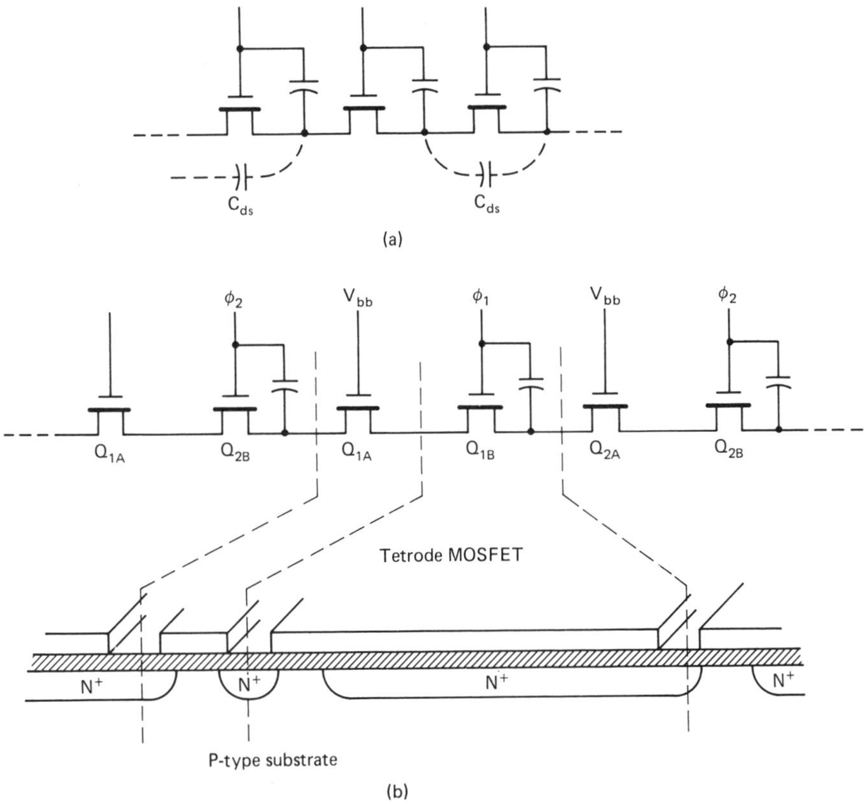

Figure 12.15 Tetrode MOSFET BBD: (a) parasitic capacitative coupling in a BBD; (b) reduction of parasitic capacitative coupling by using a tetrode MOSFET.

isolates the charge-transfer process involving this bucket-brigade stage from the other stages on either side.

12.2.2 Example of a Bucket-Brigade Device

An example of a BBD is the SAD1024 (Reticon). This device features two independent 512-stage delay sections. Total delays of from 340 μs to a maximum of 340 ms are available by variation of the clock frequency. The corresponding clock frequencies will range from 1.5 kHz to 1.5 MHz and the signal frequency 3-dB bandwidth is 200 kHz (typ). This device uses a polysilicon gate N-channel tetrode MOSFET structure.

The two 512-stage sections can be connected in series to obtain a 1024-stage device. A parallel-multiplex mode of operation is also possible in which the same analog input signal is supplied simultaneously to both 512-stage sections, as shown in Figure 12.16. The two-phase clock inputs for the two sections are cross-coupled so that the sampled analog output signals are available from the two channels on alternate clock half-periods. At the output the A-channel and B-channel signals are

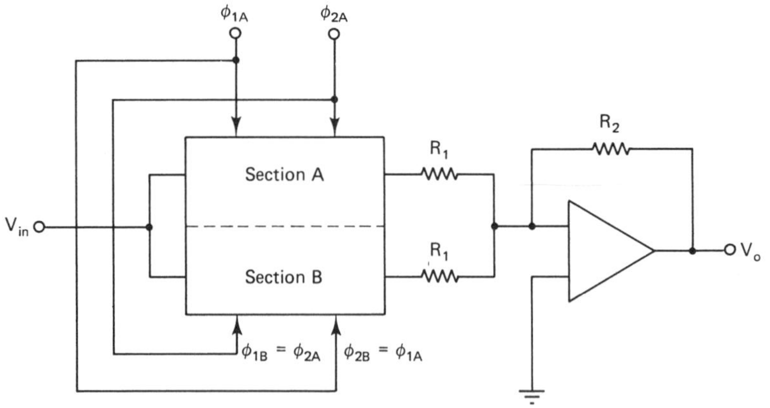

12.16 Parallel-multiplex operation of the SAD1024 BBD.

summed so that there are now two output sample per clock period rather than just one, so the maximum analog input frequency is now equal to the clock frequency.

This device offers a dynamic input range for the analog signal of 70 dB between the noise level of 630 μV and the maximum input signal level of 2 V peak-to-peak, at which point the total harmonic distortion will be up to 3%. However, for input signal levels of less than 1 V peak-to-peak, the distortion will be down to less than 0.5%.

In Figure 12.17 a circuit for using a BBD such as the SAD1024 for reverberation effects is shown, and in Figure 12.18 a circuit for vibrato effects is presented.

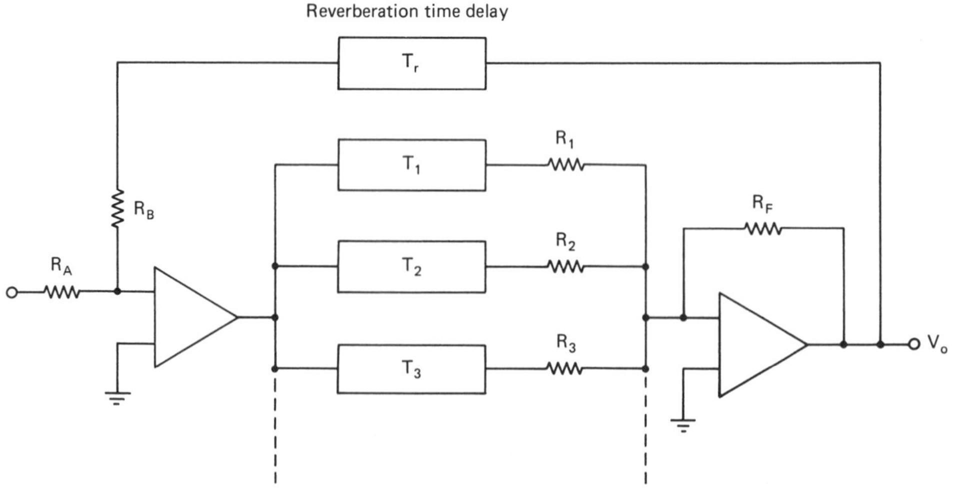

Figure 12.17 Circuit for audio reverberation effects.

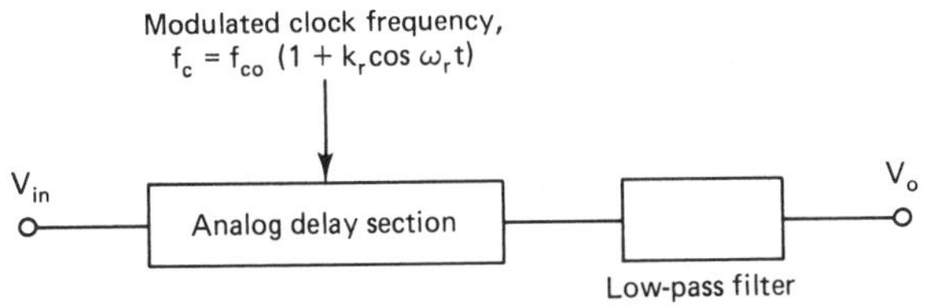

Figure 12.18 Circuit for vibrato effects.

12.3 CHARGE-TRANSFER-DEVICE SAMPLING RATE

The charge-transfer device operates as a sampled data system in which successive samples of the analog input signal are obtained and then transmitted along the array of CTD elements. The output signal will therefore be a delayed pulse-amplitude-modulated (PAM) representation of the original input signal. For the accurate reconstruction of the time-delayed analog signal, a sufficiently large sampling rate must be used.

If we consider as a simple example the unmodulated square wave of Figure 12.19a, we note that the corresponding spectrum shown in Figure 12.19b will consist of a d-c component, the fundamental frequency, f_s, and odd harmonics of the fundamental frequency at nf_s, where n is an odd integer. If an analog signal is used to modulate the amplitude of this square wave, the resulting PAM waveform will be as shown in Figure 12.19c and the corresponding frequency spectrum shown in Figure 12.19d. The PAM spectrum consists of the original square-wave components plus the upper and lower sideband frequencies at $nf_s + f_a$ and $nf_s - f_a$, where $n = 0$, 1, 3, 5, 7, . . . and f_a is the frequency of the analog modulating signal.

To recover the original signal a low-pass filter must be used to pass the signal frequency f_a and reject all of the higher-frequency components. Since the lowest of these frequency components that must be rejected will be at $f_s - f_a$, the low-pass filter must have a cutoff frequency above f_a and below $f_s - f_a$ and must have a rapid-enough roll-off characteristic to produce substantial attenuation of the $f_s - f_a$ component. Therefore, the minimum sampling frequency f_s must be such that $f_s - f_a > f_a$, so that $f_s > 2f_a$. This result is consistent with the Nyquist theorem for a sampled data system. It is usually desirable that the sampling frequency f_s be in the range of three to four times the maximum analog signal frequency, so as to provide a sufficient guard band between f_a and $f_s - f_a$ and therefore make the filtering easier.

12.4 APPLICATIONS OF CHARGE-TRANSFER DEVICES

Charge-transfer devices can be used for a wide variety of analog signal-processing applications. The charge-transfer device for most of these applications is used as an analog signal delay line. The time delays available will range from as little as 25 μs (for a 512-stage device) to as much as 100 ms. These delay times can be very precisely controlled and adjusted by the clock frequency. As a result of the accurate control

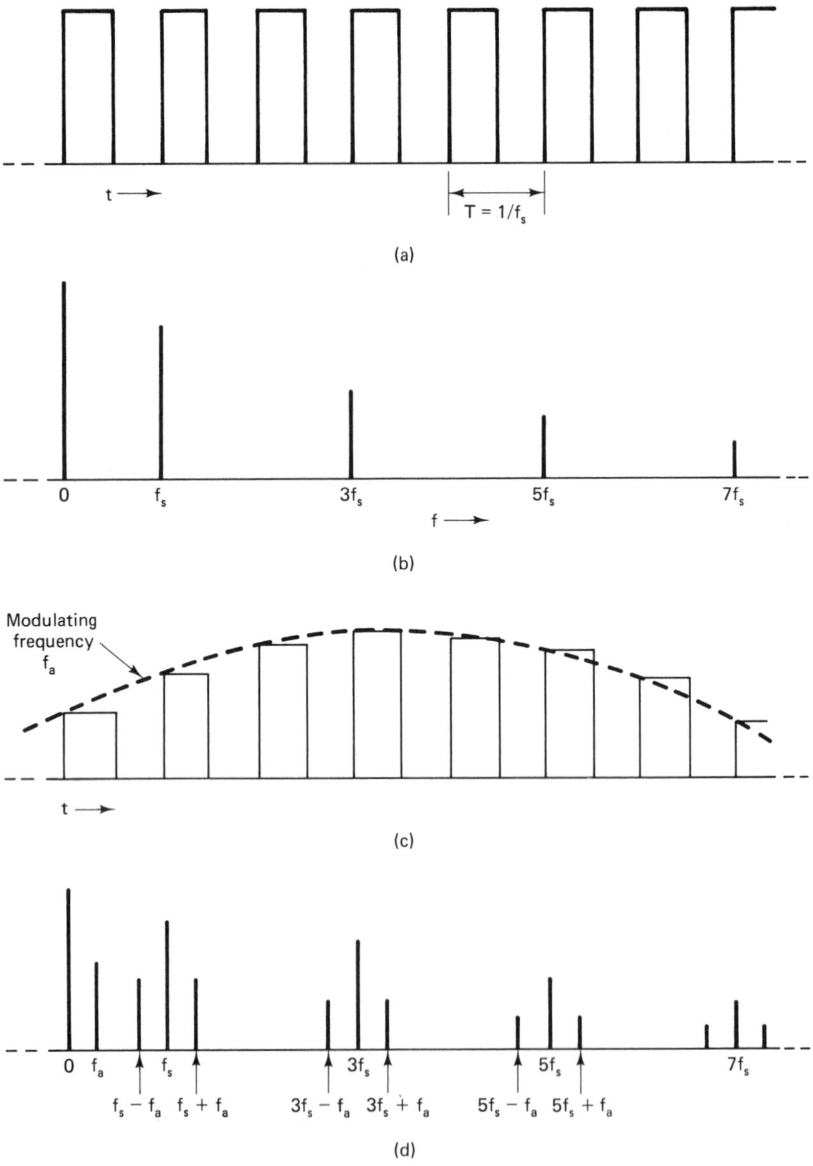

Figure 12.19 Sampling frequency requirements: (a) unmodulated square wave; (b) Fourier spectrum of unmodulated square wave; (c) amplitude-modulated square wave (PAM); (d) Fourier spectrum of amplitude-modulated square wave.

and variation of the delay time in a CTD, it can offer substantial advantages over ultrasonic delay lines.

In the case of an ultrasonic delay line the analog signal is converted to a sound wave by a piezoelectric transducer, transmitted through a suitable medium such as a quartz rod, and then reconverted back to an electric signal by a second piezoelectric transducer. The resulting delay time is, however, not adjustable as it is in the case of a CTD.

Charge-transfer devices of both the CCD and BBD type can be used for many analog signal filtering applications, such as for comb filters, recursive filters, and transversal filters. Related applications involve analog signal correlators. Special audio effects can be obtained with CTDs, such as reverberation, echo, vibrato, tremulo, and chorus effects, as well as speech compression and expansion and voice scrambling.

Charge-transfer devices can be used as analog serial memories or shift registers to provide temporary storage of an analog signal. This is useful for speed and time-base correction of audio and video tape recording systems. For videotape systems the CTD can be used for the temporary storage of one line of the video signal to provide a means of dropout compensation. If there is a partial or complete loss of signal from one line of a taped TV signal, the preceding line can be substituted and the resulting effect on the TV picture will generally not be noticeable.

Charge-transfer devices can be used as serial input–parallel output and parallel input–serial output analog shift registers for signal multiplexing, demultiplexing, and scrambling. Another applications area for CTDs is in ultrasonic systems. The electrical signal input to an array of ultrasonic transducers can be given a preprogrammed set of time delays by a number of CTDs placed in the signal paths. The ultrasonic transducers will become a phased array and the ultrasonic beam pattern, direction, and focusing can be electronically varied by control over the CTD time delays.

An important applications area for CTDs is in linear and area image sensing. In a linear image sensor, photogenerated electrons that are collected by an array of small area light-sensing areas or photodiodes are transferred to an adjacent CCD array as shown in Figure 12.20. The CCD array will operate as a parallel input–

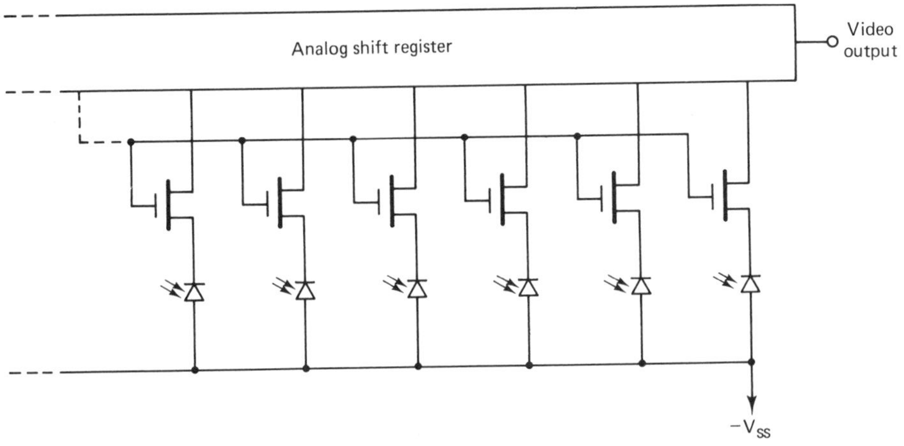

Figure 12.20 Linear image sensor.

serial output analog shift register. The photogenerated electron packets after being transferred to the CCD in parallel can then be clocked in serial fashion out of the CCD array. The output signal will then be a serial representation of the illumination pattern along the length of the array of light-sensing elements.

A area image sensor, shown in Figure 12.21, operates in a similar fashion.

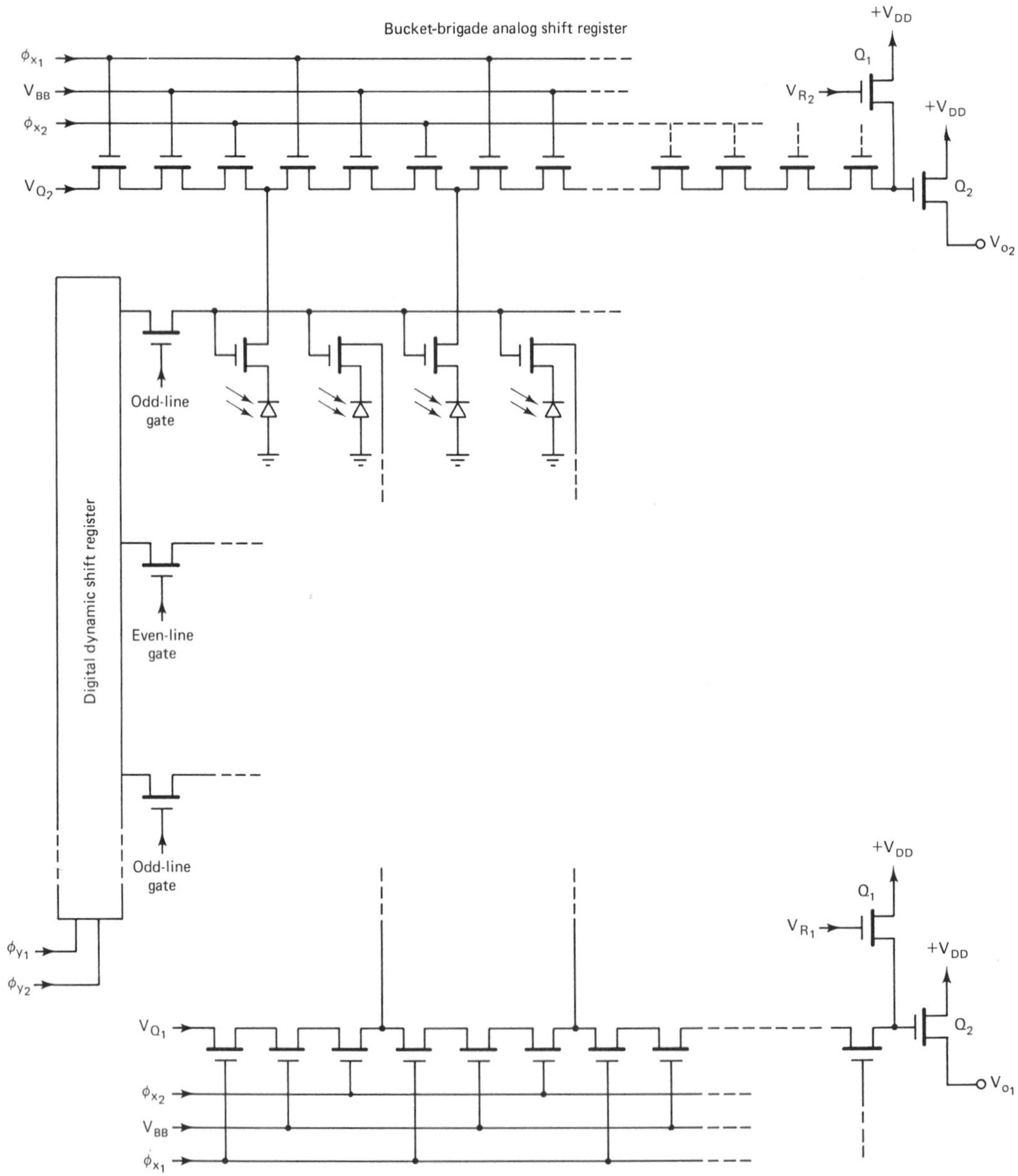

Figure 12.21 Area image sensor. Permission given by Reticon Corporation, a subsidiary of EG&G Inc. (Copyright 1977).

The photogenerated electrons that are produced in the parallel arrays of light-sensing elements are transferred to adjacent CCD arrays, which again serve as parallel input–serial output analog shift registers. The electron packets are then transferred out line by line from these interline CCD shift registers through another parallel input–serial output shift register.

We will now discuss a few of these CTD applications in more detail. Linear and area image sensors are discussed more fully in Chapter 15.

12.4.1 Comb Filter

The basic circuit for a comb filter using a CTD is shown in Figure 12.22a. The time delay T of the CTD will correspond to a phase lag of ωT radians for a sinusoidal signal. If the signals are additively combined by the amplifier and if we assume that the CTD has a transfer function magnitude of unity, the net system transfer function can be expressed as $H = V_o/V_{in} = A[1 + \exp(-j\omega T)]$. This can be rewritten as

$$H = A \exp\left(\frac{-j\omega T}{2}\right)\left[\exp\left(\frac{j\omega T}{2}\right) + \exp\left(\frac{-j\omega T}{2}\right)\right] = 2A \cos \omega T \underline{/-\omega T/2} \qquad (12.1)$$

This system transfer function is shown in Figure 12.22b. We note that there will be transmission zeros for $\omega T/2 = n\pi/2$, where n is an odd integer. Therefore, the zero transmission frequencies will be at $f = 1/2T$, $3/2T$, $5/2T$, and so on.

If the signals are subtractively combined by the amplifier, the net transfer function will become $H = A[1 - \exp(-j\omega T)]$. This can be rewritten as

$$H = A \exp\left(\frac{-j\omega T}{2}\right)\left[\exp\left(\frac{j\omega T}{2}\right) - \exp\left(\frac{-j\omega T}{2}\right)\right] = 2Aj \exp\left(\frac{-j\omega T}{2}\right) \sin \frac{\omega T}{2} \qquad (12.2)$$

$$= 2A \sin \frac{\omega T}{2} \underline{/(\pi/2 - \omega T/2)}$$

This transfer function is shown in Figure 12.22c and we note that the transmission zeros now occur when $T/2 = n\pi$, where n is an integer. The corresponding zero transmission frequencies will be at $f = 1/T$, $2/T$, $3/T$, and so on.

We see that the comb filter will have a periodic series of transmission zeros spaced at frequency intervals of $1/T$. By varying the clock rate of the CTD and therefore the delay time T, the positions of the transmission zeros can be shifted. In actual practice the transfer function will not go all of the way to zero at the transmission minima and there will also be an upper limit to the comb filter transmission characteristics as a result of the limited frequency response of the CTD.

Comb filter for color television. A good example of the use of a CTD comb filter is for the improvement of the video frequency response and hence picture quality of color TV receivers. The spectrum of a TV signal is essentially a continuous spectrum from 0 to 4.0 MHz. However, as a result of the large amount of line-to-line repetition in a TV picture, the spectral energy will be concentrated at integer multiples or harmonics of the line frequency f_L, which is 15,734 Hz for color TV and 15,750 Hz for black-and-white TV. If there were exact repetition of the video

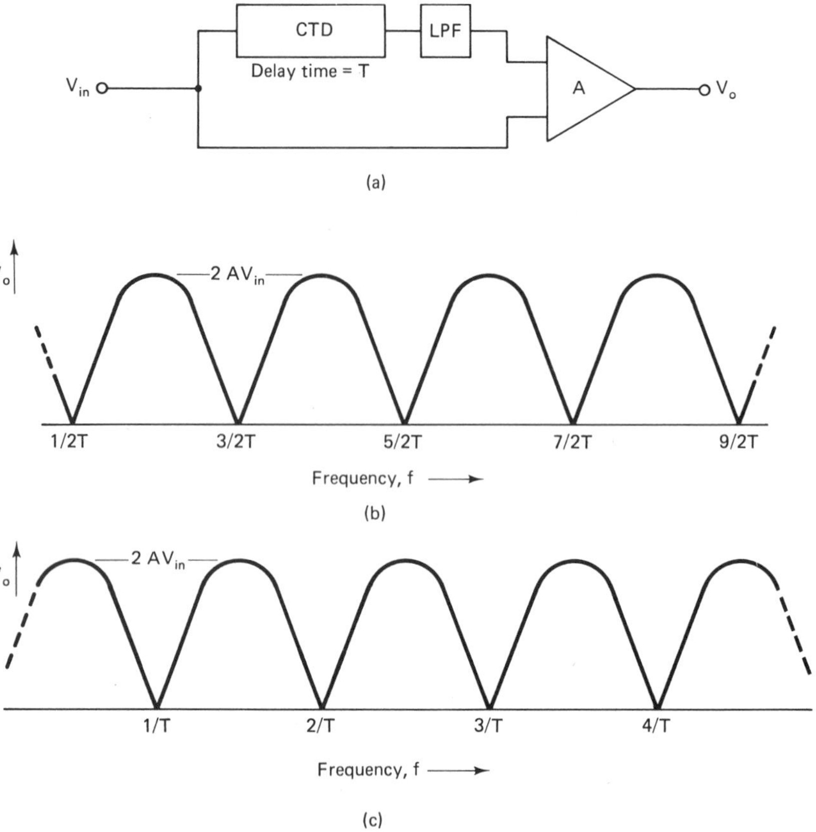

Figure 12.22 Comb filter: (a) basic circuit; (b) transfer function if amplifier inputs are added; (c) transfer function if amplifier inputs are subtracted.

signal from one line to the next, the video spectrum would be a line spectrum consisting only of harmonics of the line frequency f_L, as shown in Figure 12.23a. Due to the changes from line to line that will be present in an actual TV picture, the spectrum will be spread out over the entire video bandwidth, but there will nevertheless be a definite clustering of the spectral energy near harmonics of f_L, as shown in Figure 12.23b.

The color information in the TV signal is carried by sidebands of a color subcarrier frequency of $f_{sc} = 3.579545$ MHz, as shown in Figure 12.24. This subcarrier frequency is chosen to be an odd multiple of $\frac{1}{2}f_L$ or $227.5f_L$. As a result of this choice, the color signal that overlaps the monochrome signal will generally exhibit a polarity reversal from one line to the next and therefore will to a large extent cancel out. This cancellation will not be complete since the opposite polarity color sideband signals will be spatially one line spacing apart. Furthermore, if there is a significant change in the color signal from line to line in the vertical direction, there will not be the exact color signal polarity reversal between adjacent lines.

Since the color subcarrier is an odd multiple of $f_L/2$, the color sideband spectrum

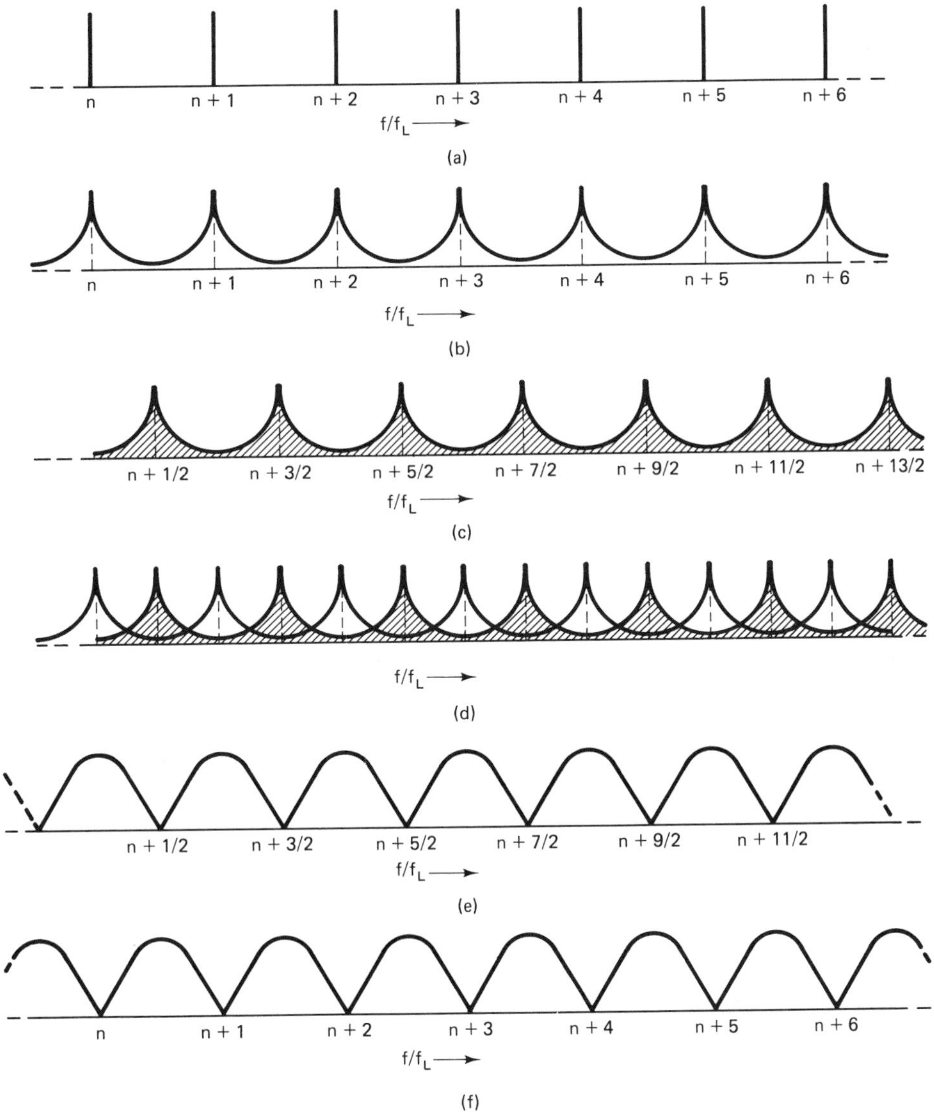

Figure 12.23 Television signal spectrum: (a) luminance (B/W) spectrum with all horizontal lines identical; (b) luminance spectrum with changes from line to line; (c) color sideband (chrominance) spectrum; (d) combined luminance and chrominance video signal spectrum; (e) comb filter transfer characteristics to filter out chrominance signal; (f) comb filter transfer characteristic to filter out luminance signal.

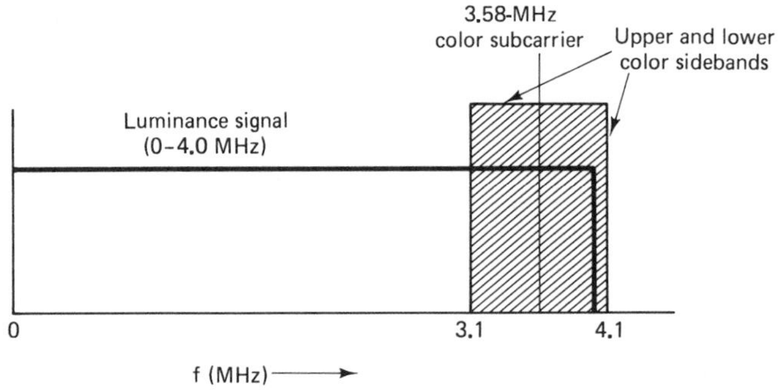

Figure 12.24 Color television signal spectrum.

will show a clustering of the spectral energy around odd multiples of $f_L/2$, as shown in Figure 12.23c. The combination of the luminance and chrominance (color) signals produces the spectrum shown in Figure 12.23d and is an example of frequency interleaving. In a conventional TV receiver the luminance (black-and-white) signal bandwidth is limited to about 3.1 MHz to prevent interference by the color sidebands. This band limiting will, however, decrease the picture resolution. To solve this problem and to allow for the full 4.0-MHz video bandwidth for the luminance signal, a comb filter can be used to filter out the color sideband components that overlap the luminance signal spectrum. This comb filter will be of the additive type using a CTD with a time delay of $1/f_L = 63.5\ \mu s$. This will produce transmission zeros at odd multiples of $f_L/2$, as shown in Figure 12.23e. In a similar fashion a comb filter can be used to filter out the luminance signal components for the chrominance circuit. This filter will be of the subtractive type, using a CTD, again with a time delay of $1/f_L = 63.5\ \mu s$. This will result in transmission zeros at integer multiples of f_L, as shown in Figure 12.23f.

12.4.2 Recursive Filter

Another filter that exhibits a periodic type of response characteristics and uses a charge-transfer device is the recursive filter. The recursive filter uses a CTD in a feedback loop, as shown in Figure 12.25a. For this circuit the output voltage V_o will be given by $V_o = V_{in} + \exp(-j\omega T)AV_o$, where the amplifier gain is restricted to values less than unity. Solving for the filter transfer function $H = V_o/V_{in}$ gives $H = V_o/V_{in} = 1/[1 - A \exp(-j\omega T)]$. This transfer function will be a maximum when $\exp(-j\omega T) = 1$ and have a value of $H_{MAX} = 1/(1 - A)$. The condition $\exp(-j\omega T) = 1$ will occur when $\omega T = 2\pi n$, where n is an integer and the corresponding frequencies will be given by $f = n/T$, as shown in Figure 12.25b. The filter transmission minima will occur when $\exp(-j\omega T) = -1$, so that $\omega T = n\pi$, where n is an odd integer, and therefore $f = n/2T$. The transmission minima will have a value of $1/(1 + A)$, so that the maximum-to-minimum transfer ratio will be $(1 + A)/(1 - A)$.

The recursive filter thus produces a periodic series of transmission peaks at a frequency spacing of $1/T$. For values of A that are close to unity, very large values

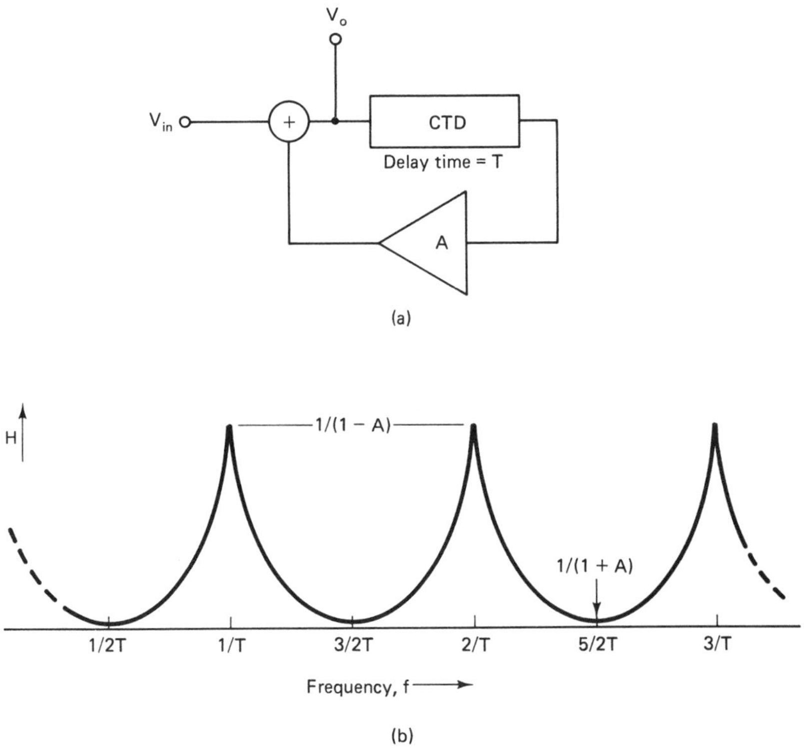

Figure 12.25 Recursive filter: (a) basic circuit; (b) transfer function.

of $H_{MAX}/H_{MIN} = (1 + A)/(1 - A)$ will be obtained and the peaks will be relatively narrow.

12.4.3 Matched Filter

A matched filter has a transfer function that is a replica of the frequency spectrum of the signal to be received. Since the frequency response of a matched filter is not flat, there will be some distortion of the signal, but the matched filter will produce the maximum obtainable signal-to-noise ratio for any given signal.

To consider a simple example of a matched filter, let us look at the waveform shown in Figure 12.26a and the spectrum of this signal shown in Figure 12.26b. The signal to be detected consists of a periodic pulse train of narrow pulse of width W and repetition frequency f_o. The matched filter for this signal will have a transfer function that is the same as the Fourier series spectrum of the signal, as shown in Figure 12.26b, and thus should have narrow transmission peaks located at integer multiples of f_o.

This matched filter can be approximated by a recursive filter with a CTD time delay of $T = 1/f_o$. It can also be approximated by a transversal of the type to be described next and shown in Figure 12.27. For the transversal filter implementation

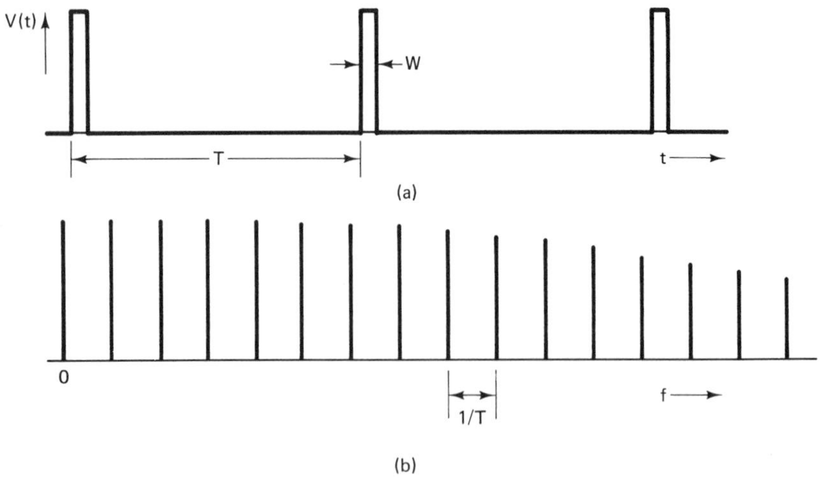

Figure 12.26 Rectangular pulse waveform: (a) rectangular pulse train; (b) Fourier spectrum.

the CTD time delays should all be equal to $1/f_o$ and the a_n coefficients should be approximately equal.

12.4.4 Transversal Filters

A basic diagram of a transversal filter is shown in Figure 12.27. The transversal filter can be used to approximate a matched filter by suitable choice of the delay times and the weighting coefficients a_n. To examine the synthesis of a filter transfer

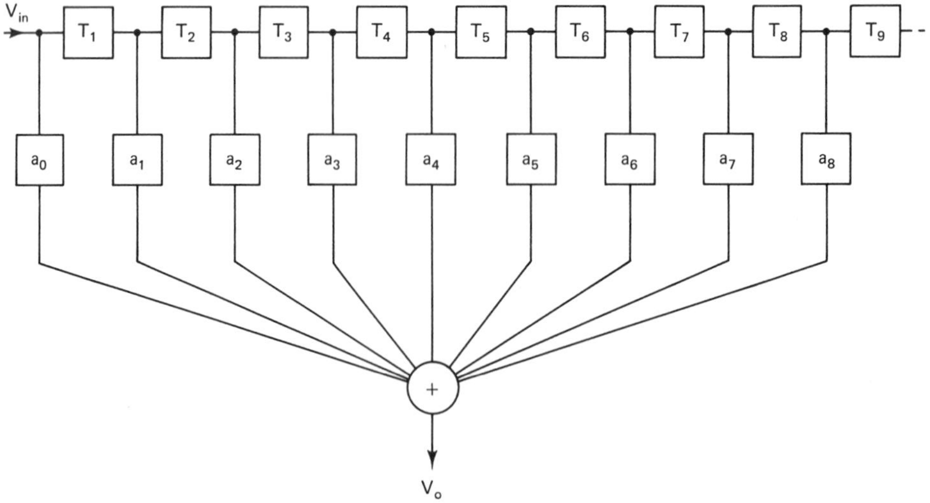

Figure 12.27 Transversal filter.

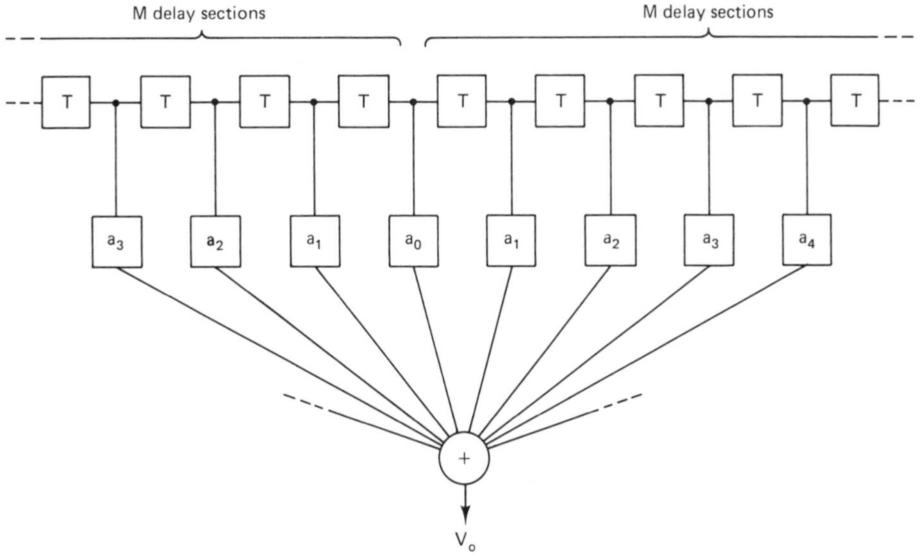

Figure 12.28 Transversal filter for Fourier response synthesis.

characteristics, let us look at the transversal filter configuration of Figure 12.28, in which all of the CTD time delays are equal.

The transfer function for this transversal filter will be given by

$$H = \frac{V_o}{V_{\text{in}}} = \cdots a_3 \exp[-j\omega(M-3)T] + a_2 \exp[-j\omega(M-2)T] + a_1 \exp[-j\omega(M-1)T + a_0 \exp(-j\omega MT) \tag{12.3}$$
$$+ a_1 \exp[-j\omega(M+1)T] + a_2 \exp[-j\omega(M+2)T] + a_3 \exp[-j\omega(M+3)T] + \cdots$$

After factoring out $\exp(-j\omega MT)$, the transfer function becomes

$$\begin{aligned} H &= \exp(-j\omega MT)[\cdots + a_3 \exp(j3\omega T) + a_2 \exp(j2\omega T) + a_1 \exp(j\omega T) \\ &\quad + a_0 + a_1 \exp(-j\omega T) + a_2 \exp(-j2\omega T) + a_3 \exp(-j3\omega T) + \cdots] \\ &= \exp(-j\omega MT)\{a_0 + a_1[\exp(j\omega T) + \exp(-j\omega T)] + a_2[\exp(j2\omega T) \\ &\quad + \exp(-j2\omega T)] + a_3[\exp(j3\omega T) + \exp(-j3\omega T)] + \cdots\} \end{aligned} \tag{12.4}$$

Since $\exp(jn\omega T) + \exp(-jn\omega T) = 2\cos n\omega T$, the preceding expression can be written as

$$H = \exp(-j\omega MT)(a_0 + a_1 \cos \omega T + a_2 \cos 2\omega T + a_3 \cos 3\omega T + \cdots) \tag{12.5}$$

The expression above can be considered to be a truncated Fourier series and by suitable choice of the a_n coefficients using the standard Fourier analysis techniques, the required filter transfer characteristics can be synthesized.

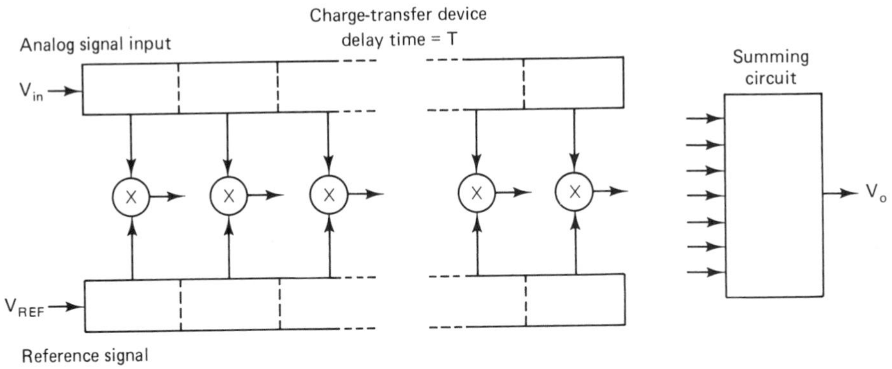

Figure 12.29 Analog signal correlator.

12.4.5 Analog Signal Correlators

A basic diagram of an analog signal correlator is shown in Figure 12.29. The maximum output voltage will be obtained when the analog input voltage waveform over time period T matches that of the reference signal. This analog signal correlator can be considered to perform a function in the time domain that is analogous to that performed by the matched filter in the frequency domain.

If an analog-to-digital converter is used to convert the input signal V_{in} to a binary digital signal and the reference input is also in digital form, the analog multipliers can be replaced by simpler and faster AND gates, as shown in Figure 12.30.

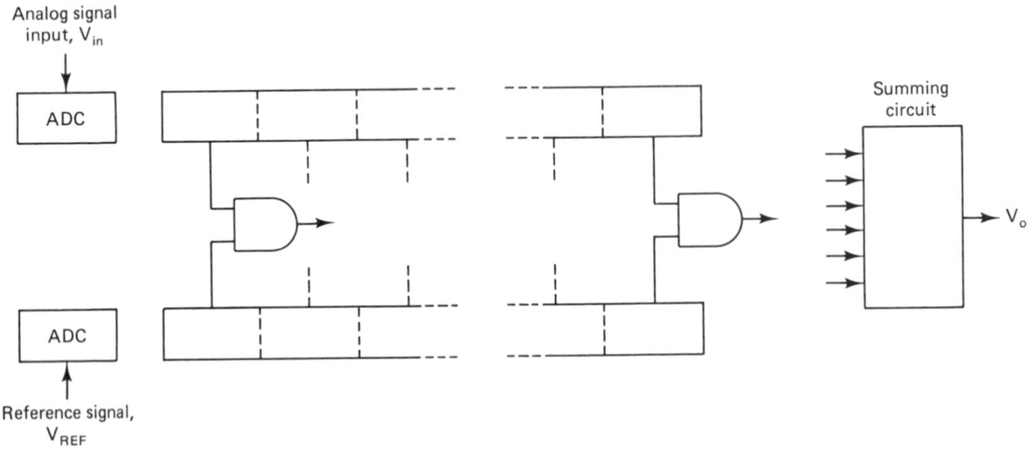

Figure 12.30 Analog signal correlator using analog-to-digital conversion.

PROBLEMS

12.1. (*CTD transfer function*) If the charge-transfer process in a charge-transfer device can be characterized by a simple exponential relationship of the form $Q(t) = Q(0)\,[1 - \exp(-t/\pi)]$:

(a) Show that for an N-stage, two-phase CTD the clock frequency f_c at which the transfer function of the CTD will be 3 dB down will be given by

$$f_c(3\text{ dB}) = \frac{1}{2\tau \ln \dfrac{1}{1 - 2^{-1/2N}}}$$

(b) If $N = 512$ and $\tau = 100$ ns, find the 3-dB clock frequency. (*Ans.*: 685 kHz)

12.2. (*Charge-coupled device*) A CCD has gate electrodes that are 10 μm × 20 μm in area and a gate oxide thickness of 800 Å. The threshold voltage for the formation of an N-type inversion layer in the P-type substrate underneath the gate electrode is +2.0 V.

(a) If the high-state gate voltage is +10 V, find the maximum charge that can be stored in the inversion layer potential well. (*Ans.*: 0.646 pC)

(b) If the thermally generated leakage current is 50 nA/cm² (at 300°K), find the time it will take for the potential wells to be filled by the thermally generated current. (*Ans.*: 6.46 s)

(c) Find the maximum output current for a clock frequency of 10 kHz. (*Ans.*: 6.46 nA)

(d) Find the output current that is due to the thermally generated leakage current for a 512-stage CCD. (*Ans.*: 51.2 pA)

(e) Find the dynamic range of the devices if this is defined as the ratio of the maximum output current to the output current due to the leakage current. (*Ans.*: 126)

(f) At what clock frequency will the dynamic range as defined above drop to unity? (*Ans.*: 79.3 Hz)

(g) If the maximum and minimum clock frequencies are 100 kHz and 1 kHz, respectively, find the minimum and maximum time delay available from this 512-stage CCD. (*Ans.*: 5.12 ms, 512 ms)

12.3. (*Comb filter*) A comb filter is to have null frequencies at odd multiples of 10 kHz. The CTD that is used for the comb filter has an analog signal 3-dB bandwidth of 1.0 MHz with a 20-dB/decade roll-off above the 1.0-MHz breakpoint frequency.

(a) Find the CTD time delay that is needed. (*Ans.*: 50 μs)

(b) The net transfer function of the CTD branch of the comb filter is adjusted to give a zero signal transmission at the first null frequency of 10 kHz. Find the signal transmission (in dB) at the following null frequencies (kHz): 30, 50, 70, 110, 150, 210, 310, 410, and 510. (*Ans.*: −68.0, −58.4, −52.4, −44.5, −39.2, −33.4, −27.0, −22.5, −19.2)

(c) Find the bandwidth between the points at which the response is down 20 dB below the maximum response. Also express the bandwidth as a percentage of the first null frequency. (*Ans.*: 637 Hz, 6.37%)

REFERENCES

BEYMAN, J. D. E., and D. R. LAMB, *Charge-Coupled Devices and Their Applications*, McGraw-Hill, 1980.

EINSPRUCH, N. G., *VLSI Electronics: Microstructure Science*, Vol. 5, Academic Press, 1982.

GLASER, A. B. and G. E. SUBAK-SHARPE, *Integrated Circuit Engineering*, Addison-Wesley, 1977.

HOBSON, G. S., *Charge-Transfer Devices*, Wiley, 1978.

MELEN, R., and DENNIS BUSS, *Charge-Coupled Devices: Technology and Applications*, IEEE Press, 1977.

MILLMAN, J., *Microelectronics*, McGraw-Hill, 1979.

SEQUIN, C. H., and M. F. TOMPSETT, *Charge Transfer Devices,* Academic Press, 1975.

YANG, E. S., *Fundamentals of Semiconductor Devices*, Chap. 11, McGraw-Hill, 1978.

Special-Function Integrated Circuits

13

13.1 INSTRUMENTATION AMPLIFIERS

An instrumentation amplifier is a difference amplifier with a very high input impedance and a low output impedance and is generally designed to amplify low level difference-mode signals in the presence of relatively large common-mode signals. They are often used to amplify the very low level output signals of various types of transducers. In the cases in which there is a very large common-mode voltage, an isolation amplifier or a combination instrumentation/isolation amplifier of the type discussed in the next section can be used. An instrumentation amplifier can be constructed with separate op amps, and an example is shown in Figure 13.1a. Instrumentation amplifiers are also available as hybrid ICs with circuitry similar to that of Figure 13.1a. These hybrid ICs include all of the resistors except for the gain setting resistor R_G. The gain of this amplifier is given by

$$V_O = \left(1 + \frac{2R_1}{R_G}\right)\left(\frac{R_3}{R_2}\right)(V_2 - V_1) \tag{13.1}$$

We see that the gain can by controlled by the variation of a single gain setting resistor R_G. Note that the output voltage is proportional to the difference-mode input voltage and is basically independent of the common-mode voltage.

One variation of the basic instrumentation amplifier circuit of Figure 13.1a is shown in Figure 13.1b in which a common-mode voltage is obtained at the junction of the two R_4 resistors and after being buffered by the optional voltage-follower A_4 is used to maintain the cable shields at the common-mode voltage level. This "guard drive" reduces the effective common-mode input capacitance and also reduces the

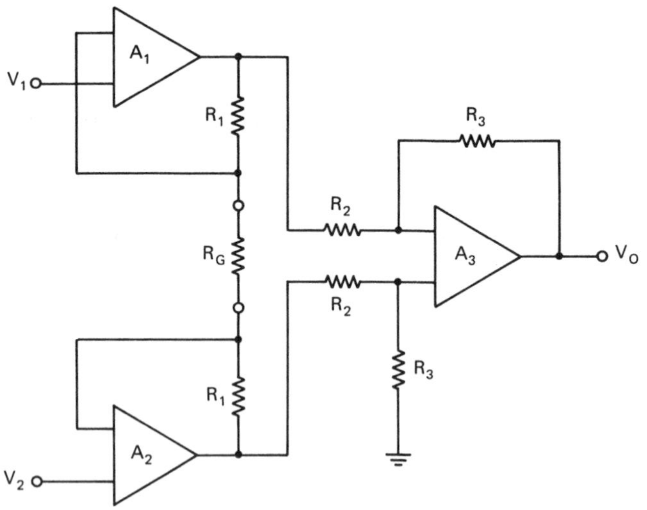

(a)

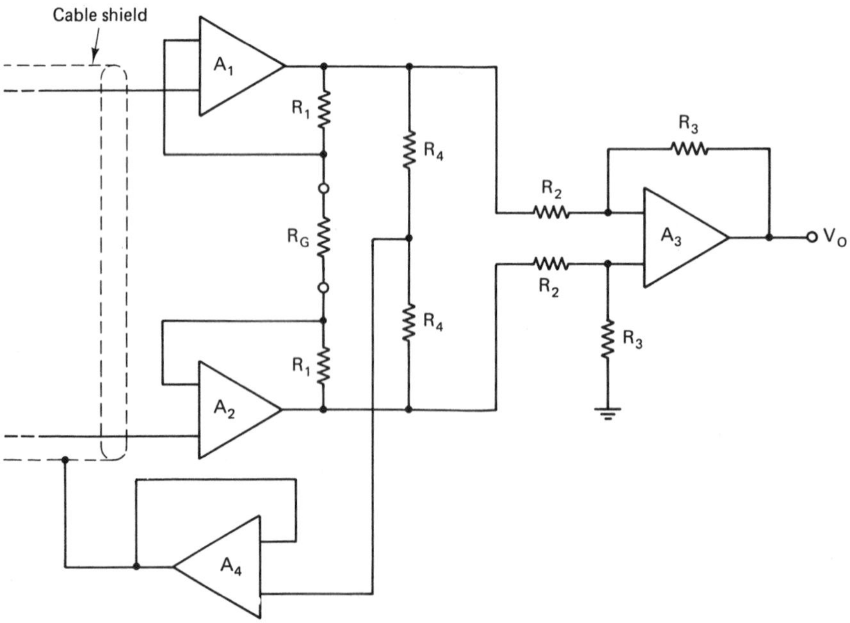

(b)

Figure 13.1 Instrumentation amplifier: (a) basic circuit; (b) instrumentation amplifier with guard drive.

input leakage currents. This feature acts to increase the common-mode rejection ratio of the system. Examples of instrumentation amplifiers of this type are the INA104 (Burr-Brown), 3630 (Burr-Brown), and LH0036 (National Semiconductor). The INA104, for example, features a common-mode rejection ratio of 106 dB minimum at 60 Hz and a differential and common-mode input impedance of 10^{10} Ω in parallel with 3 pF. The input offset voltage is just 25 μV with a temperature coefficient of only 0.25 μV/°C.

Other examples of instrumentation amplifiers of this same basic type with a guard terminal to drive an input cable shield, are the AD612 and AD614 (Analog Devices). These hybrid ICs contain a precision laser-trimmed thin film resistor network with resistance values ranging from 156 Ω to 80 kΩ. These resistors can be used for the gain setting resistor R by pin strapping that will allow the gain to be set in binary steps from 1 to 1024. As a result of the close matching of the resistor temperature coefficients and the close thermal tracking, the temperature coefficient of the voltage gain is only 10 ppm/°C. An external resistor can also be used to obtain other gain values. This is a relatively wide bandwidth instrumentation amplifier with a bandwidth of 100 kHz at unity gain, 60 kHz at a gain of 128, and 10 kHz at a gain of 1024. The common-mode rejection ratio with a 1000 Ω source impedance imbalance from d-c to 60 Hz is 74 dB minimum at unity gain and 94 dB minimum at a gain of 1024. The difference-mode and common-mode input impedance is 10^9 Ω in parallel with 3 pF.

An example will now be presented to show the advantage to be gained from the use of the common-mode feedback to the input cable shield to improve the common-mode rejection of the system. The amplifier will be assumed to have a common-mode rejection ratio (CMRR) of 106 dB and an input capacitance of 4 pF. The capacitance between each signal lead and the cable shield will be assumed to be 100 pF and a signal frequency is 10 kHz. A source impedance imbalance of just 10 Ω will cause the effective CMRR of the system to be reduced to 83 dB with the cable shield grounded. If, however, the shield is driven with the common-mode feedback voltage the CMRR will be up to 102.5 dB. A source impedance imbalance of 100 Ω results in a CMRR of 63.6 dB with the shield grounded and 90.4 dB with the common-mode guard drive. A 1000 Ω source imbalance results in a CMRR that is down to 43.7 dB with a grounded shield, but will be up to 71.8 dB with the guard drive.

13.2 ISOLATION AMPLIFIERS

An isolation amplifier is an amplifier in which there is no conductive contact between the input and output sections of the amplifier. Isolation amplifiers are often used when there is a very large common-mode voltage difference between the input and output sides of the device. This voltage difference can in some cases be in the range of several thousand volts. Another applications area is in medical instrumentation for patient safety against leakage currents. The coupling method most often used is optical, although transformer coupling is also used. Most isolation amplifiers are hybrid ICs and contain an input amplifier, a gallium arsenide (GaAs) light-emitting diode (LED), a silicon photodiode, and an output amplifier. The input signal is used to modulate the light output of an LED. The light emitted by the LED is detected by a photodiode and converted to an electrical signal.

An important characteristic of an isolation amplifier is the linearity of the input-to-output transfer characteristic. The LEDs can be a problem in this regard due to their non-linear current input-to-light output characteristics. Various means of obtaining a high degree of linearity in optically-coupled analog signal transmission systems are discussed in section 15.8 of Chapter 15. Feedback linearization circuits are shown in Figure 15.13 using a matched pair of photodiodes as in Figure 15.13a, or a matched set of LEDs and photodiode as in Figure 15.13b. In the optical coupling systems of Figure 15.14, various pulse modulation techniques are used in which the analog input signal is first converted to a digital signal and then after the optical signal transmission is reconverted back to an analog signal. The pulse modulation techniques include pulse frequency modulation as in Figure 15.14a, pulse-width modulation as in Figure 15.14b, and pulse-code modulation as in Figure 15.14c.

An example of a hybrid IC isolation amplifier is the ISO100 (Burr-Brown). This is an optically-coupled device using an LED and a matched pair of photodiodes arranged so that both photodiodes receive the same amount of light from the LED. The typical nonlinearity specification is 0.1% for the ISO100AP, 0.03% for the ISO100BP, and 0.02% for the ISO100CP. This parameter is the maximum deviation from the "best fit" straight line input-to-output transfer characteristic expressed as a percentage of the full-scale output. The isolation parameters include a d-c input-to-output maximum voltage rating of 750 V, an input-to-output isolation resistance of 10^{12} Ω and a capacitance of 2.5 pF. The small-signal bandwidth is 60 kHz and the full-power bandwidth is 6 kHz for a 20 V peak-to-peak output voltage.

The 3450–3455 series (Burr-Brown) of isolation amplifiers also uses optical coupling, but makes use of pulse width modulation rather than feedback to obtain a very high degree of linearity. The nonlinearity is specified as 0.005% maximum, 0.0015% typical for the 3450, and 0.0025% maximum, 0.005% typical for the other devices.

An example of an isolation amplifier using transformer coupling is the 3456 (Burr-Brown). A pulse-width modulation technique is used to obtain a high degree of linearity and also to minimize pickup from other units and stray magnetic fields. The typical linearity is 0.01% for gains below 100 and 0.03% for gains up to 1000. An additional feature of this device is that it is actually a combination of an instrumentation amplifier and an isolation amplifier with the input amplifier configuration being that of an instrumentation amplifier with a single external gain setting resistor. The d-c power for the input stage and pulse width modulator is obtained from the output side of the IC by means of a DC/DC converter using an oscillator, transformer, and rectifier circuit. As a result, d-c isolation can be achieved without the need for a separate power supply for the input side of the device. The peak isolation voltage rating is 8000 V and the common mode rejection ratio is 112 dB at 60 Hz. The small-signal bandwidth is 30 kHz.

Other examples of transformer coupled hybrid isolation amplifiers are the AD293 and AD294 (Analog Devices). These devices have an isolated transformer-coupled DC/DC converter to supply d-c power to the input side. These ICs feature a common-mode voltage rating of 2500 V peak for the AD293 and 8000 V peak for the AD294, and as a result are especially suitable for medical instrumentation along with other applications. The nonlinearity is specified as 0.05% maximum. This high degree of linearity is obtained by the use of a negative feedback loop for the input amplifier. The feedback voltage is produced by a feedback winding that is identical to the output winding and on the same transformer core as the output winding. The voltage induced in the feedback winding will thus be identical to the voltage produced across the output winding. This device offers very good common-mode rejection with a CMRR of 115 dB. The small-signal bandwidth is 2.5 kHZ for gains from 1 to 100.

13.3 MICROPOWER INTEGRATED CIRCUITS: TRANSISTOR OPERATION AT LOW CURRENT LEVELS

For some IC applications it is desirable to operate the circuit at very low quiescent supply current levels, often down in the range of just a few microamperes. This low-current operation is especially useful for applications in which the circuit will be powered by a battery of limited size, and in which the circuit must be operated continuously or uninterrupted for a long period.

Both bipolar transistors and field-effect transistors can be operated at very low current levels, even down into the low-nanoampere range. The major drawback inherent in operation at very low quiescent current levels is the decrease in the dynamic forward transfer conductance (g_m or g_{fs}). Since the midfrequency voltage gain is given by $A_{V(\text{MID})} = -g_m R_L$, the decrease in g_m at low current levels can lead to a substantial loss in voltage gain. In many cases the decrease in g_m can be compensated for by a corresponding increase in the size of the load resistance R_L. In the case of monolithic ICs, the very high values of R_L that may be required can be obtained by the use of an active load.

The large values of R_L that are required at low current levels to compensate for the decrease in g_m will carry with them, however, the penalty of a decrease in the bandwidth. This results from the increase in the RC time constant since the capacitance on the output (collector or drain) side of the transistor will not decrease much at low current levels.

The decrease in the dynamic forward transfer conductance at low current levels can be an especially severe problem with FETs, since the transfer conductance levels in FETs are generally much smaller than in bipolar transistors. Furthermore, the major advantage of FETs over bipolar transistors in terms of the much lower input current and higher input resistance of FETs is reduced at very low quiescent current levels.

13.3.1 Transistor Gain–Bandwidth Products at Low Current Levels

The principal drawback to the operation of transistors at very low quiescent current levels is the decrease in the gain–bandwidth product. This is due to the decrease in the transfer conductance (g_m or g_{fs}). For the bipolar transistor g_m is given by $g_m =$

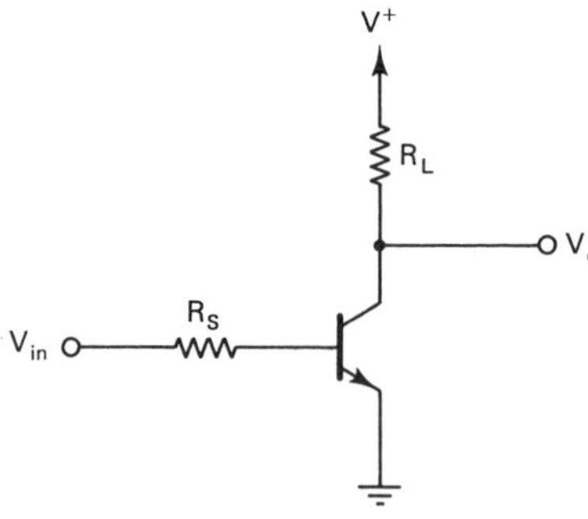

Figure 13.2 Common-emitter amplifier stage.

I_C/V_T, so we see that g_m will be directly proportional to the quiescent collector current level. Let us consider the case of a simple common-emitter amplifier stage as shown in Figure 13.2 in which R_L can represent either a passive load resistance or an active load.

The two breakpoint frequencies for the circuit of Figure 13.2 will be given by

$$f_i = \frac{1}{2\pi(r_{bb'} + R_S)C_i} = \frac{1}{2\pi(r_{bb'} + R_S)[C_{b'e} + (1 - A_V)C_{cb'}]} \tag{13.2}$$

where $A_V = -g_m R_L$, and $f_o = \dfrac{1}{2\pi R_L C_{cb'}}$. The emitter-base capacitance $C_{b'e}$ has two components, given by $C_{b'e} = C_{b'eT} + C_{b'eD}$, where $C_{b'eT}$ is the emitter–base junction space-charge region (or transition region) junction capacitance of typically about 10 to 30 pF, and $C_{b'eD}$ is the diffusion capacitance that results from the minority carriers in transit across the base region from emitter to collector. This second capacitance component will be directly proportional to the collector current I_C and will typically increase at a rate of 1 to 10 pF/mA.

If we now consider the case of a moderate-to-large voltage gain and the condition of low current levels, we will have that $(1 - A_V)C_{cb'} \gg C_{b'e}$, so that $f_i \simeq 1/[2\pi(r_{bb'} + R_S)(-A_V)C_{cb'}]$. Since $A_{V\text{(MID)}} = -g_m R_L = -I_C R_L/V_T$, at low current levels R_L will be very large, so that

$$f_o = \frac{1}{2\pi R_L C_{cb'}} \ll f_i \simeq \frac{1}{2\pi(r_{bb'} + R_S)(-A_V)C_{cb'}} \tag{13.3}$$

As a result, the 3-dB bandwidth will be given approximately by $BW \simeq f_o = 1/(2\pi R_L C_{cb'})$ and the gain–bandwidth product will correspondingly become

$$A_V \times BW \simeq \frac{g_m R_L}{2\pi R_L C_{cb'}} = \frac{g_m}{2\pi C_{cb'}} = \frac{I_C/V_T}{2\pi C_{cb'}}$$

Thus we see that at very low current levels the gain–bandwidth product will be directly proportional to the quiescent collector current level as shown in Figure 13.3.

At higher current levels R_L will be smaller such that the lowest breakpoint frequency will now become f_i. The bandwidth will now be given by

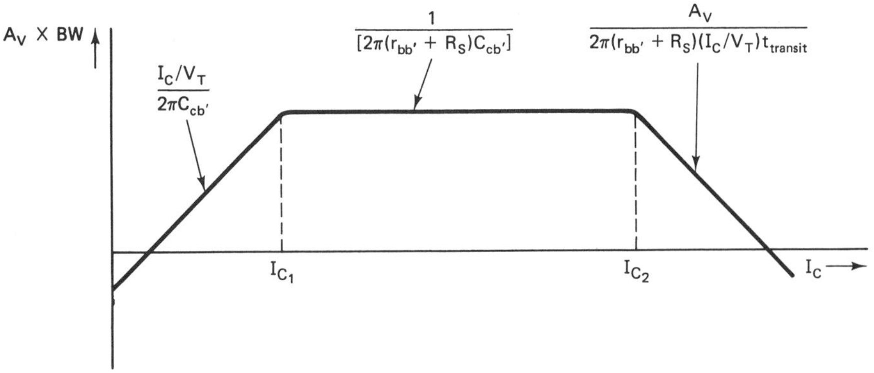

Figure 13.3 Gain-bandwidth product versus I_C.

$$BW \simeq f_i = \frac{1}{2\pi(r_{bb'} + R_S)C_i} \simeq \frac{1}{2\pi(r_{bb'} + R_S)(-A_V)C_{cb'}} = \frac{1}{2\pi(r_{bb'} + R_S)(g_m R_L)C_{cb'}} \tag{13.4}$$

and thus $|A_V| \times BW \simeq 1/[2\pi(r_{bb'} + R_S)C_{cb'}]$. In this current range the gain–bandwidth product will be relatively independent of the quiescent current level.

If we now go to the opposite extreme of large quiescent currents, $C_{b'e}$ will have increased due to the diffusion capacitance term. The diffusion capacitance will be given by $C_{b'eD} = dQ_{\text{base}}/dV_{BE} = d(I_C t_{\text{transit}})/dV_{BE} = (dI_C/dV_{BE})t_{\text{transit}} = g_m t_{\text{transit}} = (I_C/V_T)t_{\text{transit}}$, where Q_{base} = charge in transit across the base region and t_{transit} is the emitter-to-collector transit time across the base region. This transit time will be given approximately by $t_{\text{transit}} \simeq W_{\text{base}}^2/4D$, where W_{base} is the base width and $D = \mu V_T$ is the diffusion coefficient of the minority carriers in transit across the base region.

As a representative example, let us consider the case of an NPN transistor with a base width of 0.5 μm and $\mu_{n\,(\text{base})} = 1000\ \text{cm}^2/\text{V-s}$ so that

$$t_{transit} \simeq \frac{(0.5 \times 10^{-4})^2}{4 \times 25\ \text{mV} \times 1000\ \text{cm}^2/\text{V-s}} = \underline{25\ \text{ps}} \tag{13.5}$$

The diffusion capacitance for this transistor will be given by

$$C_{b'eD} = \frac{I_C}{V_T}\, t_{\text{transit}} = \frac{I_C}{25\ \text{mV}} \times 25\ \text{ps} = \underline{I_C \times 1\ \text{pF/mA}} \tag{13.6}$$

Thus in the higher current region where we now have that $C_{b'e} \gg (1 - A_V)C_{cb'}$, the bandwidth will be given approximately by

$$BW \simeq f_i \simeq \frac{1}{2\pi(r_{bb'} + R_S)C_{b'e}} \simeq \frac{1}{2\pi(r_{bb'} + R_S)C_{b'eD}} = \frac{1}{2\pi(r_{bb'} + R_S)(I_C/V_T)t_{\text{transit}}} \tag{13.7}$$

The gain–bandwidth product will be

$$|A_V| \times BW \simeq \frac{A_v}{2\pi(r_{bb'} + R_S)(I_C/V_T)t_{\text{transit}}}$$

From this last equation we see that as I_C increases, the gain–bandwidth product will decrease in this high-current region, as shown in Figure 13.3.

To consider a representative sample calculation for the variation of the gain–bandwidth product with current level, we will assume the following parameter values: $r_{bb'} + R_S = 100\ \Omega$, $C_{cb'} = 1.6$ pF, $C_{b'eT} = 15$ pF, $C_{b'eD} = I_C \times (1$ pF/mA), and a midfrequency gain of $A_{V(\text{MID})} = -100$. At low current levels we have that $|A_V| \times BW = (I_C/V_T)/(2\pi C_{cb'})$. In the "middle"-current region $|A_V| \times BW = 1/[2\pi(r_{bb'} + R_S)C_{cb'}] =$ 1000 MHz. In the high-current region $|A_V| \times BW = |A_V|/[2\pi(r_{bb'} + R_S)C_{b'eD}] = 100/[2\pi(100\ \Omega)I_C(1$ pF/mA)]. If we refer to Figures 13.3 and 13.4 we see that the transition or breakpoint currents will be given by the following conditions:

1. *At* I_{C_1}: $(I_C/V_T)/2\pi C_{cb'} = 1/[2\pi(r_{bb'} + R_S)C_{cb'}]$, so that $I_C/V_T = 1/(r_{bb'} + R_S)$ and thus $I_{C_1} = V_T/(r_{bb'} + R_S) = 25$ mV/100 Ω = 0.25 mA.
2. *At* I_{C_2}: $1/[2\pi(r_{bb'} + R_S)C_{cb'}] = A_V/[2\pi(r_{bb'} + R_S)I_C(1$ pF/mA)], so that $I_{C_2} = A_V C_{cb'}/(1$ pF/mA) = 100 × 1.6 pF/(1 pF/mA) = 160 mA.

In Figure 13.4 a graph of the gain–bandwidth product versus I_C for this example is shown. We see that although the gain–bandwidth product has a relatively high value of about 1000 MHz over the current range 250 μA to 160 mA, at low current levels it can become quite small. For example, at $I_C = 10\ \mu$A we will have that $|A_V| \times BW = (I_C/V_T)/2\pi C_{cb'} = (10\ \mu\text{A}/25\ \text{mV})/2\pi \times 1.6$ pF) = 40 MHz. At $I_C = 1.0\ \mu$A, the gain–bandwidth product will be down to 4.0 MHz, and at $I_C = 0.1\ \mu$A, it will be only 400 kHz. At this last current level and with a midfrequency gain of 50, the maximum bandwidth obtainable will be only 8 kHz.

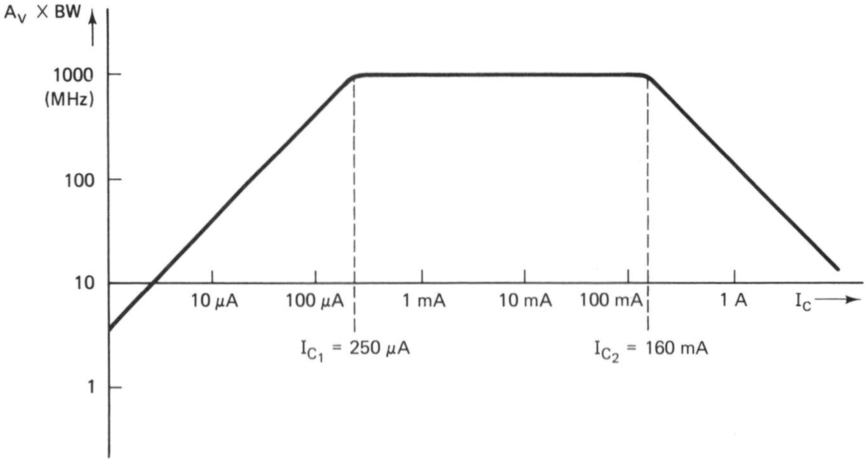

Figure 13.4 Example of gain-bandwidth product versus I_C.

13.3.2 Examples of Micropower Op Amps

An example of a micropower operational amplifier is the OP-20 (Precision Monolithics, Inc.). This device features a total quiescent supply current of only 40 μA (typ.) at a supply voltage of ± 2.5 V, and 55 μA for a ± 15-V supply.

Although the supply current is kept at a very low level, an open-loop voltage gain of 500 V/mV for a 5-V supply and 1000 V/mV for a ± 15-V supply is obtained. The slew rate will, however, be down to only 0.05 V/μs and the unity-gain frequency is only 100 kHz.

Another example of a micropower op amp is the 4132 (Raytheon), which has a quiescent supply current of only 25 μA with a ± 3-V supply and 35 μA when the supply voltage is up at ± 20 V. When operated with the ± 3-V supply the open-loop gain will be 250 V/mV, the unity-gain frequency will be 150 kHz, and the corresponding slewing rate will be 0.13 V/μs.

13.3.3 Micropower Op Amp: Programmable Operational Amplifiers

For most op amps the circuit that sets the quiescent current for the various stages of the circuit will usually draw most of the total power supply current. An example of this is shown in Figure 13.5. The biasing currents supplied by the Q_1, Q_3, and Q_4 current sources will be much smaller than I_2, due to the voltage drops across R_1, R_3, and R_4, respectively. The biasing current I_2 will be given by $I_2 = (V^+ - V^- - V_{BE})/R_2$. To reduce I_2 down into the microampere range will require very large values for R_2. These large resistance values are difficult to obtain in monolithic ICs because of the large chip area required, but they can be implemented as an off-the-chip resistor.

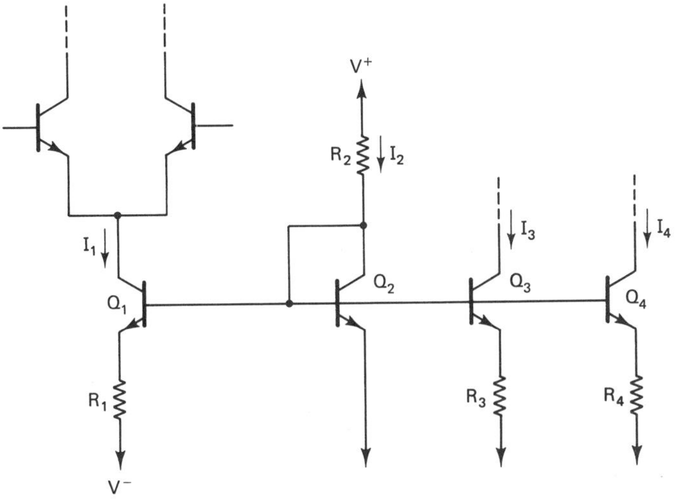

Figure 13.5 Typical operational amplifier biasing circuit.

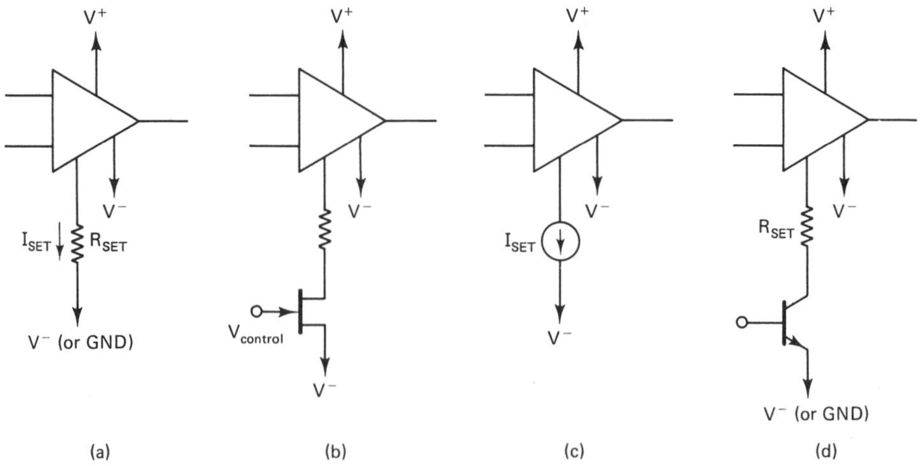

Figure 13.6 Programmable operational amplifiers: bias current setting circuits.

Programmable operational amplifiers are available in which the bias current setting resistor (such as R_2) is connected as an external component. These op amps are programmable in that the quiescent currents and therefore many of the op-amp parameters can be varied or programmed by means of an external resistor, a JFET acting as a voltage-variable resistor, or a voltage-controlled current source, as shown in Figure 13.6. An external transistor can be connected in series with the bias current setting resistor R_{SET}, as shown in Figure 13.6a to act as a strobing circuit to allow the op amp to be turned off completely. When the op amp is off, it will have a very high input impedance and a very high output impedance, so that it can act as an analog signal transmission gate. It can be connected in parallel with similar op amps as part of an analog signal multiplexing circuit, and it can also be used for a bidirectional analog signal transmission system.

The use of the programmable op amp as a micropower circuit with a total supply current down in the microampere range can easily be implemented by the use of a large ($\gtrsim$ 10 MΩ) resistor for R_{SET}. Associated with the benefits of low-power operation will, however, be the disadvantages of a (1) decreased open-loop gain; (2) a reduced unity-gain frequency, f_u; (3) a lower slewing rate and full-power bandwidth; and (4) an increased output impedance.

Examples of programmable op amps. Examples of programmable op amps are the MC1776 (Motorola), LM4250 (National Semiconductor), and OP-22 (Precision Monolithic). In the case of the MC1776 the total quiescent supply current will be approximately 10 times the bias setting current I_{SET} shown in Figure 13.7, where $I_{SET} = (V^+ - 0.6)/R_{SET}$ for single-supply operation and $I_{SET} = (V^+ - V^- - 0.6)/R_{SET}$ for the dual-supply case.

The MC1776 can easily be biased for operation in the micropower range. If, for example, $V^+ = +3$ V, $V^- = -3$ V, and $I_{SET} = 0.1\ \mu$A, the required value for R_{SET} will be $R_{SET} = (6 - 0.6)/0.1\ \mu\text{A} = 53$ MΩ if R_{SET} is connected to V^-, and 23 MΩ if R_{SET} goes to ground. The total supply current under quiescent conditions

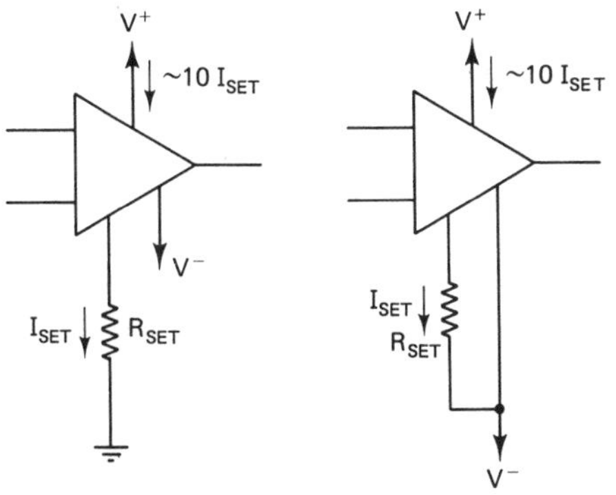

Figure 13.7 MC1776 programmable operational amplifier.

will be only about 1 μA and the power dissipation will be just 6 μW. This low-power operation does carry with it the disadvantages of a reduced A_{OL}, f_u, SR, and FPBW, as mentioned above. Listed below are some values of $A_{OL}(0)$ and f_u for various values of I_{SET}.

I_{SET}(μA)	$A_{OL}(0)$	f_u(MHz)
100	1.2×10^6	1.5
40	1.5×10^6	1.0
10	8×10^5	0.40
1.0	1.5×10^5	0.060
0.1	3×10^4	0.002

Another example of a programmable op amp that can be operated down into the micropower range is the LM4250. This op amp is also biased by an external resistor, as shown in Figure 13.6, but in this case the quiescent supply current will be approximately $5I_{SET}$. If, for example, $V^+ = +3$ V, $V^- = -3$ V, and $I_{SET} = 0.1$ μA, the required value of R_{SET} will again be 55 MΩ if R_{SET} is connected to V^- and 25 MΩ if R_{SET} goes to ground. The quiescent supply current will now be about 0.5 μA and the quiescent power dissipation will be only 3 μW. At this current level the open-loop gain will be about 20,000, f_u will be only 10 kHz, and the slewing rate will be down to 0.002 V/μs.

13.3.4 Low Voltage Operational Amplifiers

Most op amps and other ICs can operate with supply voltages down to 5 V, and many down to 3 V. There are some op amps, however, that can operate with supply voltages as low as 1.1 V. The low operating voltage together with a low-current drain makes these op amps especially suitable for single-cell battery operation.

An example of a low voltage bipolar IC is the LM10 (National Semiconductor) which contains a single supply op amp, a 200 mV temperature-compensated reference voltage circuit, and a reference amplifier all contained in one 8-pin mini-DIP package.

This IC can operate with supply voltages ranging from 40 V down to as low as 1.1 V. The quiescent supply current is 270 μA so that at the supply voltage of 1.1 V the power drain is just 300 μW.

Examples of low voltage single supply CMOS op amps are the TLC251 and TLC271 (Texas Instruments). These op amps can operate with supply voltages as low as 1.0 V and at this supply voltage the power consumption is just 100 μW. This op amp features phosphorus doped polycrystalline silicon gates for the MOSFETs. The phosphorus doping of the gate electrodes acts to immobilize the sodium ions which otherwise could drift through the gate oxide under the influence of the gate voltage and result in major shifts in the MOSFET threshold voltage. As a result of this phosphorus doping the TLC251 and TLC271 have an offset voltage temperature coefficient of only 0.7 μV/°C and a long term drift of just 0.1 μV/month. Other characteristics include a unity gain frequency of 2.3 MHz, a slewing rate of 4.5 V/μs, and an offset voltage of 2 mV.

13.4 HIGH-VOLTAGE INTEGRATED CIRCUITS

Most ICs have a maximum rated supply voltage of about 36 V (or ±18 V if a dual supply is used). This will limit the peak output voltage swing that is available to about ±16 V or 32 V peak-to-peak. The maximum supply voltage rating of ICs is based on the collector–base and collector–substrate breakdown voltages. These breakdown voltages will usually be around 50 V, so to keep well away from this critical voltage and to allow for a sufficient safety margin a maximum supply voltage rating of about 36 to 40 V is common, although many ICs will have a lower maximum voltage rating.

The breakdown voltage of a planar PN junction is determined by two principal factors: (1) the doping levels on the two sides of the junction, and (2) the junction curvature. The breakdown voltage of a flat (i.e., no curvature) abrupt PN junction is given by the approximate relationship $BV \simeq 2.7 \times 10^{12}/N^{2/3}$, where BV is the breakdown voltage (volts) and N is the net doping level as given by $1/N = (1/N_A) + (1/N_D)$, with N_A being the net doping on the P-type side and N_D being the net doping on the N-type side of the junction. For the usual case of a PN junction in which the doping level is much greater on one side than it is on the other side, the breakdown voltage will be determined principally by the doping level on the more lightly doped side and the net doping N will be given by $N \simeq N_D$ for a P^+N junction and $N \simeq N_A$ for an N^+P junction.

The junction curvature that is inherent in the planar device structure will produce a reduction in the breakdown voltage as a result of the increase in the electric field strength in the curved portion of the junction, as shown in Figure 13.8. The junction curvature can have a very major effect on the breakdown voltage. For example, if we consider a one-sided N^+P or P^+N junction with a doping level of 1×10^{15} on the more lightly doped side of the junction, the breakdown voltage for a flat junction will be about 300 V. If the junction depth is 10 μm, the breakdown voltage will be reduced to about 200 V due to the effect of the junction curvature. For a 3-μm

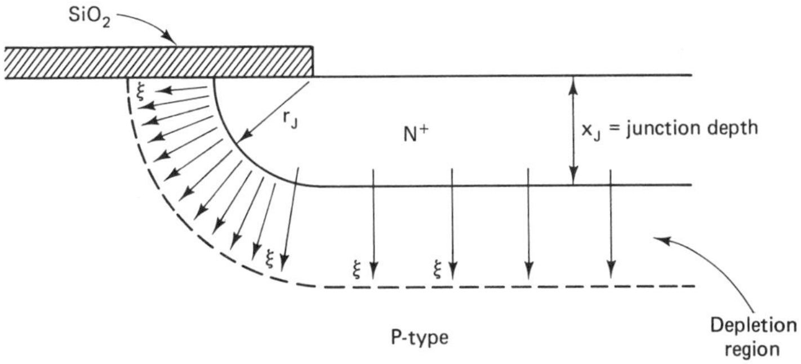

Figure 13.8 Effect of junction curvature on electric field intensity.

junction depth the breakdown voltage will be reduced to about 100 V, and if the junction depth is 1 μm, the breakdown voltage will be down to about 40 V.

To obtain high junction breakdown voltages it is necessary to have a light doping level and a deep junction. For the conventional junction-isolated monolithic IC, the light doping levels for the collector and substrate regions can cause problems due to the increased parasitic series resistance, especially for high-frequency operation. To have a high breakdown voltage it will also be necessary to increase the thickness of the N-type epitaxial layer so as to accommodate the larger depletion-layer thickness of the collector–base junction. This requirement for an increased epitaxial-layer thickness together with the requirements for greater junction depths will lead to a substantial increase in the chip area needed for the IC.

One approach that is taken for high-voltage ICs is to use a hybrid IC in which the high-voltage parts of the circuit are located on separate chips from the lower-voltage portion of the circuit. Another approach is to use a dielectric isolation IC structure. In the case of the dielectrically isolated ICs there is an SiO_2 layer between the various IC components and the common substrate so that the collector-to-substrate breakdown voltage is no longer a limiting factor in the operation of the device. The

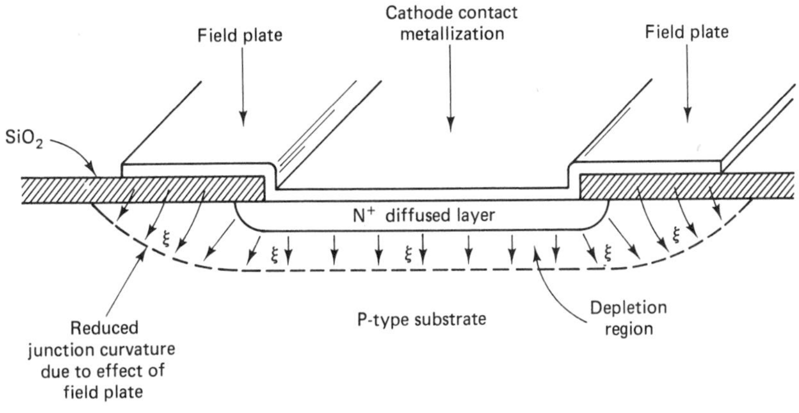

Figure 13.9 Use of a field plate to increase the breakdown voltage of a PN junction.

collector–base breakdown voltage will, however, still be a limitation for high-voltage operation.

One method of increasing the breakdown voltage of a planar junction is to use a "field plate," as shown in Figure 13.9. The electric field produced by the field plate will act to extend the depletion region laterally and acts to reduce the curvature (i.e., produce a larger radius of curvature) of the peripheral region of the junction. This can result in a very substantial increase in the breakdown voltage.

13.5 VOLTAGE-SHARING CIRCUITS

In addition to the device fabrication techniques for increasing the voltage ratings of ICs, there are some circuit design techniques that can also be applied. One interesting method for increasing the output voltage swing available from a circuit is to use the "voltage-sharing" technique of Figure 13.10. In this example the total supply voltage is 200 V. The resistive voltage divider will act to divide the output voltage V_O in equal parts across the bases of Q_2 through Q_4. Transistor Q_1 operates in the common-emitter configuration, and Q_2 through Q_4 operate as common-base transis-

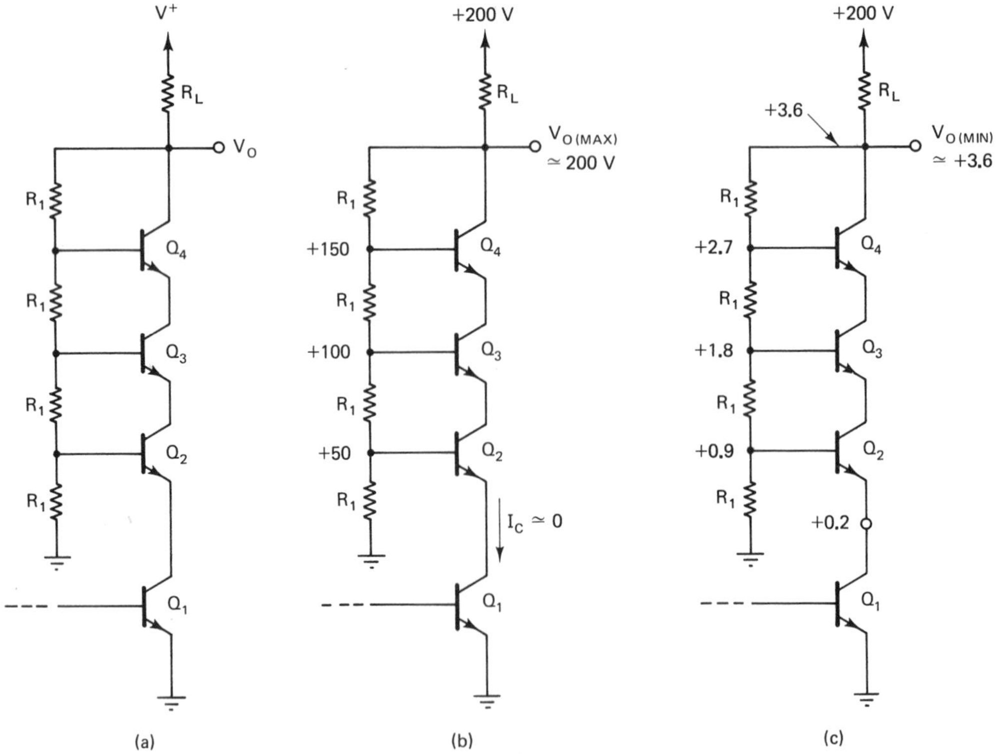

Figure 13.10 High-voltage-output circuit using voltage sharing: (a) circuit diagram; (b) voltage levels for $V_{O(MAX)}$; (c) voltage levels for $V_{O(MIN)}$.

tors. This circuit can be thought of as a modified or compound cascode circuit. The a-c voltage gain will be given approximately by $A_V = -g_m[R_L \| 4R_1] \simeq -g_m R_L$ if $4R_1 \gg R_L$ and $g_m = I_C/V_T$.

The positive peak or maximum output voltage will be given by $V_{O(\text{MAX})} = V^+ \times 4R_1/(4R_1 + R_L) \simeq V^+ = 200$ V if $4R_1 \gg R_L$, as shown in Figure 13.10b. We see that $V_{CB_1} \simeq V_{CB_2} \simeq V_{CB_3} \simeq 50 - 0.7$ V $= 49.3$ V, and $V_{CB_4} \simeq 50$ V, so that the maximum collector-to-base voltage of any transistor in the circuit will not exceed 50 V.

At the other extreme, the minimum output-voltage level is limited by the collector-to-emitter saturation voltage and the base-to-emitter forward bias voltages, as shown in Figure 13.10c. The voltage at the base of Q_2 will be limited to a minimum value of $V_{B_2} = V_{BE_2} + V_{CE(\text{SAT})_1} \simeq 0.7 + 0.2 = 0.9$ V. Since the voltage drops across all of the resistors in the voltage divider will be approximately equal, this

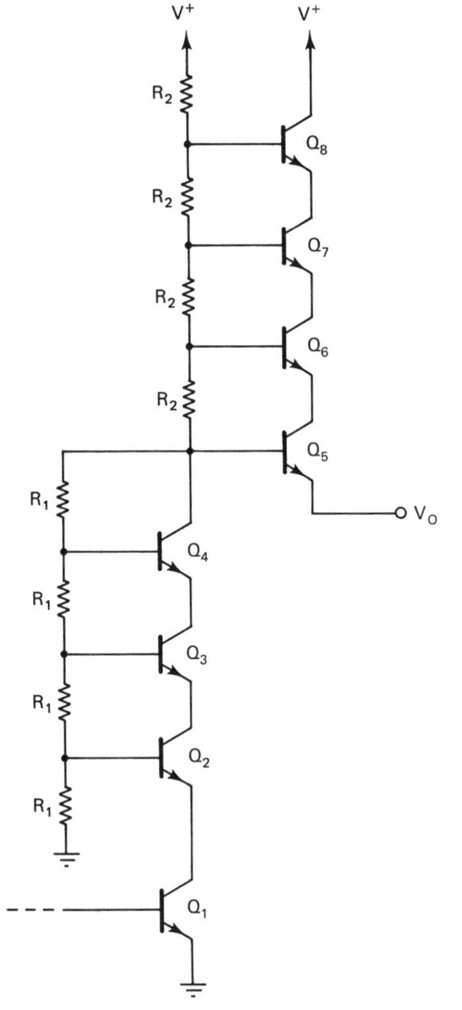

Figure 13.11 High-voltage-output stage with an emitter follower.

will result in a minimum output-voltage level of $V_{O(MIN)} \simeq 3.6$ V. As a result we see that with a 200-V supply, a peak-to-peak output-voltage swing of about 195 V is possible. At the same time, the maximum voltage drop that must be sustained by any transistor will not exceed 50 V.

In Figure 13.11 a voltage-sharing circuit with an emitter-follower output is shown. The lower part of the circuit, consisting of Q_1 through Q_4 and the associated R_1 voltage divider, operates in the same fashion as the compound cascode circuit shown in Figure 13.10. The emitter-follower part of the circuit uses Q_5 through Q_8 with the associated R_2 voltage divider. With a supply voltage of $V^+ = 200$ V and with Q_1 off the output voltage will be approximately given by $V_{O(MAX)} \simeq V^+ \times 4R_1/(4R_1 + 4R_2) = V^+ \times R_1/(R_1 + R_2)$. If $R_1 \gg R_2$, then $V_{O(MAX)} \simeq V^+ = 200$ V. At the other extreme, when Q_1 is in saturation, the voltage at the collector of Q_4 can drop to as low as about +3.6 V, so that $V_{O(MIN)}$ will be approximately $3.6 - 0.7 = 2.9$ V.

13.6 IC POWER TRANSISTORS WITH INTERNAL PROTECTION CIRCUITRY

Although power transistors can be implemented as simple discrete devices, better performance and protection from excessive power dissipation can be obtained by a monolithic IC power transistor. An example of such a device is the LM195 (National Semiconductor) and a simplified schematic diagram is given in Figure 13.12. This device can be thought of as a "triple-transistor" Darlington circuit and it has an overall current gain of about 1×10^6, requiring a base drive of only 3 μA to produce the maximum output collector current of 1.8 A.

This circuit incorporates a thermal limiting circuit that senses the chip tempera-

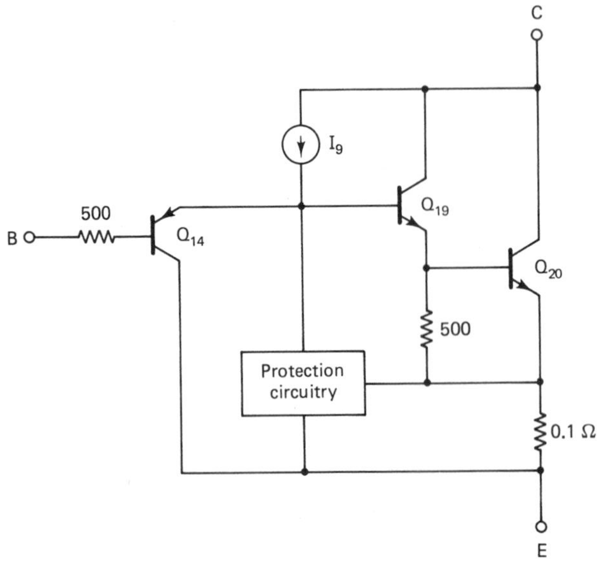

Figure 13.12 Simplified schematic diagram of monolithic IC power transistor: LM195 (National Semiconductor).

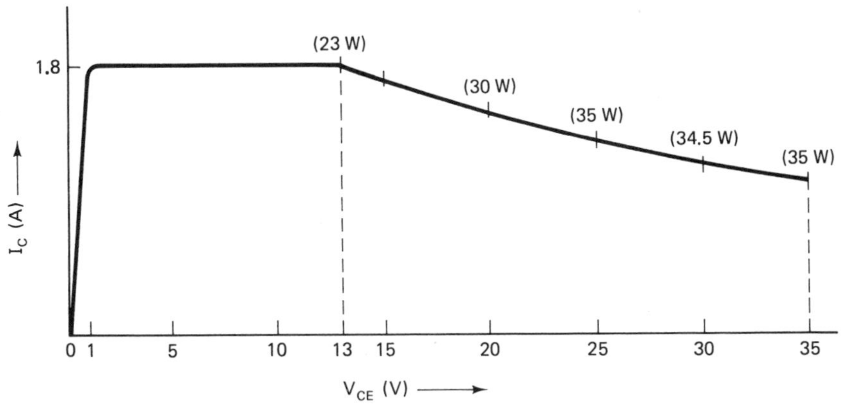

Figure 13.13 LM195 current-limiting characteristic.

ture and limits the device power dissipation when the chip temperature reaches 165°C. Current limiting is also provided. This current limiting will limit the maximum collector current to 1.8 A for V_{CE} values of less than 13 V. As V_{CE} increases above this level, the current limit decreases and so provides "safe operating area" (SOA) protection for the device. The current-limiting characteristic is shown in Figure 13.13. The maximum power dissipation rating for this device is 35 W. Note that the current-limiting characteristic will keep the power dissipation from exceeding 35 W. The maximum current is also limited to 1.8 A to protect against the fusing of the aluminum metallization and to also provide protection against the "second breakdown" effect, to be described later.

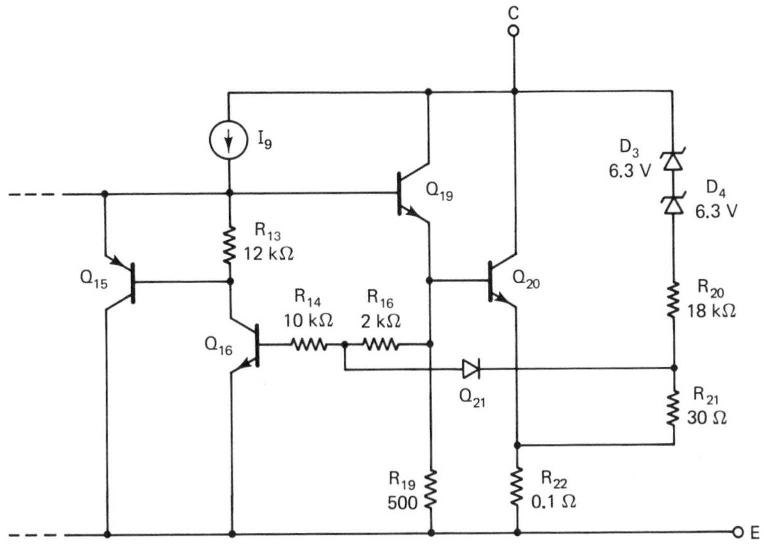

Figure 13.14 V_{CE}-dependent current-limiting circuit.

The use of a PNP transistor Q_{14} as the input stage offers two advantages. First, the net base-to-emitter voltage of this device will be given by $V_{BE} = V_{BE_{20}} + V_{BE_{19}} + V_{BE_{14}} = +0.7 + 0.7 - 0.7 = +0.7$ V, instead of about +2.1 V, which would be the case if the first transistor were an NPN transistor. The second advantage is the high emitter-to-base breakdown voltage BV_{EB} of greater than 40 V, which is inherent in the PNP transistor structure.

In Figure 13.14 a detail of the V_{CE}-dependent current-limiting circuit is shown. When the voltage drop across the current-limit resistor R_{22} (0.1 Ω) becomes large enough, transistor Q_{16} will be turned on, which in turn will turn Q_{15} on, which will divert base drive away from the Q_{19}–Q_{20} Darlington pair. Note that diode Q_{21}, in conjunction with resistors R_{14} and R_{16}, provide a "pre-bias" for Q_{16}, so that the voltage drop across R_{22} that is needed to turn Q_{16} on is only 180 mV, corresponding to a current limit of 1.8 A.

The current-limiting threshold will be lowered when V_{CE} goes above 12.6 V, for then diodes D_3 and D_4 go into breakdown. The voltage divider, comprised of R_{20} (18 kΩ) and R_{21} (30 Ω), will then add a small fraction of V_{CE} to the voltage drop across R_{22} to reduce the current through R_{22} that is required to produce current limiting.

A simplified diagram of the thermal limiting or shutdown circuit is given in Figure 13.15. The base-to-emitter voltage supplied to Q_{12} will be the $I_{11}R_9$ voltage drop that is developed across R_9. As the temperature increases, the current through Q_{12} will increase rapidly. This in turn will activate Q_{13}. The current flow through both Q_{12} and Q_{13} will increase very rapidly with increasing temperature due to the negative base-to-emitter voltage temperature coefficients ($TC_{V_{BE}}$) of the two transistors.

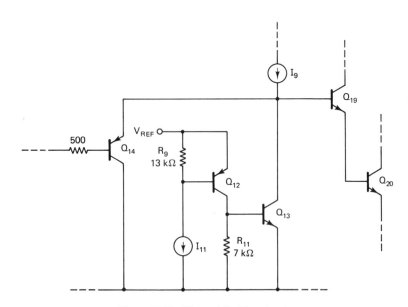

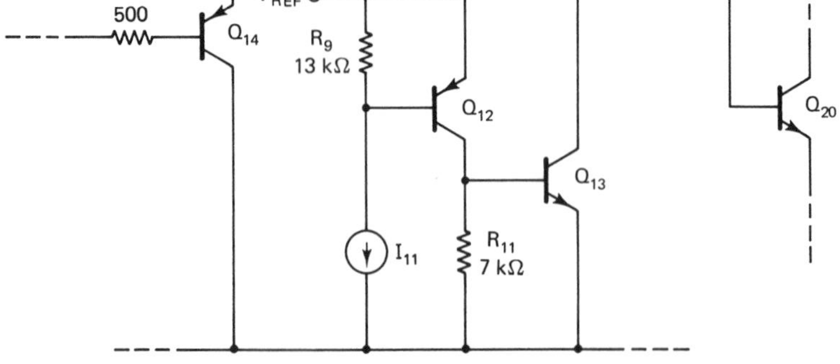

Figure 13.15 Thermal limiting circuit.

13.6.1 Second Breakdown

At high current levels in a transistor a localized current concentration can lead to the following sequence of events: localized current density increase → increased temperature in the localized region (formation of a "hot spot") → increased current density as a result of the temperature increase → and so on. This will be an electrothermal positive feedback loop which will result in the formation of current filaments of very small diameter (~10 μm) and extremely high current density (a "microplasma"). The temperature rise in the filamentary region can reach very high values, causing the alloying or fusing of the overlaying metallization and even the localized melting of the silicon. This will result in the irreversible destruction of the device and can occur at power dissipation levels that are well below the maximum power dissipation rating of the device, especially in the region where the collector current is relatively large. The region of the I_C versus V_{CE} characteristics of the device within which it will be relatively safe from damage from the second breakdown phenomenon just described is called the *safe operating area* (SOA).

13.7 TRANSISTOR GEOMETRY AND CURRENT CROWDING

The transistor top surface geometry is an important consideration for power transistors. At high collector current levels the lateral voltage drop produced by the flow of base current through the internal base resistance $r_{bb'}$ will result in the base-to-emitter voltage drop being a function of position. The V_{BE} will be higher in the peripheral regions of the junction than in the central region, as shown in Figure 13.16b, c, and d. This will result in a shift in the current distribution of the emitter-to-collector current flow from the uniform distribution of Figure 13.16a to the *current-crowding* situation of Figure 13.16d, in which most of the current flow is concentrated near the edges of the junction. An excessive amount of current crowding is bad because it leads to a decrease in the transistor current gain, and more important, increases the power dissipation density in the current-crowding regions. This localized increase in the power density will result in "hot spots," which can result in the second breakdown effect just described.

To minimize the current-crowding effect, an interdigitated transistor geometry is often used for power transistors and this geometry is used for Q_{20} in the LM195. The lateral geometry of Q_{20} is shown in Figure 13.17. The total emitter area is seen to be subdivided into many separate emitter "fingers" in order to increase the total emitter periphery. The constricted N^+ regions between each emitter region and the emitter contact strip form small-value emitter ballast resistors to help equalize the emitter current, as illustrated in Figure 13.16e.

To minimize the lateral base voltage drop a multiplicity of base contact "fingers" are used and are interdigitated with the emitter fingers. In a monolithic IC the collector contact must be taken out of the top surface. To minimize the collector series resistance the base region has been subdivided into 10 regions with an N^+ contact strip between the base regions. Each base region has six N^+ emitter areas, so that the transistor has a total of 60 separate emitter regions.

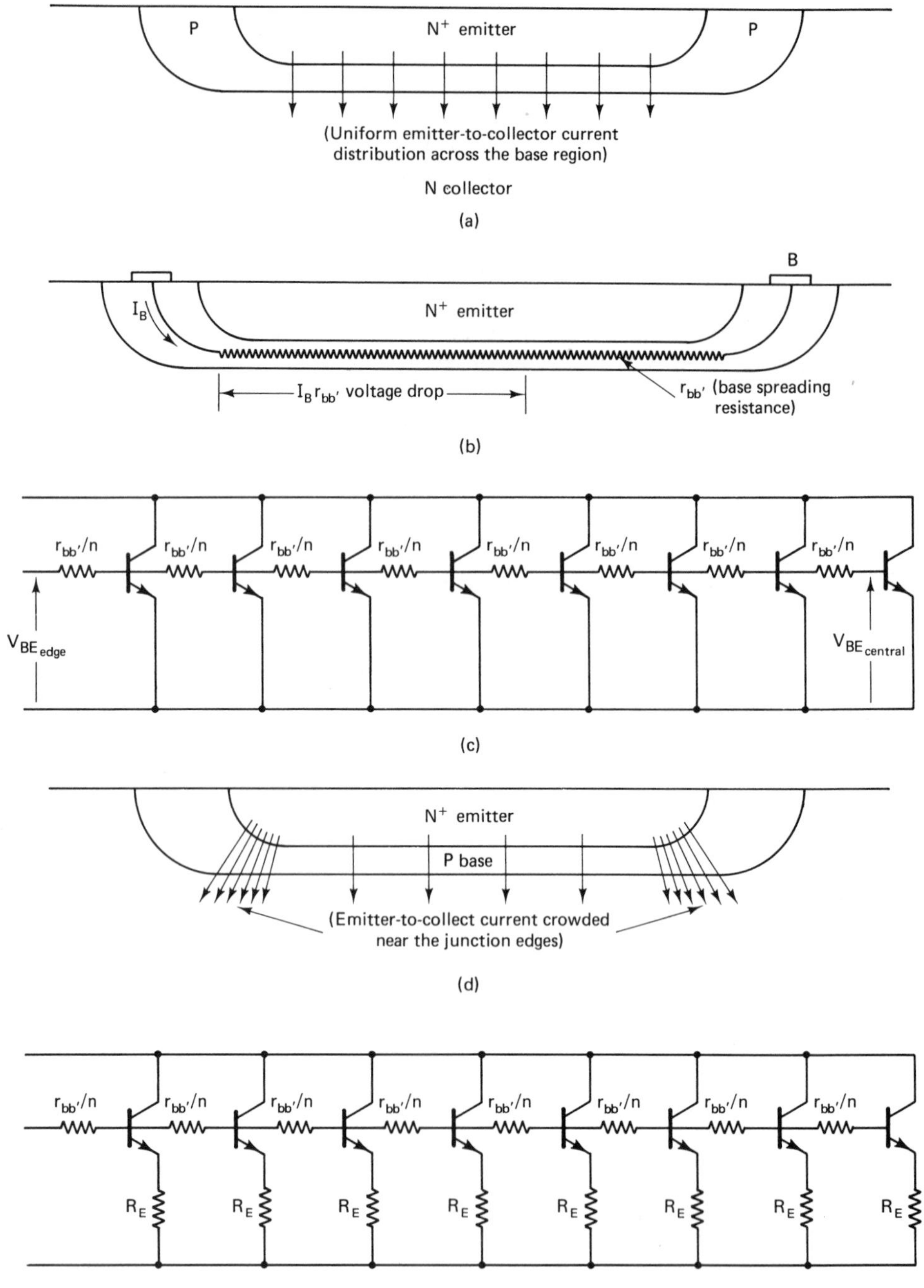

Figure 13.16 Current crowding in transistors: (a) transistor at low and moderate collector-current levels; (b) lateral voltage drop in the base region; (c) equivalent representation of transistor; (d) transistor current distribution at high collector current levels; (e) use of emitter ballast resistors to reduce current crowding.

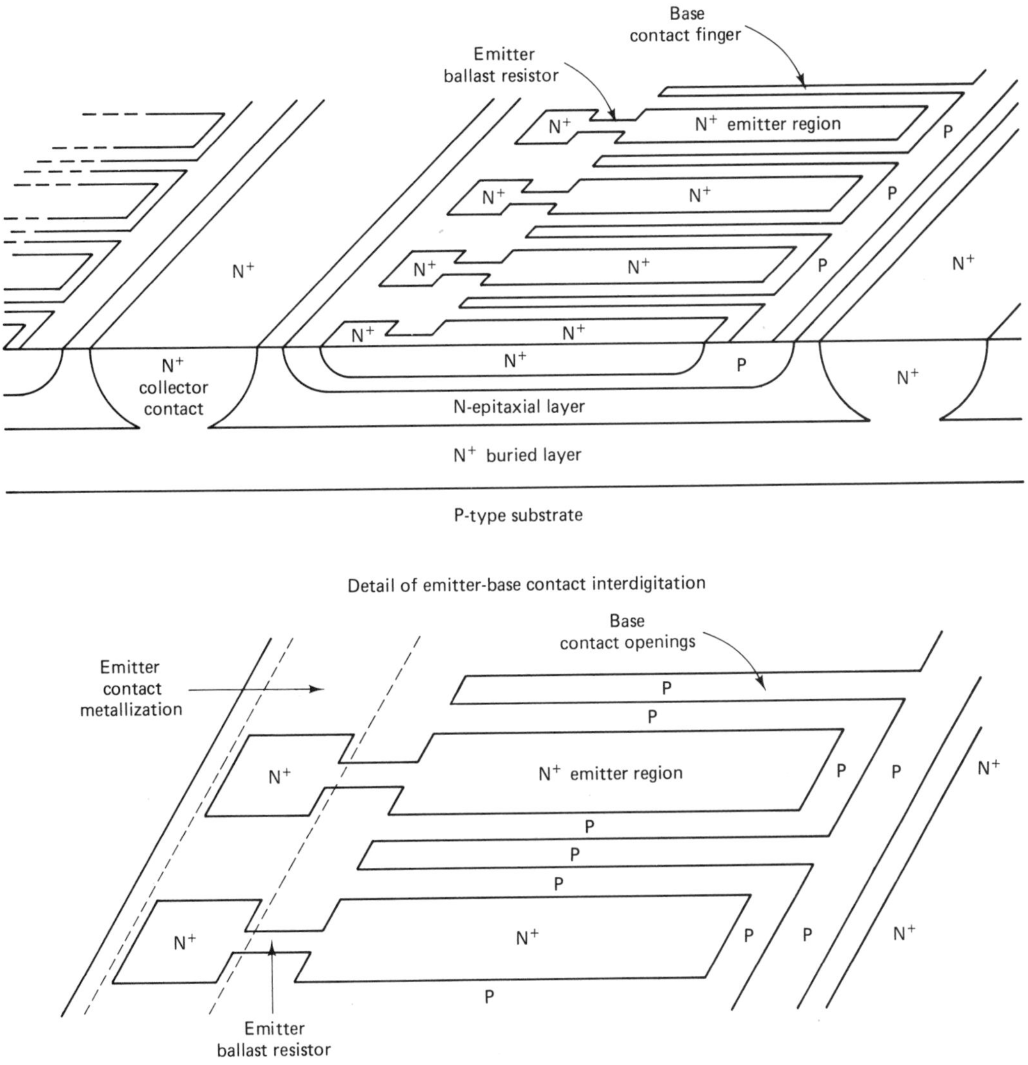

Figure 13.17 Interdigitated IC power transistor geometry.

13.8 FREQUENCY-TO-VOLTAGE CONVERTERS

A frequency-to-voltage converter is a circuit that produces an output voltage that is directly proportional to the frequency of the input voltage. A basic frequency-to-voltage converter circuit is shown in Figure 13.18. The input voltage goes into a voltage comparator, which acts as a *zero-crossing detector*. The output voltage of the comparator is a square wave with the same frequency (or period T) as the input voltage. In most cases a very limited amount of positive feedback in the comparator circuit will be desirable to produce a small amount of hysterisis. This will improve the switching speed and provide better noise immunity.

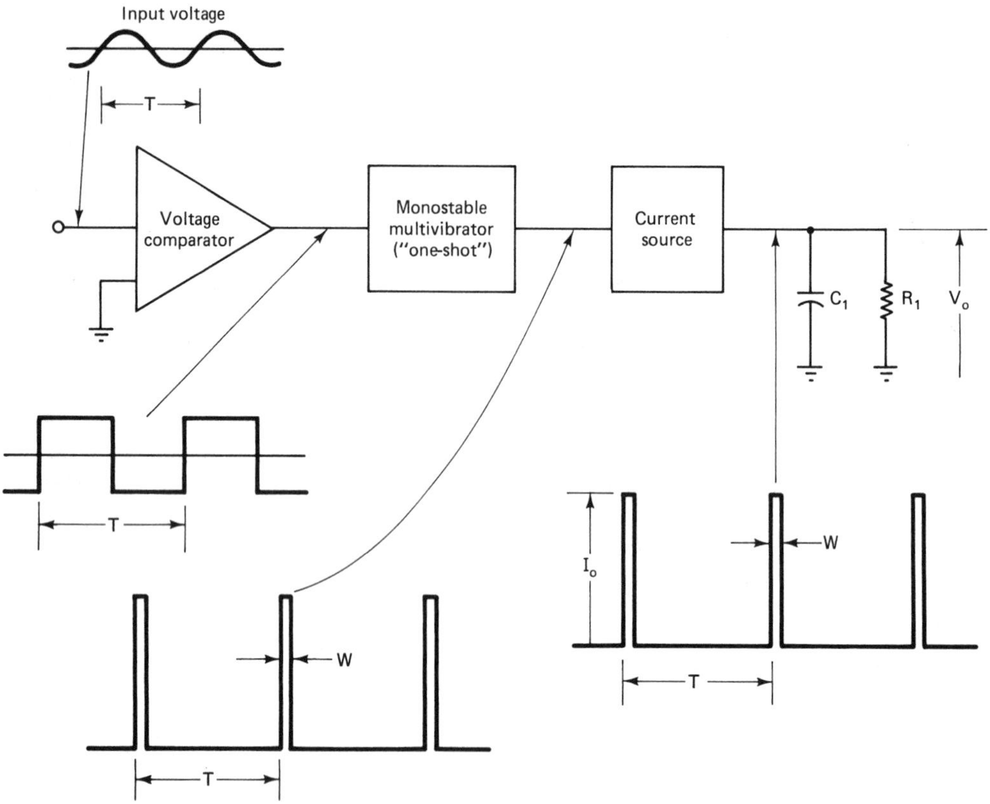

Figure 13.18 Frequency-to-voltage converter.

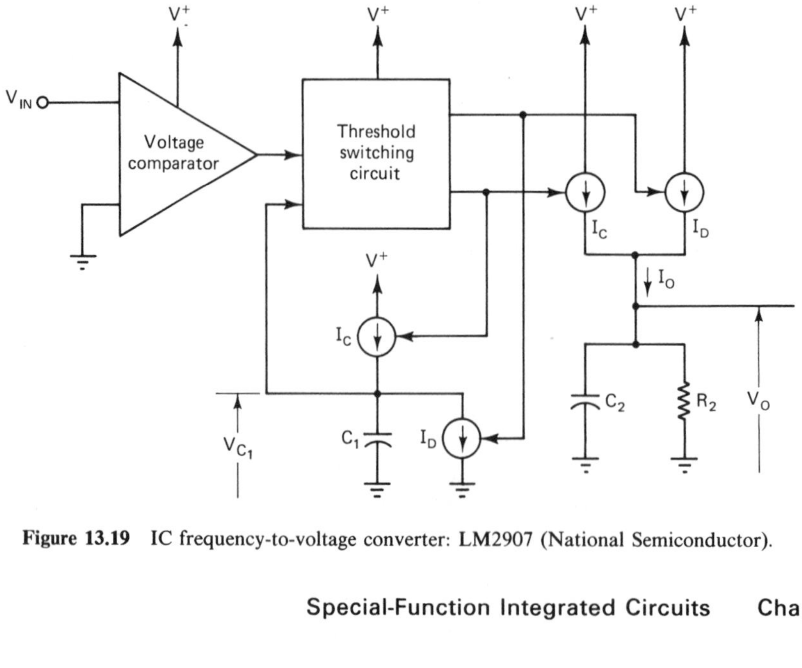

Figure 13.19 IC frequency-to-voltage converter: LM2907 (National Semiconductor).

The output voltage of the comparator drives a monostable multivibrator or "one-shot" that produces a short duration (W) pulse for every positive going transition of the comparator output voltage. This voltage pulse turns on a constant-current source of strength I_o for the duration of the pulse. This current source acts as a "charge pump" that delivers an amount of charge equal to $Q_o = I_o W$ to the R_1C_1 circuit once every period of the input voltage. The average or d-c current delivered to the R_1C_1 circuit will be $I_{dc} = Q_o/T = I_o W/T = I_o Wf$, where $f = 1/T$ is the frequency of the input voltage. The average or d-c voltage across the R_1C_1 circuit will be $V_o = I_{dc}R_1 = I_o R_1 Wf$. We therefore see that the output voltage will indeed be directly proportional to the input frequency.

The R_1C_1 time constant should be chosen to be long enough to provide a smooth output voltage waveform and should generally be in the range $R_1C_1 \gtrsim 10T = 10/f$. However, too large a value for the R_1C_1 time constant will slow down the response of the system with respect to rapid changes in the input frequency.

13.8.1 Monolithic IC Frequency-to-Voltage Converter

An example of a monolithic IC frequency-to-voltage converter is the LM2907/LM2917 (National Semiconductor). A simplified diagram of this device is given in Figure 13.19 and some waveforms are presented in Figure 13.20.

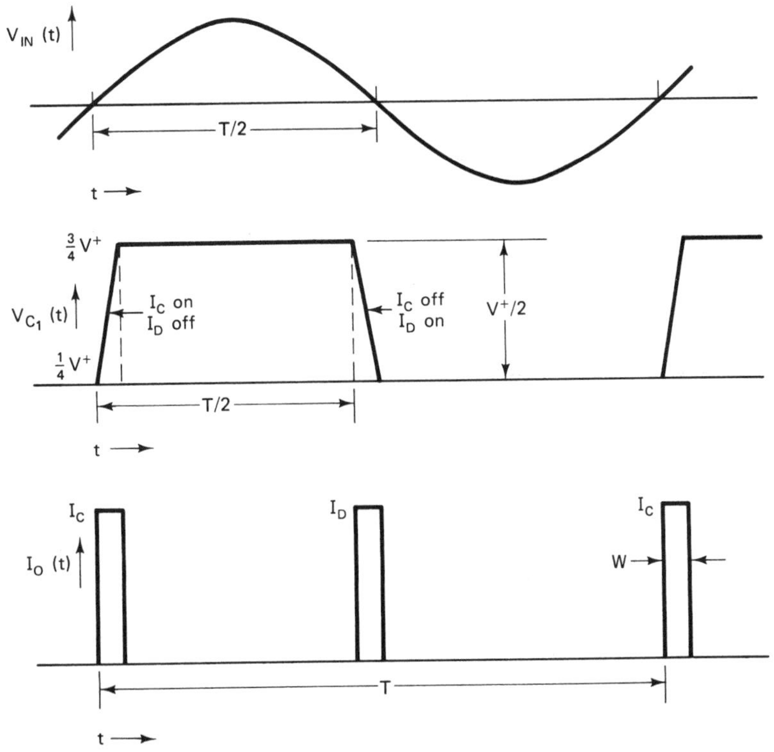

Figure 13.20 Frequency-to-voltage converter waveforms.

The voltage comparator acts as a zero-crossing detector. When the input voltage V_{IN} goes above zero, the comparator output voltage causes the threshold switching circuit to switch to the upper threshold level of $\frac{3}{4}V^+$ and the I_C current sources are turned on. This causes capacitor C_1 to charge up to the upper threshold level of $3.4V^+$, at which point the current sources are then turned off. The capacitor C_1 stays charged up at this level until V_{IN} goes negative, at which point the I_D current sources are turned on and C_1 discharges down to the lower threshold level of $\frac{1}{4}V^+$. When this voltage level is reached, the current sources are turned off and the capacitor voltage V_{C_1} remains at this lower level until V_{IN} goes positive again and the cycle then repeats.

The change in the voltage across the capacitor C_1 during the charging and discharging periods will be $\Delta V = \frac{3}{4}V^+ - \frac{1}{4}V^+ = V^+/2$. The charging and discharging time periods W will be given by $\Delta V = V^+/2 = \Delta Q/C_1 = I_C W/C_1 = I_D W/C_1$ since $I_C = I_D$. Therefore, $W = (V^+/2)C_1/I_C$. The average current delivered to the R_2C_2 circuit will be $I_{o(dc)} = I_C(W/T) + I_D(W/T) = I_C(V^+/2)C_1/I_C \times 1/T + I_D(V^+/2)C_1/I_D \times 1/T = V^+C_1/T$. The d-c voltage developed across the R_2C_2 circuit will be given by $V_O = I_{O(DC)}R_2 = V^+R_2C_1/T = V^+R_2C_1f$, where $f = 1/T$ is the frequency of the input voltage. We see that the output voltage will be directly proportional to the frequency of the input voltage.

13.9 COMPANDORS

Compandors are ICs with a nonlinear transfer characteristic that can be used to compress or expand the dynamic range of an analog signal. The signal compression is often performed at the transmitting end of a system and a complementary signal

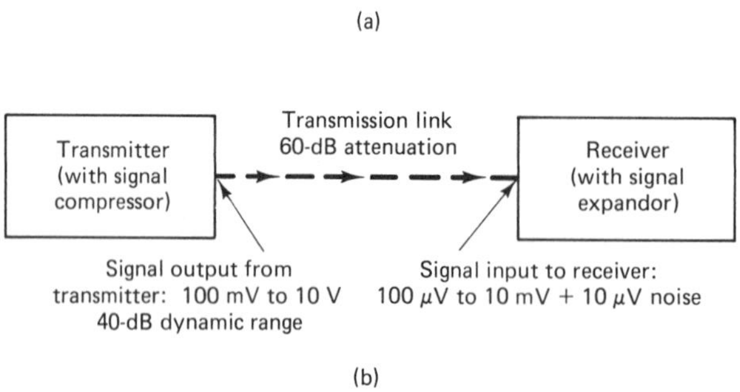

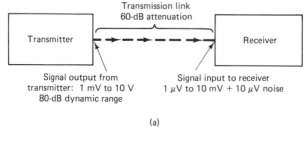

Figure 13.21 Use of compandors in signal transmission systems: (a) system with no signal compression or expansion; (b) system with signal compression and expansion.

expansion is done at the receiving end in order to improve the signal-to-noise ratio (SNR) of the received signal. To consider an example of this, let us consider the system shown in Figure 13.21a. We will assume that the signal output from the transmitter has a dynamic range of 80 dB such as from 1 mV to 10 V. If the transmission link has a total signal attenuation of 60 dB, the signal input at the receiver will have a dynamic range of from 1 μV to 10 mV. If the noise level at the receiver input is 10 μV (rms), we see that the SNR will be less than unity for the lowest 20-dB range (1 to 10 μV) of the received signal, so that this part of the signal will be essentially lost in the noise.

Now let us consider the system of Figure 10.13b, in which there is signal compression at the transmitter and signal expansion at the receiver. We will assume that the signal compressor used in the transmitter has a transfer characteristic given by $v_o \propto (v_i)^{1/2}$, and that the expandor in the receiver has the complementary transfer function of $v_o \propto (v_i)^2$. At the transmitter the signal dynamic range is compressed from the original 80 dB down to a range of 40 dB. The maximum or peak output voltage level will be kept the same at 10 V, so that now the transmitter output signal will range from 100 mV to 10 V.

At the receiver input the signal level will now range from 100 μV to 10 mV. Since the input noise level is still 10 μV, we see that the minimum value of the SNR will be 10:1, so that now all portions of the received signal will be well above the noise level. The signal expansion circuit in the receiver will then restore the signal to the full 80-dB dynamic range.

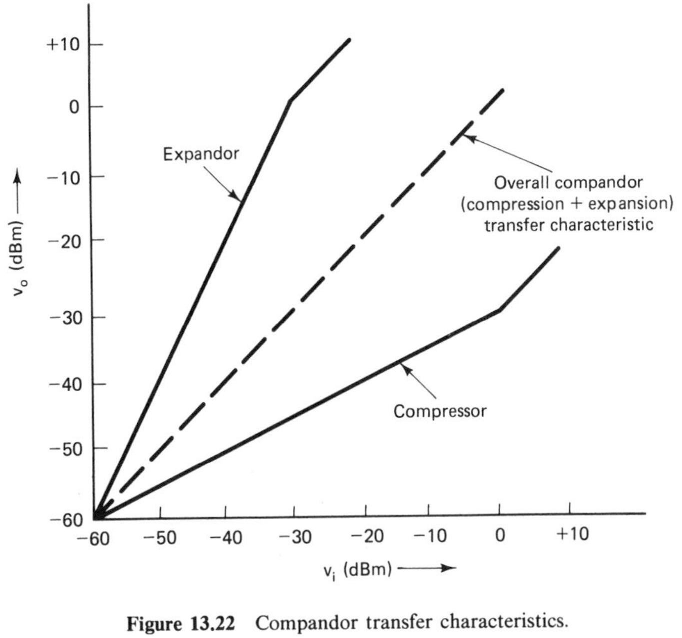

Figure 13.22 Compandor transfer characteristics.

13.9.1 Examples of IC Compandors

Some examples of analog signal compandor ICs are the LM2704 through LM2707 series (National Semiconductor). These devices feature a complementary pair of a signal compressor and a signal expandor in one IC package. In Figure 13.22 the compandor signal transfer characteristics are shown.

These devices have a dynamic range of over 70 dB. For a compandor it is desirable that the compression and expansion transfer characteristics be complementary such that the overall compression-expansion transfer characteristic will be linear and therefore the output signal of the system will be an undistorted replica of the input signal. For the LM2704–2706 devices the individual compressor and expandor transfer functions are accurate to within ± 1 dB, such that the net compandor signal distortion will be less than 0.5%.

Another example of a compandor IC is the NE570/571 (Signetics). This device has a 110 dB dynamic range. As a signal compressor it converts an input signal range of from -80 dBm (2.45 mV) to $+20$ dBm (7.75 V) to an output range of -40 to $+10$ dBm (0 dBm $=$ 1 mW across 600). As an expandor it converts an input signal range of -40 to $+10$ dBm to an output range of -80 to $+20$ dBm.

13.10 ELECTRONIC ATTENUATOR

In Figure 13.23 a schematic diagram of the MC3340 (Motorola) Electronic Attenuator is shown. This circuit can produce a variable gain or attenuation of the input signal over the range 90 dB. The gain is controlled by the voltage applied to pin 2. As the control voltage varies from 3.5 to 6.0 V the gain of this circuit will vary from a maximum of $+13$ dB (4.5) to a minimum of -77 dB (0.00014). The gain can also be controlled by a variable resistor connected between pin 2 and ground. As the external gain control resistor is varied between 4 and 30 kΩ, the gain will be varied from the maximum value of $+13$ dB down to a minimum of -77 dB.

The signal input is applied to the base of Q_9. The a-c collector current of Q_9 divides between Q_4 and Q_5, this current division being controlled by the B_4–B_5 voltage differential. The base voltage of Q_5 is obtained from the Q_2, which acts as a constant-voltage source. The circuit that supplies the base bias voltage for Q_4 is similar to that for Q_5, with Q_3 acting as a voltage source, except that this bias voltage can be varied by the control voltage applied to pin 2.

The current from Q_5 flows through the load resistance R_5. The resulting voltage drop is then buffered by the emitter follower Q_8. Note that the Q_6–Q_7 differential-amplifier pair is similar to the Q_4–Q_5 pair, but is biased by a constant-current source Q_{10}. The collectors of the two differential-amplifier pairs are cross-coupled such that the total d-c current through R_5 will remain constant, independent of the gain control voltage. This allows for a very wide range of control voltage and a correspondingly large range for the gain of this device while maintaining essentially the same quiescent conditions.

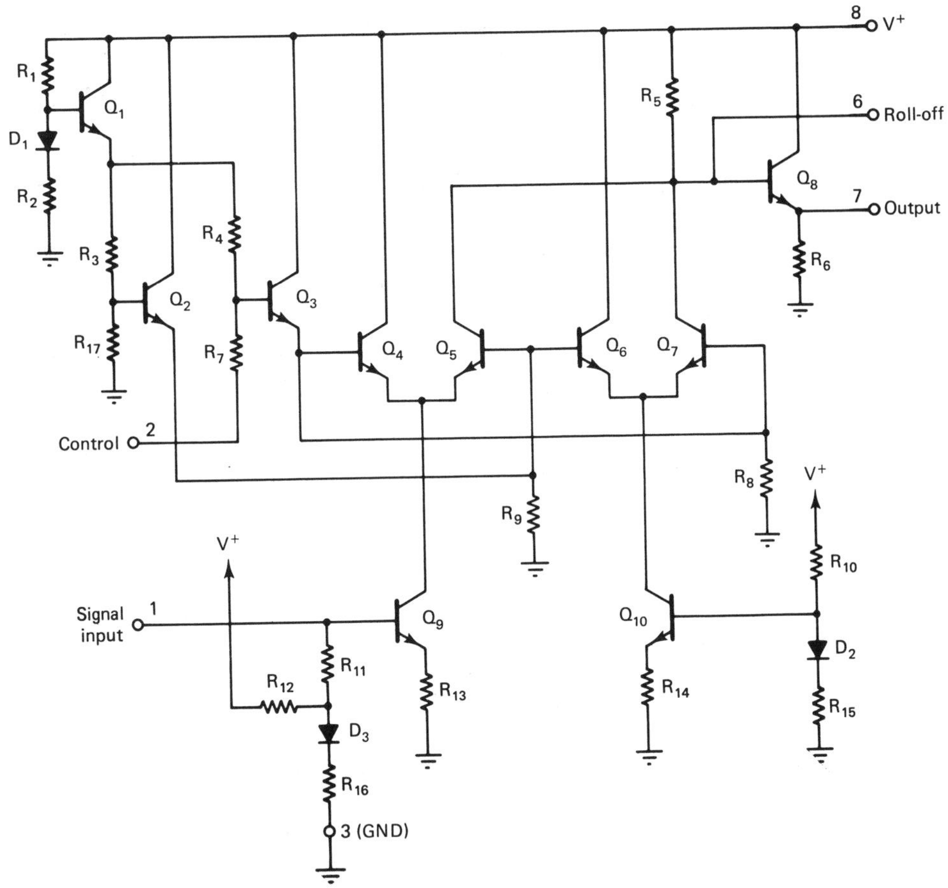

Figure 13.23 Electronic attenuator: MC3340 (Motorola Semiconductor Products).

13.11 TWO-WIRE TRANSMITTER

A two-wire transmitter is a circuit useful for remote-sensing applications in which the transmitter d-c biasing power is supplied over the same pair of wires as the signal current.

A basic block diagram of a two-wire current mode transmitter is shown in Figure 13.24. Transistor Q_1 operates as a constant-current source and produces a current given by $I_1 = (V_S/R_1)(1 + R_F/R_2)$, where V_s is the voltage produced by the sensor. The total current on the transmission line will be $I_o = I_1 + I_Q$, where I_Q is the biasing current for the amplifier and the sensor. The voltage drop across the load resistor will be given by $V_o = I_oR_L = I_QR_L + V_S(R_L/R_1)(1 + R_F/R_2)$.

This transmitter acts essentially as a current source, especially when $I_1 \gg I_Q$. This current mode of operation makes the system less affected by the voltage drop due to the transmission-line resistance and also reduces the effects of noise or

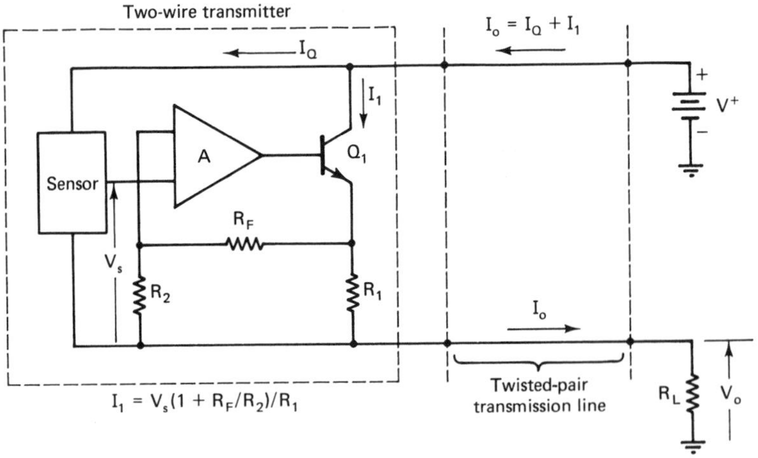

Figure 13.24 Basic circuit for a two-wire transmitter.

other types of interference that is picked up along the transmission line. The operation of a voltage-mode transmitter is compared with that of a current-mode transmitter in Figure 13.25. In the case of the voltage-mode signal transmission, the line resistance R_{LINE} and the noise and interference voltage that are induced on the transmission line will have a direct effect on the output voltage, which will be given by $V_o = (V_s + V_{\text{noise}} + V_{\text{interference}})R_L/(R_L + R_{\text{LINE}})$. In the case of the current-mode signal transmission, the line resistance and the noise and interference voltages that are induced on the line will have a very small effect on the output voltage.

An example of a two-wire current-mode transmitter IC is the LH0045 (National Semiconductor). An equivalent schematic diagram of this device is given in Figure 13.26, and a typical application is shown in Figure 13.27. Amplifier A_1 in conjunction with current source I_1 and zener diode D_2 acts as a voltage regulator and produces an output voltage of 10 V if pins 5 and 6 are open and 5 V if these two pins are

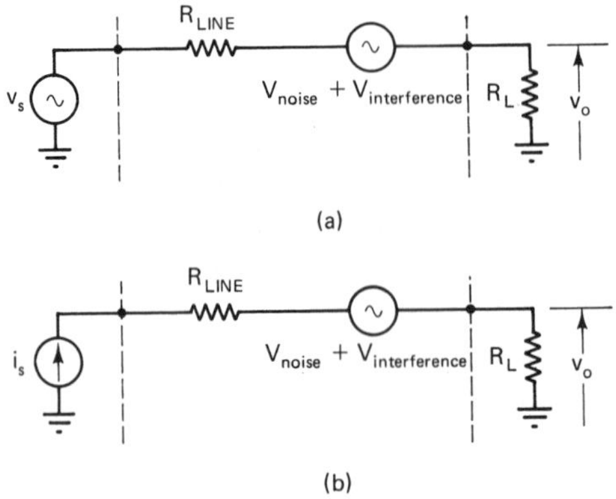

Figure 13.25 Comparison of (a) voltage-mode and (b) current-mode signal.

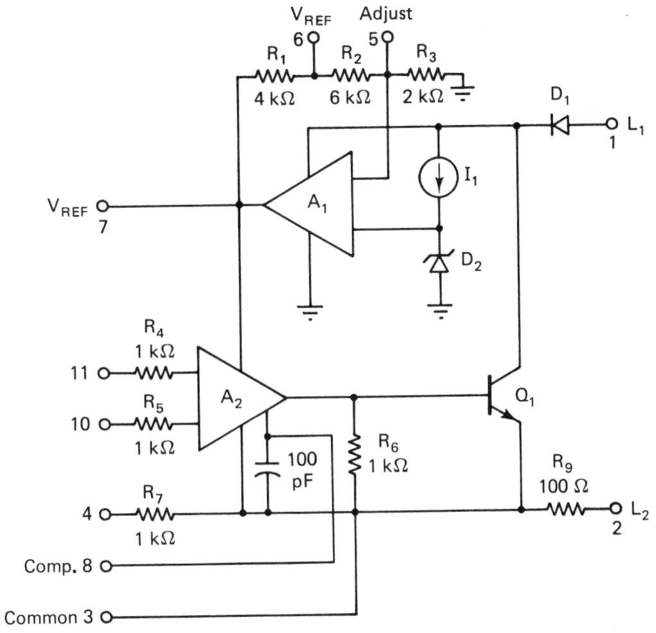

Figure 13.26 LH0045 two-wire transmitter equivalent schematic.

shorted. The output voltage of A_1 is used to bias A_2 and can also be used to bias a sensor such as the bridge circuit of Figure 13.27.

A typical application of this IC is shown in Figure 13.27. The bridge element R_{B_4} can be a pressure- or strain-sensitive resistor (i.e., a piezoresistive transducer) or a temperature-sensitive resistor such as a thermistor. For many applications the null-adjust resistor R_T would be set to give an output current level of $I_o = 4$ mA under "null conditions" of $R_{B_4} = R_{B_3}$. If R_{B_4} then decreases by 1.0 Ω, the voltage

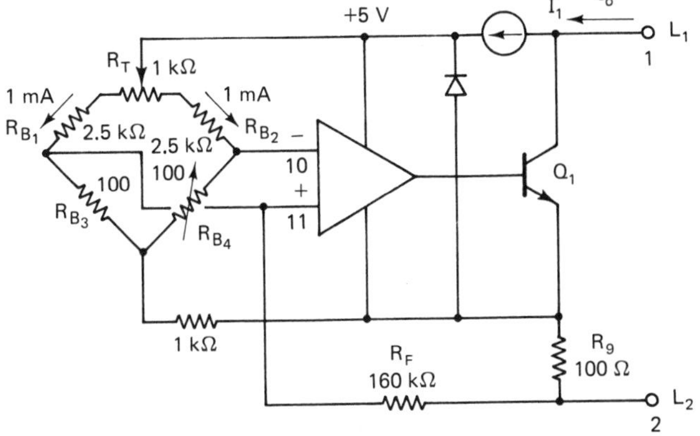

Figure 13.27 Typical application of LH0045 two-wire transmitter.

drop across R_{B_4} will change by 1.0 Ω × 1.0 mA = 1.0 mV. This will result in a change in the current through Q_1 of approximately

$$\Delta I_1 = 1 \text{ mV} \times \left(1 + \frac{R_F}{R_{B_3}}\right) \times \frac{1}{R_9} = 1 \text{ mV} \times \left(1 + \frac{160 \text{ k}\Omega}{100}\right) \times \frac{1}{100} = \underline{16 \text{ mA}} \tag{13.8}$$

so that the output current will now be at its "full-scale" value of 20 mA.

13.12 TUNED AMPLIFIER INTEGRATED CIRCUITS

Tuned amplifier ICs use externally connected *LC* tuned circuits to produce a frequency-selective or bandpass amplifier, often with a relatively narrow bandwidth. They can be used as a radio-frequency (RF) or intermediate-frequency (IF) amplifier. A common application of these ICs is as a multistage "IF strip" for radio, TV, and other communications systems. Examples of integrated-circuit IF strips are the LM172 (National Semiconductor) for AM radios, LM3089 (National Semiconductor) for FM radios, and the LM3071 (National Semiconductor) for the TV chrominance signal.

LC tuned circuits are used for frequency selectivity and can also function as impedance-transforming circuits for impedance-matching purposes. In order to have the maximum power transfer from one circuit or stage to the next, the source and load impedances must satisfy the maximum power transfer theorem, in that they should be complex conjugates of each other. An *LC* tuned circuit can be used as the coupling element between stages to produce the required frequency selectivity as well as to satisfy the impedance-matching requirement. This will result in the maximum power transfer from one stage to the next and thereby produce the "maximum available gain" (MAG) for the system.

13.13 FM SOUND CIRCUIT

The circuit shown in Figure 13.28 is available as a monolithic IC (MC1351, LM1351, etc.) and can serve as a complete FM sound circuit for TV and other applications. This IC combines the functions of an FM radio-frequency amplifier, a limiter, an FM demodulator, and an audio amplifier.

An example of an application of this circuit as a 4.5-MHz TV FM sound circuit is shown in Figure 13.29 and an output circuit is given in Figure 13.30.

The portion of the IC shown in Figure 13.28a is the FM radio-frequency amplifier and limiter. This consists of three cascaded differential-amplifier stages with an emitter-follower buffer stage connected to the output of each differential amplifier. The three differential-amplifier stages each have a load resistance of only 1 kΩ, in order to obtain a wide bandwidth.

The quiescent current of the three differential amplifiers will be set by the biasing network at $2V_{BE}/1$ kΩ = 1.4 mA. The resulting dynamic transfer conductance of the differential amplifiers will be given by $g_f = I_Q/4V_T$ = 1.4 mA/100 mV = 14 mS. The voltage gain of each differential-amplifier stage will therefore be A_v =

$g_f R_L = 14 \text{ mS} \times 1 \text{ k}\Omega = \underline{14}$. The overall voltage gain of the three differential-amplifier stages will be approximately $(14)^3 = \underline{2.7 \text{ k}\Omega}$. The actual gain of this three-stage amplifier will be somewhat less than this, about 2000, due to the voltage gain of the three emitter-follower transistors. With this large voltage gain of about 66 dB, this circuit will exhibit a limiting characteristic at an input signal level of only 80 μV (rms).

The output voltage of the FM amplifier/limiter circuit is fed to the balanced demodulator circuit of Figure 13.28b. As shown in Figure 13.28b, part of the signal is supplied directly to one differential-amplifier section of the demodulation circuit (from E_9 to B_{16}). A portion of the signal at the emitter of Q_9 (E_9) is tapped off via a 450-Ω/50-Ω voltage divider and is made available at pin 8. The signal then goes from pin 8 through a quadrature phase-shift network and is supplied to the

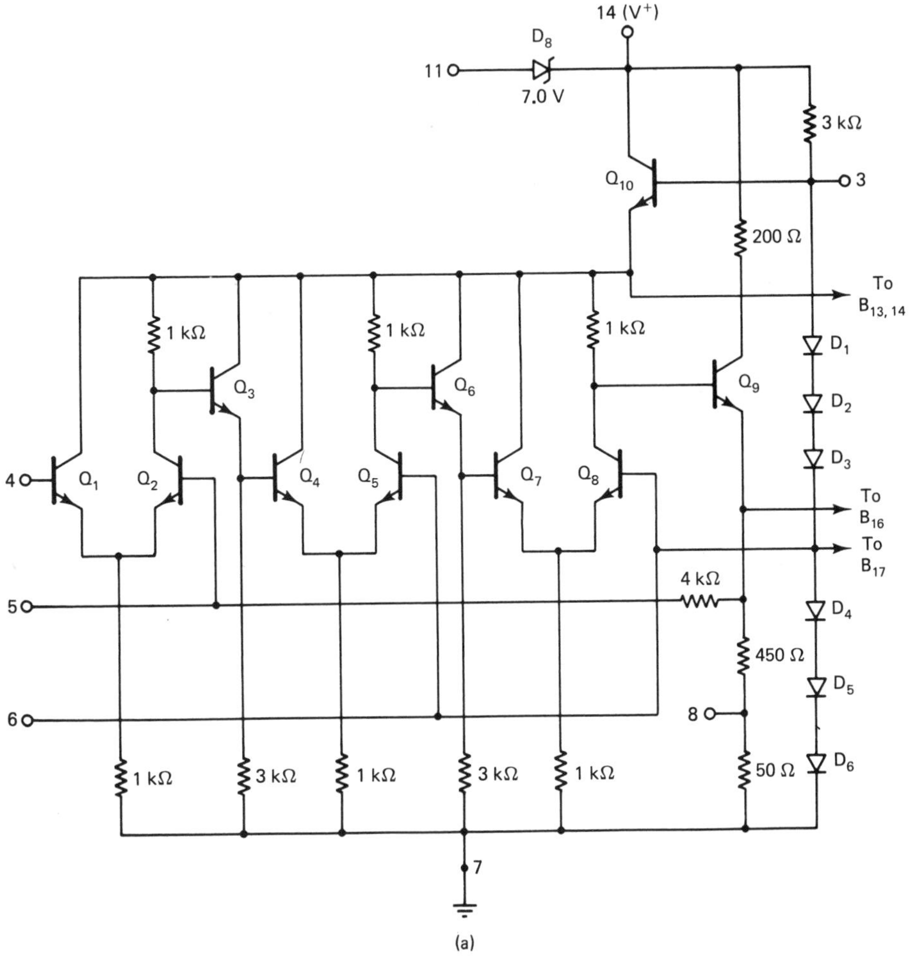

Figure 13.28 TV sound circuit: (a) FM amplifier/limiter; (b) FM demodulator; (c) audio preamplifier and driver.

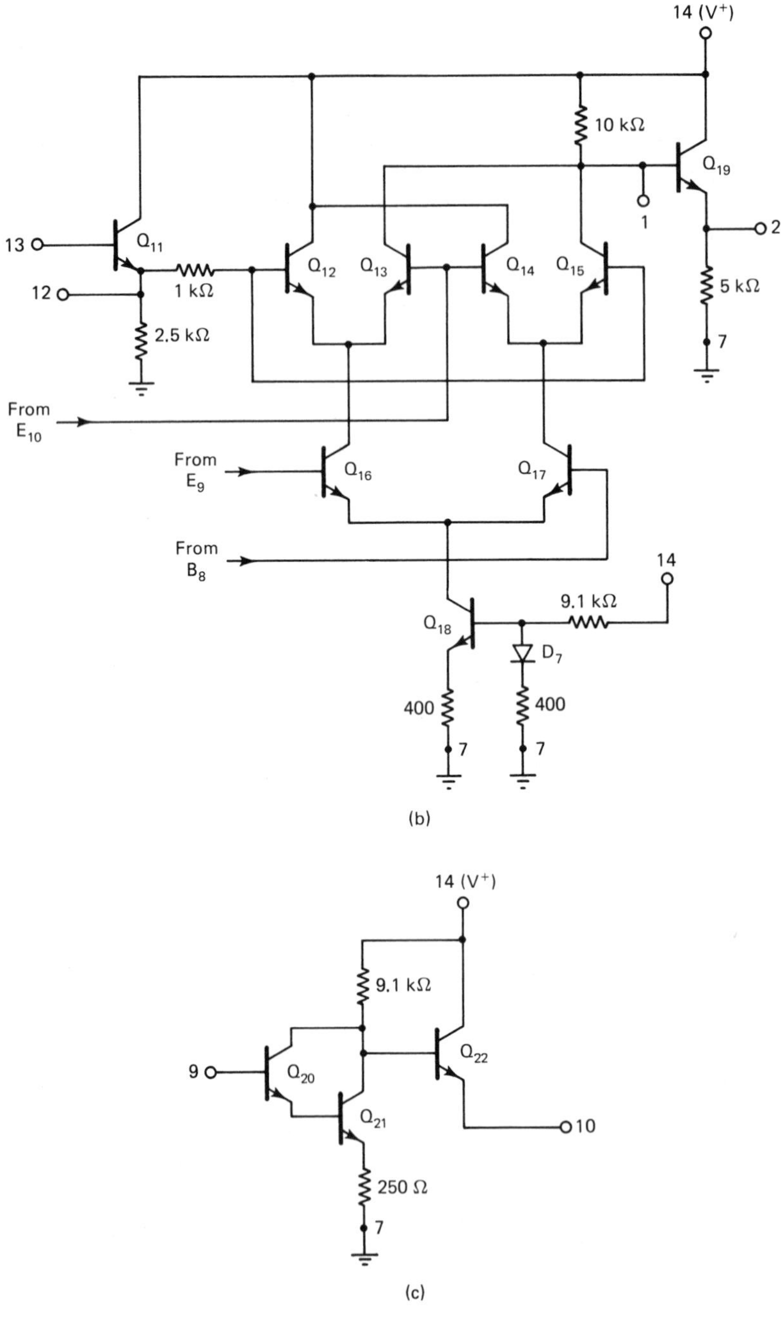

Figure 13.28 *(cont)*

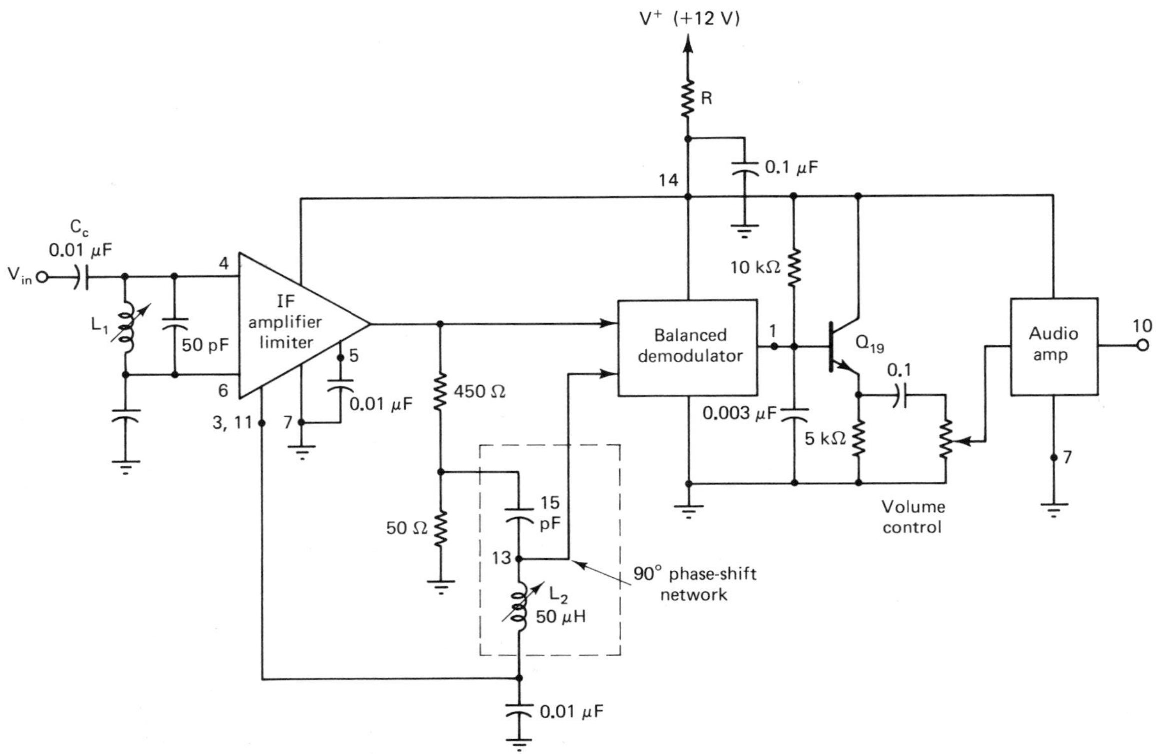

Figure 13.29 Block diagram of 4.5-MHz TV sound circuit.

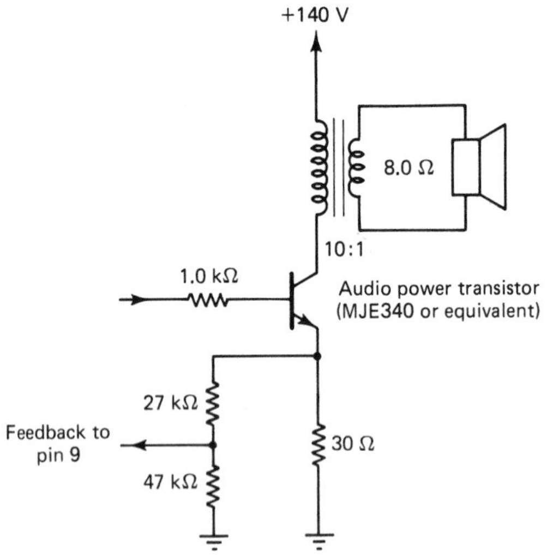

Figure 13.30 Audio power transistor output stage.

bases of Q_{12} and Q_{15} via the emitter-follower stage Q_{11}. The resonant frequency of the phase-shift network is chosen such that the phase shift will be 90° at the center frequency f_c of the FM signal.

When the signal level at the input of the demodulator reaches about 100 mV the output voltage of the circuit will no longer be dependent on the input signal level. This limiting type of characteristic is a very desirable feature for an FM demodulator system because it makes the system relatively insensitive to any amplitude modulation (AM) that may be present on the signal. This limiting characteristic will occur at an input signal level of only about 80 μV (rms). The typical AM rejection ratio for an input signal level of 20 mV (rms) with a 30% amplitude modulation and a center frequency of 4.5 MHz with a ±25-kHz FM deviation will be 45 dB.

The output voltage of the FM demodulator is filtered by a low-pass network consisting of the 10-kΩ resistor and the 0.003-μF capacitor (at pin 1) to remove all RF components. The signal is then supplied through an emitter follower (Q_{19}) and a volume-control potentiometer to the audio preamplifier stage of Figure 13.28c. This preamplifier stage is composed of a Darlington common-emitter amplifier stage and an emitter-follower output stage for driving the external audio power transistor of Figure 13.30.

13.14 FM STEREO DEMODULATOR INTEGRATED CIRCUIT

The baseband frequency spectrum for a stereo signal is shown in Figure 13.31. It is seen to consist of a monaural L + R (left + right) audio signal from about 30 Hz to 15 kHz and the L − R difference signal upper and lower sidebands. The 15-kHz L − R audio signal is combined with a 38-kHz carrier signal in a balanced modulator at the transmitter to produce the double-sideband/suppressed carrier (DSB/SC) signal shown. For the correct demodulation of the L − R audio signal a 38-kHz carrier signal must be regenerated at the receiver.

To facilitate the recovery of the carrier signal a pilot carrier at exactly one-

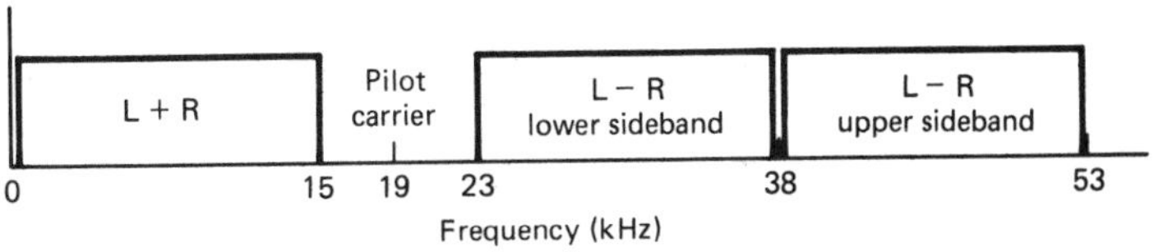

Figure 13.31 Baseband spectrum of stereo signal.

half the carrier frequency or 19 kHz is transmitted. Since this 19-kHz tone is well above the L + R signal and well outside the L − R sidebands it can easily be detected at the receiver by a phase-locked loop. This baseband signal is then used to frequency modulate an RF carrier signal to produce the FM stereo signal.

The FM stereo demodulator IC contains all of the active circuitry necessary to demodulate the L + R and the L − R audio signals at the receiver. Examples of monolithic IC stereo demodulators are the MC1310 (Motorola), LM1310, and the LM1800 (both National Semiconductor).

In Figure 13.32 a block diagram of an FM stereo receiver is shown, and a block diagram of the MC1310 is shown in Figure 13.33. It is seen to consist basically of a phase-locked loop to regenerate the 38-kHz carrier and a demodulator to obtain the L + R and L − R audio signals.

The phase-locked loop has a voltage-controlled oscillator (VCO) with a free-running frequency of approximately four times the pilot carrier frequency or 76 kHz. This frequency is then divided down twice to produce a frequency that under free-running conditions will be very close to the 19-kHz pilot carrier. The phase-locked loop can therefore easily lock in on the pilot carrier so that the VCO frequency will now become exactly equal to four times the pilot carrier frequency and therefore exactly twice the 38-kHz L − R carrier frequency. The output of the VCO following the divider will be at 38 kHz and will therefore be at exactly the correct frequency for the demodulation of the L − R signal. Note that no phase shift will be needed for the 38-kHz signal. Although there will indeed be a phase difference of approximately 90° between the 19-kHz pilot tone and the divided-down VCO signal supplied to the phase detector, the corresponding phase difference between the 38-kHz signal supplied to the L − R demodulator and the original 38-kHz carrier will be 180°. This 180° phase difference will be of no concern since it will just involve a change of the L − R signal polarity.

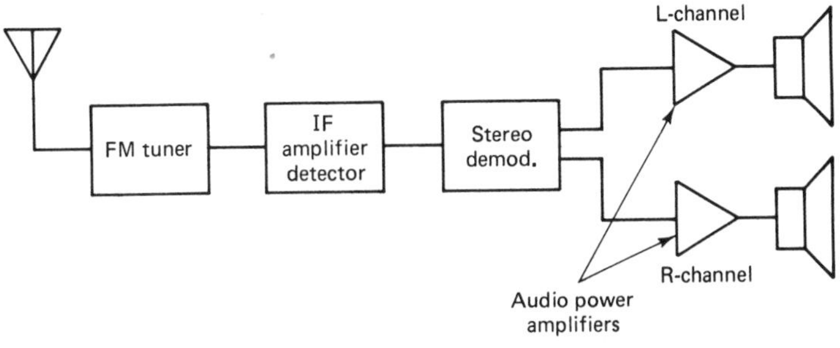

Figure 13.32 FM stereo receiver.

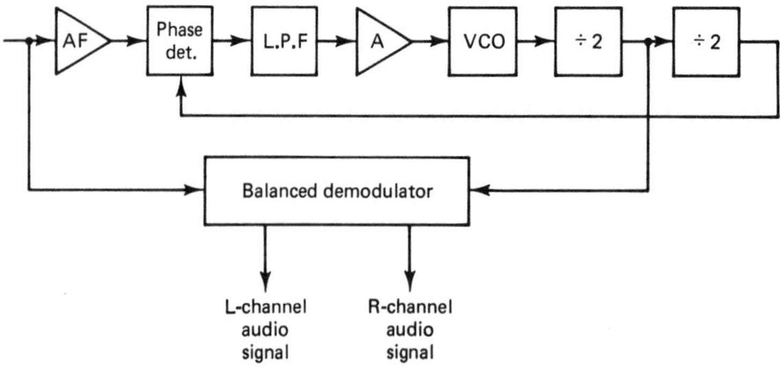

Figure 13.33 FM stereo demodulator IC block diagram: MC131.

13.15 AM RADIO SYSTEM INTEGRATED CIRCUIT

An AM radio system consisting of an RF amplifier, local oscillator, mixer, IF amplifier, AGC detector, and zener regulator is available as a monolithic IC. An example of such a system is the LM3820 (National Semiconductor) and a block diagram of a complete AM radio using this IC is shown in Figure 13.34. We see that this IC

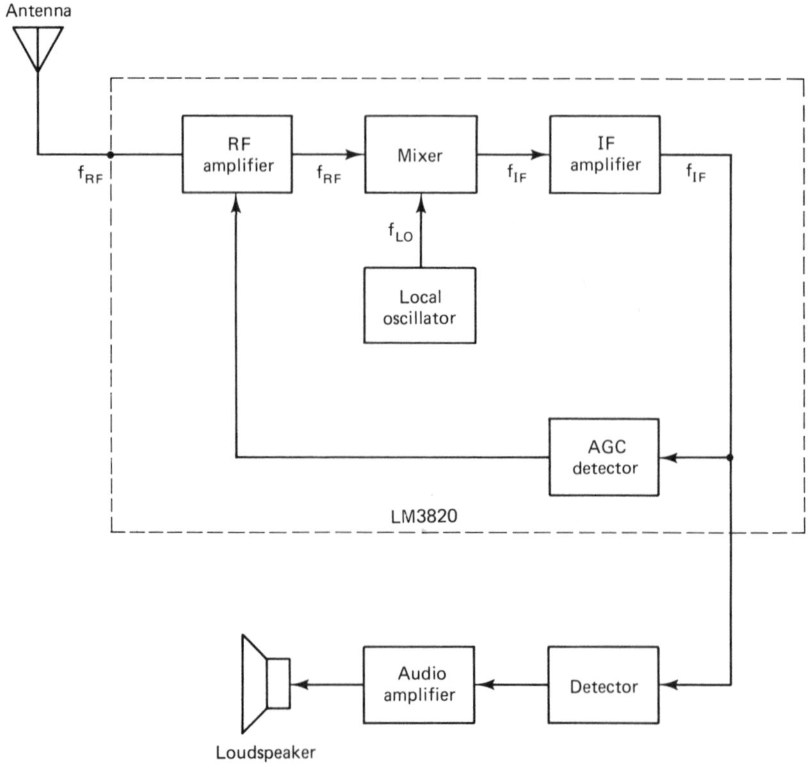

Figure 13.34 AM radio system IC block diagram: LM3820.

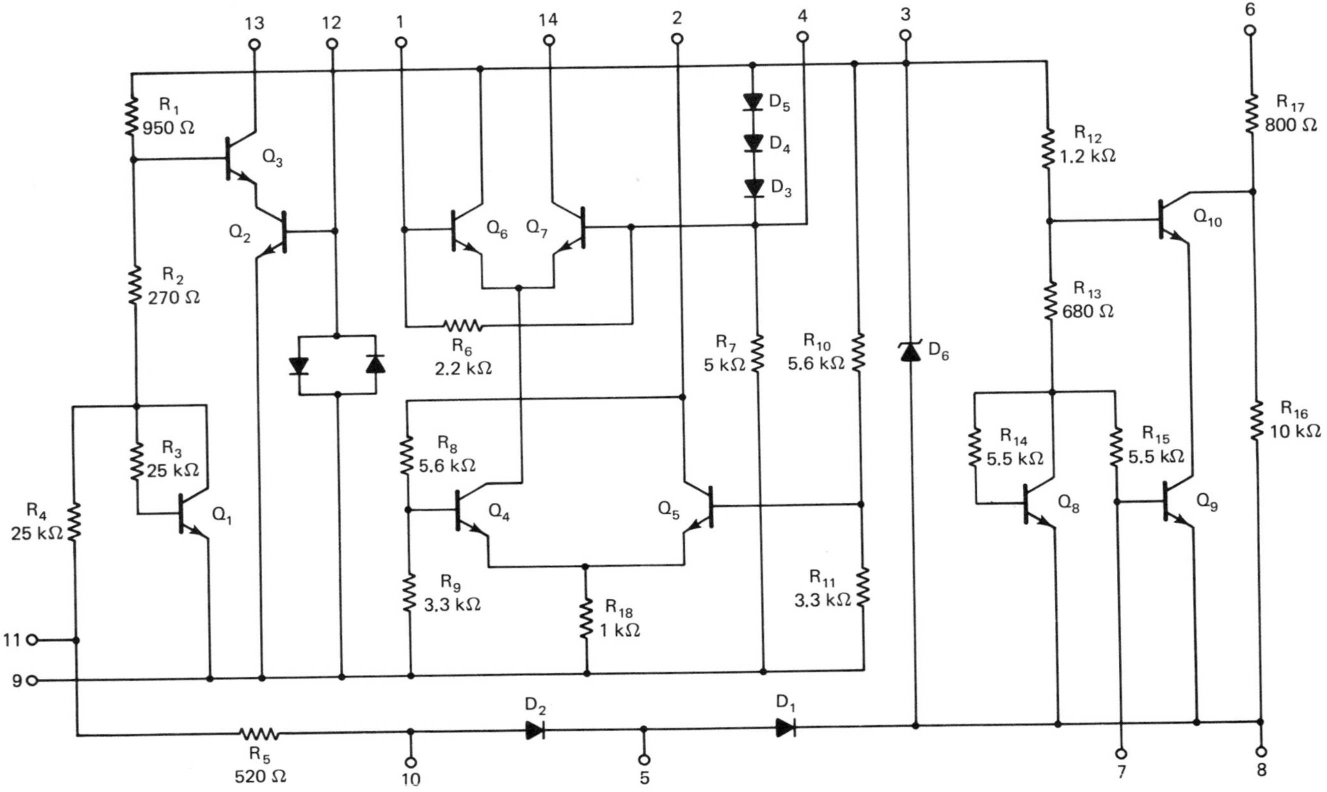

Figure 13.35 Schematic diagram of AM radio system IC: LM3820 (National Semiconductor).

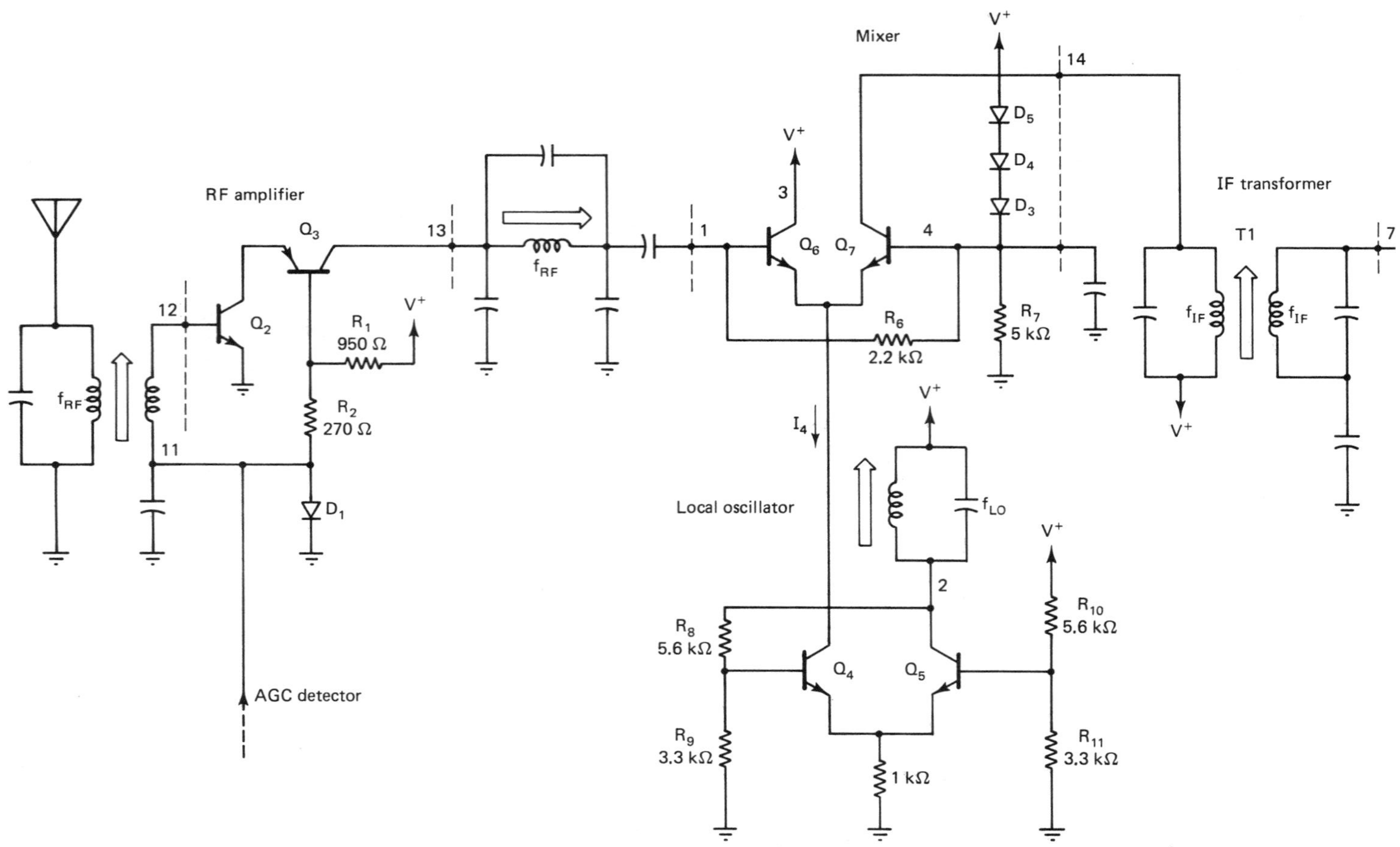

Figure 13.36 AM radio system IC: LM3820.

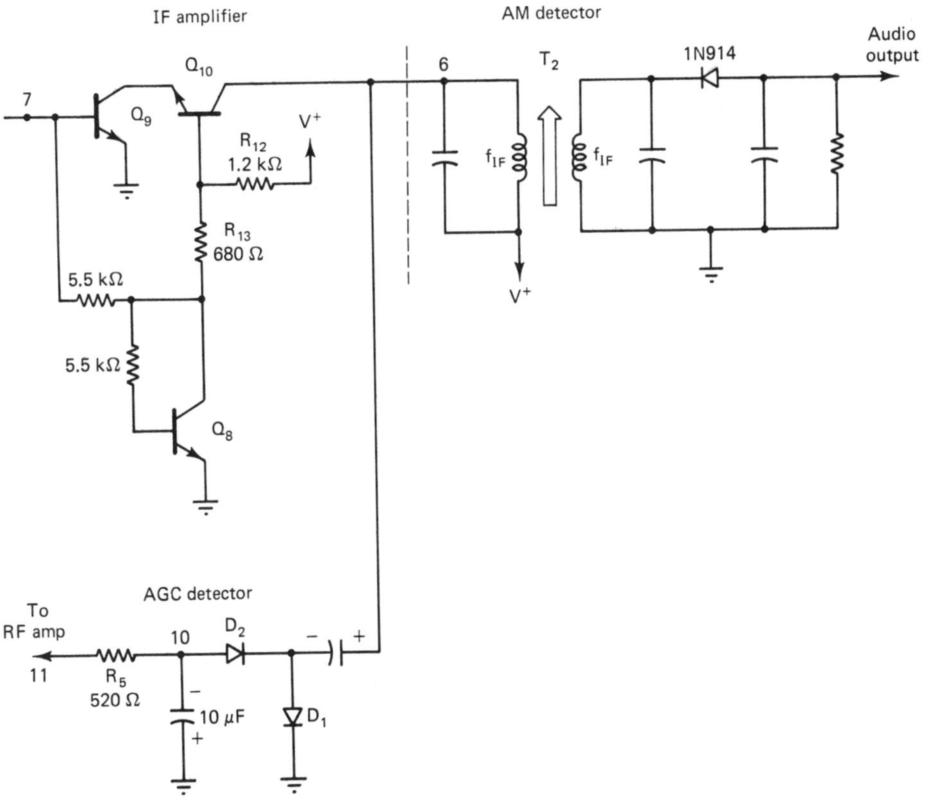

Figure 13.36 *(cont)*

provides all of the RF and IF signal processing. In Figure 13.35 a schematic diagram of this IC is given, and in Figure 13.36 the various subsections of this IC are shown together with the necessary external ("off-the chip") circuit components.

The RF amplifier sections consists of transistors Q_2 and Q_3 in a cascode configuration with the diode-connected transistor Q_1 used for the biasing of Q_2 and Q_3. The AGC voltage that is generated on the chip is supplied to the base of Q_2 to adjust the quiescent current level of the RF amplifier and thereby control the gain.

The local oscillator is composed of the Q_4–Q_5 differential amplifier pair with positive feedback from the collector of Q_5 back to the base of Q_4 via the R_8–R_9 voltage divider. Transistor Q_5 has an LC tuned circuit load and the resonant frequency of this tuned circuit will be the frequency of oscillation, f_{LO}.

The output signal from the RF amplifier section is coupled by the pi-section tuned circuit to the mixer stage. The mixer is composed of the Q_6–Q_7 differential amplifier pair with the RF signal being supplied to the base of Q_6 and the base of Q_7 will be at a-c ground potential. The biasing current for this differential amplifier is the collector current of Q_4, which is part of the local oscillator circuit. The collector current of Q_4 will have an a-c component i_{c_4} that is at the local oscillator frequency f_{LO}. The a-c collector current of Q_7 will be given by $i_{c_7} = -g_f v_{b_6} = -[(I_{C_4} +$

$i_{c_4})/4V_T]\ v_{b_6}$. Since $i_{c_4} \propto \cos \omega_{LO}t$ and $v_{b_6} \propto \cos \omega_{RF}t$ we will have that i_{c_7} will have a component proportional to $\cos \omega_{LO}t \times \cos \omega_{RF}t = \frac{1}{2} \cos (\omega_{LO} + \omega_{RF})t + \frac{1}{2} \cos (\omega_{LO} - \omega_{RF})t$. Since $\omega_{IF} = \omega_{LO} - \omega_{RF}$, we see that the IF frequency will be generated in the mixer. The output of the mixer is coupled to the IF amplifier stage by means of the IF transformer T_1, which has both primary and secondary tuned to the IF frequency.

The intermediate frequency (IF) amplifier stage uses Q_9 and Q_{10} in a cascode configuration that is biased by the diode-connected transistor Q_8. The output of this IF stage is supplied to the AM detector by means of transformer T_2, which is a tuned primary–tuned secondary transformer with both sides being tuned to f_{IF}. This transformer as well as transformer T_1 and the pi-section network serve as impedance-transforming or matching circuits in addition to being bandpass filters.

The output of the IF stage goes to the detector circuit and is also supplied via pin 6 to the AGC detector. This detector uses diodes D_1 and D_2 and is basically a peak detector that produces a d-c output voltage that is proportional to the average level of the AM signal. This automatic gain control (AGC) voltage is supplied to the RF stage via pin 1 and controls the gain of this stage so as to make the variations in the output signal level of this AM circuit less dependent on changes in the input signal level.

If this AM radio IC is combined with an LM386 audio power amplifier that has an audio-frequency gain set at 200 and is operated under the following conditions, the performance characteristics listed below will be obtained.

TABLE 13.1

Operating conditions: $V^+ = +6$ V, AM signal input with a carrier frequency of $f_c = 1000$ kHz, a modulation frequency of $f_m = 400$ Hz, and a modulation index of $m = 0.3$.

Performance characteristics:

Input signal level (μV)	Signal-to-noise ratio, SNR (dB)	Total harmonic distortion, THD (%)
10	17	2
100	37	2
1,000	50	2
10,000 (10 mV)	58	13

13.16 INTEGRATED CIRCUITS FOR TELEVISION: CHROMA DEMODULATOR

Integrated circuits can be used to good advantage in the signal processing circuitry of TV receivers. Indeed, ICs find application in almost all areas of a TV receiver except in the VHF/UHF tuner section, the high-voltage circuits, and in the power supply.

An important application of ICs is in the color signal (chroma) processing circuitry, and in particular the chroma demodulator. Some examples of chroma demodulator ICs are the MC1324 (Motorola), μA746 (Fairchild), LM746, LM1828, and LM1848 (National Semiconductor). These ICs basically contain a pair of doubly-balanced demodulator circuits for the demodulation of the I ("in-phase") and Q ("quadrature") color sidebands. The resulting I and Q chrominance output signals are then combined with the luminance signal to produce the red, green, and blue signals.

ICs can be used in other parts of the chroma processing system, such as for the regeneration of the 3.58 MHz color subcarrier and for the chroma IF amplifier. The 3.58 MHz color subcarrier is not transmitted continuously, but rather is transmitted only during the horizontal blanking interval as a short "color burst" of eight to ten cycles lasting for only 2.5 μs out of the total 63.5 μs horizontal line period. A phase-locked loop is used to lock onto this color burst with the correct phase relationship so that during the time when the color burst is not present a regenerated color subcarrier will be present. This correct phase relationship is essential for the demodulation of the chroma signal.

13.17 ACTIVE FILTER ICs

Active filter hybrid ICs which contain all of the active devices and most of the passive components needed for various types of filters are available. An example of an active filter IC is the UAF11/UAF21 (Burr-Brown). This hybrid IC contains three op amps, two 1 nF capacitors, and five 100 KΩ thin-film resistors, and with the addition of four external resistors, becomes a two-pole active filter with band-pass, low-pass, and high-pass outputs. By summing the low-pass and high-pass outputs with an external op amp, a band-reject filter can be obtained. The UAF11 can be operated over the frequency range 0.001 Hz to 20 kHz and the UAF21 can go up to 200 kHz, and both ICs offer Q-values of from 0.5 up to 500. The UAF31 and UAF41 (Burr-Brown) are similar to the UAF11 and UAF21, except that an additional op amp is included so that the band-reject function can be implemented without any external op amp being needed.

13.18 SWITCHED-CAPACITOR FILTER ICS

Switched-capacitor filter ICs are self-contained monolithic active filters that require no external resistors or capacitors. The filter capacitors are small value MOS capacitors on the IC chip. The large value resistors required are simulated by the switched capacitor technique using small MOS capacitors and MOS transistor switches, all contained on the IC chip. Band-pass, band-reject, low-pass, and high-pass filters are available. In addition to not requiring any external components, another major advantage of the switched-capacitor filters is that the center frequency of the band-pass and band-reject filters, and the 3 dB frequency of the high-pass and low-pass filters are directly proportional to the clocking frequency supplied to the device.

Examples of switched-capacitor filter ICs are the R5604, R5605, and R5606 (EG&G Reticon). These are all 6-pole Chebyshev band-pass filters. The R5604 contains three stagger-tuned 1/3 octave filters that when cascaded, cover a full octave for the pass-band. The R5605 has two stagger-tuned 1/2 octave filters that when cascaded cover a full octave, and the R5606 has a single full octave filter. For these filters, the pass-band center frequency is related to the clock frequency by $f_{center} = f_{clock}/N$, and for the R5606 the value of N is 109. For the two filter sections of the R5605, the values of N are 109 and 77.4, and for the R5604 the values of N are 136.3, 109, and 87.2. The filter center frequencies can be varied over a range of from 0.5 Hz up to 10 kHz. For all three ICs the filter insertion loss is less than ± 0.2 dB and the distortion is less than 0.1% over an 80 dB dynamic range for a 10 V peak-to-peak input signal. Other similar switched-capacitor band-pass filters are the R5614, R5615, and R5616 (EG&G Reticon) which are 1/3 octave, 1/2 octave, and full octave filters, respectively. These ratio of the clock frequency to the pass-band center frequency for these ICs is 54.5 and the center frequency can go beyond 20 kHz.

Some examples of other switched-capacitor ICs are the R5609/R5613 low-pass filters, R5611 high-pass filter and R5612 notch filter (all EG&G Reticon). These filters have cutoff or center frequencies tunable over the range 1 Hz to 25 kHz by variation of the clock frequency.

Other examples of switched-capacitor ICs are the MF4 and MF6 (National Semiconductor). The MF4 is a 4-pole Butterworth low-pass active filter in an 8-pin mini-DIP package. The MF6 is similar to the MF4 except that it is a 6-pole Butterworth low-pass filter and comes in a 14-pin DIP package. The ratio of the clock frequency to the filter cutoff frequency is 50:1 for the MF4–50 and MF6–50, and 100:1 for the MF4–100 and MF6–100. A clock input can be supplied or an external resistor and capacitor can be used to set the frequency of an internal clock. The cutoff frequency can be varied over the range 0.1 Hz to 20 kHz and the gain in the pass-band is unity so that additional MF4 or MF6 sections can be easily cascaded for higher order filtering.

REFERENCES

FAULKENBERRY, L., *An Introduction to Operational Amplifiers with Linear IC Applications*, Wiley, 1982.

FITCHEN, F., *Electronic Integrated Circuits and Systems*, Van Nostrand Reinhold, 1970.

GREBENE, A. B., *Analog Integrated Circuit Design*, Van Nostrand Reinhold, 1972.

GREBENE, A. B., *Bipolar and MOS Analog Integrated Circuit Design*, Wiley, 1984.

LENK, J. D., *Manual for Integrated Circuit Users*, Reston, 1973.

MANDL, M., *Solid State Circuit Design Users Manual*, Chap. 6, Reston, 1977.

SEIDMAN, A., *Integrated Circuits Applications Handbook*, Wiley, 1983.

Noise in Integrated Circuits and Electronic Systems

14

In any communications system, unwanted and extraneous signals which interfere with the desired signal will set a lower limit to the strength of the desired signal that can reliably and accurately be received and understood. The interfering "signals," which are of a *random* nature and are not emitted by any other communications system, are called "noise." It is the random, unpredictable nature of noise that makes it so difficult to deal with and eliminate. Interfering signals that have a reasonably fixed or predictable nature, such as having a constant frequency or band of frequencies, can be reduced by special signal-processing techniques, such as the use of bandpass and band-stop filters. Although there are techniques for noise reduction, it can never be eliminated entirely. Furthermore, the signal processing that is required for noise reduction will generally involve a trade-off of some other aspect of overall system performance. A good example of this trade-off is the reduction in the system bandwidth in order to reduce the overall noise level. The reduced system bandwidth will correspondingly reduce the information transmission rate of which the system is capable.

In an electronic communications system noise is generated internally within both the transmitter and, much more important, in the receiver, as a result of a number of random processes. These processes include the random thermal motion of electrons and holes and the random nature of the electron–hole generation and recombination processes in semiconductor devices. In addition, noise generated by external sources may enter the receiver together with the desired signal. Some examples of external noise sources are lightning discharges, electrical machinery, and the ignition systems of gasoline engines.

The most critical component of an electronic communications system from the standpoint of the ability of the system to detect weak signals is the first or input stage of the receiver. It is here that the signal is the weakest and therefore the most susceptible to interference by noise, either internally generated in the first stage or coming into the first stage together with the signal.

The ratio of the signal voltage (rms) to the noise voltage (rms) will be called the *signal-to-noise ratio* (SNR). At the receiver input there will be a certain SNR depending on the signal strength and the external noise level. The internally generated noise in the first stage will add to the noise already present, so that there will generally be a significant degradation of the SNR in the first stage. It is, of course, true that the signal is amplified by the first stage, but the noise is also amplified by the same factor, so that due to the additional noise that is generated in the first stage, there will actually be some decrease or loss in the SNR.

Following the first stage there will be further amplification of both the signal and the noise by the other stages of the receiver. In each stage there will be additional noise added to the signal due to the internally generated noise of that stage. As a result, the SNR will continue to decrease as the signal proceeds through the various stages of the amplifier. Nevertheless, it is the first stage that is generally the most important by far in determining the SNR of the receiver. If the gain of the first stage is denoted by A_1, that of the second stage by A_2, and so on, the overall amplifier gain will be $A_T = A_1A_2A_3 \cdots$. If the incoming signal level is S_i and the noise level is N_i, the SNR at the receiver input is $(\text{SNR})_i = S_i/N_i$. The noise added by the first stage will be N_1, so that the SNR following the first stage will be $A_1S_i/A_1(N_i + N_1) = S_i/N_i + N_1$.

At the output of the second stage the SNR will be given by

$$(\text{SNR})_2 = \frac{A_1A_2S_i}{A_1A_2(N_i + N_1) + A_2N_2} = \frac{S_i}{(N_i + N_1) + (N_2/A_1)} \tag{14.1}$$

where N_2 is the noise added by the second stage. Similarly, at the output of the third stage we will have

$$(\text{SNR})_3 = \frac{A_1A_2A_3S_i}{A_1A_2A_3(N_i + N_1) + A_2A_3N_2 + A_3N_3}$$

$$= \frac{S_i}{(N_i + N_1) + (N_2/A_1) + (N_3/A_1A_2)}$$

We see from this that for reasonably large gains per stage, the SNR of the first stage will largely determine the overall SNR of the receiver.

The *sensitivity* of a system is a measure of the ability of the system to detect or recover weak signals. It is usually described in terms of the lowest input signal level that will result in an acceptable SNR. In many cases the minimum SNR needed to detect the presence of a signal is equal to unity, for which case the sensitivity is the signal level that is equal to the noise present at the first amplifier stage.

In the ideal situation the amplified signal that is produced by the receiver will be an exact replica of the original signal produced by the transmitter. This will never be the case in practice due to the various nonlinearities in the system that will result in distortion and the presence of noise.

In general, in order to produce an acceptable signal level an SNR of at least around 10 (20 dB) is necessary, and for some applications SNR values as high as 30 or 40 (30 to 36 dB) are required. For example, to produce a good-quality television picture free of any apparent noise, an SNR of about 30 (36 dB) is required. If the SNR drops below 10 (20 dB), the amount of noise (or "snow") in the picture becomes quite noticeable. For SNR values of less than about 3 (10 dB), the noise will be very objectionable, and if the SNR drops below about 1 or 2 (0 to 6 dB), it will be very difficult to discern the picture at all.

There will be two basic sources of noise in an electronic amplifier system, *thermal noise* and *shot noise*. Thermal noise (or Johnson noise) is due to the random thermal motion of charge carriers (electrons and holes) in the various circuits components of the amplifier, principally the resistors and transistors. Shot noise is the result of random fluctuations in the flow of current through electronic devices. Both thermal noise and shot noise are random functions of time with a zero average value, and both will have a Gaussian probability distribution function. We will now consider these two noise sources in more detail.

14.1 THERMAL NOISE

The basic physical origin of thermal noise is the random thermal motion of charge carriers. This random motion of electrons and holes will produce random fluctuations in the voltage measured across any resistive circuit element. The average value of the thermal noise voltage is zero, but it can be characterized by its mean-squared value. The *mean-squared noise voltage per unit bandwidth* is given by the equation

$$\boxed{v_n^2 = 4kTR} \tag{14.2}$$

where k = Boltzmann's constant = 1.38×10^{-23} J/°K, T = absolute temperature (°K), R = resistance value (Ω), and v_n^2 = *mean-squared noise voltage per unit bandwidth* (V^2/Hz). This is also referred to as the *spectral density* (or spectral intensity) of the mean-squared noise voltage. At 17°C (290°K) the value of $4kT$ is 1.60×10^{-20} J, so the v_n^2 can be expressed as $v_n^2 = 1.60 \times 10^{-20}R$ (V^2/Hz). Note that the mean-squared noise voltage is directly proportional to the temperature, which is consistent with the idea of it being the result of the random thermal motion of the charge carriers.

An actual resistor can be represented for the purpose of noise calculations as an ideal "noiseless" resistor in series with an equivalent noise voltage source v_n as shown in Figure 14.1. The noise voltage v_n is the *root-mean-squared* (rms) noise voltage. The spectral density of the *rms noise voltage* is given by $v_n = \sqrt{4kTR}$ and is the square root of the mean-squared value. Note that the spectral density of the noise voltage is independent of frequency or "flat," so that this noise is said to be a *broadband* or "*white*" type of noise.

It is possible to convert the voltage source-series resistance representation of the resistor noise characteristics into a current source-parallel resistance type of equivalent circuit, as shown in Figure 14.1. The rms noise current (spectral density) will

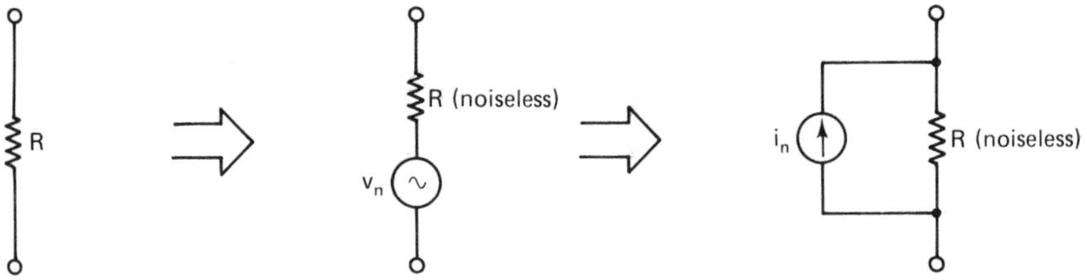

Figure 14.1 Representation of a resistor as an equivalent noiseless resistor and a voltage source or a current source.

be given by $i_n = v_n/R = \sqrt{4kTR}/R = \sqrt{4kT/R} = \sqrt{4kTG}$ (A/Hz$^{1/2}$). The mean-squared noise current spectral density will correspondingly be

$$\boxed{i_n^2 = 4kTG \text{ (A}^2\text{/Hz)}} \tag{14.3}$$

At room temperature (25°C), $\sqrt{4kT} = 1.28 \times 10^{-10}$ J$^{1/2}$ so that $v_n = 1.28 \times 10^{-10} \sqrt{R}$ and $i_n = 1.28 \times 10^{-10} \sqrt{G}$. In Table 14.1, values are given of the rms noise voltage and noise current spectral densities for various resistance values ranging from 10 Ω to 1 GΩ (10^9 Ω). It is to be noted that the noise voltages are generally in the nanovolt/$\sqrt{\text{Hz}}$ range, and the noise currents fall generally in the picoampere/$\sqrt{\text{Hz}}$ range.

TABLE 14.1 THERMAL NOISE VOLTAGE AND CURRENT VERSUS RESISTANCE

R (Ω)	G (S)	v_n (rms) (nV/Hz$^{1/2}$)	i_n (rms)
10	0.10	0.405	40.5 pA/Hz$^{1/2}$
50	0.02	0.905	18.1 pA/Hz$^{1/2}$
100	0.01	1.28	12.8 pA/Hz$^{1/2}$
1 k	1.0 mS	4.05	4.05 pA/Hz$^{1/2}$
10 k	0.1 mS	12.8	1.28 pA/Hz$^{1/2}$
100 k	10 μS	40.5	405 fA/Hz$^{1/2}$
1 M	1.0 μS	128	128 fA/Hz$^{1/2}$
10 M	0.1 μS	405	40.4 fA/Hz$^{1/2}$
100 M	0.01 μS	1280	12.8 fA/Hz$^{1/2}$
1000 M	0.001 μS	4050	4.05 fA/Hz$^{1/2}$

If the system bandwidth is B (Hz) the mean-squared noise voltage will be equal to the spectral density times the bandwidth, giving

$$\boxed{v_n^2 = 4kTRB} \tag{14.4}$$

For the mean-squared noise current, we will similarly have

$$\boxed{i_n^2 = 4kTGB} \tag{14.5}$$

14.1.1 Derivation of the Thermal Noise Equation and Noise Bandwidth

Considering the RC circuit of Figure 14.2, the average energy stored in the capacitor due to the thermal noise fluctuations in the resistor will be equal to $\frac{1}{2}kT$, which represents the thermodynamic energy of the system using the principle of the equipartition of energy for a system in thermal equilibrium. The average energy stored in the capacitor is $\frac{1}{2}C\overline{v^2}$, where $\overline{v^2}$ is the mean-squared voltage across the capacitor. We therefore have that $\frac{1}{2}C\overline{v^2} = \frac{1}{2}kT$, so that the mean-squared noise voltage will be given by $\overline{v^2} = kT/C$.

The 3-dB (or half-power) bandwidth of the RC circuit is given by $f_H = 1/(2\pi RC)$, so that $1/C = 2\pi R f_H$. If we substitute this into the expression given above for the mean-squared noise voltage, we obtain $\overline{v_n^2} = 2\pi kTRf_H$.

The effective or rectangular bandwidth of a system for the purposes of noise calculations is given by *noise effective bandwidth* $= B = \int_0^\infty |T(f)|^2\, df$, where $T(f)$ is the normalized transfer characteristic (i.e., v_o/v_i) of the system. For the RC network $T(f) = 1/[1 + j(f/f_H)]$, so that $|T(f)|^2 = 1/[1 + (f/f_H)^2]$. The noise effective bandwidth will therefore be

$$B = \int_0^\infty \frac{df}{1+(f/f_H)^2} = f_H \int_0^\infty \frac{1}{1+(f/f_H)^2}\, d\left(\frac{f}{f_H}\right) = f_H \int_0^\infty \frac{1}{1+x^2}\, dx$$

$$= f_H \tan^{-1} x \Big|_0^\infty = \frac{\pi}{2} f_H \tag{14.6}$$

Therefore, $2\pi f_H = 4B$ and thus the mean-squared noise voltage can be expressed as

$$\boxed{\overline{v_n^2} = 4kTB} \tag{14.7}$$

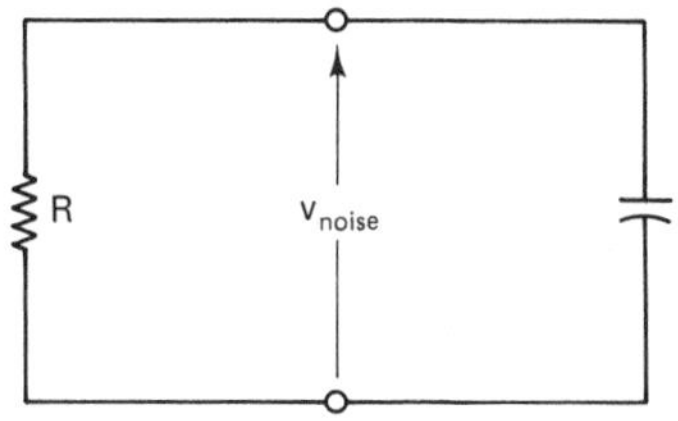

Figure 14.2 RC circuit for derivation of thermal noise equation.

where B is the noise effective bandwidth and is related to the 3-dB bandwidth f_H by $B = (\pi/2)f_H = 1.57f_H$. For a system with a transfer function of the form $T(f) = 1/[1 + j(f/f_H)]^2$, the 3-dB bandwidth will be $0.64f_H$ and the noise-effective bandwidth will be given by $B = 1.21BW$, where BW is the 3-dB bandwidth.

14.1.2 Addition of Noise Voltages

In Figure 14.3 the method of combining noise voltages and currents is illustrated. Noise voltages that arise from unrelated or uncorrelated noise sources are combined by adding the *mean-squared values* to obtain the total or net mean-squared noise voltage.

The total mean-squared noise voltage of R_1 and R_2 will be given by $\overline{v_n^2} = \overline{v_{n_1}^2} + \overline{v_{n_2}^2} = 4kTR_1 + 4kTR_2 = 4kT(R_1 + R_2)(\mathrm{V}^2/\mathrm{Hz})$. Note that this result is the same as that which would be obtained if we were first to combine R_1 and R_2 to form a total resistance of $R_1 + R_2$ and then to obtain the noise voltage of that total resistance.

In a similar fashion, uncorrelated noise currents can be combined by summing the mean-squared values to obtain the total mean-squared noise current. The mean-squared noise current of R_3 in Figure 14.3b will be $\overline{i_{n_3}^2} = 4kT/R_3 = 4kTG_3$, and that of R_4 will be $\overline{i_{n_4}^2} = 4kT/R_4 = 4kTG_4$. The total mean-squared noise current will be $\overline{i_n^2} = 4kTG_3 + 4kTG_4 = 4kT(G_3 + G_4)$. Note again that this result is the same as that which sould be obtained if we were to first combine R_3 and R_4 in parallel to obtain a net conductance of $G_3 + G_4$, and then to obtain the noise current of that net conductance.

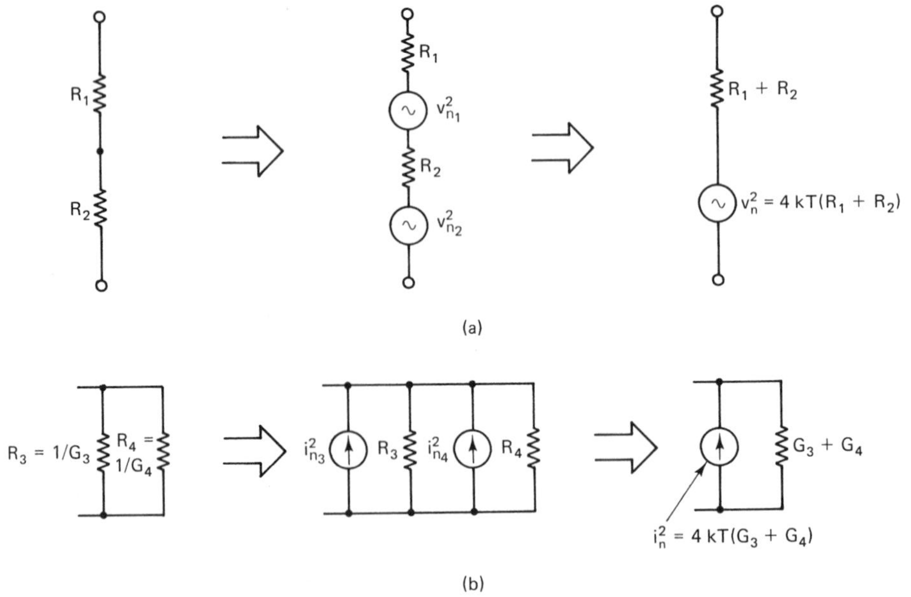

Figure 14.3 Combining methods: (a) combination of noise voltages; (b) combination of noise currents.

14.2 SHOT NOISE

The flow of electrons and holes across a forward-biased PN junction in a diode or transistor is an example of a random process. For a potential barrier of height $V_J = \phi - V_F$ at the junction, only the more energetic of the charge carriers will be able to climb this potential hill and make it over to the other side of the junction. The kinetic energy of any individual electron or hole is not fixed or constant, but rather is given by a probability distribution function, as is the entire assemblage of electrons and holes. As a result, the flow of electrons and holes across the junction will not be absolutely constant with time, but will exhibit small fluctuations.

The *mean-squared deviation* of a large number of random events is equal to the average or mean number of events in the time period under consideration. The flow of electrons and holes across a PN junction can be considered to be a random process involving a very large number of charge carriers, so that this statistical theorem will be applicable.

The average or d-c current of a device is related to the number of charge carriers passing through the device by $I = \bar{n}q/T$, where $\bar{n}$ is the average number of charge carriers passing through the device in observation time T and q is the charge on the electron (or hole). Since the mean-squared fluctuation in a large number of random events is equal to the average number of events, we have that $\overline{(\Delta n)^2} = \overline{(n - \bar{n})^2} = \bar{n}$, where $\overline{(\Delta n)^2}$ is the mean-squared fluctuation or deviation, n is the number of events in the period of observation, and $\bar{n}$ is the average number of events as observed over many observation times.

If $\bar{n}$ represents the average number of charge carriers passing through the device in an observation time T as obtained by averaging over a very large number of observation times, we will have that the mean-squared fluctuation in the number of charge carriers will be given by $\overline{(\Delta n)^2} = \bar{n} = (I/q)T$. The corresponding mean-squared fluctuation in the current flow that results from this fluctuation in the flow of charge carriers will thus be given by $\overline{(\Delta I)^2} = \overline{(\Delta n)^2}\,(q/T)^2 = (I/q)T(q/T)^2 = qI/T$. Note that this is the mean-squared deviation or fluctuation in the average current flow over the observation period T from that average or d-c current that is obtained over a period of time that is very long compared to the observation time.

The mean-squared deviation or fluctuation in the current flow is the mean-squared shot noise $\overline{(i_{sn})^2}$ of the device so that we have that

$$\boxed{\overline{(i_{sn})^2} = \frac{qI}{T}} \qquad (14.8)$$

Note that as the period of time over which the current is averaged increases, the mean-squared deviation decreases.

From the sampling theorem in communications theory a sampling or observation time T in the time domain is equivalent to a bandwidth $B = 1/2T$ in the frequency domain. Therefore, for a system with a bandwidth B, the mean-squared shot noise will be

$$\overline{i_{sn}^2} = 2qIB \tag{14.9}$$

The spectral density of the shot noise is therefore

$$\overline{i_{sn}^2} = 2qI \qquad (\text{A}^2/\text{Hz}) \tag{14.10}$$

Like the thermal noise, shot noise has a flat spectral density, so that it is a broad-band or "white" type of noise.

14.3 COMPARISON OF SHOT NOISE AND THERMAL NOISE

The mean-squared spectral density of the shot noise of diodes and transistors is given by $\overline{i_{sn}^2} = 2qI$, and the mean-squared spectral density of the thermal noise of a resistance R is $\overline{i_{th}^2} = 4kTG = 4kT/R$. We will now compare these two noise currents to see under what conditions one or the other will be the dominant noise source. If we equate the two noise currents given above, we obtain $2qI = 4kT/R$, so that when $R = 2(kT/q)/I = 2V_T/I \simeq 50\ mV/I$, the two noise currents will be equal. For resistance values less than this, the thermal noise will be the dominant noise source if the resistance is considered to be connected in parallel with the shot noise current source. This is shown in Figure 14.4. The thermal noise current and the shot noise current can be combined by taking the summation of the mean-squared values to obtain the total mean-squared noise current. Thus, for the circuit of Figure 11.4, if the d-c device current is $I = 1.0$ mA, the thermal noise will be the dominant contributor to the total noise current for resistance values of less than 50 mV/1.0 mA = 50 Ω.

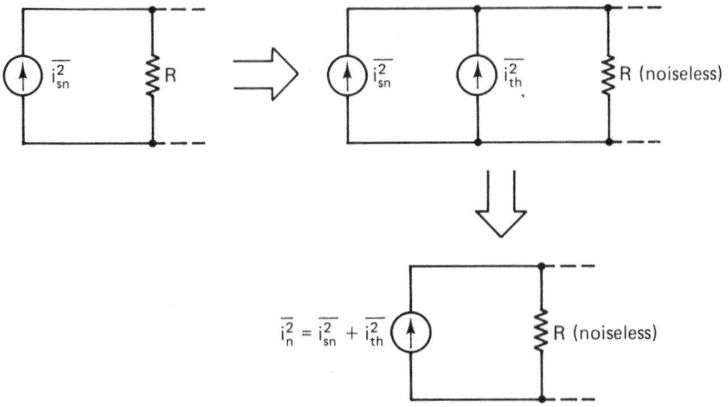

Figure 14.4 Combination of shot noise current and thermal noise current.

14.4 TRANSISTOR NOISE

In many communications systems the dominant noise source is most likely to be the noise generated in the amplifier, and in particular, the noise generated by the first transistor stage of the amplifier. As a result, it is of interest to examine the noise produced by transistors, both of the bipolar and field-effect types.

14.4.1 Bipolar Transistor Noise

For a bipolar transistor, the mean-squared shot noise of the collector current will be given by

$$\overline{(i_{C\,(\text{shot noise})})^2} = 2qI_C \tag{14.11}$$

where $\overline{(i_{C\,(\text{shot noise})})^2}$ is the spectral density (A^2/Hz) of the mean-squared collector current shot noise. Under small-signal conditions the a-c collector current is related to the a-c input voltage, v_{be}, by $i_C = g_m v_{be}$, where g_m is the dynamic transfer conductance as given by $g_m = I_C/V_T$. The shot noise of the collector current can be expressed as an equivalent input noise voltage of

$$v_{i\,(\text{noise})} = \frac{i_{C\,(\text{shot noise})}}{g_m} \tag{14.12}$$

In terms of the mean-squared spectral density value, this can be written as

$$\overline{(v_{i\,(\text{noise})})^2} = \frac{2qI_C}{(I_C/V_T)^2} = \frac{2qV_T^2}{I_C} \tag{14.13}$$

The thermal noise voltage of the base spreading resistance, $r_{bb'}$, will also contribute to the total input noise voltage. The spectral density of the mean-squared value of this thermal noise voltage will be given by $\overline{(v_{th\,(r_{bb'})})^2} = 4kTr_{bb'}$. One other contribution to the input noise voltage is the voltage drop produced by the flow of the shot noise component of the base current through the base spreading resistance, $r_{bb'}$.

The mean-squared value of the base current shot noise (spectral density) is

$$\overline{(i_{B\,(\text{shot noise})})^2} = 2qI_B = \frac{2qI_C}{\beta} \tag{14.14}$$

The mean-squared voltage drop produced by the flow of this current through $r_{bb'}$ will be

$$\overline{(v_{\text{noise}})^2} = \overline{(i_{B\,(\text{shot noise})}r_{bb'})^2} = 2qI_B r_{bb'}^2 = 2q\frac{I_C}{\beta}(r_{bb'})^2 \tag{14.15}$$

If we now combine all of the mean-squared noise voltage components given above, we will obtain the *total* mean-squared equivalent input noise voltage of the transistor, which will have a spectral density (V^2/Hz) given by

$$\overline{(v_{i\,(\text{noise})})^2} = \frac{2qV_T^2}{I_C} + 4kTr_{bb'} + 2qI_B(r_{bb'})^2 \tag{14.16}$$

If we note that the thermal voltage, V_T, is $V_T = kT/q$, this equation can be rewritten as

$$\overline{(v_{i\,(\text{noise})})^2} = 2kT\frac{V_T}{I_C} + 4kTr_{bb'} + \frac{2kTI_B(r_{bb'})^2}{V_T} \tag{14.17}$$

so that

$$\boxed{\overline{(v_{i\,(\text{noise})})^2} = 4kT\left[\frac{V_T}{2I_C} + r_{bb'} + \frac{I_B}{2V_T}(r_{bb'})^2\right]} \tag{14.18}$$

Since the quantity $4kT$ appears so very often in noise calculations, it is worthwhile noting its numerical value, which at $T = 290°\text{K}$ (17°C) is given by $4kT = 1.60 \times 10^{-20}$ J. The temperature of 290°K is one that is very often used for noise calculations and in the specifications of the noise characteristics of electronic devices and systems.

The transistor can now be represented as shown in Figure 14.5 as a noiseless device in combination with equivalent input noise voltage and noise current sources. In Figure 14.5 it is to be understood that the shot noise of the base current is to be considered to flow only toward the source and not back into the transistor.

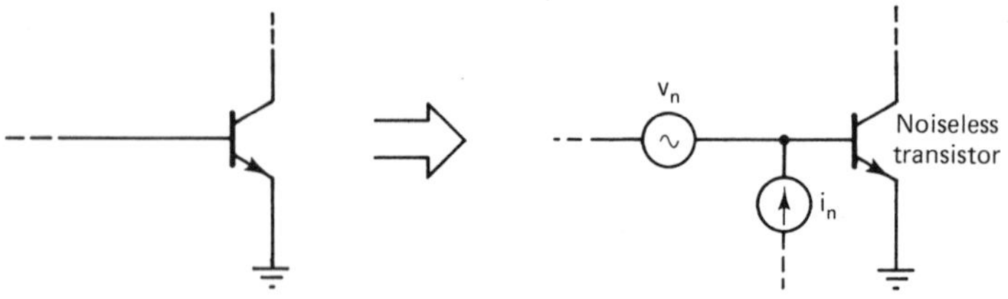

Figure 14.5 Representation of a transistor in terms of an equivalent "noiseless" transistor and noise voltage and current sources.

The net resistance looking back toward the signal source is R_S, so that the base current shot noise flowing through R_S will produce a mean-squared noise voltage given by $(2qI_B)(R_S)^2$ in terms of the spectral density. In addition to this, the source resistance itself will produce a noise voltage given in terms of the mean-squared value as $(v_{th\,(R_S)})^2 = 4kTR_S$, as shown in Figure 14.6. As a result, the total mean-squared noise voltage appearing at the input terminal of the equivalent "noiseless" transistor due to both R_S and the noise produced by the transistor itself will be given by

$$\begin{aligned}\overline{(v_{\text{noise}})^2} &= \overline{(v_{i\,(\text{noise})})^2_{\text{transistor}}} + 2qI_B(R_S)^2 + 4kTR_S \\ &= \frac{2qV_T^2}{I_C} + 4kT(r_{bb'} + R_S) + 2qI_B(r_{bb'} + R_S)^2\end{aligned} \tag{14.19}$$

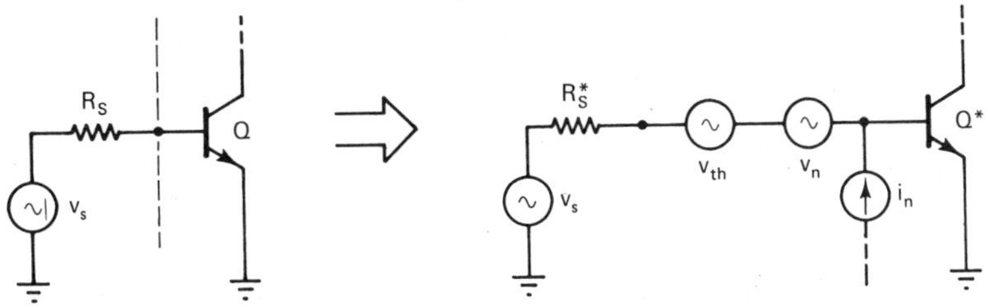

Figure 14.6 Representation of a transistor and source resistance in terms of a noise source equivalent circuit: R^*, "noiseless" resistance; Q^*, "noiseless" transistor.

so that

$$\overline{(v_{\text{noise}})^2} = 4kT\left[\frac{V_T}{2I_C} + (r_{bb'} + R_S) + \frac{I_B}{2V_T}(r_{bb'} + R_S)^2\right] \tag{14.20}$$

Note that the last term in this equation is given as $(r_{bb'} + R_S)^2$ rather than $(r_{bb'})^2 + (R_S)^2$, since the noise voltages produced by the flow of the shot noise component of the base current through $r_{bb'}$ and R_S are completely correlated (unity correlation).

We see that the total noise voltage is a function of the quiescent (d-c) collector current, I_C. The value of collector current that will result in minimum noise and therefore maximum signal detection sensitivity can be obtained by taking the derivative of the expression for $\overline{(v_{i\,(\text{noise})})^2}$ and setting it equal to zero, and then solving for I_C. Doing this gives $4kT[-V_T/2I_C^2 + (r_{bb'} + R_S)^2/\beta 2V_T] = 0$, so that the value of I_C for minimum noise is $I_{C\,(\text{opt})} = V_T\sqrt{\beta}/(r_{bb'} + R_S)$. For example, if $r_{bb'} = 50\ \Omega$, $R_S = 50\ \Omega$, and $\beta = 150$, the collector current for minimum noise will be 3.06 mA.

If the transistor is indeed biased at the I_C value that gives minimum noise, namely $I_C = I_{C\,(\text{opt})}$, then the mean-squared input noise voltage can be written as

$$\overline{(v_{i\,(\text{noise})})^2_{I_C = I_{C\,(\text{opt})}}} = \frac{4kT(r_{bb'} + R_S)}{\sqrt{\beta}} + 4kT(r_{bb'} + R_S) \tag{14.21}$$

Since $V_T = kT/q$, $qV_T = kT$, so that

$$\overline{(v_{i\,(\text{noise})})^2} = 4kT(r_{bb'} + R_S)\left(1 + \frac{1}{\sqrt{\beta}}\right) \simeq 4kT(r_{bb'} + R_S) \tag{14.22}$$

since $\beta \gg 1$. We thus note that when I_C has a value that is equal, or close to, $I_{C\,(\text{opt})}$, the dominant transistor noise source will be the thermal noise voltage of $r_{bb'}$.

The *noise figure* (NF) is a measurement of the degradation of the signal-to-noise ratio (SNR) by the noise due to the transistor, and will under these conditions be given as

$$NF = 10 \log_{10} \frac{\overline{(v_{i\,(\text{noiseTOTAL})})^2}}{\overline{(v_{th\,(RS)})^2}}$$

$$= 10 \log_{10} \frac{r_{bb'} + R_S}{R_S} \tag{14.23}$$

$$= 10 \log_{10} \left(1 + \frac{r_{bb'}}{R_S}\right)$$

If $r_{bb'} = 50\ \Omega$, the minimum noise figure that can be obtained for the transistor with respect to a 50-Ω source will be 3.0 dB. With respect to a 100-Ω source resistance, the NF value is only 1.76 dB, and is down to only 0.7 dB with respect to a 300-Ω source resistance.

In Figure 14.7 a generalized graph of the total mean-squared noise voltage (on a logarithmic scale) as a function of the total resistance, $R_S + r_{bb'}$, which is also on a logarithmic scale, is presented. At the breakpoints that mark the intersection of the various asymptotic response lines, the actual mean-squared noise voltage is approximately twice the value obtained from the intersection of the asymptotes. From this graph we note that for small $R_S + r_{bb'}$ values, the dominant noise component

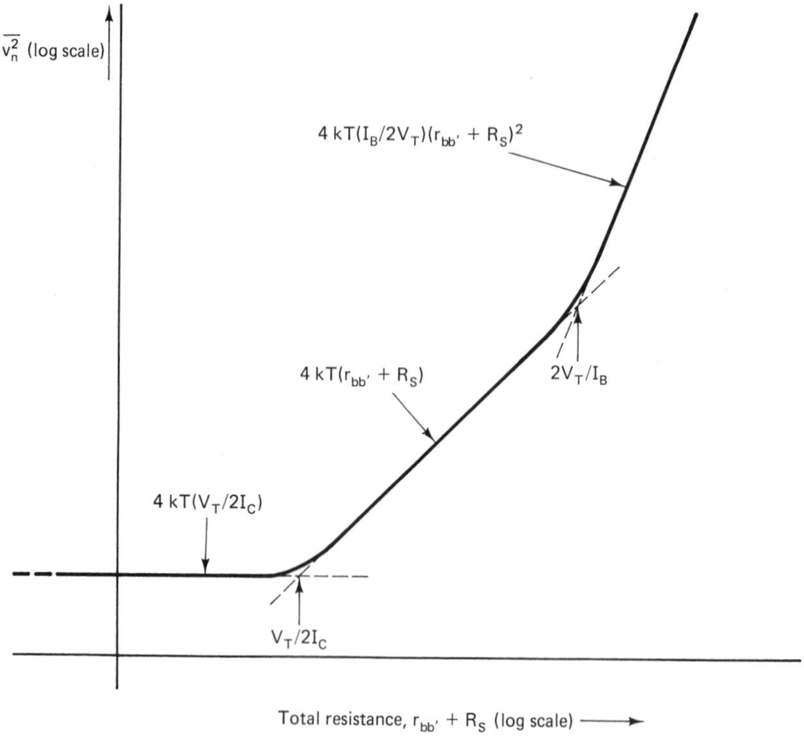

Figure 14.7 Total mean-squared noise voltage spectral density for a bipolar transistor with source resistance R_S.

is the collector-current shot noise. For resistance values bounded by $(V_T/2I_c) < R_S + r_{bb'} < (2V_T/I_B)$, the thermal noise of $R_S + r_{bb'}$ will be the dominant noise source, and only for large values of resistance such that $R_S + r_{bb'} > 2V_T/I_B$ will the noise due to the base current shot noise flowing through $R_S + r_{bb'}$ be the dominant noise component.

If, for example, $I_C = 0.10$ mA and $\beta = 200$, then for $R_S + r_{bb'} < 125\ \Omega$, the collector-current shot noise will be the dominant noise source, for $R_S + r_{bb'} > 100\ \text{k}\Omega$ the base current shot noise will be the dominant component, and in the region in between, the thermal noise voltage of $R_S + r_{bb'}$ will be the most important source of noise in the circuit.

14.4.2 Noise in Field-Effect Transistors

The mean-squared input noise voltage of a field-effect transistor (FET) due to the resistance of the source-to-drain channel is given by $\overline{v_i^2} = 4kT\delta/g_{fs}$, where δ is a numerical factor, typically around $\frac{2}{3}$, and g_{fs} is the dynamic (common-source) transfer conductance of the FET. If the net resistance looking back toward the signal source is R_S, then the total mean-squared noise voltage spectral density will be given by

$$\begin{aligned}\overline{(v_{\text{noise}})^2} &= \frac{4kT\delta}{g_{fs}} + 4kTR_S + 2qI_G(R_S)^2 \\ &= 4kT\left(\frac{\delta}{g_{fs}} + R_S + \frac{I_G}{2V_T}R_S^2\right)\end{aligned} \tag{14.24}$$

where I_G is the gate leakage current, which is generally in the range of 30 pA to 3 nA for JFETs.

The transfer conductance of a JFET can be written as $g_{fs} = 2\sqrt{I_{DS}I_{DSS}}/V_P = g_{fs_0}\sqrt{I_{DS}/I_{DSS}}$, where $g_{fs_0} = 2I_{DSS}/V_P$. In the preceding equations, V_P is the pinch-off voltage, I_{DSS} is the drain-to-source current in the saturated region with $V_{GS} = 0$, and g_{fs_0} is the value of g_{fs} when $V_{GS} = 0$. The expression for the total noise voltage can be rewritten as

$$\begin{aligned}\overline{(v_{\text{noise}})^2} &= \frac{4kT(2/3)}{2(I_{DSS}/V_P)\sqrt{I_{DS}/I_{DSS}}} + 4kTR_S + 2kT\frac{I_G}{V_T}(R_S)^2 \\ &= 4kT\left[\frac{V_P}{3I_{DSS}}\sqrt{\frac{I_{DSS}}{I_{DS}}} + R_S + \frac{I_G}{2V_T}(R_S)^2\right]\end{aligned} \tag{14.25}$$

The noise voltage will be a minimum when the JFET is biased such that $I_{DS} = I_{DSS}$, which corresponds to $V_{GS} = 0$. Under these conditions the spectral density of the noise voltage will be given by

$$\overline{(v_{\text{noise}})^2} = 4kT\left[\frac{V_P}{3I_{DSS}} + R_S + \frac{I_G}{2V_T}(R_S)^2\right] \tag{14.26}$$

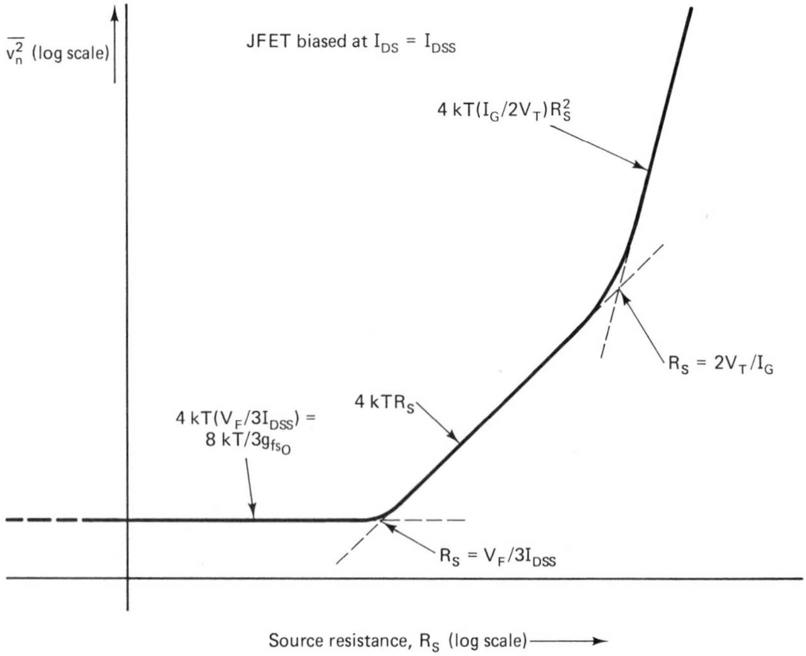

Figure 14.8 Total mean-squared noise voltage spectral density for a JFET with a source resistance R_S.

In Figure 14.8 a generalized graph of the total mean-squared noise voltage (spectral density) as a function of the source resistance is given. We note that for source resistances less than $V_P/3I_{DSS}$ the dominant noise source will be the JFET channel resistance. For larger values of R_S the thermal noise of the source resistance will be dominant, and only for very large values of R_S, generally in excess of 30 MΩ, will the shot noise of the gate current be the dominant noise factor. To consider an example, if $V_P = 4.0$ V, $I_{DSS} = 4.0$ mA, and $I_G = 1.0$ nA, then only for $R_S <$ 330 Ω will the JFET channel resistance be the dominant noise component. From $R_S = 330$ Ω up to $R_S = 50$ mΩ, the dominant noise source will be the thermal noise of the source resistance, and only for R_S values above 50 MΩ will the shot noise of the gate leakage current become an important factor.

14.4.3 Comparison of the Noise Characteristics of the Bipolar Transistor with the JFET

The question often arises as to whether to use a bipolar transistor or a JFET for a particular low-noise application. In Figure 14.9 a graphical comparison is made of the noise voltages produced by these two different types of transistors in conjunction with a source resistance R_S. Since the pinch-off voltage, V_P, is generally in the range 3 to 10 V, whereas V_T is 25 mV and I_C and I_{DSS} are comparable quantities, we see that generally the condition that $V_T/2I_C \ll V_P/3I_{DSS}$ will be satisfied. As a result,

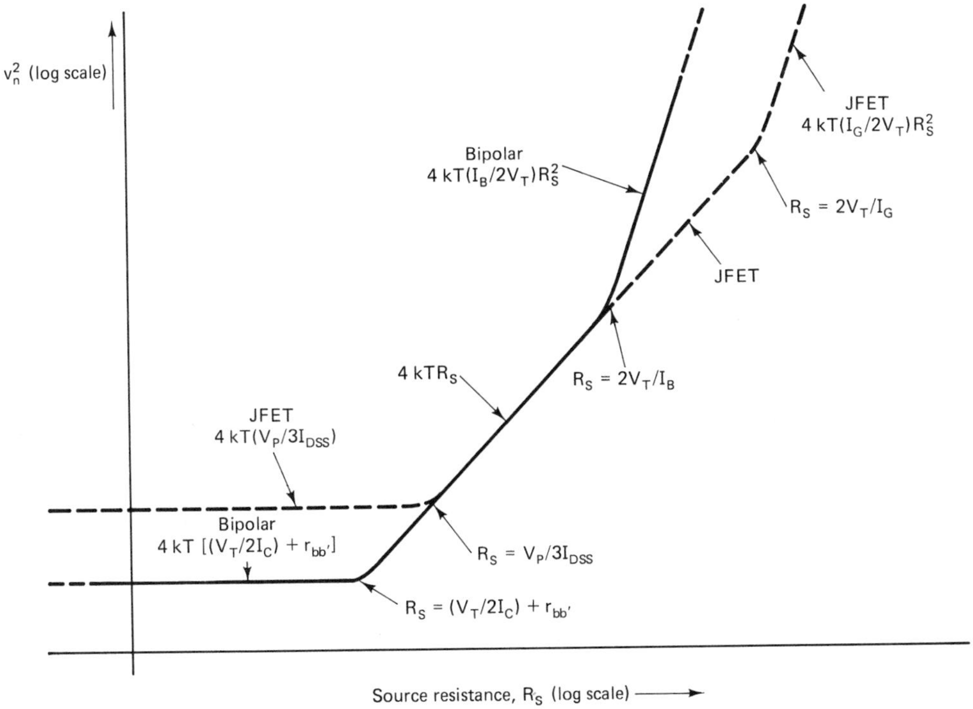

Figure 14.9 Comparison of the total mean-squared noise voltage spectral density of a JFET with that of a bipolar transistor.

for small values of source resistance the bipolar transistor may prove to be preferable.

For moderate values of source resistance the dominant noise source will be the thermal noise of R_S, so that the noise performance will not be very dependent on the choice of transistor. However, for large values of source resistance such that $R_S > 2V_T/I_B$, the JFET will become the clear choice.

Let us, for an example, consider the case of a bipolar transistor that has $r_{bb'} = 60\ \Omega$ and $\beta = 150$ at a quiescent collector current level of $I_C = 1.0$ mA. We will compare this transistor with a JFET that has $V_P = 5.0\ V$, $I_G = 2.0$ nA (max.) and is operated at a quiescent point such that $I_{DS} = I_{DSS}$, where $I_{DSS} = 2.5$ mA. Since $V_P/3I_{DSS} = 667\ \Omega$, whereas $V_T/2I_C = 12.5\ \Omega$ and $r_{bb'} = 60\ \Omega$, so that $(V_T/2I_C) + r_{bb'} = 72.5\ \Omega$, we see that for source resistance values below 660 Ω the bipolar transistor circuit will result in a substantially lower overall noise. The noise voltage of the bipolar transistor will be lower than that of the JFET by a factor of $\sqrt{667/72.5} = 3.0$, or 9.6 dB in this range of small R_S (i.e., $R_S \ll 660\ \Omega$).

If we now look at the other extreme of source resistance values we see that since $2V_T/I_B = 7.5\ \text{k}\Omega$, for values of R_S larger than this the JFET circuit will result in less noise. For example, if $R_S = 1.0\ \text{M}\Omega$, the noise voltage of the bipolar transistor circuit will be greater than that of the JFET circuit by a factor of $I_B R_S/2V_T = 11.5$, which corresponds to 21.2 dB.

14.4.4 Low-Noise Transistors

An example of a very low-noise JFET is the 2N6550. The low-noise characteristics of this device is the result of its high value of transfer conductance [40 mS (typ.)], which is, in turn, related to the high value of the zero gate voltage drain current, I_{DSS} [100 mA (typ.)], and the low value for the pinch-off voltage, V_P [1.5 V (typ.)], shown.

If we use the minimum g_{fs} value specified for this device, which is 25 mS, the value of the equivalent input noise voltage as obtained from the equation $v_{i\,(\text{noise})} = \sqrt{4kT(\delta/g_{fs})}$ is 0.7 nV/Hz$^{1/2}$. Since $\delta/g_{fs} = 27\ \Omega$ (max.) we see that the JFET noise is equivalent to the thermal noise voltage of a resistance of only 27 Ω.

In Figure 14.10 a graph of the short-circuit (i.e., $R_S = 0$) input noise voltage of the 2N6550 JFET is given. We see from this graph that for frequencies above 3 kHz the noise voltage is close to the value given above. At lower frequencies, however, the noise voltage (on a per unit bandwidth basis) increases substantially. This is the low-frequency or "$1/f$" noise, which has its origin in the trapping of charge carriers (electrons and holes) at surface states in the region where the junction intersects the surface. The changes in the occupancy of these surface states due to the capture and the release of charge carriers produces random current impulses. The result of this will be a noise component whose mean-squared value has a spectral density that is inversely proportional to frequency.

The gate leakage current for this device is specified as 0.1 nA (typ.) and 3.0 nA (max.) at 25°C. The shot noise component of this current will therefore be 6 fA/Hz$^{1/2}$, which agrees favorably with the manufacturer's specified value of 10 fA/Hz$^{1/2}$ (typ.).

As a result of these characteristics, it turns out that for source resistances in the range 30 Ω to about 160 MΩ, the thermal noise of the source resistance will be the dominant source of noise. Only for very small source resistances ($R_S < 20\ \Omega$) will the noise due to the JFET channel resistance be the dominant noise component, and only for very large source resistance values ($R_S \gg 200$ MΩ) will the shot noise component of the gate leakage current be the most important source of noise.

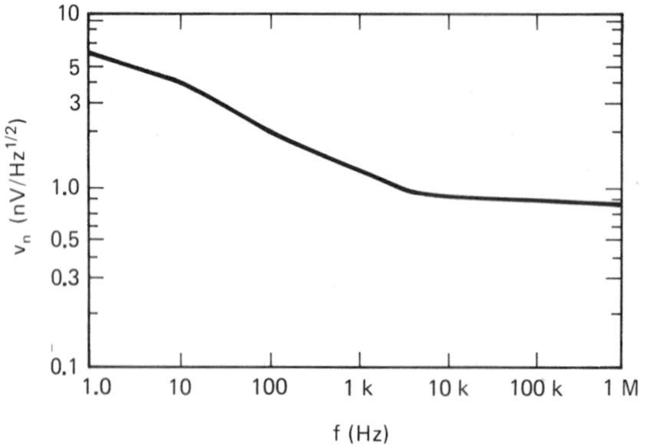

Figure 14.10 Input noise voltage versus frequency for the 2N6550 JFET (Teledyne Crystalonics).

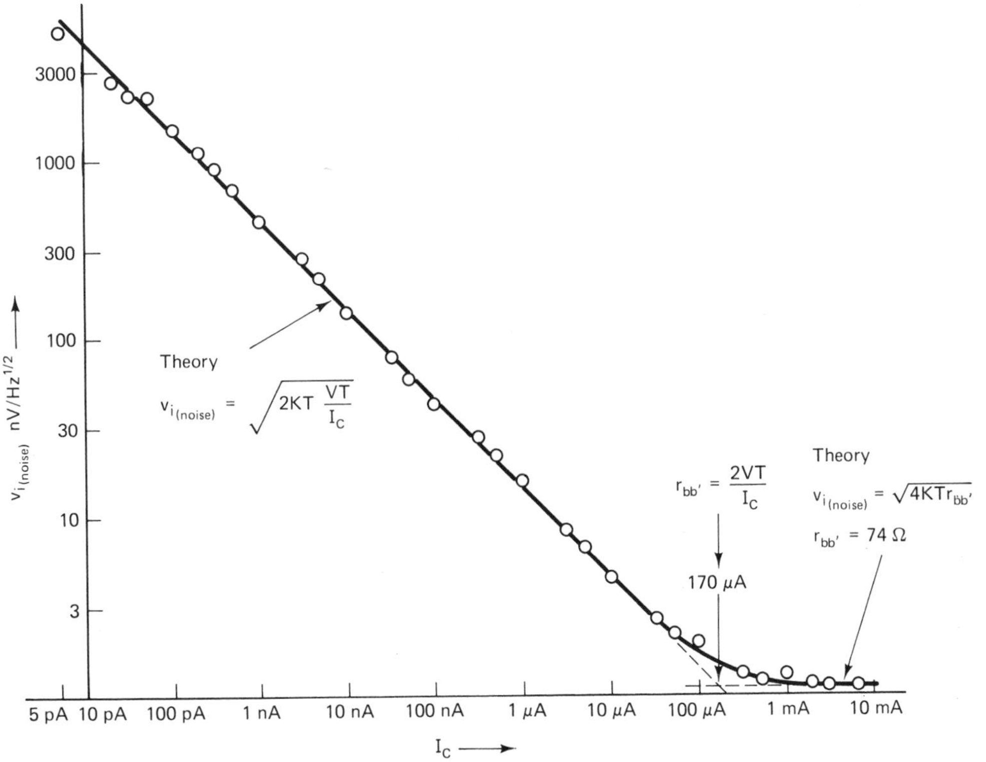

Figure 14.11 Equivalent input noise voltage versus collector current: 2N4124 transistor.

In Figure 14.11, a graph of the equivalent input noise voltage versus collector current for a 2N4124 NPN transistor is shown. Note the variation of the equivalent input noise voltage with collector current follows the theory very closely. For currents below 170 μA the dominant noise source is the collector current shot noise. Above 170 μA the noise will be due principally to the thermal noise of the base spreading resistance $r_{bb'}$. The value of this resistance, as determined from the noise measurements, is about 74 Ω. The noise is down at a minimum value of only 1.1 nV/$\sqrt{\text{Hz}}$. At higher currents in excess of about 100 mA, the noise voltage will start to increase again due to the voltage drop produced by the flow of the base current shot noise through $r_{bb'}$. An example of a transistor with an even lower input noise voltage is the 2N4403 with an equivalent input noise voltage of only 0.8 nV/$\sqrt{\text{Hz}}$, which corresponds to a base-spreading resistance of 40 Ω.

14.5 NOISE OF A DIFFERENTIAL-AMPLIFIER CIRCUIT

In many electronic systems, especially those utilizing IC operational amplifiers or IC video amplifiers, the input stage of the amplifier is a differential amplifier.

The differential amplifier shown in Figure 14.12 can be split down the axis of

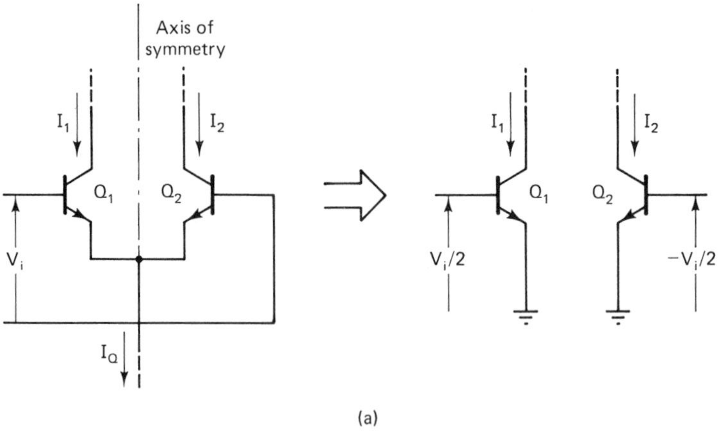

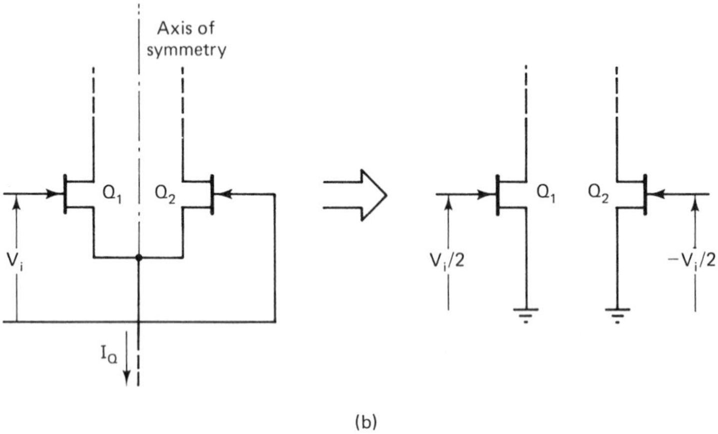

Figure 14.12 Differential amplifier noise analysis: (a) bipolar differential amplifier; (b) JFET differential amplifier.

symmetry so that each half looks like an ordinary single-ended transistor amplifier as shown in Figure 14.12a. Note, however, that the input voltage applied to each side will be one-half of the total (i.e., base-to-base) input voltage.

The mean-squared noise voltage of each half-circuit will be the same as given earlier, namely

$$\overline{(v_{\text{noise}})^2} = 4kT\left[\frac{V_T}{2I_C} + (r_{bb'} + R_S) + \frac{I_B}{2V_T}(r_{bb'} + R_S)^2\right] \tag{14.27}$$

However, since there is zero correlation between the instantaneous noise voltages of each half of the differential amplifier, the total (base-to-base) mean-squared noise voltage of the differential amplifier will be *twice* that of a single transistor. The equivalent input noise voltage of the differential amplifier will therefore be given as

$$\overline{(v_{i\,(\text{noise})})^2_{\text{DIFF AMP}}} = 8kT\left[\frac{V_T}{2I_C} + (r_{bb'} + R_S) + \frac{I_B}{2V_T}(r_{bb'} + R_S)^2\right] \quad (14.28)$$

Note that this noise voltage does not depend on whether a single-ended or a balanced output is taken from the amplifier. We see therefore that a differential amplifier will have an input noise voltage that is larger than that of a single-ended transistor stage, operated with the same collector current, by a factor of $\sqrt{2}$ corresponding to 3.0 dB.

For a JFET differential amplifier, the same analysis as given above for the bipolar case holds true, as shown in Figure 14.12b, with the input noise voltage being given by

$$\overline{(v_{i\,(\text{noise})})^2_{\text{DIFF AMP}}} = 8kT\left[\frac{V_P}{3I_{DSS}}\left(\frac{I_{DSS}}{I_{DS}}\right)^{1/2} + R_S + \frac{I_G}{2V_T}(R_S)^2\right] \quad (14.29)$$

14.6 NOISE OF A DARLINGTON COMPOUND TRANSISTOR

For the Darlington direct-coupled compound-transistor configuration as shown in Figure 14.13, the collector current $I_C = I_2$ is related to the input voltage by $I_C = I_{TO}\exp(V_{BE}/2V_T)$, where V_{BE} is the voltage between the base of Q_1 and the emitter of Q_2. The dynamic transfer conductance will therefore be $g_f = dI_C/dV_{BE} = I_C/2V_T$. This is to be compared to that of a single transistor, which is $g_m = I_C/V_T$. We see that the two expressions are similar except that the V_T for the single-transistor case is replaced by $2V_T$ for the Darlington configuration.

The total equivalent mean-squared input noise voltage for the Darlington case can be obtained from the expression for the single-transistor case by replacing the $V_T/2I_C$ term by $2V_T/2I_C = V_T/I_C$, giving

$$\overline{(v_{\text{noise}})^2} = 4kT\left[\frac{V_T}{I_C} + (r_{bb'} + R_S) + \frac{I_B}{2V_T}(r_{bb'} + R_S)^2\right] \quad (14.30)$$

The current gain β of the Darlington pair is the product of the individual transistor current gains as given by $\beta = \beta_1\beta_2$. This overall current gain will be

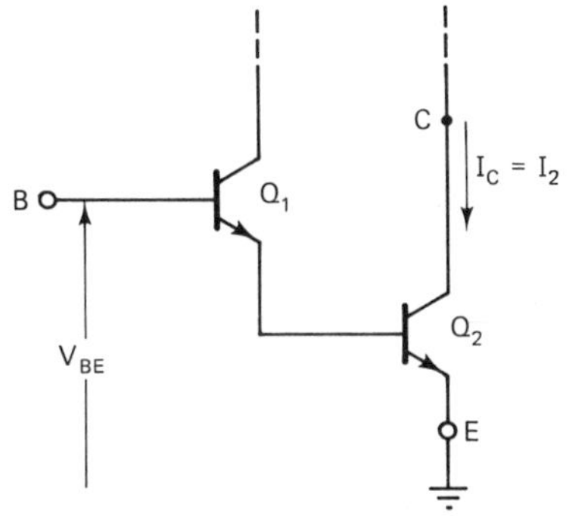

Figure 14.13 Darlington compound transistor.

very large. As a result the base current will be very small and the last term in the expression above for the noise voltage will generally be negligible.

We see that the noise characteristics of the Darlington will be similar to that of the single-transistor case. For small values of $r_{bb'} + R_S$ the Darlington configuration will be "noisier" than the single transistor due to the replacement of the $V_T/2I_C$ term by V_T/I_C in the noise equation. However, for very large values of $r_{bb'} + R_S$ the noise performance of the Darlington configuration will be superior to that of the single transistor as a result of the much smaller base current I_B in the Darlington case.

14.7 MOSFET NOISE CHARACTERISTICS

The MOSFETs tend to be much noisier than JFETs or bipolar transistors due to the much larger $1/f$ noise component in MOSFETs. The large $1/f$ noise of MOSFETs is the result of the random nature of the charge trapping and release process at the silicon–oxide interface, which is immediately adjacent to the surface inversion layer, as shown in Figure 14.14. The MOSFET is particularly affected by this process due to the contiguity of the very thin (~100 Å) conducting channel (inversion layer) to the oxide–silicon interface and the consequent close interaction of electrons (or holes for PMOS) in the channel with the gate oxide.

The *1/f noise corner frequency* is the frequency at which the $1/f$ noise becomes equal to the midband noise, which is the broadband thermal and shot noise. The $1/f$ noise corner frequency for MOSFETs is typically in the range of about 100

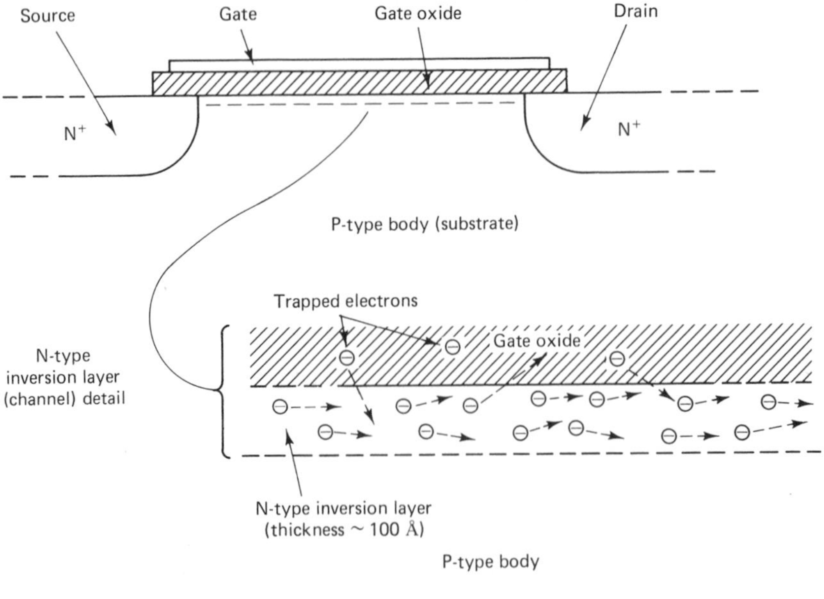

Figure 14.14 Noise in MOSFETs.

kHz to 1 MHz, and so at low frequencies very large $1/f$ noise voltages may occur, such as values of around 100 to 300 nV/Hz$^{1/2}$ at 100 Hz. This is to be compared to the $1/f$ noise corner frequency in the range 100 Hz to 10 kHz for bipolar transistors and JFETs under typical bias conditions.

14.8 OP-AMP NOISE ANALYSIS

Let us consider the op-amp circuit shown in Figure 14.15. In Figure 14.15b an equivalent circuit for noise analysis is shown in which the op amps and the resistors have been replaced by a "noiseless amplifier" and "noiseless resistors" and the noise produced by the amplifier and the resistors is represented by equivalent noise voltage

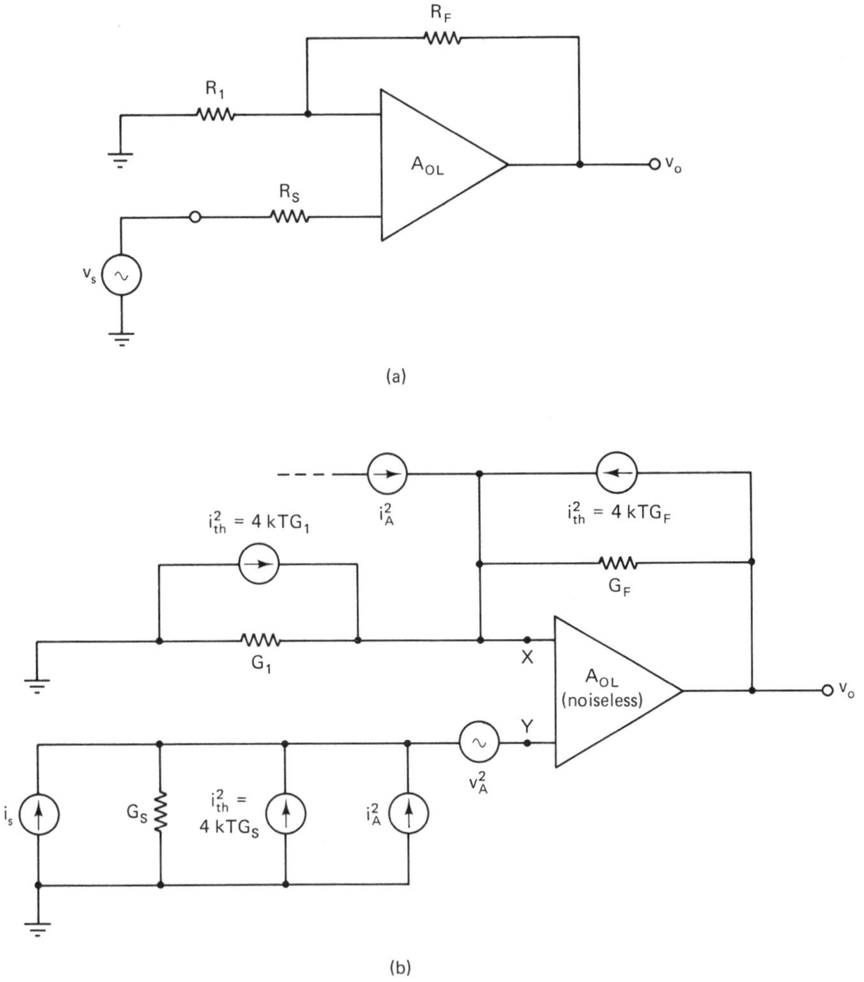

Figure 14.15 Operational-amplifier noise analysis: (a) op-amp circuit; (b) equivalent circuit for noise analysis.

and current sources. For purposes of analysis and for the ease in combining these sources, the mean-squared spectral density values of the noise voltages and currents will be used.

At node Y the total mean-squared noise voltage (spectral density) will be

$$\overline{v_Y^2} = \overline{v_A^2} + \overline{i_A^2}R_S^2 + (4kTG_S)R_S^2 = \overline{v_A^2} + \frac{\overline{i_A^2}}{G_S^2} + \frac{4kT}{G_S} \tag{14.31}$$

where v_A and i_A are the equivalent input noise voltage and current of the amplifier (spectral density), respectively.

At node X we will have

$$\overline{v_o^2}G_F^2 + 4kTG_F + 4kTG_1 + \overline{i_A^2} = \overline{v_X^2}(G_1 + G_F)^2 \tag{14.32}$$

For the usual case of a very large open-loop gain such that $A_{OL} \gg 1$, we have that $v_X \simeq v_Y$, so that

$$\overline{v_o^2}G_F^2 + 4kT(G_1 + G_F) + \overline{i_A^2} = \left(\overline{v_A^2} + \frac{\overline{i_A^2}}{G_S^2} + \frac{4kT}{G_S}\right)(G_1 + G_F)^2 \tag{14.33}$$

For bias current cancellation the condition is that $R_1 \| R_F = R_S$, or equivalently $G_1 + G_F = G_S$. If we use this condition in the equation above and note that the noise currents on the two sides of the equation are *uncorrelated* so that they do not cancel out, but rather the mean-squared values are additive, we obtain

$$\overline{v_o^2}G_F^2 + 4kTG_S + \overline{i_A^2} = \overline{v_A^2}G_S^2 + \overline{i_A^2} + 4kTG_S \tag{14.34}$$

and thus after combining the mean-squared noise currents, we obtain

$$\overline{v_o^2}G_F^2 = \overline{v_A^2}G_S^2 + 2\overline{i_A^2} + 8kTG_S \tag{14.35}$$

Solving for the mean-squared output noise voltage (spectral density) $\overline{v_o^2}$, we now obtain

$$\overline{v_o^2} = (v_A^2 G_S^2 + 2i_A^2 + 8kTG_S)R_F^2 \tag{14.36}$$

The closed-loop voltage gain of this amplifier circuit will be given by

$$A_{CL} = 1 + \frac{R_F}{R_1} = 1 + \frac{G_1}{G_F} = \frac{G_F + G_1}{G_F} = \frac{G_S}{G_F} \tag{14.37}$$

since $G_F + G_1 = G_S$ for bias current cancellation. Therefore, $A_{CL} = G_S/G_F = G_S R_F$ and the equation for the output noise voltage can be rewritten as

$$\begin{aligned}\overline{v_o^2} &= v_A^2(A_{CL})^2 + 2i_A^2R_F^2 + 8kTR_S(A_{CL})^2 \\ &= (A_{CL})^2(v_A^2 + 2i_A^2R_S^2 + 8kTR_S)\end{aligned} \tag{14.38}$$

The output voltage produced as a result of applying a signal to the noninverting input will be $v_{o\,(\text{signal})} = A_{CL}v_{i\,(\text{signal})}$. The output mean-squared noise voltage is obtained by multiplying $\overline{v_o^2}$ given above, which is the mean-squared noise voltage spectral density by the effective noise bandwidth B so that $\overline{v_{o\,(\text{noise})}{}^2} = \overline{v_o^2} B$. The *signal-to-noise ratio* SNR will therefore be given by

$$(\text{SNR})^2 = \left(\frac{v_{o\,(\text{signal})}}{v_{o\,(\text{noise})}}\right)^2 = \frac{v_{i\,(\text{signal})}{}^2 A_{CL}^2}{A_{CL}^2 (v_A^2 + 2i_A^2 R_S^2 + 8kTR_S)\, B} \tag{14.39}$$

and thus

$$(\text{SNR})^2 = \frac{v_{i\,(\text{signal})}{}^2}{(v_A^2 + 2i_A^2 R_S^2 + 8kTR_S)\, B} \tag{14.40}$$

In Figure 14.16, a graph of the output noise voltage of a 741 type of op amp versus the 3-dB bandwidth is given. The closed-loop gain of the op amp circuit is 10,000. From this graph the equivalent input noise voltage spectral density can be determined to be approximately 25 nV/$\sqrt{\text{Hz}}$.

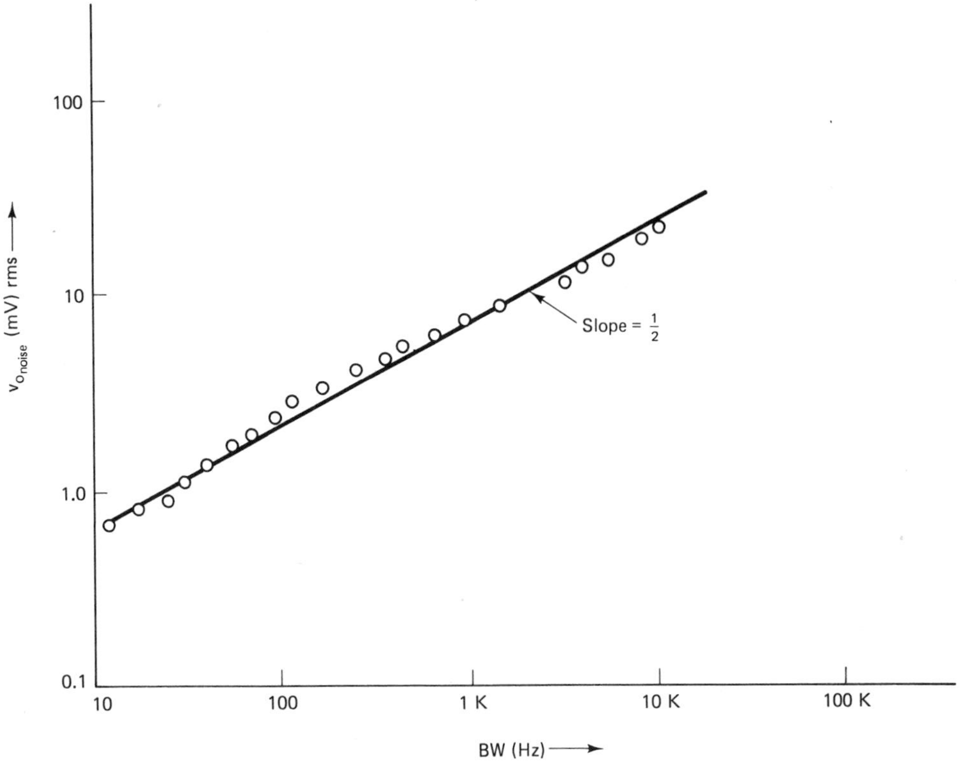

Figure 14.16 Operational amplifier output noise voltage versus bandwidth (741-type).

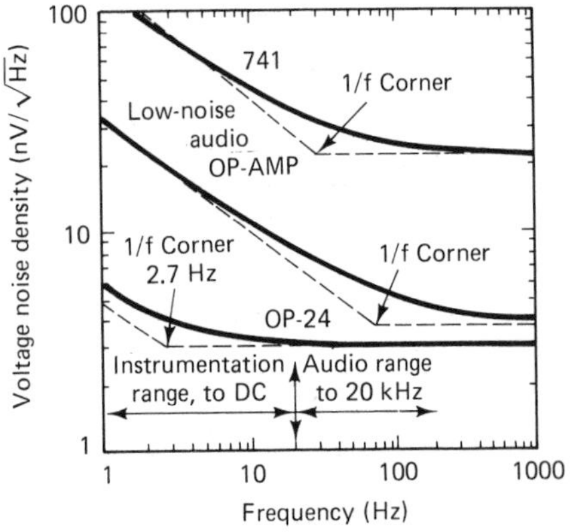

Figure 14.17 Input noise voltage versus frequency for low-noise op amp (Precision Monolithics, Inc.).

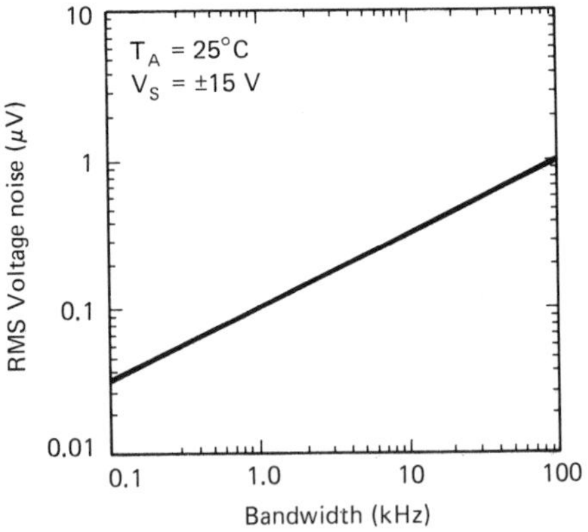

Figure 14.18 Input noise voltage versus bandwidth for low-noise op amp (Precision Monolithics, Inc.).

14.9 LOW-NOISE OP AMPS

There are operational amplifiers that are especially designed to obtain low-noise performance. Some examples of low-noise op amps are the OP-24/27/34/37/227 series (Precision Monolithics Inc.). These operational amplifiers feature an input noise voltage spectral density of 3.5 $nV/Hz^{1/2}$(typ.) at 10 Hz, 3.1 $nV/Hz^{1/2}$(typ.) at 30 Hz, and only 3.0 $nV/Hz^{1/2}$(typ.) at frequencies of 1000 Hz and up.

A graph of the input noise voltage versus frequency for these devices is given in Figure 14.17. It is noted that the $1/f$ corner frequency is at only 2.7 Hz. In Figure 14.18 the input noise voltage as a function of bandwidth is given. The bandwidth is from 0.1 Hz up to the frequency indicated. We see that for a 100-kHz bandwidth the rms noise voltage will be only 1 μV.

These devices also feature low values for the input noise current. In Figure

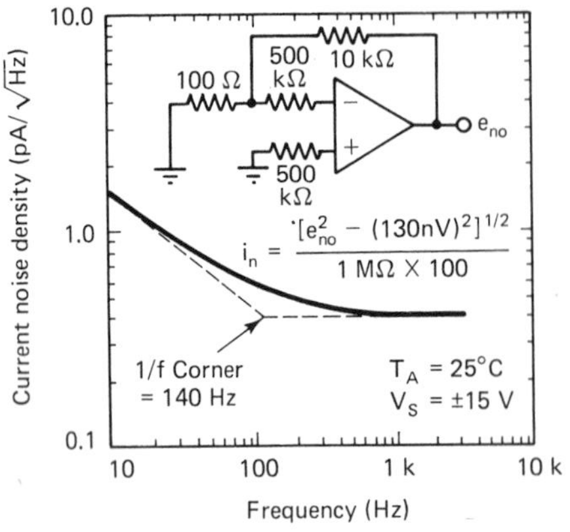

Figure 14.19 Input noise current spectral density versus frequency for low-noise op amp (Precision Monolithics, Inc.).

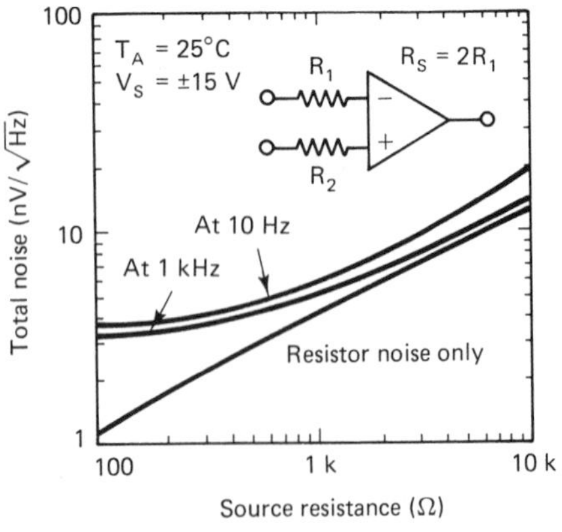

Figure 14.20 Total input noise voltage spectral density versus source resistance for low-noise op amp (Precision Monolithics, Inc.).

14.19 a graph of the input noise current spectral density versus frequency is shown. The noise current levels off at 0.4 pA/Hz$^{1/2}$ for frequencies above 1000 Hz and the $1/f$ corner frequency is only 140 Hz.

In Figure 14.20 a graph is given of the total input noise voltage spectral density versus source resistance. The input noise voltage now includes the thermal noise due to the source resistance and the noise voltage produced by the flow of the input noise current through the source resistance. The operational amplifier input noise voltage of 3 nV/Hz$^{1/2}$ is equal to the thermal noise produced by a 560-Ω resistor. For source resistance values above this, up to about 100 kΩ, the thermal noise of the source resistance will be the dominant noise source. Beyond a source resistance of 100 kΩ the dominant noise source will be the noise voltage produced by the flow of the input noise current through the source resistance.

PROBLEMS

For all problems, use $T = 290°K$.

14.1. Referring to Figure P14.1, find the rms noise voltage and noise current produced by the following resistances:

(a) 50 Ω (*Ans.*: 0.895 nV/Hz$^{1/2}$; 17.9 pA/Hz$^{1/2}$)
(b) 1.0 kΩ (*Ans.*: 4.0 nV/Hz$^{1/2}$; 4.0 pA/Hz$^{1/2}$)
(c) 100 kΩ (*Ans.*: 40 nV/Hz$^{1/2}$; 400 fA/Hz$^{1/2}$)
(d) 10 MΩ (*Ans.*: 400 nV/Hz$^{1/2}$; 40 fA/Hz$^{1/2}$)

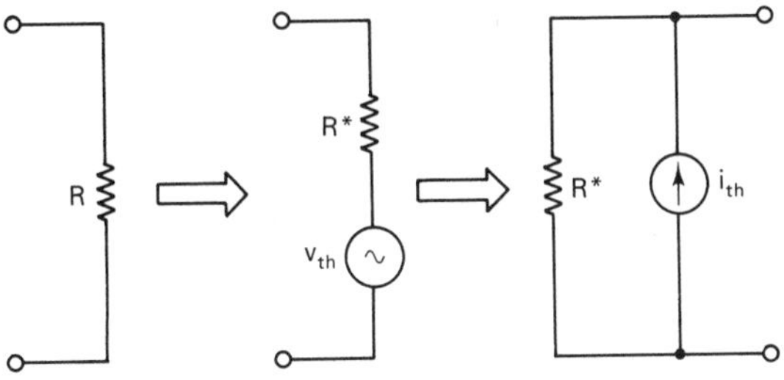

R* = "noiseless" resistor of value R

Figure P14.1

14.2. Given a transistor (Figure P14.2) with $r_{bb'} = 100\ \Omega$, $\beta = 100$, and $I_C = 1.0$ mA, find:

(a) Shot noise current (rms) of I_C. (*Ans.*: $i_{sn} = 17.9$ pA/Hz$^{1/2}$)
(b) Thermal noise voltage of $r_{bb'}$. (*Ans.*: 1.265 nV/Hz$^{1/2}$)

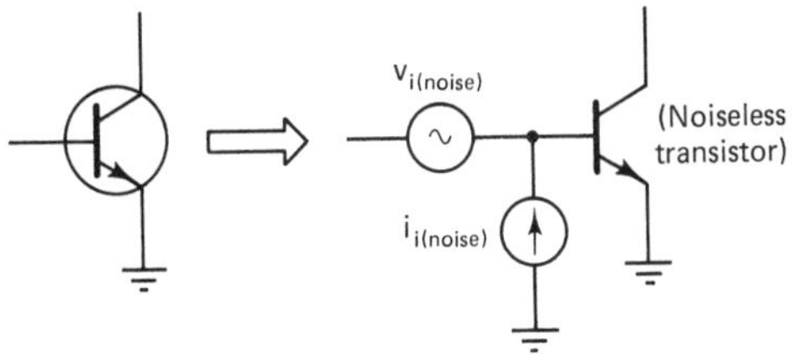

Figure P14.2

(c) Equivalent input noise voltage, $v_{i\,(\text{noise})}$. (*Ans.*: 1.35 nV/Hz$^{1/2}$)

(d) Equivalent input noise current, $i_{i\,(\text{noise})}$ if $\beta = 100$ (min.). (*Ans.*: $i_{i\,(\text{noise})} = 1.8$ pA/Hz$^{1/2}$)

14.3. Repeat Problem 14.2 for $I_C = 100$ mA. [*Ans.*: (a) $i_{sn} = 179$ pA/Hz$^{1/2}$; (b) $v_{th} =$ 1.265 nV/Hz$^{1/2}$; (c) $v_{i\,(\text{noise})} = 2.19$ nV/Hz$^{1/2}$; (d) $i_{i\,(\text{noise})} = 18$ pA/Hz$^{1/2}$]

14.4. Repeat Problem 14.2 for $I_C = 10$ μA. [*Ans.*: (a) $i_{sn} = 1.79$ pA/Hz$^{1/2}$; (b) $v_{th} =$ 1.265 nV/Hz$^{1/2}$; (c) $v_{i\,(\text{noise})} = 4.65$ nV/Hz$^{1/2}$; (d) $i_{i\,(\text{noise})} = 179$ fA/Hz$^{1/2}$]

14.5. (a) Show that if a transistor is driven from a source of resistance R_S, the value of quiescent collector current for maximum sensitivity (i.e., minimum noise) is given by

$$I_C = \frac{V_T\sqrt{\beta}}{R_S + r_{bb'}}$$

(b) If $\beta = 200$, $r_{bb'} = 50\ \Omega$, and $R_S = 50\ \Omega$, find I_C for maximum sensitivity. (*Ans.*: $I_C = 3.5$ mA)

(c) What will v_{NOISE} be in this case? (*Ans.*: 1.265 nV/Hz$^{1/2}$)

14.6. Refer to Figure P14.6.

(a) If the system bandwidth is 10 kHz (single-pole response), find the value of v_s for a unity signal-to-noise ratio. (*Ans.*: 177 nV)

(b) Find the noise figure (NF) of the transistor with respect to the 50-Ω source resistance. (*Ans.*: NF = 3.95 dB)

(c) If the net load resistance driven by this transistor is 5 kΩ, find the noise figure when the thermal noise added by this load resistance is taken into account. [*Ans.*: NF = 3.9529 dB versus 3.9485 dB when the thermal noise of the load resistance is not considered, as in part (b); this is indeed a negligible change]

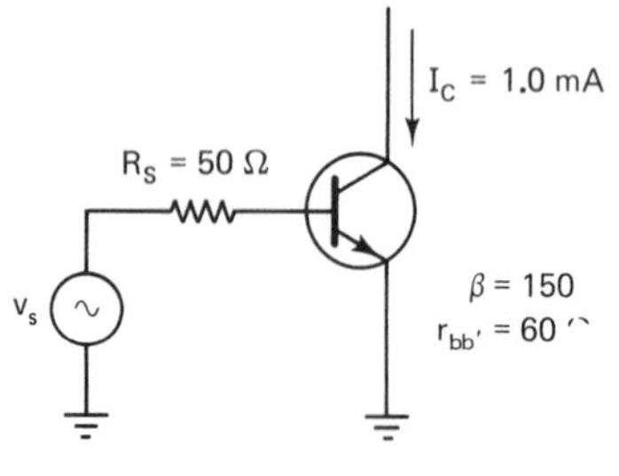

Figure P14.6

14.7. Given a differential amplifier with $r_{bb'} = 100\ \Omega$, $\beta = 100$, and $I_Q = 10$ μA.

(a) Find the equivalent input noise voltage, $v_{i\,(\text{noise})}$. (*Ans.*: 9.0 nV/Hz$^{1/2}$)

(b) Find the equivalent input noise current, $i_{i\,(\text{noise})}$. (*Ans.*: 128 fA/Hz$^{1/2}$)

(c) Repeat part (a) for $I_Q = 1.0$ mA. (*Ans.*: 2.0 nV/Hz$^{1/2}$)

(d) Repeat part (b) for $I_Q = 1.0$ mA. (*Ans.*: 1.27 pA/Hz$^{1/2}$)

14.8. An amplifier has $v_{i\,(\text{noise})} = 2.0$ nV/Hz$^{1/2}$ and $i_{i\,(\text{noise})} = 1.0$ pA/Hz$^{1/2}$.

(a) For a 3-dB bandwidth (single-pole) of 1.0 MHz and a source resistance of 50 Ω, find the sensitivity (SNR = 1) of the amplifier. (*Ans.*: 2.74 μV)

(b) What would the sensitivity be for the system above if the amplifier were a noiseless amplifier? (*Ans.*: 1.12 μV)

(c) Find the *noise figure* of the amplifier with respect to the 50-Ω source resistance- (*Ans.*: 7.81 dB)

(d) Repeat part (a) for a source resistance of 1000 Ω. (*Ans.*: 5.74 μV)

(e) Repeat part (b) for a source resistance of 1000 Ω. (*Ans.*: 5.0 μV)
(f) Repeat part (c) for a source resistance of 1000 Ω. (*Ans.*: 1.176 dB)

14.9. Given op amp shown in Figure P14.9 $v_{i\,(\text{noise})} = 20\ \text{nV/Hz}^{1/2}$ and $i_{i\,(\text{noise})} = 2.0\ \text{pA/Hz}^{1/2}$.

(a) Find the sensitivity (SNR = 1) for R_S = 1.0 kΩ and a bandwidth of 10 kHz. (*Ans.*: 2.63 μV)
(b) Repeat part (a) for R_S = 10 kΩ. (*Ans.*: 4.89 μV)
(c) Repeat part (a) for R_S = 100 kΩ. (*Ans.*: 36.4 μV)
(d) Repeat part (a) for R_S = 1.0 MΩ. (*Ans.*: 355 μV)

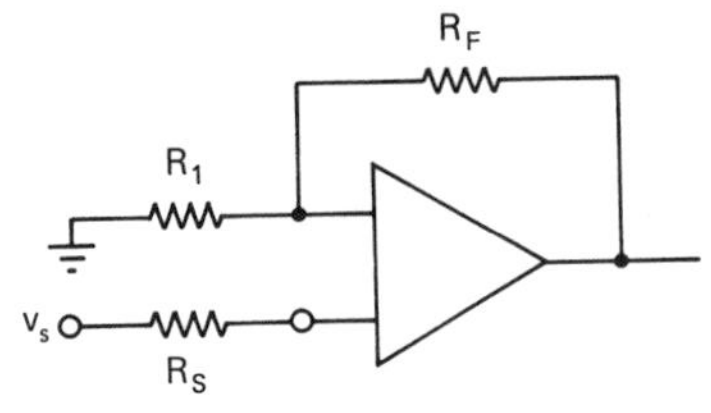

Figure P14.9

14.10. Given a LF355 JFET input op amp (Figure P14.10).

(a) Find the sensitivity (SNR = 1) for the amplifier configuration shown above for a bandwidth of 10 kHz. (*Ans.*: 286 μV)
(b) What is the noise figure for the amplifier? (*Ans.*: NF = 5.1 dB)
(c) Why is it important to use a FET input op amp for this application?

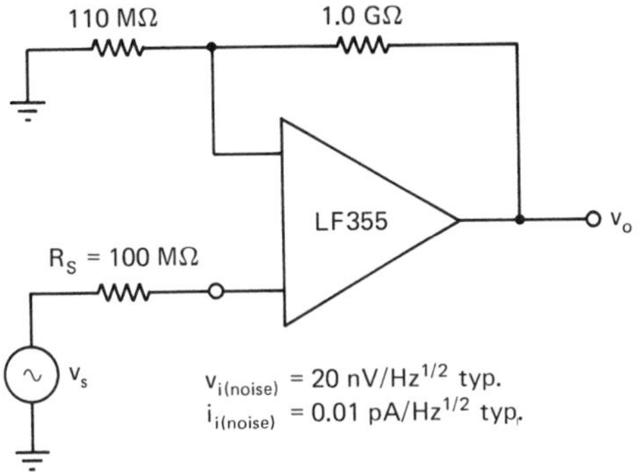

Figure P14.10

14.11. For the op amp circuit of Figure 14.15a, the equivalent input noise voltage is 20 nV/Hz$^{1/2}$ and the input noise current is 0.1 pA/Hz$^{1/2}$. The 3-dB bandwidth is kHz. Find the input signal (rms) needed for a 10:1 signal-to-noise ratio for the following values of source resistance R_S:

(a) 100 Ω (*Ans.*: 25.2 μV)
(b) 1000 Ω (*Ans.*: 26.0 μV)
(c) 10 kΩ (*Ans.*: 33.7 μV)
(d) 30 kΩ (*Ans.*: 46.5 μV)
(e) 100 kΩ (*Ans.*: 77.2 μV)

14.12. Given a 2N4869 N-channel silicon JFET with $g_{fs_0} = 1300\ \mu S$ (min.) and $4000\ \mu S$ (max.) $I_{GSS} = 250$ pA (max.). Find:

(a) Equivalent input noise voltage at $I_{DS} = I_{DSS}$. [*Ans.*: $v_{i(\text{noise})} = 1.6\ \text{nV/Hz}^{1/2}$ (min.), $2.9\ \text{nV/Hz}^{1/2}$ (max.)]

(b) Equivalent input noise voltage at I_{DS}. [*Ans.*: $v_{i(\text{noise})} = 2.4\ \text{nV/Hz}^{1/2}$ (min.), $4.3\ \text{nV/Hz}^{1/2}$(max.)]

(c) Equivalent input noise current, $i_{i(\text{noise})}$. [*Ans.*: $i_{i(\text{noise})} = 9.0\ \text{fA/Hz}^{1/2}$ (max.)]

REFERENCES

COWLES, L. G., *Sourcebook of Modern Transistor Circuits*, Chap. 7, Prentice-Hall, 1976.

GIACOLLETTO, L. J., *Differential Amplifiers*, pp. 161–172, Wiley, 1970.

GRAY, P. R., and R. G. MEYER, *Analysis and Design of Analog Integrated Circuits*, Wiley, 1984.

HALL, C., *Questions and Answers about Noise in Electronics*, Howard W. Sams, 1973.

KRAUSS, H. L., C. W. BOSTIAN, and F. H. RAAB, *Solid State Radio Engineering*, Wiley, 1980.

MOTCHENBACKER, C., and F. C. FITCHEN, *Low Noise Electronic Design*, Wiley, 1973.

OTT, H. W., *Noise Reduction Techniques in Electronic Systems*, Wiley, 1976.

RISTENBATT, M. P., *Semiconductor Circuits*, Chap. 11, Prentice-Hall, 1975.

ROBINSON, E. N. H., *Noise and Fluctuations in Electronic Devices and Circuits*, Oxford, 1974.

STOUT, D. F., *Handbook of Microcircuit Design and Applications*, Chap. 3, McGraw-Hill, 1980.

UNITED TECHNICAL PUBLICATIONS, *Modern Applications of Integrated Circuits*, Tab Books, 1974.

VAN DER ZIEL, A., *Fluctuation Phenomena in Semiconductors*, Academic Press, 1959.

VAN DER ZIEL, A., *Noise: Sources, Characterization, and Measurement*, Prentice-Hall, 1970.

Optoelectronic Integrated Circuits and Systems

15

In most of the integrated circuits and systems considered up to this point, both the input and output signals have been electrical. In the optoelectronic integrated circuits considered in this chapter, an optical signal will be involved either on the input side or on the output side.

Both monolithic and hybrid ICs are widely used in optoelectronic systems. The simplest form of optoelectronic IC is the phototransistor, which is an integrated combination of a photodiode and a transistor. At the other extreme of complexity are the linear and area image sensors, which can contain more than 100,000 photosensing and charge-transfer diodes and transistors.

Whereas very sensitive light-sensing devices can be made with silicon, this material makes very inefficient light-emitting devices. For light-emitting devices (LEDs) various III–V binary and ternary compound semiconductors such as GaAs, GaAsP, and GaAlAs are used. Therefore, optoelectronic ICs that contain both light emitters and sensors cannot be monolithic ICs, but can be only in the form of hybrid ICs. Examples of these are optically coupled isolators (OCIs), reflective sensors, and light interruption sensors. These devices contain an LED and a silicon photosensor in the same package.

15.1 APPLICATIONS OF OPTOELECTRONICS

The two basic applications areas for optoelectronic devices and systems are for light sensing and communications. In the sensing area optoelectronic devices can be used for the sensing of the position and movement of objects. Linear and area image sensors can be used to obtain a video signal representation of an illumination pattern such as for use in a video camera. Emitter and sensor pairs can be used to detect the presence and motion of objects for such applications as intrusion detection and object counting. An important applications area for reflective sensors is for product code readers.

For the communications area, optically coupled isolators are used when the signal source and receiver are in close proximity ($\lesssim$1 cm), and the principal advantage to be gained is the excellent common-mode electrical isolation obtained as well as the almost total lack of any reverse signal feedback. For other applications in which the spacing between the signal source and the receiver is limited to less than about 30 m, a free-space or unguided optical link can be used for such applications as remote controls for TVs, video tape recorders, and other appliances.

For long-distance communications links of as long as 100 km, a fiber optic (FO) link can be used in which the optical wave is guided by a solid, small-diameter ($\lesssim$1 mm) glass fiber. The FO system offers many advantages over coaxial systems. These include a much greater signal bandwidth, relative immunity from electrical interference, and a lighter weight and smaller size. The FO system can be used to

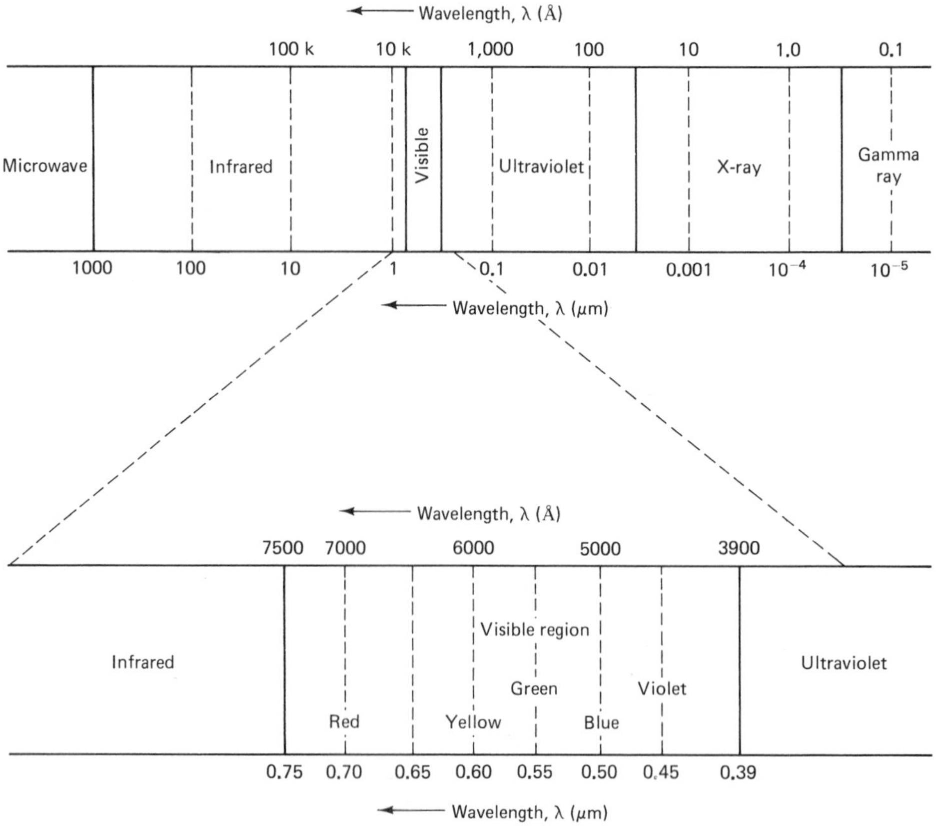

Figure 15.1 Electromagnetic spectrum.

great advantage in high-density telephone links, where the wide bandwidth and lower cost, weight, and size offer the net advantages of a much lower overall systems cost than that of a coaxial or twisted-pair system. Fiber optic systems can also be used to great advantage in avionics, where the lower weight and immunity from electrical interference are principal advantages.

Some representative IC optoelectronic devices and applications will be presented. Optoelectronic devices are electronic devices that can be used for the emission or sensing of optical radiation. Devices that are used for the emission of light include light-emitting diodes (LEDs) and laser diodes, and the light-sensing or light-detecting devices include photodiodes and phototransistors. Optically coupled isolators have both an LED and a light-sensing device (a photodiode or phototransistor) in the same package.

In optoelectronic systems a light beam is used for the communication or transfer of information from a light sensor to a light detector. A good example of such a system is a fiber optic communication system in which an LED or laser diode is used as the light source and a photodiode is used as the light sensor. A small-diameter highly transparent glass fiber is used as an optical waveguide to direct the light from the emitter to the detector. The length of a fiber optic link can in some cases be as great as 10 km, and with repeater the fiber optic link can extend over very long distances.

Semiconductor devices can be used for both light sensing and light emission. The portions of the electromagnetic spectrum that are usually of interest for optoelectronic devices and systems are in the infrared (IR), visible, and ultraviolet (UV) regions, as shown in Figure 15.1. The spectral range of greatest interest is from the near-IR region through the visible region, from about 1.5 μm wavelength down to about 0.5 μm.

15.2 PHOTODIODES

Silicon is a light-sensitive semiconductor, but the change in the conductivity resulting from illumination will often be too small to be measured conveniently or accurately. For these cases the light sensing can be done by means of the change in the reverse current of a PN junction that results from photon illumination.

A photodiode is a diode that is specifically designed for light-sensing applications and is placed in a package that has a transparent window, as shown in Figure 15.2a. A photodiode has a basic construction similar to that of an ordinary diode except that is of usually much larger junction area than an ordinary diode, generally ranging from around 1 mm^2 up to several cm^2 in area. In addition, the top surface metallization is restricted so as to allow most of the incident light to enter the semiconductor, as shown in Figure 15.2b.

A principal component of the reverse current of a diode is the flow of minority carriers down the potential hill or barrier at the junction as shown in Figure 15.3. Note that the holes fall downhill, whereas the electrons fall uphill. Under unilluminated ("dark") conditions the reverse current of a diode will be very small, often in the

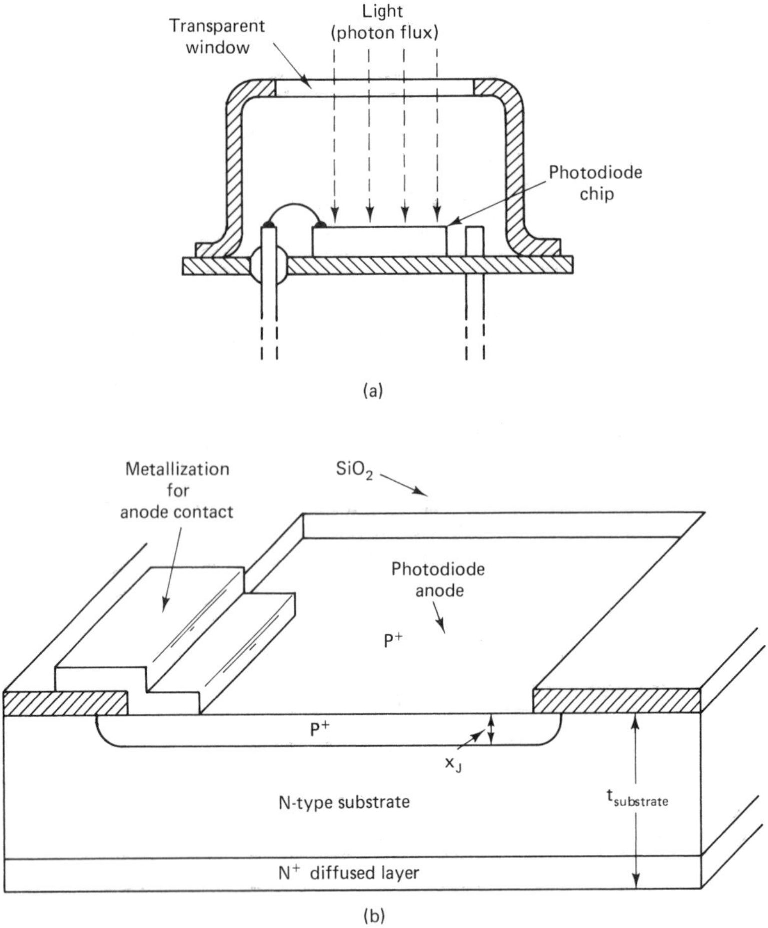

Figure 15.2 Photodiode: (a) photodiode package with transparent window; (b) photodiode chip (cross-sectional perspective view).

range 1 nA/mm². This is due to the very small density of minority carriers on both sides of the junction. Upon illumination, however, the minority carrier density can be increased by several orders of magnitude. The increase in the majority carrier density will be exactly equal to the increase in the minority carrier density, but in percentage terms it will be extremely small due to the much higher density of majority carriers under dark conditions. Correspondingly, the percentage change in the conductivity or resistivity will be very small.

The large percentage increase that can be obtained in the minority carrier density upon illumination will result in a correspondingly large increase in the reverse current of the device. The increase in the reverse device current that results from the illumination and photogeneration process is called the photocurrent I_L.

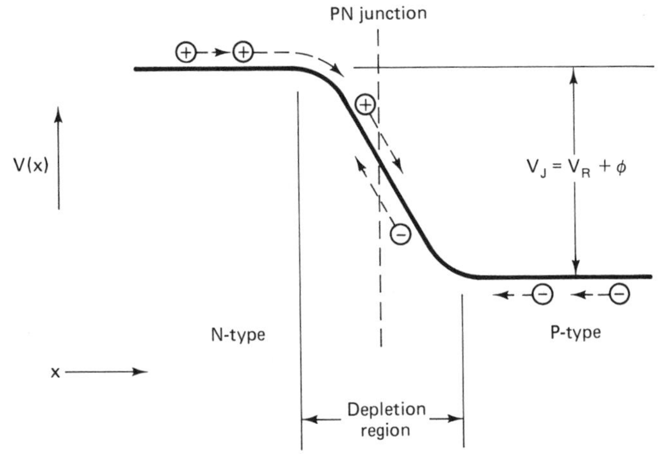

Figure 15.3 Flow of minority carriers across a reverse-biased PN junction.

15.2.1 Current Responsivity

The current responsivity $\mathcal{R}$ of a photodiode is the ratio of the photocurrent to the optical power incident on the device that produces the photocurrent, and will be given by *responsivity* $= \mathcal{R} = I_L/P$, where P is the optical power (watts). An ideal photodiode will be defined as a photodiode in which every incident photon is absorbed and produces a *photogenerated minority carrier* (PMC), which in turn reaches the PN junction and passes over to the other side (i.e., is "collected" by the junction). Every PMC that is collected by the PN junction will result in the flow of an electron around the external circuit.

The photon flux is related to the optical power P by $P =$ photon flux (photons/second) $\times$ energy per photon (joules), and the photocurrent I_L is related to the photon flux for the ideal photodiode case by $I_L =$ photon flux (photons/second) $\times$ q, where q is the electronic charge. We will therefore have that

$$\boxed{\begin{aligned}\mathcal{R} &= \frac{I_L}{P} = \frac{q}{\text{energy/photon}} = \frac{q}{hc/\lambda} \\ &= \frac{\lambda}{\text{hc/q}} = \frac{\lambda}{1.239\ \text{V}\mu\text{m}} = \frac{\lambda\ (\mu\text{m})}{1.239}\ \text{A/W}\end{aligned}} \tag{15.1}$$

In Figure 15.4 the current responsivity versus wavelength characteristic of an ideal silicon photodiode is shown. The energy gap of silicon is 1.1 eV, so that only photons with energies greater than this can be absorbed and thereby produce a contribution to the photocurrent. Since $E_{\text{photon}} = 1.239$ eV-μm/λ, the *critical wavelength* or *long-wavelength limit* (or *absorption edge*) for silicon will be given by $\lambda_c = 1.239$ eV-μm/1.1 eV $= 1.13$ μm, so that only photons with wavelengths such that $\lambda <$

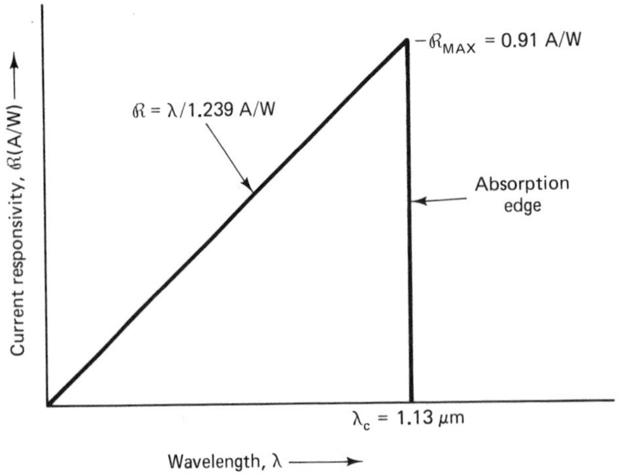

Figure 15.4 Current responsivity $\mathcal{R}$ of an ideal photodiode.

$\lambda_c = 1.13\ \mu$m will be absorbed. The maximum current responsivity for the ideal case will occur at λ_c and will be given by $\mathcal{R}_{MAX} = \mathcal{R}(\lambda_c) = \lambda_c/1.239$ (A/W) $= 1/E_G = 1/1.1$ V $=$ 0.91 A/W. For actual silicon photodiodes the peak current responsivity will generally occur at wavelengths in the region 0.8 to 0.9 μm and will be around 0.5 or 0.6 A/W. If, for example, the current responsivity of a silicon photodiode is 0.5 A/W at a wavelength of 0.9 μm and the active area is 1 cm^2, the photocurrent produced by a radiant power density of 10 mW/cm^2 at 0.9 μm will be $I_L = 0.5$ A/W $\times$ 10 mW/cm^2 $\times$ 1 cm^2 = 5 mA.

The current responsivity of an actual photodiode will be less than the value of an ideal device due to several loss factors, which are:

1. The partial reflection of light at the various optical interfaces, and in particular at the air/silicon interface
2. The incomplete absorption of photons in the semiconductor
3. The recombination of the PMCs before they reach the PN junction

15.3 PHOTOTRANSISTORS

A phototransistor is an integrated combination of a photodiode and a transistor. In Figure 15.5 a phototransistor circuit symbol is shown together with an equivalent representation as a separate photodiode and transistor. From Figure 15.5b we see that the photocurrent I_L of the photodiode becomes the base current of the transistor. This is amplified by the current gain β of the transistor to become the collector current of βI_L. The total phototransistor current thus becomes $I = (\beta + 1)I_L$. The phototransistor thus provides an internal current gain of $\beta + 1$. Since the β value of phototransistors will normally range from 100 up to values in excess of 1000, we see that very large gains can indeed be obtained.

In Figure 15.6 a diagram of the phototransistor structure is shown. We see that the structure is very similar to that of an ordinary double-diffused NPN epitaxial

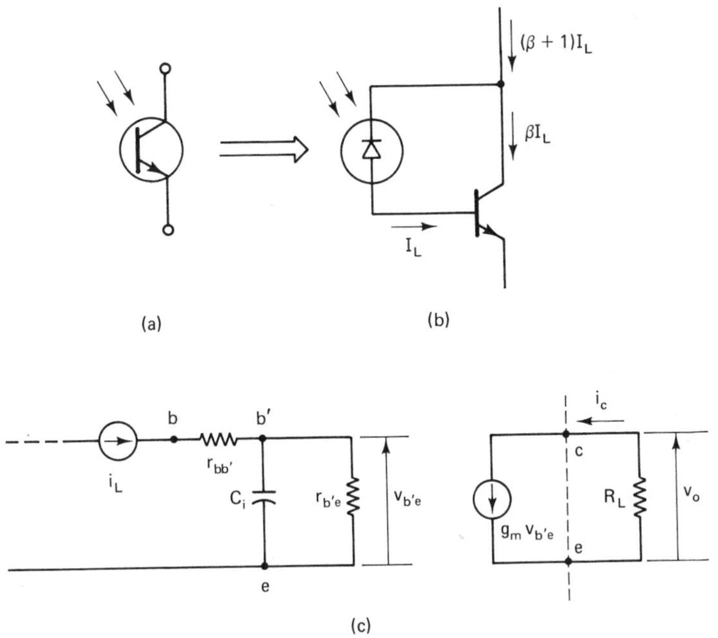

Figure 15.5 Phototransistor: (a) phototransistor symbol; (b) equivalent circuit; (c) a-c small-signal equivalent circuit for frequency response analysis.

planar transistor except that the area of the P-type base region has been greatly increased. This extended base region in combination with the N-type epitaxial layer will constitute the photodiode part of the phototransistor structure. The transistor portion of the device will normally occupy only a small fraction of the total device area.

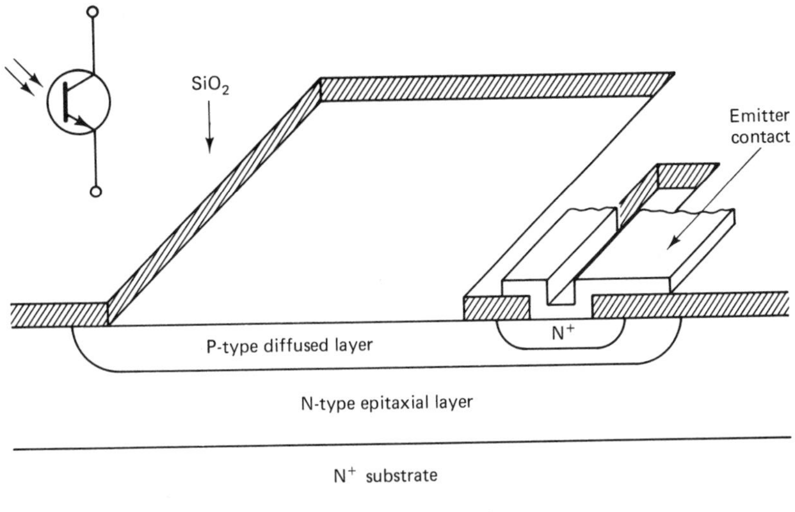

Figure 15.6 Phototransistor.

The cost and size of a phototransistor is about the same as that of an equivalent photodiode. The phototransistor offers the substantial advantage of a very large internal current gain. There are, however, two important drawbacks to the use of this device. First, the current gain β will not be a constant, but will vary with current level as is the case with all transistors. As a result, there will no longer be the exact linearity between the optical power and the resulting output current as was the case for the photodiode. In general, the phototransistor current will vary with the optical power level as $I \; \alpha \; (P_{\text{optical}})^n$, where the exponent n will be about $\frac{2}{3}$ at low-to-moderate power levels, and may decrease to as low as $\frac{1}{2}$ at very low illumination levels and only at relatively high light levels will n approach unity.

The second and even more serious drawback to the use of a phototransistor is the much poorer frequency response of this device compared to that of a photodiode.

15.3.1 Photodarlington Transistor

A photodarlington transistor is an integrated combination of a photodiode and a Darlington transistor configuration, as illustrated in Figure 15.7. From this diagram we see that the photocurrent produced by the photodiode part of the structure is multiplied by the current gains of both transistors so that the resulting device current will be approximately given by $I \simeq \beta_1\beta_2 I_L$. The photodarlington transistor thus has the advantage of providing an extremely large internal current gain. Since the individual transistor current gains will usually be in the range of about 100 to 1000, the overall current gain will be about 10,000 to as much as 10^6.

In Figure 15.8 the integrated structure of a photodarlington transistor is shown. Note that both transistors will share a common N-type collector region. As in the case of the phototransistor the transistor active or emitter areas will occupy only a relatively small fraction of the total chip area.

We have seen that the photodarlington transistor offers the advantage of a very large internal current gain and therefore will have a correspondingly high current responsivity with respect to the incident optical power. The drawbacks of this device,

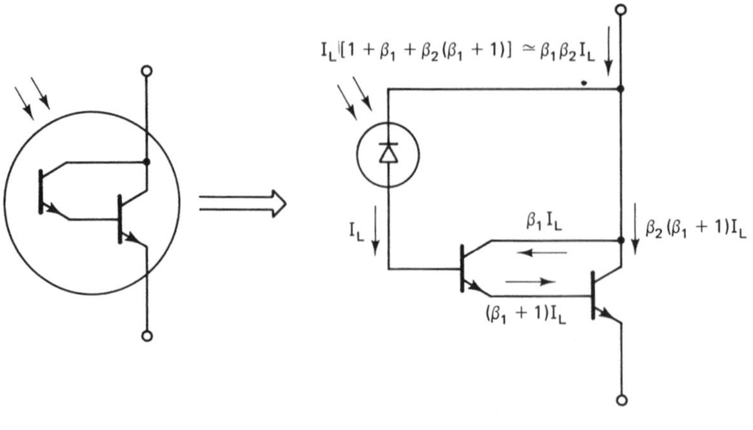

Figure 15.7 Photodarlington transistor.

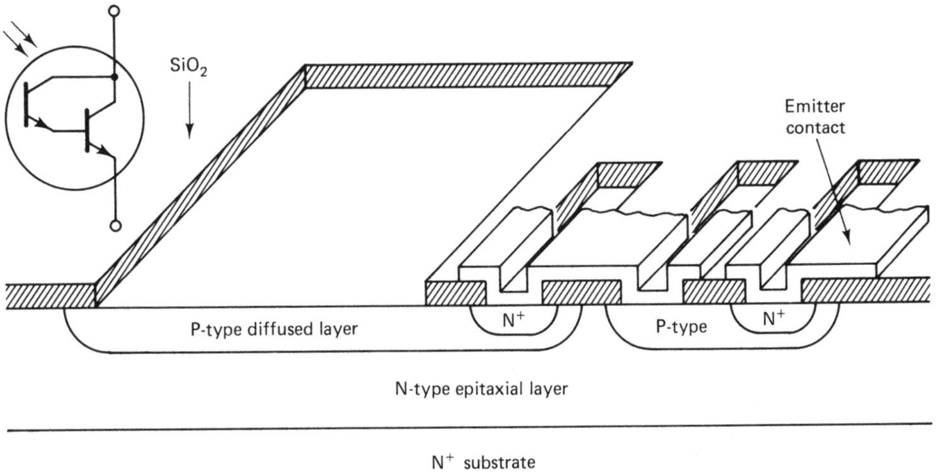

Figure 15.8 Photodarlington transistor.

however, are the same as for the phototransistor. The variation of the transistor current gains with current level will result in a very nonlinear response characteristic. The frequency and time-domain response will be similar to that of the phototransistor, except that it will be worse by a factor approximately equal to the transistor current gain (β_1). In Figure 15.9 the variation of 3-dB bandwidth with load resistance is shown for a representative photodarlington transistor (2N5777). A light-emitting diode is used as the light source. The light-emitting diode is driven by a current that has

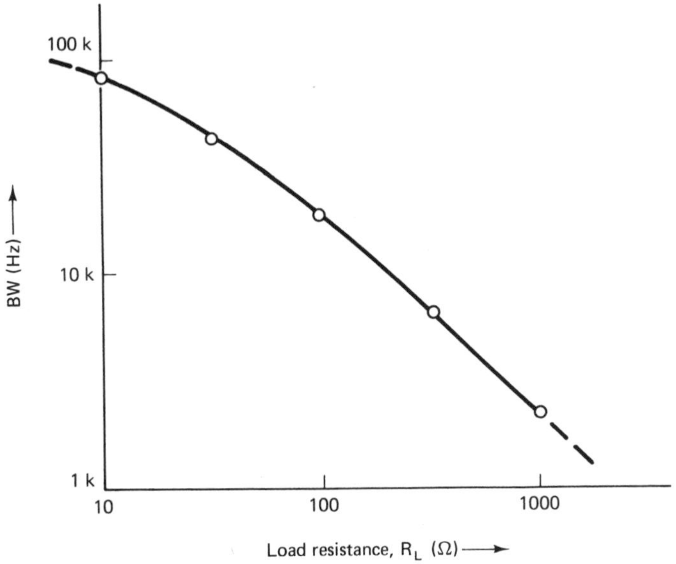

Figure 15.9 Photodarlington transistor (ZN5777) bandwidth versus load resistance (I_C = 10 mA, V_{CE} = +10 V, GaAs light-emitting-diode light source).

a d-c component plus an a-c component whose frequency can be varied so that the resulting light output will be modulated in amplitude. We see that even for very low load resistance values of around 10 Ω, the bandwidth will still be less than 100 kHz. At a load resistance of 1 kΩ the bandwidth is down to only about 3kHz.

15.4 RADIATION DETECTORS

Ionizing radiation consists of high-energy particles and photons such as those produced by nuclear reactions. The high-energy particles include α-particles (helium nuclei), β-particles (high-energy electrons), protons, and other nuclear fission products. High-energy photons include x-rays and gamma rays.

Each high-energy particle can generate a large number of free electrons and holes when absorbed by a semiconductor. These radiation-generated charge carriers can then be collected by a PN junction and the resulting current pulse can be used to measure the particle energy. For high-energy radiation the principal energy loss mechanism in semiconductors will be the generation of free electrons and holes. The energy loss per electron–hole pair will be 3.6 eV in silicon and 2.8 eV in germanium. Therefore a 3.6-MeV particle entering silicon will produce 10^6 free electrons and holes, so that very large quantum yields can indeed be obtained.

The high-energy particles will also have a very large penetration depth or range. For 10-MeV particles the range in silicon will be 60 μm for α-particles, 800 μm for protons, and 20 mm for electrons. Consequently, the collecting volume of a semiconductor radiation detector must be large. This large collecting volume can be obtained by the use of PIN diodes with very wide, high-resistivity base regions. One way of doing this is to use lithium doping to compensate for the P-type base region doping. With lithium doping, base region depletion-layer thicknesses of up to 5 mm are possible with silicon diodes and even larger thicknesses in germanium diodes.

The very wide depletion-layer thicknesses are made possible by a lithium drift process, as shown in Figure 15.10. Lithium is diffused into the silicon surface for a few minutes at 400 to 500°C. A reverse-bias voltage is then applied across the diode at a temperature of 130 to 150°C. Lithium ions are very small and can travel interstitially in silicon. The Li^+ ions will drift across the silicon wafer under the influence of the electric field produced by the reverse bias voltage, and after about 5 to 20 h can reach the opposite side. The Li^+ ions will become distributed uniformly throughout the boron-doped P-type base region in such a fashion as to neutralize the B^- acceptor ions by the formation of stable $Li^+ - B^-$ pairs. This results in a compensated, high-resistivity base region that has a very small net doping level. The wide base region of this lithium-drifted diode can now be fully depleted with the application of only a moderately small reverse-bias voltage.

Let us consider a fully depleted silicon PIN radiation detector diode with an active area of 10 cm² and a thickness of 4mm. The device capacitance will be 25 pF. A 3.6-MeV particle absorbed by this diode will produce 10^6 electron–hole pairs, so that the charge collected by the PN junction will be 0.16 pC. If we assume an amplifier input capacitance of 5 pF such that the total shunt capacitance is 30 pF, the voltage developed across this shunt capacitance will be $\Delta V = \Delta Q/C = 0.16$

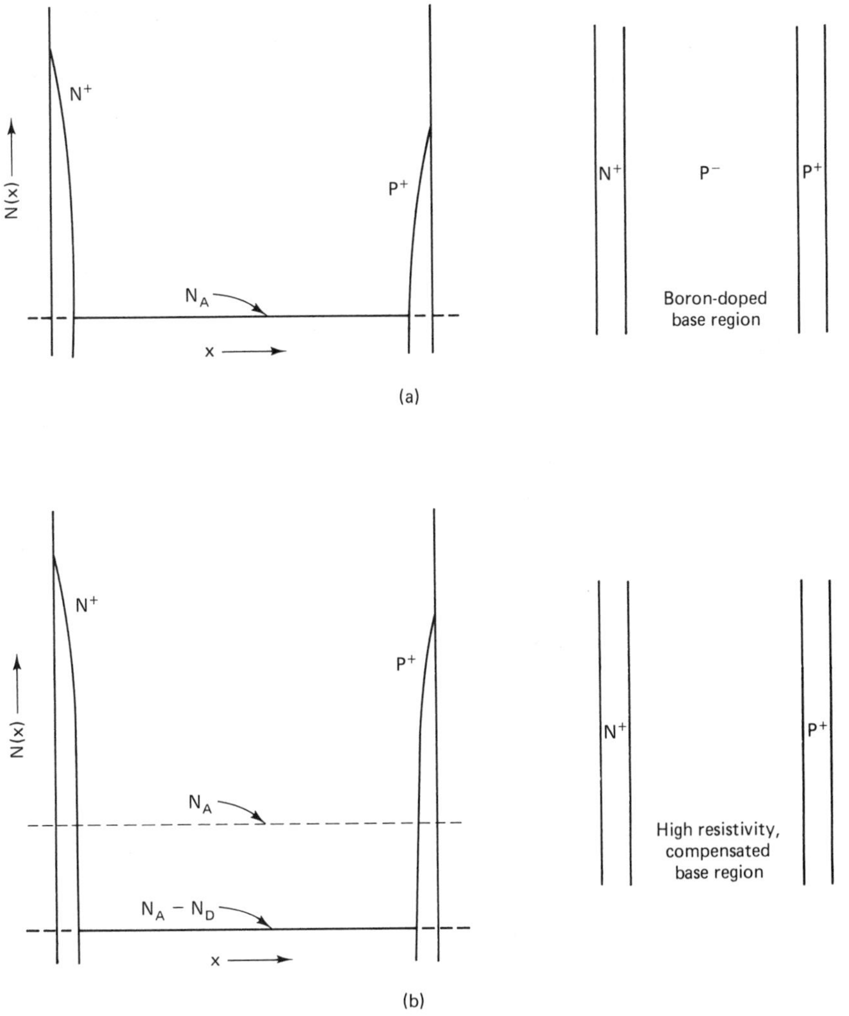

Figure 15.10 Lithium-drifted semiconductor radiation detector: (a) before lithium ion drift; (b) after lithium drift process.

pC/30 pF = 5 mV. The resolution of this radiation detector for energy spectroscopy can therefore be expressed as 5 mV mV/3.6 MeV = 1.5 mV/MeV or 15 μV/keV. If the amplifier input noise is 1 μV, then particle energy resolution available will be about 1 keV.

15.5 RADIATION DAMAGE

High-energy particles will dissipate most of their energy in a semiconductor by producing a very large number of free electron–hole pairs. The high-energy particles can also displace atoms from their normal crystal lattice position and produce vacancy–

interstitial atom pairs or Frenkel defects. This damage to the crystallographic structure of the semiconductor will produce a lower minority carrier lifetime, which will result in a lower current gain for bipolar transistors and an increased junction leakage current for all devices. There will also be a decrease in the charge carrier mobility values and therefore a change in the resistivity. This will produce an increase in the resistance values for the IC resistors.

In addition to the long-term radiation damage effects, the exposure of integrated circuits and other semiconductor devices to a pulse of ionizing radiation will produce a very large transient increase in the junction reverse currents. This current pulse can temporarily interfere with or disable operation of the circuit. The radiation-generated current pulse can be a particular problem in the case of the conventional junction-isolated monolithic integrated circuits. This is due to the relatively large volume of the common P-type substrate. Radiation-generated electrons produced in the substrate can diffuse to the various devices on the IC chip and produce a momentary disruption of the operation of the circuit.

The effect of the radiation-generated current pulse can be lessened to some extent by careful design of the circuit. A simple example of a circuit technique for the reduction of the effect of a radiation-generated current pulse is shown in Figure 15.11. Transistor Q_2 is a compensation transistor of the same size as Q_1 and located close to Q_1. The radiation pulse produces a transient increase in the collector–base current of Q_1 of amount I_{RG_1}. If Q_2 were not present, this current pulse will produce a change in the base voltage of Q_1 of amount $\Delta V_{B_1} = I_{RG_1} R_S$. With the compensation transistor in the circuit the current pulse through R_S will be reduced by I_{RG_2} to $I_{RG_1} - I_{RG_2}$, so that the change in the base voltage of Q_1 will now be $\Delta V_{B_1} = (I_{RG_1} - I_{RG_2})R_S$. Since Q_1 and Q_2 are of similar geometry and are close to each other, the two radiation-generated currents will be approximately equal, so that the change in the base voltage of Q_1 will be greatly reduced.

One of the most effective ways to increase the radiation resistance of integrated circuits is to use dielectric isolation. The insulating SiO_2 layer between the substrate and the various IC devices will block the flow of radiation-generated electrons and holes from the substrate to the active parts of the circuit.

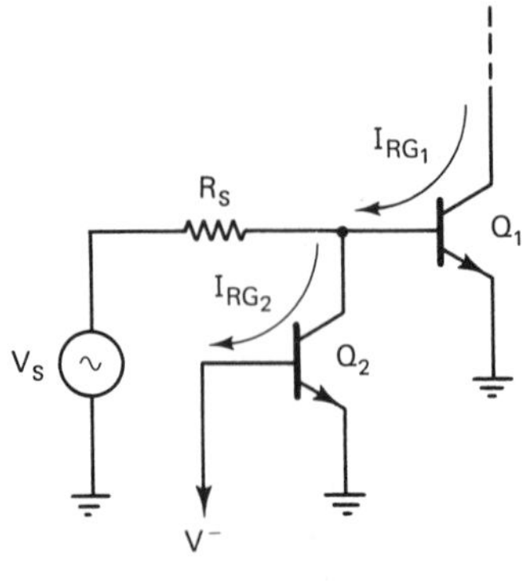

Figure 15.11 Circuit to compensate for radiation-generated current pulse.

15.6 OPTICALLY COUPLED ISOLATORS

An optically coupled isolator (OCI) is a combination of a light-emitting diode (GaAs LED) and a light-detecting device, usually a silicon phototransistor, photodiode, or phototransistor in a single package for the purpose of coupling an electrical signal from the input port to the output port with a minimum of coupling in the reverse direction and a minimum of common-mode coupling. Schematic representations of LED-phototransistor, LED-photodiode, and LED-photodarlington OCIs are shown in Figure 15.12. In all three cases the input current, which is the forward current of the LED, results in the emission of light by the LED. This light is detected by the photodetector and produces the output current. The *current transfer ratio* (CTR) is the ratio of the output current to the input current (I_F) of the OCI and is typically

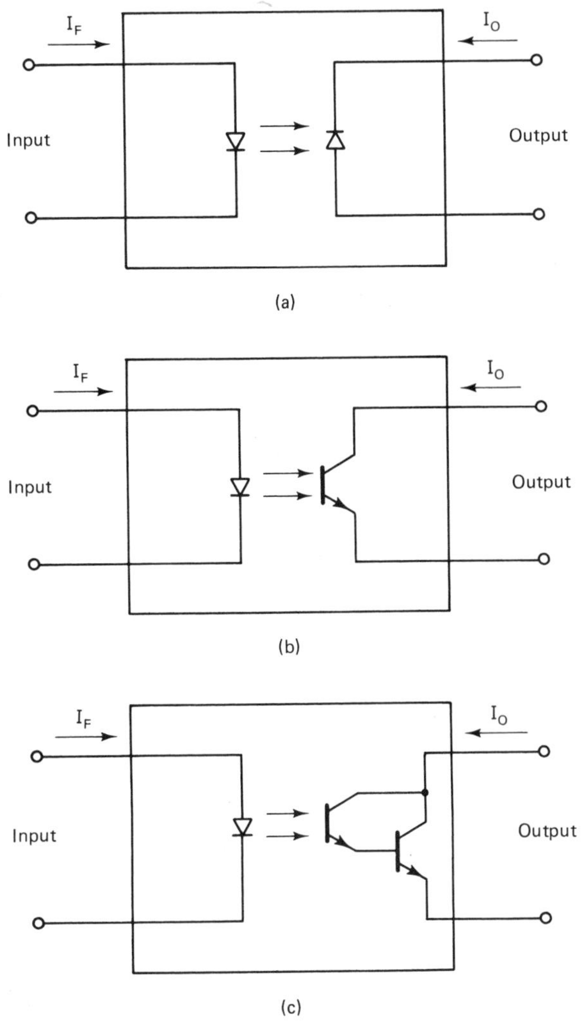

Figure 15.12 Optically coupled isolators: (a) LED-photodiode OCI; (b) LED-phototransistor OCI; (c) LED-photodarlington OCI.

of the order of 1 to 3% for the LED-photodiode type, 10 to 100% for the LED-phototransistor type, and 100 to 500% for the LED-photodarlington type.

The coupling in the OCI is solely by means of the light emitted by the LED and detected by the photodetector. There is no direct electrical connection between the input and output of the device. Since the photodetector is inherently incapable of light emission there is no reverse signal transmission in the device, other than by means of the very small parasitic capacitance between the input and output of the device. This capacitance is very small, usually about 1 pF. There is also a leakage resistance between the input and output parts of the device, but this is very large, generally of the order of 100 GΩ (10^{11} Ω) or more.

Since the light output of the LED is a function of the forward current of the device, which is produced by the application of a forward-bias voltage across the input terminals of the device, a signal component that is common to the input terminals (i.e., a common-mode input) will not be coupled to the output.

Optically coupled isolators come in a variety of packages, the most common being the mini-dual-in-line (or mini-DIP) six-pin package. In this package two of the pins on one side are for the anode and cathode of the LED and the three pins on the other side are for the photodetector, usually the emitter, base, and collector of the phototransistor. This package is very convenient to use and relatively inexpensive, but limited to a maximum input-to-output voltage difference (isolation voltage) generally in the range 1000 to 2500 kV. Isolators are also available in tubular-type packages with the input and output leads at opposite ends, with isolation voltage ratings of ≥10 kV. Generally, however, with a higher isolation voltage the current transfer ratio will be less, due to the greater separation of the detector from the emitter.

15.7 OPTOELECTRONIC ANALOG SIGNAL TRANSMISSION

An analog signal can be transmitted over an optical link with an LED at the transmitting end and a photodiode or phototransistor at the receiving end. The emitter and sensor can be close together, as in the case of an optically coupled isolator, or may be many kilometers apart, as in the case of a fiber optic system. The two most important characteristics of the analog signal transmission system will be the speed or bandwidth and the overall linearity such that the output waveform will be an accurate replica of the input signal.

A phototransistor exhibits poor linearity and is very slow compared to a photodiode and so is usually not used for analog signal transmission. A photodiode, on the other hand, can be very fast, with response times as small as 1 ns and also will exhibit excellent linearity. The LED, however, will have a considerable amount of nonlinearity. The variation of optical power output P_O with forward current I_F for the LED will be of the form $P_o \; \alpha \; I_F^n$ where $1 \leq n \leq 2$ and is typically in the range 1.6 to 1.8.

To obtain an acceptably linear transfer characteristic for an optoelectronic system there are three basic techniques that can be employed. The simplest technique is to bias the LED at some suitable d-c operating point and to limit the a-c signal current through the LED to a relatively small fraction of the d-c bias current. This approach has the major disadvantage of a very limited dynamic signal range.

A second basic technique is to use feedback as shown in Figure 15.13. In Figure 15.13 a pair of matched photodiodes is used to receive light from the LED. At the inverting input terminal of the operational amplifier we will have that $-V_{in}/R_1 + I_{L_1} = 0$ so that $I_{L_1} = V_{in}/R_1$. Since the current produced by photodiode PD_2 will

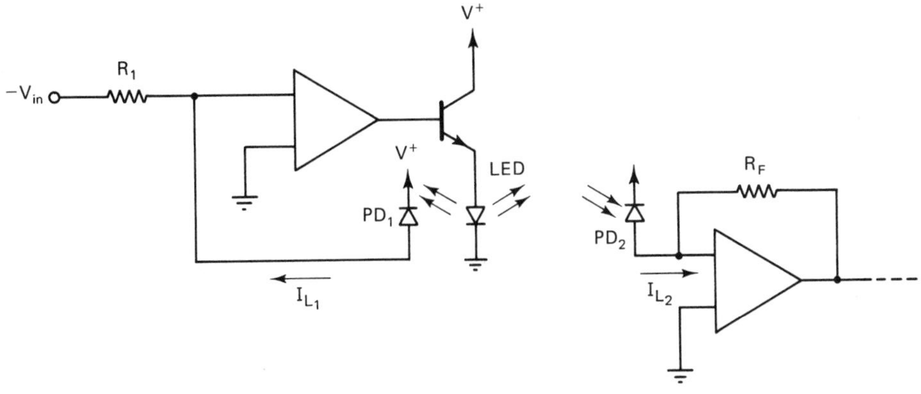

(a)

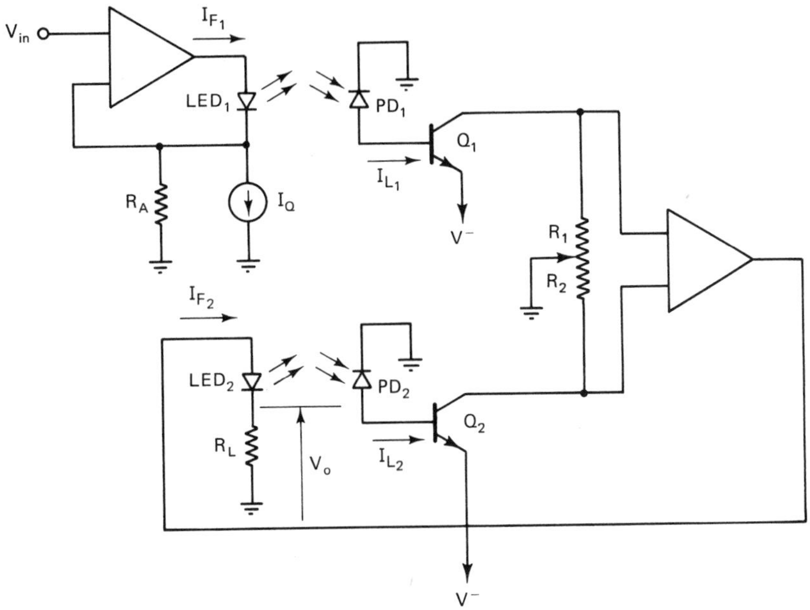

(b)

Figure 15.13 Feedback linearization of optoelectronic analog signal transmission: (a) linearization circuit using a matched pair of photodiodes; (b) linearization circuit using a matched set of emitters and sensors.

be linearly related to the current of photodiode PD_1, we see that I_{L_2} will be linearly related to the input voltage V_{in} and that overall system linearity will thus be obtained.

Another feedback method for achieving linearity is shown in Figure 12.33b. In this case two matched emitter-detector pairs are used. Operational amplifier A_2 will produce a current flow through LED_2 that will result in a current in PD_2 such that $\beta_2 I_{L_2} R_2 = \beta_1 I_{L_1} R_1$. If the balance potentiometer is adjusted to make $R_1 = R_2$, then $I_{L_1} = I_{L_2}$. Since the two emitter-detector pairs have identical characteristics we will therefore have that $I_{F_1} = I_{F_2}$ for the LEDs. For I_{F_1} we have that $I_{F_1} = V_{in}/R_A + I_Q$ and V_o will be given by $V_o = I_{F_2} R_L$, so that we obtain $V_o = V_{in}(R_L/R_A) + I_Q R_L$. We see that a linear input–output relationship is produced.

In practice it may be desirable to adjust the R_1–R_2 balance potentiometer to compensate for the op-amp offset voltage and to cancel out the $I_Q R_L$ term such that the output voltage becomes simply $V_o = V_{in}(R_L/R_A)$. The cancellation of the I_Q term will, however, be at the expense of a small increase in the linearity error.

The third basic technique for linear signal transmission is shown in Figure 15.14. The analog signal is converted into a pulse waveform at the transmitting end and is converted back to an analog signal at the receiver. A number of different pulse conversion methods can be used, including pulse-frequency modulation, as shown in Figure 15.14a. In this case a voltage-to-frequency (V/F) converter is used to produce

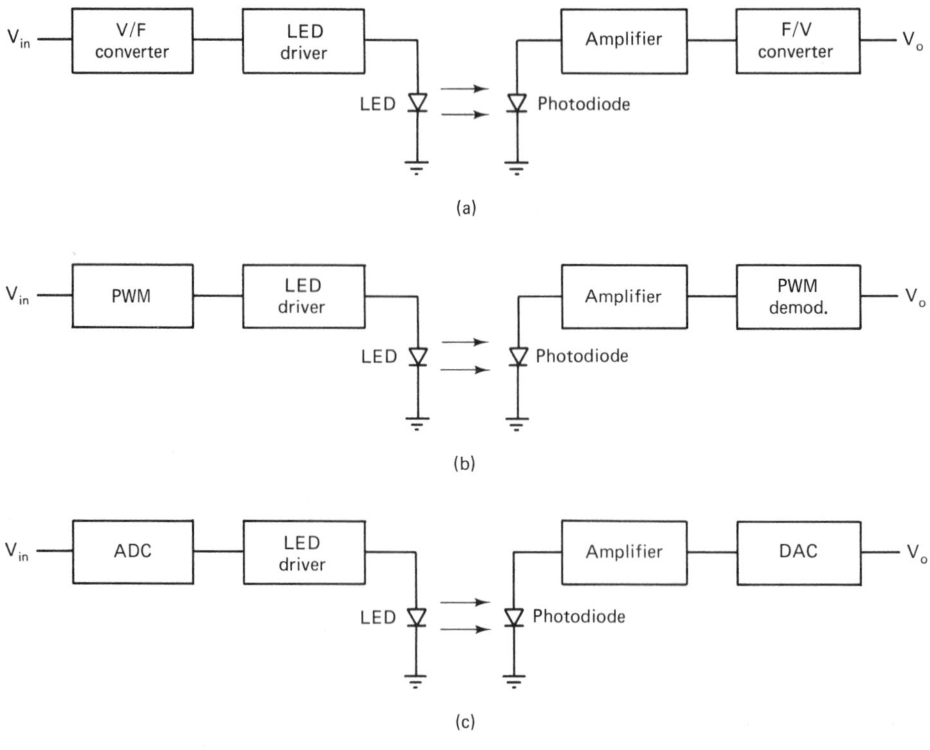

Figure 15.14 Optoelectronic analog signal transmission using pulse modulation: (a) pulse-frequency modulation; (b) pulse-width modulation; (c) pulse-code modulation.

a pulse train whose repetition frequency is proportional to the input signal amplitude. At the receiver a frequency-to-voltage (F/V) converter is used to convert the pulse train back into an analog signal.

In the system of Figure 15.4b a pulse-width modulator (PWM) is used to convert the input signal to a pulse train. This pulse train will have a constant repetition frequency, but the pulse width will be proportional to the input signal. At the receiver a pulse-width demodulator is used to recover the analog signal waveform.

A binary pulse code modulation (PCM) system is shown in Figure 15.14c. An analog-to-digital converter (ADC) is used to convert the input signal to a binary digital signal, and at the receiver a digital-to-analog converter (DAC) is used to convert the digital signal back to the original analog waveform.

These pulse transmission techniques can be used to produce a system with a very high degree of analog signal transmission linearity. A linearity error of under 0.1% can usually be achieved, and in the case of the PCM system linearity errors of less than 0.01% are obtainable.

15.8 SLOTTED AND REFLECTIVE EMITTER-SENSOR MODULES

Closely related to optically coupled isolators are the slotted and reflective emitter-sensor modules. A slotted module or light interruption sensor, shown in Figure 15.15 can be used for such applications as shaft encoders, sector sensors, level indicators, and end-of-tape indicators.

An example of a slotted module is the TIL32 (Texas Instruments), which uses a GaAs LED and an NPN phototransistor. This device has a 3.2-mm gap between the emitter and the sensor, and for an LED current of 35 mA the phototransistor collector current will be 4 mA.

A basic diagram for an optical reflective sensory is shown in Figure 15.16. This device can be used for such applications as bar code (product code) scanners, line location, tachometry, object sizing, and pattern recognition.

An example of a reflective sensor is the HEDs-1000 (Hewlett-Packard), which contains an LED, photodiode, and transistor in one module. The maximum response is obtained for a reflective surface at a distance of 4.3 mm from the device reference

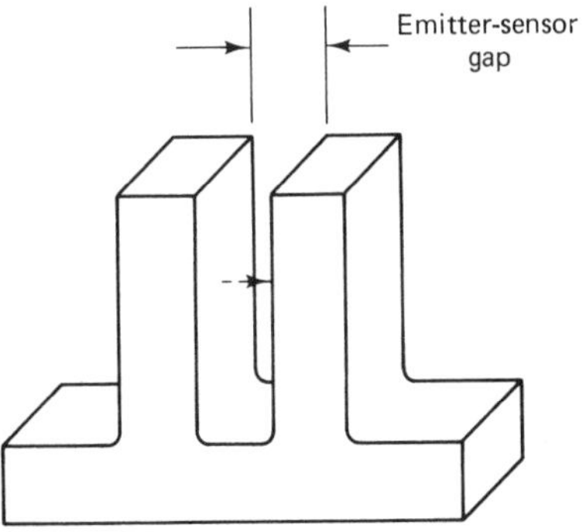

Figure 15.15 Slotted emitter-sensor module.

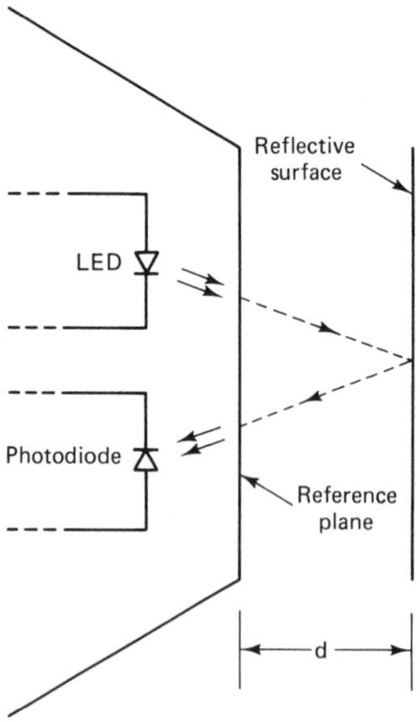

Figure 15.16 Reflective emitter-sensor module.

plane. If the LED current is 35 mA, the maximum photodiode current will be 180 nA. The reflective edge discrimination is such that the 10% to 90% step edge response distance is 1.6 mm.

15.9 FIBER OPTICS

A beam of light can be transmitted from a source to a sensor through air, or any other suitably transparent medium without the need of a conduit, guide, or any other type of supporting or guiding structure. This type of transmission is called "free-space propagation" and is similar to the broadcasting of a radio or television signal from a transmitting antenna.

The free-space transmission of the light beam is the simplest means of transmitting an optical signal from a source to a sensor but suffers from some severe drawbacks and limitations. First light travels in a straight line, so that there must exist a clear line-of-sight path between the light source and the sensor with no intervening objects that may block or deflect the light beam. In some cases the clear line-of-sight path may be subject to intermittent interruptions by various objects so that the free space communication link may be of limited reliability. Furthermore, variations in the atmospheric absorption due to smoke, smog, rain, snow, dust, and so on, may cause severe problems, even for very short-distance communications links.

In the case of the free-space transmission of a light beam, the spreading of the beam will result in the radiant power density at the detector surface being inversely proportional to the square of the distance between the source and the detector. This decrease in the power density, together with the attenuation of the light beam in the transmission medium, can be a very severe limit on the maximum source to the detector spacing.

Additional problems with free-space light transmission have to do with the susceptibility of the system to noise and other types of interference, either natural or human-made, since the detector will be responsive to any light signals within its field of view. Furthermore, since the transmitted light beam spreads out in all directions, the communications link is not secure, in the sense that it is subject to eavesdropping.

The problems with a free-space communications link noted above can be eliminated by the use of a light guide between the light source and the detector. The light guide serves as a conduit for the light beam, guiding it around obstacles and keeping it from spreading out so that the optical power density decreases with distance at a much slower rate than for the free-space propagation case. Such a light guide could be a rod made from transparent materials, or in the most useful form is a composite guide made from a package of tightly spaced thin fibers. An individual fiber optic light guide consists of a small-diameter core of some transparent material, usually glass, although various plastic materials are often used. The fiber optic core has a refractive index, n_1, and is surrounded by a thin sheath or cladding of lower index of refraction, n_2, such that $n_2 < n_1$. A typical fiber optic light guide, shown in Figure 15.17, consists of a glass core of diameter usually in the range 50 to 100 μm, clad with a plastic or glass sheath a few micrometers thick. Surrounding this is a thicker plastic layer to give the light guide mechanical strength and to protect it from mechanical damage. As a result of the small diameter of the glass core, the light guide is flexible and can be bent with a relatively small radius of curvature.

The light beam is guided through the core by means of *total internal reflection* (TIR) at the boundary between the core and the cladding as shown in Figure 15.18. Snell's law for the refraction of a light beam at the interface between two optical media is given by $n_1 \sin \theta_1 = n_2 \sin \theta_2$. Since the maximum value of θ_2 is 90°, if $n_1 \sin \theta_1 > n_2$, there will be no refracted beam in medium 2. What will happen is that there will be a total reflection of the incident beam at the interface between medium 1 and medium 2. The critical angle, θ_c, for total internal reflection is given by the condition that $n_1 \sin \theta_c = n_2$, so that $\sin \theta_c = n_2/n_1$. Note that since the maximum value of $\sin \theta_c$ is unity, total internal reflection can occur at the core–cladding boundary only if the index of refraction of the cladding is less that of the core, so that $n_2 < n_1$. Thus if the angle of incidence θ_i is greater than θ_c, the

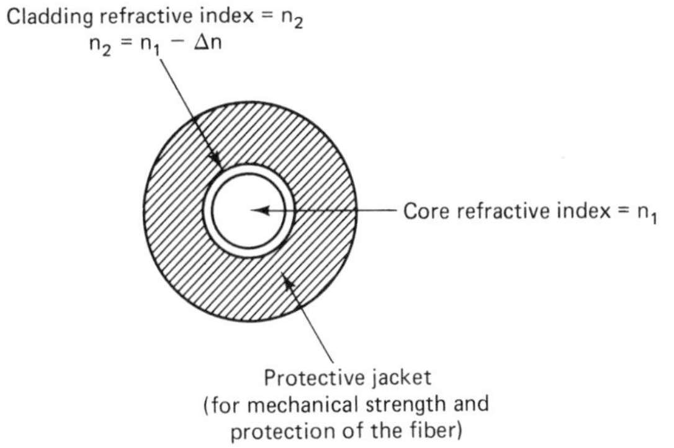

Figure 15.17 Optical fiber: cross-sectional view.

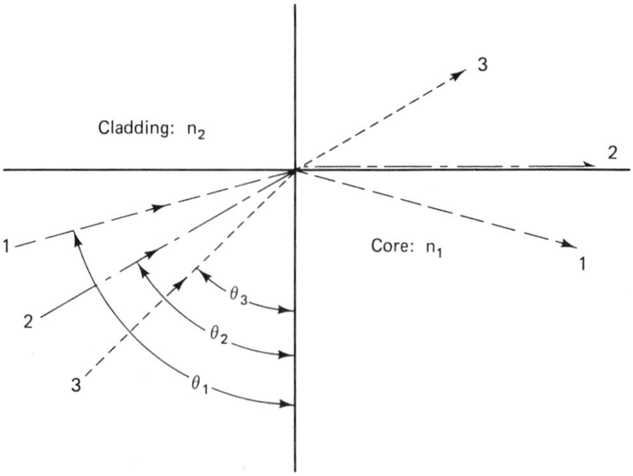

Figure 15.18 Critical angle for total internal reflection at the core–cladding interface. Ray 1: $\theta_1 > \theta_c$, so that this ray will undergo total internal reflection and there will be no refracted ray; ray 2: $\theta_2 = \theta_c$, so that the refracted ray will be parallel to the core–cladding interface; and ray 3: $\theta_3 < \theta_c$, so that this ray will be partially refracted and partially reflected.

beam will undergo total internal reflection every time it reaches the core–cladding interface, and as a result will stay within and be guided by the core, as shown in Figure 15.19. We have seen that light rays that have angles of incidence greater than θ_c will propagate through the core of the fiber optic light guide. Those rays with smaller angles of incidence, however, will be partially transmitted (refracted) into the cladding material at every bounce, so that these rays will very rapidly "leak" out of the core and after a very short distance will be lost almost completely.

Instead of using a dielectric sheath cladding it might be thought possible to use a metallic coating on the core to produce the reflections and thus confine the light beam to the core. It turns out, however, that the reflectivity of the metal–glass core boundary will not be 100%, but rather, there will be a small amount of optical losses (a few percent). As a result, at every reflection the light ray will become progressively weaker and after a very short distance will be almost completely lost.

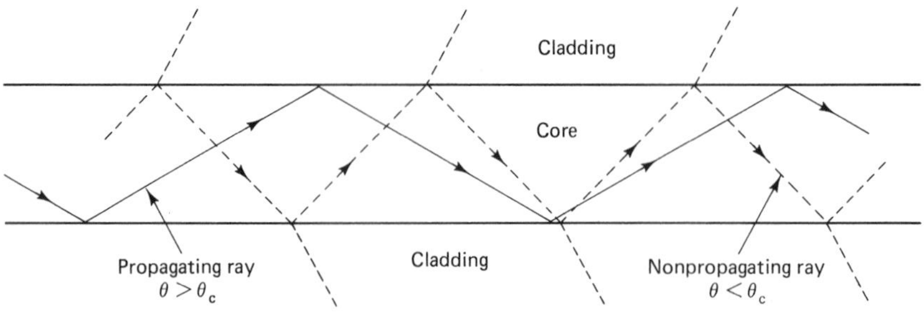

Figure 15.19 Propagation of a light beam through an optical fiber.

On the other hand, the total internal reflection process involves very little reflection loss, the reflectivity at the core–cladding interface being virtually 100%.

It has been indicated that only those light rays that have an angle of incidence greater than θ_c will undergo total internal reflection at the core surface and thus be propagated down the fiber optic light guide. This restriction, in turn, will limit the angles of incidence of the light rays at the end of the light guide that can be propagated through the guide. If we refer to Figure 15.20, we see that at the air–core interface, the maximum angle of incidence for a light ray that can propagate down the guide will be related to the critical angle θ_c by Snell's law as

$$\begin{aligned}\sin\phi &= n_1 \sin(90 - \theta_c) \\ &= n_1 \cos\theta_c = n_1\sqrt{1-\sin^2\theta_c}\end{aligned} \tag{15.2}$$

Since $\sin\theta_c = n_2/n_1$ we have

$$\sin\phi = n_1\sqrt{1-\left(\frac{n_2}{n_1}\right)^2} = \sqrt{n_1^2 - n_2^2}$$

The quantity $\sin\phi$ is called the *numerical aperture* (N.A.) of the light guide, and ϕ represents the maximum *acceptance angle* for propagation of all rays. Only those light rays that are incident on the end of the core and lie within a cone of half-angle ϕ can be propagated through the light guide. If the medium through which the light travels before entering the light guide has an index of refraction n_0, the equation above becomes, $n_0 \sin\phi = \sqrt{n_1^2 - n_2^2}$, so that $\sin\phi = \sqrt{(n_1^2 - n_2^2)}/n_0$, so that we see that with any medium other than air, the acceptance angle will be reduced. In many cases the difference between the core and cladding refractive indices will be small, so that $\sin\phi$ will be small. As a result, the approximation that $\sin\phi \simeq \phi$ can be used, giving N.A. $\simeq \phi = \sqrt{n_2^2 - n_1^2}$. Since $\Delta n = n_2 - n_1$ is small, we can furthermore say that

$$\sqrt{n_2^2 - n_1^2} = \sqrt{(n_2 - n_1)(n_2 + n_1)} \simeq \sqrt{\Delta n(2n_1)}$$

so that N.A. $\simeq \phi \cong \sqrt{2n_1\,\Delta n}$. For example, an optical fiber with a glass core refractive index of $n_1 = 1.62$ and a cladding index of $n_2 = 1.48$ will have a critical angle given by $\sin\theta_c = 1.48/1.62 = 0.9135$, so that $\theta_c = \underline{66.0°}$. The acceptance angle will be given by $\sin\phi = \sqrt{n_1^2 - n_2^2}$, so that $\phi = \underline{41.2°}$ and the numerical aperture is N.A. = $\underline{0.66}$.

In the example just given the difference in the indices of refraction between

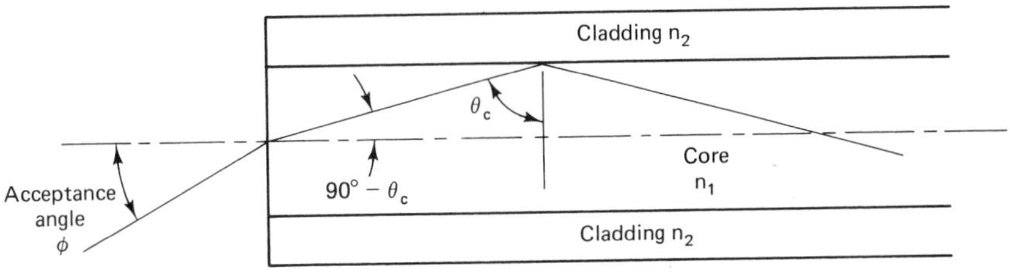

Figure 15.20 Acceptance angle.

the core and the cladding was relatively large (8.6%), so that a large acceptance angle was obtained. Although a large acceptance angle is desirable from the standpoint of the light-gathering ability of the fiber, there are some disadvantages to a wide acceptance angle, principally from the standpoint of signal distortion and the bandwidth capability of the optical fiber.

15.9.1 Examples of Fiber Optic Hybrid Integrated Circuits

The FOT110KG-IR (Burr-Brown) fiber optic transmitter when used with a FOR110KG (Burr-Brown) receiver and a low-attenuation (~2 db/km) optical fiber can be used to provide an optical link of up to 7.4 km without repeaters. The signal transmitted can be an analog signal of up to 1 MHz bandwidth or a digital signal at a 2-Mbit/s NRZ data rate.

The transmitter can supply 90 μW (-10.5 dBm typ.) into a 200-μm-diameter fiber at 880 nm. For a fiber diameter of 63 μm, the optical power into the fiber will be about 8 μW (-21 dBm).

The receiver is capable of a bit error rate (BER) of 10^{-9} at an input optical power level of 15 nW (-48 dBm). If the input power is increased to 17 nW, the BER will drop to 10^{-11}, and at a power level of 20 nW, the BER will be down to 10^{-14}. This last BER corresponds to only one error in 3 years at a 1-Mbit/s data rate.

For a 63-μm fiber the optical power launched into the fiber is about 8 nW (-21 dBm) and for a BER of 10^{-14}, the optical power level at the receiver end of the link must be 20 nW or -47 dBm. If a low-loss silica fiber with an attenuation per unit length of 3 dB/km is used, the link length can be as much as 8 km long.

Simplified schematic diagrams of the FOT110KG-IR transmitter and the FOR110KG receiver are shown in Figure 15.21. For the transmitter, exclusive-or gates are used for the control and enabling of the digital data input. Transistors Q_2 and Q_3 constitute a ratioed current mirror for the control of the LED current. When the external resistor R_{ext} is at zero, the LED current will be a maximum at 100 mA. An analog signal input is also provided. Analog and digital signals can be transmitted simultaneously with this FO system.

In the FOR110KG receiver circuit amplifier A_1 operates as a current-to-voltage converter or transimpedance amplifier. The output of A_1 goes to one input terminal of the comparator and also to the peak detector. The output voltage of the peak detector is divided in half by the R_1–R_2 voltage divider and is then supplied to the other input terminal of the comparator. This serves as the reference voltage for the determination of the 0 and 1 digital logic levels by the comparator. For analog signal transmission the output of A_1 can be used directly.

In Figure 15.22a a FO voice link using the FOT110KG and FOR110KG combination is shown. In Figure 15.22b an analog signal transmission link that offers a high degree of overall system linearity is shown. The analog signal is converted to a frequency-modulated pulse waveform by the voltage-to-frequency (V/F) converter at the transmitter. At the receiver a frequency-to-voltage (F/V) converter is used

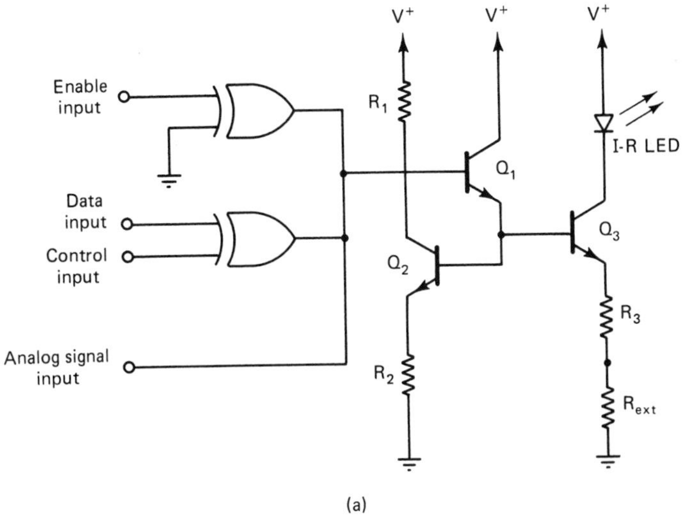

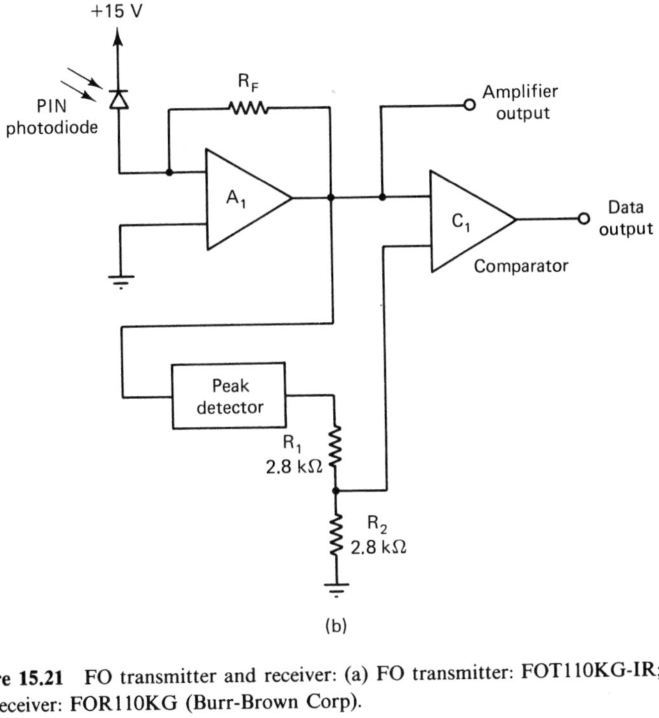

Figure 15.21 FO transmitter and receiver: (a) FO transmitter: FOT110KG-IR; (b) FO receiver: FOR110KG (Burr-Brown Corp).

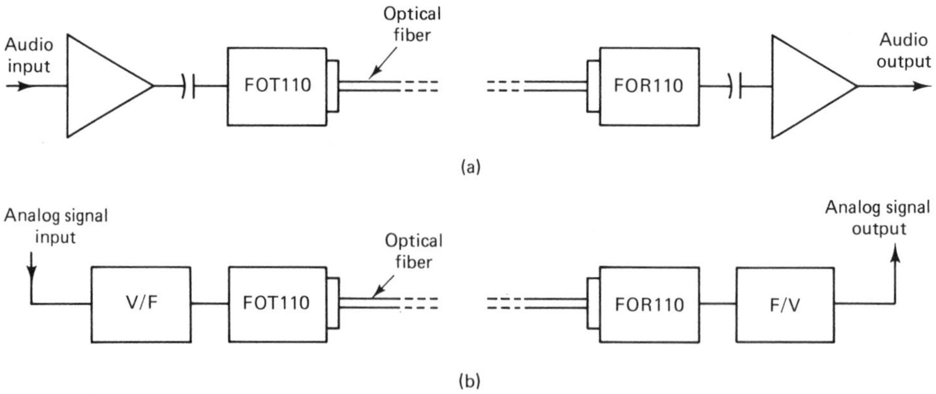

Figure 15.22 Fiber optic analog signal transmission links: (a) voice transmission link; (b) high-linearity analog signal transmission link.

to convert the pulse waveform back to an analog signal. The overall linearity of this system will be determined by the linearity of the V/F and F/V converters.

A hybrid IC V/F and F/V converter that can be used in this application and that offers very good linearity is the VFC52 (Burr-Brown). This IC can be operated as either a V/F or a F/V converter and at frequencies up to 100 kHz. The linearity error is only 0.025% typ. and 0.05% max. over the full-scale frequency range of 0.1 Hz to 100 kHz. Thus when using two of these devices in an FO link, the net system linearity error will be less than 0.1%.

15.10 IMAGE SENSORS

We will now consider linear and area solid-state image sensors, in which an array of image-sensing photoelements is electronically scanned to produce a video output signal. The photoelements can be arranged in a linear array of from as few as 64 photoelements to as many as 4096 photoelements. Circular arrays are also available with up to 720 photoelements. Area image sensor arrays with as many as 185,000 sensing elements are available for use in video camera systems and other applications to produce two-dimensional video pictures.

These image sensors can be used for many applications, especially in the areas of industrial process control and inspection. They can be used for object positioning, including edge and width centering and angular adjustment. Height, width, and diameter control as well as surface defect and contaminant monitoring can also be implemented with image sensors. An important applications area is pattern recognition for robotics and various other automated industrial systems. A related use of image sensors is for optical character recognition. Linear image sensor with large numbers of photoelements can be used for facsimile scanning of documents.

There are two basic types of photoelements for the self-scanned image sensors, the PN junction photodiode and the MOS capacitor-potential well photoelement. We will consider both types of image sensors, starting with the photodiode type.

15.10.1 Photodiode Image Sensor Elements

Let us consider the photodiode circuit shown in Figure 15.23. The MOS transistor is an N-channel device and is fabricated in the same P-type substrate as the photodiode. We note that the N^+ source region of the MOSFET is a continuation of the cathode region of the photodiode. The photodiode anode is the common P-type substrate region of the photodiode and the MOS transistor. There is no external electrical contact made to the photodiode cathode.

When the gate-to-source voltage of the MOSFET is positive and greater than the threshold voltage the transistor will be turned on. For this case the switch shown in the equivalent circuit of Figure 15.23b will be in the closed position and the

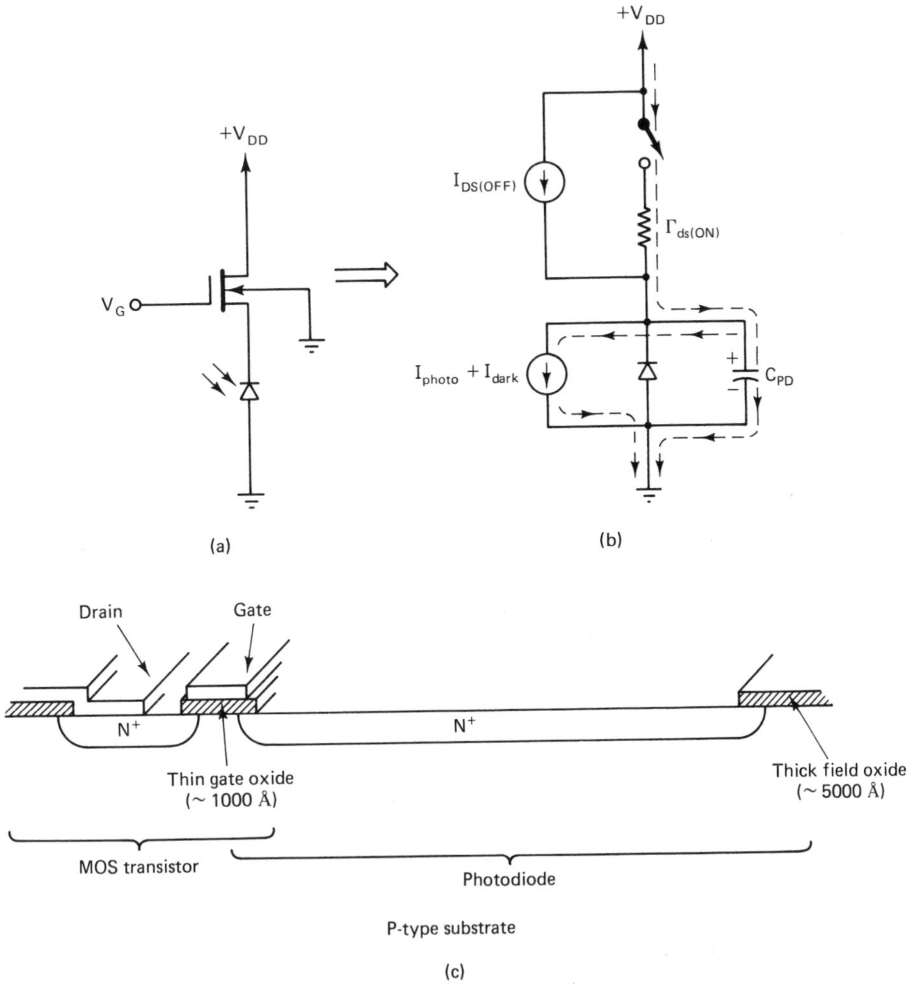

Figure 15.23 Photodiode and MOS switch for photocurrent integration: (a) photodiode and MOSFET; (b) equivalent circuit; (c) integrated photodiode-MOS transistor circuit.

MOSFET will look like a small resistance, $r_{ds\,(\mathrm{ON})}$, which generally will be in the range 100 to 1000 Ω. Under these conditions the photodiode capacitance C_{PD} will be charged from the $+V_{DD}$ supply through the MOSFET drain-to-source channel resistance $r_{ds\,(\mathrm{ON})}$. The voltage across C_{PD} will asymptotically approach the voltage level of $V_G - V_{\mathrm{threshold}}$, where $V_{\mathrm{threshold}}$ is the MOSFET threshold voltage for channel formation. The photodiode capacitance will generally be of the order of 10 pF so that an RC time constant of around 10 ns is a typical value for the charging of C_{PD}. After about 50 ns C_{PD} will be essentially fully charged.

When the gate voltage of the MOSFET goes low (OV) the MOSFET will be turned off. Now it can be represented as a current source $I_{DS\,(\mathrm{OFF})}$, which will be a very small current, generally in the range of 1 pA.

The illumination of the photodiode will produce photogenerated electrons in the P-type substrate and holes in the N^+ diffused layer. These photo-generated minority carriers, together with the thermally generated minority carriers, will diffuse and drift across the PN junction. The results in a current flow of $I_{\mathrm{photo}} + I_{\mathrm{dark}}$, which acts to discharge C_{PD}. If the MOSFET is kept off for a time t_{OFF}, the change in the charge stored in C_{PD} at the end of this time period will be given by the time integral of the combination of the photocurrent I_{photo}, the junction dark reverse leakage current I_{dark}, and the MOSFET leakage current $I_{DS\,(\mathrm{OFF})}$. At the end of the charge integration period t_{OFF}, the change in the stored charge ΔQ will be $\Delta Q = \int_0^{t_{\mathrm{OFF}}} (I_{\mathrm{photo}} + I_{\mathrm{dark}} - I_{DS\,(\mathrm{OFF})})\, dt$, and the corresponding change in the voltage across C_{PD} will be $\Delta V = \Delta Q / C_{\mathrm{PD}}$.

At the end of the integration period the MOSFET is gated on and the photodiode capacitance is recharged back up to its original level. The total charge that flows through the capacitor and around the circuit during this recharge time t_{ON} will be equal to the charge lost by C_{PD} during the integration time t_{OFF}. We note that since the photocurrent is directly related to the radiant power incident on the photodiode, this charge ΔQ will be a function of the time integral of the radiant power incident on the photodiode.

Some of the voltage and current waveforms of interest are shown in Figure 15.24. We note that even though the photodiode sampling or readout time t_{ON} is very short compared to the storage or integration time t_{OFF}, the photodiode will be active all of the time due to the charge storage capability of the photodiode capacitance. As a result, the total charge flowing around the circuit during the sampling (recharge) time will be a function of the radiant energy received by the photodiode during the entire cycle time period of $T = t_{\mathrm{ON}} + t_{\mathrm{OFF}}$.

In Figure 15.25 a generalized graph of the discharge of the photodiode capacitance is presented. Under dark conditions the photodiode capacitance will discharge slowly and if the discharge time is long enough the capacitance can become completely discharged. If we define this self-discharge time as t_{SAT}, we see that this will set an absolute upper limit on the integration time t_{OFF} since for times longer than t_{SAT} the circuit will not be able to respond to any variations in the illumination as a result of the capacitance being fully discharged. Indeed, it is usually desirable that the integration time t_{OFF} be very short compared to t_{SAT} in order to minimize the effect of the dark leakage current on the output signal.

To do an order-of-magnitude calculation for t_{SAT}, let us consider the case of

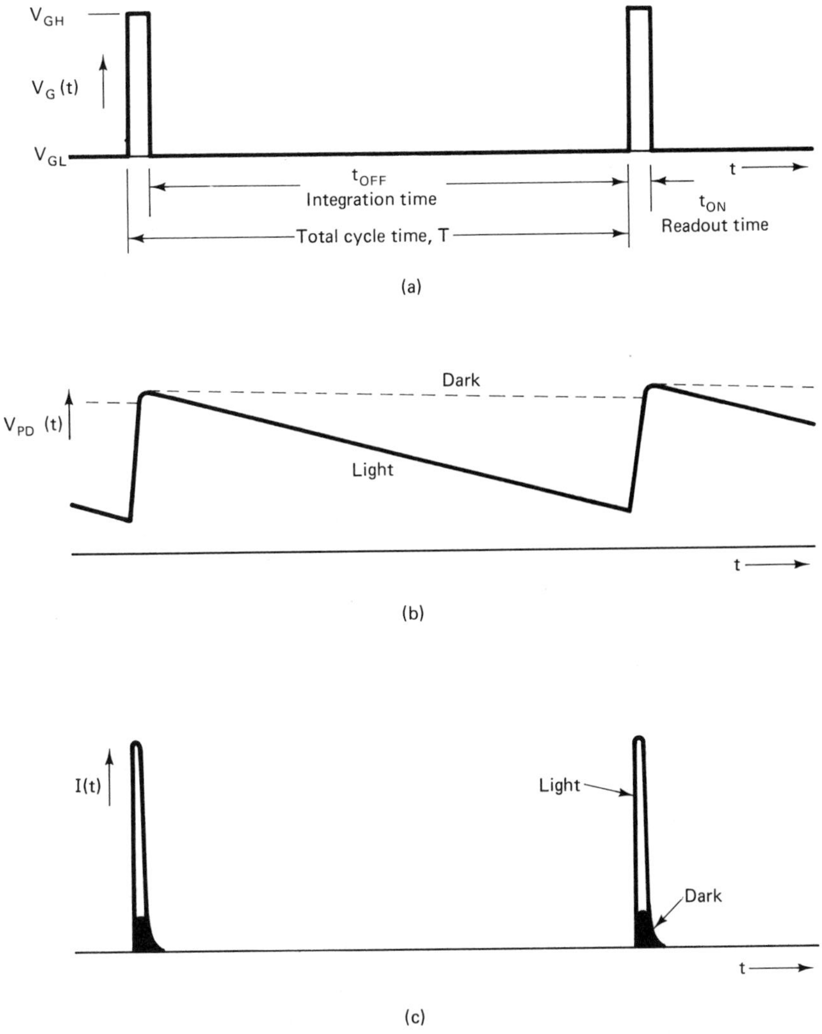

Figure 15.24 Voltage and current waveforms for photodiode operated circuit in the charge storage mode: (a) gate voltage of MOSFET; (b) voltage across photodiode capacitance; (c) recharge current flow through the MOSFET.

an N^+P abrupt junction photodiode for which the charge stored in the PN junction depletion region capacitance is $Q = qNWA$, where N is the substrate doping, W is the width of the depletion region, and A is the junction area. The dark leakage current of the device will be due primarily to the thermal generation of minority carriers in the depletion region. This current will be given approximately by $I_{\text{dark}} = qn_i WA/\tau$, where n_i is the intrinsic carrier density and τ is the sum of the electron and hole lifetimes in the depletion region. If we solve for t_{SAT}, we obtain that $t_{\text{SAT}} = Q/I_{\text{dark}} = (N/n_i)\tau$. For silicon at room temperature (300°K) the value of n_i is 1.4×10^{10} cm^{-3}. As a representative example, let us assume a substrate

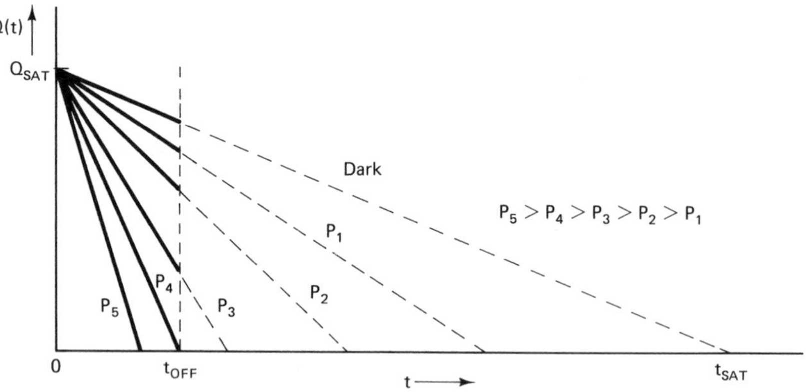

Figure 15.25 Photodiode capacitance discharge curves.

doping level of $N = 3 \times 10^{15}$ cm^{-3} and a net carrier lifetime value of $\tau = 10\ \mu$s. With these values we obtain $t_{SAT} = 2.1$ s. In general, the values of t_{SAT} will be of the order of 1 to 10 s at room temperature, but will decrease exponentially with increasing temperature. We note that t_{SAT} is proportional to the $N\tau$ product, so that for large values of t_{SAT} a moderately large value of substrate doping should be used and the device processing and silicon starting material should be such that a high value for the carrier lifetime is obtained.

It is of interest now to evaluate the initial charge $Q(0)$ stored in the photodiode capacitance at the beginning of the charge integration period. This initial charge is important because it will determine the saturation exposure, which is the maximum amount of radiant energy that can be received by the photodiode during the integration time before the diode capacitance becomes fully discharged. If we again assume the case of an abrupt junction N$^+$P photodiode, the value of $Q(0)$ and the corresponding depletion layer width will be given by $Q(0) = qNWA$ and $W = \sqrt{2\epsilon V_J/qN}$. In the last equation $V_J = \phi + V_R$, where V_J is the total junction voltage, ϕ is the contact potential of the junction (~0.8 V), and V_R is the reverse-bias voltage applied across the junction at the end of the recharge time. We will again choose the substrate doping N to be $N = 3 \times 10^{15}$ cm^{-3}. If we let $V_J = 5.0$ V and choose a diode junction area of 50 μm $\times$ 50 μm, we obtain an initial photodiode charge of $Q(0) =$ 1.7 pC. The corresponding value of dark current based on a net depletion region lifetime of 10 μs will be 0.8 pA and the self-discharge time will be 2.1 s.

The photocurrent I_{photo} is related to the optical power density or irradiance P by $I_{\text{photo}} = PA\mathcal{R}_c$, where $\mathcal{R}_c$ is the current responsivity. The relationship between the saturation exposure and the initial charge $Q(0)$ will be obtained from $I_{\text{photo}}t_{ON} = PA\mathcal{R}_c t_{ON} = Q(0)$. If $\mathcal{R}_c$ has a typical value of 0.5 A/W at a wavelength of 900 nm, we obtain for the saturation exposure a value given by

$$\text{saturation exposure} = \frac{Q(0)}{A\mathcal{R}_c} = \underline{1.4 \times 10^{-7}\ \text{J/cm}^2} = \underline{0.14\ \mu W\text{-s/cm}^2} \qquad (15.3)$$

We should note here that since $Q(0)$ is directly proportional to the photodiode area, the value of the saturation exposure will be independent of the device area.

If the radiant energy source is an incandescent tungsten lamp at a color temperature of 2870°K, an appropriate current responsivity value will be about 0.1 A/W. The corresponding saturation exposure level will be 0.71 μW–s/cm², and in photometric terms this corresponds to an exposure of 0.013 fc-s.

If the photodiodes are read out at a rate of 30 times per second the corresponding integration time will be approximately 33 ms. The optical power density corresponding to a saturation exposure level will be 4.2 μW/cm² at a wavelength of 900 nm and 21 μW/cm² for the incandescent light source. For the latter case this will correspond to an illumination level of 0.405 fc.

In Figure 15.26 a graph of the charge output ΔQ during the readout time as a function of the exposure is given based on the example above. The characteristics for both the 900-nm monochromatic light source and the incandescent light source are shown.

The lower end of the dynamic operating range of this device will be set by the noise developed in the system. It is of interest, however, to determine the radiant power density that will produce a charge output ΔQ equal to that produced by the dark current. We will use the dark current value of 0.8 pA as calculated in a previous example. The optical power density that will produce a photocurrent that is just equal to this dark current will be 64 nW/cm² at 900 nm and 320 nW/cm² for the incandescent source. For an integration time of 33 ms the corresponding exposure levels are 2.1 nW-s/cm² and 10.7 nW-s/cm², respectively. Since the corresponding saturation exposure levels are 140 nW-s/cm² and 710 nW-s/cm², we note that the ratio of the saturation exposure level to the "dark current" exposure level is 66 in both cases. This corresponds essentially to the ratio of the saturation time to the integration time.

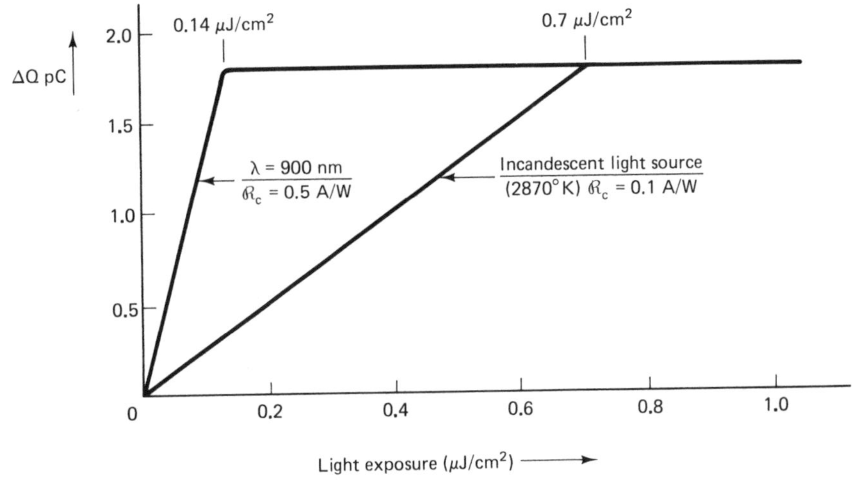

Figure 15.26 Charge output as a function of exposure.

15.10.2 MOS Capacitor to Increase Saturation Time

The value of the saturation or self-discharge time of the photodiode can be increased by the addition of a MOS capacitor to the circuit as shown in Figure 15.27. The expression for t_{SAT} has previously been given as $t_{SAT} = Q(0)/I_{dark}$. By adding a MOS capacitor in parallel with the photodiode, the value of the initial stored charge $Q(0)$ can be substantially increased without a corresponding increase in the dark leakage current, this being due to the excellent insulating properties of the thin SiO_2 layer that forms the dielectric layer of the MOS capacitor.

As an example, let us consider the same photodiode as in the earlier examples and now add a MOS capacitor of area equal to the photodiode area. With an oxide thickness of 1000 Å the MOS capacitance will be given by $C_{MOS} = \epsilon_{ox}A/t_{ox} = 3.8 \times 8.85 \times 10^{-14}\ \text{F/cm}^2 \times (50\ \mu\text{m})^2/(1 \times 10^{-5}\ \text{cm}) = \underline{0.84\ \text{pF}}$. For a voltage across the capacitance of 5 V at the start of the integration period the MOS capacitor will store an initial charge of 4.2 pC. Since the charge stored in the photodiode junction capacitance is 1.7 pC, the total stored charge will now be 5.9 pC. The value of the self-discharge time will now be $t_{SAT} = (Q_{PD} + Q_{MOS})/I_{dark} = 5.9\ \text{pC}/0.8\ \text{pA} = \underline{7.1\ \text{s}}$. Thus, by the addition of the MOS capacitor the self-discharge time has been increased from 2.1 s to 7.1 s. The corresponding increase in the stored

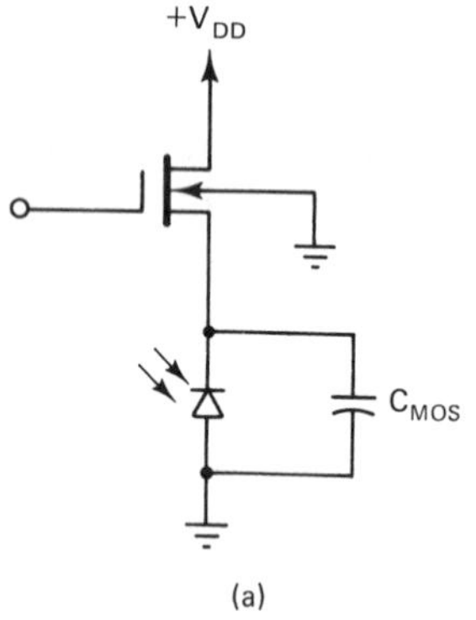

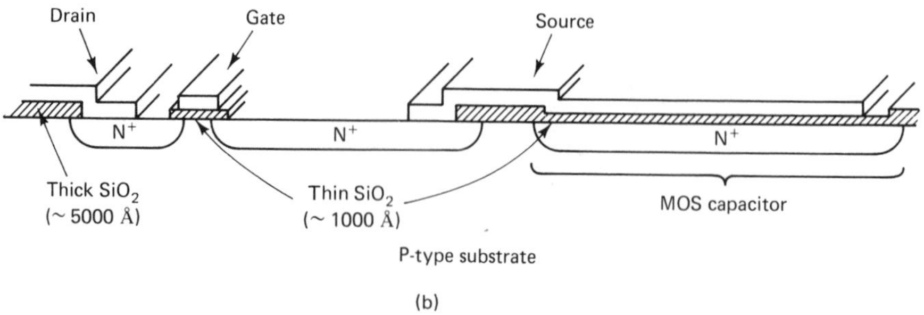

Figure 15.27 Addition of MOS capacitor to photodiode: (a) photodiode-MOS transistor-MOS capacitor circuit; (b) photodiode-MOS capacitor-MOS transistor structure.

charge from 1.7 pC to 5.9 pC will increase the saturation exposure level and the dynamic range by a factor of 3.5.

The basic trade-off involved in the use of the MOS capacitor to increase the initial stored charge is the additional chip area that is required. For a linear image sensor this may be acceptable since the MOS capacitors can be placed parallel to the photodiode array so that the photodiode area, the photodiode center-to-center spacing, and the total length of the photodiode array can remain unchanged. For an area image sensor, however, the MOS capacitors cannot be added to the two-dimensional array without affecting the photodiode active area and the center-to-center spacing. As a result, the use of MOS capacitors to increase the initial stored charge is generally used only for linear image sensors.

15.10.3 Self-Scanning Photodiode Linear Image Sensor

A basic circuit for a self-scanned photodiode line sensor is shown in Figure 15.28. This linear image sensor consists of an array of N^+P photodiodes on a common P-type silicon substrate. Associated with each photodiode is a MOS transistor switch, the gate electrode of which is connected to a digital shift register. The clock pulses applied to the shift register will result in one MOSFET at a time being turned on which will connect the corresponding photodiode to the common video signal bus. Since this video signal bus is essentially at ground potential, the photodiode capacitance C_{PD} will be charged to a voltage equal to V_{SS} in such a direction as to provide a reverse-bias voltage across the PN junction.

After the MOSFET is turned off, the photodiode capacitance will be become partially discharged due to the combination of the photocurrent and the dark leakage current. Associated with this partial discharge of the capacitance there will be a decrease in the voltage across the photodiode from V_{SS} to $V_{SS} - \Delta V$, where $\Delta V = \Delta Q/C_{PD}$. The next time the MOSFET is switched on, the photodiode capacitance will again be recharged so that the voltage across it is brought up to V_{SS}. In order to do this an amount of charge ΔQ equal to that lost by C_{PD} during the integration period must be supplied to the photodiode capacitance. There will accordingly be a short pulse of current flowing from the video signal bus through the MOSFET and the photodiode during the sampling time. This current pulse will flow through the charge-to-voltage converter circuit, which is basically a current integrator, and produce an output voltage pulse that is proportional to the charge ΔQ.

As the shift register sequentially turns on the various MOSFETs of the image sensor array, a sequence of charge pulses will be delivered to the charge-to-voltage converter. The output of this circuit will be an overlapping sequence of pulses. The amplitude of each pulse will be proportional to the time integral of the radiant power incident on a corresponding photodiode during the integration time.

Example of linear image sensors. We will now consider some examples of linear image sensors that use photodiodes operating in the integration mode with the charge being stored in the photodiode junction capacitance. A series of linear image sensor arrays of this type are made by Reticon with devices having 64, 128, 256, 1728, 2048, and 4096 photodiode elements being available. The center-to-center

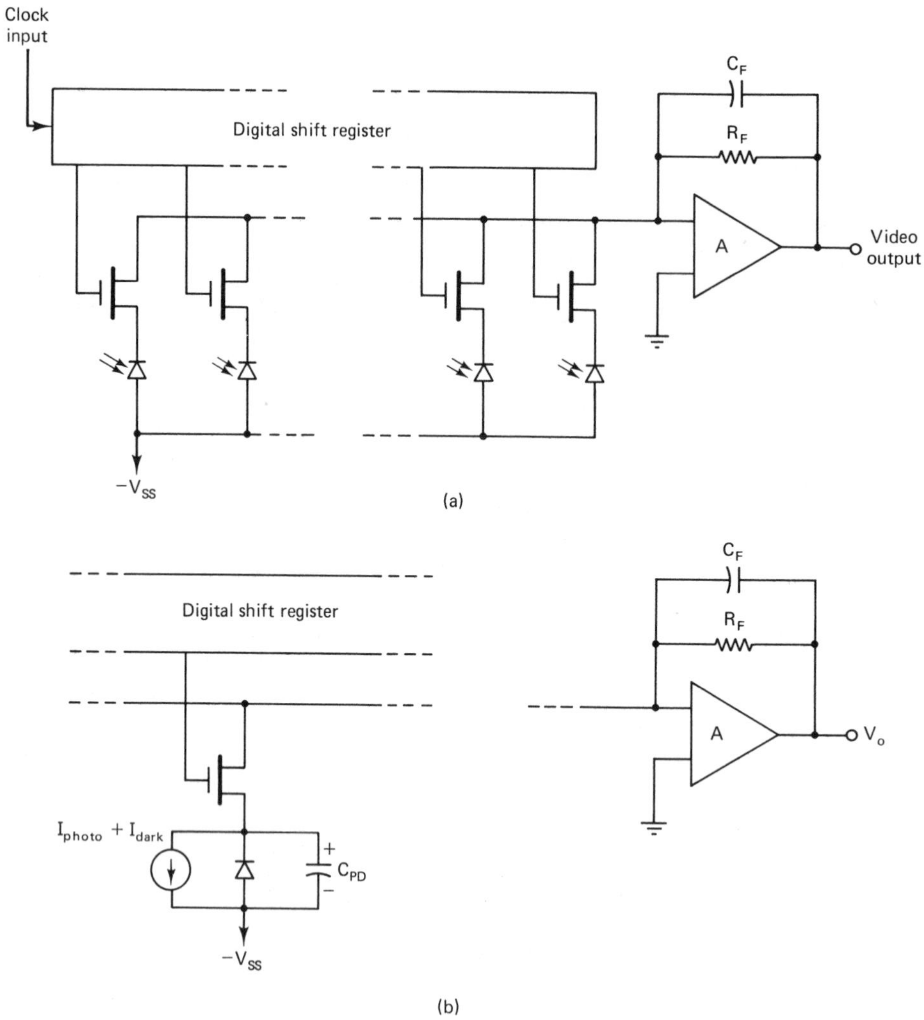

Figure 15.28 Photodiode line scanner: (a) basic circuit; (b) line scanner showing photodiode equivalent circuit.

element spacings range from 15 to 50 μm and the widths range from 16 μm to as much as 2.5 mm. For these devices the charge stored by the photodiodes is read out in serial form by a two-phase digital shift register, as shown in Figure 15.28.

The shortest array is the RL64A with 64 elements that have a 50-μm center-to-center spacing and a 50-μm width. The maximum sampling rate is 10 MHz. The longest array is the RL4096, with 4096 elements that have a center-to-center spacing of 15 μm for a total length of 61 mm for the array. Two element widths are available, 16 μm and 508 μm. This device also has a maximum sampling rate of 10 MHz. The large number and small size of the photoelements of this device make it useful for facsimile scanning and related applications.

Circular image sensor arrays are also available and are useful for such applications as focusing, angle, and rotation measurements. An example of a circular array is the RL64 (Reticon), which has 64 elements on 100-μm centers and a 100-μm width located on a circle with a diameter of 2 mm. The maximum sampling rate is 2.5 MHz. The RL720B (Reticon) is a circular image sensor array with 720 elements that have a 31-μm center-to-center spacing and a width of 200 μm. The photodiode array is located on a circle with a diameter of 7.2 mm, and the photodiode element spacing corresponds to angular increments of only 0.5°. The maximum sampling rate for this array is 1.0 MHz.

15.10.4 Image Sensors Using Analog Shift Registers

The linear image scanners that have been discussed thus far have the photodiodes connected to a common video output line via the MOS multiplexing transistors. As a result, the total capacitance between this video output line and ground can be quite large, especially for the case of large arrays. For example, for the case of the RL128G (Reticon), which has 128 photodiodes, the video line capacitance is 5 pF. This goes up to 10 pF for the RL256G, 20 pF for the RL512G, 30 pF for the RL768F, and reaches 40 pF for the 1024G. For area image sensors with many thousands of photodiodes the capacitance will be even much higher than these values. This video output line capacitance can limit the video bandwidth of the system, especially for the case of very large linear arrays and area image sensor arrays.

The problem of a high video line capacitance can be solved by the use of an analog shift register, as shown in Figure 15.29. In this linear image scanner all of the MOS switches are turned on at the same time during the short sampling period once each scanning cycle. During this short sampling time the photodiode capacitances are recharged and the corresponding charge deficiency is transferred to the analog shift register. This analog shift register can be in the form of a charge-coupled device (CCD) or a bucket-brigade device (BBD). During the following integration time these

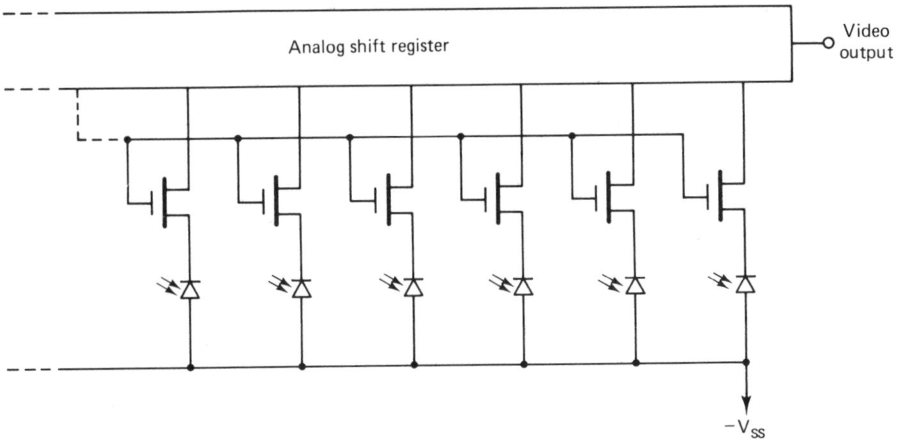

Figure 15.29 Image sensor using an analog shift register.

charge packets will be transferred through the shift register to the video output. The charge packets supplied by the individual photodiodes to the shift register will then appear at the output in serial form.

We note that the video output line is connected only to the output terminal of the shift register. As a result of the much reduced capacitance, video sampling rates in excess of 5 MHz are possible.

15.10.5 Area Image-Sensing Devices

We will now consider area image sensor arrays that use photodiodes in the charge storage mode. We will first consider the system of Figure 15.30, showing the use of MOSFET switches to provide for the multiplexing of a two-dimensional array of photodiodes to a common video output line. In this circuit an individual photodiode is connected to the video output line only when the MOSFET switches connected to the selected x-address and y-address lines are turned on simultaneously.

This image sensor system has the advantage of not requiring an analog shift register for the temporary storage of the video signal. However, the video output line capacitance will be relatively large since it is connected to all of the x-address line MOSFETs.

Examples of this type of area image sensor are the RA32x32A (Reticon) with 1024 photodiode image-sensing elements and the RA50x50A (Reticon) with 2500 elements. For both devices the photodiode image-sensing elements have a 100-μm center-to-center spacing in both the x and y directions. The maximum photodiode sampling rate is 5 MHz. The video output line capacitance is 100 pF for the RA32x32A and 250 pF for the RA50x50A, so that the load resistance must be limited to about 600 Ω for the RA32x32A and 250 Ω for the RA50x50A in order to obtain a 2.5-MHz video bandwidth.

A diagram of an area image sensor that uses an analog shift register is shown in Figure 15.31. The stored charge accumulated by the photodiodes is transferred line by line into the two analog shift registers. The shift registers are of the two-phase tetrode MOSFET bucket-brigade type, with the odd-numbered photodiodes of each line being connected to the top shift register and the even-numbered elements being connected to the bottom shift register.

The digital shift register will select one line of the photodiode array at a time. When the odd line gate is high, only the odd-numbered lines will be subject to selection. After all of the odd-numbered lines have been successively read out, the odd-line gate voltage goes low and the even-line gate goes high. The even-numbered lines will then be read out into the analog shift registers. This scanning of the odd-numbered lines and then the even-numbered lines can be used to produce a television picture with two interlaced fields per frame.

As each line is selected there will be a transfer of the stored charge from the odd-numbered photodiodes to the upper analog shift register and from the even-numbered photodiodes to the lower shift register. After this charge transfer has taken place, the charge packets are transferred through the bucket-brigade shift registers to the video output transistors Q_2. Transistor Q_1 is used to reset the gate voltage

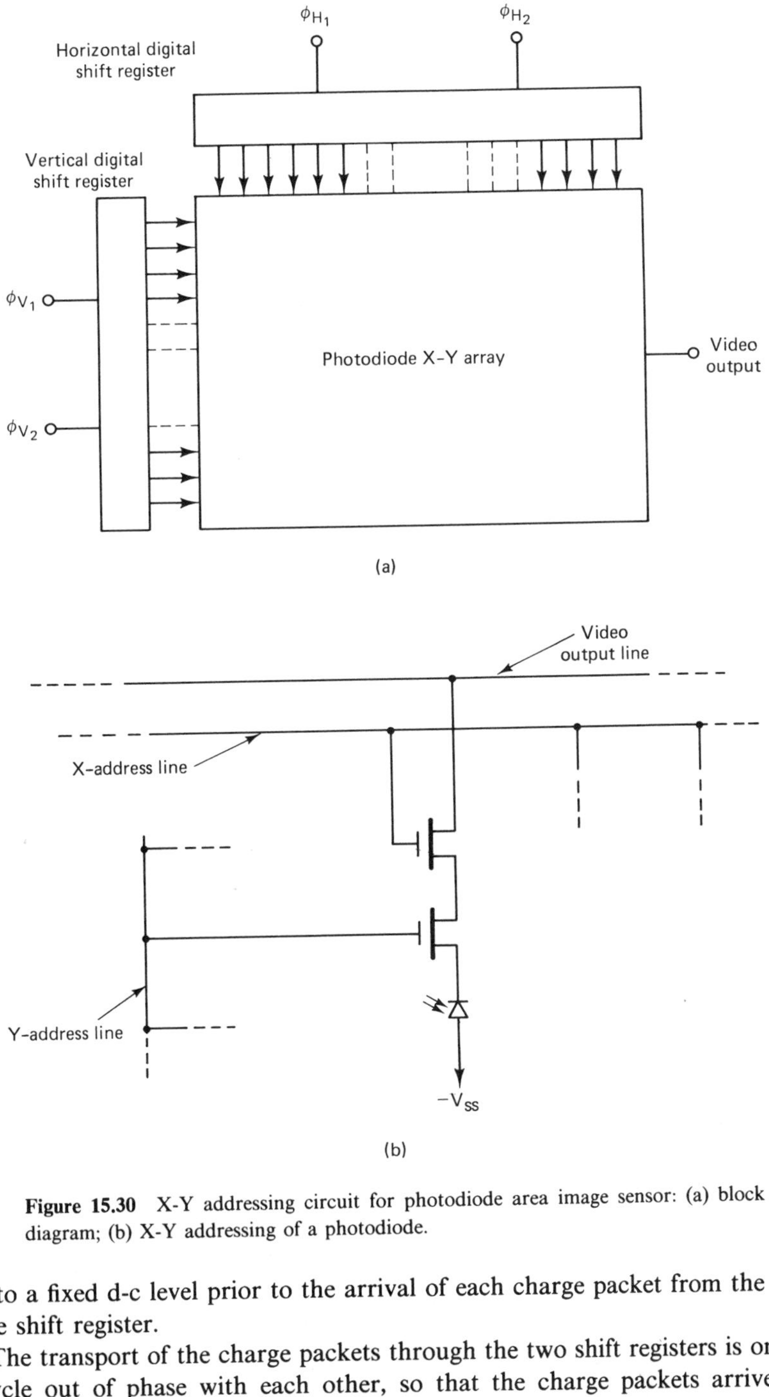

Figure 15.30 X-Y addressing circuit for photodiode area image sensor: (a) block diagram; (b) X-Y addressing of a photodiode.

of Q_2 to a fixed d-c level prior to the arrival of each charge packet from the bucket-brigade shift register.

The transport of the charge packets through the two shift registers is one clock half-cycle out of phase with each other, so that the charge packets arrive at the two video outputs on alternate clock phases. The two output voltages, V_{o1} and V_{o2},

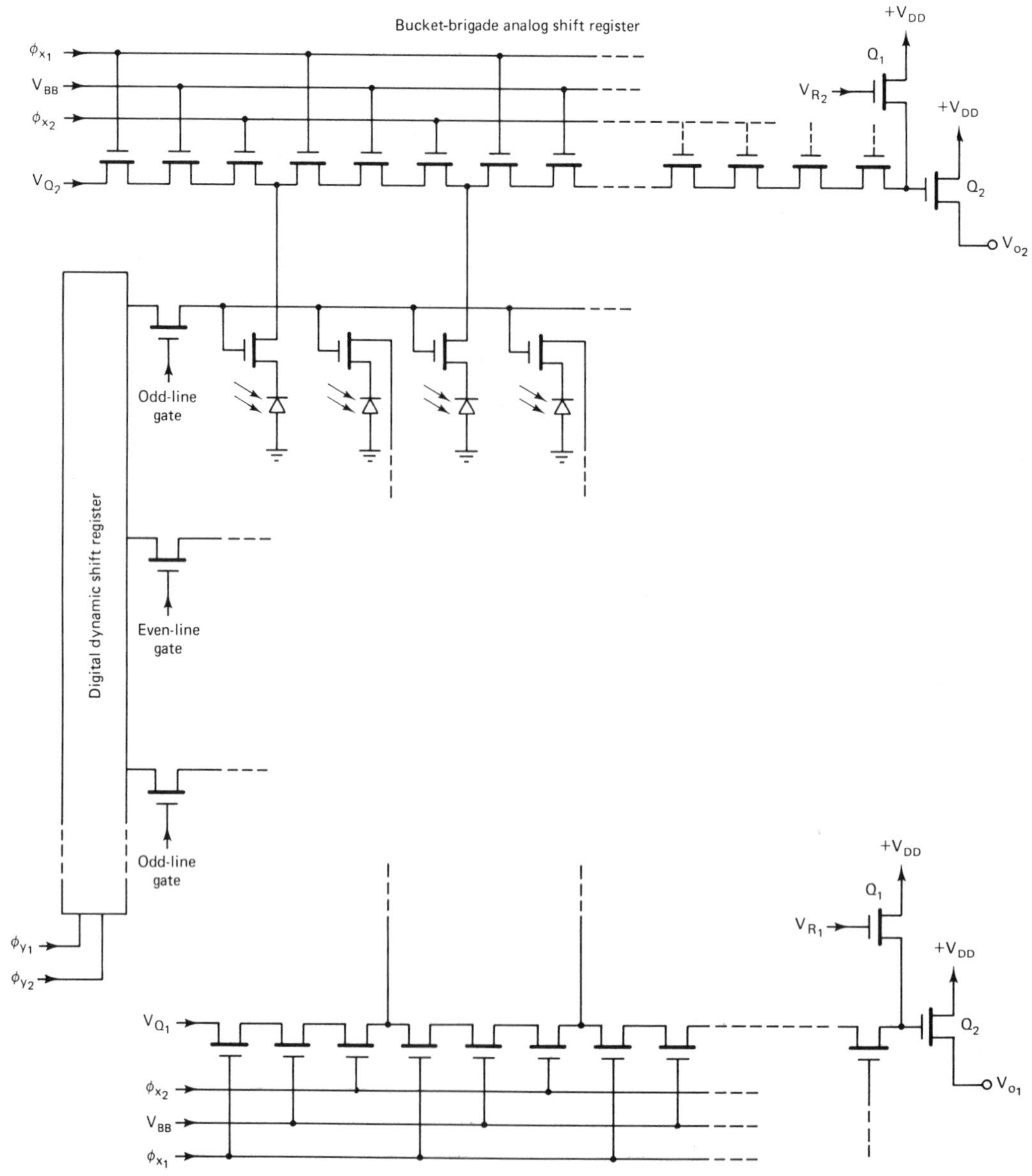

Figure 15.31 Image sensor (Reticon). Permission given by Reticon Corporation, a subsidiary of EG&G Inc., (Copyright 1977).

can therefore be combined to obtain the total video output signal from both the even- and odd-numbered photodiodes of each line.

Examples of area image sensors that use photodiodes as the sensing elements and analog shift registors are the RA100x100A with 10,000 elements, the RA128x128 with 16,384 elements, and the RA256x256 with 65,536 elements, all manufactured by Reticon. The first two image sensor arrays have photodiode sensing elements on a 60-μm center-to-center spacing in both x and y directions, and for the RA256x256 the spacing is 40 μm. The maximum sampling rate for all three devices is 5 MHz.

15.11 CHARGE-COUPLED DEVICES FOR IMAGE SENSING

In this section the application of charge-coupled devices (CCDs) to image sensing will be discussed. The CCDs are used as parallel input–serial output analog shift registers to produce a serial readout of the charge accumulated by an array of photoelements. The basic operation of CCDs has been discussed in Chapter 12. The photoelements used for the CCD image sensors are usually of the MOS capacitor-potential well type, which will be discussed next.

15.11.1 MOS Photoelements

The MOS photoelement uses the potential well produced by the MOS capacitor structure of Figure 15.32a. Electrons that are produced in the depletion region or in the adjacent P-type substrate region will diffuse or drift into the potential well near the silicon surface and be accumulated there. One source of these electrons is the thermal generation of electron–hole pairs, and the other and more important source is the photogeneration process. The photons for this second process can enter the device through the back side or more commonly through a thin polycrystalline silicon gate electrode, as shown in Figure 15.32a.

In Figure 15.32b a diagram is shown of the variation of the potential energy of electrons as a function of distance from the silicon surface for the MOS photoele-

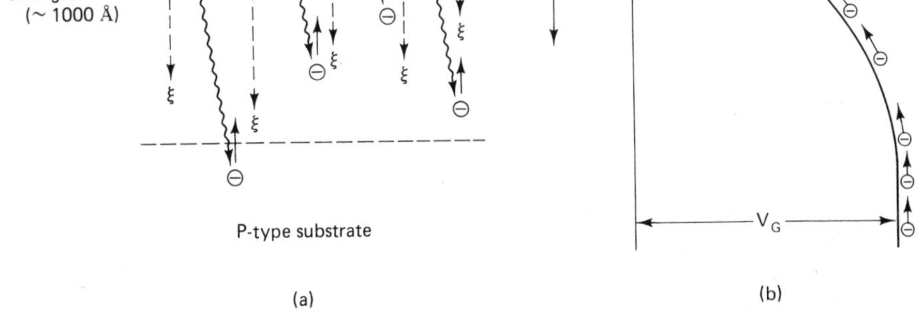

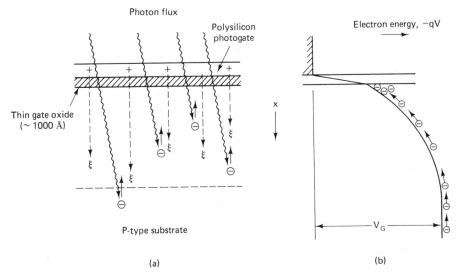

Figure 15.32 MOS photosite: (a) MOS capacitor photosite; (b) potential well diagram.

ment. We note that at the same time that the holes are repelled from the surface regions the electrons will be drawn to this same region. The surface regions will act as a potential well for electrons. Electrons will diffuse into this potential well and eventually fill it up. The supply of electrons is limited, so that will happen gradually. The silicon substrate is P-type, so that the electrons will be minority carriers and the thermal equilibrium electron concentration will be extremely small. Nevertheless, electrons will be continuously generated due to the thermal generation process in the P-type substrate region and in the depletion region, so that the potential well will become filled up eventually. The filling up of the potential well can be substantially accelerated by the photogenerated electrons that result from the illumination of the photoelements.

As the potential well fills up with electrons, the depletion region capacitance becomes discharged, the voltage across the depletion region will decrease, and correspondingly the width of the depletion region will become smaller. The voltage drop across the depletion region will not decrease all of the way to zero, since this would completely wipe out the potential well and there would be nothing to hold the accumulated electrons. The voltage drop across the depletion region will decrease to a value corresponding to that needed for the maintenance of the potential well. This will be about 500 to 700 mV for a completely filled well. If the voltage applied between the gate electrode and the P-type substrate is 15 V, we see that when the potential well is filled almost all of the applied voltage will be dropped across the oxide layer. Under the equilibrium situation of a filled well, the flow of electrons into the well will be exactly balanced by the outward diffusion of electrons from the well back into the P-type substrate.

The thickness of the gate oxide will typically be about 1000 Å. For an oxide of this thickness, the capacitance between the gate electrode and the N-type surface inversion layer will be 3.4×10^{-8} F/cm^2. For the case of a MOS photoelement with dimensions of 20 μm $\times$ 20 μm, the oxide capacitance will be 0.134 pF. If the gate voltage is 10 V, the maximum charge Q_{SAT} in the surface inversion layer when completely filled will be 1.34 pC.

The thermal generation of electrons in the P-type substrate and in the depletion region will correspond to a dark current density generally in the range 10 to 100 nA/cm^2. For the example under consideration the total dark current will therefore be in the range 0.04 to 0.4 pA. Using the saturation charge density of $Q_{SAT} = 1.34$ pC, the time required for the potential well to fill up completely under dark conditions will be given by $t_{SAT} = Q_{SAT}/I_{dark}$. This saturation or self-discharge time will be in the range 3 to 30 s.

15.11.2 Integration Time

The photon flux integration time is the time interval during which the photogenerated electrons are accumulated in the potential wells at the silicon surface. At the end of this integration time the accumulated electron charge packets are transferred to an adjoining CCD analog shift register array. As long as this integration time is short compared to the self-discharge time t_{SAT}, the potential well will not become saturated with electrons resulting from the dark current. It is usually desirable to limit the integration time to such values that the charge in the inversion layer due to the dark current is no more than about 1% of the saturation level Q_{SAT}. We see therefore that the integration time should generally be limited to a maximum of about 30 ms. If this is done, the electron charge stored in the potential well at the end of the integration time will be proportional to the time integral of the photon flux density incident on the device during the integration period. An exception to this is under very low-light-level conditions, for which the dark current can represent a substantial fraction of the accumulated charge.

The self-discharge time for the MOS photoelements is comparable to that of the photodiodes described earlier. We also note that again the self-discharge time will be relatively independent of device area.

15.11.3 CCD Image Sensor Charge Storage and Transfer

The CCD image sensor will have an array of MOS photoelements on a common silicon substrate. At the end of a photon flux integration period each photoelement will have stored in it a packet of electrons trapped in the potential well at the silicon surface. The net charge stored in these potential wells will be directly proportional to the radiant energy received by the individual photoelement during the integration time. The MOS photoelements perform the same basic photon flux integration and charge storage function that is done by the photodiode arrays described earlier.

A CCD analog shift register can perform the functions of both photon flux integration and charge transfer. However, as a result of the time that is required to shift the charge packets through the CCD array, the individual charge packets reaching the end of the array will contain contributions from the incident photon flux all along the length of the CCD array. The charge packets will not be representative of the radiant energy received by the individual MOS photoelements of the array, but will be some smeared representation of this due to the additional photogenerated charge received by the charge packet as it is being transferred along the array. As a result, it is usually found to be desirable to separate the two functions of photon flux integration and charge transfer. The CCD image sensor examples to be considered in the next section are representative of this separation of functions.

15.11.4 CCD Linear Image Sensors

An example of a CCD linear sensor is the CCD111 (Fairchild). This sensor has 256 image-sensing elements that are each 13 μm long and 17 μm wide with a 13-μm center-to-center spacing as shown in Figure 15.33. The photoelements are MOS capacitors using polycrystalline silicon gate electrodes, so front-surface illumination can be used. The MOS photoelements are defined in the width direction by the photogate electrode and in the length direction by the P^+-channel stop-diffused layers, which are 5 μm wide.

The organization of this image sensor is shown in Figure 15.34. The image-sensing photoelements are used only for charge storage and not as part of the CCD analog shift register. The CCD analog shift register is shielded from the light by an aluminum metallization layer so that image smearing effects are minimized.

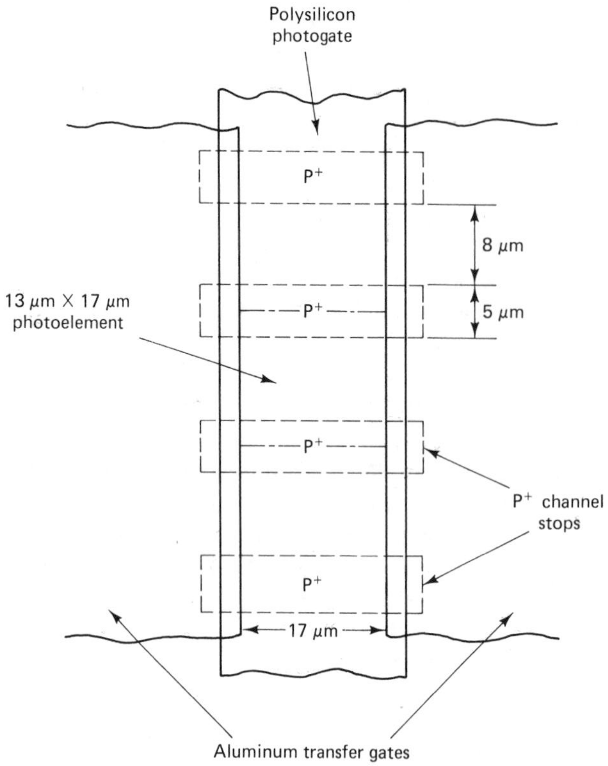

Figure 15.33 MOS photoelement dimensions: CCD111 (Fairchild CCD Imaging).

The charge accumulated by the 256 photoelements are transferred to the two 128-bit CCD shift registers by the transfer gates. During the photon flux integration time the transfer gates are low (~0.5 V). The photogate which is the polycrystalline silicon electrode over the photoelements is always kept high at +10 V. The silicon substrate is P-type, so that this photogate voltage will produce a potential well for the accumulation of the photogenerated electrons.

The CCD shift register is a buried-channel device having a very thin N-type phosphorus ion-implanted layer near the surface so that the potential well minimum will not be right at the Si/SiO_2 interface, but rather at a small distance (~0.1 μm) from the silicon surface. The resulting slight separation of the electron charge packets from the surface will minimize the trapping of electrons by surface states at the Si/SiO_2 interface and will result in a higher value for the charge-transfer efficiency for the CCD shift register. This will allow the shift register to run at a 5.0-MHz clock transfer frequency.

At the end of the photon flux integration time the transfer gates go high (+8 V) and the charge stored in the photoelements is transferred to the two analog shift registers. The charge packet from each photoelement will go to the adjoining CCD shift register element that is in the high state (+10 V). When the transfer gate is high, the ϕ_{1A} and ϕ_{1B} shift register elements will be high, and the ϕ_{2A} and ϕ_{2B} elements will be low. The arrangement of the two shift registers is such that the ϕ_{1A} elements in the top shift register are opposite the odd-numbered photoelements

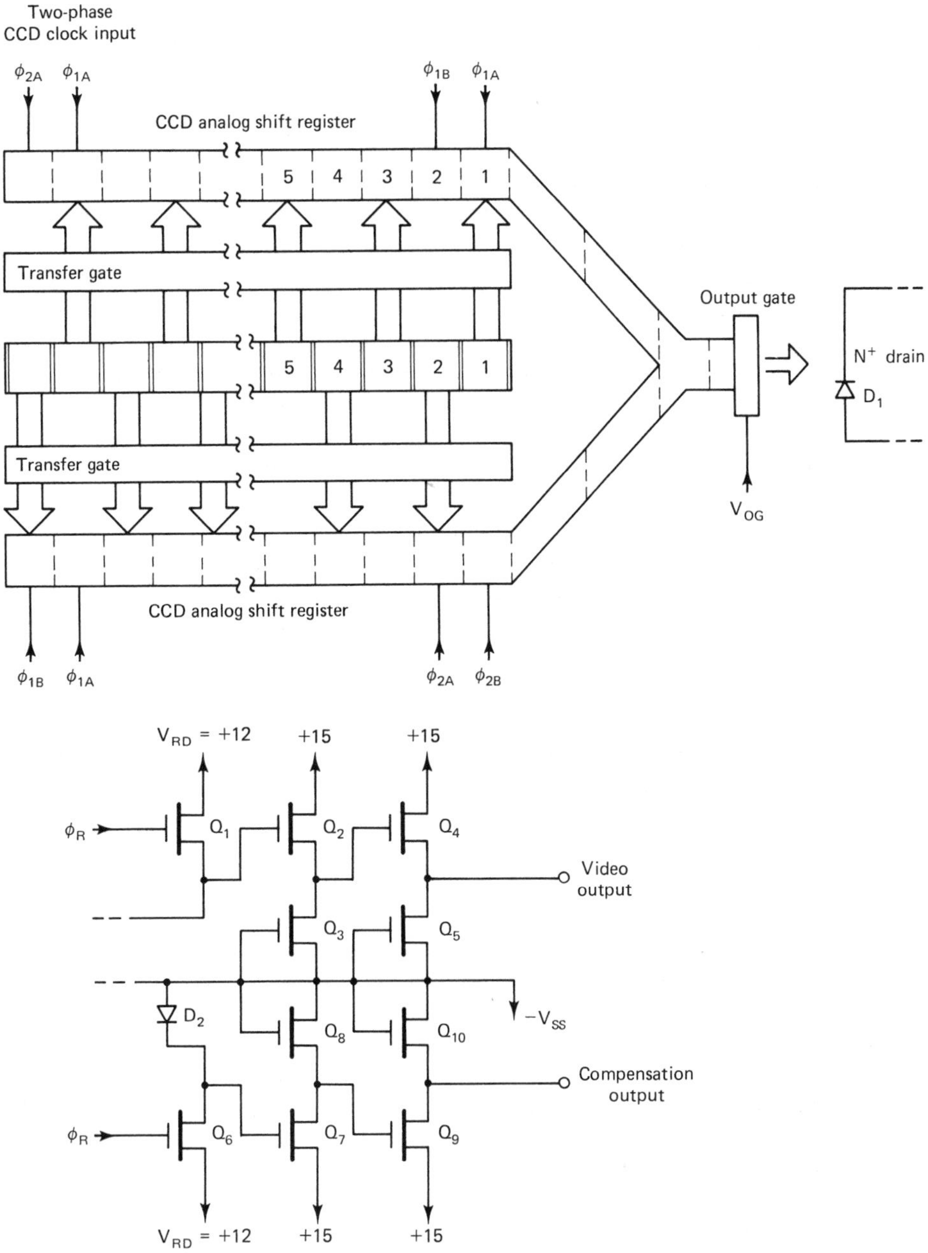

Figure 15.34 Linear scan CCD image sensor: CCD111 (Fairchild CCD Imaging).

and the ϕ_{1B} elements in the bottom shift register are opposite the even-numbered photoelements. The charge packets from the odd-numbered photoelements will therefore go to the top shift register and the charge packets from the even-numbered photoelements will go to the bottom shift register.

After the charge packets have been transferred to the two shift registers, the transfer gate goes low and the next integration period begins. The charge that has been loaded into the shift register is then transferred to the N^+ drain region of the output diode D_1. The two phase-shift registers operate in synchronism with $\phi_{1A} = \phi_{1B}$ and $\phi_{2A} = \phi_{2B}$. The charge packets from the two shift registers are combined in the N^+ drain region and appear on alternate clock half-cycles. As a result, the combined video information will now appear at a rate equal to twice the shift register clock frequency. With a maximum shift register clock frequency of 5.0 MHz the rate at which the video output pulses will appear will be 10 MHz. The corresponding maximum video signal bandwidth will be 5 MHz.

After the charge packets have been transferred through the two CCD shift registers they pass through a common channel that is formed in the substrate by the output gate. The output gate voltage V_{OG} is always kept high at +5 V, so that this channel is always open to charge packets from both shift registers. The charge packets are then collected by the N^+ region of the readout diode D_1.

The output charge packets are supplied to the gate of transistor Q_2. The reset transistor Q_1 is used to periodically drain off the charge from the gate of Q_2. The reset clock pulses ϕ_R are applied to the gate of Q_1, which has a constant drain voltage V_{RD} of +12 V. When the reset clock ϕ_R is high (+8 V), the reset transistor will be on and the junction capacitance of the readout diode D_1 charges up to V_{RD}. Then when the reset clock goes low (+0.5 V) the reset transistor will be off and the junction capacitance of the readout diode will start to discharge. This discharge will be due to the combination of the dark leakage current and the electron charge packets coming into the N^+ drain region of D_1 from the two shift registers. As the electron packets enter the drain region the voltage across the readout diode will decrease by an amount $\Delta Q/C$, where ΔQ is the charge contained in the electron packet delivered by shift register and C is the sum of the diode junction capacitance and the capacitances resulting from Q_1 and Q_2.

The reset transistor is turned on prior to every ϕ_1 and ϕ_2 clock pulse, so that the readout diode capacitance starts off fully charged before the arrival of the electron charge packet.

The voltage across the readout diode D_1 is fed to the gate of Q_1, which is connected as a source follower and uses Q_3 as an active load. This source-follower stage is followed by a second source-follower stage that consists of Q_4 with Q_5 being used as an active load. This cascaded source-follower configuration helps to isolate the readout diode from the load and provides for an output impedance of 1000 Ω.

There will be some capacitative feedthrough of the reset clock pulses to the video output. This feedthrough of the reset pulses can be substantially canceled out by the compensation circuit consisting of diode D_2 and transistors Q_6 through Q_{10}. This compensation circuit is a mirror image of the video output circuit just discussed above. The only difference is that the readout diode D_2 in this circuit does not receive any charge packets from the CCD shift registers. The reset pulse feedthrough in the compensation circuit will be approximately the same as in the video signal circuit. In addition, the effect of the dark leakage currents of the readout diodes on the d-c output level will also be approximately the same. By combining the video output with the compensation output in a difference amplifier the reset clock feedthrough can to a large extent be eliminated as well as the d-c level shift due to the leakage current of the readout diode.

Performance characteristics. The minimum clock frequency is related to the effects of the dark current. As the clock frequency decreases, the integration time will increase and the charge due to the dark current will become a larger fraction of the total charge stored in the photoelements. In Figure 15.35 a graph is presented of the average dark output signal as a function of the integration time for the CCD111. We note the very rapid increase of the dark signal with temperature. The saturation output voltage level has a value of 900 mV (typ.), which corresponds to a completely filled potential well. This is the output voltage that is produced when the stored charge is at its maximum value of Q_{SAT}.

At 25°C the average dark signal level is 1.0 mV for a 2-ms integration time. Since the saturation output voltage is 750 mV, which corresponds to a full potential well, we see that the self-discharge time t_{SAT} will be approximately 1.5 s. At 35°C the average dark signal will be up to 4 mV for the same 2-ms integration time so that the self-discharge time is now 0.4 s and at 45°C it will be down to only 0.1 s.

For a dynamic range of 100:1 such that the saturation output voltage level is 100 times larger than the average dark signal, the integration time must be limited to a maximum of about 15 ms at 25°C. This will correspond to a minimum shift register clock frequency of 58 kHz. If the device temperature goes up to 35°C, the integration time will have to be shortened to about 4 ms, which will correspond to a clock rate of 218 kHz.

Another factor that will be involved in deciding on the integration time and clock rate is the optical power or irradiance level. With a high irradiance level a

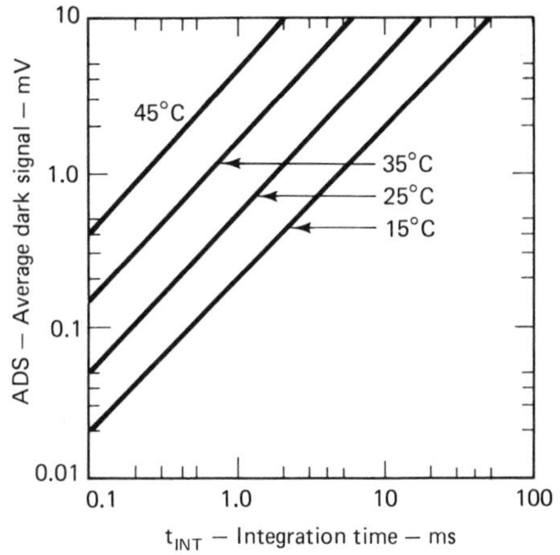

Figure 15.35 Average dark output signal versus integration time for the CCD111 (Fairchild CCD Imaging).

short integration time may be desirable to prevent the saturation of the potential wells by the photogenerated electrons. The minimum integration time is controlled by the maximum analog shift register clock frequency. The maximum clock frequency of 5.0 MHz for the CCD121H corresponds to an integration time of 173 μs. The saturation exposure of this device is 1.0 $\mu J/cm^2$ for an incandescent (2854°K) light source. This will correspond to a saturation irradiance level of (1.0 $\mu W\text{-}s/cm^2$)/173 $\mu s = 5.8$ mW/cm², which in photometric units corresponds to 120 fc.

In Figure 15.36 the spectral response characteristics of the CCD121H is presented. We note that the maximum responsivity value of 0.30 A/W is somewhat lower than what would be obtained from a silicon PN junction photodiode. This is due to the photon absorption in the polycrystalline silicon gate electrodes as well as optical losses due to multiple reflections at the polycrystalline silicon/SiO_2/silicon interfaces. Evidence for the latter is shown by the fluctuations in the spectral response curve due to the effects of constructive and destructive interference as the wavelength is varied.

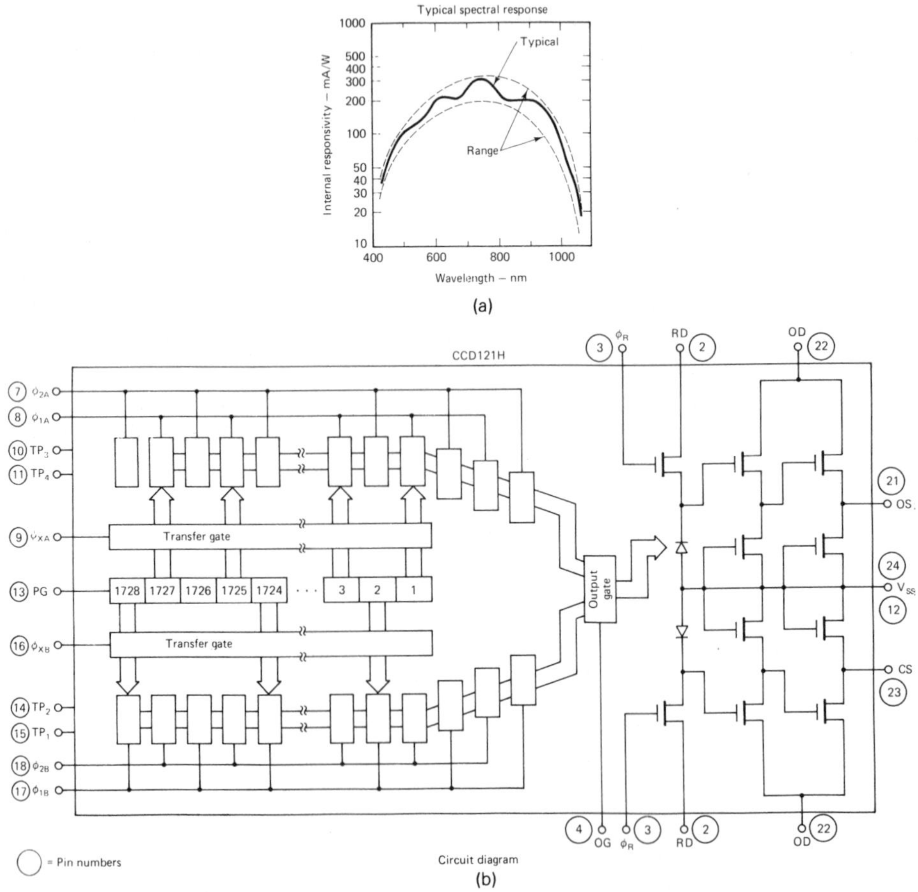

Figure 15.36 (a) Typical spectral response; (b) circuit diagram (Fairchild CCD Imaging).

15.11.5 CCD Area Image Sensors

An example of a CCD area image sensor is the CCD222 (Fairchild). The CCD222 has 185,440 elements in a 488 × 380 array. The basic organization of this device is shown in Figure 15.37. The individual photoelements measure 12 μm horizontally by 18 μm vertically. The center-to-center spacing is 30 μm horizontally and 18 μm vertically as shown in Figure 15.38. We note that the photoelements are separated by a 3-μm P^+-channel stop diffusion in the vertical direction and are separated by an 18-μm gap in the horizontal direction. This gap is needed for the two-phase vertical analog CCD shift register. The overall array dimensions are 8.8 × 11.4 mm.

The MOS photoelements use a thin polycrystalline silicon gate electrode so that front-surface illumination is possible, as was the case with the CCD121H linear image sensor considered in the preceding section. Again in this case the photoelements are used only for the photon flux integration and charge storage function and do not constitute part of the CCD shift register.

During the photon flux integration time the photogate voltages are high

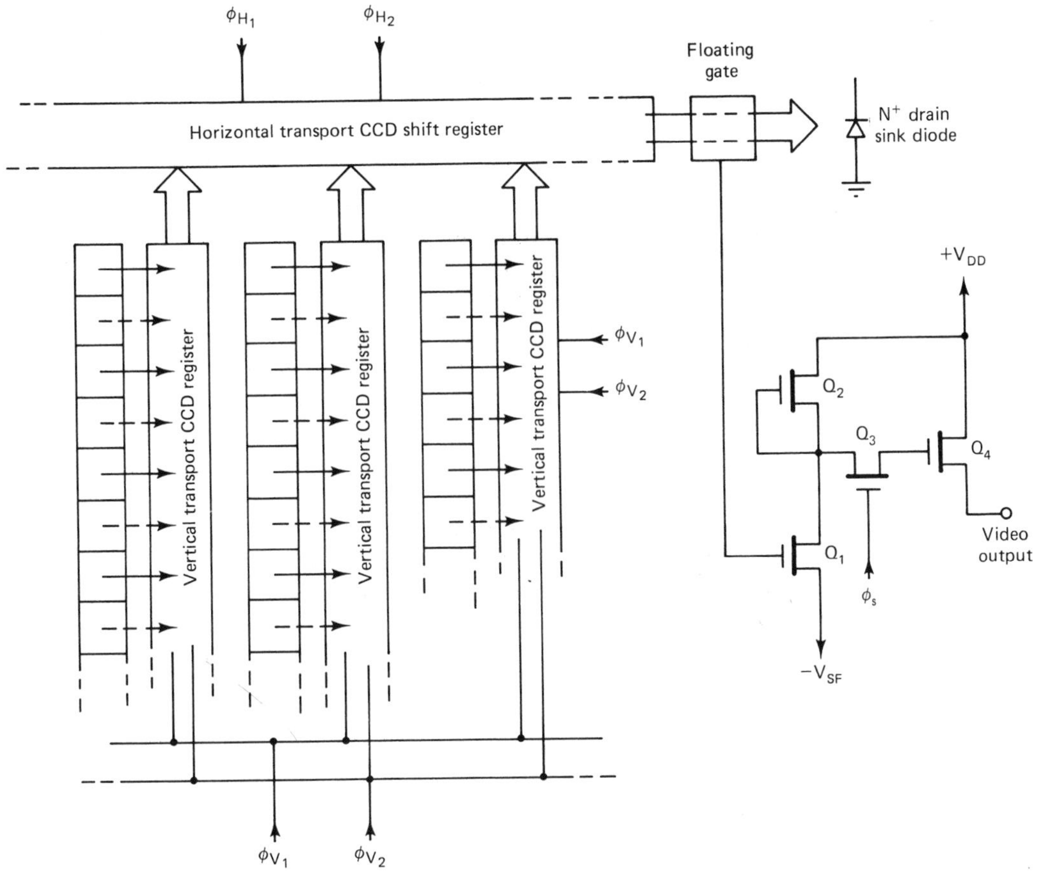

Figure 15.37 CCD area image sensor: CCD222 (Fairchild CCD Imaging).

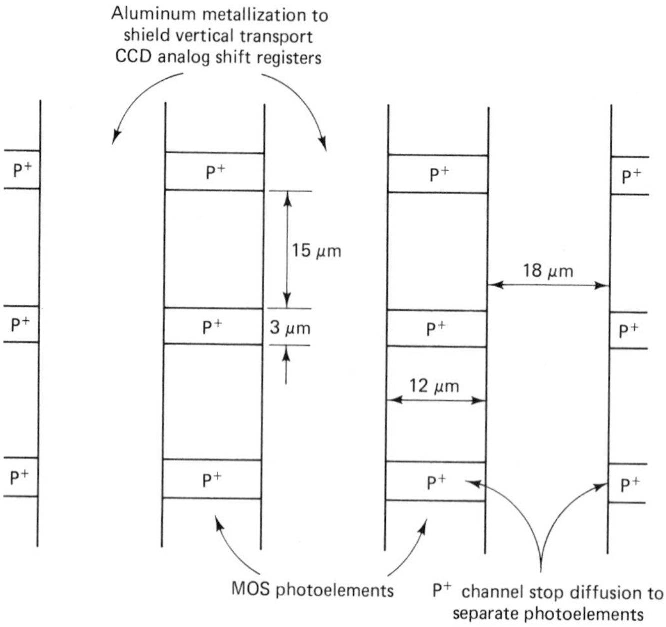

Figure 15.38 MOS photoelement dimension: CCD222 (Fairchild CCD Imaging).

($\phi_P = +5$ V), so that potential wells are formed in the P-type silicon underneath the gate where photogenerated electrons can be collected. At the end of the integration time the photogate voltage goes low ($\phi_P = 0$) and the transfer of charge from the photoelements to the vertical analog shift register will take place. This charge transfer does not occur for all of the photoelements at the same time. In order for the charge transfer to take place, the gate of the shift register stage that is adjacent to the photoelement must be high ($\phi_V = +7$ V). If the gate is low with $\phi_V = 0$, the charge transfer will not occur and the electron charge packet will remain in the photoelement. As a result of the two-phase clocking of the vertical shift register, only one-half of the photoelements will have their charge packets delivered to the vertical shift register during any field transfer interval. Thus at the beginning of the odd field scanning cycle, the photogate voltage will be low at $\phi_P = 0$ V, and at the same the ϕ_{V_1} elements of the vertical shift register will be high at +9 V and the ϕ_{V_2} elements will be low at 0 V. As a result, the 122 odd-numbered photoelements in each vertical column that are adjacent to the ϕ_{V_1} shift register elements will have their charge packets transferred to the shift register. At the end of this transfer period the photogate voltage will go high (+5 V) and a new integration period for the odd-numbered photoelements will begin.

The charge packets that have been transferred to the 190 vertical shift registers will then be shifted into the horizontal analog shift register. After the transfer of a charge packet from each of the 190 vertical shift registers into the horizontal register, the corresponding horizontal line of video information is shifted through the horizontal register to the output. This same process will be repeated until all of the charge packets in the vertical shift registers have been transferred to the horizontal register and then shifted out through the horizontal register. Thus the video signal of the odd field will appear at the output, horizontal line by horizontal line, for the 122 lines of the odd field.

After the entire field of charge packets from the odd-numbered photoelements has been transferred out of the shift registers, the same process will be repeated with the even field. This is initiated by the transfer of the charge packets from the even-numbered photoelements into the vertical shift registers at the beginning of the even-field transfer cycle. During this time the photogate voltage will be low and the ϕ_{V_2} elements of the vertical shift register will be high. Since the even-numbered photoelements of the photosensor array are adjacent to the ϕ_{V_2} shift register elements, the charge transfer can now take place from these photoelements to the shift register. The net result of this alternate transfer and shifting out of the charge packets from the odd-numbered photoelements and then from the even-numbered photoelements will be an interlaced scan. The interlaced scan will have a frame consisting of two fields. One field will be the result of the scanning of the odd-numbered photoelements and the second field will be the result of the scanning of the even-numbered photoelements.

The electron charge packets that reach the end of the horizontal shift register are delivered to the N^+ drain region of what in other image sensors would be the readout diode. For this image sensor this diode is called a sink diode and its function is solely to provide a sink back to the substrate for the electron charge packets. The actual video signal sensing is accomplished by the *floating gate* electrode. As the charge packets pass underneath this electrode, a voltage is induced in the floating gate by means of the capacitance between this gate and the channel underneath the oxide layer.

The floating gate electrode is connected to the gate of a MOS common-source amplifier Q_1. This N-channel MOSFET uses Q_2 as an active load and drives Q_4, which is a source-follower output stage. Transistor Q_3 operates as a sample-and-hold switching transistor.

The source voltage V_{SF} of the floating gate amplifier Q_1 is at a voltage of +7 V and the drain supply voltage V_{DD} is +15 V. As a result, the floating gate can be at a positive voltage of about +13 V, so that a conducting N-type channel can be maintained underneath the floating gate to allow for the passage of the electron charge packets from the horizontal shift register to the N^+ drain region of the sink diode.

Typical performance characteristics. The maximum horizontal shift register clock frequency for the CCD222 is 20 MHz. This will correspond to a maximum frame rate of 20 MHz/185,440 elements = 108 Hz.

The standard U.S. television format is a 30-Hz frame rate with each frame consisting of two interlaced fields. There are 525 lines per frame so that the horizontal or line frequency will be 15,750 Hz. A clock rate of 7.16 MHz will produce picture elements (pixels) at a 7.16-MHz rate which corresponds to a video bandwidth of 3.58 MHz. Under these conditions the saturation output voltage level at a 0°C chip temperature will be 700 mV with an output impedance of 1000 Ω.

With reference to an incandescent (2854°K) light source the saturation exposure level is 0.28 $\mu J/cm^2$ and the responsivity is 2.5 $V/(\mu J/cm^2)$. The dynamic range between the noise level (SNR = 1) and the saturation exposure is typically 1000:1.

With a 30-Hz frame rate the photon flux integration time will be 1/30 s. The saturation exposure level of 0.28 $\mu J/cm^2$ will correspond to a saturation irradiance of 0.28 $\mu J/cm^2/\frac{1}{30}$ s = 8.4 $\mu W/cm^2$. For a 100-W incandescent lamp at 2854°K with an isotropic radiation pattern this saturation irradiance will correspond to a source-to-sensor distance R given by $100\,W/(4\pi R^2) = 8.4\ \mu W/cm^2$, so that R = 9.73 m for the saturation level and $R = 9.73\text{ m} \times \sqrt{1000} = 308$ m for the unity signal-to-noise ratio condition. From this last result we see that this device can indeed be used under very low-light-level conditions.

CCD Area Image Sensor: SID504A. Another example of a CCD image sensor is the SID504A (RCA), which can be used for producing standard interlaced 525-line television pictures. This device has a total of 206,336 image-sensing elements organized in an array of 512 rows by 403 columns. The individual photoelement size is 30 $\mu m \times 30\ \mu m$ and the overall chip size is 12.7 mm × 19.05 mm, of which the image-sensing area occupies an area of 7.3 mm × 9.75 mm, which is 30% of the total chip area.

The basic organization of this device is shown in Figure 15.39. The image-sensing area consists of an array of 403 parallel vertical columns of three-phase CCD analog shift registers. Each CCD column has 512 image storage sites. The substrate is P-type silicon and the storage sites are produced by the application of a positive gate voltage ϕ_{VA} (+1.5 V) to the appropriate gate electrodes with respect to the substrate, which is at a voltage of $V_{BB} = -3$ V. This produces the potential wells for the collection of the photogenerated electrons. The gates are thin polycrystalline silicon electrodes, so that front-surface illumination can be used.

The photon flux integration time is typically $\frac{1}{60}$ s. During this integration time the photogenerated electrons are accumulated and stored under the 256 electrodes in each CCD column that have the gate voltage ϕ_{VA} in the high state. At the end of the integration time the charge packets are transferred up to the storage area, which has the same organization as the image-sensing area. This transfer of the charge packets from the image-sensing area occurs during the vertical blanking time, which lasts for 1.3 ms. The charge transfer process itself takes only about 0.2 ms out of a total integration time of 16.7 ms, so we see that there will not be much image smearing during this transfer process.

After the transfer to the storage area has been completed, the charge packets in the storage area are shifted upward line by line into the horizontal shift register. After the transfer of a charge packet from each of the 403 vertical shift registers into the horizontal register the charge packets are then shifted out of the horizontal register in a time of about 53 μs to produce one horizontal line of the TV picture. This process is repeated until the entire field of 256 × 403 picture elements has been read out.

During this readout of the field of picture elements in the storage area the picture information of the next field is being accumulated and stored in the image sensor area. The position of the storage sites is slightly shifted from that of the

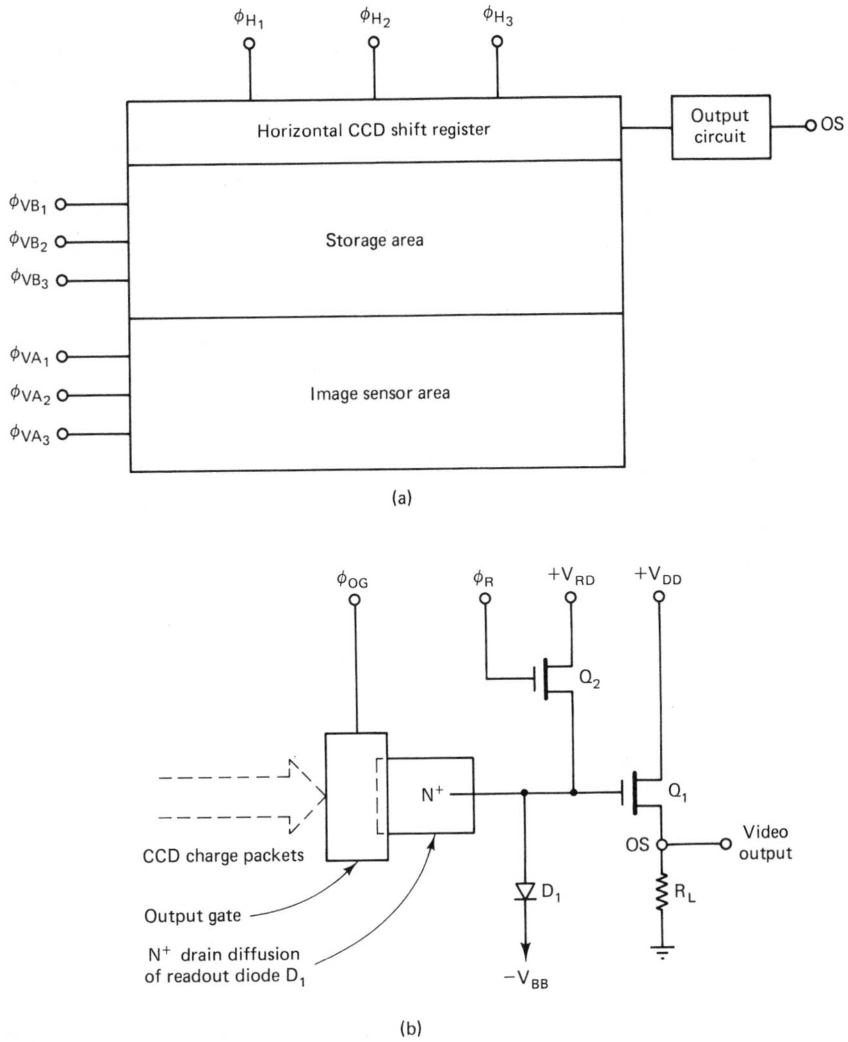

Figure 15.39 CCD area image sensor: SID504A (a) block diagram; (b) video output circuit (RCA New Products Division, Lancaster, PA).

previous field. For the first field the image storage sites were located under the ϕ_{VA_3} gates, which were biased high at + 1.5 V, and not under the ϕ_{VA_1} and ϕ_{VA_2} gates, which were biased low at −5.0 V. For the next field the charge accumulation sites will be underneath the ϕ_{VA_2} gates, which will now be biased high, and the ϕ_{VA_1} and ϕ_{VA_3} gates will be low. Thus the position of the imaging sites will be shifted up or down by an amount equal to one picture line for each successive field. This will produce an interlaced television picture with the equivalent of 512 lines of picture information. Each line will have 320 picture elements, corresponding to the 320 CCD columns in the image-sensing and storage areas.

The CCDs in this device are of the surface charge structure, with the potential well minima being right at the Si/SiO_2 interface. To minimize the trapping of the photogenerated electrons that are collected in the potential well by the surface states at the Si/SiO_2 interface, a "fat zero" minimum charge level is used. This fat zero minimum accumulated charge level is used to keep the surface states close to a saturated level, so that the trapping of additional electrons will be minimized. The fat zero d-c bias condition is provided in the image-sensing area by a uniform d-c background illumination. This can be accomplished by using some LEDs arranged to give a reasonably uniform illumination over the image-sensing area. This fat zero produced by the uniform illumination will result in a d-c component in the output video signal which can be compensated for electronically. To produce a fat zero in the horizontal shift register which is shielded from the light, there is a bias charge circuit to inject a fat zero charge packet into the source end of the horizontal register.

The video output circuit is shown in Figure 15.39. The charge packets that reach the end of the horizontal shift register are collected by the N^+ drain region which is connected to the gate of the video output transistor Q_1. As the charge packets are collected by the N^+ drain region, the gate voltage of Q_1 will change by an amount proportional to the size of the charge packet. The reset transistor Q_2 is turned on prior to the arrival of each charge packet to reset the voltage at the gate of Q_1 to a fixed level and then Q_2 is turned off. The video output signal can be obtained from Q_1 by using a source-follower configuration with a load resistor connected between the source terminal (OS) and ground.

PROBLEMS

Optoelectronics

15.1. A light source produces a radiant power output of 1.0 W at a wavelength of 1000 nm. Find the photon energy and the total photon flux. (*Ans.*: 1.239 eV, 5.05×10^{18} photons/s)

15.2. If the light source in Problem 15.1 is an isotropic radiator, find the photon flux density at a distance of 2.0 m from the source. (*Ans.*: ϕ = photon flux density = 1.00×10^{13} photons/s-cm²)

15.3. If the radiator in Problem 15.2 is not isotropic, but has a directivity of 25, find the axial intensity. (*Ans.*: axial intensity = 2.0 W/sr)

15.4. Find the axial radiant power density and the photon flux density at a distance of 200 cm from the radiator of Problem 15.3. (*Ans.*: 50 μW/cm², $\phi = 2.5 \times 10^{14}$ photons/s-cm²)

15.5. If the radiant power from the light source in Problem 15.4 is incident on a silicon photodiode (distance = 200 cm) that has an active area of 1.0 mm² and a current responsivity of 0.45 A/W at 1000 nm wavelength, find the resulting photocurrent. (*Ans.*: 224 nA)

15.6. Show that if a source of radiant energy has a hemispherical radiation pattern described by $I(\theta) = I(0) \cos^n \theta$, where $I(\theta)$ is the radiant intensity and $I(0)$ is the axial intensity, the axial intensity will be related to the total radiant power output by $I(0) = (n + 1)P_{total}/2\pi$.

15.7. Show that for an isotropic radiator, $I(0) = P_{total}/4\pi$.

15.8. The directivity of a source of radiant energy is defined as the ratio of the maximum (axial) radiant intensity to the radiant intensity that would be produced by an isotropic radiator of the same total power output. Show that the directivity D of a radiant energy source with a $\cos^n \theta$ radiation pattern will be given by $D = 2(n + 1)$.

15.9. Find the directivity of Lambertian ($n = 1$) radiator. (*Ans*.: $D = 4$)

15.10. The radiation pattern for a source of radiant energy with a half-power beam angle of θ_{50} (i.e., total half-power beam width of $2\theta_{50}$) can be approximated as $I(\theta) = I(0)$ for $\theta < \theta_{50}$, and $I(\theta) = 0$ for $\theta > \theta_{50}$.

(a) Show that based on this approximate description of the radiation pattern, the corresponding approximation for the axial intensity will be given by

$$I(0) \simeq \frac{P_{total}}{2\pi(1 - \cos\theta_{50})}$$

(b) Show that the directivity will be given approximately by $D \simeq 2/(1 - \cos\theta_{50})$.

(c) Show that for radiant energy sources with narrow beamwidths such that $\theta_{50} \lesssim 0.1$ rad $= 5.7°$, the axial intensity can be expressed approximately as $I(0) \simeq P_{total}/$ $\pi_{total}/\pi\ \theta_{50}^2$, where θ_{50} is expressed in radians.

(d) Show that the expression for the directivity for the narrow-beamwidth case will be given approximately by $D \simeq 4/\theta_{50}^2$, where θ_{50} is the half-power angle expressed in radians. If the half-power angle is expressed in degrees the equation for directivity becomes $D \simeq 13{,}000/\theta_{50}^2$.

15.11. An LED chip has a light-emitting surface area of 0.25 mm × 0.25 mm. The LED emits 100 mW of radiant power and has a Lambertian radiation pattern. What is the *radiance* (axial intensity per unit emitting area) of the LED chip surface? (*Ans*.: radiance = 51 W/sr-cm^2)

15.12. An LED chip has a light-emitting surface with a radiance of 10 W/sr-cm^2 and a Lambertian radiation pattern. If the light-emitting area is 0.25 mm in diameter, what is the total radiant power output of the LED? (*Ans*.: $P_{total} = 15$ mW)

15.13. An LED has a radiation pattern that is approximately of the form $I(\theta) = I(0)\cos^n\theta$.

(a) If the total beamwidth between the half-power points of the radiation pattern is 60°, find the value of n in the equation above and the corresponding directivity. (*Ans*.: $n = 4.82$, $D = 11.6$)

(b) Repeat part (a) for the case of a total beamwidth of 50° between the half-power points. (*Ans*.: $n = 7.05$, $D = 16.1$)

(c) Repeat part (a) for a total beamwidth between the half-power points of 20°. (*Ans*.: $n = 45.3$, $D = 92.6$)

15.14. An LED has a radiation pattern corresponding to part (b) of Problem 15.13 and has a total radiant power output of 5.0 mW.

(a) Find the axial radiant intensity, $I(0)$. [*Ans*.: $I(0) = 6.40$ mW/sr)

(b) Find the radiant power density at a distance of 100 cm from the LED along the optical axis of the device. (*Ans*.: power density = 640 nW/cm^2)

(c) If a silicon photodiode with a current responsivity of 0.40 A/W at the wavelength of interest is located on the optical axis of the LED at a distance of 100 cm, find the resulting photocurrent. (*Ans*.: 256 nA)

15.15. An LED has a peak emission wavelength of 660 nm. If the total radiant power output of this device is 50 μW, what is the total luminous flux output? (*Ans*.: 2.0×10^{-3} lm)

15.16. The radiation pattern for the LED in Problem 15.15 has half-power points at an angle of ±42° from the optical axis of the device for a total half-power beamwidth of 84°. Find the approximate directivity of this device and the *axial luminous intensity*. [*Ans.*: $D \simeq 7.8$, luminous intensity $\simeq 1.24 \times 10^{-3}$ lm /sr = 1.24×10^{-3} candelas (cd) = 1.24 mcd]

15.17. What will the luminous flux density be at a distance of 20 cm from the LED of Problem 15.16 along the optical axis? (*Ans.*: luminous flux density = 3.1×10^{-6} lm/cm² = 0.031 lm/m² = 0.031 candle-m = 0.0029 lm/ft² = 0.0029 fc)

15.18. A 100-W tungsten lamp ($T \simeq 2600$°K) has a luminous efficiency of 2.1%.

(a) Find the luminous efficacy. (*Ans.*: 14.3 lm/W)

(b) Find the total luminous flux output. (*Ans.*: 1428 lm)

(c) If the radiation pattern is approximately that of an isotropic radiator, what is the luminous intensity (candlepower) of the lamp? (*Ans.*: luminous intensity = 114 lm/sr = 114 candelas)

(d) Find the luminous flux density at a distance of 2.0 m from the lamp. (*Ans.*: 28.4 lm/m² = 2.64 lm/ft² = 2.64 fc)

15.19. What fraction of the light at normal incidence will be reflected at a GaAs/air interface, and what fraction will be transmitted? Use $n = 3.6$ for GaAs. (*Ans.*: *reflectance* = 32%, *transmittance* = 68%)

15.20. Find the critical angle θ_c for total internal reflection (TIR) at the GaAs/air interface. (*Ans.*: $\theta_c = 16.1°$)

15.21. Assuming that the photon emission process within GaAs is isotropic:

(a) Show that the fraction of the emitted radiant power contained in a cone of half-angle θ_c will be given by

$$\frac{A_{\text{CONE}}}{A_{\text{TOTAL}}} = \frac{1}{2}\left(1 - \sqrt{1 - \frac{1}{n^2}}\right) \simeq \frac{1}{4n^2}$$

where n is the index of refraction of the light emission medium (GaAs).

(b) Find this fraction for GaAs. (*Ans.*: 0.0197 or 1.97%)

15.22. Assuming that there is no internal optical absorption losses, approximately what fraction of the internally generated photon flux will be emitted by a GaAs LED assuming a flat surface and no antireflective coating? (*Ans.*: 1.3%)

15.23. If this LED produces a radiant power output of 0.737 mW when $I_F = 50$ mA and the peak emission wavelength is 940 nm, find the emitted photon flux. (*Ans.*: 3.5×10^{15} photons/s)
Find the external quantum efficiency. (*Ans.*: Q.E. = 1.12%)

15.24. Using the results of the preceding two problems, find the internal quantum efficiency. (*Ans.*: internal Q.E. = 86%)

15.25. If an LED has a total radiant power power output of 1.0 mW and has a total beamwidth between the half-power points of 20°, find the *axial intensity*, $I(0)$. (*Ans.*: 10.5 mW/sr)

15.26. Find the radiant power density along the optical axis of the LED in Problem 15.25 at the following distances from the LED.

(a) 10 cm (*Ans.*: 105 μW/cm²)

(b) 1.0 m (*Ans.*: 1.05 μW/cm²)

(c) 10 m (*Ans.*: 10.5 nW/cm²)

(d) 100 m (*Ans.*: 105 pW/cm²)

15.27. A GaAs LED has a total radiant power output of 4.0 mW at a peak emission wavelength of 940 nm and at a forward current level of $I_F = 100$ mA. At this current level the forward voltage drop across the diode is $V_F = 1.4$ V. What is the photon energy? (*Ans.*: $E_{\text{photon}} = 1.32$ eV)

15.28. What is the photon flux emitted by the LED? (*Ans.*: 1.9×10^{16} photon/s)

15.29. What is the radiant power efficiency of the LED? (*Ans.*: 2.86%)

15.30. If the LED in Problem 15.27 has an axial intensity of 10 mW/Sr, find the "gain" or directivity of this LED over an isotropic radiator. (*Ans.*: 31.4)

15.31. What is the external quantum efficiency of the LED in Problem 15.27? (*Ans.*: 3.03%)

15.32. Find the axial radiant energy density at a distance of 10 cm from the LED in Problem 15.30 with $I_F = 100$ mA. (*Ans.*: 100 μW/cm^2)

15.33. Find the axial photon flux density ϕ at a distance of 10 cm from the LED in Problem 15.30. (*Ans.*: $\phi = 4.74 \times 10^{14}$ photons/s-cm^2)

15.34. What will the current responsivity of an ideal photodiode be at a wavelength of 940 nm? (*Ans.*: 0.7576 A/W)

15.35. If an uncoated photodiode has a current responsivity of 0.39 A/W at 940 nm, what will the responsivity be if the surface reflectance is reduced to just 4% by an antireflective coating? (*Ans.*: 0.535 A/W)

15.36. If the active area of this photodiode is 1 mm × 1 mm, find the *radiation sensitivity* S_R of the device at 940 nm and with an antireflective coating. The *radiation sensitivity* is the photocurrent produced per unit *irradiance* (radiant power density). (*Ans.*: $S_R = 5.35$ μA/(mW/cm^2)

15.37. Repeat Problem 15.36 for:

(a) A phototransistor of the same active area and optoelectronic parameters as the photodiode and a current gain of $\beta = 250$ (typ.). [*Ans.*: $S_{R(CEO)} = 1.34$ mA/(mW/cm^2)]

(b) A photodarlington transistor with the same active area and optoelectronic parameters as the photodiode and a net current gain of 15,000 (typ.). [*Ans.*: 80 mA/(mW/cm^2)]

15.38. For the photodiode of Problem 15.36, what will the photocurrent be at a distance of 10 cm from the LED of Problem 15.32? (*Ans.*: 437 nA)

15.39. The dark current of a photodiode is 500 pA (typ.) at $V_R = 10$ V. Find the shot noise current in terms of:

(a) The spectral density. (*Ans.*: 13 fA/VHz$^{1/2}$)

(b) A 3-dB (single pole) bandwidth of 1 kHz. (*Ans.*: 515 fA)

(c) A 3-dB (single-pole) bandwidth of 10 MHz. (*Ans.*: 51.5 pA)

15.40. A photodiode has a current responsivity of 0.535 A/W at 940 nm and a dark reverse current of 500 pA at $V_R = 10$ V as above. Find the *noise equivalent power* (the optical signal power required to produce a unity signal-to-noise ratio) for the following 3-dB (single-pole) bandwidths (neglect the noise contributions of the load resistance and the amplifier):

(a) 1 Hz (*Ans.*: 30.5 fW)

(b) 1 kHz (*Ans.*: 963 fW)

(c) 10 MHz (*Ans.*: 96 pW)

15.41. Find the thermal noise current produced by a 1.0-MΩ resistor. (*Ans.*: 128 fA/Hz$^{1/2}$)

15.42. Find the NEP of a photodetector system using the photodiode of Problem 15.40 and a 1.0-MΩ load resistor, assuming that the noise contribution of the amplifier at 3-dB bandwidth is negligible at:

(a) 1Hz (*Ans*.: 241 fW)

(b) 1 kHz (*Ans*.: 9.53 pW)

15.43. Repeat Problem 15.42 for the case of an amplifier with an equivalent input noise voltage of 20 nV/Hz$^{1/2}$. (*Ans*.: 305 fW, 9.65 fW)

15.44. An LED as described in Problem 15.32 is used as the light source for the photodetector system of Problem 15.43. Find the distance at which an SNR of 10 will be obtained with a 3-dB bandwidth (single pole) of 1.0 kHz. (*Ans*.: 10.3 m)

15.45. If the LED is operated under low-duty-cycle pulsed conditions such that the peak radiant power is increased by a factor of 10 over what is obtained under CW conditions, find the distance for an SNR of 10. (*Ans*.: 31 m)

15.46. A photodiode has a capacitance of 10 pF and the amplifier input capacitance is 2.0 pF. What is the largest value load resistance that can be used for a 3-dB bandwidth of 10 MHz? (*Ans*.: 1.33 kΩ)

15.47. **(a)** Show that the sensitivity of a photodetector circuit can be no better than NEP = $\sqrt{8\pi kTC}\,BW/\mathcal{R}$, where C is the total shunt capacitance, BW is the 3-dB bandwidth, and $\mathcal{R}$ is the current responsivity.

(b) Find the NEP for a 3-dB bandwidth of 10 MHz, a total capacitance of 10 pF, and a responsivity of 0.535 A/W. (*Ans*.: NEP = 19 nW)

(c) At what distance from an LED with an axial intensity of 10 mW/Sr will an SNR of 10 be obtained if the photodiode active area is 1 mm^2? (*Ans*.: 72.5 cm)

15.48. **(a)** A photodiode has a dark reverse current of 500 pA. For what values of load resistance R_L will the thermal noise of R_L become the dominant contributor to the total noise current? (*Ans*.: $R_L < 100$ MΩ)

(b) Show that, in general, for load resistance less that $R_L = 2V_T/I_{DR}$, the dominant contribution to the total noise current will be thermal noise of the load resistance.

15.49. A GaAlAs LED light source and a silicon photodiode is to be used in a fiber optic communications link with a 10-MHz 3-dB bandwidth. The LED has a radiant power output of 10 mW at 850 nm, and the photodiode has a current responsivity of 0.40 A/W at this wavelength. The photodiode has a capacitance of 5 pF and a dark reverse current of 1.0 nA. The amplifier input capacitance is 5 pF. Find the maximum load resistance that can be used across the photodiode. (*Ans*.: 1.6 kΩ)

15.50. Find the thermal noise current of the resistor. (*Ans*.: 12.7 nA)

15.51. Find the shot noise current of the photodiode of Problem 15.49. (*Ans*.: 71 pA)

15.52. If the amplifier has an equivalent input noise voltage of 5 nV/Hz$^{1/2}$, find the equivalent noise current. (*Ans*.: 12.5 nA)

15.53. Find the optical power input to the photodiode for SNR = 1. (*Ans*.: 44.5 nW)

15.54. The input coupling loss (LED to optical fiber) is 20 dB and the output coupling loss (fiber to photodiode) is 3 dB. The optical fiber has an attenuation of 10 dB/km at 850 nm. Find the length of the link between repeaters for an SNR of 10. [*Ans*.: 2.05 km (max.)]

Image Sensors

15.55. A MOS photoelement is 15 μm $\times$ 15 μm in area and has a 750-Å gate oxide. Find the maximum electron charge Q_{SAT} that can be stored in the potential well at the silicon surface for a photogate voltage of +15 V. Use 3.8 for the dielectric constant of the oxide layer. (*Ans.*: 1.51 pC)

15.56. If the dark leakage current density is 30 nA/cm^2, find the self-discharge time of the MOS photoelements. (*Ans.*: 22.4 s)

15.57. If the current responsivity of the MOS photoelements is 0.10 A/W for an incandescent light source, find the saturation exposure level. (*Ans.*: 6.73 μJ/cm^2)

15.58. For a frame rate of 30 Hz, find the saturation irradiance. (*Ans.*: 202 μW/cm^2)

15.59. If the incandescent light source has an isotropic radiation pattern and the total radiant power output is 100 W, at what source-to-sensor distance will the saturation irradiance level be reached? (*Ans.*: 1.99 m)

15.60. Using the dark leakage current density of 30 nA/cm^2, find the corresponding shot noise current spectral density. Find the shot noise current for a 3-dB bandwidth of 5.0 MHz. (*Ans.*: 1.47 A/Hz$^{1/2}$, 0.412 pA)

15.61. What irradiance level will produce a signal-to-noise ratio of unity (i.e., the NEP)? (*Ans.*: 1.832 μW/cm^2)

15.62. The dynamic range of this image sensor is the ratio of the saturation irradiance level to the irradiance level that produces a unity signal-to-noise ratio. Find the dynamic range. (*Ans.*: 110)

15.63. For the 100-W isotropic incandescent light source of the previous problems, what source-to-sensor distance will result in a unity signal-to-noise ratio? (*Ans.*: 20.8 m)

15.64. If the photoelement area is doubled, what effect will this have on the following?

(a) Saturation irradiance (*Ans.*: none)

(b) Dark current (*Ans.*: doubles)

(c) Shot noise current (*Ans.*: increases by $\sqrt{2}$)

(d) Dynamic range (*Ans.*: increases by $\sqrt{2}$ to 155.8

(e) Source-to-sensor distance for unity signal-to-noise ratio. (*Ans.*: increases by $2^{1/4}$ to 24.8 m)

15.65. This image sensor is to use a two-phase 512-bit analog shift register. The overall transfer function is to be at least 0.90 at a 5.0-MHz clock frequency. What must the transfer efficiency per stage be? If the charge transfer from one element of the CCD array to the next is characterized by a simple exponential function with a single time constant, what must the value of the time constant be? [*Ans.*: 0.999897, 21.8 ns (max.)]

REFERENCES

BAR-LEV, A., *Semiconductors and Electronic Devices*, Prentice-Hall, 1979.

BARNOSKI, M. K., *Fundamentals of Optical Fiber Communications*, Academic Press, 1981.

CHAPPELL, A., *Optoelectronics*, McGraw-Hill, 1978.

ELION, G., *Fiber Optics in Communications Systems*, Marcel Dekker, 1978.

ELION, G. R., AND H. A. ELION, *Electro-Optics Handbook*, Marcel Dekker, 1979.

HERMAN, M. A., *Semiconductor Optoelectronics*, Wiley, 1980.

HOWES, M. J., AND D. MORGAN, *Optical Fiber Communications*, Wiley, 1980.

KAO, C. K., *Optical Fiber Systems: Technology, Design, and Applications*, McGraw-Hill, 1982.

KARP, S., *Optical Communications*, Wiley, 1976.

KUECKEN, J. A., *Fiberoptics*, Tab Books, 1980.

LENK, J. D., *Handbook of Electronic Circuit Design*, Prentice-Hall, 1976.

MELEN, R., AND D. BUSS, *Charge-Coupled Devices: Technology and Applications*, IEEE Press, 1977.

MILLER, S. E., AND A. G. CHYNOWETH, *Optical Fiber Telecommunications*, Academic Press, 1979.

MIMS, F. M., *Light-Beam Communications*, Howard M. Sams, 1975.

PANKOVE, J. I., *Optical Processes in Semiconductors*, Prentice-Hall, 1971.

SEIPPEL, R. G., *Optoelectronics*, Reston, 1981.

SZE, S. M., *Physics of Semiconductor Devices*, Wiley, 1969.

WOLF, H. F., *Handbook of Fiber Optics: Theory and Applications*, Garland, 1979.

Physical Constants, Conversion Factors, and Parameters

Appendix

Angstrom unit	Å	1 Å = 10^{-4} μm = 10^{-8} cm = 10^{-10} m
Boltzmann constant	k	$k = 1.380 \times 10^{-23}$ J/K = 8.62×10^{-5} eV/K
Electron charge	q	$q = 1.602 \times 10^{-19}$ C
Micron	μm	1 μm = 10^{-6} m = 10^{-4} cm = 10,000 Å
Mil		1 mil = 0.001 in. = 25.4 μm
Nanometer	nm	1 nm = 10^{-9} m = 10^{-3} μm = 10 Å
Permittivity of free space	ϵ_0	$\epsilon_0 = 8.854 \times 10^{-14}$ F/cm
Permeability of free space	μ_0	$\mu_0 = 4\pi \times 10^{-9}$ H/cm
Planck's constant	h	$h = 6.625 \times 10^{-34}$ J-s
Thermal voltage	V_T	$V_T = kT/q = 25.85$ mV at 300K (27°C)
Velocity of light in free space	c	$c = 2.998 \times 10^{10}$ cm/s

	Silicon	Germanium	GaAs	SiO_2
Dielectric constant, ϵ_r (relative permittivity)	11.8	16.0	10.9	3.8
Energy gap, E_G (eV at 300 K)	1.11	0.67	1.43	
Electron drift mobility, μ_n ($cm^2/V\text{-}s$ at 300 K)	1350	3900	8500	
Hole drift mobility, μ_p ($cm^2/V\text{-}s$ at 300 K)	500	1900	400	
Intrinsic carrier concentration, n_i (cm^{-3} at 300 K)	1.4×10^{10}	2.1×10^{12}	1.1×10^{7}	
Electron saturation velocity, v_{sat} (cm/s)	0.8×10^{7}	0.6×10^{7}	2×10^{7}	
Saturation electric field, E_{sat} (V/cm)	2×10^{4}	3×10^{3}	2×10^{3}	

Index

A

B

C

M

N

O

P

Q

R